Please return to Bill Burdick

Love Does Not Condemn

Absence from Felicity: The Story of Helen Schucman and Her Scribing of A Course in Miracles

"Christian Psychology in *A Course in Miracles*"

The Fifty Miracle Principles of A Course in Miracles

Forgiveness and Jesus: The Meeting Place of A Course in Miracles *and Christianity*

Glossary-Index for A Course in Miracles

The Obstacles to Peace

"A Talk Given on *A Course in Miracles*"

A Vast Illusion: Time According to A Course in Miracles

Awaken from the Dream (co-author, Gloria Wapnick)

LOVE DOES NOT CONDEMN

The World, the Flesh, and the Devil
According to Platonism, Christianity,
Gnosticism, and *A Course in Miracles*

Kenneth Wapnick

Foundation for "A Course in Miracles"

Foundation for "A Course in Miracles" Roscoe, NY 12776

Printed in the United States of America

95 94 93 92 91 90 5 4 3 2 1

Excerpts from *The Jerusalem Bible*, © 1966, 1967, and 1968 by Darton, Longman and Todd, Ltd and Doubleday, a division of Bantam, Doubleday, Dell Publishing Group, Inc. Reprinted and used by permission of the publishers.

Excerpts from *The Nag Hammadi Library* edited by James Robinson. © 1978 by E. J. Brill. Reprinted by permission of Harper & Row, Publishers, Inc. and E. J. Brill.

Reprinted from *New Testament Apocrypha*: Volume I: Gospels and Related Writings, by Edgar Hennecke; edited by Wilhelm Schneemelcher; English translation by R. McL. Wilson. © 1959 J.C.B Mohr (Paul Siebeck), Tubingen; English translation © 1963 Lutterworth Press. Reprinted and used by permission of the Westminster/John Knox Press and Lutterworth Press.

Reprinted from *New Testament Apocrypha*, Volume II, edited by Wilhelm Schneemelcher and Edgar Hennecke, English translation edited by R. McL. Wilson. Published in the U.S.A. by The Westminster Press, 1966. © 1964 J.C.B. Mohr (Paul Siebeck) Tubingen. English translation © 1965 Lutterworth Press. Reprinted and used by permission of Publisher.

Excerpts from *Gnosis: A Selection of Gnostic Texts*, Volumes I and II, edited by Werner Foerster, 1972, 1974. Used by permission of Artemis Publishers.

Portions of *A Course in Miracles* © 1975, "Psychotherapy: Purpose, Process and Practice" © 1976, "The Song of Prayer" © 1978, *The Gifts of God* © 1982 used by permission of the Foundation for Inner Peace, Inc.

Library of Congress Cataloging in Publication Data

Wapnick, Kenneth
   Love does not condemn : the world, the flesh, and the Devil according to Platonism, Christianity, Gnosticism, and a Course in miracles / Kenneth Wapnick.
        p.   cm.
        Bibliography: p.
        Includes index.
        ISBN 0-933291-07-8
        1. Course in miracles. 2. Platonists. 3. Gnosticism.
4. Christianity. I. Title.
BP605.N48F68 suppl. 10
299'.93--dc20
                                   89-16887
                                   CIP

To all "Gnostics"—past, present and to come—who seek to know God through understanding this world's purpose, striving to realize, in the words of the oft-quoted Valentinian formula, that "what liberates is the knowledge of who we were, what we became; where we were, whereinto we have been thrown; whereto we speed, wherefrom we are redeemed; what birth is, and what rebirth" (Excerpta ex Theodoto).

The body was not made by love. Yet love does not condemn it and can use it lovingly, respecting what the Son of God has made and using it to save him from illusions.

A Course in Miracles

CONTENTS

PART II-A THE BASIC MYTH:
PLATONISM, CHRISTIANITY, GNOSTICISM

PART II-B THE BASIC MYTH: *A COURSE IN MIRACLES*

PART III SUMMARY AND CONCLUSIONS

APPENDIX

NOTATIONS

References

The complete reference for works cited appears in the Appendix: Works Cited.

Textual Signs

For ease of reading, parentheses enclosing material supplied by the editor or translator are the only textual signs which have been retained in the tractates and writings cited in this book. Other textual signs such as above-the-line strokes, brackets, and braces have been omitted.

Translations and Editions

ARISTOTLE: *The Basic Works of Aristotle*, ed. Richard McKeon; *Problems* I, trans. W. S. Hett, The Loeb Classical Library.

AURELIUS, MARCUS: *Meditations*, ed. Moses Hadas.

THE BIBLE: *The Jerusalem Bible*

MANDEAN TEXTS: References to Mandean texts are from Werner Foerster's *Gnosis: A Selection of Gnostic Texts*. Consult Abbreviations for further explanations of Mandean references.

NAG HAMMADI TRACTATES: *The Nag Hammadi Library*, first edition, 1977 (= *NHL*). References are identified by the Nag Hammadi codex number, followed by the page and line number from the Coptic manuscripts, then the page number in *NHL*.

Tractates from the Berlin Gnostic Codex 8502 (= BG) are listed by the tractate title used in *NHL* followed by the page and line number from the Coptic manuscript, then the page number in *NHL*.

ORIGEN: *On First Principles*, trans. by G. W. Butterworth. All other works: *Origen*, trans. Rowan A. Greer.

PHILO: Unless otherwise noted, all works cited are from The Loeb Classical Library edition of the works of Philo.

PLATO: *Republic* and *Timaeus*, trans. Desmond Lee. The following works are from *Plato: Collected Dialogues*, edited by Edith Hamilton and Huntington Cairns: *Phaedo*, trans. Hugh Tredennick; *Phaedrus*, trans. R. Hackforth;

xv

PLATO (cont.): *Theaetetus, Parmenides,* trans. F. M. Cornford; *Statesman,* trans. J. B. Skemp; *Epinomis,* trans. A. E. Taylor.

PLOTINUS: *The Enneads,* seven volumes, trans. A. H. Armstrong, The Loeb Classical Library.

ST. AUGUSTINE: *Confessions,* trans. John K. Ryan. Citations from the following works are from *The Essential Augustine,* edited by Vernon J. Bourke: *City of God,* trans. Marcus Dods; *Enchiridion,* trans. Marcus Dods; *Literal Commentary on Genesis,* trans. Vernon J. Bourke; *On Admonition and Grace,* Nicene trans.; *On Music,* trans. Tafford P. Maher, S.J.; *Sermon,* trans. Vernon J. Bourke; *The True Religion,* trans. C. A. Hangartner, S.J.; *The Nature of the Good,* trans. Marcus Dods.

ABBREVIATIONS

Scriptural References
(In Biblical Order)

OLD TESTAMENT

Gn	Genesis	2K	2 Kings
Ex	Exodus	Ps	Psalms
Lv	Leviticus	Pr	Proverbs
Nu	Numbers	Ws	Wisdom
Dt	Deuteronomy	Is	Isaiah

NEW TESTAMENT

Mt	Matthew	2 Th	2 Thessalonians
Lk	Luke	1 Tm	1 Timothy
Jn	John	2 Tm	2 Timothy
Ac	Acts	Tt	Titus
Rm	Romans	Heb	Hebrews
1 Co	1 Corinthians	1 P	1 Peter
2 Co	2 Corinthians	2 P	2 Peter
Ga	Galatians	1 Jn	1 John
Ep	Ephesians	2 Jn	2 John
Ph	Philippians	Jude	Jude
Col	Colossians	Rv	Revelations
1 Th	1 Thessalonians		

The Nag Hammadi Library (= *NHL*)

Allog.	"Allogenes"
ApocAdam	"Apocryphon of Adam"
1 ApocJs	"The First Apocalypse of James"
2 ApocJs	"The Second Apocalypse of James"
ApocPaul	"The Apocalypse of Paul"
ApocPt	"The Apocalypse of Peter"
ApocryJohn	"The Apocryphon of John"
ApocryJs	"The Apocryphon of James"
APt 12	"The Acts of Peter and the Twelve Apostles"
Ascl.	"Asclepius"
Auth. Teach.	"Authoritative Teaching"
Conc. Great Power	"The Concept of Our Great Power"
Dial. Savior	"The Dialogue of the Savior"
Disc. Eighth Ninth	"Discourse on the Eighth and Ninth"
Exeg. Soul	"The Exegesis on the Soul"
GEgypt	"The Gospel of the Egyptians"
GM	"The Gospel of Mary"

The Nag Hammadi Library (Continued)

GPh .... "The Gospel of Philip"
Gr. Seth .... "The Second Treatise of the Great Seth"
GT .... "The Gospel of Truth"
GTh .... "The Gospel of Thomas"
Hypos. Arch. .... "The Hypostasis of the Archons"
Interp. Kn. .... "The Interpretation of Knowledge"
Mel. .... "Melchizedek"
Orig. Wld. .... "On the Origin of the World"
Para. Shem .... "The Paraphrase of Shem"
Pt Ph .... "The Letter of Peter to Philip"
Sophia .... "The Sophia of Jesus Christ"
Silv. .... "The Teachings of Silvanus"
3 St. Seth .... "The Three Steles of Seth"
Test. Tr. .... "The Testimony of Truth"
Thanks. .... "Prayer of Thanksgiving"
Th Cont. .... "The Book of Thomas the Contender"
Treat. Res. .... "The Treatise on Resurrection"
Tri. Prot. .... "Trimorphic Protennoia"
Tri. Tract. .... "The Tripartite Tractate"
Val. Expo. .... "A Valentinian Exposition"
Zostr. .... "Zostrianos"

Related Literature

Aa .... *Acta apostolorum apocrypha*
AA .... "The Acts of Andrew"
Adv. haer. .... *Adversus haereses* (Irenaeus)
Adv. Marc. .... *Adversus Marcionem* (Tertullian)
AJ .... "The Acts of John"
AP .... "The Acts of Paul"
APt .... "The Acts of Peter"
ATh .... "The Acts of Thomas"
BG .... Berlin Gnostic Codex 8502
Corp. herm. .... *Corpus Hermeticum*
CV .... *Codex Vaticanus* 808
Eccles. Hist. .... *Ecclesiastical History* (Eusebius of Caesarea)
Eden .... *The Forgotten Books of Eden*
Excerpta .... *Excerpta ex Theodoto*
F I, II .... Foerster, *Gnosis: A Selection of Gnostic Texts*, Volumes I, II
GB .... "The Gospel of Bartholomew"
GEve .... "The Gospel of Eve"
GH .... "The Gospel of the Hebrews"
GL, GR .... Left Ginza, Right Ginza: two parts of the Mandean *Ginza*
GPt .... "The Gospel of Peter"
Haer. .... *Haereses* (Epiphanius)

Related Literature (Continued)

HG .... *Haran Gawaita* (Mandean)
Jb. .... *Johannesbuch* - "The Book of John" (Mandean)
Ker. Pet. .... "The Kerygmata Petrou"
Konai .... "Commentary" of Theodore bar Konai
Liv. Gosp. .... "The Living Gospel"
Lost Books .... *The Lost Books of the Bible*
ML .... *Mandäische Liturgian;* Qolasta = ML Qol;
    Oxford Collection = ML Oxf.
Narr. .... *Narratio* ("The Acts of Andrew")
NTA I, II .... *New Testament Apocrypha* Volumes One and Two
Panar. .... *Panarion* (Epiphanius)
Praes. adv. Haer. .... *Praescriptio adversus Haereticos* (Tertullian)
Ref. .... *Refutatio omnium haeresium* (Hippolytus)
Strom. .... *Stromata* (Clement of Alexandria)
Sum. Theol. .... *Summa Theologiae* (St. Thomas Aquinas)

Platonists

ORIGEN
First Princ. .... *On First Principles*
Homily .... *Homily XXVII on "Numbers"*
Martyrdom .... *An Exhortation to Martyrdom*
Prologue .... *The Prologue to the Commentary on "The Song of Songs"*

PHILO
Alleg. Interp. .... *Allegorical Interpretation*

PLATO
Epin. .... *Epinomis*
Parm. .... *Parmenides*
Rep. .... *Republic*
States. .... *The Statesman*
Theaet. .... *Theaetetus*
Tim. .... *Timaeus*

PLOTINUS
Enn. .... *Enneads*

ST. AUGUSTINE
Conf. .... *Confessions*
Contra epist. fund. .... *Contra epistulam fundamenti*
de haer. .... *de haeresibus ad Quodvultdeum*
Enchir. .... *Enchiridion*
Lit. Com. Gen. .... *Literal Commentary on Genesis*

PREFACE

A litany from the seventeenth-century Book of Common Prayer of the Church of England contains this petition: "From fornication, and all other deadly sin; and from all the deceits of the world, the flesh, and the devil, Good Lord, deliver us" (*Oxford Dictionary of Quotations*, 3d ed., p. 385, #16). "The world, the flesh, and the devil" have been pre-occupations of world religions ever since people began reflecting on their existential situation of feeling alone and vulnerable in a world that could be perceived as harmful, evil, and uncaring. Religions, thus, can be seen as attempts to render sensible this otherwise inexplicable and meaningless phenomenal world. They have sought answers to the question of how a separated and physical world, apparently under the benevolent guidance of a loving and non-physical God, can arise in the first place, and then continually manifest pain and suffering. They address the problem of how one is to live in a world of the body, while trying to recall and identify with one's spiritual Self.

In the Western philosophical world, this problem has been addressed since the time of the pre-Socratics in ancient Greece, with Plato being the first to develop an elaborate cosmogony (study of the origin of the world) and cosmology (study of the nature of the world), and then an ethical system and theory of society that was derived from this. His work became the foundation for over two thousand years of theoretical speculation about the nature of spiritual reality and its relation to the world of the body, not to mention having presented a problem that has perplexed Platonists for centuries and centuries. American classicist and Greek scholar John Dillon has stated it this way:

> Perhaps the chief problem that faces any religious or philosophical system which postulates, as does the Platonic, a primary state or entity of pure and unitary perfection, is that of explaining how from such a first principle anything further could have arisen. Any further development, after all, from a perfect principle must necessarily be a declination of some sort, and it is not easy to see why the supreme principle, if omnipotent, should want this to occur.... [There] is a further problem. Accepting that a world or universe of some sort is thus brought into being, how can we further explain the imperfect and disorderly nature of *our* world as it now exists? Something, surely, has gone wrong somewhere. There must at some stage, over and above the basic creation, have been a declination, a Fall (in Layton, p. 357).

This book presents two primary approaches to this problem--Gnosticism and *A Course in Miracles*--and discusses them within the context

1

of the Platonic and Christian traditions. Before proceeding any further, however, a few introductory remarks may be helpful for those relatively unfamiliar with the Course.

A Course in Miracles was the result of a decision made in 1965 by two New York psychologists, Helen Schucman and William Thetford, to join with each other to find "another way" (more loving) of relating to people. That moment of joining (what the Course would later term a "holy instant") served as a signal that triggered off a series of visionary, dream, and psychic experiences in Helen that culminated in her hearing an internal voice, identified as Jesus, who began to "dictate" the three books--text, workbook for students, manual for teachers-- that comprise the Course. The dictation was begun in the fall of 1965, completed seven years later, and published in 1976.

Briefly stated, the Course teaches that the forgiveness of our projected guilt is the means whereby we remember our oneness with each other, our true Self, and with the God who created us. This teaching comes within a non-dualistic metaphysical framework wherein God did not create the phenomenal, material world, a term which includes the *entire* physical universe. Rather, the world and the body are seen to have arisen from the projection of the fundamentally illusory thought and belief that we could separate ourselves from God, and make a world wherein the opposite of Heaven seems to have been accomplished. This belief in the reality of the separation is called the ego by the Course.[1] The world then serves the purpose of protecting the ego thought system of separation and usurpation within its shadows of guilt that ostensibly keep God the "Enemy" away. Thus, our entire experience in this world, within our bodily and psychological selves, is part of an illusory thought system we believe to be reality, yet which remains nothing more than a dream. Salvation is attained through hearing the Voice of the Holy Spirit, awakening us from the dream of separation by teaching us to join with others through forgiveness. This is the process of Atonement, which principle is that the separation never truly occurred.

Though A Course in Miracles teaches that the world is illusory, it does not advocate avoidance of this world, nor its rejection as evil or sinful. Rather, it emphasizes that the mistakes of separation be corrected at the level of our experience here. It urges us to look within our most intimate and meaningful relationships, asking the Holy Spirit--our internal Teacher--to heal them for us. What is encouraged, therefore, is gratitude for our involvement in the world because of its potential to teach us that there is no world. Under the Holy Spirit's guidance we

---

1. The word "ego" is used, here and elsewhere in the book, synonymously with the "false self," a usage that is consistent with the spiritualities of the East.

become grateful for the classroom that is our bodily experience, and for His teaching us the lessons that are found here. Thus, the *metaphysics* of non-duality is reconciled with our *experience* of duality.

One final note on the Course: Its contextual framework is Christian, with its language and terminology coming from the Judaeo-Christian world of the Bible. Thus, although the nature of God is obviously beyond gender, we shall in this book remain within the Judaeo-Christian tradition by utilizing masculine terminology to denote God, Christ, and the Holy Spirit. In addition, the term "Son of God" is consistently used to denote both Christ (our spiritual Self that God created) as well as the separated self (the ego) asleep within the dream.[2] However, the Course's message clearly transcends sectarian concerns and, in fact, can be seen as an attempt to correct some of the misconceptions that have held such prominence in Western religious thought for centuries. These misconceptions will be discussed later in this book. They include:

1) the belief in the sacredness of physical life because God created it, as well as in the sacredness of certain places, structures, objects, acts, and persons that sets them apart from other material and behavioral forms; this error of "spiritual specialness" also includes viewing the Bible as the literal Word of God, and the only authentic revelation that has been given to the world.
2) the atonement role of suffering and sacrifice.
3) the exclusive divinity of Jesus.
4) the special place Jews or Christians have in God's plan for salvation.

Thus, in presenting its universal vision within a specific form--i.e., the Judaeo-Christian tradition--we find another reflection of the Course's emphasis on the practical application of its universal principles.

It is my contention that concurrent with the rise and spread of Christianity ran a strong thread of truth, closer to the message of the living Jesus and counter to the orthodox Christian position. The roots of this thread in the Western world are traceable back to Plato and before, and extend through the great Gnostic and Neoplatonic thinkers to the present day, where *A Course in Miracles* is among its clearest and purest exponents. This thread reflects a unified spirit, despite its disparate voices. It is the spirit of a wisdom that recognizes the alienation of living in a world that does not correspond to the pure oneness of God, the voice of one *experiencing* the paradox of the unbridgeable gulf between the perfection of God and His creation, set

---

2. The Course retains the capitalization of "Son" throughout to accentuate the all-inclusive nature of the Sonship, not exclusively identifying it with Jesus.

against the obvious imperfections of this world that are so foreign to one's true Self. And yet it is a voice that sees salvation from this world as possible if not inevitable.

In many ways, therefore, *A Course in Miracles* can be seen as integrating the Platonic, Christian, and Gnostic traditions, while at the same time correcting and extending them through a far more inclusive vision that utilizes the insights of contemporary psychology to support its universal message of salvation. My earlier book, *Forgiveness and Jesus: The Meeting Place of* A Course in Miracles *and Christianity*, dealt with many of the similarities and differences between Christianity and the Course. The current book explores this comparison in greater depth, more specifically focusing on the behavioral implications of the respective positions of these and the Gnostic and Platonic thought systems regarding the origin and nature of the body and the phenomenal world; in other words, how to meet the challenge stated in John's gospel of being in the world yet not of it (Jn 15:19; 17:14,16,18).

Increased light is shed on the differences between Christianity and the Course when the Gnostic stance is considered. The first major attempt to present an alternative to the orthodox view, Christian Gnosticism developed, in part, as a movement *within* the emerging Church to correct what the Gnostics considered the orthodox Church's misunderstandings of the nature of the world and God's relation to it. This most prominent of all Christian "heresies" arose in the first century A.D., flowered in the second century, and was then for all intents and purposes eradicated by the more powerful Church in the fourth, fifth, and sixth centuries when St. Augustine and others sounded the death knell for Manicheism, Christian Gnosticism's virtual last hurrah. *A Course in Miracles* can be seen as a further correction within a larger context of the Holy Spirit's correction--the Atonement-- of our belief in the reality of the separation from God. Indeed, the history of Christianity can be understood in terms of the attempts of all generations, from the first followers of Jesus to the present, to make sense of his life, death, and resurrection, which were the manifest demonstrations of the principle of the Atonement.

Our point of departure is the conviction that *A Course in Miracles* represents the highest level of contemporary spiritual thought and, even more specifically, of Christian thought. The Course alone, of all the explanations that present the meaning and message of Jesus' life, presents a theology--both abstractly *and* practically--that is without contradiction. This book's principal argument, to be developed in the succeeding chapters, is that a theology or philosophy that begins with the premise that this phenomenal world is *in any way* the manifestation of the Will of God, must inevitably fall into the paradoxical trap of placing within the omni-benevolent God an inherent flaw that contains

4

the tendency towards evil, suffering, and death or, at least, a Will that allows it to happen, the traditional Christian theological position. This paradox has been the basic tension underlying the whole Platonic tradition, to which we shall return again and again. We see it not only in Plato, but in the great Neoplatonists--Philo, Origen, Plotinus, and St. Augustine--all of whose work is so decisive in understanding the philosophical and religious thought of the early Christians, orthodox and Gnostic alike.

Therefore, while there is no adequate rational or empirical means for explaining how this world arose--nor does the Course attempt one-- any thought system that concludes that this world is ontologically real, faces the insoluble dilemma noted above. It then must either resort to theological "mysteries" as explanations, or somehow to positing a duality of good and evil within God. On the other hand, American Judaic and Hellenistic scholar David Winston makes an important statement in his introduction to an anthology of Philo's writings, challenging all theorists within the Platonic tradition, from antiquity to the present:

> As a matter of fact, no philosophy that declares the intelligible [spiritual] alone to be real and all else relatively unreal . . . has ever successfully bridged the gap between these two realms (*Philo of Alexandria*, p. 11).

This gap *can* never be bridged by the human mind, limited by its rootedness in the spatial-temporal world. In a panel discussion held at Yale University, Hans Jonas, one of the most distinguished scholars in the field of Gnosticism, responded to a question:

> You say that I have given no answer to the fundamental question of why God was bestirred from his eternal existence into activity. The answer must be that, in the nature of things, there can be no answer to such a primordial query. As Immanuel Kant said, the thought that the Godhead should have rested for aeons and then bestirred itself to the creation of a world staggers the human mind and makes it helpless. . . . we cannot ask why in the first place some part of eternity is no longer eternity or why time began (in Layton, p. 348).

In his excellent study of Plotinus, the French scholar Emile Bréhier poses the same question:

> The intelligible world, in its turn, granting its existence, is explained by the One. But why should the lower stages of reality exist? Why did the One not remain in its solitude, and why did it give birth to an in-

telligible world, and the intelligible world to a soul? Why, in short, do the many proceed from the One? (Bréhier, p. 48)

One of the basic premises of this book is that *A Course in Miracles*, although not bridging this unbridgeable gap, has nonetheless successfully resolved the paradox of the One and the many, eternity and time, without the inherent inconsistencies in attitude, if not theory, that have plagued all Platonists, and have marred the history of Judaism and Christianity from their inception. The Course accomplishes this by presenting its thought system on two basic levels.[3] The first of these is metaphysical, contrasting the spiritual reality of Heaven with the illusory, phenomenal world of the ego. The second, remaining only within this world, contrasts two ways of interpreting what is perceived: the ego's condemnatory judgment of sin vs. the Holy Spirit's vision of a forgiving classroom in which we learn to see all thoughts and actions as either expressing love or calling for it. Thus, the material world is seen as illusory but not evil, serving the Holy Spirit's purpose of correcting *our* purpose in having made it. As is stated in the following passage from the text, which provided this book with its title:

> The body was not made by love. Yet love does not condemn it and can use it lovingly, respecting what the Son of God has made and using it to save him from illusions (text, p. 359).

By declaring the phenomenal universe to be the work of the illusory ego, though *not* inherently evil or sinful, the Course gently resolves the great Platonic paradox of living in an imperfect, visible, and material world, yet knowing of a spiritual world whose Source is perfect and good.

The Gnostic schools of the second century, most especially the Valentinian, recognized the incongruity existing between believing in a God of love who yet was responsible for this imperfect and unloving world. As one Gnostic text comments: "What kind of a God is this?" Joachim of Fiore, a twelfth-century Italian mystic, also observed this seemingly ambivalent nature of God in *The Article of Belief*.

> David the Psalmist says, "Taste and see how sweet the Lord is" (Ps 33:8), but for Paul "It is a fearful thing to fall into the hands of the living God" (Heb 11:31). Since almost every page of scripture proclaims both how lovable and how terrifying God is, it is perfectly right for people to ask how such great opposites can be put together,

---

3. For further discussion of these two levels, *see* my *Forgiveness and Jesus*, pp. 20-24, and *Glossary-Index for* A Course in Miracles, pp. 7-9.

so that a person can rejoice for love's sake in his fear and tremble with dread in the midst of love. But according to scripture, the just and loving God is like fire, for it says: "Hear O Israel, your God is a consuming fire" (Dt 4:24). Why is the fire which so frequently burns homes and whole cities sought out with such eagerness by those trapped in darkness? Why is it so cherished by anyone who has endured real cold? If one and the same material reality can be so loved and feared, why is it that Almighty God in whom we live and move and have our being (Ac 17:28) is not both cherished for his indescribable loveliness and still feared for his transcendent greatness? (In McGinn, p. 112)

Yet the Gnostics, too, fell prey to inconsistencies, as they sought to draw certain practical and moral implications from their metaphysical position: While on the one hand denying the reality of the phenomenal world, they then proceeded psychologically to establish its reality in their minds by making the world the locus of sin. *A Course in Miracles*, then, coming in our sophisticated age of psychology, strips away the inconsistencies, yet retains the metaphysical understanding of the mutually exclusive nature of Heaven and earth.

One of the important stimulants for this book has been the widespread confusion surrounding these teachings of the Course, even though its published history spans only thirteen years (as of this writing). These errors basically reflect the confusion of the two levels of the Course's system--the metaphysical and the practical--and will be taken up in detail in Part III. Suffice it for now, however, to restate that the entire thought system of *A Course in Miracles* rests on the metaphysical teaching that God did not create the phenomenal universe, which was rather part of the ego's defensive war against God. Therefore, all problems and concerns about our world and our bodies are but smokescreens thrown up by the ego to confuse us as to where the true problem is, i.e., in our minds. This non-dualistic view is the foundation for the Course's understanding of forgiveness, and is the primary focus of this book. When seen from this metaphysical perspective, the Course's teachings on the everyday applications of forgiveness and the role of the Holy Spirit in our lives are suddenly transformed in our understanding. We come to recognize that the traditional language of *A Course in Miracles* is a veil that but barely conceals the truly radical teachings that are contained behind the words, and whose truths can be discerned in many of the great thinkers of ages gone by. Thus the Course is like an onion, and its layers of language can be gradually peeled away to reveal the core of its central teaching.

Traditional Christian theologians--Catholic and Protestant alike-- may assert that *A Course in Miracles* is not truly Christian, for indeed it does overturn most of the basic Christian tenets. In fact, in a written communication to me, Father Bede Griffiths--a Benedictine priest from England who has lived in an Indian ashram for over thirty years, devoting himself to bridging the gap between East and West--observed, and correctly so from my point of view, that the Course and biblical Christianity cannot be reconciled. Another prominent Christian thinker, Father Norris Clarke, S.J., a neo-Thomist philosopher, has declared in a filmed interview that even the claim that the Course is a correction for Christianity is unfounded, as correction implies maintaining the basic framework of what is to be corrected. *A Course in Miracles*, as he rightly points out, refutes the very foundation of the traditional Christian framework. Nonetheless, this book holds that because of its logical consistency--from a metaphysical ontology to a practical psychology-- the Course, having Jesus as its source, is the closest we have ever come to knowing the message he brought to the world, the two-thousand-year-old teaching of the Churches notwithstanding.

We shall thus compare the Gnostic position with *A Course in Miracles*, with special reference to the theology of the early Church in its relation to Gnosticism, as well as to its Platonic antecedents and concomitants. To the student of the Course unfamiliar with these philosophical antecedents, such comparison will help clarify the importance of the Course's metaphysical and practical teachings in light of the history of philosophy and theology. It is therefore my hope that the reader of this book will come away with at least three benefits: 1) a fuller understanding of the principles of the Course, especially recognizing the important interface of its metaphysics of an illusory world with the direct implications of this metaphysics for our living in this world under the principle of forgiveness; 2) an awareness of the importance of the Platonic and Neoplatonic traditions--with special emphasis on Plato and Plotinus--which serve as the backdrop for the Course's metaphysical and practical stance; and 3) a newer appreciation of the contribution of the Gnostics towards the development of a Christian theology that does full justice to the teachings of Jesus who loved us as no one else has ever done, and who left to our alien though illusory world the message of forgiveness as the means for accepting his love here on earth, to remember at last the totally transcending love that is our true home.

This book has three parts: Part I is a general introduction for readers coming to this material for the first time. In effect, it presents the essential "cast of characters": the Gnostics, Platonists, and early Christians.

Part II presents a seven-stage myth, which forms the basis for comparing and contrasting the position of Gnosticism and *A Course in Miracles*, with special reference to Platonism and Christianity. This Part, the largest in the book, presents the teachings of these traditions, and comprises as it were the basic data for this study. This Part is divided in half: in Part A each of the seven stages is discussed from the Neoplatonic, Christian, and Gnostic position; in Part B the Course's teachings relating to these stages are presented without pause.

Part III discusses the information presented in Part II, highlighting its bearing on the God-world paradox. This is followed by a discussion of the errors and distortions that have already begun to surface regarding *A Course in Miracles*. These are specifically treated as similar to the Gnostic errors of the early Christian centuries, and also as they are found in the Platonic and Christian traditions.

The Appendix includes the complete text of "The Gospel of Truth," one of the most important of the Gnostic writings, a glossary of technical terms cited in the book, a table of dates, a list of works cited, a selected bibliography, and several indices.

A Note on Theology

A Course in Miracles states that "The world was made as an attack on God" (workbook, p. 403), a statement that succinctly expresses a whole theological point of view, contains within it the seeds of salvation, and reflects one of the crucial consonances of the Course with Gnosticism, albeit in psychologically more sophisticated terms. At the same time, as we have already seen, this statement represents a principal point of divergence from the Judaeo-Christian tradition, not to mention from Platonism and Neoplatonism.

While the Course teaches that "a universal theology is impossible" (manual, p. 73), it is nonetheless true that its thought system most definitely does express a theology, and one which is distinguished from many others. Such distinctions are inevitable in any system of thought, be it economics, psychology, philosophy, or religion. Often people confuse the Course's emphasis on non-judgment with over-looking differences on the level where differences do exist, seeking to blur its distinctions from other thought systems. This enhances none of the systems, and reflects a confusion of the two levels--the meta-physical and the practical--that comprise the Course's theoretical position. The recognition and avoidance of this confusion is central to the basic thesis of this book, and we shall return to it over and over in subsequent chapters.

To state that there are theological (or philosophical) differences between *A Course in Miracles* and other spiritual paths is not to make a judgment based on value or worth, nor to condemn or reject other teachings. Rather, these differences are simply identified. The Course addresses its reader in this regard:

9

> Time has been saved for you because you and your brother are together. This is the special means this course is using to save you time. You are not making use of the course if you insist on using means which have served others well, neglecting what was made for *you* (text, p. 363).

Helen Schucman, the "scribe" of the Course, in the midst of an angry mental outburst against someone she judged to be assuming a spurious spirituality, heard this message from Jesus: "Do not take another's path as your own; but neither should you judge it." The lesson here for all of us is clear. We are asked not to adopt an attitude of "spiritual specialness"--which we shall discuss in more depth in Chapters 8 and 19--which includes the belief that our spiritual path is better than another's. Rather, we are urged to remain non-judgmentally involved with the path we feel is our own. In this regard, a comment need be made about the opening lines of the text of *A Course in Miracles*: "This is a course in miracles. It is a required course." Sometimes incorrectly interpreted to mean that the Course is required for *all* spiritual seekers, these lines originally were meant for Helen Schucman and William Thetford, reminding them that this Course was the better way they had asked for, and thus *for them A Course in Miracles* was required. For the general audience this statement can be understood to mean that if the Course is a person's path it should be followed; however, if it is not a suitable path, another would be found to serve the same purpose.

As the Course says of itself in the manual for teachers:

> This is a manual for a special curriculum, intended for teachers of a special form of the universal course. There are many thousands of other forms, all with the same outcome (manual, p. 3).

In this book, therefore, we are concerned with understanding exactly what this "special curriculum" teaches, and its relationship to earlier forms that share many of the same ideas and goals, yet also present very different means of attaining these goals.

At a workshop I gave on the Course several years ago, I was asked about Mother Teresa, the Albanian nun who was awarded the Nobel Peace prize for her work among the poor in India and the world. The questioner wondered how I reconciled Mother Teresa's guidance from Jesus with his dictation of *A Course in Miracles*. The question specifically centered on the difference between Mother Teresa's path of suffering and sacrifice within the context of the Roman Catholic Church, and the Course, which makes sacrifice central to the ego's thought system and not God's, not to mention the Course's giving no exclusive salvific role to any one religious institution.

Having met Mother Teresa several times, and being very impressed by her sincerity, integrity, and the unmistakable spiritual and peaceful presence that emanated from her, I responded that I did believe Jesus was inspiring her, even though her path, on the level of form, was certainly not in accord with *A Course in Miracles*. Moreover, I had no difficulty in accepting that Jesus would guide certain people one way, and others another. There can be no denying the tremendous effect Mother Teresa has had on the world. For millions of people she has become a symbol of God's love and peace, even among non-Christians or those claiming to be atheists. Similarly, there can be no denying the effect the Course has already had--even though it is still in its infancy--on those who have been exposed to it. It would seem clear that Heaven is indifferent to how people return to it. Thus, its messengers will use whatever means is most effective for those who seek the peace of God. As the Course's companion pamphlet "Psychotherapy" states:

> If healing is an invitation to God [i.e., the Christ in the person] to enter into His Kingdom, what difference does it make how the invitation is written? Does the paper matter, or the ink, or the pen. Or is it he who writes that gives the invitation? God comes to those who would restore His world, for they have found the way to call to Him ("Psychotherapy," p. 6).

A passage in the writings of Mani, the influential Gnostic prophet of the third century whose life and work we shall consider later, expressively states the same idea, using the simile of royal couriers:

> The countries and the tongues to which they are sent are different from one another; the one is not like the other. So it is likewise with the glorious Power which sends out of itself all the Apostles: the revelations and the wisdom which it gives them, it gives them in different forms, that is, one is not like the other, for the tongues to which they are sent do not resemble each other (*Kephalaia* Ch. 154, in Jonas, p. 206n).

All theologies are illusory, since they must use concepts and words which, as the Course states, are ". . . but symbols of symbols. They are thus twice removed from reality" (manual, p. 51). Therefore, according to the Course, they must be unreal since they are "removed from reality." In the end, theologies will disappear when they have served their purpose of leading us to God--in experience, not thought. The Course teaches that its central teaching of forgiveness, too, is illusory, since its purpose is to undo illusions; in Heaven, the only state of truth, forgiveness is unknown for it is not needed. Similarly St. Thomas Aquinas, in the midst of completing the third part of his *Summa* near the end of his life--after writing some forty volumes of theology--had

what most Church historians consider to have been a mystical experience. Unable to continue in his work, he said to a good friend who
sought an explanation for this sudden shift: "All that I have written
seems to me like straw compared to what has now been revealed to
me" (in Weisheipl, p. 322).

If only *one* form of truth were needed in the world, there would be
but one form. The presence of "many thousands" of spiritual paths--
many of which conflict theologically with the others--reflects our need
for multiple pathways in a world of multiplicity. The Course states
further:

> God knows what His Son needs before he asks. He is not at all
> concerned with form, but having given the content [love] it is His Will
> that it be understood. And that suffices. The form adapts itself to
> need; the content is unchanging, as eternal as its Creator (manual, p.
> 79).

The ancient Hindu saying that truth is one but sages know it by many
names reflects this same principle.

Therefore, for our purposes, this discussion of the Course, compared
and contrasted with Platonism, Christianity, and Gnosticism, is meant
to present the Course's position on the world and the body as a distinct
approach and solution to the God-world problem discussed earlier.
The theological tenets of *A Course in Miracles* form the basis for its
whole theory of salvation and, specifically, the meaning and purpose
of forgiveness. When salvation's plan--the Atonement--is complete,
systems of thought fall away. Together, as the united Child of our
Creator, we leave the world of illusion entirely to enter Heaven "and
disappear into the Heart of God" (workbook, p. 469). To help us reach
this goal, however, different paths or theologies are necessary.

Personal Note

In *Forgiveness and Jesus* I began with some autobiographical reflections, ending with my discovery of *A Course in Miracles* in 1973. By way
of introducing the topics to be discussed in the present book, I shall
continue that narrative with my developing interest, subsequent to
that date, in Christian theology and Gnosticism.

Much of my work--therapy and lecturing--in the years immediately
following my introduction to the Course focused on Roman Catholics
in and around New York City. These included priests, members of religious orders, the laity, and religious communities. I was already
developing an interest in Christian thought and scripture, but my
work within the New York Archdiocese made it imperative that I be-

come more familiar with the history and theology of Christianity, not to mention the New Testament, and the interface between them and *A Course in Miracles*. I recognized that such study would help me bridge the gap between orthodox Christian thinking and the Course for those who were coming to the Course from this tradition. As the Course states:

> It would indeed be strange if you were asked to go beyond all symbols of the world, forgetting them forever; yet were asked to take a teaching function. You have need to use the symbols of the world a while. But be you not deceived by them as well. . . . They become but means by which you can communicate in ways the world can understand, but which you recognize is not the unity where true communication can be found (workbook, p. 337).

And from the manual for teachers:

> If you would be heard by those who suffer, you must speak their language (manual, p. 61).

It was during this period that I wrote "Christian Psychology in 'A Course in Miracles.'" This pamphlet attempted to be such a bridge by discussing the many similarities found in both teachings. It did not, however, aim at an exhaustive comparison *or* contrast between the two.

I continued to study, and enlisted the aid of some Catholic friends who were scripture scholars and theologians. Their book recommendations were of great assistance in directing my research. As this process continued, I began to realize, even more than previously, how specifically *A Course in Miracles* was addressing certain important theological issues. Among others, these included the exclusive divinity of Jesus, various sacraments, and the sacrificial theology of the crucifixion. I saw that the Course's choice of language was deliberate as well. Words such as "sin," "sacrifice," "forgiveness," "salvation," "Atonement," "Christ," etc., had been deliberately chosen by Jesus to redefine and correct the more traditional thinking. *Forgiveness and Jesus*, one of the fruits of this period of study, lecturing, and practice of psychotherapy, discussed this aspect of the Course's teaching in more depth.

As the Course and my work in New York Catholic circles became more widespread, so did interest in the Course increase in these circles, both positively and negatively. For some theologians, the Course presented serious problems. In general, these concerns tended to center on the issue of Gnosticism, whose spectre has remained for centuries the reddest of all flags that could be waved in front of someone committed to orthodoxy. The extreme defensiveness I began to encounter when this issue surfaced piqued my curiosity and interest still further, for I recognized that something of importance must be present in the Gnostic material if only because it had aroused such antagonism and resistance in the past, and continued to do so in the present.

As my prior knowledge of Gnosticism was superficial, based primarily on reading Jung for whom the Gnostics held a special attraction, I began to explore the subject for myself. I discovered to my surprise and great interest that indeed the Course and many Gnostic writers shared much in common, most especially the Valentinian understanding that the phenomenal world was inherently illusory--a product of our misthought--and therefore had not been created by God. On the other hand, the differences between these two thought systems were as important as the similarities, notably in the implications for our everyday living that were drawn from the shared metaphysical principles of Gnosticism and *A Course in Miracles*.

I discussed this with interested friends, and one of them, the transpersonal psychologist (and psychiatrist) Roger Walsh, suggested I write an article on the relationship between the Course and Gnosticism. From time to time Roger renewed his suggestion, and I planned to write such an article once I had completed the two books I was working on. These were finally finished by the summer of 1983, and I began to re-read some of the Gnostic literature in preparation for the article. My reading expanded in scope, embracing Plato and the Neoplatonists, and, not atypically, the article rapidly grew in theme and substance into the current book.

This book, consequently, is considerably larger, both in size and scope, than originally planned. Despite its linear arrangement, on another level the book, similar to *A Course in Miracles*, is constructed symphonically. Its major themes are continually presented and re-presented, developed through many forms and variations. This is a demanding book on the reader, not only because of its difficult philosophical material but, even more to the point, because of its underscoring concepts that radically alter how we understand and experience God, our individual selves, and the world. As already indicated, *A Course in Miracles'* true teachings, not always immediately apparent, seem to belie some of its own words. Thus, the material covered in this book serves to substantiate this deeper understanding of the Course, helping the reader recognize its truly profound contribution to the world.

These preliminaries out of the way, we can begin the journey through a veritable treasure-house of philosophical and spiritual gems. In the words of the Viennese conductor Erich Leinsdorf, speaking of first-time listeners to Wagner's great music-drama *Die Walkuere*: "I envy all those yet to make its acquaintance."

Acknowledgments

I am grateful to the many people who have contributed to the birth of this book. Countless friends, too numerous to mention, have over the years provided or recommended books and articles helpful to my research, and I thank them all.

I especially wish to thank Rosemarie LoSasso, formerly Chairperson of the Philosophy Department of Molloy College and now Administrative Director of Publications for the Foundation for "A Course in Miracles," not only for her aid in procuring books and articles otherwise difficult to acquire, but for her invaluable assistance in the various stages of the writing, and the very careful and loving attention she paid to the compilation of the Index and the final preparation of the manuscript.

Finally, I am grateful, as always, to my wife Gloria. The love and dedication she has felt--probably being herself an old Gnostic lover of Jesus--for the theme of this book was an important part of the process-- in spirit and form--of its being written, from its pre-beginnings through the final editing.

PART I

INTRODUCTION

INTRODUCTION TO PART I

Part I has three chapters. The first is a general introduction to Gnosticism, discussing its source material, origins, and characteristics; its four leading figures: Basilides, Marcion, Valentinus, and Mani; and its later history.

The second chapter presents an overview of Platonism, with specific reference to its treatment of the relationship between the spiritual and physical worlds. This chapter begins with the pre-Socratics and continues with Plato, Aristotle, Middle Platonism and Philo, Origen, Plotinus, and St. Augustine.

The third chapter has two sections, the first dealing with the Gnostic (or proto-Gnostic) and anti-Gnostic elements in the New Testament, and the second with a history of the orthodox Church's struggle against what it perceived to be the Gnostic threat and heresy.

Part I thus provides the introductory material for the in-depth discussion in Part II of the Gnostic version of the myth as compared and contrasted to Platonism, orthodox Christianity, and *A Course in Miracles*.

Chapter 1

GNOSTICISM

Primary and Secondary Sources

As interested readers begin to investigate the area of Gnosticism, they are immediately confronted by almost as many theories about what it is, where it originated, and who belongs in its group, as there are scholars debating these questions. These debates, incidentally, have been renewed and greatly stimulated by the 1945 discovery at Nag Hammadi, Egypt (though not published in English until 1977) of a virtually intact monastic library of Gnostic writings. It is beyond the scope of the present book, however, to discuss the issues of origin that scholars have been debating for almost a century. Rather, our concern is with the general philosophical ideas that cluster around a basic system of thought that we can properly call "Gnostic." In this regard, the work of Hans Jonas, specifically his book *The Gnostic Religion*, is perhaps the single best reference for the lay reader to consult. The combination of dispassionate scholarship with passionate interest in the material makes his work both unusual and inspiring. Another recommended general source is *Gnosis* by Kurt Rudolph, a fine updated summary of the Gnostic literature. Elaine Pagels' popular *The Gnostic Gospels* is a somewhat polemic account of the history of the Church-Gnostic conflict in the second century, and lacks an in-depth treatment of what the Gnostics actually believed.

For primary sources there is the aforementioned *Nag Hammadi Library* edited by James Robinson. This unique volume is the culmination of almost three decades of scholarship exercised in the midst of an embarrassing plethora of political and academic intrigue. Robinson's introduction to the book provides some of the background to this strange story, as does Pagels in her book. In what is considered one of our most important contemporary archaeological finds, equaling that of the discovery of the Dead Sea Scrolls at Qumran a little over a year later, the Nag Hammadi library offers us a window to the Gnostic world that had heretofore seemed forever lost to the scholar's gaze.

The library presumably belonged to the monastery founded by St. Pachomius in the Egyptian desert, and was probably buried by some of the monks in the middle of the fourth century A.D. in fear of its discovery and destruction, perhaps by Roman authorities who by this time had become Christian. Since the early Christian Church and its leaders felt extremely threatened by Gnostic teachings, as we shall see later, they were obliged to attack and destroy all Gnostic ideas. A letter has survived from Bishop Athanasius, dating from this period, that warns against the "apocryphal" books of these heretical "seducers," as Church Fathers usually referred to the Gnostics:

> Since, however, we have spoken of the heretics as dead but of ourselves as possessors of the divine writings unto salvation, and since I am afraid that . . . some guileless persons may be led astray from their purity and holiness by the craftiness of certain men and begin thereafter to pay attention to other books, the so-called apocryphal writings, being deceived by their possession of the same names as the genuine books (Athanasius, "Festal Letter" XXXIX, in *NTA* I, p. 59).

Athanasius then lists the "authentic" scriptures of the Old and New Testaments, including the extra-canonical books (the Apocrypha) approved by the Church Fathers. These are contrasted to the apocryphal writings of the Gnostics, which are

> a fabrication of the heretics, who write them down when it pleases them and generously assign to them an early date of composition in order that they may be able to draw upon them as supposedly ancient writings and have in them occasion to deceive the guileless (ibid., pp. 59f).

Some of the Nag Hammadi writings appear to date originally from as early as the second century, and it is presumed that they were recopied in the fourth century. The evident care with which this copying was done attests to the value the monks placed on these manuscripts. The strongly ascetic teachings of these texts suggest that the monks who compiled the library were themselves ascetics, as would be expected from a monastic community of that period. With few exceptions, this library constitutes our only primary source of Christian Gnostic material.

Gnosis: Volume II, edited by Werner Foerster, contains excerpts from the Nag Hammadi library, as well as an excellent collection of Mandean Gnostic texts. Though currently out of print, it is available in certain theological libraries. Primary Manichean Gnostic sources are difficult to come by, but one can consult Robert Haardt's *Gnosis: Character and Testimony*, which offers a small selection of actual Manichean texts, in addition to other Gnostic material. Over 300 Manichean psalms can be found in Allberry's edited and out-of-print collection. *Foester's Gnosis: Volume III* is devoted solely to the Manicheans, but as of this writing has not yet been translated into English.

An excellent reference of secondary sources is *Gnosis: A Selection of Gnostic Texts: Vol. I: Patristic Evidence*, also edited by Foerster. This compendium presents the writings of the heresiologists (nowadays called "heresy hunters") of the early Church, notably Irenaeus, Hippolytus, and Epiphanius, which for centuries have remained the only source for the extensive body of Gnostic literature. Interestingly enough, given the overtly antagonistic stance of these writers toward the group they considered to be heretical children of the devil, the recent discoveries have substantiated much of what these Fathers reported. Unfortunately, both Foerster Volumes I and II are currently out of print.

Origins and Characteristics

Despite recent public interest, Gnosticism remains for most people a relatively unknown area of thought. It has been concealed behind the "Iron Curtain" of ecclesiastic heresy hunters who attacked the Gnostic teachings and teachers, destroying its primary literature and thereby wrapping it in the mysterious veils of the esoteric writings of antiquity, seemingly lost forever. Thus almost all of the actual writings of Basilides, Marcion, and Valentinus, the three great second-century Gnostic teachers, have been destroyed. Gnosticism's ultimate origins are in part shrouded in these veils, and the clearest statement we can make is that it has multiple roots, including Hellenistic, Babylonian, Egyptian, Persian (Iranian), and Judaic elements. As Jonas has pointed out, however, these syncretistic elements do not argue for a strictly composite origin of Gnosticism. Its "autonomous essence" stands beyond the mere combining of these cultural and religious influences.

Two camps of scholars have evolved, centering on the issue whether Gnosticism is essentially a pre-Christian or post-Christian phenomenon. Recent scholarship has still not settled the question of whether one can indeed speak of an authentically pre-Christian Gnosticism. However, even those scholars holding to the belief that there is a pre-Christian Gnostic tradition admit that there is no conclusive empirical evidence for this position. All the extant Gnostic literature comes after the beginning of the Christian era. As we shall see, there are many writings, including parts of the New Testament, that seem to contain Gnostic elements, but in this case the part does not necessarily make the whole, and we must wait for the second century to observe any fully developed Gnostic system. Thus, many of those Gnostic traditions that are non-Christian would seem to postdate Christianity. As some scholars have asserted: non-Christian does not mean pre-Christian. What is important for our purposes, however, is the general Gnostic characteristic--its "autonomous essence"--regardless of its form of expression, whether pre- or post-Christian in origin.

While Gnostic expressions differ widely, we may still attempt a basic summary which, in general, introduces some of the key Gnostic ideas. The chief Gnostic concern is with the soul, the part of our being that has somehow fallen from the heavenly world of light--the Pleroma (meaning fullness)--into an alien world of darkness and materiality in which it is trapped in the body. The soul still retains a spark of the heavenly light, its true Self, which needs to be reawakened by the light of the Pleroma before it can return home. This light is the *gnosis*, or knowledge, brought by the Redeemer, sent by the light into the darkness. (Bultmann, pp. 163-71)

Some of the key differences among Gnostic thought systems center on the mythological treatment of these themes. In addition, the source of the fall divides Gnostic teachings into two principal groups, following Jonas' discussion to which we shall return in Part II. The non-dualistic ("Syrian-Egyptian") school, including Basilides and Valentinus, is basically the more sophisticated of the two groups, and posits the fall as coming from within the Godhead itself. By this is meant the exclusion of any *external* causative agent such as evil or darkness; rather the fall comes from *within* the beings of the Pleroma or, in the words of *A Course in Miracles*, from within the mind of the Sonship. In its more mature form, as in the Valentinian, this school understood the fall in psychological terms. The dualistic ("Iranian") school, of which Manicheism and Mandeanism are the principal exponents, speaks of an inexplicable ontological dualism of coexisting good and evil, light and darkness.

The soul is referred to by the Valentinians as Sophia, from whom eventually comes the material world, a product of her ignorance and error. The world's actual creator (or in the Course's language, mis-creator) is the progeny of Sophia, and is variously called the Demiurge, Ialdabaoth, or other corruptions for the name of the Old Testament God, for whom they are taken to be synonymous. The world is seen as being under the rule of the archons ("rulers") who seek to hold the tiny sparks of light prisoner. The Redeemer--in Christian Gnosticism of course he is Jesus--comes to the world, announces his identity, presents his message to those able to hear it (the Gnostics), who then in turn present it to the world. In time the "saved" return to the Pleroma, while those unredeemed are destroyed in the great conflagration with which the world will end.

Thus we may isolate the two distinguishing characteristics of Gnosticism: 1) the belief in an absolutely transcendental and transmundane God who remains separate and alien from a physical world He did not create; this belief leads to an anti-cosmic attitude wherein the physical world--including the planets and stars--is perceived as evil and sinful, a place in which humanity feels alienated and homeless, imprisoned by the hostile forces of the Demiurge and his archons; 2) a body of revealed truth (*gnosis* or knowledge) that was given only to a select few (the perfect ones, the Gnostics) who would be saved at the end of time, while the remainder of the world would be destroyed.

Three subsidiary characteristics, not common to all Gnostic systems, also directly led to confrontation with the early Church. These, to be treated in Part II-A, are docetism, the resurrection as a non-physical event, and the redeemer myth. Docetism comes from the Greek word meaning "appear," and refers to Jesus' not truly living in the flesh, yet *appearing* to do so. Following from the docetic view, the resurrection was seen not as a physical event (since Jesus was not truly in the body in the first place, a physical resurrection after his *seeming* death would make no sense), but rather as a psychological event that had already occurred for those who truly believed in the message of light; namely, the Gnostics. Finally, the redeemer is sent by God into the world of darkness to retrieve the lost souls. He "puts on the beast" (i.e., the body) to confuse the demonic archons, announces himself ("I am the good shepherd," for example), awakens the sleeping souls and reminds them of their true home. He then presents them with the necessary information (passwords, etc.) to survive the perilous journey past the archons, ascends to Heaven, thus preparing the way for others to follow. These ideas will be presented and re-presented throughout the book, where they shall be discussed in greater depth.

We shall see below that the Gnostic teachings on salvation differ radically from their Greek and orthodox Christian counterparts. Salvation is attained for the Gnostic, not through the pursuit of reason and virtue, nor from the historical revelation present in the incarnational and crucified Jesus, as orthodox Christianity taught, but only through a revealed *gnosis* that awakens knowledge of the innermost Self. The philosophical and orthodox Christian traditions are thus rendered virtually superfluous and irrelevant. We turn now to the four great Gnostic teachers: the second-century Basilides, Marcion, and Valentinus, and the third-century Mani.

The Great Gnostic Schools

Whatever different scholars may maintain are the origins of Christian Gnosticism--pre-Gnostic or proto-Gnostic--none could deny that the emergence of Gnosticism as a fully developed system of thought came in the second century A.D. Of the actual writings of this period, however, practically nothing remains. Until recently, therefore, students of this period were forced to rely almost exclusively on the excerpts and analyses found in the writings of the early Church Fathers, as mentioned above. The history of Gnosticism thus reaches

25

its pinnacle in the second century, where its achievements are dominated by the figures of three of its foremost theologians: Basilides, Marcion, and Valentinus. Of them it can be said that *Basilides* was the first of the great Gnostic teachers, one who saw himself as a Christian theologian. He was considered by Hegel to be one of the most distinguished Gnostic representatives, while Jung thought of him as his spiritual ancestor. *Marcion,* a contemporary of Basilides, without question presented the greatest single danger to the Church of the second century. Placing himself within the Pauline tradition, he attempted to establish his own church, the only Gnostic to have proceeded in this manner until the third-century Mani. *Valentinus* was the founder of the greatest Gnostic school. Having stimulated a long list of distinguished Gnostic teachers, he had by far the largest influence of any Gnostic theologian. The core of his teaching, as we shall see below, remains one of the brightest stars in the classical firmament of metaphysical thought.

Our fourth theologian, *Mani,* comes a century later and is actually in a class by himself. He is the one Gnostic who consciously saw himself as a founder of a world religion, one that would supplant not only Christianity, but Buddhism and Zoroastrianism as well. Some commentators, in fact, classify Manicheism among the world's major religions because of its over-reaching influence, even if it ultimately failed and is no longer extant.

1. Basilides

Of Basilides' life we know practically nothing, not even the years of his birth or death. Although his birthplace remains unknown, it is commonly accepted that he lived in Alexandria under the reign of the Roman emperors Hadrian and Antonius Pius (117-161). Save for a few fragments, nothing remains of his actual writings, which are thought to have included a gospel, an exegesis of some twenty-four books, and a group of psalms. His school seemed to have had little influence outside of Egypt, but lasted at least into the fourth century, where it is mentioned by Epiphanius of Salamis, the notorious fourth-century Church heresiologist. Thus, we are almost entirely at the mercy of Basilides' opponents for information regarding his theology. Moreover, the issue is confounded for the historian by the fact that the two richest patristic sources--Irenaeus and Hippolytus--provide differing accounts of his teachings. It is possible, however, as Rudolph suggests, that both heresiologists are correct. We have already seen that the Gnostics generally were not systematic theologians who rigidly insisted on the truth of their own particular set of dogmas. Thus, their disciples were free to modify, expand, or even refute certain aspects of their teacher's system. Moreover, Basilides' own thinking may have evolved over the years. Thus, the sources used by the second-century Irenaeus and the third-century Hippolytus may reflect differing interpretations of what was never truly one cohesive system anyway.

Irenaeus presents an essentially dualistic ontology, which reflects the influence of Middle Platonism that we shall explore in the next chapter. The Basilidean system begins with the unbegotten Father, from whom emanate six pairs of spiritual powers. From the final pair, Sophia (wisdom) and Dynamis (power), there come 365 heavenly powers (or aeons) to which correspond of course the worldly year. The last of these powers created the world, and their leader, the Jewish God, is called Abraxas. This name is derived from the numerical value of the number 365. Since the Hebrew word for "four" is "Arba," Abraxas may also have etymological roots with the Tetragramaton, the four consonants of God's Name: YHWH. To free His children from the tyranny of Abraxas, who "wished to subject the other nations to his own men, that is, to the Jews," the true Creator-God sent Christ (one of the original six emanations) into the world, manifesting himself in Jesus. In order to fool the world, Jesus, at the time of the crucifixion, substitutes his image for Simon of Cyrene and vice versa. Those who believed that the real Jesus suffered and died on Calvary were thus in error, and worthy of Jesus' derisive laughter as he stood watching from a nearby tree. Only those who knew the truth were saved from the rulers of the world. Irenaeus, writing about the Basilidean Gnostics, states:

> Salvation is for their soul alone; the body is by nature corruptible. He [Basilides] says that even the prophecies themselves came from the rulers who made the world, and that the law in particular came from their chief, him who led the people out of the land of Egypt. They despise things sacrificed to idols and think nothing of them, but enjoy them without any anxiety at all. They also enjoy the other [pagan] festivals.... They also engage in magic, conjuring of the dead, spells, calling up of spirits, and all the other occult practices.... Not many, either, can know these [doctrines], but one in a thousand and two in [ten thousand].[4] They say they are no longer Jews, but not yet Christians; and their secrets must not be uttered at all, but they must keep them concealed by silence (*Adv. haer.* I.24.5-6, in F I, pp. 59-61).

---

4. *See* the interesting numerical parallel in the Mandean version of the Last Judgment found in "The Book of John II," where the Scales judge: "Out of a thousand, one it chooses, one it chooses out of a thousand, two out of ten thousand. It selects and brings up the Souls which are ardent, and show themselves worthy of the Place of Light" (in Haardt, p. 388).

The system of Basilides given in Hippolytus reads differently, and is an essentially monistic theology that is more the exception rather than the rule in Gnostic teaching, and also reflects its Platonic antecedents. Here, the ineffable God deposits a "world-seed" from which emanates the material universe. This emanation has three components, which specifically gives this system its Gnostic flavor and similarities to the account we have in Irenaeus. We find here also the set of three groups that is characteristic of many Gnostic systems, also reflecting its Platonic antecedents. The first is the least dense (containing the most light), and speedily returns to God; the second is only able to return through the help of the Holy Spirit; while the third, the most coarse of the three, must remain below until it is purified.

From the world-seed there also arose the rulers of the stars and the planets, and here we see similarities with the Greek veneration of the cosmos. The other non-dualistic Gnostic systems do not share this "cosmic piety," however. In order to save the third group that is trapped in the material world, the Gospel (Christ) is sent through the layers of the world until it descends upon Jesus, enlightening him. This system then follows the traditional gospel narratives, including the sufferings that befell Jesus' body until he leads the sonship back to its home in the celestial spheres, and order is once again restored.

2. Marcion

To this day, Marcion remains a controversial figure when one attempts to place him within a specific category, for in many ways his teaching stands outside Gnosticism, embracing the more traditional Christian-Pauline theology. Yet, his teaching also shares many of the Gnostic ideas we find in other theologians. Thus, he has as it were a foot in both camps.

The year of Marcion's birth is unknown, though it probably falls toward the end of the first century A.D. He was born in Asia Minor, and supposedly grew up in a Christian environment (one report states that his father was a local bishop). Later on he is said to have taught in the Asia Minor cities of Smyrna and Ephesus, two well-known Gnostic centers of learning. The intervening years are unclear, but it is certain that he was in Rome around 140 where he was involved in a local Christian church. Under the influence of the Syrian Gnostic philosopher Cerdo he finalized his theology, which included the prominent Gnostic idea that the Old Testament Creator God is the enemy of the true God. He presented his views to the Roman synod in 144 but was rejected, and this marks the beginning of Marcion's church. Recorded history fails us from this point, and we know only that Marcion labored to expand his church and promulgate his theology, dying around 160.

Marcion firmly believed that it was his mission to expose the false thinking of the orthodox Church and present the truth of his message. As Nigg has written:

> ... he felt he understood true Christianity, while the acknowledged Church with its corrupted version of Christianity was an assembly of plotters who employed cunning means to undermine truth.... he felt called upon to expose the criminal conspiracy. Unmasking the plotters became the great aim of his life, a task at which he labored with bitter passion (Nigg, pp. 64f).

To solidify the basis for his theology and to strengthen his community of believers, Marcion established a New Testament canon, the first to do so. As did the later Church Fathers, he selected those elements and books that supported his theology, rejecting those which did not. For example, he only admitted a "purified" version of Luke's gospel, excluding all the other gospels. The Old Testament, the book of the Jewish Creator God, was of course rejected outright. As Irenaeus wrote:

> ... Marcion circumcises the gospel according to Luke and takes out everything written about the generation of the Lord [the opening two chapters which establish Jesus' divine and Davidic ancestry], as well as many items about the teaching of the Lord's words in which the Lord is most plainly described as acknowledging the Creator of this universe as his Father. He persuaded his disciples that he himself was more trustworthy than the apostles who transmitted the gospel; but he delivered to them not the gospel but a particle of the gospel. Similarly he abridged the epistles of the apostle Paul, taking out whatever was clearly said by the apostle concerning that God who made the world as well as whatever the apostle taught when he mentioned passages from the prophetic writings which foretell the Lord's coming (*Adv. haer.* I.27.2, in Grant, p. 45).

Paradoxically, then, Marcion taught the literal interpretation of the Old Testament, as opposed to the allegorical interpretations made by some of the Church Fathers such as Clement and Origen who, through their ingenious efforts, sought to reconcile the older texts with the new revelation of Jesus. Thus, Marcion took the biblical words as literally true--the words of the Creator God--yet not from the true God who alone was divine. Ironically, it was Marcion's unorthodox canon that, more than any other influence, pushed Bishop Irenaeus and other Church authorities to establish their own canon and dogma.

Marcion's church did expand, not only to Egypt, Syria, Armenia, and Asia Minor, but into the East as well. He was actively combatted by the Church Fathers, however, who, among other things, denounced him as being the "First-Born of Satan," "the devil's mouthpiece," "a raging beast," and the "mouth of godlessness" (*Adv. haer.* III.3; I.27, in Nigg, pp. 58f). Nonetheless, the church of Marcion survived the persecutions of Rome until the fourth century when the Christianized Roman rulers issued edicts against the Gnostics whom they classified as heretics. Remnants of the Marcion church can be traced beyond this to East Syria and the Orient, but little is heard of them after the fifth century. Finally, it can be seen that the Marcion ecclesiology paved the way for Manicheism, the most organized and powerful of any of the non-orthodox churches. In many instances, moreover, the Marcionites merged with their more successful brothers.

The key element in Marcion's system is the antithesis between what he called the God of the Law and the God of salvation. This latter is the true God, "good" and "strange," whose essence of perfection is totally beyond this world, in which he is unknown. In contrast to Him is the imperfect and despicable God of creation, the Cosmocrator. This is the false God of the Old Testament who created the phenomenal world and rules it through the Law, which is both just and vengeful. It is only the true God who is merciful.

While the juxtaposition of the Law and Goodness is an integral part of Pauline theology, Marcion wreaks havoc on the apostle's system by splitting off the two attributes that Paul saw present in the one God, placing them into two mutually exclusive deities. Thus, this complete denigration of the Old Testament God of the Law and the created world--Marcion sees the world as petty, weak and inconsistent: this "puny cell in its Creator"--is certainly more akin to the Gnostic position. In the words of Tertullian, the second- to third-century Church Father who is our most extensive source of Marcion's teachings: "... turning up their noses the utterly shameless Marcionites take to tearing down the work of the Creator: 'Indeed,' they say, 'a grand production, and worthy of its God, is this world!'" (*Contra Marc.* [= *Adv. Marc.*] I.13, in Jonas, p. 141).

Despite the good God's total lack of involvement in the world, He nonetheless, according to Marcion, sends his son Jesus into the world as savior and redeemer. Marcion thus calls this purely good and merciful One the God of salvation, and Tertullian states about his theology:

> This *one* work suffices *our* God, that he has liberated man by his supreme and superlative goodness, which is to be preferred to all grasshoppers [another instance of Marcion's contempt for the created world] (ibid., I.17, in Jonas, p. 142).

The nineteenth-century German Harnack, the leading scholar of Marcion's work, summarizes Marcion's radical view of the redemption: "He [Jesus] has saved us from the world and its god in order to make us children of a new and alien God" (in Jonas, p. 139).

Marcion believed that Jesus' body was a "phantasm," thus exhibiting characteristics of the docetic strand of Gnosticism. Jesus' crucifixion was ordained by the Creator God, and Marcion did believe, in contrast with Basilides, that the savior died on the cross. Thus, despite his docetic strain, Marcion shared the Pauline view that Jesus "redeemed us from the curse of the Law" (Ga 3:13), purchasing our salvation by his own death. In contradistinction to Paul, however, Marcion held that the "purchase price" of Jesus' blood was not as ransom for our sins, nor was his bloody sacrifice reflective of a vicarious atonement reminiscent of Isaiah's Suffering Servant. Rather, Jesus' death was to cancel out the Creator God's claim to what had been truly his. The crucifixion was, in effect, the "paying off" of the Creator God for the human souls he created. Properly compensated, this Old Testament God released humanity to the true God, who has now rightfully and legally purchased its salvation.

Marcion also taught that Jesus descended into the underworld to save the entrapped souls. Yet, in true Gnostic fashion Jesus releases just those who had been condemned by the Old Testament God, while the "righteous" remain condemned below. Irenaeus reports:

> [Marcion assumes] the role of the devil . . . saying everything contrary to the truth. When the Lord descended to Hades, Cain and those like him, the Sodomites, the Egyptians, and those like them, and in general all the peoples who have walked in every compound of wickedness, were saved by him. . . . But Abel, Enoch, Noah, and the rest of the righteous, and the patriarchs related to Abraham, along with all the prophets and those who pleased God, did not participate in salvation (*Adv. haer.* I.27.3, in Grant, p. 46).

One can well imagine the reaction of the orthodox Church leaders to this clever and polemic reversal of biblical teaching.

Finally, Marcion reflects his Gnostic influences not only in his devaluation of the world and the body, but in the pronounced ascetic implications he drew from such an anti-cosmic theology. As history has shown, this asceticism--in Marcion and other Gnostic teachers--made its way into orthodox ascetic spirituality and the desert monasticism that arose in the fourth and fifth centuries. We shall discuss this asceticism in more depth in Part II-A. However, Marcion departs from the other Gnostics in seeing not only the *body* as alien from God, but the *soul* too. In his system, the soul is derived from the false Creator God and not, as in all other Gnostic systems, from the God of the Pleroma. Thus, both body and soul share in the evil of the Cosmocrator. Unlike other Gnostics who taught that our true home is in God, Marcion held that our home was here in the evil world of the Creator God. As Jonas writes of Marcion's theory:

> He [the true God] does not gather lost children from exile back into their home but freely adopts strangers to take them from their native land of oppression and misery into a new father's house (Jonas, p. 139).

Thus we can see the influence of Paul's teaching that we are adopted sons of God, Jesus being the only true Son (Ga 4:4; Ep 1:5). Humanity is therefore totally corrupt, and can be saved only through the omni-beneficence and mercy of the true God who intervenes by sending Jesus, teaching those with ears to listen to transform their evil souls.

As a final illustration of Marcion's independence from Gnosticism, we find the total lack of any mythological speculation--e.g., no aeons emanating from the Father, a characteristic of almost all other Gnostic systems. He limits himself solely to the biblical narrative and characters. Thus we have in Marcion a strikingly original and independent thinker, who freely borrowed from both traditions--biblical and Gnostic--to fuse his own theology.

3. Valentinus

Valentinus is the third of our second-century Gnostic teachers, and certainly the most influential. As with Basilides and Marcion, little is known biographically of him, although he and his school were preoccupations of the Church Fathers for three centuries. He was born in Egypt, probably around the turn of the second century, and was educated in Alexandria where he embraced Christianity, albeit most likely in a form that was intermingled with Gnostic ideas. Valentinus claimed to have received his teaching from a certain Theudas, not the zealot mentioned in Acts 5:36, but probably, according to scholars, the disciple of Paul mentioned in the apocryphal "Acts of Paul" (NTA II, p. 336). Like his two Gnostic counterparts, Valentinus never saw himself outside the Christian tradition. In fact, though no connection between the two is ever reported, he was studying and teaching in Alexandria roughly at the time that Basilides did. Valentinus then travelled to Rome around 140, the period of Marcion's Roman stay. Valentinus, too, was repudiated as a heretic, yet he was more success-ful in Rome than was Marcion, and remained there for about twenty years where his school apparently flourished. Tertullian wrote that Valentinus had aspirations to the bishopric which, if true, reflects Valentinus' self-estimation as a Christian within the Church. One report states that he remained in Rome until his death around 160; another that he left for Cyprus.

Even the heresiologists were forced to admit his great gifts as teacher and poet. As St. Jerome wrote: "No one can bring a heresy into being unless he is possessed, by nature, of an outstanding intellect and has gifts provided by God. Such a person was Valentinus" (in F I, p. 121). Unfortunately, precious little has remained of his writings, save for some isolated fragments. We are told, however, that his work included sermons, hymns, and letters. Much of his teaching was done orally and, until recently, was available to us solely through the reports of the Church heresiologists. The Nag Hammadi documents substantiate considerably what the Church Fathers have provided, and indicate the wide range of Valentinian teaching. His pupils--such as Ptolemaeus and Heracleon--were obviously comfortable with disagreeing with their mentor, elaborating on and often changing different aspects of the original system.

We shall spend considerable time later discussing the specific components of the Valentinian *Gnosis*, and so will confine ourselves here to a brief outline of the system. It appears that all the Valentinians concurred that the Pleroma (Heaven) consisted of at least fifteen pairs of aeons (worlds) or emanations, of which the first two tetrads or Ogdoad are primary. The Valentinians differed among themselves on whether God was alone before the emanations, or whether the aeons coexisted with Him from the beginning. The final aeon is Sophia (Wisdom), who "falls" through striving to know the Unknown and Unknowable Father, seeking to create like Him. Her error, known as Ignorance, ultimately results in the creation of the material world by the Demiurge, sometimes called Ialdabaoth (the Gnostic corruption for Ya and Sabaoth, Old Testament appellations for God). As in many of the Gnostic systems, Ialdabaoth is characterized by ignorance and arrogance.

The events that follow from Sophia's error occur both within and without the Pleroma. The Valentinians differ here in many of the details, but the following summary of the system, based largely on Rudolph (pp. 320-22), can be taken as representative. In order to restore the disturbance within the Pleroma, created by what is sometimes referred to as Sophia's folly, the Father creates an additional pair of aeons, Christ and the Holy Spirit, who lead the errant Sophia back into harmony. This restored aspect is called the upper Sophia, which becomes separated from the lower Sophia which consists of her original passion to be like her Father. The lower part falls outside the Pleroma and is the object of salvation. Jesus is brought forth as "the perfect fruit of the Pleroma," and is the savior who brings knowledge (the correction for the original ignorance). The Valentinian Jesus corresponds closely to the orthodox view, in that Valentinus taught that Jesus had suffered and died in the flesh.

Finally, there is the Valentinian threefold division of the world, similar to Basilides. From Sophia's passion arises the *hylic*, the material world and the body; from her repentance comes the *psychic*, or the mind; and from the purified Sophia is the *pneuma*, or the spirit. These divisions, which categorize the people of the world, are thus ontologically rooted in the original activity of the Pleroma.

In summary, the Valentinian system renders the fall and redemption of the mythological Sophia as psychological constructs, occurring within the mind. This system is summarized in the sophisticated "formula" found in "The Gospel of Truth":

> Since the deficiency came into being because the Father was not known, therefore when the Father is known, from that moment on the deficiency will no longer exist (GT I.24.28-32, in *NHL*, p. 41).

In Part II we shall consider in greater depth the error of moving from knowledge to ignorance, and the subsequent correction and return to knowledge.

4. Mani

Mani was born in A.D. 216 in Babylonia (southern Mesopotamia) to Persian parents, said to be of noble descent. Mani's early environment was permeated with Gnostic ideas, as his father was a member of a Gnostic baptist sect, the Jewish-Christian Elkesaites, while the Mandeans also constituted an important part of this community. When he was about twelve years old Mani had the first of several visions which eventually led him to oppose these baptist communities, culminating in his expulsion along with his father and two disciples.

While little is known of the details of his later life, Mani quite clearly saw himself as an "apostle of light," called by God to bring His message to the world. In a hymn, Mani describes his apostleship:

> I am a grateful hearer
> who was born in the land of Babylon
> . . . .
> and I am set up at the gate of the truth.
> I am a singer, a hearer,
> who has come from the land of Babylon
> . . . .
> to send forth a call in the world.
> (In Rudolph, p. 330)

Mani began to extend his ministry outside of Persia, himself travelling to India, while his missionaries spread his message to the Western provinces:

> I have (sown) the corn of life . . . from East to West; as you see (my) hope (has) gone towards the East of the world and (all) the regions of the globe [i.e., the West], to the direction of the North and the (South). None of the apostles has ever done this . . . (in Rudolph, p. 330).

Manicheism flourished for a while under favorable Persian rulers, successfully holding off the Zoroastrian priestly caste. However, eventually a new king took the throne who sympathized with the Zoroastrians in their struggle against this insurgent new religion. Mani's attempts to gain this king's favor failed, and he was thrown into prison where he died in 276. As was the custom with heretics, his body was mutilated and put on public display. This was taken by his followers as an example of the martyrdom which preceded his ascension into light. The Manichean church then entered into a difficult period, with persecutions from without and schisms from within storming its citadels. It continued to have its influence, however, for at least another two centuries (St. Augustine, interestingly enough, joined this "teaching of light" in North Africa in the years 373-382) before it began to wane and eventually disappear as a religious form in the sixth century. Its influence continued, however, for centuries to come, extending from China to Spain, leading Jonas to comment that "from the point of view of the history of religions Manicheism is the most important product of Gnosticism" (Jonas, p. 208).

Scholars have commented on the identification Mani probably made between himself and the apostle Thomas, whom legend taught also travelled to India where he was martyred. For Mani, therefore, Thomas acted as a mediating figure between Jesus and himself. The extreme dualism and severe asceticism of "The Acts of Thomas," the early third-century Gnostic text we shall consider in greater detail in Part II-A, were a great influence on Manicheism. In addition, we find the collected sayings of Jesus in "The Gospel of Thomas" quoted in several Manichean sources.

While the Manicheans quoted from the four canonical gospels—there is an extensive quotation by Mani himself of the Matthean parable of "The Last Judgment"—they also availed themselves of the non-canonical Gnostic gospels, including those attributed to Peter, Philip, and Thomas. In addition, there is a gospel reportedly written by Mani himself, "The Living Gospel," which apparently contains the Manichean system as well as perhaps a correction for the canonical gospels. Only two brief fragments of this gospel have survived, however.

Therefore, as with the other Gnostic systems, it is difficult to know exactly what the founder of Manicheism taught. The following summary is based upon Rudolph's distillation (pp. 336-39) of various sources which include some recently discovered original writings, as well as the anti-heretical Church writings of the fourth, fifth, and eighth centuries. The purpose of the summary is to provide a general orientation to the Manichean theology. Later chapters will elaborate on certain aspects of the system.

Mani's theology shares the basic Gnostic dualism that opposes spirit and body, light and darkness, and underscores the salvation of the light from enslavement in the darkness. Mani's emphasis was eminently practical, concentrating on this salvation rather than on cosmological issues. He begins with an ontological duality of light and darkness, good and evil. These coexist from the beginning, a principle different from the basic Valentinian position that saw evil arising from *within* the good.

There is a boundary between these two worlds, which the agitated Darkness eventually penetrates. Called into action against this "invasion," the God of Light responds by creating beings, from whom comes Ormuzd, Primal Man. Ormuzd does battle with the Darkness, is defeated, and leaves his "soul" behind. In response, the God of Light sends the Living Spirit to awaken the sleeping Ormuzd. This action is successful, yet the soul is still imprisoned in the darkness. Thus, the Living Spirit creates the material world from particles of light *and* darkness for the soul's deliverance. (This differs from most Gnostics, yet is similar to Origen's notion that God created the world *after* the fall, as a means--classroom--to return to God.) Next is set in motion what we may call a cosmic ferris wheel, consisting of the zodiac. Herein the trapped particles of light are released and borne above where they are safely deposited in the world of light.

To fight against this activity which would deprive it of the light particles, the Darkness devises a plan to entrap the light still further. This plan involves sexuality which combines the seeds of light and darkness, fertilizes them, and gives rise to the plant and animal kingdoms. The culmination of this plan is the creation of man and woman (Adam and Eve) by two demons chosen by the Darkness. Sex thus serves the specific purpose of ensuring that souls continue to remain trapped in bodies through the process of reproduction. This tactic is now countered by the light's calling on "Jesus Splendor" (a mythological, not the historical figure), who is sent to enlighten man's soul through the knowledge of the light, which is spirit, as opposed to the dark evil of the body. This is the plan of redemption which awaits the awakening of the soul. If this does not occur at death, the soul must return again and again until its final redemption. Humanity, therefore, needs messengers of light to bring this message to it, and these are the great religious prophets of history, beginning with Seth and Noah, including the Old Testament holy men, Buddha, Zoroaster, Jesus, Paul, and then finally Mani who, according to himself, is the consummatory fulfillment of all the past religions. After him there will be no other.

The Manichean church was thus the community of salvation, whose responsibility was to look after the light in the world and purify it of contamination by evil matter. This led to a strong asceticism which, when practiced in the extreme, led to an almost total passivity.

The Fifth Century and Beyond

Having cut off the historical connection with Jesus that the apostolic Church provided through the transmission of the New Testament and the authority of the bishops, the Gnostics were not able to build a popular base of support. In addition, they were not in the main really interested in establishing religious structures with clergy, sacraments, etc., but rather in having schools. Thus they promoted individual expressiveness rather than conformist thinking or behavior, and this was not conducive to building large institutions that met the security needs of the population.

The Gnosticism of the fourth and fifth centuries largely survived through Manicheism, which in time also did not meet the social and religious needs of the people that required a more conservative and popularized gospel. Largely through the efforts of St. Augustine, as we shall see in the next chapter, this Gnostic religion virtually disappeared from history, the victim of persecution and wholesale destruction of its documents. With the demise of Manicheism, ancient Gnosticism died out as well. As Rudolph comments:

> . . . the Christian Church, by adapting to its environment, and by accepting the legitimate concerns of gnostic theology into its consolidating body of doctrine, developed into a forward-looking ideology and community structure, which ultimately made it heir to the religions of antiquity. By avoiding extremes and by transforming the radical traits of the early Christian message into a form acceptable to the world, thus not persisting in mere protest but at the same time accepting the cultural heritage of antiquity, it increasingly reduced the influence of Gnosis until it ultimately, after having been invested with the authority of the state (in the 4th century), succeeded in mobilizing the physical political power against it which the remaining adherents could not resist for any length of time (Rudolph, p. 367).

How one traces Gnosticism from this time on depends on one's definition, and

> it is difficult to prove continuity in any detail, as the connecting links often are "subterranean" channels, or else the relationships are based on reconstructions of the history of ideas which have been undertaken especially in the realm of the history of philosophy (Rudolph, p. 368).

Some scholars have extended the history of Gnosticism to include Boehme, Schelling, Schleiermacher, Hegel, Heine, and Goethe, even Marx, not to mention twentieth-century figures such as Jung and Weil, among many, many others. One source even included Plato, Virgil, Kant, Beethoven, and Schopenhauer as Gnostics, while some modern day writers have attempted to organize esoteric, astrological, and Jungian elements around a medieval or even contemporary Gnosticism. All these have made for more rather than less confusion, for the definition of Gnosticism becomes hopelessly diluted by calling Gnostic almost any philosophical or artistic genius who contains even a twinge of rebelliousness. This radically shifts the focus of Gnosticism, wrenching it from the original definition of the early Christian centuries that gave this ancient tradition its primary identity: a systematized body of thought representing the radically transcendental and transmundane view of God and the human spirit.

For the purposes of this book, therefore, we have adopted the more traditional understanding, which restricts Gnosticism to its classical expression, deriving its primary definition from an anti-cosmic dualism. In this vein the most important heirs are the Bogomils who arose in Bulgaria in the tenth century and obviously owed their debt to Manicheism. The Bogomils penetrated Italy and France in the eleventh century, and metamorphosed into the Cathars and Albigensians. Their neo-Manichean church was finally vanquished by the Inquisition in the fourteenth century. But obviously, as pointed out in the Preface, the Church has never totally shaken itself of what it has always considered to be its greatest threat. Rudolph summarizes the situation of the Church:

> One can almost say that Gnosis followed the Church like a shadow; the Church could never overcome it, its influence had gone too deep. By reason of their common history they remain two--hostile--sisters (Rudolph, p. 368).

The sole exception to this concluding history of Gnosticism is the Mandeans, an extant Gnostic community of approximately 15,000 in Iraq, whose roots date back to the beginnings of Gnosticism. Their origins, if not pre-Christian as claimed by some scholars, certainly date from at least the first century of the Christian era. Thus they can almost be termed an "historical relic." Their strong anti-Jesus, pro-John the Baptist mentality distinguished them from their Christian counterparts, and it has led many scholars to assert that they originally began as an heretical Jewish group who followed the Baptist.

The Mandeans fled Palestine after the Roman destruction of Jerusalem in 70, which the Mandeans believed was divine punishment for the Jewish persecution of their community. They fled further persecution and moved North and East, making their way to what was then northwest Iran, and then on to Baghdad; and it was in Iraq that the Mandeans finally settled and remain to this day. They were constant victims of persecutions, suffering at the hands of the Christians and Moslems, among others.

The Mandeans, therefore, escaped the fate of other Gnostic groups, and a surprisingly large body of Mandean literature is extant, which does not always provide a logical or consistent theoretical presentation of the Mandean theology. It has been the burden of scholars for over a century to make sense of the Mandean corpus, to sift out from the many historical layers of literature what is closest to the Mandean belief system. Basically, the Mandeans (the name means those who know, i.e., Gnostics) fall into the dualistic camp we shall address in Part II-A, of which Mani is the most important figure. In fact, as was mentioned above, Mani had contact with the Mandeans, though with some resultant theological disagreements. We shall draw from their impressive body of literature below.

Chapter 2

PLATO AND THE PLATONIC TRADITION

We have already presented as a key Gnostic belief that God did not create this world. Moreover, in almost all Gnostic teachings the world is seen as inferior or evil. While this world-denigration was revolutionary as far as the Judaeo-Christian milieu in which Gnosticism flourished was concerned, it did have important philosophical antecedents, most especially in the Greek philosophical schools of the preceding centuries. The influence of Plato is so direct in the great Gnostic schools of Alexandria that it is impossible to evaluate them properly without consideration of him and the Platonic tradition. As Rudolph comments:

> In the question of the construction of the world and of theology, the Alexandrine gnosis was an important link in the tradition of Middle Platonism which united early and late Platonism (Rudolph, p. 284).

As was emphasized in the Preface, we are exploring the central philosophical issues of how the perfect unity of the Divine can lead to the imperfect sensory world of multiplicity, and the implications of this "descent" for individuals living in the phenomenal world. A paradox is found in almost all Platonic and Neoplatonic attempts to reconcile the "irreconcilable"--the ontological reality of good and evil, the One and the many, the perfect and imperfect: The material cosmos is good because it emanated from the Godhead, yet the material body, a product of the same emanation, is evil because it imprisons the soul.

These issues, as we shall see, are absolutely central to Gnostic thought, and in this chapter we shall explore some of its Greek philosophical antecedents, as well as its Middle Platonic and Neoplatonic contemporaries. This will lead to greater appreciation of one of the important cultural milieus in which Gnosticism, especially its Valentinian variety, arose. For much of this discussion I am indebted to A. H. Armstrong's *An Introduction to Ancient Philosophy*, which provides a succinct yet cogent overview of the principal themes that run through the cradle of Western philosophy, from the pre-Socratics to St. Augustine.

Pre-Socratics

We begin with Orphism, whose origins trace back to the sixth century B.C.. Information about this movement's beginning--its legendary prophet is Orpheus--is mostly lacking. Among its central teachings is a dualistic view of man--the divine soul and earthly body. Orphism advocated elaborate rites of purification and ascetic norms to free the soul from its prison that it might return to its home in the nonmaterial world. We shall see the influence of Orphism in some of the Gnostic texts and groups witnessed to by the Church Fathers. However, its influence in philosophical history was more directly felt in the rise of Pythagoreanism, and through that movement into Plato.

Pythagoras (*ca.* 571-497), about whom and his teaching very little is known, essentially built upon the Orphic dualism of the soul as divine and good, and the body as an evil prison. The Pythagorean school further elaborated this view by identifying the good with the intellect, and with the order and harmony of the universe. It was the contemplation of the musical harmony of the spheres that liberated the soul (male) from its corporeal prison (female) and returned it to its divine state. The basic Pythagorean question, so Gnostic in its feeling, can be stated thus:

> How may I deliver myself from the body of this death, from the sorrowful weary wheel of mortal existence and become again a god? (Armstrong, p. 1)

The early-fifth-century B.C. Parmenides (dates unknown) taught that all reality is one, immovable and unchanging. He thus placed himself in opposition to his older contemporary Heraclitus, who emphasized perpetual change and conflict as the basic attribute of life. According to Parmenides, this One is undivided yet also limited in that it is contained in the form of a perfect sphere. Anything else that *seems* real is denied and defies the logic of the One. Thus, Parmenides is the first Greek philosopher to posit an unbridgeable gulf between this reality and the material world of appearance, "this strange universal mirage" (Armstrong, p. 14). Some of his successors attempted to bridge this gap by having the One evolve into the many, yet remaining undivided and unchanged. It remained for Plato, however, to develop the more complete philosophical system to account for this "descent."

Plato

Plato's teacher was Socrates (469-399), whose principal focus was not metaphysics--which was left to his illustrious pupil and immediate successor--but rather ethics or, more specifically, the pursuit of virtue or the Good. Socrates' Good was a universal principle, of an unchanging and non-relative nature, and was in sharp contrast to the teachings of his Sophist opponents. One finds this voice of Socrates, incidentally, echoed in *A Course in Miracles*, where the first law of chaos (the ego's laws as opposed to the Holy Spirit's principles of miracles) states that truth is relative (text, p. 455).

Plato (427-348), who was twenty-eight when his teacher was killed, was never able to forgive the rulers and citizens of Athens for Socrates' death through poisoning. This unforgiveness found its way into his philosophy of the State, and the depiction of the world as containing evil seeds which must be expunged. A basic and unresolved dichotomy permeated Plato's work: On the one hand he saw the cosmos as good, if not divine, while on the other hand he could never escape a deep distrust and even hatred for the world of the body. We shall explore this in greater depth as we continue our discussion, for it becomes central to our book's theme of the philosophical and theological attempt to integrate reality and illusion, spirit and the flesh.

Pythagoras' teachings of the eternal reality beyond our senses, and the corporeal imprisonment of the divine soul, were a major influence on Plato. Plato taught that there was a world of Ideas or Forms, perfect and eternal, that transcended the phenomenal world we perceive, and which Ideas are totally independent of the individual minds that seek to know them. These unchanging Ideas are in sharp distinction to what we perceive here in the sensory and imperfect world, where no true knowledge can ever be attained. Moreover, the things of the visible world are the mere reflections or shadows of these perfect Ideas.

There is thus a universal Idea to correspond to every category we perceive here, both material (a bed, tree, etc.) and abstract (justice, virtue, etc.). As Socrates is asked in the *Parmenides*:

> Have you yourself drawn this distinction you speak of and separated apart on the one side forms [abstract ideas] themselves and on the other the [material] things that share in them? Do you believe that there is such a thing as likeness itself apart from the likeness that we possess, and so on with unity and plurality and all the terms? . . . Is there, for example, a form [idea] of rightness or of beauty or of goodness, and of all such things? . . . And again, a form [idea] of man, apart from ourselves and all other men like us. . . . Or a form [idea] of fire or of water? . . . or mud or dirt or any other trivial and undignified objects? . . . Then each thing that partakes receives as its share either the form [idea] as a whole or a part of it? (*Parm.* 130b,131)

The collective grouping of these perfect Ideas (or Forms) is a radiant world, resplendent with beauty.

The source of the Ideas is the Good. Though Plato employs different metaphors that we shall examine later, he nowhere truly defines the Good in any writings that are extant. Near the end of his life, however, it is reported that he delivered a lecture at his Academy in which he stated that the "Good is One," a principle that certainly found its way into the teachings of the great third-century Neoplatonist Plotinus.

The Good is an absolutely transcendent Idea. It is the cause of the world of Ideas, yet is not the cause nor the sustainer of the world of the senses, which for Plato was always there, a given that could never be explained. It is the soul, as it were, that is the mediator between these two worlds. The soul, seen in three descending parts--reason, emotion, and the appetites--must be trained to look past the appearance of the material forms in this world to the perfect Ideas beyond. The soul is immortal and divine, has pre-existed physical birth, and will survive beyond the grave. It must be freed from its attachment to the world of the senses, and sex and death were seen by Plato to be the greatest hindrances to the soul's release as it strives to be re-united with the Good. Plato actually conceived of two aspects to the phenomenal world, the world of the heavenly bodies which he considered to be divine, fixed and unchanging, in great distinction to the lower world of the body which is the seat of change and evil. The soul must become free of this lower attachment, and make its home in the greater world of the cosmos, a divine and living creature.

The pre-existent soul, as we have seen, is totally alien to the shadow world below and, in fact, can never be known through the senses belonging to this lower world, for there is nothing in the world of the body that is like its nature. Incidentally, how the soul became embodied here is never explained by Plato, and there is nothing in his metaphysics, contrary to his Pythagorean forerunners (or Christian and Gnostic successors) that deals with this. It is simply a fact to be reckoned with. The divine world, therefore, can only be known by the soul through a process of remembering (*anamnesis*) its true home while it is imprisoned here. It is this remembering that is the function of reason and education, helping the soul recall its divine origins by recognizing those aspects of this world that "participate" in the divine Ideas. This is discussed in great detail in the sections on education in the *Republic*. What is important here, especially in contrast to Plato's pupil Aristotle, is that the sensory apparatus, despite appearances, is not really involved in attaining knowledge of the Good. The senses are but incidental to the mind's proper perception of the reality that is *beyond* the senses. Plato's famous Allegory of the Cave, which depicts this process, will be discussed in Part II-A.

This bridge between the two worlds--the world of Ideas and that of sense-perception--was of primary concern for Plato. Based on Pythagorean models, his thinking evolved to the belief that the soul was the prime mover of the material universe and was responsible for bringing its warring and discordant parts into harmony with the

higher world of the Ideas. This can be most
cosmogony of the *Timaeus*, one of Plato's last dia

The key figure in the making of the visible wo
who fashions it out of the pre-existing matter, k
Ideas. The Demiurge is also called a god, maker,
it is this last designation that most approximates h
templates the Ideas, and then with the skill of a con
fashions the physical universe from the raw mate
benevolent work, based on a wholly generous per:
out by Armstrong, this Craftsman falls midway l
unpleasantness of the Greek pantheon and the pei
ness of the Judaeo-Christian Creator. This view of
an important preparation for the Greeks' acceptai
message when it was presented to them four cent

It is important for our later discussion of the Gno
see that the Craftsman, though good and just, is n
with the ultimate Good, in which we might otherwi
God. It is from the Good that the world of Ideas e
turn, is "copied" by the Craftsman when he makes t
material substance. Thus the Demiurge-Craftsman
ian Gnostic system, is the creator of "heaven and ea
is *not* the ultimate divine principle, for he is obvious
pattern of the Ideas and by his material.

Of special interest is Plato's understanding of the
sickness in the world. Clearly, they cannot have
pattern of Ideas which are divine and perfect, or
himself, since he is only good. Rather, evil originat
material itself, which can be defined as all that i
universe. Matter, which is constantly changing
found within a space--the Receptacle or Nurse--wh
thrown about by the constant chaotic motion of wh.
which is the task of the Craftsman to harness and p

While Plato certainly placed responsibility for th
with matter, he never specifically identified evil w
stance. Rather, matter was disordered and thus in
order of the Good. From this disorder evil arose. Th
to Pythagoras who did see matter as evil, expres
dualism that was such an important influence or
schools. It was this dualistic thought that held
embodiment of evil that found its way into much of N

Plato hardly shared the later Gnostic denigratio
quite to the contrary. Though making a clear distinc
Good, the world of Ideas, and the visible world--the
place of evil and imperfection--he nonetheless sa

, as it was the product of the Demiurge, the good god. On the
hand, Plato also saw the embodied soul as entrapped in the body
o, foreshadowing Freud, he viewed life as a rehearsal for death.
e *Phaedo* Plato writes that

ιe body provides us with innumerable distortions in the pursuit of
ur necessary sustenance, and any diseases which attack us hinder
ur quest for reality. . . . We are in fact convinced that if we are ever
ɔ have pure knowledge of anything, we must get rid of the body.
. . [and] avoid as much as we can all contact and association with the
ody. . . . keeping ourselves uncontaminated by the follies of the
ody. . . . the corporeal is heavy, oppressive, earthly, and visible. So
he soul which is tainted by its presence is weighed down and
lragged back into the visible world . . . (*Phaedo* 66b-d; 67a; 81c).

ʾlato would not have shared Freud's pessimistic outlook, for he
d people to transcend the phenomenal world and attain the vision
e Good.

s denigration of the body, however, did not lead Plato to advocate
ᴇ of physical purity or extreme asceticism, as did the earlier
ιics and Pythagoreans, or Neoplatonists such as Plotinus. More-
, Plato emphasized, especially in the *Republic*, that the philoso-
-king had as his sacred duty to live in the world, guiding it
ιgh reason to the contemplation of the world of Ideas. This guid-
was more a form of persuasion, just as the Craftsman "per-
ιed" the unstable matter to enter into the best form possible. This
ιuasion comes through education, guiding, and controlling the
r emotions and lusts. On the individual level we again see a
shadowing of Freud's system, wherein the ego had the responsi-
y of harnessing the raw drives of the id.
summary, we may say that Plato did not recognize the inconsis-
y of his position in having the Demiurge create both the higher
ld of the cosmos, seen as divine and therefore real, as well as the
ᴇr and inferior world of the body. Thus, he never truly resolved the
ɔlem of reconciling the perfect, divine cosmos with the imperfect,
ɔle world.

Aristotle

ʾe continue our discussion with the towering figure of Aristotle
-322 B.C.), with apologies for the otherwise scanty space given to
philosophic giant, the intellectual co-equal of his teacher Plato.
ιtrasting Plato with Aristotle helps to clarify still further the essen-

tial Platonic teaching. It was these differences with Plato, not to mention with those who succeeded him as head of the Academy, that led Aristotle eventually to found his own school called the Lyceum. While Aristotle certainly did not disagree with his master regarding the presence of objective universals, he most definitely differed in seeing the relation between these and the specifics of the visible world.

We have seen that Plato's unchanging, perfect, and eternal immaterial Ideas were independent and transcendent of the things of the visible world. These Ideas--all that are truly real--were the only beings capable of being known, and were in sharp distinction to the changing material world which cannot truly be known, for its contents are but reflections of what is real. On the other hand, Aristotle taught that the objects of our physical senses were very real, and through their careful and systematic study one would be led to the unchanging universals. These latter are seen therefore as characteristics of, and immanent in, the visible and real objects. They do not exist separately in a transcendent world.

It is because of this difference that Christians made such a distinction between the two philosophers, seeing Aristotle, understood later through the great theology of St. Thomas Aquinas, as theologically materialistic, while Plato, mediated through the Neoplatonic Greek theologians such as St. Gregory of Nyssa, St. Basil, and the pseudo-Dionysius, as more mystical and spiritual. While it is true that later in his life Plato moved closer to serious study of the phenomenal world, understanding it as mediated through the soul, he nonetheless emphasized the "other-worldly," with an accompanying de-emphasis on the body. This sowed the ascetic seeds for seeing the body as the locus of sin and source of evil. For Aristotle, on the other hand, the spiritual principle was, again, immanent in matter.

These two philosophers likewise differed in their understanding of the soul. For Aristotle the soul was inextricably joined with the body, as it was the soul that established and maintained the body's life. For Plato, as we have seen, the soul was imprisoned in the body, and its pure state, which alone was real, was outside the corporeal. Thus, again, Aristotle opposed Plato's teaching that truth can only be known through the apprehension of the transcendent Ideas, and advocated instead the search for knowledge and truth in this physical world by scientific study mediated through our physical senses. He believed that the specifics of our world were real, and were hardly the shadow forms of Plato's transcending and abstract reality.

The only immaterial substance Aristotle recognized was the Mind, which he called the Unmoved Mover. This notion metamorphosed through the later Christian centuries into God, the uncreated Creator. This Divine Mind, unknowing of anything that is not itself, and eternally active within itself--a single thought ("thinking upon thinking")--nonetheless became an object of love from the heavenly spheres, which initiated the motion that parallels the world's being. Armstrong has summarized this process:

> How, then, does this remote and self-contained being act as the universal first cause of motion? Not by any action on its part, for this would detract from its perfect self-sufficiency. There is, therefore, according to Aristotle, only one way in which it can cause motion, and that is by being an object of love or desire. The first heaven, the sphere of the fixed stars, which seems to be thought of as itself alive and intelligent, desires the absolute perfection of the Unmoved Mover and by reason of its desire imitates that perfection as best it can by moving everlastingly with the most perfect of all motions, that in a circle (Armstrong, pp. 88f).

Thus we find in Aristotle a positive evaluation of the striving for the perfection of the Divine--"the most perfect possible actuality"--that in Valentinian thought became Sophia's error, from which arose all deficiency including the physical universe. The Aristotelian process becomes complicated, however, by the fact that the differing motions of the sun, moon, and the planets led him eventually to postulate fifty-five (!) Unmoved Movers to account for these differences. Though Aristotle never worked this hierarchy through, it would certainly seem from his overall teleology that he would have seen these other Movers as subordinate to or proceeding from the original Unmoved Mover. We find here, as in Plato, the positive evaluation of the divine cosmos--"cosmic piety"--that also found prominence, in sharp distinction from the cosmic denigration of the Gnostics, in Judaeo-Christian thought.

Middle Platonism - Philo

Middle Platonism, whose dates span the first century B.C. to the second century A.D., is the term given to the revival of interest in the philosophy of Plato. It played an important role in the evolution of Christian theology in its early centuries, not to mention its strong influence on Gnostic thought, especially as it evolved in the first and second centuries in Alexandria. While Middle Platonism is not a coherent philosophical system, some basic notions can be isolated that are important for the development of our theme of reconciling the perfect spiritual reality with the world of materiality.

One of the most important elaborations and extensions of Middle Platonic thought was the placing of the divine Ideas *within* the Mind of

God, or the Good, whereas Plato saw these Ideas as outside the Good, though coeternal with it. The Middle Platonic Ideas were thus conceptualized as Thoughts within this Mind. We are not far removed here, incidentally, from *A Course in Miracles*, which sees God's Thoughts as part of His Mind, never having left their Source: The Sons of God--His Thoughts--are Ideas in the Mind of God.

Like Plato, the Platonists of this period maintained the doctrine of the remoteness of this Mind, or Supreme Principle, from the visible world, identifying Mind with Plato's Good. The Mind is transcendent, and has no direct contact with the phenomenal universe, though the Middle Platonists did posit intermediate beings such as the stars and daemons, some of whom were the rulers of the physical universe. In these philosophers, as in Plato, the cosmos or world was considered to be a living being.

For the Middle Platonists, the transcendent Mind, so removed from this world, made the apprehension of such Mind practically an impossibility. Their best hope was to have a fleeting awareness or intuition of this Divine Presence. This is in marked contrast to those who took a more "optimistic" view of Plato, and believed that knowledge of the Good was attainable by those who applied themselves to its pursuit through the proper use of reason. The Middle Platonist belief that only indirect knowledge of God was possible was a primitive forerunner of what has come to be known in the mystical tradition as the "negative theology." This holds that God cannot be truly known by the senses or conceptual thinking, but only through direct mystical experience, which comes through negating all that He is *not*. In the East, this is expressed by the Hindu notion of going to all things in the phenomenal universe saying, "Neti, Neti"--"God is not this, not that." What then remains is God Himself. We shall return to the "negative theology" in Part II.

The leading Middle Platonist was Philo of Alexandria, the first-century Jewish philosopher (*ca.* 20 B.C.-*ca.* A.D. 50) who sought to reconcile biblical and Platonic thought. Following closely this Platonic tradition, Philo contrasted the immaterial soul with the material body, continually urging his readers to see the soul's purpose as separate from the body. Like Plato, however, he did not end up advocating asceticism, but a more moderate approach to life in the body, not too different, as we shall see, from the attitude found in *A Course in Miracles*. Philo thus advised involvement in the world rather than flight from it, and his ideal was the true philosophers (Plato's philosopher-kings) who would be able to transcend the imprisonment of the soul in the body.

Philo shared Plato's teaching that mind (*nous*) is divine, and not inherently part of this lower material world. *Nous* actually is a part of God and can thus transcend this world through the practice of reason.

Inheriting the Platonic tradition that God or the Divine Principle was remote from the phenomenal world, Philo was faced with the dilemma of reconciling this transcendent God with the biblical Creator who not only created the visible world, but remained involved with it. Middle Platonism offered Philo his solution through its doctrine of intermediary powers: The God who rules the world has created it only through divine powers lower than Himself. Thus, by removing God from being the *direct* source of the world, Philo was able to retain the integrity of the Divinity's transcendence and yet maintain the biblical view. He did this, incidentally, by allegorically interpreting the Old Testament, a practice enlarged on by the later Alexandrians Clement and Origen.

While Philo is never strictly consistent in his presentation of the divine intermediaries, he does speak often of the Logos, which is usually identified with the Platonic Ideas: the pattern that God subsequently uses for creation. The Logos then is the divine instrument through which the world is created, as well as later serving as the intermediary through which the purified soul returns to its Creator. The world was created by God out of pre-existent matter, as was anticipated by Plato, although Philo never clarifies the issue of where the matter came from. It does seem clear, however, that matter was not directly created by God, for the Platonic Philo could never have God directly create anything that was inherently disorderly and chaotic, as was the state of matter before it was molded by the Logos. Thus, Philo remains consistent in his Platonic denigration of matter, albeit at times subtly so.

With Philo we have come to the beginnings of the Christian era and the gradual emergence of Gnosticism, which we briefly surveyed in the preceding chapter. We shall leave for the next chapter a discussion of the possible Gnostic and Platonic influences on the New Testament and early patristic writings, and continue our survey with the Neoplatonists.

Origen

We skip two centuries now to the figure of Origen (A.D. 185-254) a Christian theologian who, like Philo, attempted to integrate Platonic thought with his faith. Interestingly enough, even though he attacked the Gnostics, Origen's thinking did not escape the anti-cosmic Gnostic influence of his native Alexandria. Always a devout Christian, he nonetheless avidly pursued studies in Greek philosophy, and evidently studied under Plotinus' teacher Ammonius Saccas. From his youth Origen was recognized as a brilliant scholar, and a reference by Porphyry indicates that Origen even attended a lecture of Plotinus, who felt he had nothing to teach the brilliant Alexandrian (in *Plotinus*, pp. 41, 43).

Origen's Christian-Platonist integration made him a controversial teacher and preacher during his lifetime, and such controversy continued long after his death. Epiphanius, the fourth-century Church Father, spoke of him as "the visionary who far preferred to introduce into life the products of fantasy than the truth" (in Nigg, p. 55), while Abbot Pachomius "testified before the face of God that every man who reads Origen and accepts his writings will fall into the pits of hell," and he advised his monks to take no notice of the "foolish babble" of this blasphemer and apostate (in Nigg, p. 56). Such attack culminated after Origen's death in his denunciation by the sixth-century Second Council led by Justinian. His influence, nonetheless remained strong, especially in the more mystical Greek Fathers such as Gregory of Nyssa. Always ascetic in his practice and teachings, Origen, according to the third-century Eusebius, castrated himself "both to fulfill the Savior's saying (Mt 19:12), and also that he might prevent all suspicion of shameful slander on the part of unbelievers" (in *Origen*, p. 3). Though a prolific writer, especially in his biblical commentaries, few of Origen's writings survived the Church's "book-burning" wars against heresy.

Origen's theology begins, in true Neoplatonic fashion, with an absolutely transcendent and unified God who is beyond time and space. God is immaterial, and Origen emphatically refutes the contention that Heaven is a place where God resides as a body:

> ...no one should allow that God is in a corporeal place, since it would follow that He is Himself corporeal...and He will be thought to be divisible, material and corruptible (*On Prayer* XXIII.3).

> God therefore must not be thought to be any kind of body, nor to exist in a body, but to be a simple intellectual [i.e., spiritual] existence (*On First Principles* I.1.6).

A corporeal God was a scandalous thought for any Platonist, and the immateriality of the Neoplatonic God was extremely influential, as we shall see below, in Augustine's liberation from the Manicheans, whose God lacked the abstract purity found in Neoplatonism.

Origen's theology of the Trinity is an example of Subordinationism, the downward procession of the Son from the Father, and the Holy Spirit from the Son. The Son is basically equated with Plato's Demiurge (with whom Plotinus later equated the Mind), through whom creation of the "rational beings" occurs, a process antedating the onset of time and matter. These "beings" constitute our true identity as a spiritual

Self. Jesus likewise is a rational being, but one who does not fall. Thus he becomes united with the Son (or Logos) who, for Origen, is thus the Mediator between God and creation. Though bound by Catholic doctrine to assert the unity of Father and Son, the Platonist in Origen nonetheless upheld the absolute distinctness of the Father, whose Son is subordinate to Him. Only the Father, according to Origen, has His power extending to all created things, while the power of the Son and the Holy Spirit is limited to rational beings. In his Introduction to *Origen*, Greer summarizes:

> Thus, the Father is archetype with respect to the Word, while the Word is archetype with respect to the rational beings. In this way life and knowledge are radiated from the Father through the Son [and in the Holy Spirit] to the rational beings (*Origen*, p. 11).

It was this notion, among others, that led to Origen's condemnation by the Church. Origen's teaching of the Son's subordination to the Father is reflected in the following quotes from his discussion of prayer and the Agony in the Garden, where Jesus is portrayed as wishing to avoid his impending crucifixion, yet ends up submitting his will to that of the Father:

> Now if we are to take prayer in its most exact sense, perhaps we should not pray to anyone begotten, not even to Christ Himself, but only to the God and Father of all, to whom even our Savior Himself prayed (*On Prayer* XV.1).

> But this was not the Father's will, which was wiser than the Son's will, since He was ordering events by a way and an order beyond what the Savior saw (*Martyrdom* XXIX).

In his *On First Principles* Origen writes:

> But if the Father comprehends all things, and the Son is among all things, it is clear that he comprehends the Son. But someone will inquire whether it is true that God is known by himself in the same way in which he is known by the only-begotten, and he will decide that the saying, "My Father who sent me is greater than I" (Jn 14:24,28), is true in all respects; so that even in his knowledge the Father is greater, and is known more clearly and perfectly by himself than by the Son (*First Princ.* IV.4.8).

Though the rational beings share in God's immateriality, they nonetheless are distinct from Him by their capacity for change. Herein lies the capacity for turning away from God and the Son, Origen's version of original sin. As with all other theologies, including *A Course in Miracles*, Origen does not attempt any true explanation as to how or why this occurred, other than to suggest that its cause was boredom and negligence. Such turning away, however, occurred while the rational beings, or souls, were still disembodied. The physical world was not created until after the fall, when it became necessary as a place where the fallen souls could do penance and make restitution for their sinfulness.

These fallen souls (formerly the rational beings) were then "assigned" to bodies, each according to their state of sin. Even the heavenly bodies were part of this plan, for they too contained sinful spirits. The more dignified bodies--such as the sun, planets, and human beings--belonged to those who had fallen less than those found in "lower" forms of animal and vegetable life. Origen thus can be placed among the Gnostic, Platonic, and Christian views: He did not see the world as evil in itself, as did the Gnostics; but he also did not hold that the world was necessary, as did Plotinus, nor *inherently* good, as did the orthodox Church. In Armstrong's words, Origen believed that "it would have been much better if there had never been any need for it" (Armstrong, p. 173); for him, rather, the world was a classroom in which the fallen souls learn (Plato would have said remember) their true nature and origin.

This notion of souls learning in the classroom of the world, grade by grade, expresses Origen's belief in reincarnation, similar to Plato, wherein souls continue to come into different bodily forms until able to undo their sinful and corporeal natures. Finally, every soul completes the process, and is restored to the original purity and perfection of spirit. Origen made no exceptions to this process of return, and so hell had no place in his system. Here, too, he differs from the Gnostics, who taught that only the true believers--the Gnostics--would be restored to their home in the Pleroma. The remainder would die in the final conflagration.

Being Christian, Origen believed that redemption is brought about only through Jesus and the Church. However, the follower of Jesus must facilitate the process by a life of ascetic withdrawal from the material world and the body--"the earthly tent that hinders us, weighs down the soul, and burdens the thoughtful mind" (*Martyrdom* XLVII)-- and contemplate the truths of the intelligible (spiritual, non-material) world. Martyrdom specifically was encouraged by Origen, who himself suffered torture under the Emperor Decius, not to mention jealousy and condemnation by Church authorities.

Plotinus

In Plotinus we have, after Plato, the most important non-Gnostic figure in our book. He lived in the third century A.D., and was most reticent about his personal life. Porphyry, his pupil and editor, wrote that Plotinus

> seemed ashamed of being in the body. As a result of this state of mind he could never bear to talk about his race or his parents or his native country (in *Plotinus*, p. 3).

Nonetheless, we know that Plotinus was born in Egypt, spent his formative intellectual years in Alexandria, and the last twenty-five years in Rome, where he founded his own school. We can see in Plotinus an almost logical progression of Platonic thought, as it developed from the beginnings of the Academy through the Middle Platonism of Philo to Plotinus' high level of Neoplatonism.

Plotinus is our only true non-Christian critic of the Gnostics from the early centuries A.D., though paradoxically he was within the same Platonic tradition that inspired the great Gnostic teachers. He is certainly the foremost Neoplatonist, and is perhaps the clearest expression of the dilemma that has faced all Platonists from the time of Plato's Academy. This dilemma strikes at the heart of this book, for Plotinus presents a dualistic system which on the one hand clearly denigrates the body as the virtual embodiment of evil, while on the other hand venerates the "higher" cosmos--the celestial spheres--as being divine. Plotinus, ascetic in his teaching and personal practice (in clear distinction to Plato and Philo, for example), was never truly able to bridge the gap between the two worlds of the spiritual and material. Armstrong summarized the situation:

> And we can sometimes detect a conflict . . . between that attitude of respect for the visible world . . . and the sharply other-worldly Pythagorean temper . . . which regards embodiment as an evil, a falling below the highest (Armstrong, p. 195).

The One, the First Principle of Plotinus' Divine Triad (One, Mind, Soul)--best understood vertically, proceeding in descending order-- stands absolutely transcendent of anything else. It thus comes closest to the apophatic, indescribable God of the great Christian mystics, most especially seen in the early Greek Fathers and later in Meister Eckhart. This One is total unity, absolutely perfect and good, what Eckhart termed the Godhead beyond God. This total transcendence of the One is unique in Greek philosophical thought. Interestingly enough, for the orthodox Church has always considered Plotinus to be a pagan, this apophaticism brings Plotinus very close to the more mystical Christian concepts of the God who is the Source of all Being, yet totally different and Other from what has emanated from Him. While the Middle Platonists also spoke of this Principle as transcendent, they nonetheless identified it with the Mind, influenced by Aristotle's notion of the Unmoved Mover. Plotinus, on the other hand, understood the One as non-dualistic, beyond all thought and, in fact, beyond all Being. The One is the Source of the Divine Mind, and subsequently, therefore, of the world of Ideas.

It is from the One, the true and unadulterated reality, that all being is sequentially derived: the Divine Mind (the *Nous*), the Soul, and finally the material world. This process of emanation is inevitable, given the nature of Plotinus' spiritual reality, and is a procession that is eternal and beyond time. However, as we shall see in later chapters, our words, rooted in a temporal and spatial framework, cannot but convey a sequential process. Plotinus wrote:

> Things that are said to have come into being did not just come into being (at a particular moment) but always were and always will be in process of becoming . . . (*Enn.* II.9.3).

To describe this process of necessary emanation, Plotinus uses the metaphor of the radiation of light from the sun, a metaphor which he derived from Plato.

The Divine Mind for Plotinus is the counterpart for Plato's world of Ideas. It is the One-Being, also known as the All (conceptually distinct from the One, which is beyond all being). Within it is the perfect unity of Mind and thought. The Divine Mind is thus the highest level of being, and everything below it in the visible world is only a shadow of this reality. As with Plato, the Soul is the mediating principle between the higher, spiritual world of the Ideas, and the lower, visible world.

Plotinus' Soul has essentially two aspects: the higher and lower. The lower soul emanates from the higher, as the higher Soul has emanated from the Mind, paralleling the emanation of the Mind from the One. This higher or Universal Soul is thus transcendent. Its immanent aspect is the lower soul, which is confined to the body according to the laws of the Universal Soul. The purpose of the lower soul's living in the body, once it has fallen, is to be in a spirit of contemplation beyond the cares and concerns of the material world, re-uniting with the higher or Universal Soul, and eventually to be restored to Its place in the Divine Mind. Plotinus taught that when the soul descends into the body, part of Itself remains in the Mind, and thus the lower soul re-unites with Itself. In Part II-A we shall see this unique idea expressed in the Gnostic notion of the Redeemed Redeemer, part of whose self becomes trapped in the body, requiring its own redemption. Rarely, the Soul may pass beyond the Mind and enjoy the ecstatic union with the One, and this is possible while the lower soul still remains in the body.

Plotinus conceived of this lower soul's activity as being within a dream; only the higher Soul and, of course, the Divine Mind, is awake. The emanations from the sleeping soul are "dead," unable within themselves truly to contemplate the higher realms of being. They are the end-product of the process of emanation and are the lowest on the ladder of being. This is matter as manifest in bodies. Similar to Plato, Plotinus saw matter as a formless darkness, awaiting the activation of the Soul. This darkness is inherently negative, resistant within itself to any change. Thus, Plotinus considered matter to be the source of evil and, in some passages, he describes it as being evil itself.

However, while the basic stuff of matter is evil, the cosmos is most definitely not. Plotinus did concede that the material universe is the lowest form of being, yet he believed that it is nonetheless the best of all possible material universes, and does in fact possess a soul. We shall explore this in Part II-A when we consider Plotinus' diatribe against the Gnostics on the issue of the divinity vs. evilness of the cosmos.

Again, we can denote in Plotinus the basic tension we have already observed. On the one hand, he shared Plato's veneration for the cosmos, as seen for example in the Athenian's *Timaeus*, while on the other hand, Plotinus shared the Pythagorean notion, as did Plato in the *Phaedo*, that being in a body constituted a fall, a descent into evil. Even though Plotinus never clearly articulated that life in a human body was a sin, it was very much a part of his thinking in his later years that the soul found itself in an infra-human body (animal or vegetable) because of its own sinful nature. Embodiment thus became for Plotinus a necessary evil, and one which the truly spiritual would do their best to escape through a life of ascetic detachment from the materiality of the visible world, identifying more and more with the noble being of the intelligible world of the Ideas. Thus, a life of suffering and conflict was inevitable, and it was the fate of the enlightened person--the Sage--to struggle through this inherent tension of physical existence and attain the truth of the spiritual world beyond it.

St. Augustine

The final Neoplatonist to be discussed is St. Augustine, Bishop of Hippo (A.D. 354-430). Augustine is of particular interest for this study, not only for his contribution to our history of the Platonic paradox, but because of his early association and subsequent break with Manicheism. Sometimes known as the Christian Plato he is, along with Origen, the most important example of an orthodox Christian's attempt to integrate Christian doctrine with the Platonic tradition. It was, in fact, to his reading of the Neoplatonists, especially Plotinus with his emphasis on the absolute non-materiality of God, that Augustine attributed his deliverance from the evils of Manichean thought:

> ... after reading those books of the Platonists and being instructed by them to search for incorporeal truth, I clearly saw your [God] invisible things which "are understood by the things that are made." ... I was made certain that you exist, that you are infinite ... that you are truly he who is always the same, with no varied parts and changing movements, and that all other things are from you (*Conf.* 7.20.26).

In the *City of God* Augustine favorably compared the Platonists (Idealists) to the Stoics, Epicureans, and other materialists who

> having their mind enslaved to their body, supposed the principles of all things to be material. ... [they must] give place to the Platonic philosophers who have recognized the true God as the author of all things, the source of the light of truth, and the bountiful bestower of all blessedness (*City of God* 8.5-6).

However, when he discovered the Bible, Augustine keenly felt the absence in pagan thought of the incarnation and redemptive work of Jesus. Nonetheless, he remained positive in his estimation of Plotinus, and compared his and the Neoplatonists' thought to the gold that the children of Israel were allowed to take out of Egypt on their way to the Promised Land.

> I had come to you [God] from among the Gentiles, and I set my mind on that gold which you willed your people to take out of Egypt, for it was yours wherever it was (*Conf.* 7.9.15).

We will specifically focus on Augustine's understanding of the relationship between God and the world, as well as the nature of the soul and the body.

As with Plotinus' One, Augustine's God is beyond all attempts at description. Pure and unlimited Being, He is yet beyond being as we know it in the world. However, the Augustinian God includes not only Plotinus' One, but also his "Second Person" or Divine Mind, for within God dwell all the eternal principles, roughly equivalent to the Platonic Ideas. These Ideas are totally immutable and share God's immutability. Thus, while insisting on the absolute unity of God, Augustine nonetheless does not assume for God the extreme undifferentiated unity of Plotinus' One, which transcends even the divine Ideas.

Crucial to the distinction between the Plotinian and Augustinian First Principle (the Godhead) is that despite his insistence on God as pure Being, Augustine nonetheless also insisted on the personal love of God, a characteristic impossible for the totally impersonal One. This becomes directly relevant in discussing the origin of the material universe. For Plotinus, as we have seen, the cosmos is a natural result of the One's activity of emanation, an act that is inevitable because of what the One is. Augustine, however, does not see the world as inevitable at all, but rather as having come into being as a direct result of God's generosity towards His creations, expressed through the divine love of His Son. Clearly, however, the Christian Augustine is very much in agreement with the non-Christian Plotinus in affirming the essential goodness of the cosmos, and in sharp disagreement with the Gnostic cosmic antipathy:

> Some people read books in order to find God. Yet there is a great book, the very appearance of created things. Look above you; look below you! Note it; read it! God, whom you wish to find, never wrote that book with ink. Instead, He set before your eyes the things that He had made. Can you ask for a louder voice than that? Why, heaven and earth cry out to you: "God made me!" (*Sermon*, in Bourke, p. 123).

God created the specific things of the material universe by implanting the Ideas on the already planted seeds in matter:

> Lord, you made the world out of formless matter. . . . Out of this unordered and invisible earth, out of this formlessness, out of this almost-nothing, you made all things, of which this mutable world stands firm (*Conf.* 12.8.8).

Moreover, matter is inherently good because it comes from God, as must be everything in the universe. Evil, on the other hand, is not an inherent property of matter, as is expressed, albeit at times indirectly, in Platonic thought. Rather, evil is defined by Augustine as the absence of good, which should be present in all creation. Moral evil, however, is an imperfection introduced by the free choice of the soul. It is this proclivity towards evil or sin that must be transcended by humanity if it is to remember its Source. Thus, Augustine, as did his Platonic predecessors, urged the transcendence of the physical world, not only of the evil tendencies of the soul.

Creation thus is the outpouring of God's love through Jesus, and His love can be truly known only through the Trinity--Father, Son, Holy

Spirit--three Persons in one. Further, this knowledge of the Trinity can come only through the grace of God, one of the pillars of Augustinian teaching. The doctrine of grace emphasized the insufficiency and helplessness of fallen humanity to redeem itself, a belief that Augustine strongly upheld against the Pelagian "heresy" that God is generally not necessary for salvation. Before the fall, for Augustine, individuals were as God created them to be. After Adam's sin this innate perfection became thoroughly corrupted, and could only be undone through the active love and grace of God and the redemptive work of Jesus, His Son.

Augustine's position is in marked contrast to the Plotinian insistence of knowing the One only through the negation and transcendence of all else, *including* the Divine Mind. Plotinus shared the basic belief of Greek antiquity that the person of reason, through the consistent pursuit of virtue and a life of purity, could in fact attain the vision of truth and even ascend to the experience of the ultimate union with the One. In one passage, which can perhaps be taken as an allusion to Christianity (his only one), Plotinus criticizes the notion of vicarious salvation wherein Jesus is sent by God to die so that humanity is saved:

> But it is not lawful for those who have become wicked to demand others to be their saviors and to sacrifice themselves in answer to their prayers, nor furthermore, to require gods to direct their affairs in detail, laying aside their own life . . . (*Enn.* III.2.9).

The Gnostics in this respect are closer to the traditional Christian stance than the Greek philosophers, since they emphasized the necessity for reception of the divine *gnosis* (revelation) for redemption from the material world.

The soul for Augustine, as for his Platonic predecessors, is essentially independent of the body. However, unlike the soul for Plato and Plotinus, the Augustinian soul is not divine, although it is defined as a spiritual substance, a "trace" of the reality of the Idea, an image of God. It is an active spiritual essence that is used by the Creator for the ruling of the body, yet in its essence is totally unaffected by the body. The body is used as the means whereby the soul can correct its fallen nature and return to the vision and experience of God: ". . . is it not so fashioned, as to indicate that it was made for the service of a reasonable soul?" (*City of God* 22.24.24). Nonetheless, the body is perceived as an impediment to spiritual progress, as is seen in this passage reminiscent of Plato's *Phaedo*:

> I was borne up to you [God] by your beauty, but soon I was borne down from you by my own weight. . . . This weight was carnal

custom.... "For the corruptible body is a load upon the soul, and the earthly habitation presses down upon the mind that muses upon many things" (Ws 9:15) (*Conf.* 7.17.23).

Thus we find in Augustine the basic Platonic tension of seeing the material world as good because it was created by God, and yet emphasizing, if not the evil nature of matter, certainly the urgent need to leave the world and the body to strive for the truth of the inner reality of spirit. Like Plotinus before him, Augustine conceived that continually choosing sin was a choice for the lower reality of the visible world, against ascending to the higher truth of the intelligible and spiritual world of God. The Mind of Jesus Christ remains the only source of truth in our minds while we are here in the world. The light of this truth shines into our minds and illuminates them, freeing them from the shackles of sin that bind us to the body. Parallel to Plato's notion of *anamnesis*, the soul "remembers" where it came from and where it belongs. The crucial difference, again, is that this remembrance for Augustine cannot occur without divine grace, which allows humanity to exercise its free will on behalf of God, and turn away from sin.

Chapter 3

GNOSTICISM AND THE EARLY CHURCH

First Century: New Testament

Much scholarly blood has been shed on the issue of Gnostic elements in the New Testament, for it is one of the more controversial and contested issues in contemporary scripture scholarship. While a detailed examination of this issue would be beyond the scope of this book, some comment is necessary in this historical overview.

Rudolph Bultmann contended that the New Testament was basically an adaptation of pre-Christian Gnostic ideas, leading him to see Gnostic elements all through the New Testament, especially in John and Paul:

> . . . it [is] abundantly clear that it [Gnosticism] was really a religious movement of pre-Christian origin, invading the West from the Orient as a competitor of Christianity. . . . All its forms, its mythology and theology, arise from a definite attitude to life and an interpretation of human existence derived therefrom. In general, we may call it a redemptive religion based on dualism.[5] This is what gives it an affinity to Christianity. . . . Consequently, Gnosticism and Christianity have affected each other in a number of different directions, from the earliest days of the Christian movement (Bultmann, p. 162; *see also* pp. 193-95).

While Bultmann's highly influential thesis has fallen out of favor with recent scholars, it nonetheless continues to stimulate tremendous research in this area. The interested reader may consult Rudolph, pp. 299-307, and Yamauchi, pp. 13-55, 190-99, for a more thorough discussion of this topic from opposing points of view. Rudolph, whose views are heavily influenced by Bultmann and his school, has summarized this position:

> The process which is plain from the New Testament itself is twofold, the Christianizing of Gnosis and the gnosticizing of Christianity. The result of both processes is the canonizing of Christianity as an orthodox Church on the one hand, and the elimination of Gnosis as a heresy on the other (Rudolph, p. 300).

However, Simone Pétrement's summation may be taken to reflect the general scholarly consensus:

---

5. *See below*, pp. 111ff; *see also* Appendix: Glossary.

> No decisive proof of the non-Christian origins of Gnosticism has yet
> been found in the New Testament, in the Nag Hammadi library, or
> in any other source. No Gnostic text has been discovered which was
> certainly, or even probably, written before the emergence of Christi-
> anity (Pétrement, "Sur le problème du gnosticisme," in Hanratty, p.
> 218).

We must also keep in mind that the New Testament as we have it
today is the end product of a long period of the Church's rejecting,
selecting from, and editing of, the many gospels and epistles that
sprang forth during the first and second centuries. Thus, what remains
is a decidedly biased sample of the texts of that period. Since many of
these rejected texts (and portions of texts) were destroyed, scholars
can only work with what evidence is available, both primary as well as
subjective secondary sources.

As scholars have cautioned, we must not jump to conclusions based
on scriptural terminology that later on became more specifically
focused as Gnostic. In the first century, the best we can speak of is a
pre-, proto-, or incipient Gnosticism, but hardly any developed Gnostic theology or community. The later polemicized polarity between the
orthodox and Gnostic Christians was non-existent earlier, and there
was instead a cross-fertilization that did find fruits in the New Testament, notably in the epistles and the Johannine writings. Therefore,
opponents of the Bultmannian position warn against inferring Gnostic
teachings from language that suggests Gnostic thought, such as the
Essene and Platonic, but is not exclusive to Gnosticism itself. Dissident
or heterodox elements only later focalized in the second century into
what we now call Gnosticism. In *Gnosis and the New Testament*, Scottish
scholar R. McL. Wilson states that

> ... we need to pay greater attention to questions of chronology, for
> sometimes it would appear that scholars have formulated a synthesis
> on the basis of second or third century sources, and have then
> proceeded to force the New Testament writings into the resultant
> mold, on the assumption that the hypothetical pre-Christian gnosis
> which they postulate was identical with their reconstruction from the
> later documents. ... To sum up: the problems of Gnosticism, and in
> particular the problem of Gnostic origins, are more complex than is
> sometimes recognized. Particular motifs and concepts can be traced
> far back into the pre-Christian period, but it is not clear that such
> motifs can be truly classed as Gnostic except in the context of the
> developed Gnostic systems. Attempts to derive the whole movement
> from any single source comes to grief (Wilson, pp. 9,143).

Thus, most scholars today would agree that there did exist what we may call a proto-Gnosticism, to be distinguished from the more fully developed schools of the second century. These Gnostic elements in the early decades of Christianity (extending into the second century), regardless of their origin, began to become expressed *within* the emerging churches, so that at times it would be difficult to know where one ended and the other began. Yet these remain only Gnostic tendencies. There are, for example, no instances of the denigration of the Old Testament Creator God that is so common in later Gnostic teachings, and certainly nothing that denies this God His role as Creator of the world. This fact, in and of itself, would mitigate against speaking of a genuine New Testament Gnosticism. Nonetheless, we can certainly see the battle lines beginning to form in the later New Testament writings.

New Testament evidence for the influence of proto-Gnostic ideas can therefore be grouped into two basic categories: those texts which reflect proto-Gnostic elements, and those which specifically refute these elements. We shall treat the Johannine writings (the gospel and epistles of John) separately, as they reflect a different stance regarding the Gnostics.

1. Proto-Gnostic Elements in the New Testament (Non-Johannine)

The earliest Christian witness is St. Paul (*ca.* 10-67), in whom we find (as well as in the later letters falsely attributed to him, though belonging to his school) not only opposition to the Gnostic influences he felt were contaminating his churches, but also great sympathy for many ideas later embraced by the Gnostics. These ideas included: 1) the antipathy of the powers of light and darkness, the true God versus the god of the world; 2) the anti-corporeal dualism of flesh and spirit; and 3) the redeemer Christ who descends from Heaven, delivers the world from the powers of evil, and finally ascends back to God uniting all believers. We first examine the evidence in the authentic Pauline letters: Romans, Corinthians, Galatians, Philippians, and Thessalonians.

1) In Second Corinthians Paul warns against the "god of this world," whom the later Gnostics termed the Demiurge or Ialdabaoth:

> If our gospel does not penetrate the veil, then the veil is on those who are not on the way to salvation; the unbelievers whose minds the god of this world has blinded, to stop them seeing the light shed by the Good News of the glory of Christ, who is the image of God (2 Co 4:3f).

63

In Galatians Paul equates this world god (*not* the Creator God, as in Gnosticism) with the Law, whose purpose is to rule and judge in the world, acting through intermediate figures. These angelic figures, though not perceived by Paul as evil, are nonetheless considered inferior to the supreme God, the Father of Jesus. Here, by the way, we find ourselves in the philosophical world of Middle Platonism, with which Paul was certainly familiar:

> What then was the purpose of adding the Law? This was done to specify crimes, until the posterity came to whom the promise was addressed. The Law was promulgated by angels, assisted by an intermediary. Now there can only be an intermediary between two parties, yet God is one. . . . The Law was to be our guardian until the Christ came and we could be justified by faith. Now that that time has come we are no longer under that guardian, and you are, all of you, sons of God through faith in Christ Jesus. . . . Now before we came of age we were as good as slaves to the elemental principles of this world. . . . Once you were ignorant of God, and enslaved to "gods" who are not really gods at all; but now that you have come to acknowledge God--or rather, now that God has acknowledged you-- how can you want to go back to elemental things like these, that can do nothing and give nothing, and be their slaves? (Ga 3:19-27; 4:3-9).

The world is seen as the realm of darkness, while Jesus came from Heaven with the light. Darkness and light are irreconcilable enemies and we are urged to become sons of light and spirit, renouncing the unspiritual darkness, a theme we also find prominently expressed in the Essene literature. Some Pauline examples are:

> But it is not as if you live in the dark, my brothers, for that Day to overtake you like a thief. No, you are all sons of light and sons of the day: we do not belong to the night or to darkness, so we should not go on sleeping, as everyone else does, but stay wide awake and sober. Night is the time for sleepers to sleep and drunkards to be drunk, but we belong to the day and we should be sober (1 Th 5:4-8).

> . . . you know "the time" has come: you must wake up now: our salvation is even nearer than it was when we were converted. The night is almost over, it will be daylight soon--let us give up all the things we prefer to do under cover of the dark; let us arm ourselves and appear in the light (Rm 13:11f).

2) The issue of the world is obviously an ambivalent one for Paul, and there are many passages in which his antipathy for the flesh adumbrate the later Gnostic denigration of the material world.

... flesh and blood cannot inherit the kingdom of God: and the perishable cannot inherit what lasts for ever (1 Co 15:50).

We are always full of confidence, then, when we remember that to live in the body means to be exiled from the Lord, going as we do by faith and not by sight—we are full of confidence, I say, and actually want to be exiled from the body and make our home with the Lord (2 Co 5:6-8).

In First Corinthians Paul cautions against marriage as being, in effect, a waste of time for one focused only on God:

I would like to see you free from all worry. An unmarried man can devote himself to the Lord's affairs, all he need worry about is pleasing the Lord; but a married man has to bother about the world's affairs and devote himself to pleasing his wife. . . . [likewise with an unmarried woman] (1 Co 7:32-34).

Sex, too, is considered a dangerous distraction:

Yes, it is a good thing for a man not to touch a woman; but since sex is always a danger, let each man have his own wife and each woman her own husband. . . . This is a suggestion, not a rule: I should like everyone to be like me [i.e., celibate], but everybody has his own particular gifts from God. . . . There is something I want to add for the sake of widows and those who are not married: it is a good thing for them to stay as they are, like me, but if they cannot control the sexual urges, they should get married, since it is better to be married than to be tortured (1 Co 7:1-9).

3) Finally, we see in Paul an emphasis on the heavenly Christ as opposed to the earthly Jesus, an emphasis that foreshadows the Johannine Christ, and in turn anticipates some of the second-century Gnostic teachings (*see* Bultmann's Redeemer Myth, Yamauchi, pp. 29f). Paul's Christology reflects a mid-point between the "low" Christology of the Synoptic gospels (Matthew, Mark, Luke) and the "high" Christology of the Fourth Gospel (John), whose Christ (Logos) is pre-existent with the Father. Paul writes to the Corinthians:

... still for us there is one God, the Father, from whom all things come and for whom we exist; and there is one Lord, Jesus Christ, through whom all things come and through whom we exist. . . . The first man, Adam, as scripture says, became a living soul; but the last Adam [Jesus] has become a life-giving spirit. The first man, being from the earth, is earthly by nature; the second man is from heaven. As this earthly man was, so are we on earth; and as the heavenly man is, so are we in heaven. And we, who have been modeled on the earthly man, will be modeled on the heavenly man (1 Co 8:6; 15:45-49).

The famous Philippian hymn, probably taken by Paul from an unknown source, poetically summarizes this Pauline view of the cosmic Christ:

His state was divine, yet he did not cling to his equality with God but emptied himself to assume the condition of a slave, and became as men are; and being as all men are, he was humbler yet, even to accepting death, death on a cross. But God raised him high and gave him the name which is above all other names so that all beings in the heavens, on earth and in the underworld, should bend the knee at the name of Jesus and that every tongue should acclaim Jesus Christ as Lord, to the glory of God the Father (Ph 2:6-11).

The post-Pauline letters of Colossians and Ephesians (*ca.* 80) also reflect the influence of these proto-Gnostic ideas. In Colossians we have the interesting example of "Paul" combating a heresy which seems to have been an early form of Jewish Gnostic asceticism, while at the same time utilizing ideas and language that have much in common with an incipient Gnosticism. The Colossians are warned:

Make sure that no one traps you and deprives you of your freedom by some secondhand, empty, rational philosophy based on the principles of this world instead of on Christ.... Do not be taken in by people who like grovelling to angels and worshipping them; people like that are always going on about some vision they have had, inflating themselves to a false importance with their worldly outlook. ... It may be argued that true wisdom is to be found in these, with their self-imposed devotions, their self-abasement, and their severe treatment of the body; but once the flesh starts to protest, they are no use at all (Col 2:8,18,23).

Käsemann has commented:

We thus arrive at the peculiar fact that heresy in Colossians is combatted by a confession of faith, the formulation of which has itself been very strongly conditioned by heterodox views (in Yamauchi, p. 45).

On the other hand, in the hymn in Colossians we find the cosmic Christ who is "the image of the unseen God and first-born of all creation, for in him were created all things in heaven and on earth..." (Col 1:15f), and who, suggestive of Gnostic dualism--perhaps as Rudolph suggests, an example of the Christianizing of Gnostic ideas--

overturns the powers of darkness, leading us to abandon the flesh and the Law:

> He [Christ] has overridden the Law, and canceled every record of the debt that we had to pay; he has done away with it by nailing it to the cross; and so he got rid of the Sovereignties and the Powers. . . . Let your thoughts be on heavenly things, not on the things that are on the earth. . . . That is why you must kill everything in you that belongs only to earthly life: fornication, impurity, guilty passion, evil desires and especially greed. . . all this is the sort of behavior that makes God angry. . . . You have stripped off your old behavior with your old self, and you have put on a new self which will progress toward true knowledge the more it is renewed in the image of its creator. . . (Col 2:14f; 3:2,5f,9f).

In Ephesians we find reference to themes--light and darkness, awakening from the sleep of the dead--we found in the earlier epistles:

> You were darkness once, but now you are light in the Lord; be like children of light. . . . Try to discover what the Lord wants of you, having nothing to do with the futile works of darkness but exposing them by contrast. . . . Wake up from your sleep, rise from the dead, and Christ will shine on you (Ep 5:8,10f,14).

We also find here allusions to the cosmic Christ who freed the world from the divisions created by the Law. He is the head of the Church, to which he is joined. The following are some representative passages:

> But now in Christ Jesus, you [the pagans] that used to be so far apart from us have been brought very close, by the blood of Christ. For he is the peace between us, and has made the two into one and broken down the barrier which used to keep them apart, actually destroying in his own person the hostility caused by the rules and decrees of the Law. This was to create one single New Man in himself out of the two of them. . . to unite them both in a single Body and reconcile them with God. . . . When it says, "he ascended," what can it mean if not that he descended right down to the lower regions of the earth. The one who rose higher than all the heavens to fill all things is none other than the one who descended. . . . who is the head, by whom the whole body [of Christ] is fitted and joined together. . . (Ep 2:13-16; 4:9f,15f).

2. Anti-Gnostic Elements in the New Testament (Non-Johannine)

We come now to texts that refute the dissident voices in the churches; voices that contained proto-Gnostic elements in the earlier epistles, and a more pronounced and specific Gnosis in the later ones. One may infer that these proto-Gnostic elements were in Paul's mind when he issued this warning to the elders of the church of Ephesus while in Miletus, as reported by Luke in the Acts of the Apostles, writing around A.D. 80:

> Be on your guard for yourselves and for all the flock of which the Holy Spirit has made you the overseers. . . . I know quite well that when I have gone fierce wolves will invade you and will have no mercy on the flock. Even from your own ranks there will be men coming forward with a travesty of the truth on their lips to induce the disciples to follow them (Ac 20:28-30).

In fact, Paul's letters are replete with denunciations and warnings against what he considered to be false doctrines. The clearest example comes in Paul's letters to the people of Corinth, which seemed to be a stronghold of what appears to have been proto-Gnostic teachings and practices. As the American scholar R. M. Grant has written:

> Though the ability of modern scholars to recover Paul's opponents' ideas may be over-estimated, it would appear that a movement like the one which later became Gnosticism was probably present in Corinth (Grant, p. 157).

The following statement in Chapter 2 of Paul's first letter to the Corinthians could very likely be aimed against those proto-Gnostics who believed "hidden wisdom" was the truth:

> As for me, brothers, when I came to you, it was not with any show of oratory or philosophy. . . . During my stay with you, the only knowledge I claimed to have was about Jesus. . . . The hidden wisdom of God which we teach in our mysteries is the wisdom. . . that none of the masters of this age have ever known. . . . Therefore we teach, not in the way in which philosophy is taught, but in the way that the Spirit teaches us: we teach spiritual things spiritually (1 Co 2:1f,7f,13).

In Chapters 10 and 11 of the second letter to the Corinthians, Paul defends himself against enemies who could include these proto-Gnostic groups, presumably of Jewish origin (11:22).

> We demolish sophistries, and the arrogance that tries to resist the knowledge of God. . . . Face plain facts. Anybody who is convinced that he belongs to Christ must go on to reflect that we all belong to Christ no less than he does. . . . I am afraid that. . . your ideas may get corrupted and turned away from simple devotion to Christ. Because any newcomer has only to proclaim a new Jesus, different from the one that we preached. . . and you welcome it with open arms. As far

as I can tell, these arch-apostles have nothing more than I have. . . . These people are counterfeit apostles. . . disguised as apostles of Christ. . . . Hebrews, are they? So am I. Israelites? So am I. Descendants of Abraham? So am I (2 Co 10:4,7; 11:3-5,13,22).

As we have seen, one Gnostic strand was docetism, the belief that Jesus never truly inhabited a body, though he *appeared* to. Thus, the cosmic or spiritual Jesus was sometimes emphasized at the expense of the earthly man. It likely is this incipient docetism that Paul observed in Corinth:

> I want you to understand that on the one hand no one can be speaking under the influence of the Holy Spirit and say, "Curse Jesus" [i.e., the earthly Jesus], and on the other hand, no one can say, "Jesus is Lord," unless he is under the influence of the Holy Spirit (1 Co 12:3).

Some of the later Gnostic schools taught that the resurrection has *already* occurred in us with the acquisition of knowledge, and is not to be exclusively identified with the corporeal resurrection of Jesus. This teaching seems to have made its way into the Corinth community, as witness to Paul's emphasis on the actual resurrection of Jesus and our *future* resurrection:

> Now if Christ raised from the dead is what has been preached, how can some of you be saying that there is no resurrection of the dead? If there is no resurrection of the dead, Christ himself cannot have been raised, and if Christ has not been raised then our preaching is useless (1 Co 15:12-14).

> For we know that when the tent [body] that we live in on earth is folded up, there is a house built by God for us, an everlasting home not made by human hands, in the heavens. . . . Yes, we groan and find it a burden being still in this tent, not that we want to strip it off, but to put the second garment over it and to have what must die taken up into life. This is the purpose for which God made us, and he has given us the pledge of the Spirit (2 Co 5:1, 4f).

Finally, in Paul's warnings against the sexual excesses of the Corinthians (1 Co 5:1-13; 6:9,15-20) we find pre-echoes of the patristic concerns with the Gnostic libertines.

In the later canonical writings, coming about the turn of the century, we find the attack on the Gnostics becoming more pointed. These include "Paul's" two letters to Timothy, one to Titus, the letter of Jude, the second letter of "Peter," and Revelation. At this time there were almost definitely Gnostic circles, although the great schools--Basilides, Marcion, Valentinus--were yet to come. Wilson has commented:

> [the] cumulative effect of a number of features shared with the later Gnostics by the opponents attacked in these documents . . . makes us think of an incipient Gnosticism as the heresy in view. But there is nothing . . . to suggest that this incipient Gnosticism had as yet advanced very far in the direction of later developments (Wilson, p. 42).

These teachings were considered a threat to the emerging Christian churches, as is seen in the following excerpts from these epistles. One can hear in these writings the beginning voices of what would emerge several decades later as the "official" Church's denunciation of this "Gnosis, falsely so-called" (1 Tm 6:21). As Rudolph states:

> The process of separation of orthodoxy and heresy, Church and sect, begins to make itself felt; the early Catholic Church declares itself (Rudolph, p. 303).

The "enemy" is clearly identified as Gnostic:

> My dear Timothy, take great care of all that has been entrusted to you. Have nothing to do with the pointless philosophical discussions and antagonistic beliefs of the "knowledge" [gnosis] which is not knowledge at all; by adopting this, some have gone right away from the faith (1 Tm 6:20f).

The authors of these letters continually warn against the dangers of affiliating with these sects, specifically identifying them by their extensive mythologizing, a salient characteristic of many of the later Gnostic schools:

> As I asked you when I was leaving for Macedonia, please stay at Ephesus, to insist that certain people stop teaching strange doctrines and taking notice of endless myths and endless genealogies; these things are only likely to raise irrelevant doubts instead of furthering the designs of God which are revealed in faith (1 Tm 1:3f).

> The time is sure to come when, far from being content with sound teaching, people will be avid for the latest novelty and collect themselves a whole series of teachers according to their own tastes; and then, instead of listening to the truth, they will turn to myths (2 Tm 4:3f).

> So you will have to be severe in correcting them, and make them sound in the faith so that they stop taking notice of Jewish myths and doing what they are told to do by people who are no longer interested in the truth (Tt 1:13f).

Specific teachers are even mentioned:

> Some people have put conscience aside and wrecked their faith in consequence. I mean men like Hymenaeus and Alexander, whom I have handed over to Satan to teach them not to be blasphemous (1 Tm 1:19f).

> Have nothing to do with pointless philosophical discussions—they only lead further and further away from true religion. Talk of this kind corrodes like gangrene, as in the case of Hymenaeus and Philetus, the men who have gone right away from the truth and claim that the resurrection has already taken place. Some people's faith cannot stand up to them (2 Tm 2:16-18).

Aside from the extensive mythologizing of this Jewish-Gnostic sect, another characteristic emerged that outraged the early Christian Church; namely that women played an important role in the community (although this was not always the prevailing Gnostic practice):

> During instruction, a woman should be quiet and respectful. I am not giving permission for a woman to teach or to tell a man what to do. A woman ought not to speak, because Adam was formed first and Eve afterwards, and it was not Adam who was led astray but the woman who was led astray and fell into sin (1 Tm 2:11-15).

This deutero-Pauline argument is modeled after Paul's sexist teaching in Corinth (1 Co 11:3-16), which concludes: "To anyone who might still want to argue: it is not the custom with us, nor in the churches of God."

In Part II-A we shall explore the strict asceticism that ran through many Gnostic groups. Here at the turn of the century we can hear warnings against such practices. Ironically, the Church in the following centuries increasingly adopted the Gnostics' pronounced anti-corporeal stance, culminating in the emergence of an ascetic monasticism.

> The Spirit has explicitly said that during the last times there will be some who will desert the faith and choose to listen to deceitful spirits and doctrines that come from the devils; ... they will say marriage is forbidden, and lay down rules about abstaining from foods which God created to be accepted with thanksgiving by all who believe and who know the truth.... You should give up drinking only water and have a little wine for the sake of your digestion and the frequent bouts of illness that you have (1 Tm 4:1,3; 5:23).

The other side of the Gnostic morality coin was also present. The writer of Jude warns the faithful against the Gnostic libertines, who will be repaid by the Old Testament's promise of vengeful judgment:

> Certain people have infiltrated among you, and they are the ones you
> had a warning about, in writing, long ago, when they were con-
> demned for denying all religion, turning the grace of our God into
> immorality. . . . in their delusions they. . . defile their bodies and dis-
> regard authority. . . . May they get what they deserve. . . . It was with
> them in mind that Enoch. . . made his prophecy when he said, "I tell
> you, the Lord will come with his saints in their tens of thousands, to
> pronounce judgment on all mankind and to sentence the wicked for
> all the wicked things they have done. . . . ["These unspiritual and
> selfish people"] are mischief-makers, grumblers, governed only by
> their own desires, with mouths full of boastful talk (Jude 4,8,11,16).

In the letters to the churches that we find in the second chapter of
Revelation (*ca.* A.D. 100), there is a specific attack against Gnostics
whose influence was spreading throughout Ephesus, Smyrna, Per-
gamum, and Thyatira. This was a decidedly libertine group named the
Nicolaitans:

> It is in your favor. . . that you loathe as I [Jesus] do what the
> Nicolaitans are doing. . . . I know the trials you have had. . . and the
> slanderous accusations that have been made by the people who
> profess to be Jews but are really members of the synagogue of Satan.
> . . . I know where you live, in the place where Satan is enthroned.
> . . . you are encouraging the woman Jezebel [a Nicolaitan] who claims
> to be a prophetess, and by her teaching she is luring my servants away
> to commit the adultery of eating food which has been sacrificed to
> idols. . . . Now I am consigning her to bed, and all her partners in
> adultery to troubles that will test them severely, unless they repent of
> their practices; and I will see that her children die. . . (Rv 2:6,9,13,20,22f).

The Nicolaitans were believed by the later Church Fathers to have been
named after the deacon Nicolas of Antioch, mentioned in Acts 6:5. As
Irenaeus wrote:

> The Nicolaitans have as teacher a certain Nicolaus, one of the seven
> who were first ordained to the diaconate by the Apostles. . . . They live
> in promiscuity. Who they are is revealed quite clearly in the
> Revelation of St. John. . . since they teach that adultery, or the eating
> of meat sacrificed to idols, is a matter of indifference (*Adv. haer.* I.26.3,
> in Haardt, p. 63).

In what is generally conceded by scholars to be the latest New
Testament book, the Second Letter of Peter, we have one of the most
vicious denunciations of these Gnostic "heretics." The author, obvi-

ously not the apostle, virtually copies out Jude's letter in his second chapter, but adds to the vituperation against "those who are governed by their corrupt bodily desires and have no respect for authority" (2 P 2:10), and warns those in his circle not to be lured away from the true faith:

> ...these people...are...simply animals born to be caught and killed, and they will quite certainly destroy themselves by their own work of destruction, and get their reward of evil for the evil that they do. They are unsightly blots on your society: men whose only object is dissipation all day long... with an infinite capacity for sinning, they will seduce any soul which is at all unstable. Greed is the one lesson their minds have learnt. They are under a curse.... People like this are dried-up rivers... and the dark underworld is the place reserved for them. With their high-flown talk, which is all hollow, they tempt back the ones who have only just escaped from paganism, playing on their bodily desires with debaucheries.... anyone who has escaped the pollution of the world once by coming to know our Lord and savior Jesus Christ, and who then allows himself to be entangled by it a second time and mastered, will end up in a worse state than he began in.... What he has done is exactly as the proverb rightly says: The dog goes back to his own vomit [Pr 26:11] and: When the sow has been washed, it wallows in the mud (2 P 2:12-22).

In words that foreshadow the patristic diatribes against the later Gnostics for their treatment of scripture, "Peter" writes:

> ...these are the points [in "our brother Paul"] that uneducated and unbalanced people distort, in the same way as they distort the rest of scripture--a fatal thing for them to do (2 P 3:16).

3. Gnostic Elements in the Johannine Writings

We come now to the gospel of John and the three epistles written in his name, and find the same paradox we observed in Paul: an anti-Gnostic polemic in a framework that exhibits some decidedly Gnostic characteristics. However, as we have already observed, the presence of themes that would later emerge in second-century Gnosticism does not decisively show Gnostic influence, but perhaps another example of the cross-fertilization we have observed before. As Yamauchi writes:

> One need not subscribe to Bultmann's theory to recognize that the author of the Gospel of John used concepts which occur in Gnostic literature and that the Gospel was popular among Gnostics.... [It] has recently [been] argued that the Gospel of John illustrates diver-

sity and development rather than any conscious heterodoxy or orthodoxy.... There is none the less still a great gulf between both the concepts and the language used by John and the Gnostic texts as recovered in the Nag Hammadi library (Yamauchi, p.34).

In *The Epistles of John*, scripture scholar I. H. Marshall comments:

These false teachers were forerunners of the heretics who were responsible for the developed Gnostic sects of the second century. The seeds of Gnosticism were already to be found in the New Testament period, although it is misleading to use the actual term "Gnosticism" to describe the incipient Gnosticism or "pre-gnosticism" of this period (in Yamauchi, p. 199).

It certainly appears that John drew upon a pre-existent tradition, shared by many different groups, and that this tradition later extended into the second century when the orthodox and heterodox split in terms of their relation to this tradition. We shall return to this idea at the end of this chapter. Some of the more obvious proto-Gnostic elements in John include 1) dualism; 2) Christology; and 3) the resurrection.

1) A strong dualism permeates the gospel, although one never finds the radical anti-cosmic feeling as in the Gnostics. The Prologue, in fact, quite clearly states that the world was created by the Divine Logos: "Through him [the Word] all things came to be, not one thing had its being but through him" (Jn 1:3). Nonetheless, a dualism similar to what we observed in the Pauline writings is present, as seen in the following passages when Jesus speaks of overcoming the prince of this world (the devil):

Now sentence is being passed on this world; now the prince of this world is to be overthrown (Jn 12:31).

I shall not talk with you any longer, because the prince of this world is on his way. He has no power over me, but the world must be brought to know that I love the Father... (Jn 14:30f).

And when he [the Advocate, i.e., the Holy Spirit] comes, he will show the world how wrong it was... about judgment: proved by the prince of this world being already condemned (Jn 16:8,11).

In his conversation with Nicodemus, the Johannine Jesus enunciates this duality:

I tell you most solemnly, unless a man is born from above, he cannot see the kingdom of God.... unless a man is born through water and the Spirit, he cannot enter the kingdom of God: what is born of the flesh is flesh; what is born of the Spirit is spirit (Jn 3:3-6).

The Last Discourses continually return to this theme of the contrast between heaven and this world:

If the world hates you, remember that it hated me before you. If you belonged to the world, the world would love you as its own; but because you do not belong to the world, because my choice withdrew you from the world, therefore the world hates you (Jn 15:18f).

I came from the Father and have come into the world and now I leave the world to go to the Father.... I have conquered the world (Jn 16:28,33).

I have made your [God] name known to the men you took from the world to give me.... I pray for them; I am not praying for the world but for those you have given me, because they belong to you.... I passed your word on to them, and the world hated them, because they belong to the world no more than I belong to the world (Jn 17:6,9,14).

In John's first epistle we read words of Jesus' hatred for the world that could just as easily have come from a second-century Gnostic text:

You must not love this passing world or anything that is in the world. The love of the Father cannot be in any man who loves the world, because nothing the world has to offer--the sensual body, the lustful eye, pride in possessions--could ever come from the Father but only from the world (1 Jn 2:15f).

Jesus repeatedly contrasts his heavenly gifts with those of the world, as with the woman at the well:

If you only knew what God is offering and who it is that is saying to you: "Give me a drink," you would have been the one to ask, and he would have given you living water.... Whoever drinks this water will get thirsty again; but anyone who drinks the water that I shall give will never be thirsty again... (Jn 4:10-14).

To the disciples requesting food, Jesus replies:

I have food to eat that you do not know about.... my food is to do the will of the one who sent me, and to complete his work (Jn 4:32-34).

Light and darkness are common symbols of this duality:

> The light will be with you only a little longer now. Walk while you have the light, or the dark will overtake you; he who walks in the dark does not know where he is going. While you still have the light, believe in the light and you will become sons of light (Jn 12:35f).

And in the first epistle:

> God is light; there is no darkness in him at all. If we say that we are in union with God while we are living in darkness, we are lying because we are not living the truth. But if we live our lives in the light, as he is in the light, we are in union with one another (1 Jn 1:5-7).

John's gospel is a polemic tract, clearly separating out the Johannine community from the world. The dualism thus is not only between the light of Heaven and the darkness of the world, but also between their representatives on earth: the Johannine community and those it considered its enemies, even including fellow Christians. Raymond Brown, one of this generation's leading Johannine scholars, has enumerated six groups perceived by the Johannine community as falling within this category: the world, the Jews, the followers of John the Baptist, the crypto-Christians (Jews remaining in the synagogue), the Jewish-Christians (Jews who left the synagogue but did not accept the high Christology of John's community), and other Christians who also did not accept the Johannine Christology (Brown, pp. 168f).

2) The Christology in the Johannine writings is loftier than in the Synoptics, and in time became the dominant view of the Church. The Synoptic focus is on Jesus' miraculous birth into this world, while in John, despite the explicit statements that Jesus was human and did come in the flesh, the overriding emphasis remains on the pre-existent, cosmic Christ who is but barely human, prefiguring the Gnostic Revealer: "The stress is on the glory of God which shines through this humanity" (Brown, *Community of the Beloved Disciple*, p. 114). The cosmic Christ who descends and ascends, foreshadowed in the Pauline hymns, here finds its grandiloquent expression:

> In the beginning was the Word: the Word was with God and the Word was God. He was with God in the beginning. Through him all things came to be, not one thing had its being but through him. All that came to be had life in him and that life was the light of men, a light that shines in the dark, a light that darkness could not overpower. ... The Word was the true light that enlightens all men and he was coming into the world.... The Word was made flesh, he lived among

us, and we saw his glory, the glory that is his as the only Son of the Father, full of grace and truth (Jn 1:1-5,9,14).

This theme is carried through the whole gospel, where Jesus makes statements about himself not found previously in the New Testament. These include:

No one has gone up to heaven except the one who came down from heaven, the Son of Man who is in heaven; ... For God sent his Son into the world not to condemn the world, but so that through him the world might be saved (Jn 3:13,17).

All that the Father gives me will come to me, and whoever comes to me I shall not turn him away; because I have come from heaven, not to do my own will, but to do the will of the one who sent me (Jn 6:37f).

I tell you most solemnly, before Abraham ever was, I Am (Jn 8:58).

The Father and I are one. ... the Father is in me and I am in the Father (Jn 10:30,38).

Now, Father, it is time for you to glorify me with that glory I had with you before ever the world was. ... Father, I want those you have given me to be with me where I am, so that they may always see the glory you have given me because you loved me before the foundation of the world (Jn 17:5,24).

In Chapter 6, this idea of the cosmic Christ is expressed in the context of John's version of the Eucharist, which moves away from the remembrance aspects of the Last Supper ("Do this as a memorial of me" Lk 22:19), focusing more on the body and blood as nourishers of eternal life. Jesus says:

I am the living bread which has come down from heaven. Anyone who eats this bread will live forever. ... I tell you most solemnly, if you do not eat the flesh of the Son of Man and drink his blood, you will not have life in you. Anyone who does eat my flesh and drink my blood has eternal life, and I shall raise him up on the last day. For my flesh is real food and my blood is real drink. He who eats my flesh and drinks my blood lives in me and I live in him (Jn 6:51-56).

Brown has discussed how John's pre-existence Christology colored his portrait of Jesus' earthly life, and we excerpt from his succinct summary that treats how, based on this coloration, the gospel *could have* been read by these later docetic Gnostic groups:

77

The Johannine Jesus seems scarcely to eat or drink in the normal sense, for when he discusses food (4:32), bread (6:33ff), or water (4:7-14; 7:38; 9:7), they are symbolic of spiritual realities. He loves Lazarus but with a love strangely lacking in human sympathy (11:5-6,11-15,33,35).... The Johannine Jesus knows all things (16:30), so that he cannot ask for information. When he says to Philip, "Where shall we ever buy bread for these people to eat?" (6:5), the evangelist feels impelled in the next verse to insert parenthetically: "Actually, of course, he was perfectly aware of what he was going to do, but he asked this to test Philip's reaction." [Likewise with his foreknowledge of Judas' betrayal].... The Johannine Jesus is one with the Father (10:30), and so he cannot really pray to the Father in the sense of seeking a change in the divine will. When he speaks to God on the occasion of the raising of Lazarus, he says, "Father I thank you because you heard me. Of course, I knew that you always hear me; but I say it because of the crowd standing around, that they may believe that you sent me." ... [In contrast to the Synoptics' Jesus in Gethsemane praying to have the cup pass from him,] the Johannine Jesus has a very different attitude: "What should I say?--'Father, save me from this hour?' No, this is precisely the reason why I came to this hour. 'Father, glorify your name!'" (12:27f). In other words the Johannine Jesus refuses to pray in the manner in which the Synoptic Jesus prays because... there is no distinction between Jesus' will and the Father's will, and the Father's name has been given to Jesus (Brown, *Community of the Beloved Disciple*, pp. 114-16).

It is interesting to consult Origen's conclusions based upon the very different Synoptic version of the scene in Gethsemane. (*See* p. 52.)

Moreover, the view of the crucified Jesus differs too. The Synoptic as well as Pauline Jesus is very much the victimized savior (Isaiah's Suffering Servant) (see *Forgiveness and Jesus*, pp. 221-27). In John, however, Jesus willingly chooses a death in which he is in full control, a death of triumph, hardly humiliation:

He is in such control that only when he affirms, "It is finished," does he bow his head and hand over his Spirit (19:20). This sovereign affirmation is far from the cry of the Marcan Jesus, "My God, my God, why have you forsaken me?" (15:34)--a cry that would have been inconceivable on the lips of the Johannine Jesus who claimed in the face of desertion by his disciples, "I am never alone because the Father is with me" (16:32) (Brown, *Community of the Beloved Disciple*, pp. 118f).

Brown concludes his discussion by quoting Johannine scholar Forestell:

The cross of Christ in John is evaluated precisely in terms of revelation in harmony with the theology of the entire Gospel [i.e., his divine glory], rather than in terms of vicarious and expiatory sacrifice for sin [i.e., his suffering humanity] (ibid., p. 119).

3. We have seen how one of the key differences between the orthodox and Gnostic communities was the view of the resurrection (*see again,* 2 Tm 2:16-18). John's gospel, established in the late second century as orthodox, here sets forth a view decidedly different in emphasis from the Synoptic gospels and the epistles, which stressed the physical resurrection of Jesus. John's Jesus, however, stresses the internal resurrection of those who believe:

> I tell you most solemnly, whoever listens to my words, and believes in the one who sent me, has eternal life; without being brought to judgment he has passed from death to life. I tell you most solemnly, the hour will come--in fact it is here already--when the dead will hear the voice of the Son of God, and all who hear it will live (Jn 5:24f).

Before calling Lazarus forth from the grave, Jesus tells Martha:

> I am the resurrection. If anyone believes in me, even though he dies he will live, and whoever lives and believes in me will never die (Jn 11:25f).

The later Gnostics believed they were especially called out by God (or Jesus). Many Gnostics referred to themselves as "pneumatics," (i.e., those who received or were filled with the Holy Spirit), and we find that idea of "spiritual specialness" presaged here in John's first letter:

> Whoever keeps his commandments lives in God and God lives in him. We know that he lives in us by the Spirit that he has given us. . . . anyone who has been begotten by God has already overcome the world; this is the victory over the world--our faith (1 Jn 3:24; 5:4).

4. Anti-Gnostic Elements in the Johannine Writings

Despite these expressions of proto-Gnostic themes and a leaning towards a moderately docetic Christology, we find strong anti-Gnostic statements in both the gospel and letters. These focus not only on 1) docetism, but also on 2) the assertion of these dissident groups that they were sinless.

1) The dissident groups did not hold fully to a docetic view of Jesus, but they greatly downplayed his human life in terms of having any

salvific significance. Brown has summarized their position:

> For the secessionists [i.e., dissident groups] the human existence was only a stage in the career of the divine Word and not an intrinsic component in redemption. What Jesus did in Palestine was not truly important for them nor the fact that he died on the cross; salvation would not be different if the Word had become incarnate in a totally different human representative who lived a different life and died a different death. The only important thing for them was that eternal life had been brought down to men and women through a divine Son who passed through this world. In short, theirs was an incarnational theology pushed to exclusivity (Brown, *Community of the Beloved Disciple*, pp. 113f).

We shall see in Part II-A how closely this view approximates the later teachings of many of the Gnostic groups.

With this understanding of the opposition, gleaned from the gospel and epistles, we can better understand the counter-arguments--a strong statement of witness--found in the first letter of John which attempted to offset a docetic interpretation of the gospel. Though the gospel does lean towards the idea of a divine Christ, a docetism such as is seen in many second-century Gnostics is avoided: Jesus remains human as well as divine. Thus, the Johannine statements that Jesus came in the flesh and was perceived by the flesh were a distinct rebuttal to the already strong docetic tendencies of these proto-Gnostics.

> Something which has existed since the beginning, that we have heard, and we have seen with our own eyes; that we have watched and touched with our hands: the Word, who is life--this is our subject. That life was made visible: we saw it and we are giving our testimony... (1 Jn 1:1f).

Later, the author issues a similar warning, re-emphasizing that "The word was made flesh, he lived among us, and we saw his glory" (Jn 1:14). Thus, whatever docetism was present, was certainly not the extreme form found in the later Gnostic groups:

> It is not every spirit, my dear people, that you can trust; test them, to see if they come from God, there are many false prophets, now, in the world. You can tell the spirits that come from God by this: every spirit which acknowledges that Jesus the Christ has come in the flesh is from God; but any spirit which will not say this of Jesus is not from God, but is the spirit of Antichrist, whose coming you were warned about (1 Jn 4:1-3).

The author of the first letter reinforces his argument by stating:

Jesus Christ who came by water and blood, not with water only, but with water and blood (1 Jn 5:6).

Water and blood signify the baptism and death of Jesus, and they are stressed here not only to denote Jesus' humanness, but the beginning and end of his ministry of salvation. Thus the author of the epistle highlights what had only been in the background of the gospel: the saving act of the crucifixion:

> This has taught us love--that he gave up his life for us; and we, too, ought to give up our lives for our brothers. . . . this is the love I mean: not our love for God, but God's love for us when he sent his Son to be the sacrifice that takes our sins away (1 Jn 3:16; 4:10).

These teachings seem directed against those proto-Gnostic groups who would have sought to emphasize only the docetic aspects to the gospel, minimizing his suffering and salvific death.

In the second letter we find the same warning as in the first:

> There are many deceivers about in the world, refusing to admit that Jesus Christ has come in the flesh. They are the Deceiver; they are the Antichrist. Watch yourselves, or all our work will be lost and not get the reward it deserves. If anybody does not keep within the teaching of Christ but goes beyond it, he cannot have God with him: only those who keep to what he taught can have the Father and the Son with them. If anyone comes to you bringing a different doctrine, you must not receive him in your house or even give him a greeting. To greet him would make you a partner in his wicked work (2 Jn 7-11).

Returning to the gospel, the story of the doubting Thomas--who would not believe unless he sees "the holes that the nails made in his [Jesus'] hands and can put my finger into the holes they made, and unless I can put my hand into his side" (Jn 20:25), and then is allowed to do so by the risen Jesus--seems directed to this anti-docetic argument.

2) The first letter also repudiates those perfect ones--the proto-Gnostics--who believe that they cannot sin:

> If we say we have no sin in us, we are deceiving ourselves and refusing to admit the truth; but if we acknowledge our sins, then God who is faithful and just will forgive our sins and purify us from everything that is wrong. To say that we have never sinned is to call God a liar and to show that his word is not in us (1 Jn 1:8-10).

However, later in the epistle the author himself states that

> No one who has been begotten by God sins; because God's seed remains inside him, he cannot sin when he has been begotten by God. . . . the begotten Son of God protects him, and the Evil One does not touch him (1 Jn 3:9; 5:18).

The difference between these two statements appears to be that the Johannine position maintains sinlessness as an obligation to be met by the true Christian (i.e., the Johannine Christian), and one which can always be returned to:

> I am writing this, my children, to stop you sinning; but if anyone should sin, we have our advocate with the Father, Jesus Christ, who is just; he is the sacrifice that takes our sins away, and not only ours, but the whole world's (1 Jn 2:1f).

The opponents, on the other hand, presaging the more developed Gnostic position, seemed to believe that their sinlessness was true. This was but a short step away, as Brown points out (*Community of the Beloved Disciple*, p. 127), from the later Gnostic belief in an ontological sinlessness, wherein the Gnostics saw themselves pre-existent with Jesus. This perfection was guaranteed by their divine heritage as pneumatics, children of the spirit.

In the decades that followed its writing around the turn of the century, John's gospel became for the Church the most controversial book of scripture. The Gnostics claimed it as their own, and forged from its Gnostic leanings justification for their own beliefs. The second-century Fathers were thus hesitant to draw upon the Fourth Gospel, and we find no specific mention of it in Ignatius, Polycarp, or Justin Martyr. On the other hand, the noted Valentinian teacher Heracleon gave us the first known commentary on the gospel and, in fact, it was among the most favored scriptural books for the Valentinians. As Brown summarizes:

> The fact that these secessionists brought the Johannine Gospel with them offered to the docetists and gnostics, whose thought they now shared, a new basis on which to construct a theology--indeed, it served as a catalyst in the growth of Christian gnostic thought. The Great Church, which had accepted elements of the Johannine tradition when it accepted the Johannine Christians who shared the author's views, was at first wary of the Fourth Gospel because it had given rise to error and was being used to support error. Eventually, however, having added the Epistles to the Gospel as a guide to right interpretation, the Great Church. . . championed the Gospel as orthodox over against its gnostic interpreters (ibid., pp. 146f).

Thus the first Johannine letter, by showing how the gospel could be read non-docetically, "saved" it from the embrace of the Gnostics and "returned" it to the orthodox Church.

The division within the churches, already expressed in these later New Testament writings, hardened as the second century began. What had begun as disagreements within essentially the same Christianity, now emerged as a virtual state of war between the orthodox Church and the Gnostic "heretics."

Second Century: The Church vs. Gnosticism

1. The Beginning Stages: Fluidity of Doctrine

When the Gnostic systems began to flourish in the middle of the second century there was no organized Church. There was, to be sure, a Church hierarchy, but an authorized canon to instruct the faithful about which gospel or epistle was truly the Word of God was lacking; nor was there a prescribed body of dogmas to lead and instruct. When the Gnostic teachers formed their schools and attracted disciples unto themselves they had no thought of opposing the Church. These teachers identified as Christians and, as noted above, both Marcion and Valentinus presented themselves before the Roman bishops. Thus, to reiterate our earlier discussion, the rigid typological distinctions that have been made between the orthodox and Gnostic groups were not generally valid in the beginning stages, for the two were not as discretely separate as they were to become. It was only as the polemic grew among the Church Fathers that the differences became more pronounced. Wilson has written:

> At this stage the situation is still fluid, the lines of division not yet clearly drawn. . . . it is by no means uncommon for "heretic" and "orthodox" to live in peaceful coexistence for a period, for the men of one generation to tolerate with equanimity ideas and conceptions, theories and doctrines, which a later generation will denounce as heretical. It is only in the light of subsequent developments that we can determine which was to become the "orthodox" position and which the "heretical." We have therefore to guard against the danger of judging by the standards of a later age, of transferring the clear distinctions of a later period back into a situation in which the final cleavage had not yet taken place and the full implications of a particular theory had not yet been realized (Wilson, p. 32).

Clement of Alexandria (A.D. 150-211) is one example of a theologian who bridged this orthodox-Gnostic gap. Considered by some a Father of the Church and by others a near heretic, he wrote:

> For in the doctrines of the schools of heretics, in so far as they have not
> become totally obtuse. . . are to be found many things which,
> dissimilar as they appear, agree in category with the Wholeness of
> truth (*Strom.* I.xiii.57, in Nigg, p. 28).

Such bridging led to the German theologian Hornschuh's coining of
the term "semi-gnosis," which stood "in the midst between early
Catholicism on the one hand and extreme Gnosis on the other" (in *NTA*
II, p. 84).

The mid-second-century "Gospel of Peter" exemplifies this difficulty in categorization. Its mythological rather than historical treatment of the death and resurrection of Jesus led Maurer to state that
these references

> show no articulated Gnostic theology, but they indicate that such a
> theology is already on the way, since the representation is taken out
> of the framework of the divine act of revelation and set in that of a
> Gnostic myth. Thus the Gospel of Peter stands on the one hand
> through its comparative sobriety nearer to the canonical Gospels than
> to the later Gnostic embellishments, but on the other hand it prepares
> a way for them (in *NTA* I, p. 182).

Schneemelcher and Saeferdiek, introducing the five apocryphal (i.e.,
non-canonical) "Acts of the Apostles" (John, Peter, Paul, Andrew, and
Thomas) which date from the second and third centuries, have written:

> The circles from which the apocryphal Acts took their origin have
> been. . . a subject of sharp dispute. The controversy on this problem
> has been handicapped by the fact that Gnosticism and primitive
> Catholicism have been contrasted as if they were fixed quantities, and
> the origin of the apocryphal Acts has been sought in terms of an
> "Either-Or". But the boundaries between the two phenomena,
> Gnosticism and primitive Catholicism, remained fluctuating for a
> considerable period. . . (*NTA* II, pp. 176f).

The second-century "Acts of Andrew," which we shall explore later,
exhibits some definite Gnostic characteristics; e.g., a dualism (though
not the radical cosmic dualism we find in true Gnostic systems), a
certain antipathy towards a world seen as transitory and illusory, and
a goal of realizing one's true being by returning to the One. That these
Gnostic elements could be incorporated in a text that originated within
the existing Church of the second half of the second century is yet again
another example of the fluid boundaries between Gnostic and orthodox Christians. These elements, as we have seen, could also reflect the
Middle Platonism that influenced some of the orthodox.

84

The late-second-century "Acts of Peter," most decidedly not Gnostic, nonetheless exhibits definite Gnostic traits of extreme asceticism and docetism, as seen in the following teachings:

> And hearing [from Peter] the preaching of purity and all the words of the Lord they were cut to the heart and agreed with each other to remain in purity, renouncing intercourse . . . . And many other women besides fell in love with the doctrine of purity and separated from their husbands, and men too ceased to sleep with their own wives since they wished to worship God in sobriety and purity . . . . You who hope in Christ, for you the cross must not be this thing that is visible; for this passion [Peter's imminent martyrdom], like the passion of Christ, is something other than this which is visible [i.e., reflecting the docetic view that the crucifixion was illusory] (APt II.9.33,37 in *NTA* II, pp. 316f,319).

Finally, the "Acts of Thomas" presents the interesting phenomenon of a decidedly Gnostic work of third-century Syria that found favor with the Church, which then proceeded to Christianize it one or two centuries later by deleting the offensive Gnostic elements and substituting more orthodox Catholic teaching. We shall examine some of these changes in Part II-A.

2. The Emerging Polarity: "We - They"

The fluid situation, of course, did not remain this way, a loss for *all* Christians, "orthodox" and "heterodox" alike. Without the ego's investment in separateness, all Christian groups could have remained united in their devotion to Jesus, yet accepting of differing interpretations. Gnosticism could have infused the Catholic understanding with a greater profundity, while the orthodox could have grounded the speculative Gnostic theorizing in a more compassionate application of the gospel to everyday living. Brown has penetratingly criticized the "we-they" mentality of the Johannine corpus, suggesting that the Church's hatred of its opponents found its justification in John's gospel and epistles which, in effect, sowed the seeds for the later struggles between the orthodox and heterodox. He comments:

> Here we come upon the great anomaly of the First Epistle. No more eloquent voice is raised in the NT [New Testament] for love within the Christian brotherhood and sisterhood; . . . Yet that same voice is extremely bitter in condemning opponents who had been members of his community and were so no longer. They are demonic, antichrists, false prophets, and serve as the embodiment of eschatological lawlessness or iniquity.... Although the members of the com-

munity are exhorted to love one another, the way they should treat dissenters is illustrated by 2 Jn 10-11: "If anyone comes to you who does not bring this teaching, do not receive him into your house, for whoever greets him shares the evil he does. . . ." The Matthean Jesus says, "Love your enemies and pray for those who persecute you" (Mt 5:44), but there is no such maxim in the Johannine tradition. The command to love is *not* in terms of love of neighbor. . . but in terms of loving *one another*. . . and John 15:13-15 allows that "one another" to be interpreted in terms of those who are disciples of Christ and obey the commandments. The attitude of the Johannine Jesus who refused to pray for the world (17:9) is easily translated in the First Epistle (5:16) into a refusal to pray for other Christians who have committed the deadly sin by apostasizing from the Johannine community. . . . When we discussed the Gospel, we found a sense of estrangement, of "us" against "them," especially toward those who had made the Johannine Christians suffer. As understandable as this sense is, its dualistic articulation is dangerous; and in fact it encouraged Christians of later centuries to see a dualistic division of humankind into believers [Christians] and non-believers, into an "us" who are saved and a "them" who are not. Inevitably such a dualistic outlook will shift over to divisions within the "us," and the cannons that once pointed outwards to protect the fortress of truth against the world will be spun around to point inwards against those betraying the truth from within [for whom there is always a more special hatred]. Those who believe that God has given His people the biblical books as a guide should recognize that part of the guidance is to learn from the dangers attested in them as well as from their great insights. . . . the author of the Epistles did the church a great service in preserving for it the Fourth Gospel; he did this by showing that the Gospel did not have to be read the way the secessionists [i.e., the proto-Gnostics] were reading it. In his struggle against the secessionists he had to take stern means. Nevertheless, one must recognize that his defense of the truth as he saw it was at a price. In his attitude toward the secessionists in a passage like 2 Jn 10-11 he supplied fuel for those Christians of all times who feel justified in hating other Christians for the love of God (Brown, *Community of the Beloved Disciple*, pp. 132-35).

On one level, therefore, John's gospel was written to counteract the groups that the Johannine Church identified as threatening, as Brown explains. However, this included not only dissident Christians, such as the emerging Gnostic tendencies within the Church but, among others, the Jewish groups that opposed these early Christians. Thus, we read in John these words of Jesus to the Jews:

You are from below; I am from above. You are of this world; I am not of this world. I have told you already: You will die in your sins. Yes, if you do not believe that I am He, you will die in your sins. . . . If God were your father, you would love me, since I have come here from God....Do you know why you cannot take in what I say? It is because you are unable to understand my language. The devil is your father and you prefer to do what your father wants.... A child of God listens to the words of God; if you refuse to listen, it is because you are not God's children (Jn 8:23f,42-47).

Only the most conservative fundamentalist would maintain today that these were the actual words of the Prince of Peace, whose message of God's love for *all* His children literally saved these children from the ego's belief in the "world, the flesh, and the devil," and the ego's God who seeks to punish us for our mistaken beliefs.

It would take us beyond the theme of this book to discuss the Johannine literature in any greater detail. However, this literature is instructive not only to illustrate the interface of the early Church and Gnosticism, but also to point out the "we-they" mentality that Brown has isolated in the gospel and epistles, and how it has provided "divine" justification for a theology of hatred. Obviously it was a practice that both sides embraced, to the detriment of all who through the centuries sought to follow the loving example and teachings of Jesus.

3. One Church: The Bible and the Apostolic Tradition

This defensiveness and fear of the Gnostic threat led to the establishing of the *regula fidei*, the rule of faith, as the means of establishing once and for all the norm for the true interpretation of the gospel. Such a rule, being "divinely inspired," automatically rejected all dissident teachings as false or heretical, originating from the devil. Schneemelcher summarized the situation:

> This is bound up with the historical development of the Church from a multiplicity into a visible unity. In the early period the multiplicity of doctrines and opinions was no hindrance to faith in the one *ecclesia catholica* [Catholic Church], which certainly was an element of the faith. But in the 2nd century, as a defense against an all-subversive syncretism, it became necessary to search for uniform norms for life and doctrine, for the compass of Scripture and for worship, and thus to make membership of the *one* Church visible and manifest. In the course of this development it came about in various places and countries that what hitherto had been recognized as "orthodox," i.e., as Christian, now all at once became "heretical" and had to be rejected. As a designation that could express unmistakably what ecclesiastically was now obligatory the word "canon" [given in Greek, meaning "rule"] presented itself (*NTA* I, p. 23).

In distinction from the first-century Paul, for example, whose standard for God's truth was his own experience of Jesus, the third-century Christian's standard was set by the Church. By the middle of the fourth century the books of the Old and New Testaments, as we know them today, were firmly established as canonical (*NTA* I, p. 24), the culmination of the process that began two centuries earlier.

The guiding force in this "counter-Gnostic" movement was Bishop Irenaeus, who decided in the latter half of the second century that the best defense against the perceived Gnostic threat was to choose those gospels and epistles that corresponded to the Church's understanding of Jesus and God's plan of salvation, and to announce that all other texts were false or apocryphal. Perkins discusses this action:

> The brilliance of Irenaeus' counterattack was to see that such arguments [based upon each individual Gnostic's *gnosis*] have no conclusion and to move the locus of authority onto new ground. This move required that the teaching community be associated with a smaller group which had come to have responsibility for Christian churches. It also required what they were to teach to be regulated by a fixed, normative text that would be subject to certain standards of interpretation. The full flowering of this move was not yet realized in Irenaeus' time. But it fit into the larger pattern of religious developments that would dominate the third through the fifth centuries (Perkins, p. 203).

The Church's need to solidify the Christian message was of course heightened by the ending of the age of the apostles--presumed to be the only authentic witnesses to Jesus--and the increased proliferation of the Christian message. Schneemelcher continues:

> Here lies the proper starting point of the formation of the canon, but here there must also be seen the beginnings of the association of the problem of the canon with that apostolicity. The need of genuine authority and of certainty in the proclamation led to the formation of a canon. Only what in the opinion of the churches in the 2nd century had authority was canonized and this authority was determined by apostolicity (*NTA* I, p. 37).

As each side vied for the correctness of its position, it sought authority in the apostolic tradition. The Church Fathers accused the Gnostics of claiming that they had special and superior knowledge that had been given to them alone, the "perfect ones," and lifted them above the benighted Church faithful. Irenaeus wrote:

> Jesus, they [the Valentinian Marcosians] say, spoke in a mystery to his disciples and apostles privately, and charged them to hand these

things on to the worthy and those who assented.... [The disciples did not understand Jesus, but after his resurrection] to a few of his disciples whom he knew to be capable of such great mysteries he taught these things. ... They claim that they have more knowledge than all others, and that they alone have attained the greatness of the knowledge of the ineffable power. They claim that they are in the heights beyond every power . . . (*Adv. haer.* I.25.5; 30.13; 13.6, in F I, pp. 38,93,202).

According to Irenaeus, as well as many of the Church Fathers, the source of all Gnostic heresy was Simon Magus, Peter's opponent mentioned in the biblical Acts of the Apostles.

All those who in any way corrupt the truth, and harm the teaching of the church, are the disciples and successors of Simon Magus of Samaria.... They put forth, indeed, the name of Jesus Christ as a kind of lure, but in many ways they introduce the impieties of Simon. . . spreading to their hearers the bitter and malignant poison of the great serpent [Satan], the great author of apostasy (*Adv. haer.* I.27.4 in Pagels, p. 55).

The Gnostics' appeal to the apostolic tradition was to a more esoteric source of revelation, which usually included only those apostles specifically called out by the Lord as able to receive his *gnosis*--Peter, James, John, Philip, and Paul were among the Gnostic favorites--not to mention those special ones who were able to receive this secret teaching. Basilides asserted a connection with Peter through Glaucias, an alleged interpreter of Peter, while Valentinus claimed to have been instructed into the secret teachings of Jesus by Theudas, a disciple of Paul. The late-second-century Clement of Alexandria, one of the first and foremost of the "orthodox" Christian Gnostics, also reflects the Gnostic apostolic tradition of transmission of the secret teachings, which he set down from the

instructive lectures of those holy and remarkable men whom it was his [Clement] privilege to hear and who held fast the true "tradition of the blessed doctrine" originating directly from the holy apostles Peter, James, John and Paul, and received by them "as by a son from his father." "And by God's grace they reach into our time to sow in us those apostolic seeds inherited from the fathers. ... This knowledge has descended from the apostles in unbroken sequence to *a few only* through oral tradition." Clement thus claims to have access to secret teaching traditions. . . . Only few of the believers of the succeeding generations, those namely "who are capable of grasping it" were found worthy of initiation into the secret wisdom. To the rank and file of Christians the approach to it is closed (compiled and paraphrased by Hornschuh, *NTA* II, pp. 79f, my italics).

The third-century Gnostic "Gospel of Bartholomew" contains a strong statement of this theme of "a few only" who understood the true gospel. It is interesting to note that the string of name calling, so common in Church attacks on the Gnostics, is here used aggressively by a Gnostic author against the Church:

> Jesus answered him: Bartholomew, my beloved, entrust them [the revealed mysteries] to all who are faithful and can keep them for themselves. For there are some who are worthy of them; but there are also others to whom they ought not to be entrusted, for they are boasters, drunkards, proud, merciless, idolaters, seducers to fornication, slanderers, teachers of falsehood, and doers of all the works of the devil, and therefore they are not worthy that they should be entrusted to them . . . (GB IV.67, in *NTA* I, pp. 501f).

In their own blindness, however, the Church Fathers failed to realize that they were guilty of the same "spiritual specialness" that was reflected in the gospel of Bartholomew. They believed that their special status as bishops and church leaders was conferred upon them by Jesus himself, through the line of apostolic succession. This was clearly expressed in a number of texts, scriptural and apostolic, which reflect the importance placed on the oral apostolic tradition. Hornschuh has summarized this principle, highlighting the teaching of *A Course in Miracles*: projection makes perception. *Wanting* to believe that there was a single line extending from Jesus to themselves, the Fathers *perceived* the gospels and epistles to be expressing a unity:

> In view of the existing differences in doctrine, of the great number of tendencies and opinions, as also of the increasing Gnostic peril, recourse to the beginnings of the Christian faith seemed to provide the only sure guarantee of a verdict as to the truth. This thought took for granted the supposition that originally Christianity had been of a *dogmatically uniform mould*. In the beginning there was unity; subsequently multiplicity developed as a depravation of what was historically original. The recovery and full establishment of unity could therefore take place only through a return to what was early, i.e., by way of a faithful bringing back of the original mould, consequently of the Christian faith in the form in which it was revealed by the Lord. . . . On the basis of the conception of tradition thus characterized there grew up in the second century the doctrine of an apostolic succession of bishops. An attempt was made to connect the tradition backwards by drawing up a series of bishops for each of the chief places, and so to bind the present to the beginning. . . [i.e.] an actual connection of the doctrine with the apostles; these lists prove that the church is in the place where the original truth is taught (in *NTA* II, pp. 74f, my italics).

In the canonical Acts of the Apostles, Luke (the same Luke who authored the third gospel) states that the early Christians "remained faithful to the teaching of the apostles.... The many miracles and signs worked through the apostles made a deep impression on everyone" (2:42f). The letter of Jude exhorts the faithful to remember "what the apostles of our Lord Jesus Christ told you to expect" (v. 17), while "Peter" writes:

> That is why I am continually recalling the same truths to you.... I am sure it is my duty... to keep stirring you up with reminders.... and I shall take great care that after my own departure you will still have a means to recall these things to memory. It was not any cleverly invented myths that we were repeating when we brought you the knowledge of the power and the coming of our Lord Jesus Christ; we had seen his majesty for ourselves (2 Pt 1:12f,15f).

Clement, Bishop of Rome (not to be confused with the later Clement of Alexandria), wrote to the Corinthians at the end of the first century in the earliest extant non-biblical statement of this apostolic philosophy of the Church:

> The Apostles have preached to us from the Lord Jesus Christ; Jesus Christ from God. Christ therefore was sent by God, the Apostles by Christ; so both were orderly sent, according to the will of God. For having received their command.... they went abroad... preaching through countries and cities, they appointed the first fruits of their conversion to be bishops and ministers over such as should afterwards believe, having first proved them by the Spirit.... So... our Apostles knew by our Lord Jesus Christ, that there should contentions arise, upon account of the ministry. And therefore having a perfect fore-knowledge of this, they appointed persons, as we have before said, and then gave direction, how, when they should die, other chosen and approved men should succeed in their ministry (Clement "First Epistle to Corinthians" XIX.1-7, in *Lost Books*, pp. 131f).

At the beginning of the second century St. Ignatius, Bishop of Antioch, wrote a series of letters upholding the same principle. To the Trallians he wrote:

> I exhort you therefore... that ye use none but Christian nourishment; abstaining from pasture which is of another kind, I mean heresy. For they that are heretics, confound together the doctrine of Jesus Christ, with their own poison: whilst they seem worthy of belief.... Wherefore guard yourselves against such persons.... continue inseparable from Jesus Christ our God, and from your bishop, and from the commands of the Apostles. He that is within the altar is

pure; but he that is without, that is, that does anything without the bishop, the presbyters, and deacons, is not pure in his conscience (Ignatius "Trallians" II.1-5, in *Lost Books*, p. 177).

Finally, in his treatise against the Gnostics, St. Irenaeus, within a declaration of the Catholic faith which became more formally adopted by the later Church councils as the true believer's creed, made the following statement of the *one* church:

> The Church. . . throughout the world. . . carefully preserves the faith that she received from the Apostles and from their disciples, believing in *one* God, the Father Almighty. . . . The Church. . . having received this message and this faith, diligently guards it, as though she inhabited but *one* house; and her faith is conformable to these doctrines, as though she had but *one* soul and *one* heart; and she preaches these things harmoniously, and teaches and hands them on, as though she had but *one* mouth. For, dissimilar as the languages of the world may be, still the power of the tradition is *one* and the same. . . . But as the sun, the creature of God, is *one* and the same in all the world, such also is the preaching of the truth in its universal phase, enlightening all men who wish to approach the knowledge of the truth. He that among the Bishops of the Church is mightiest in the word speaks no other doctrine than this, for none is above his Master (*Adv. haer.* I.10.1,2, in Mansel, pp. 241f, my italics).

Moreover, we next see Irenaeus giving the most succinct statement of this principle that was rapidly becoming the Church doctrine:

> One must obey the priests who are in the church--that is. . . those who possess the succession from the apostles. For they receive simultaneously with the episcopal succession the sure gift of truth. . . . One must hold in suspicion others who depart from the primitive succession, and assemble themselves in any place at all. These one must recognize as heretics. . . or as schismatics. . . or as hypocrites. All of these have fallen from the truth (*Adv. haer.* IV.26.2, in Pagels, p. 54).

4. "We - They": The Church

Armed now, as it perceived itself, with apostolic justification for the truth of its position, the orthodox Church launched an embarrassing barrage of vituperation against the Gnostics. Hanratty has written that

> since the many-sided heresy threatened the faith and order of the Church, it is understandable that care was taken in the suppression and destruction of the theological devotional texts which were

composed by the Gnostics. . . . even more crucial were the apologetic concerns which led the Fathers to highlight those features of the Gnostics' speculation which threatened the unity and continuity of the Church. For polemical purposes too, the Fathers concentrated on the fractious nature of the movement and on the exorbitant claims of the most spectacular Gnostic teachers. Yet, the Fathers always insisted that the numerous Gnostic sects shared certain fundamental philosophico-religious attitudes and ideas which were incompatible with the apostolic tradition (Hanratty, pp. 214f).

Jean Guitton is an example of a Catholic writer who has preserved his objectivity and has, in fact, exposed the Church Father's preoccupation with the "heretical" thinking of their opponents, providing some telling comments about the heresiologists' attitude towards the doctrine of their "enemy" and their "mystery of iniquity":

> . . . in most of the ancient treatises, even in. . . [some contemporary] works. . . the passages that deal with gnosticism spread out before us an array of absurd and extravagant doctrines, and read like a catalogue of theological monstrosities (Guitton, p. 52).

Of these writers, Guitton states,

> the heresy, like a Platonic idea, seems to have always existed in the realms of shadows and temptations; as though it had come down to earth by settling in an agitated and obstinate brain to become visible among men's minds. . . it was the clandestine history of all conspiracies; orthodoxy has exposed to the bright light of day a traitor who had always existed in its bosom (Guitton, p. 14).

Abundant examples will be found throughout the heresiological literature cited in Part II-A, so we shall confine ourselves here to only a few illustrations. Eusebius (*ca.* A.D. 264-339), the first true though hardly objective Church historian, wrote:

> Like brilliant lamps the churches were now shining throughout the world, and faith in our Savior and Lord Jesus Christ was flourishing among all mankind, when the devil who hates what is good, as the enemy of truth, ever most hostile to man's salvation, turned all his devices against the church. Formerly he had used persecutions from without as his weapon against her, but now that he was excluded from this he employed wicked men and sorcerers, like baleful weapons and ministers of destruction against the soul, and conducted his campaign by other measures, plotting by every means that sorcerers and deceivers might assume the same name as our religion and at one time lead to the depth of destruction those of the faithful

whom they caught, and at others, by the deeds which they undertook, might turn away from the path to the saving word those who were ignorant of the faith (*Eccles. Hist.* IV.7, in Rudolph, pp. 275f).

Eusebius then turned to the Gnostic heresy beginning with the "sorcerer" Simon Magus; from his disciple, Menander, came Saturninus and Basilides like "a double-tongued and double-headed serpent," who founded "ungodly heretical schools"; and on and on Eusebius' "history" went.

Bishop Irenaeus, in the preface of his five-volume denunciation of the Gnostic heretics, stated that its purpose was to

> set forth the views of those who are now teaching heresy . . . to show how absurd and inconsistent with the truth are their statements . . . I do this so that . . . you may urge all those with whom you are connected to avoid such an abyss of madness and of blasphemy against Christ (*Adv. haer.* in Pagels, p. xvii).

And later:

> . . . in the same way have I shown . . . what is wicked, deceitful, seductive, and pernicious, connected with the school of the Valentinians, and all those other heretics who promulgate wicked opinions respecting the Demiurge [the Creator God of the Old Testament]. . . (*Adv. haer.* II.19.8, in Layton, p. 152).

Bishop Hippolytus, writing in the early part of the third century, claimed that the theories of the heretics were "stolen from the inventions of heathen men" (Mansel, p. 275); while Tertullian, the late-second- to early-third-century convert who became among the most vociferous of the heresiologists, and then later, ironically, joined the heretical Montanist sect, viciously depicted the Gnostics in the following passage, as summarized by Mansel:

> . . . our duty is to avoid them as we would some deadly sickness. . . they are the offspring of a perverse will and idle curiosity, doctrines of demons, borrowed from heathen philosophy, with which Christians ought to have nothing to do. . . . the Church has a rule of faith to be accepted without further seeking. . . . the faith was committed by Christ to the Apostles and their successors, and no other teachers should be sought than those who were instructed in all truth by Christ and the Holy Ghost, and who taught no secret doctrine beyond that which has been handed down by the Church. . . . [The heretics] not being Christians, they have no share in the Christian Scriptures; . . . they have perverted and mutilated the Scriptures; . . . their teaching is from the Devil, introducing profane imitations of Christian rites (in Mansel, pp. 251-53).

The Gnostic groups of the aforementioned Epiphanius seemed to be an amalgam of various sects, some of which already were the product of the process of deterioration, far from the speculative heights of the great second-century teachers. His principal work, the "Medicine Chest" (*Panarion*) led to Epiphanius being recognized as the "Patriarch of Orthodoxy." Rudolph describes his opus this way:

> The basic idea of this book is to portray all the heretics as fierce and venomous wild beasts [especially as serpents] . . . whose poison endangers the purity of the faith; in its defense and as an antidote for those already bitten he offers his "medicine chest." . . . For Epiphanius all heretics are. . . "worthless" and "evil-minded"; their apostasy from the pure apostolic doctrine of the church condemns them to destruction. . . . His attempt to adduce as many sects or names of sects as possible [eighty in all, based on the eighty concubines mentioned in The Song of Songs, 6:8] makes him act quite uncritically in his treatment of the facts, and even seduces him into invention and quite improbable reports. By this he brought the history of early Christian heresy into great confusion, and critical research has first laboriously had to separate the wheat from the chaff, a task which even today is not complete. . . (Rudolph, pp. 19f).

The "Epistula Apostolorum" ("Letter of the Apostles"), dating from the early part of the second century, was a strong anti-Gnostic (yet nonetheless docetic) text as can be seen in these excerpts:

> [It] was written because of the false apostles Simon and Cerinthus, that no one should follow them--for in them is deceit with which they kill men–that you may be established and not waver, not be shaken and not turn away from the word of the Gospel that you have heard. As we have heard it, kept it, and have written it for the whole world, so we entrust it to you (Epistula Apostolorum, in *NTA* I, pp. 191f).

Interestingly enough, the "Epistula" also reflected the Gnostic myth of the descent and ascent of Jesus (*see* Chapter 6). The strange forms in which this myth expressed itself evidently led to this controversial text being suppressed by the Church, in such an effective manner that its existence was not even known to scholars until its discovery at the end of the nineteenth century.

The ninth-century Photius described the five Acts of the Apostles-- many of which contain strong Gnostic teachings--with words such as: "corrupt," "stuffed with foolishness, inconsistency and incongruity," "invents foolish absurdities," "concoct[s] senseless and childish [stories]", and concludes:

> In short, this book contains innumerable childish, improbable, ill-

conceived, false, foolish, self-contradictory, profane and godless things; and if anyone called it the source and mother of all heresies he would not be far from the truth (in *NTA* II, pp. 178f).

These Acts, probably organized by the Manicheans in the fourth century, also brought down the expressed condemnation of Pope Leo the Great in the fifth century:

The apocryphal writings, however, which under the names of the Apostles contain a hotbed of manifold perversity, should not only be forbidden but altogether removed and burnt with fire (in *NTA* II, p. 193).

One of the most Gnostic of these Acts, as we shall consider in Part II-A, is John, and this led to the following pronouncement of the Nicene Council of A.D. 787:

No one is to copy this book: not only so, but we consider that it deserves to be consigned to the fire (in *NTA* II, p. 193).

The late-second-century "Acts of Paul," including apocryphal letters from and to the Corinthians, is decidedly not Gnostic and, in fact, takes a strong position against various Gnostic ideas, including the rejection of the Old Testament, denial of the physical resurrection, docetism, and tendencies towards libertinism. This text provides still another example of the vituperative vengeance the Church felt towards the Gnostics who disagreed with them. The Corinthians write to Paul, complaining of Gnostic teachers who seem to reflect the teachings of Basilides and Marcion:

Two men are come to Corinth named Simon and Cleobius, who pervert the faith of many through pernicious words, which thou shalt put to the test. For never have we heard such words, either from thee or from the other apostles; but what we have received from thee and from them, that we hold fast (AP I.2, in *NTA* II, p. 374).

Paul responds:

Since I am in many tribulations, I do not wonder that the teachings of the evil one are so quickly gaining ground. . . . And whoever abides by the rule which he received through the blessed prophets and the holy Gospel, he shall receive a reward. . . . But he who turns aside therefrom—there is fire with him and with those who go before him in the way, since they are men without God, a generation of vipers; from these turn ye away in the power of the Lord . . . (AP 8.3.2,36,37, in *NTA* II, pp. 374-77).

In the fourth- to fifth-century non-canonical "Apocalypse of Paul," in which the apostle is given a vision of Paradise and hell, we find, antedating Dante by several centuries, that the Church's enemy (here, of course, the Gnostic) is confined to the fiery inferno:

> Then when the well was opened there came up immediately a disagreeable and very evil smell which surpassed all punishments. And I looked into the well and saw fiery masses burning on all sides.... And I said [to the angel]: Who are these, sir, who are sent into this well? And he said to me: They are those who have not confessed that Christ came in the flesh and that the Virgin Mary bore him, and who say that the bread of the Eucharist and the cup of blessing are not the body and blood of Christ (ApocPaul V.41, in *NTA* II, pp. 785f).

The Manicheans certainly received their share of vituperation as well, as seen in these three brief examples: Aphraates, a fourth-century Syrian Church Father, refers to the Manicheans as "the children of darkness, the doctrine of the wicked Mani, who dwell in darkness like serpents, and practice Chaldeism [i.e., astrology], the doctrine of Babel" (*Enc. of Religion and Ethics*, Vol. 8, p. 394). Augustine--who again was first a follower of Mani, and then a convert to Christianity and later Bishop of Hippo--refers to the "insane doctrine" of Mani (in Haardt, p. 341), and, in what is probably the earliest diatribe against the Manicheans, a parish letter from Theonas, Bishop of Alexandria (282-300), we read:

> As I stated above, I have quoted this briefly from a document of the Manichaean delusion, which came into my hands, so that we may be on guard against those who penetrate into houses with deceiving and lying words, and especially against women, who call them [the Manicheans] Elect, and hold them in honor, apparently because they require their menstruation blood for the abomination of their delusion (in Haardt, p. 336).

As indicated in the Preface, the maligning hardly ended in the ancient period. Writing in the late nineteenth century, the influential German scholar Harnack, who did some of the important pioneering work in contemporary Gnostic scholarship from the perspective of a believer in the New Testament, stated that the Gnostics "distorted the Christian message, and propagated false, hybrid forms of Christian teaching [meaning the Platonic influence]" by what he referred to as the "acute Hellenizing of Christianity" (in Pagels, p. xxxi). The contemporary British scholar Nock agreed, asserting that Gnosticism was "Platonism run wild" (in Pagels, p. xxxi). Wilson has cited another British scholar, Robert Law, who observed that the emergence of Gnosticism "forms one of the dimmest chapters in Church history"

(Wilson, p. 1). The highly influential twentieth-century German scholar Rudolph Bultmann, in discussing the influence of Gnostic ideas in first-century Christianity, not to mention Judaism, writes also from the perspective of the orthodox Church:

> Christian evangelism was thus faced from the beginning with the *danger* of absorbing not only pieces of Gnostic terminology, but also Gnostic types of problem and speculation, and the *danger* was increased by the fact that Jewish circles were already *infected* (Bultmann, p. 41, my italics).

Claude Tresmontant, a French Catholic twentieth-century philosopher, dismisses the Gnostics in this way:

> It is the character of reason, balance and wisdom which impresses me personally, in the great stream of patristic thought. Faced with systems that depreciate and despise matter, the body, the world and creation, Christian thought teaches the excellence of this creation, and rejects the notions accepted by modern psychopathology: these are notions that trouble the sick. Someday Gnosticism and Manicheism should be subjected to psychoanalysis. The psychologist and psychotherapist should realize that Christian orthodoxy is found on the side of balance, wisdom and sanity (Tresmontant, pp. 120f).

Finally the contemporary Hanratty, writing in a two-part article discussing the Gnostics, but from the point of view of the Church looking at an ancient heresy and its influence, falls into the same polemic exaggeration as did the earlier Church Fathers. He writes:

> The Gnostics frequently taught that the process of regeneration and divinization was accomplished by astrological, magical and alchemical techniques which they borrowed from various esoteric traditions. Complementing the Fathers' denunciations of these techniques, there are extant accounts of the use of magical "passwords" and "seals". . . (Hanratty, p. 289).

The reader unfamiliar with the Gnostic literature would understandably find little appeal in such descriptions, as well one might who knew nothing of the often profound theological and Christological discussions found in the great Gnostic schools.

5. "We - They": The Gnostics

These ego beliefs and motives, however, were not restricted to the early Church. One can see in many second-century Gnostics the same tendency to attack and contemptuously exclude the other side as we find in the patristic sources. According to Irenaeus, although hardly an objective source, the Valentinian Marcus and his disciples believed that "none could equal the extent of their knowledge, not even if you were to mention Paul or Peter, or any other of the apostles" (*Adv. haer.* I.13.6, in F I, p. 202); the Ophites stated that the disciples did not recognize nor understand Jesus:

> When the disciples saw that he had risen, they did not know him; they did not even know Christ himself, through whom he rose from the dead.... the greatest error which arose among his disciples was that they thought he had risen in a worldly body, and did not know that "flesh and blood do not possess the kingdom of God" (1 Co 15:50) (*Adv. haer.* I.30.13, in F I, pp. 92f).

In the apocryphal "Acts of Peter" we hear the infidel Simon Magus, enemy to Peter, quote Jesus as saying: "Those who are with me have not understood me" (APt 4.10, in *NTA* II, pp. 292f); while the anti-Jewish Marcion "can only see people [the apostles] who in their indiscretion have adulterated the teaching of Jesus with Judaism" (Bauer, in *NTA* II, p. 41).

The Nag Hammadi texts likewise furnish examples of such Gnostic vituperation. The third-century "Apocalypse of Peter" reflects a rather advanced stage of the conflict between the Gnostics and the orthodox Church. In this particular Gnostic circle Peter is seen as recipient of the *gnosis* revealed by Jesus:

> But you yourself, Peter, become perfect in accordance with your name with myself, the one who chose you, because from you I have established a base for the remnant [the Gnostics] whom I have summoned to knowledge (ApocPt VII.71.15, in *NHL*, p. 340).

This remnant is contrasted to the orthodox who will

> praise the men of the propagation of falsehood, those who will come after you. And they will cleave to the name of a dead man [i.e., worshipping the crucified body of Jesus instead of his resurrected spirit], thinking that they will fall into a name of error, and into the hand of an evil, cunning man and a manifold dogma, and they will be ruled heretically.... Some who do not understand mystery speak of things which they do not understand, but they will boast that the mystery of the truth is theirs alone. And in haughtiness they shall grasp at pride.... And there shall be others of those who are outside our number who name themselves bishop and also deacons, as if they have received their authority from God. They bend themselves under the judgment of the leaders. Those people are dry canals (ApocPt VII.74.10-20; 76.25-35; 77.1; 79.20-30, in *NHL*, pp. 340-43).

This last phrase, "dry canals," is taken from 2 Peter 2:17, where the orthodox Church of the early second century is decrying false prophets and teachers, a group which certainly would have included the Gnostics, who here are using the "enemy's" own words against it.

The author of "The Testimony of Truth," probably dating from the third century, likewise attacks the orthodox Christians:

> The foolish—thinking in their heart that if they confess, "We are Christians," in word only but not with power, while giving themselves over to ignorance to a human death, not knowing where they are going nor who Christ is, thinking that they will live, when they are really in error—hasten towards the principalities and the authorities [i.e., the evil rulers of the world] (Test. Tr. IX.31.23-31f, in *NHL*, p. 407).

6. Martyrdom

A major issue on which the orthodox Church and the Gnostics tangled was martyrdom. Identifying with the sufferings of Jesus was clearly central to the orthodox Church's understanding of the gospel, for it was seen as the ultimate expression of the disciples' love for their Lord. Such suffering, whether in the form of the ascetic turning away from the pleasures of the world, or actively seeking to suffer and die in the name of Jesus, was all seen as the Will of God.

One of the scriptural cornerstones of this apostolic tradition of suffering martyrdom was the boastings of Paul to the Corinthians, whereby he proved his superiority over other Christian witnesses, and unfortunately lay the quantitative standard for future Christians to evaluate theirs and others' fidelity to Jesus:

> because I have worked harder, I have been sent to prison more often, and whipped so many times more, often almost to death. Five times I had the thirty-nine lashes from the Jews; three I have been beaten with sticks; once I was stoned; three times I have been shipwrecked and once adrift in the open sea for a night and a day. Constantly travelling, I have been in danger from rivers and in danger from brigands, in danger from my own people and in danger from pagans; in danger in the towns, in danger in the open country, danger at sea and danger from so-called brothers. I have worked and labored, often without sleep; I have been hungry and thirsty and often starving; I have been in the cold without clothes (2 Co 11:23-27).

St. Ignatius of Antioch proved worthy of Paul's example, as witnessed to in his rather graphic letter to the Romans, written while in Syria awaiting death in the amphitheater:

Wherefore ye cannot do me a greater kindness, than to suffer me to be sacrificed unto God, now that the altar is already prepared. . . . I am the wheat of God; and I shall be ground by the teeth of the wild beasts, that I may be found the pure bread of Christ. . . . [by my suffering] I shall then become the freeman of Jesus Christ, and shall rise free. . . . Let fire and the cross; let the companies of wild beasts; let breakings of bones and tearing of members; let the shattering in pieces of the whole body, and all the wicked torments of the devil come upon me; only let me enjoy Jesus Christ. . . . Permit me to imitate the passion of my God (Ignatius "Romans" I.6; II.3; II.7; II.13; II.16, in *Lost Books*, pp. 179-181).

Many Gnostics, too, emphasized martyrdom as being part of salvation. Since they were the targets of the Church Fathers, it logically follows, as it did for the orthodox who were attacked by the synagogue and the Romans, that they would lift the experience of a suffering victimhood to a spiritual ideal. One representative Gnostic text that took on the Church is "The Second Treatise of the Great Seth," a Christian document in spite of its title:

After we went forth from our home [the Gnostic believers who left the Pleroma, i.e. Heaven], and came down to this world. . . in bodies, we were hated and persecuted, not only by those who are ignorant, but also by those who think that they are advancing the name of Christ, since they were unknowingly empty, not knowing who they are, like dumb animals. They persecuted those who have been liberated by me [Jesus], since they hate them--those who, should they shut their mouth, would weep with a profitless groaning because they did not fully know me (Gr. Seth VII.59.19-61, in *NHL*, pp. 333f).

In "The Testimony of Truth" which, as we have already seen, contains a bitter attack on the orthodox Church, we find the following polemic against the Church's emphasis on martyrdom:

They are blind guides, like the disciples. . . . These are empty martyrs, since they bear witness only to themselves. And yet they are sick, and they are not able to raise themselves.

But when they are "perfected" with a martyr's death, this is the thought that they have within them: "If we deliver ourselves over to death for the sake of the Name we will be saved." These matters are not settled in this way. But through the agency of the wandering stars they say that they have "completed" their futile "course." . . . They do not have the word which gives life (Test. Tr IX.33.21,25; 34.1-10.25, in *NHL*, p. 408).

The late-second-century Heracleon, called by Clement of Alexandria the "most celebrated of Valentinus' school," is more subtle than the author of "The Testimony of Truth," though yet unmistakably *un*impressed by the embrace of martyrdom. As reported by Clement, Heracleon comments on two kinds of confession, or profession of faith: that made by one's faith and conduct, the other simply by mouth. This latter

> the multitudes consider to be the only confession, but not correctly, for even the hypocrites can make this confession. But it will be found that this word was not spoken universally. For not all who are saved made the confession by mouth, among whom are Matthew, Philip, Thomas, Levi, and many others (*Strom.* IV.9, in F I, p. 182).

The "multitudes" of course refers to the orthodox church, and the references to the disciples are, as Pagels has pointed out, conspicuous by the absence of the prominent apostolic martyrs such as Peter and Paul. Clement continues:

> What is universal is the one he [Heracleon] now mentions, the one in works and actions which correspond to faith in him [Jesus] .... For the latter [confession by mouth] . . . deny him, since they do not confess him in action. Only those who live in confession and action which conform to him confess "in him," and in their case he confesses himself, since he has grasped them and is held by them so that they can never deny him (ibid.).

Thus, while the orthodox emphasis on martyrdom is never directly attacked, it is certainly devalued by this prominent Gnostic teacher who considers the daily Gnostic life of witnessing to the truth of Jesus' words as the higher salvation path.

The Fathers of the Church were obviously not silent on this subject. Martyrdom struck right at the heart of their understanding of the Christian message, and they felt that the position of many Gnostic groups opposing martyrdom, as in the above quotation, was a direct attack on themselves. This "attack" was perceived to be the strongest from those Gnostics who adopted a docetic position. This in effect stated that since Jesus' body was illusory, not to mention his suffering, there was nothing with which to identify. The aforementioned great martyr Ignatius was quite explicit in his repudiation of such "false teachings":

> Be not deceived with strange doctrines. . . . For they that are heretics, confound together the doctrine of Jesus Christ, with their own poison. . . . Who was truly born and did eat and drink; was truly persecuted under Pontius Pilate; was truly crucified and dead. . . . But if, as some who are Atheists, that is to say infidels, pretend, that he only seemed to suffer: [they themselves only seeming to exist] why

then am I bound?--Why do I desire to fight with beasts?--Therefore do I die in vain: therefore I will not speak falsely against the Lord. Flee therefore these evil sprouts which bring forth deadly fruit; of which if any one taste, he shall presently die. For these are not the plants of the Father. . . . (Ignatius "Epistle to the Magnesians" III.1; "Epistle to the Trallians" II.2,11,13, in *Lost Books*, pp. 174,177f).

Once again, Irenaeus attacks the Gnostics as

false brethren . . . [who] have reached such a pitch of audacity that they even pour contempt upon the martyrs, and vituperate those who are killed on account of confessing the Lord, and who . . . thereby strive to follow in the footsteps of the Lord's passion, themselves bearing witness to the one who suffered (*Adv. haer.* III.18.5, in Pagels, pp. 104f).

Tertullian extols the virtue of martyrdom in face of the rampant persecution, and explains away the Gnostic stance as nothing but a cowardly response to the situation:

You must take up your cross and bear it after your Master. . . . The sole key to unlock Paradise is your own life's blood. . . . This among Christians is a time of persecution. When, therefore, the faith is greatly agitated and the church on fire. . . then the gnostics break out; then the Valentinians creep forth; then all the opponents of martyr-dom bubble up. . . for they know that many Christians are simple and inexperienced and weak, and. . . they perceive that they will never be applauded more than when fear has opened the entries of the soul, especially when some terrorism has already arrayed with a crown the faith of martyrs (Tertullian *De Anima* 55; *Scorpiace* 1, in Pagels, p. 106).

7. Conclusion

The Church's ruthless destruction of virtually the entire Gnostic literature must remain as one of the sadder elements in Christian history, and rank among history's greatest losses. Further, it points to a fundamental ego dynamic that insidiously thwarts the avowed goal of most religions to be instruments of God's love. To believe that the destruction and obliteration of a thought system different from one's own is to one's benefit, or that such attacks protect truth and advance God's plan for the salvation of His children, is part of the same ego insanity that leads one to believe that destruction of a people different from one's own serves a "noble" or "holy" purpose. Religious fanaticism and political demagoguery are but different forms sharing identical premises. The Orwellian nightmare world of *1984* has always been with us, however subtle or catastrophic its forms of expression have been throughout history.

The second-century Church did believe that attack under the guise of "heresy hunting" was serving the cause of love, holiness, and the Kingdom of God. Irenaeus was clearly sincere in his upholding the truth of God, teaching that there was only *one* Church and, outside of that Church, "there is no salvation" for only the members of that one Church are true Christians. It is tempting on the one side to condemn such belief as malicious and evil, or on the other to ascribe the oblitera- tion of the Gnostic literature to lofty spiritual motives that were guided by the Holy Spirit. The truth lies, however, in the recognition that these Church leaders merely followed the same ego plan for salvation we all do. In order to maintain itself, as the ego counsels every last one of us, the early Church had to create an enemy. Thus the Gnostics became, for all intents and purposes, agents of the devil, and for the next century the theological and political life of the Church was dominated by the need to eliminate the Satanic influence of the enemy, perceived to be *outside* the "true" Church.

As answer to this ancient (though still widely held) Church position, the fresh breeze of a Christian voice that opens wide the doors of dogmatic truth to inquiry and personal experience is heard in *The End of Religion* by Dom Aelred Graham, a Benedictine monk. Writing of the history of the Church and Gnosticism, Graham says:

> In this way Christianity itself partook of the prevailing religious syn- cretism; for a time the boundaries between the Church and the contemporary cults were ill-defined. The door was open to the so- called Gnostic movement and the adoption of Christianity into the various syncretistic systems. At the same time, the Church was be- coming aware of the danger that threatened it from the encroachment of foreign beliefs and the need to make clear its uniqueness at the cost of a life-and-death struggle.... The Church took its stand on its uni- versality. By the strict enforcement of unity in creed and worship it sought to make its Catholic character more manifest. There was es- tablished a "rule of faith" [regula fidei]—an authoritative standard of belief by which all innovations could be tested. From this arose the formal creeds of succeeding times, which still remain the test of orthodoxy. Slowly the official canons of both the Old and New Testament scriptures were formulated, largely, in both cases, for controversial purposes: to provide ammunition for the anti-Gnostic polemic rather than as a result of calm reflection on the nature of the Christian religion and what might be compatible with the future spiritual needs of the faithful (Graham, pp. 85,89).

As it was inherent to Gnostic systems to resist institutionalization, emphasizing instead individual revelation (or *gnosis*), these systems, as we have seen, proved no match for the heavy structure of Church teaching and authority. Perkins has commented that the Gnostics saw themselves as an "inner circle" of Christianity. In this role, therefore, they resisted any kind of adaptation to social and religious needs, in contrast to the ecclesiastical authorities, and were "unable to move into the new world of stable, local Christian communities" (Perkins, p. 204). Moreover, judging from the literary evidence we do possess, the Gnostic theology that reached its pinnacle in the great schools of the second century seemed to deteriorate rapidly in the centuries that followed into an anti-Church polemic, and an extensive mythologizing that often strikes the modern reader as simply silly. These Gnostic writings seem merely to regurgitate, as it were, the teachings of the great teachers that preceded them, without creatively adding to their systems. Therefore, through its hatred and systematic destruction of virtually all the Gnostic literature, coupled with the Gnostic loss of true creative inspiration, the Church had won, emerging virtually as the sole voice in Christendom.

PART II-A

THE BASIC MYTH:

PLATONISM, CHRISTIANITY, GNOSTICISM

INTRODUCTION TO PART II-A

Regardless of their particular emphases and differences, all religions tell a myth or story that reveals a common base, for all people share the same Source, as well as a belief in separation from that Source. These myths begin with God--Creator, Source, Father--in and from whom all life begins and emanates. At some point there is a fall or separation from this Source, setting into motion a cosmic crisis which entails a long and wearying journey away from God into a world variously seen as sin, separation, and materiality. Salvation consists of the journey back, usually with the help and/or example of a redeemer figure. One major exception is in classical Greek thought--referred to by Christianity as pagan--where there is no redeemer, as reason alone is seen as necessary for the return. Thus we journey home to the God that had been forsaken, although religions differ as to who specifically does ultimately return, a point we shall address later. This myth can be divided into the following seven stages.

1) The Nature of God and His Heaven: The Pre-Separation State
2) The Separation from God
3) The Origin and Nature of the World
4) The Nature of Humanity: Spirit, Mind (Soul), Body
5) The Meaning of Salvation
6) The Redeemer - Jesus
7) Practical Implications

Throughout these chapters we shall in greater detail continue our examination of the God-world paradox in light of these stages of the myth; in other words, how the basic cosmogonic premises of any theology (essentially discussed in Chapters 5, 6, and 12, 13) determine the understanding of the body, world, and the process of redemption or salvation (Chapters 7, 8, 10, and 14, 15, 17). Thus the in-depth treatment of these stages in Part II will enable us in Part III to compare and contrast Gnosticism with *A Course in Miracles*, in the historical context of Neoplatonic and Christian thought. Our discussion is not exhaustive, though it is representative of these traditions. However, since for most readers the Gnostic literature is relatively unfamiliar, and the work of Plotinus practically unknown to all but philosophers, a more generous selection from their writings is provided than this book's theme would otherwise require.

Chapter 4

THE NATURE OF GOD AND HIS HEAVEN:
The Pre-Separation State

We begin our story, as did Alice, at the beginning. One's view of God and the state of Heaven--dualistic or non-dualistic, perfect non-dualism or partial--leads inevitably to the succeeding aspects of the myth, which follow logically from how the Source and its creation is perceived. As we shall see much later, only *A Course in Miracles* follows this logic consistently from beginning to end. Again, it is the burden of Part II to present the data upon which this conclusion can be understood in Part III.

Duality vs. Non-Duality

Hans Jonas has divided the multitudinous Gnostic systems into two essential categories, what he has termed the Iranian and Syrian-Egyptian speculations or schools, designations based upon the primary locus of its adherents. The former presents a dualistic metaphysics that traces back to the Persian Zoroastrianism of approximately 1000 B.C., and which later became part of the Gnostic scene. Examples include Mandeanism, the *Poimandres* (originally attributed to the legendary and pre-Christian Hermes Trismegistus, later dated in the second and third centuries A.D.), and finally in its most complete form the new religion founded by Mani. The latter non-dualistic category, stands in sharp contrast to the former, and comprises by far the greater number of Gnostic adherents. Of these, the most fully developed is the Alexandrian Valentinian school, followed (though not chronologically) by the Syrian Basilides, hence Jonas' term: Syrian-Egyptian.

In this book we shall utilize Jonas' categories, but will simply refer to them as dualistic and non-dualistic. It should be mentioned at the outset, to be elaborated as we proceed, that these designations refer basically to the origin of what becomes essentially in almost all Gnostic systems a strictly dualistic view of the world. The dualistic systems begin with two pre-existent states, from which evolve the dualistic view of the world; the non-dualistic systems posit an original monism, out of which arises an opposing system, *after which* is found the characteristic Gnostic duality of spirit and matter.

Basically, the dualistic systems posit a pre-existent Light *and* Darkness, which constitute the pre-separation (or pre-fall) state. In contrast, the non-dualistic schools write only of Light or God as pre-

111

existing. The Darkness emerges later, in what the Judaeo-Christian tradition has called sin, but the Gnostics (especially the Valentinian school) called ignorance. This position has its counterpart in the teachings of the East where, for example, in the Vedanta philosophy the non-dualism is called *advaita*. This distinction between these two systems becomes crucial, in fact, for one of the principal points of this book: The original premise of what is ontologically real directly affects one's understanding of salvation and, even more importantly, one's attainment of this salvation. Thus, within the metaphysical framework we have adopted, we can state that if only God is ontologically pre-existent, then only He is real and everything else must be illusory. Recognizing this truth (which recognition was called *gnosis*) is salvation. If, on the other hand, the Darkness (or evil or sin) shares in God's ontological reality, then it too is real and cannot be denied: Sin's presence would always be among us, and salvation from it therefore would ultimately be impossible. We shall build to this understanding slowly and logically, as the thesis of the book is developed.

Duality

Dualism is essentially a primitive and less sophisticated thought system than its non-dualistic counterpart, despite its most complete emergence in Mani a century later than Valentinus. It has several modes of expression, all of which reflect this essential duality of pre-existing forces of good and evil, light and darkness.

Zoroastrian dualism found its most pronounced and influential expression in the system of Mani, which gave rise to the religion that bore his name, Manicheism. It is the foundation of Mani's system and, despite the many different accounts of his teaching, this dualism remains constant throughout. Here, in a passage taken from what appears to be Mani's own words to a disciple in the "Epistula Fundamenti," we read one of its clearest statements:

> These in the primeval beginning [before the existence of heaven and earth] were the two substances separated from one another. God the Father ruled over the Light, eternal in his holy descendants, glorious in his power, by nature true, forever rejoicing over his eternity. In himself he contained wisdom and the living forces of the spirit by which he also embraces the twelve Members [i.e., Aeons] of his Light, which are the abounding riches of his rule. In each of his members, however, thousands of countless and immeasurable treasures are concealed. The Father himself, exalted in his glory and incomprehensible in his greatness, had joined with himself blessed and illustrious Aeons, whose number and extent cannot be estimated. . . . Near the

one section, but on one side of that elevated and holy land, was situated the Land of Darkness, deep and of immeasurable extent; in it resided fiery bodies, baneful breeds. [Jonas has added in his account: "The world of Light borders on that of Darkness without a dividing wall between the two" (Jonas, p. 211).] Here, out of the same principle, came a boundless and incalculable darkness, together with its abortions. On the other side [of the Darkness] lay filthy whirling waters with their inhabitants . . . .Next follows another fiery Region a prey to destruction, with its leaders and peoples. In the same way there lived inside it a breed filled with dark and smoke, in which the horrible Ruler and Leader of all [these worlds] dwelt, who had congregated around himself innumerable Princes, the origin and spirit of all of whom was he himself. And these were the five Natures of the corruption-bearing Land (in Haardt, pp. 297f).

From the Manichean psalms, composed within a century of Mani's death, we read from the Psalms of Thomas:

When the Holy Spirit came he revealed to us the way of Truth and taught us that there are two Natures, that of Light and that of Darkness, separate one from the other from the beginning. The Kingdom of Light, on the one hand, consisted in five Greatnesses [elsewhere named Reason, Knowledge, Thought, Imagination, Reflection], and they are the Father and his twelve Aeons and the Aeons of the Aeons, the Living Air, the Land of Light; the great Spirit breathing in them, nourishing them with his Light. But the Kingdom of Darkness consists of five storehouses, which are Smoke and Fire and Wind and Water and Darkness; their Counsel creeping in them, moving them and inciting them to make war with one another (in Allberry, p. 9).

Central to this teaching is the identification of the evil Darkness with materiality. Where the Persian and Arabic Manichean sources personify Darkness (Ahriman and Iblis, the latter being derived from the Greek *diabolos*, meaning devil), the Greek sources use the word *Hyle*, which means matter. It is this word that is found in the Syriac, Latin, and Coptic writings, and evil was certainly rendered this way by Mani himself. Thus we are speaking not only of an abstract philosophic concept, but an active principle, co-existent with God: The Darkness has "powers, movements, and striving of its own which differ from those of God only by being evil" (Jonas, p. 211). Some Manichean sources teach that the Devil was created out of pre-existing elements of the Darkness. As an example of this, Jonas quotes an early seventh-century Christian formula which opposed this heresy to the Christian teaching that Satan originally was "created a good angel by God and changed afterwards by his own perversity" (Jonas, p. 211n).

113

These two co-eternal states exist side by side, though separate and disconnected. The Light, for its part, wants nothing to do with the Darkness, being content to let it be itself; it is indifferent to the Darkness' raging and tormented turbulence. In the following chapter we shall return to this point in the Manichean myth and consider the succeeding stages in its development.

The Mandean literature offers many rich examples of this dualistic system, parallel to the Manichean. The Light consists of:

> The great Lord of all kings [the "kings" are elsewhere called "uthras," literally riches, our identity as emanations of the supreme principle]: nothing was when he was not and nothing would be were he not to be; he is under no obligation to death and destruction means nothing to him. His light illuminates and his radiance irradiates all the worlds, and the kings . . . stand before him and shine in their radiance and in the great light which rests upon them. . . . He is the Light, in whom is no darkness, the Living One, in whom is no death, the Good One, in whom is no malice, the Gentle One, in whom is no confusion and anger, the Kind One, in whom is no venom or bitterness (GR I.4-37 [selections], in F II, pp. 148f).

The Mandean world of Light is summarized in the following psalm:

> The world, in which he (the King of Light) stands, cannot pass away: A world of radiance and light, in which there is no darkness, a world of gentleness, in which there is no rebellion, a world of integrity, in which there is no disorder or confusion, a world of fragrance, in which there is no vile odor, a world of eternal life, in which there is no demise or death, a world of living waters, in whose aroma kings rejoice, a world of goodness, in which there is no malice, a world of truth and faith, in which there is no deceit or lying; it is a pure world, without evil admixtures (GR I.41, in F II, p. 151).

Next comes the extension of the Light, the aforementioned kings or emanations.

> He [the King of Light] spoke with great power and with mighty utterance: and there came into being kings of light of pure radiance and great light which passes not away. Kings of praise blossomed, came into being, and were set up, for whom there is no end, number or transitoriness. They are all full of praise and stand there, praising the sublime King of Light . . . (GR I.40, in F II, p. 157).

Other passages describe the emanations of the world of Light in terms of stages, the First, Second, Third, and Fourth Lives. It is the Fourth Life from which comes the imperfection and deficiency--"and uproar broke out in the world"--which we shall describe in the next chapter. The world of darkness, pre-existent, endless and eternal, is described thus:

> Beyond the earth of light downwards and beyond the earth Tibil southwards is that earth of darkness. It has a form which differs in kind and deviates from the earth of light, for they both deviate from each other in every characteristic and form. Darkness exists through its own evil nature, is a howling darkness, a desolate gloom. . . . But the King of Light . . . perceived that evil was there, but he did not want to cause it harm, just as he said: "Harm not the wicked and the evil, until it has done harm itself." . . . From the black water the King of Darkness was fashioned through his own evil nature and came forth. He waxed strong, mighty, and powerful, he called forth and spread abroad a thousand thousand evil generations without number and ten thousand times ten thousand ugly creations beyond count. Darkness waxed strong and multiplied through demons, devs, genii, spirits . . . Satans, all the detestable forms of darkness . . . gloomy, black, clumsy . . . poisonous, filthy, and stinking. Some among them are dumb, deaf, mute, stupid, stuttering, unhearing . . . insolent, hot-headed, violent, debauched . . . of flashing fire, and devastating conflagration. . . . They are master-builders of every wickedness, instigators of oppression who commit murder and shed blood with no pity or compassion. They are artists of every hideous practice . . . (GR XII.6, in F II, pp. 159f).

As with the Manicheans, we shall await the next chapter before continuing the saga.

A variation of the dualistic systems is the Three Root Principle, though these principles essentially rest on the duality of light and darkness. The *Nag Hammadi Library* provides a few examples of the triadic schools, and one of the clearest statements for these positions is in "The Paraphrase of Shem," a non-Christian Gnostic text, albeit in a Christianized form, almost certainly known to Hippolytus, the third-century heresiologist. It was once thought to have had roots dating back to pre-Christian times. The context of the tractate is a revelation to Shem (Seth) by Derdekeas, the son of the Light.

> I heard a voice saying to me, Shem . . . hear and understand what I shall say to you first concerning the great Powers who were in existence in the beginning, before I appeared. There was Light and Darkness and there was Spirit between them. Since your root fell into forgetfulness—he who was the unbegotten Spirit--I reveal to you the truth about the Powers. The Light was mind full of attentiveness and reason. They were united into one form. And the Darkness was wind in . . . waters. He possessed the mind wrapped in a chaotic fire. And

the Spirit between them was a gentle humble light. These are the three roots. They reigned each in themselves, alone. And they covered each other, each one with its power (Para. Shem VII.1.16-2.10, in *NHL*, p. 309).

Reporting on the Sethians, Hippolytus provides the clearest statement of this Three Root Principle:

> Let us now see what the Sethians say. They think that the universe has three clearly defined principles, and each principle has an infinite number of powers. . . . But the essential natures of the principles, he says, are light and darkness; and in between them is a pure spirit (*Ref.* V.19.1-2, in F I, p. 300).

But the spirit is ethereal ("like a scent of myrrh . . . a subtle power"), with no real energy of its own; however, it is infused by the light above:

> But since the light is above and the darkness below, and between them, as I said, the spirit which is of this kind, and since the light, like a ray of the sun, was such as to shine from above on the darkness below, and again the fragrance of the spirit, which is situated between them, extends and diffuses everywhere . . . since this is the power of the [elements] divided into three, the power of the spirit and of the light is present together in the darkness that is situated below them (ibid., 4-5).

Thus, with spirit and light now combined, we end up with an essentially dualistic system.

Non-Duality: God

The non-dualistic story begins with God, and with God alone. Almost all these Gnostic writers affirm that God is unknowable and ineffable. In this they share in the Christian apophatic mystical tradition, which has its roots in the same soil as does Christian Gnosticism. All thus have the similar theological perspective that God is perfect and that His essence is spirit. Where these theologies differ, and differ sharply, is in what can be termed the transmundane quality of God that is central to the Gnostic position, yet is clearly an unacceptable idea in orthodox Christian theology. This belief in God's transmundane nature--that He is independent of the phenomenal or physical world He did not create--marks one of the principal divergences between the Gnostics and their Christian contemporaries, not to mention other philosophical traditions such as Neoplatonism, with which Gnosticism would otherwise have much in common. We shall return to this transmundane aspect of God when we discuss the nature of the world. Apophaticism has been described by Lossky as

> the perfect way, the only way which is fitting in regard to God, who is of His very nature unknowable. . . . God is beyond all that exists. In order to approach Him it is necessary to deny all that is inferior to Him, that is to say, all that which is. . . . It is by *unknowing* that one may know Him who is above every possible object of knowledge. Proceeding by negations one ascends from the inferior degrees of being to the highest, by progressively setting aside all that can be known, in order to draw near to the Unknown in the darkness of absolute ignorance. . . . which is the only way by which one can attain to God in Himself. . . . [Apophaticism] is, above all, an attitude of mind which refuses to form concepts about God. Such an attitude utterly excludes all abstract and purely intellectual theology which would adapt the mysteries of the wisdom of God to human ways of thought (Lossky, pp. 25,38f).

Lossky quotes and paraphrases pseudo-Dionysius, the anonymous mystic who lived around the fifth or sixth century, who prays to the Holy Spirit to lead him

> "to the supreme height of mystical writings, which is beyond what is known, where the mysteries of theology, simple, unconditional, invariable, are laid bare in a darkness of silence beyond the light." . . . It is necessary to renounce both sense and all the workings of reason, everything which may be known by the senses or the understanding, both that which is and all that is not, in order to be able to attain in perfect ignorance to union with Him who transcends all being and all knowledge. . . . One must abandon all that is impure and even all that is pure. . . . It is only thus that one may penetrate to the darkness wherein He who is beyond all created things makes his dwelling (Lossky, p. 27).

A modern expression of apophaticism is seen in this poetic passage from Thomas Merton:

> Desert and void. The Uncreated is waste and emptiness to the creature. Not even sand. Not even stone. Not even darkness and night. A burning wilderness would at least be "something." It burns and is wild. But the Uncreated is no something. Waste. Emptiness. Total poverty of the Creator: yet from this poverty springs *everything*. The waste is inexhaustible. Infinite zero. Everything wants to return to it and cannot. For who can return "nowhere"? But for each of us there is a point of nowhereness in the middle of movement, a point of nothingness in the midst of being: the incomparable point, not to

be discovered by insight. If you seek it you do not find it. If you stop seeking, it is there. But you must not turn to it. Once you become aware of yourself as seeker, you are lost. But if you are content to be lost you will be found without knowing it, precisely because you are lost, for you are at last, nowhere (*Cables to the Ace*, 84).

We begin now by presenting the Gnostic treatment of the ineffability of God. In his introduction to the discussion of the important second-century Gnostic document "The Apocryphon of John," Jonas writes in words that could apply to almost all the Gnostic descriptions of God:

... here we meet with the kind of emphatic and pathetic verbosity which the "ineffable" seems to have incited in many of its professors: the over four pages of effusive description devoted to the very indescribability of the divine Absolute--expatiating on the theme of His purity, boundlessness, perfection, etc., being beyond measure, quality, quantity, and time; beyond comprehension, description, name, distinction; beyond life, beatitude, divinity, and even existence–are typical examples of the rising "negative theology" [i.e., apophaticism] whose spokesmen did not tire for centuries of the self-defeating nature of their task (Jonas, p. 199).

A few examples will suffice, and we begin with a condensation of the "effusive . . . verbosity" of "The Apocryphon of John," where Jesus reveals the truth to his chosen disciple:

The Monad is a monarchy. . . . who exists as God and Father of everything. . . . he did not lack anything that he might be completed by it. But at all times he is completely perfect in light. He is illimitable because there is no one prior to him to limit him. He is unsearchable because there exists no one prior to him to examine him. He is immeasurable because there was no one prior to him to measure him. He is invisible because no one saw him. He is eternal who exists eternally. He is ineffable because no one could comprehend him to speak about him. He is unnameable because there is no one prior to him to name him.
He is the immeasurable light which is pure, holy, and immaculate. He is ineffable, being perfect in imperishability, not in perfection nor in blessedness nor in divinity, but being far superior. He is not corporeal nor incorporeal. He is not great and not small. It is not possible to say, "What is his quantity" or "What is his quality," for no one can know him. He is not one of the existing ones, but is far superior. . . . For the perfect one is majestic; he is pure and immeasurable greatness. He is an aeon-giving Aeon, life-giving Life, a blessedness-giving Blessed One, knowledge-giving Knowledge, goodness-giving Goodness, mercy and redemption-giving Mercy, grace-giving Grace, not because he possesses it, but because he gives immeasurable and incomprehensible light.

How shall I speak with you about him? His aeon is indestructible, at rest and being in silence, reposing and being prior to everything He is the head of all the aeons, and it is he who gives them strength through his goodness (ApocryJohn I.2.27-4.15, in *NHL*, pp. 100f).

Basilides, whose life and teachings we summarized in an earlier chapter, taught, according to Hippolytus, that Being

is not simply something ineffable which is named [indicated]; we call it ineffable, but it is not even ineffable. For what is not [even] inexpressible is called "not even inexpressible," but is above every name that is named (*Ref.* VII.20.3, in F I, 64).

To Basilides this Being is the "non-existent God" (ibid., 21.1), for he is beyond existence; a distinction, incidentally, one also finds articulated in *A Course in Miracles*.[6]

The neo-Valentinian "Tripartite Tractate" describes God the Father as

without beginning and without end; for not only is he without end– he is immortal for this reason, that he is unbegotten–but he is also invariable in his eternal existence.... Not one of the names which are conceived, spoken, seen, or grasped, not one of them applies to him, even if they are exceedingly glorious, great, and honored.... it is impossible for mind to conceive him, nor can any work express him, nor can any eye see him, nor can any body grasp him, because of his inscrutable greatness, and his incomprehensible depth, and his immeasurable height, and his illimitable will.... he possesses this constitution, without having a face or a form, things which are understood through perception, which the incomprehensible one transcends. If he is incomprehensible, then it follows that he is unknowable.... namely, the inconceivable, ineffable, the incomprehensible, unchanging one... (Tri. Tract. I.52.6-10; 54.2-55.15, in *NHL*, pp. 56f).

"Allogenes," a Neoplatonic Gnostic document possibly dating from the third century, speaks thus of "the ineffable and Unknown God":

... if one should know [him] completely one would be ignorant of him.... He is endowed with blessedness and perfection and silence– not the blessedness nor the perfection--and stillness. Rather it [this triad] is a reification of him that exists, which one cannot know, and

6. "All it [the ego] can offer is a sense of temporary existence.... Against this ... spirit offers you the knowledge of permanence and unshakable being.... Existence... is specific in how, what and with whom communication is judged to be worth undertaking. Being is completely without these distinctions. It is a state in which the mind is in communication with everything that is real" (text, pp. 55,64).

which is at rest. Rather they are all unknown reifications of him.
... he is unknown, he is an airless place of the limitlessness (Allog.
XI.61.17; 63.34-64.2; 66.23, in *NHL*, pp. 449-51).

Near the end of the first edition of *The Gnostic Religion*, Jonas includes
two Gnostic hymns, of which we quote the second, by Gregorius the
Theologian:

> O thou beyond all things
>   what else can it be meet to call thee?
> How can speech praise thee?
>   for thou art not expressible by any speech.
> How can reason gather thee?
>   for thou art not comprehensible by any mind.
> Thou that art alone ineffable
>   while thou engenderest all that is open to speech.
> Thou that alone art unknowable
>   while thou engenderest all that is open to
>   thought.
>   . . . .
> End of all things art thou
>   and one and all and none,
> Not being one nor all, claiming all names
>   how shall I call thee?
>   (In Jonas, p. 289)

By way of concluding his discussion Jonas writes of the Gnostics'
"Unknown God,"

> whose acosmic essence negates all object-determinations as they
> derive from the mundane realm; whose transcendence transcends
> any sublimity posited by extension from the here, invalidates all
> symbols of him thus devised; who, in brief, strictly defies description.
> ... The knowledge of him itself is the *knowledge of his unknowability*;
> the predication upon him as thus known is by negations: thus arises
> the *via negationis*, the negative theology, whose melody, here first
> sounded as a way of confessing what cannot be described, hence
> swells to a mighty chorus in Western piety (Jonas, p. 288).

Thus, in all these Gnostic descriptions we can see the attempts to
anthropomorphize God and the process of creation, attempting to put
into words what their own theory teaches is totally ineffable.

Before concluding this section, let us consider some Platonic notions
of God. Plato, of course, was not a strict non-dualist; however, the
Pythagorean influence on his thought certainly lay the seeds for the
non-dualism we find later in Gnosticism.

We have already seen that Plato never truly defined the Good, the highest Idea, yet he did describe it as

> the end of all endeavor, the object on which every heart is set, whose existence it divines, though it finds it difficult to grasp just what it is (*Rep.* VI 505e).

Plato uses the metaphor of the sun to describe the Good: Just as the sun is the source of light in the visible world, making possible perception of the things of this world, giving the power of sight to the eye, so is the Good the source of reality and truth, which renders intelligible these Ideas, and gives the mind the power to know their perfection. We shall return to this metaphor when we consider the Allegory of the Cave in Chapter 8. However, we can comment briefly on the relation between the Good and the other Ideas, such as knowledge and truth, as Plato discussed them in the *Republic*:

> Then what gives the objects of knowledge their truth and the knower's mind the power of knowing is the form [Idea] of the good. It is the cause of Knowledge and truth, and you will be right to think of it as being itself known, and yet as being something other than, and even more splendid than, knowledge and truth, splendid as they are. And just as it was right to think of light and sight as being like the sun, but wrong to think of them as being the sun itself, so here again it is right to think of knowledge and truth as being like the good, but wrong to think of either of them as being the good, whose position must still be ranked higher.... The good therefore may be said to be the source not only of the intelligibility of the objects of knowledge, but also of their being and reality; yet it is not itself that reality, but is beyond it, and superior to it in dignity and power (*Rep.* VI 508e; 509b).

We have already seen Origen's insistence on the immateriality of God, to which we can add His absolute Oneness:

> Having then refuted ... every interpretation which suggests that we should attribute to God any material characteristics, we assert that in truth he is incomprehensible and immeasurable. ... he is far and away better than our thoughts about him.... And among all ... incorporeal things, what is there so universally surpassing, so unspeakably and immeasurably excelling, as God, whose nature certainly the vision of the human mind, however pure or clear to the very utmost that mind may be, cannot gaze at or behold? ... God therefore ... is Unity ... Oneness throughout, and the mind and fount from which originates all intellectual existence or mind (*First Princ.* I.1.5,6).

We turn now to Plotinus. In him we find almost classic statements

121

of apophaticism in describing that which totally transcends the limited experience of this phenomenal world:

> Whenever we say "the One" and whenever we say "the Good," we must think that the nature we are speaking of is the same nature, and call it "one" not as predicating anything of it but as making it clear to ourselves as far as we can (*Enn.* II.9.1).

> For when you think of him as Intellect or God, he is more; and when you unify him in your thought, here also the degree of unity by which he transcends your thought is more than you imagined it to be; for he is by himself without any incidental attributes. But someone could also think of his oneness in terms of self-sufficiency. For since he is the most sufficient and independent of all things, he must also be the most without need (*Enn.* VI.9.6).

> Therefore, when you have said "The Good" do not add anything to it in your mind, for if you add anything, you will make it deficient by whatever you have added. Therefore you must not even add thinking, in order that you may not add something other than it and make two, intellect and good (*Enn.* III.8.11).

> But this "what it is like" must indicate that it is "not like": for there is no "being like" in what is not a "something." But we in our travail do not know what we ought to say, and are speaking of what cannot be spoken, and give it a name because we want to indicate it to ourselves as best we can. But perhaps this name "one" contains (only) a denial of multiplicity.... But if the One--name and reality expressed--was to be taken positively it would be less clear than if we did not give it a name at all: for perhaps this name (One) was given it in order that the seeker, beginning from this which is completely indicative of simplicity, may finally negate this as well, because, though it was given as well as possible by its giver, not even this is worthy to manifest that nature; since that cannot be heard, nor may it be understood by one who hears, but, if at all, by one who sees. But if the seer tries to look at a form, he will not know even that (*Enn.* V.5.6).

The Platonic St. Augustine echoes his master in *The Nature of the Good*:

> The highest good, than which there is no higher, is God, and consequently He is unchangeable good, hence truly eternal and truly immortal. All other good things are only from Him, not of Him. For what is of Him, is Himself (in Bourke, p. 48).

Non-Duality: The Pleroma

The next stage in the "story" of God is His extension of Himself; in *A Course in Miracles* this extension of God includes Christ and the creations of Christ. It must be emphasized, as was discussed earlier, that this process occurs on a plane that transcends time and space. Thus we can never truly explain what cannot be understood on the phenomenal level. Indeed, according to the Course, creation exists before the separation and the birth of the rational and logical mind that was developed specifically to preclude the experience of a non-rational and *a*logical awareness. The problem that the Gnostics had to address at this point was the procession from the perfect unity of God to the imperfect multiplicity of the phenomenal world. The Gnostics attempted to resolve this problem by mythologically introducing many aeons or divine beings, almost as a psychologically unconscious way of putting distance between the good God and the subsequent evil world, for it is the last of the aeons that is the responsible agent for the fall.

The totality of God's extension is called Heaven, what in the Gnostic lexicon is known as the Pleroma, etymologically derived from the Greek word meaning fullness. Thus we are discussing the fullness of God, as manifest in the extension of His being or spirit. There are many divergences in Gnostic writings about the nature of the Pleroma and the process by which it came into being, but the differences among the various Gnostic schools are not as important for our purposes as what they share in common. The Pleroma is frequently referred to as "aeons"; in Neoplatonic thought these were called emanations. Some of the characteristics of the Pleroma are what it shares with its Creator: an undivided and eternal unity, and a nature of pure spirit.

We begin with the Valentinian school, the most advanced and highly developed of the Gnostic systems. Irenaeus wrote of this school:

> Let us now consider the inconsistent teaching of these men, for although there are only two or three of them they do not speak with one voice on the same points, but with reference to the subject-matter and the names put forward opposing views (*Adv. haer.* I.11.1, in F I, p. 194).

To be sure, there seems to be enough documentation to support Irenaeus' contention, for the nature of the Pleroma--the sequence of the emanations, their number and composition, etc.--appeared to be a major source of conflict within the Valentinian circle. However, the finer distinctions that these Gnostics drew in their intramural controversies--was God solitary or not?--need not concern us here since such controversy does not bear on our central theme. Besides, as we observed before about the teachings of *A Course in Miracles*, "No one on earth can grasp what Heaven is, or what its one Creator really means" (manual, p. 56).

"The Gospel of Truth," a Nag Hammadi tractate formerly considered by some scholars to be the work of Valentinus himself, is one of the most important Valentinian documents in our possession.[7] In it we read:

> Now the name of the Father is the Son. It is he who first gave a name to the one who came forth from him, who was himself, and he begot him as a son. He gave him his name which belonged to him; he is the one to whom belongs all that exists around him. . . . Since the Father is unengendered, he alone is the one who begot a name for himself before he brought forth the aeons in order that the name of the Father should be over their head as lord, that is, the name in truth (GT I.38.8-39.1, in *NHL*, p. 47).

And of the extensions of the Son:

> . . . all the emanations of the Father are pleromas and the root of all his emanations is in the one [i.e., Christ] who made them all grow up in himself (ibid., 41.15, p. 48).

One is reminded of lesson 183 in the Course: "I call upon God's Name and on my own," which recalls to us our Identity in Him:

> God's Name is holy, but no holier than yours. To call upon His Name is but to call upon your own. . . . Your Father's Name reminds you who you are, even within a world that does not know; even though you have not remembered it. . . . Repeat the Name of God, and call upon your Self, Whose Name is His (workbook, p. 334).

Incidentally, one reads an almost identical statement in the third-century Valentinian "Gospel of Philip":

> One single name is not uttered in the world, the name which the Father gave to the Son, the name above all things: the name of the Father. For the Son would not become Father unless he wears the name of the Father (GPh II.54.5, in *NHL*, p. 133).

Irenaeus summarizes the position of Ptolemaeus, one of the leading

---

7. The entire text of this valuable document can be found in the Appendix.

Valentinian disciples, yet one who deviated from his teacher in certain theological issues:

> Along with him [God] there existed also Ennoia [Thought], whom they also name Grace and Silence [Sige]. Once upon a time Bythos [the Primal Cause or God] determined to produce from himself the beginning of all things and, like a seed, he deposited this production which he had resolved to bring forth, as in a womb, in that Sige who was with him.... [This process continues on until it] makes up the first and original Pythagorean Tetrad, which they also call the root of all things: Primal Cause and Silence, then Nous and Truth.
> When the Only-begotten [Nous] perceived for what purpose he had been produced he himself brought forth Logos and Life.... From the union of Logos and Life there was produced another pair, Man and Church. This constitutes the primordial Ogdoad, the root and substance of all things.... These aeons, brought forth for the glory of the Father, themselves desired to praise the Father by their own efforts, and they produced emanations by means of uniting. Logos and Life, after having brought forth Man and Church, produced ten other aeons.... Man with the Church also produced twelve aeons. ... These are the thirty aeons ... concerning whom silence prevails and consequently they are not known. This is the invisible and spiritual Pleroma which is divided into three, namely, an Ogdoad, a Decad, and a Duodecad (*Adv. haer.* I.1-3, in F I, pp. 127f).

The Valentinian system recorded in Bishop Hippolytus shares the same basic spirit we find in the earlier account by Irenaeus, but with certain discrepancies. The process of emanations or creations does not begin with the Dyad—Primal Cause and Silence--but from the Monad, the Father. Moreover, God is not included in the counting of the aeons, and thus we end up with twenty-eight, as opposed to the thirty that are usually found in the Valentinian excerpts. Briefly, Hippolytus sees the process this way:

> He [the unbegotten Father] was alone, solitary ... and reposing in isolation within himself. But since he was productive, he decided once to generate and bring forth the fairest and most perfect that he had in himself, for he was not fond of solitariness. Indeed, he was all love, but love is not love if there is nothing which is beloved. Thus the Father himself, since he was alone, brought forth and produced Nous and Truth, that is, a Dyad, which was mistress, beginning and mother of all the aeons which they number within the Pleroma (*Ref.* VI.29.5-7, in F I, p. 186).

The process continues along lines similar to what we saw in Irenaeus, and concludes:

> These are, according to Valentinus, the primary roots of the aeons:
> Nous and Truth, Logos and Life, Man and Church; ten from Nous
> and Truth, twelve from Logos and Life, and twenty-eight in all (ibid.,
> 30.3, p. 187).

The system of Basilides presents a different process from the Valentinians, and ends with 365 aeons. "A Valentinian Exposition," probably attributable to Heracleon, another Valentinian disciple, speaks of 360 aeons. In the world of myth, as in dreams, what is essential is the "latent content" or meaning, not the "manifest content" or form. All such descriptions of the Pleroma are symbolic attempts to render the inexpressible: the "actuality" of the non-corporeal God and His creation.

In "Zostrianos," one of the examples of a non-Christian Gnostic text from the *Nag Hammadi Library*, we read of the one who is saved from the world of matter. This text is of interest because of its discussion of the "glories," who seem to occupy a position in salvation similar to the Course's "creations," discussed below in Chapter 11:

> Therefore, powers are appointed over the salvation of them, and
> these same powers exist in the world. Within the Hidden Ones
> corresponding to each of the aeons stand glories, in order that he who
> is in the world might be safe beside them. The glories are perfect
> thoughts living with the powers; they do not perish because they are
> models of salvation by which each one is saved when he receives
> them.... In that world are all living beings existing individually, yet
> joined together. The knowledge of the knowledge is there... (Zostr.
> VIII.46.15-26; 117.1-5, in *NHL*, pp. 380f, 389).

The "glories" also appear in the Sethian, late-second-century "Trimorphic Protennoia," which shares the Barbeloite (a pre-Valentinian Gnosticism where the figure of Barbelo is the first aeon of the Father) expression of "The Apocryphon of John" (the occasional Christian terminology found here seems secondary to what was probably originally a non-Christian text). The heavenly redeemer Protennoia states at the close of the tractate:

> I hid myself within them all until I revealed myself among my
> members [Sons of the Light], which are mine, and I taught them about
> the ineffable ordinances, and about the brethren.... These are the
> glories that are higher than every glory, that is, the Five Seals
> complete by virtue of Intellect. He who possesses the Five Seals of
> these particular names has stripped off the garments of ignorance
> and put on a shining Light. And nothing will appear to him that
> belongs to the Powers of the Archons [the evil rulers of the world]
> (Tri. Prot. XIII.49.20, in *NHL*, p. 470).

We look briefly now at the theory of emanation belonging to Plotinus, the great third-century Neoplatonist, to return to it in subsequent chapters. The Divine Mind proceeds from the One, and does not affect its Source nor change it in any way:

> For this which we call primary being proceeded, so to speak, a little way from the One, but did not wish to go still further, but turned inwards and took its stand there, and became substance and hearth of all things. . . . He does not need the things which have come into being from him, but leaves what has come into being altogether alone, because he needs nothing of it, but is the same as he was before he brought it into being. He would not have cared if it had not come into being; and if anything else could have been derived from him he would not have grudged it existence; but as it is, it is not possible for anything else to come into being: all things have come into being and there is nothing left (*Enn.* V.5.12).

This process of emanation is ongoing and eternal, and in this sense is necessary since it cannot be conceived that it would not happen, for it is inevitable and inherent in the very being of the One. However, what is produced (or created) must be somewhat inferior to what created it, and we shall return to this idea in the next chapter. The One and Mind of Plotinus are parallel to the Gnostic God and His emanations (the Pleroma).

Central to Plotinus' system is the "reversal" of the emanation, wherein what has emanated returns to its Source through contemplation. Thus Plotinus posits a two-movement view of the cosmos: an emanation or descent--"the automatic creativity of the higher which generates the lower as a necessary reflex action of its own contemplation" (Armstrong, p. 178)--and a return or ascent, which is the reuniting of the Soul with the Mind--the very heart of the spiritual life. We shall explore this process in the chapters to come. For now it should be pointed out that the mind contains Ideas--"living intelligences,"--and each Idea is part of all the Ideas: "Each form [idea]-Intelligence thinks the whole World of Forms [Ideas] and so becomes it; so that There the part is the whole and the whole is in every part, and there is no separation or division" (Armstrong, p. 188). As Plotinus wrote:

> But certainly when the true Intellect thinks itself in its thoughts and its object of thought is not outside but it is itself also its object of thought, it necessarily in its thinking possesses itself and sees itself: and when it sees itself it does so not as without intelligence but as thinking. . . . we must lay down that there is one intellect, unchangeably the same, without any sort of decline, imitating the Father as far as is possible to it (*Enn.* II.9.1,2).

> So we must not go after other first principles but put this first, and
> then after it Intellect, that which primally thinks, and then Soul after
> Intellect [for this is the order which corresponds to the nature of
> things]: and we must not posit more principles than these in the
> intelligible world, or fewer (*Enn.* II.9.1).

In terms of the problem stated at the beginning of this section of
proceeding from the perfect One to the imperfect world of multiplicity,
and the Gnostic introduction of multiple aeons between God and the
world, we find a similar attempt made by the Neoplatonists who
followed Plotinus. Plotinus himself, as we have seen, kept his system
relatively free from such intermediaries, positing just the One and the
emanation of the Divine Mind. However, the fifth-century Syrianus
and his disciple Proclus spoke of the Divine Henads, which come from
the One and form, as it were, the bridge to the multiplicity of the world.
They are the rough counterpart to the pantheon of gods found in the
ancient Greeks, though philosophically far more abstract than the very
human gods. The attempt, however, hits up against the same problem,
for it cannot really explain how these Henads proceed from the strict
undifferentiated unity of the One.

Summarizing once again the material in this chapter, we may
understand the pre-separation state in two ways: duality vs. non-
duality. The former position holds a coexisting light and darkness,
good and evil, while the latter monistically speaks only of the one
principle of light, good, or God. To the former category belongs
ancient Zoroastrianism, reformulated by Mandeanism and Manicheism; while in the latter are found the majority of the Gnostic systems
and Neoplatonists. It has also been observed that the monistic if not
apophatic position was very similar to that of the traditional Christian
mystics. We shall see in the next chapter, however, that what appears
in Christianity on one level to be a strictly monistic view of God and
Heaven is really closer to the dualistic systems we have considered.
This dualism emerges when we enter the next stage of our story: the
fall or separation from God.

Chapter 5

THE SEPARATION FROM GOD

We now build upon the respective theologies of the two metaphysical categories--duality and non-duality--we introduced in the preceding chapter, considering how they explain the separation or fall.

No aspect of our story is more problematic nor paradoxical, nor more demanding of the ingenuity of its theorists--especially the non-dualists--than attempting to explain how a separated and imperfect material world could have come from the oneness of Heaven, the perfect unity of Creator and created. The theologies or theories that have been constructed to account for this phenomenon are more than idle philosophical speculations. The very nature of these speculations has determined, however intricate or even convoluted their lines of development have been, the specific ways of living and behaving in this post-separation world, not to mention the codes of morality that have arisen to govern such behavior. Thus we must pay careful attention to how our four approaches--Platonism, Gnosticism, Christianity, and *A Course in Miracles*--have handled this problem, for these approaches are based on premises upon which an entire thought system and morality rest. Moreover, as indicated earlier, the theological myths that account for the separation are expressing the inner conflict between God and the ego that is common to *all* separated minds, regardless of their particular religious or philosophical persuasion.

By far the simplest of Gnostic explanations for the separation belongs to the dualistic schools. Since their view presupposes a duality of light and darkness, it presented no philosophical difficulty for them to account for the fall from Light or God, since it arose from an external influence, the pre-existent Darkness. Its adherents, then, simply had to confine themselves to describing how the light became trapped in the darkness. The non-dualistic view, however, most thoroughly developed by the Valentinian school, begins with monism, or one system. Thus, the fall occurred *within* the Godhead itself, and is thus purely an internal process. Consequently the separation here demands a more intellectualized if not ingenious explanation. As Jonas summarizes:

> The really important difference [between these two approaches] rests, not so much in the pre-existence or otherwise of a realm of Darkness independent of God, but in whether the tragedy of the divine is forced upon it from outside or is motivated from within itself (Jonas, p. 130).

Duality

As in Chapter 4, we begin with the dualistic speculation, and we shall discover that the basic structure of its myth is similar to the process we will observe later in the story of Adam and Eve. The myth has several modes of expression, all of which reflect this essential dualism of pre-existing forces of good and evil, light and darkness. We shall examine different representatives of this group here, including "The Hymn of the Pearl," the *Poimandres* of "Hermes Trismegistus," the Sethian corpus, and finally its most important and influential exposition in the work of Mani.

The so-called "Hymn of the Pearl" (its name was given by modern commentators) is part of the larger "Acts of Thomas," an apocryphal and Gnostic writing from the second (or possibly early third) century. It was originally written in Syriac and, though definitely pre-Manichean, the "Acts" was subsequently used by Mani and his followers. The Hymn does not seek to explain nor even describe the fall; it begins with the premise that it has already occurred, and then proceeds from there. Its primary symbol is the Pearl, which can be likened to the soul or self that is trapped in the world and must be redeemed. It is the task of the King's son, the narrator, to retrieve it:

> When I was a little child and dwelt in my kingdom, the house of my father . . . from the East, our homeland, my parents provisioned and sent me. . . . And they made with me a covenant and wrote it in my heart, that I might not forget: ". . . go down to Egypt and bring the one pearl which is in the midst of the sea, in the abode of the loud-breathing serpent" (ATh 108, in *NTA*, II, pp. 498f).

The triadic symbol of Egypt, sea, and serpent in Gnostic literature represent respectively the world of ignorance and matter, the world of darkness, and the principle of evil that rules the world. This, then, is the darkness of materiality into which the spiritual Pearl has fallen.

Even though the author does not concern himself with how the Pearl was trapped, we can use the Hymn as an example to contrast our two schools of Gnostic thought. A Valentinian, for example, would have had the challenge of explaining how the Pearl fell through its own devices and, indeed, this school would have seen that the Darkness--Egypt, sea, and serpent--was a direct outgrowth of its error. A dualist, however, would begin by positing the dual existence of both the Pearl *and* the Darkness, and would have described how the serpent stole the Pearl. "The Hymn of the Pearl," as we have seen, falls into this latter category, even though its author does not involve himself in the details of the theft. He begins rather with the pearl having already been stolen, and then concerns himself with the process of its being regained by the Prince.

The *Poimandres* is perhaps the best-known part of the Hermetic literature, the Hellenistic body of writings dating from the second to the fourth centuries A.D., and which centers about the revealer figure of Hermes Trismegistus ("Thrice Great Hermes"), reminiscent of the Egyptian God Thoth. This tradition is pagan, unlike the bulk of the Gnostic literature, and contains no Judaic or Christian references. However, some familiarity with the Bible is reflected, especially, as we shall see, when these writings consider creation. Although these Hermetic writings do not express a purely Gnostic viewpoint, enough Gnostic ideas are found, especially in the *Poimandres*, to warrant inclusion here.

The text consists of a revelation from the figure of Poimandres, "the Nous [Mind] of the Absolute Power." The visionary requests of Poimandres "to be taught about the things that are and understand their nature and know God." Poimandres' response constitutes the virtual entirety of the text. It begins with an experience of total Light:

> I saw an immeasurable view, everything is light, (a light) serene and gay, and I loved the sight. Shortly after there was a darkness, tending downwards, following in its turn, frightful and horrible, wound in a coil; it appeared to me like a snake. Then the darkness changed into something moist, unspeakably confused, giving off smoke as from a fire, and uttering an inexpressibly doleful sound. Then an inarticulate cry issued from it, such that I supposed it came from the fire. And from the light a holy Logos [Word] came upon the Nature, and pure fire shot up from the moist Nature to the height. For it was light . . . and the air, being light, followed the spirit, as it ascended from earth and water up to the fire. . . . But earth and water remained mixed together by themselves, so that I did not see the earth for water. But they were stirred through the spiritual Logos which stirred upon them, so that it became audible (*Corp. Herm.* I.4, in F I, p. 329).

Poimandres explains the vision:

> That light . . . is I, the Nous, your God, who was there before the moisture which appeared from the darkness. The luminous Logos which came forth from the Nous is the Son of God. . . . "Whence then," said I, "did the elements of Nature come into existence?" To this he again replied: "From the will of God. . ." (ibid. I.6,8, pp. 329f).

What concerns us here is the temporal and causal relationship between the Light and the Darkness, the two primeval principles. Interestingly, we discover here a mixture of both types of speculations we have been considering. Clearly, before the "fall" of the Light into the Darkness, the existence of the Darkness is presupposed--the dualistic view--although the Darkness comes *after* the Light. And where does the Darkness originate? Poimandres' answer is "from the will of God," reflecting our non-dualistic view of which the Valentinian is the chief representative. We also find the strong influence of the Judaeo-Christian (biblical) dualism that sees that the Will of God (Logos) "stirred upon" the elements, bringing order out of chaos. Still later in our discussion we shall see the practical importance of these apparently abstract and erudite distinctions.

The *Nag Hammadi Library* provides a few examples of this school, and one of the clearest statements for this position is found in "The Paraphrase of Shem," which we considered in the previous chapter as an example of the Three Root school. The context again is the revelation to Shem by Derdekeas, the son of the Light, and we pick up the narrative where we had left it, with the coexistence of Light and Darkness, and Spirit in between. What we observe is similar to the Manichean view, in that the Darkness begins the crisis in the Light by attacking the Spirit, in whose superiority it sees its own inherent inferiority. It does not know of the Light until it later perceives it in the Spirit.

> But the Light, since he possessed a great power, knew the abasement of the Darkness and his disorder, namely that the root was not straight. But the crookedness of the Darkness was lack of perception, namely (the illusion that) there is no one above him. . . . And when he stirred, the light of the Spirit appeared to him. When he saw it he was astonished. He did not know that another Power was above him. And when he saw that his likeness was dark compared with the Spirit, he felt hurt. And in his pain he lifted up to the height of the members of Darkness his mind which was outside the bitterness of evil. He caused his mind to take shape in a member of the regions of the Spirit, thinking that, by staring down at his evil, he would be able to equal the Spirit. But he was not able. For he wanted to do an impossible thing (Para. Shem VII.2.10-17; 3.1-17, in *NHL*, pp. 309f).

In Hippolytus' version, the same dynamic is expressed this way:

> But the darkness is a dreadful water, into which the light, together with the spirit, is drawn and transferred into this element. Now the darkness is not without intelligence, but cunning in all respects, and it knows that if the light is taken away from the darkness, the darkness remains deserted, dark, without light, without power, inert, and feeble. So it exerts itself with all its cunning and intelligence to keep in its possession the brilliance and the spark of light with the fragrance of the spirit. . . . the light and the spirit seek to possess their

own power; and they hasten to remove and recover for themselves their own powers that have been mingled with the dark and dreadful water that lies beneath (*Ref.* V.19.5-7, in F I, pp. 300f).

We consider now the Manichean system, the most elaborate of the dualisms. We begin the narrative at the point in the preceding chapter which described the coexistent state of the Light and the Darkness. It is here, more than in any other aspect of Gnosticism, that we see the important distinction between the two schools. To introduce the discussion, we again quote from the "Epistula Fundamenti":

> You have turned to me, my dearest brother Patticius, to inform me that you wish to know in what manner Adam and Eve came into existence, whether they were brought forth through the Word or were begotten from a body. To this you shall receive an appropriate reply. . . . The true situation in this matter is therefore misunderstood by almost all peoples and by all who have discussed the subject at length and in detail. . . . In order to penetrate to (the heart of) of this mystery however, beyond any ambiguity, one must of necessity set forth other facts in addition. In the first place, therefore, if you will, hearken to what was before the world came into existence, and how the struggle was conducted, so that you may be able to distinguish the nature of the Light and the Darkness (in Haardt, pp. 296f).

The Light is content to remain as it is, and there is no conflict or turbulence within its realm. The problem enters from without: in the Darkness below. The continual unrest within the limits of the Darkness pushes itself upwards until it finally perceives the Light, which in its jealous coveting, it begins to attack. In Psalm CCXX, we read of

> the obscure abyss wherein there was creeping the Darkness with its five. . . . The Original One of Sin, the enemy of God, do thou make him less? . . . They arose, they that belong to Matter, the children of Error, desiring to uproot thy [Jesus] unshakable tree and plant it in their land; they strove at the matter, they did not succeed, those creatures of shame (in Allberry, pp. 3f).

Drawing from several sources, almost all of which were unfortunately unavailable to me, Jonas has formed a composite narrative of the Darkness' attack. I quote from this summary when other references are lacking.

> The Darkness was divided against itself. . . . Strife and bitterness belong to the nature of its parts . . . and each destroys what is close to him.
> Yet it was their very tumult which gave them the occasion to rise up

to the worlds of Light. . . . Thus aroused and mutually incited they fought and devoured one another, and they did not cease to press each other hard, until at last they caught sight of the Light. For in the course of the war they came, some pursued and some pursuing, to the boundaries of the Light, and when they beheld the Light a sight wondrous and glorious, by far superior to their own--it pleased them and they marveled at it; and they assembled—all the Matter of Darkness—and conferred how they could mingle with the Light. . . . they cast a mad glance upon it from lust for the spectacle of these blessed worlds, and they thought it could become theirs. And carried away by the passion within them, they now wished with all their might to fight against it in order to bring it into their power and to mix with the Light their own Darkness. They united the whole dark pernicious Hyle and with their innumerable forces rose all together, and in desire for the better opened the attack (Jonas, pp. 213f).

As Jonas points out, the model for Mani's account traces back to ancient Zoroastrianism, but it was Mani's unique contribution to describe the fierce intra-mural warfare that eventually led to perceiving the Light, which in turn united the fratricidal forces of the Darkness. In looking beneath the mythological *form* of Mani's description, interestingly enough, one can note similarities on the level of *content* to *A Course in Miracles'* descriptions of the ego's vicious conflict within itself.

The attack now stirs the Light into action, yet it is basically unable to respond in kind:

God had nothing evil with which to chastise Matter, for in the house of God there is nothing evil. He had neither consuming fire with which to hurl thunder and lightning, nor suffocating water with which to send a deluge, nor cutting iron nor any other weapon; but all with him is Light and noble substance, and he could not injure the Evil One (Jonas, pp. 215f).

In this statement, incidentally, we find Mani's rejection of the vengeful God of the Old Testament, in true Gnostic style, not to mention his rejection of the gods of other civilizations. We also find a very interesting parallel to the basic principle of forgiveness found in *A Course in Miracles*: defenseless non-opposition in the face of seeming attack. The parallel ends with the Deity, however, for the narrative continues with the "Father of Greatness" then saying, as quoted by the eighth-century heresiologist Theodore bar Konai:

I shall not send any of these five dwelling-places, which are my Aeons, into battle, for I created them for quiet and for peace, rather shall I myself go and fight (Konai, in Haardt, p. 290).

"Rather shall I myself go and fight" means that He will create a Son to represent Him, and this in fact leads to the creation of several divine figures. The scene is depicted thus in Manichean Psalm CCXXIII:

> Now as they were making war with one another they dared to make an attempt upon the Land of Light, thinking that they would be able to conquer it. But they know not that which they have thought to do they will bring down upon their own heads. But there was a multitude of angels in the Land of the Light, having the power to go forth to subdue the enemy of the Father, whom it pleased that by his Word that he would send, he should subdue the rebels who desired to exalt themselves above that which was more exalted than they (in Allberry, p. 9).

At this point we are on familiar territory, for we are dealing with the Gnostic emanations we saw in Chapter 4, the counterpart to Christ and His creations spoken of in *A Course in Miracles*. The important difference, however, is that in Manicheism the creation comes in reaction to the external situation, while in the other Gnostic systems creation is the natural process of the Pleroma, occurring without necessity.

This Son is called Primal Man (we are still in a pre-physical dimension) or Ormuzd, who in Manicheism is no longer identified, as in Zoroastrianism, with the God of Light Himself, but is rather His first lieutenant, as it were. Armed with his five Sons (or Light emanations; also called Living Soul), he descends to the world of Darkness to do battle with the Arch-devil and his five Sons. (It is left to the reader's imagination, incidentally, from where these five Sons of Light and Darkness have indeed come, although they appear to have had their origins in each of the five attributes of the Gods of Light and Darkness.) Eventually, Man is overcome, a process narrated again by bar Konai:

> Thereupon the Primal Man with his five sons gave himself to the five sons of darkness, as food, just as a man who has an enemy, mixes a deadly poison in a kitchen and gives it to him. And he says: When they [the sons of darkness] had consumed them [the sons of Primal Man] the five light-gods lost their reason. Through the poison of the sons of darkness they became like unto a man who has been bitten by a mad dog or snake (Konai 11, in Haardt, p. 290).

The five parts of Light now become mixed with, and held captive by, the five parts of Darkness, and by the "evil mother of all demons," who from the

> impurity of the he-demons and from the filth of the she-demons . . . formed this body, and she herself entered into it. Then from the five

135

Light-elements, Ormuzd's armor, she formed the good Soul and fettered it in the body. She made it as if blind and deaf, unconscious and confused, so that at first it might not know its origin and kinship (Konai, in Jonas, p. 341).

Thus is the soul--the spiritual nature of humanity--the innocent and passive victim of the force of evil, darkness, and matter: trapped in a world it did not seek, from which it needs to be saved. The first Manichean Psalm of Thomas contains a moving portrait of these events, albeit somewhat different in content, which we now excerpt:

Where did the Son of Evil see them [the Aeons]--the poor one who has nothing, no riches in his treasure, no Eternity in his possession. . . . He rose up saying, May I be one like them. He caught the hand of his seven companions and his twelve helpers. . . . he looked to them. . . in order that, if any should fall and come down, he might go and be one like them. The Great Father therefore took the first step. He strengthened all his Angels, saying "Assemble, all of you, and guard yourselves from the eye of the Evil one which has looked up." One of the Sons of Light looked from on high and saw him: he said to his rich brethren: "O my brethren, the Sons of Light, in whom there is no waning or diminution: I looked down to the abyss, I saw the Evil one, the Son of Evil . . . desiring to wage war. . . . I saw the poor wretches . . . thinking to wage war. . . . I saw them reclining, drinking stolen wine, eating plundered flesh." The Little one . . . stepped forth, he armed himself and girt his loins, the son of the Brightnesses and the Richnesses armed himself and girt his loins, he leapt and sped down into the abyss . . . he came into their midst that he might make war with them, he humbled the Son of Evil and his seven companions and his twelve ministers, he uprooted their tent and threw it down, he put out their burning fire, he fettered the poor wretches that were at hand. . . he rolled up his wealth, he took it, he took it up to the Land of Rest (in Allberry, pp. 203-205).

The next stanza repeats the same story, this time from the perspective of the trapped soul:

The wretches that belong not to the house of my Father rose, they took arms against me . . . fighting for my holy robe, for my enlightening Light, that it might lighten their Darkness, for my sweet Fragrance, that it might sweeten their foulness. . . . A part therefore went forth from my robe, it went, it lightened their Darkness. . . . They did not stir from warring with me until they had made a wall against me . . . the wretches thinking in their heart that I was a man for whom none would seek. I therefore was looking towards my Father, that he might send aid, looking towards my brethren, the sons of Light, that they might come, tracking me. My Father therefore sent the aid to me, my brethren arose, they became one with me. Through a cry only which my brethren uttered, their wall tottered and fell.... the demons ran to the Darkness, trembling seized their Archon [Ruler] entirely (in Allberry, pp. 205f).

We shift now to the traditional Judaeo-Christian understanding of the separation (more usually called the "fall"), since the Gnostic ideas--especially the non-dualistic variety--developed in large measure as a response to this theocentric and essentially dualistic view. The cosmic drama begins with the decision to listen to the non-divine voice--the temptation of the serpent--and unfolds from that point. This aspect of the Judaeo-Christian myth is found in the beginning of the third chapter of Genesis, and we quote it now:

The serpent was the most subtle of all the wild beasts that Yahweh God had made. It asked the woman, "Did God really say you were not to eat from any of the trees in the garden?" The woman answered the serpent, "We may eat the fruit of the trees in the garden. But of the fruit of the tree in the middle of the garden God said, 'You must not eat it, nor touch it, under pain of death.'" Then the serpent said to the woman, "No! You will not die! God knows in fact that on the day you eat it your eyes will be opened and you will be like gods, knowing good and evil." The woman saw that the tree was good to eat and pleasing to the eye, and that it was desirable for the knowledge that it could give. So she took some of its fruit and ate it. She gave some also to her husband who was with her, and he ate it. Then the eyes of both of them were opened and they realized that they were naked (Gn 3:1-7a).

Key to the Western understanding of creation is the notion that God created us with free will. Sometimes this idea is explained as an expression of God's love, in that He imbued His children with the freedom to choose against Him. Thus, they would love Him freely, without coercion. The "fall," therefore, is the result of the free choice of Adam and Eve (the prototypes for all of us) to think and act independently of God. A third protagonist in this cosmic drama is the devil (symbolized by the serpent), conceived as an external force of evil, real and present, coexistent with God. We are speaking here, therefore, of a dualistic system in which good and evil, God and the devil, end up for all practical purposes occupying positions of equal power.

Christian theology does teach that in the beginning there was only God and His host, which was good. However, for reasons that have been the object of theological speculation for millennia, one of God's angels, Lucifer, turned against Him and was cast out of Heaven. Thus, even though we might say, following Jonas' non-dualistic framework, that the fall occurs within the Godhead (i.e., is not due to any *external* intervention, as was the case in Mani's system, for example), Lucifer's rebellion, as with Adam's choice, is really theologically understood as occurring *outside* of God. Furthermore, once the fall occurs, evil is accorded the same ontological reality as its coexistent, good. God and the devil become antagonists, continually vying for the affections and loyalty of humanity, as we see for example in the late mythic story of Job. In fact, throughout the Old Testament, God is continually portrayed as reacting to His people's sins, and thus on one level is always the "victim" of the power of evil as mediated through His sinful children.

As we see, therefore, the creation story as understood by Judaeo-Christian theology does not go into the origins of the devil or evil at all; he is accepted as already being in existence. Adam, the First Man, has before him therefore the possibility of choosing one or the other, as both potentials coexist in his mind. As with the rebellion of Lucifer, no explanation is ever truly offered as to why Adam chose to trust the offering of the serpent as opposed to that of God, other than describing in mythological terms that it *did* happen. Different means of description have been variously set forth to "explain" the fall, as for example the traditional view of human pride, or the Augustinian notion of concupiscence (sexuality). None of these "explanations," however, goes beyond post-hoc descriptions for something that has *already happened, without explanation.*

For all intents and purposes, therefore, good and evil are ontological, coexisting realities, personified in the persons of God and the serpent-devil. Adam and Eve "inherit" both realities and can freely choose to identify with one or the other. Clearly, from the Judaeo-Christian view, Adam and Eve chose "wrongly" for, as is taught, sin entered the world through their disobedience. With sin, in the classical Pauline formulation, death also entered into the world (Rm 5:12; 6:23). Adam and Eve's specific sin was to eat of the fruit of the tree that grants knowledge of good and evil. For God had commanded: "You may eat indeed of all the trees in the garden. Nevertheless of the tree of the knowledge of good and evil you are not to eat, for on the day you eat of it you shall most surely die" (Gn 2:16f). Yet the serpent counseled: "No! You will not die! God knows in fact that on the day you eat it your eyes will be opened and you will be like gods, knowing good and evil" (Gn 3:4f). It can thus even be said that God established the dualism--the tree of the knowledge of good and evil--which posits an already inherent dualism of good and evil within His Mind.

To the orthodox Church, Adam committed the sin of pride and was deceived; to some Gnostics, however, who delighted in turning the Old Testament upside down, Adam's "sin" was his salvation. In the

Gnostic "Testimony of Truth," for example, we find the following "midrash" (commentary) on the story of the fall:

> But of what sort is this God [the Old Testament Creator God]? First he envied Adam that he should eat from the tree of knowledge. And secondly he said, "Adam, where are you?" And God does not have foreknowledge, that is, since he did not know this from the beginning. And afterwards he said, "Let us cast him out of this place, lest he eat of the tree of life and live for ever." Surely he has shown himself to be a malicious envier. And what kind of a God is this? For great is the blindness of those who read, and they did not know it. And he said, "I am the jealous God; I will bring the sins of the fathers upon the children until three and four generations." And he said, "I will make their heart thick and I will cause their mind to become blind that they might not know nor comprehend the things that are said." But these things he has said to those who believe in him and serve him!
>
> And in one place Moses writes, "he made the devil a serpent for those whom he has in his generation." In the other book which is called "Exodus," it is written thus (cf. 7:8-12): "He contended against magicians, when the place was full of serpents according to their wickedness; and the rod which was in the hand of Moses became a serpent, and it swallowed the serpents of the magicians."
>
> Again it is written (Nu 21:9), "He made a serpent of bronze and hung it upon a pole ... which ... for the one who will gaze upon this bronze serpent, none will destroy him, and the one who will believe in this bronze serpent will be saved."
>
> For this is Christ; those who believed in him have received life. Those who did not believe will die (Test. Tr. IX.47.14-49.10, in *NHL*, p. 412).

In characteristic Gnostic fashion, this author has reversed the tale so that the creator God is seen as the evil agent, while the serpent is representative of Jesus, the great Gnostic Redeemer who is sent into the world to bring the saving *gnosis*. It is this false god who would keep Adam and Eve from attaining this knowledge (eating the fruit of the tree of knowledge) that Jesus is offering to them, and successfully so.

The apocryphal "Kerygmata Petrou" ("Proclamations of Peter"), written about A.D. 200, also contains a telling passage that expresses the Gnostic horror at considering the Old Testament God as the real Creator. We find here a long enumeration of the very human traits (the italicized words are all biblical) that the Old Testament gives as belonging to God. The author basically asks throughout: If these are the characteristics of the good God, to whom then can we go, for what kind of God is this?

On this account be it far from us to believe that the Lord of all, who has made heaven and earth and all that is in them, shares his authority with others or that he *lies*, (for if he lies, who then is truthful?) or that he *puts to the test* as if he was ignorant (for who then has foreknowledge?) If he *is grieved* or *repents*, who then is perfect and of immutable mind? If he is *jealous*, who then is satisfied with himself? If he *hardens hearts*, who then makes wise? If he *makes blind* and *deaf*, who then has given sight and hearing? If he counsels robberies, who then requires that justice be done? If he *mocks*, who then is without deceit? If he is powerless, who then is omnipotent? If he acts unjustly, who then is just? If he *makes what is wicked*, who then will work what is good? If he longs for a *fertile hill*, to whom then do all things belong? If he *lies*, who then is truthful? If he dwells in a *tabernacle*, who then is incomprehensible? If he craves after the steam of fat, *sacrifices, offerings, sprinklings*, who then is without need, holy, pure and perfect? If he takes delight in *lamps* and *candlesticks*, who then set in order the luminaries in the firmament? If he dwells in *shadow, darkness, storm and smoke*, who then is light and lightens the infinite spaces of the world? If he draws near with *flourish of trumpets, war-cries, missiles* and *arrows*, who then is the rest that all long for? If he loves *war*, who then desires peace? If he *makes what is wicked*, who then brings forth what is good? If he is cruel, who then is kind? If he does not make good his promises, who then will be trusted? If he loves the unjust, *adulterers* and *murderers*, who then is a just judge? (Ker. Pet. H II.43.1-44.12, in *NTA* II, pp. 120f).

The great Gnostic teacher Marcion, from basically the same texts, likewise sees the Old Testament God as, in the words of Nigg, merciless, stern, cruel, full of passion, fanatic, wrathful, partisan, petty, formalistically just, self-contradictory, vacillating, morally questionable, an instigator of wars, breaker of promises, and a master of malice (Nigg, p. 43). We shall return to this important Gnostic theme of denigrating the God of the Old Testament when we consider the creation of the world in the next chapter.

Returning to the traditional Christian understanding of the fall, or what has been called "original sin," we see that we are presented with a psychological reality. While only an ardent fundamentalist would hold that the Genesis story of creation and fall is literally true, contemporary Christianity has maintained that its mythological treatment reflected this ontological truth of sin and the need for redemption. Parallel to this, we note that after impressively presenting the evidence for not taking the infancy narratives in Matthew and Luke as literally true--showing how and why the Matthean and Lucan churches presented the birth of Jesus as they did, and often contradictorily so-- Raymond Brown in *The Birth of the Messiah* concludes that while not *historically* true, these infancy narratives nonetheless remain *theologically* true. He does not think it

> possible to maintain intelligently that the two infancy narratives as they now stand are totally historical . . . . as belonging to the literary genre of factual history. . . . Be this as it may, I do not think that the approach to the infancy narratives [previously described] . . . imperils either the fundamental message of the infancy narratives [that Jesus was God's Son from his conception] or the insight that God guided the composition of Scripture for the instruction of His people . . . . there are ways other than history by which a people can be instructed (Brown, *The Birth of the Messiah*, p. 562).

Therefore, the traditional churches teach that we have indeed fallen from God: our sin against our Creator is real. Moreover, our sinfulness has caused a life of pain, suffering, and death. God created the body and the physical world, but our sin has introduced death into it. The Gnostic view is quite the opposite and, as we shall see, its totally different set of premises should have led to totally different behavioral conclusions. That it did not will be the subject of a later chapter.

Non-Duality

1. Valentinus

We turn now to the form of Gnostic speculation that in many respects was the stimulus for this entire book. The greatest of the Gnostic teachers, Valentinus, seemed indeed to have been the recipient of a genuine *gnosis*, as he claimed. As reported by Hippolytus, Valentinus stated that

> he saw a small child, newly born, and asked him who he was, and he answered that he was the Logos (*Ref.* VI.42.3, in F I, p. 243).

Valentinus' metaphysical explanations for the separation seem to have no antecedents--philosophical or religious--and more than any other system of thought--from antiquity through the modern era--seems to have reflected the same metaphysical-psychological explanation we find in *A Course in Miracles*. It should be mentioned that while we will continue to speak of Valentinus' specific contribution, citing many different sources--primary as well as heresiological--it is impossible to know exactly how what Valentinus himself taught differs from his students' teachings. Very, very little actually remains of Valentinus' original work. However, there is sufficient Valentinian literature to furnish a reasonably accurate portrait of the basic tenets of Valentinianism which, we may assume, ultimately can be traced to the one acknowledged as its founding teacher. In the end, however, as with the problem of Shakespeare's identity, it is the work that is important, not the identity of the specific source.

What remains unique in Valentinus' work is the transfer of the problem from an external or moral source, such as the devil or an ontological tendency towards evil, to a purely internal or psychological state. It is not that the divine Light has become trapped in the Darkness that had an existence independent of the Light, as an almost natural phenomenon; rather the fall from perfection is an event that an aspect of the Light willed, from within its own mind. Everything that follows from this "fall," therefore, i.e., matter and the phenomenal universe, must also share in its ultimate nature of being a psychological aberration, with no true reality outside of this mind. The world, then, is considered to be a basic epiphenomenon of this fundamental psychological mistake (or misthought). Jonas writes:

> In this way, matter would appear to be a function rather than a substance on its own, a state or "affection" of the absolute being, and the solidified external expression of that state: its stable externality is in truth nothing but the residual by-product of a deteriorating movement of *inwardness*, representing and as it were fixating the lowest reach of its defection from itself (Jonas, p. 174).

By placing the fall or separation squarely within the mind of the Pleroma (specifically the aeon Sophia), having no ontological reality outside it as we shall see, Valentinus allows for the solution also to be within this mind, although not without some intervening variables. Redemption thus consists in correcting this mistake in the mind, correspondingly correcting the problem of the world. We may summarize the Valentinian position therefore as being that the basic problem of the world is the psychological state of ignorance (or forgetfulness) of our origin, while the principle of salvation is the knowledge that undoes the underlying ignorance. Jonas, again:

> It [ignorance] is thus a derivative state, therefore revocable, and so is its external manifestation . . . : materiality (Jonas, p. 175).

Bianchi has likewise written of the purely internal nature of the Valentinian understanding of the problem, as opposed to the clearly dualistic Platonic view:

> This Valentinian pleroma is a novelty and a complication, if compared to the dualistic schema of the Platonic ontology, in the sense

that the Platonic opposition between an inferior realm (of mutability, sensation, and *genesis*) and a superior realm (that of eternity and stability) is shifted up by Valentinus into the very interior of the pleroma, whose periphery, as expressed by the hypostasis Sophia, is open to crisis and alienation--with the consequence that the Valentinian cosmos is only an epiphenomenon where those intra-pleromatic tensions are so to speak finally discharged (Bianchi, "Religio-Historical Observations on Valentinianism," in Layton, pp. 104f).

We shall return to the salvation aspect of Valentinianism in Chapter 8, as we await the following chapter for an elaboration of the origin and nature of the world of matter. It is sufficient for now, however, to restate that the two principal themes of Valentinianism that concern us in this and the chapters to come are how the Sophia principle fell, and how the material world logically and inevitably followed from this mental aberration.

2. Platonism - Plotinus

The foregoing remarks having been made, it is nonetheless the case that the general outline of the Valentinian system can be seen as falling within a tradition of antecedent systems, however unelaborated they are, that share the same general theme of the fall coming from within the Godhead. It was Valentinus' inspired genius to highlight this intra-divine fall, focusing on its specific psychological characteristics yet within a mythological framework, laying the foundation for a process of correcting or reversing this error under the same psychological principle. The parallels with *A Course in Miracles* are striking indeed, and will be the focus of discussion later in the book. We have already discussed the strong Platonic elements in Valentinian Gnosticism, and will begin this section by examining this influence in more detail. Our treatment of this Platonic tradition is chronological, even though Valentinus falls in the middle of this development.

What we have called the Platonic paradox, the problem of imperfection proceeding from perfection, is our emphasis here. In general, Platonists considered that any deviation from the purity of the divine and non-material Ideas in the direction of multiplicity was a descent into impurity. It is interesting to note that Plato's nephew and his successor as head of the Academy, Speusippus, differed from his uncle in seeing multiplicity as expressive of a second divine principle, and thus as ontologically good, as would be the material derivatives of such a principle. We shall see just below his influence on later Platonism.

Plato was ambivalent about the nature of matter and its connection with evil. Found throughout the dialogues are references to an inherent disorder in matter, implying that matter is intrinsically evil. In the *Theaetetus*, for example, Socrates states:

> Evils... can never be done away with, for the good must always have its contrary; nor have they any place in the divine world, but they must needs haunt this region of our mortal nature. That is why we should make all speed to take flight from this world to the other, and that means becoming like the divine [i.e., non-corporeal] so far as we can (*Theaet.* 176a).

In the *Statesman*, Plato, speaking through the voice of the Stranger, instructs on the chaos of the cosmogony--"its clamors and confusion ... great upheaval ... utter chaos of disorder"--and relates it to "the bodily element in its constitution." It is thus the corporeal that interferes with the will of God, who is the world's "maker and father":

> The bodily factor belonged to it [the world] in its most primeval condition, for before it came into its present order as a universe it was an utter chaos of disorder. It is from God's act when he set it in its order that it has received all the virtues it possesses, while it is from its primal chaotic condition that all the wrongs and evils arise in it-- evils which it engenders in turn in the living creatures within it (*States.* 273b).

And finally in the *Timaeus*, which we shall examine in more detail in the next chapter, Plato reflects this ambivalence in the world's origins. God, the Craftsman, is only able "to wish all things to be as like himself as possible ... wishing that all things should be good, and so far as possible nothing be imperfect... " (*Tim.* 29e; 30a). The phrase "in the best way possible" recurs a third time later in the dialogue as well. A struggle between "reason and necessity" (necessity being equated with matter) is the ultimate cause of the creation of the world:

> For this world came into being from a mixture and combination of necessity and intelligence. Intelligence controlled necessity by persuading it for the most part to bring about the best result, and it was by this subordination of necessity to reasonable persuasion that the universe was originally constituted as it is (*Tim.* 48a).

The whole problem of evil, here almost tangentially considered by Plato, becomes more crucial in the later centuries with the Gnostic teachings, and was also picked up by Plotinus in the third century: Is evil superimposed on the world by sin, or is it inherent in matter and thus the world? In other words, is evil a moral problem, or is it a problem inevitable in the very existence of matter and the world. For the Gnostics it was of course the latter, for the absolute existence of the world is identical to the origin and existence of evil. As the nineteenth-century Mansel, Dean of St. Paul's Cathedral in London, commented:

> Contemplated from this point of view, evil is no longer a moral but a natural phenomenon; it becomes identical with the imperfect, the relative, the finite; all nature being governed by the same law and developed from the same principle, no one portion of its phenomena can itself be more evil, more contrary to the law, than another; all alike are evil only so far as they are imperfect; all alike are imperfect so far as they are a falling off the perfection of the absolute. Thus contemplated, the problem of the origin of evil is identified with that of the origin of finite and relative existence; the question how can the good give birth to the evil, is only another mode of asking how can the absolute give birth to the relative; the two great inquiries of philosophy are merged into one, and religion and morality become nothing more than curious questions of metaphysics (Mansel, p. 13).

Mansel has thus put his finger on one of the fundamental issues the orthodox Church raised against the Gnostics: the absence of morality. We return to that issue in Chapters 10 and 17.

In his paper, "The Descent of the Soul in Middle Platonic and Gnostic Theory," the previously quoted American scholar John Dillon has commented on the Gnostic-Platonic solution of introducing a female principle that has arisen from the male supreme being: "This is a principle of negativity, boundlessness and lack, and provokes the generation of the multiplicity of creation" (in Layton, p. 357). Whether such process is a degeneration or merely the natural outgrowth--positive and benevolent--of the laws of spirit is a moot point among the Platonists, although it does seem to reflect the prevailing denigration of women in many Platonic and Gnostic circles.

Thus, we see two essential ways that the Platonists viewed the "separation": one positive, the other negative. The first is an extension of the divine will, however differently that will is conceived; the second a willful choice on the part of the soul, the product of some form of sin, what Origen termed sloth and negligence. Dillon concludes his discussion with the following summary:

> There does . . . seem . . . to be in Gnostic theory, as in Platonism--represented most clearly by Plotinus--a tension between two views of the soul's lot, a conviction that a conscious transgression of some sort has taken place, and an equally strong conviction that somehow God willed all this, and that thus it is all, if not for the best, at least an inevitable consequence of there being a universe at all (in Layton, p. 364).

Let us briefly consider a positive view. The Syrian Iamblichus, one of the leading post-Plotinian Neoplatonists, writing around A.D. 300, gives two explanations for the descent of the soul from its state of perfection:

> The Platonists of the school of Taurus say that souls are sent down by the Gods to earth--some of them, following the *Timaeus*, declaring it to be for the completion of the universe, so that there should be as many living things in the cosmos as there are in the noetic realm, *others* describing the purpose of the descent as being the manifestation of divine life. For this, they say is the will of the Gods, to make their divinity manifest through the medium of souls; for the gods advance to a visible state and reveal themselves through the pure and uncontaminated life of souls (quoted by Dillon in Layton, p. 359).

An opposite point of view is advanced by the second-century Middle Platonist Albinus, whose views are much closer to the denigration of the soul's descent we have already seen in the Gnostics. As quoted by Dillon, Albinus, cited by Iamblichus, attributes the soul's "derangement" to "the mistaken judgment of a free will" (in Layton, p. 360). From this, of course, the resultant material world is also seen in a negative light. These Middle Platonists also had a notion of the alternatives open to the soul once it had become incarnate, and this looked back to Philo. We shall examine these in Chapter 7.

We come now to Plotinus' view of the descent. As the process of emanation proceeds from the One, there is a corresponding loss of purity. The Divine Mind, the first emanation from the One, still retains the unity of its Source, yet it has already within it a plurality of unity, as it were: the world of Ideas or archetypes. Furthermore, the emanation of the higher Soul becomes a further descent from the One into the world of multiplicity, reaching the "bottom" which is matter and, as we shall see presently, the home of evil. The higher Soul is yet part of the divine world of Ideas, yet it is also the link between these spiritual Ideas and the material expressions that constitute the visible world. Here, the Soul's function is similar to that of the Holy Spirit, as set forth by *A Course in Miracles*: It both is part of the Divine Mind (Christ Mind), at the same time being involved in the world of materiality (the separated ego mind), where it rules and orders it. We shall return to the function of the Soul in Chapter 6, when we more specifically consider the origins of the phenomenal world. For now, we shall quote Plotinus:

> And that one part of our soul is always directed to the intelligible realities, one to the things of this world, and one is in the middle between these; for since the soul is one nature in many powers,

sometimes the whole of it is carried along with the best of itself and of real being, sometimes the worse part is dragged down and drags the middle with it; for it is not lawful for it to drag down the whole. . . . It is probably not worth enquiring into the reason for this self-caused turning towards the worse; for a deviation which is slight to begin with, as it goes on in this way continually makes the fault wider and graver; and the body is there too, and necessarily, its lust. And the first beginning, the sudden impulse, if it is overlooked and not immediately corrected, even produces a settled choice of that into which one has fallen (*Enn.* II.9.2; III.2.4).

Plotinus' understanding of evil is a conflicting one. On the one hand he treats evil as a reality, housed in matter. On the other hand he sees that evil cannot exist in itself, but rather is a half-existence; being the final effort and end-product of the emanations of the Good, the point when the Good no longer exists or has basically petered out. MacKenna, the early-twentieth-century English translator of the *Enneads*, has provided an interesting summary of the Plotinian view:

If this seems too violent a paradox to be even mentioned among us, we must remember that it is to some degree merely metaphorical, like so much in Plotinus: it is the almost desperate effort to express a combined idea that seems to be instinctive in the mind of man, the idea that Good is all-reaching and yet that it has degrees, that an infinitely powerful Wisdom exists and operates and casts an infinite splendor on all its works while we ourselves can see, or think we see, its failures or the last and feeblest rays of its light (MacKenna, pp. xxixf).

Plotinus himself states:

If, then, these [all that is of the Good or the One] are what really exists and what is beyond existence, then evil cannot be included in what really exists or in what is beyond existence; for these are good. So it remains that if evil exists, it must be among non-existent things, as a sort of form of non-existence, and pertain to one of the things that are mingled with non-being or somehow share in non-being. Non-being here does not mean absolute non-being but only something other than being . . . like an image of being or something still more non-existent (*Enn.* I.8.3).

But how then is it necessary that if the Good exists, so should evil? Is it because there must be matter in the All? This All must certainly be composed of contrary principles; it would not exist at all if matter did not exist. "For the generation of this universe was a mixed result of the combination of intellect and necessity [from Plato's *Timaeus*]." What comes into it from God is good; the evil comes from the "ancient nature" (Plato means the underlying matter, not yet set in order by some god). . . . One can grasp the necessity of evil in this way too. Since not only the Good exists, there must be the last end to the process of going out past it . . . and this last, after which nothing else can come into being, is evil. Now it is necessary that what comes after the First should exist, and therefore that the Last should exist; and this is matter, which possesses nothing at all of the Good. And in this way too evil is necessary. . . . For matter masters what is imaged in it and corrupts and destroys it by applying its own nature which is contrary to form . . . its shapelessness to the shape and its excess and defect to that which is measured, till it has made the form belong to matter and no longer to itself. . . . If then the body is the cause of evils, matter would be in this way too the cause of evils (*Enn.* I.8.7,8).

Thus, one cannot have good without evil, according to Plotinus, since the good *must* emanate to evil, and it is inherent in the process of emanation that the lesser follow what has been before. To wish to remove evil must then also be the wish to remove the good ("providence"):

But how did he [man] originally become worse, and how did he fall? It has often been said that all things are not of the first rank but all things which are second and third class have a lesser nature than those before them. . . . And because there are better things, there must be worse as well. Or how could there be anything worse in a multiform thing if there was not something better, and how could there be anything better if there was not something worse? So one should not blame the worse when one finds it in the better but approve the better because it has given something of itself to the worse. And altogether, those who make the demand to abolish evil in the All are abolishing providence itself (*Enn.* III.3.4,7).

However, the evil nonetheless ends up imprisoning the soul, which

. . . has false opinions because it has come to be outside absolute truth.
. . . This misfortune befalls it because it does not remain in the noblest, where the soul remains which is not a part . . . (*Enn.* I.8.15; II.9.2).

Plotinus then asks how this evil has come about, and answers in words that prefigure *A Course in Miracles'* emphasis on the ego's nature to be on its own and other than God: self-created rather than God-created:

The beginning of evil for them [the souls] was audacity and coming to birth and the first otherness and the wishing to belong to themselves. Since they were clearly delighted with their own independence, and made great use of self-movement, running the opposite course and getting as far away as possible, they were ignorant even

that they themselves came from that world [God's ''higher world'']
(*Enn.* V.1.1).

How the soul remembers its origin in the "higher world" remains for
a later chapter.

3. Pre-Valentinianism

We continue now with some pre-Valentinian Gnostic representatives. As mentioned earlier, Bishop Irenaeus stated that the first
Gnostic was Simon Magus ("from whom all the heresies take their
origin" [*Adv. haer.* I.23.2, in F I, p. 30]), the magician who is mentioned
in the canonical Acts of the Apostles as having been converted by
Philip and denounced by Peter for his spiritual greed (Ac 8:9-24). His
system, what we know of it, is prototypic of the general school of non-
dualism, wherein the eventual duality originates within the ontologically unitary divinity. Thus, it begins with

> one Power [i.e., God], divided into upper and lower, begetting itself,
> increasing itself, seeking itself, finding itself, being its own mother, its
> own father. . . its own daughter, its own son. . . One, root of the All
> (Hippolytus *Ref.* VI.17.1, in Jonas, p. 104).

This Power, also called Silence, becomes Mind, from which emanates
Thought (Ennoia or Epinoia). It is Ennoia that eventually creates the
angels and the world, loses control over what she created and falls. In
the words of Irenaeus:

> This Ennoia, leaping forth from him [the Power] and knowing what
> her father willed, descended to the lower regions and gave birth to
> angels and powers by whom . . . this world was made. But after she
> had given birth to them, she was detained by them out of envy,
> because they did not wish to be considered the progeny of any other.
> . . . Ennoia . . . suffered every contumely from them, that she might
> not return again to her father, even to the point that she was shut up
> in a human body and through the centuries, as from one vessel to
> another, migrated into ever different female bodies (*Adv. haer.* I.23.2,
> in F I, p. 30).

The remainder of Simon's system need not concern us here, except
to note that Simon, according to the heresiologists, proclaimed himself
as God, coming to earth to free his Ennoia and offer redemption to the
world. He was said to have kept as his constant companion the
"whore" Helena, whom he claimed to be the fallen Ennoia. If nothing

else, taking the Church Fathers at their word, Simon was not only the first but among the most original and daring of all the Gnostics.

It is not until Basilides that we encounter the extensive genealogies of the emanations that place increasing distance between the supreme God and the material world. We can understand these to be, as mentioned above, the psychological means of dissociating the goodness and purity of the spiritual Godhead from what the Gnostics considered to be the evil filth of the body. These descending ladders were described by Jonas as "a kind of metaphysical 'devolution' ending in the decadence that is this world" (Jonas, p. 133). As we saw in the preceding chapter, Basilides deduced no less than 365 emanations. The final one is inhabited by the angels who made the physical world: "But those angels who possess the last heaven, which is the one seen by us, set up everything in the world and divided between them the earth and the nations upon it. Their chief is the one known as the God of the Jews [called "Abraxas" in another report]. . ." (Adv. haer. I.24.3, in F I, p. 60). We shall return to the Old Testament God in the next chapter. Suffice it for now to comment that it is this god who imprisons the fallen spirit.

Our final pre-Valentinian example comes from perhaps the most well-known and best-documented Gnostic text, "The Apocryphon of John." This dates from approximately the middle of the second century and has been available in four extant copies: two long and two short. The Apocryphon is an example of what is termed Barbelognosis, of which according to Irenaeus there were many adherents: ". . . there has arisen a multitude of Barbelognostics, appearing like mushrooms out of the ground" (Adv. haer. I.29.1, in F I, p. 104). Their name is taken from the character Barbelo who, as we have seen, is the first aeon or Pronoia of the Father. From Barbelo there emanate the now familiar series of aeons which completes the Pleroma, concluding with Sophia. We now quote directly from this ancient text, as found in the *Nag Hammadi Library*:

> And the Sophia of the Epinoia, being an aeon, conceived a thought from herself with the reflection of the invisible Spirit and foreknowledge. She wanted to bring forth a likeness out of herself without the consent of the Spirit--he had not approved--and without her consort and without his consideration. . . . And because of the invincible power which is in her, her thought did not remain idle and a thing came out of her which was imperfect and different from her appearance, because she had created it without her consort. And it was dissimilar to the likeness of its mother for it has another form.
>
> And when she saw the consequence of her desire, it had changed into a form of a lion-faced serpent. And its eyes were like lightning fires which flash. She cast it away from her, outside that place that

no one of the immortal ones might see it, for she had created it in ignorance. And she surrounded it with a luminous cloud and she placed a throne in the middle of the cloud that no one might see it except the holy Spirit who is called the mother of the living. And she called his name Yaltabaoth [Ialdabaoth--the Old Testament God] (ApocryJohn II.9.26-31; 10.1-20, in *NHL*, pp. 103f).

Thus, Sophia's fall comes from the wish to create like her Father (in this text referred to as Spirit), yet separate from Him. As has been stated, Sophia is part of the Pleroma, the Heavenly host, and so the error occurs *within* part of the Godhead.

4. Valentinianism: The Fall of Sophia

We turn now to the Valentinian system, which elaborates on the cosmogony of the Apocryphon, yet brings to it a more sophisticated understanding that is the pinnacle of Gnostic thought.

The lengthy report in Irenaeus, from which part of this summary is taken, is based on the teachings of Ptolemaeus who lived in the latter half of the second century, roughly Irenaeus' contemporary. Another major source we shall draw upon is the presentation of Hippolytus, which differs in some areas, yet retains the similar principles underlying the fall of Sophia. Finally, we shall quote from some of the newly discovered Valentinian manuscripts in the *Nag Hammadi Library*.

The Pleroma develops along the lines we have already seen, culminating in the creation of Sophia. In the Valentinian system the Pleroma is not composed of equal members. There is God the Source, called Fore-Father, who is known only by His only-begotten Nous. As Irenaeus writes:

> This Forefather of theirs . . . was known only to the Only-begotten who came into existence from him, that is, to Nous, while to all others he was invisible and incomprehensible. And Nous alone took pleasure in beholding the Father and rejoiced in perceiving his immeasurable greatness (*Adv. haer.* I.2.1, in F I, p. 126).

Nous was stopped by Silence--the Father's consort or Ennoia--because of the Father's Will who wanted the other aeons to desire Him without knowing Him. Thus,

> the rest of the aeons quietly wished to see the one who had produced their seed and to acquire knowledge of the root which had no beginning (*Adv. haer.* I.2.1, in F I, pp. 128f).

At this point, according to Hippolytus, the story takes a dramatic turn:

> Now when the . . . youngest of all the twenty-eight aeons, a female, Sophia [Wisdom] by name, observed the quantity and power of the aeons brought into being, she hastened back into the depth of the Father and perceived that all the other aeons, being begotten, were procreating pairs, but that the Father alone was procreating without a partner. She wished to emulate the Father and to produce offspring of herself alone, without a partner, in order that she might achieve a work which would not be in any way inferior to that of the Father. She did not know that he, being uncreated, the beginning of all things . . . is capable of procreating alone, but that Sophia, being begotten and born only after many others, cannot have the power of the unbegotten one. In the unbegotten . . . all things exist simultaneously, but in the begotten the female brings forth the substance, while the male gives form to the substance brought forth by the female. So Sophia brought forth that of which she was capable, an unformed and incomplete substance [what is later called an abortion] (*Ref.* VI.29.6-8, in F I, p. 187).

Irenaeus' narrative adds that Sophia's passion

> is said to be the search after the Father, for she wished . . . to comprehend his greatness. Since she was unable to do this, because she had undertaken an impossible task, she was in very deep distress, because of the greatness of the depth and the inscrutability of the Father, and because of her love for him (*Adv. haer.* I.2.2, in F I, p. 129).

Sophia began to grieve, and "wept and bewailed greatly over the abortion which had been produced by her." Her terror, anguish, torment, and especially the pangs of her agony were compared by the Valentinians to Jesus' on Calvary. God took pity on her, as well as listening to the anguished cries of the other aeons over what had occurred and might as yet occur as a result. Through the aeons of Nous and Truth, Christ and the Holy Spirit were created

> for the sake of the formation and the separation of the abortion, and for the consolation of Sophia and her release from her groaning (*Ref.* VI.29.5, in F I, p. 188).

And so, to prevent any further extension of Sophia's folly as well as to end the torment, the Cross (or Horos or the Limit) is created:

> In order that the formlessness of the abortion may not at all be manifest to the perfect aeons, the Father produces again a further aeon, the Cross. . . . He is called Horos (Limit) because he separates

from the Pleroma the deficiency [the abortion] outside . . . but Cross because he is fixed unwaveringly and immovably, with the result that nothing of the deficiency can come near the aeons within the Pleroma (*Ref.* VI.29.5, in F I, p. 188).

Thus, according to Irenaeus, Sophia's perfection as an aeon is restored by

the power which supports all things and keeps them outside the unutterable greatness. . . . So she laid aside her original purpose, together with the passion which had arisen from that stupefied wonder. . . . [Thus she] was purified, established, and restored to her partner, for when the desire had been separated from her, along with the supervening passion, she herself remained within the Pleroma, but her desire, with the passion, was separated from her by Horos, fenced off, and left outside it [the Pleroma]. It was indeed a spiritual substance, since it was the natural instinct of an aeon, but it was without shape and form, because it understood nothing. Therefore they call it a frail and female fruit (*Adv. haer.* I.2.3,4, in F I, p. 129).

The account of the Valentinian system given by Hippolytus decades later differs from Irenaeus' in some of the details concerning the development of the Pleroma, especially whether the emanations begin from a single Father, or a pair. In fact, it appeared that this--whether the original Cause was solitary or dyadic--was a source of great contention among the Valentinians, as already mentioned. This issue, however, is beyond our concern, which is the fate of Sophia; and here Hippolytus is in basic agreement with his predecessor.

The Barbeloites distinguished between the upper and lower Sophia, which is a distinction we may find helpful in summarizing the essential aspects of the Valentinian system. The former is the restored Sophia, perfect once again, as is the integrity of the Pleroma; while the latter is the Sophia now placed outside the Pleroma, the product of the aborted attempt to create and to be like the Father. Thus, it cannot be undone, for the thought (or what Jonas terms her Intention) is already in existence, and therefore has effects. This separation of "upper" from "lower" is the means for expressing this dynamic, which becomes important in the ultimate undoing of the error. The part of Sophia that is in error--passion, thought, Intention--now becomes, in Jonas' term, a "hypostasized spiritual substance," still without form. This is the "abortion" spoken of above, and in the literature is usually referred to as Sophia. In some accounts, however, the name Achamoth (derived from the Hebrew word "chochma," meaning wisdom) is used.

Crucial to this system is the role of the Limit, which has a dual function. Within the Pleroma he is called the Cross, and essentially his task is to protect the aeons from any effects of Sophia's fall, as well as to be the boundary between themselves and the Father. Outside the Pleroma he is called Limit, for he serves to protect the aeons from any entry of the now split-off passion of Sophia. The necessity of the Cross-Limit is the result of "Sophia's folly," which has brought about the crisis in the Pleroma. It is the function of the Cross to restore peace and rest which, of course, was not needed prior to the separation. As Jonas summarizes:

> Thus the Limit was not planned in the original constitution of the Fullness [Pleroma], i.e., of the free and adequate self-expression of the godhead, but was necessitated by the crisis as a principle of consolidation and protective separation. The appearance of the figure itself is therefore a symbol of the beginning dualism as it dialectically arises out of original Being itself (Jonas, p. 184).

We find here the interesting notion that Sophia became split into two--the upper and lower Sophia--illustrative of the ambivalence felt in Valentinian circles. Sophia could not be perceived as totally evil, nor, by the way, as totally good. Both qualities have become incorporated by way of this division. In the aforementioned "Kerygmata Petrou" we find this variation of the Sophia myth, which portrays the fallen aeon in the worst possible light:

> . . . she [Sophia] steals the seed of the male, envelops them with her own seed of the flesh and lets them . . . come forth as her own creations. . . . She not only ventures to speak and hear of many gods, but also believes that she herself will be deified; and because she hopes to become something that contradicts her nature, she destroys what she has. Pretending to make sacrifice, she stains herself with blood at the time of her menses and thus pollutes those who touch her (Ker. Pet. H III.23.3; 24.1, in *NTA*, II, p. 117).

The narrative continues with Sophia giving birth to Cain who was "a murderer and a liar and did not wish to cease to sin once he had begun to do so." From his descendants come adulterers and warriors.

There is a parallel to the Valentinian understanding of the Cross-Limit in the "Acts Of John," a text we have already discussed. This again highlights the strong connection between this document and the Valentinian brand of Gnosticism. The passage comes immediately after the "Hymn of Jesus," which we shall consider in Chapter 9. While Jesus is being crucified he appears to John on the Mount of Olives:

...he showed me a Cross of Light firmly fixed.... And I saw the Lord himself above the Cross, having no shape but only a kind of voice ... one that was sweet and gentle and truly of God, which said to me, "... This Cross of Light is ... the distinction of all things, and the strong uplifting of what is firmly fixed out of what is unstable, and the harmony of wisdom.... But there are places on the right and on the left, powers.... authorities... demons ... Satan and the inferior root from which the nature of transient things proceeded.

This Cross then is that which has united all things by the word and which has separated off what is transitory and inferior, which has also compacted all things into one" (AJ 98-99.1, in *NTA* II, pp. 232f).

Interestingly enough, as we have noted, the documents unearthed at Nag Hammadi substantiate much of what we have read in the Church Fathers, despite their evident biases and at times gross distortions. In the third-century "Hypostasis of the Archons," we read: "Within limitless realms dwells Incorruptibility. Sophia, who is called Pistis [Faith], wanted to create something, alone without her consort; and her product was a celestial thing" (Hypos. Arch. II.94.5, in *NHL*, p. 157).

In a parallel document to the "Hypostasis," "On the Origin of the World," we find first a polemic reference to those Gnostics of what Jonas called the Iranian school. Since this is probably dated in the late third century at the earliest, it can be surmised that the Manicheans are meant:

Since everyone–the gods of the world and men--says that nothing has existed prior to Chaos, I shall demonstrate that they all erred, since they do not know the structure of Chaos and its root. Here is the demonstration: If it is agreed by all men concerning Chaos that it is a darkness, then it is something derived from a shadow. It was called darkness. But the shadow is something derived from a work existing from the beginning. So it is obvious that it [the first work] existed before Chaos came into being, which followed after the first work. Now let us enter into the truth, but also into the first work, from whence Chaos came; and in this way the demonstration of truth will appear (Orig. Wld. II.97.24-98.11, in *NHL*, p. 162).

Thus we see our author categorically denying the pre-existence of the Darkness of Chaos, claiming that it must have arisen from "the first work," which is the Pleroma. The narrative continues then with the account of Sophia:

After the nature of the immortals was completed out of the boundless one, then a likeness called "Sophia" flowed out of Pistis. She wished that a work should come into being which is like the light which first existed, and immediately her wish appeared as a heavenly likeness, which possessed an incomprehensible greatness, which is in the middle between the immortals and those who came into being after them, like what is above, which is a veil which separates men and those belonging to the sphere above.

Now the aeon of truth has no shadow within it because the immeasurable light is everywhere within it. Its outside, however, is a shadow. It was called "darkness" (ibid. 11-27).

The initial action of Sophia is thus seen positively; however, it sets up a situation of opposites, which ultimately leads to the Darkness and, as we shall see in the following chapter, to the creation of this world.

The late-second-century or early-third-century Gnostic dialogue, "The Letter of Peter to Philip," has Valentinian overtones as we see in this excerpt:

First of all concerning the deficiency of the Aeons, this is the deficiency. And when the disobedience and the foolishness of the mother [Sophia, in our other versions] appeared without the commandment of the majesty of the Father, she wanted to raise up aeons. And when she spoke, the Authades (Arrogance) followed. And when she left behind a part, the Authades laid hold of it, and it became a deficiency (Pt Ph VIII.135.9-20, in *NHL*, p. 396).

"A Valentinian Exposition" is perhaps the only original account of the Sophia myth that we have from the Valentinian school, although it appears that it is not from the Master himself, nor Ptolemaeus (the account given in Irenaeus). Rather it is from Heracleon's school that is presented in Hippolytus, the evidence being the statement that the Father is alone, rather than creating with a consort, and that Sophia's error was in attempting to create alone, like her Father. Unfortunately the manuscript is a mutilated one and so one must speculate on some of what was contained there. Too much is missing to reconstruct the actual fall, but immediately after her folly it is said of Sophia:

... and she repented and she besought the Father of the truth, saying, "Granted that I have left my consort. Therefore I am beyond confirmation as well. I deserve the things (passions) I suffer. I used to dwell in the Pleroma putting forth the Aeons and bearing fruit with my consort." And she knew what she was and what had become of her (Val. Expo. XI.34.23-34, in *NHL*, pp. 438f).

Finally, in "The Tripartite Tractate"--so named because it is written in three parts--we find an interesting Valentinian text that nonetheless differs markedly from the central teaching of the school. Here the author holds that it is the divine Logos (not Sophia!) who devolutes and eventually creates the world, but all in accord and in the fulfillment of the Father's will. It is speculated by the editors that this possibly came in response to negative reactions of the Church. The text reads like this:

> It came to one of the aeons that it should attempt to grasp the incomprehensibility. . . . Since he is a Logos of the unity, he is one, though he is not from the Father of the Totalities [i.e., the aeons]. . . . The intent of the Logos was something good. When he had come forth, he gave glory to the Father, although he had attempted an act beyond his power, wishing to bring forth one who is perfect, from a harmony in which he had not been, and without having a command. . . . he acted magnanimously, from an abundant love, and set out for the one who is within perfect glory, for it was not without the will of the Father that the Logos was produced, which is to say, not without him [the Father] does he [the Logos] go forth. But the Father himself had brought him forth for those of whom he knew that it was fitting that they should come into being (Tri. Tract. I.75.17-24; 76.2-30, in *NHL*, pp. 67f).

Once the Logos acted in this way the Limit comes into existence:

> The Father and the Totalities drew away from him, so that the limit, which the Father had set, might be established--for it is not from the attainment of incomprehensibility but by the will of the Father--and furthermore they withdrew so that the things which have come to be might become a system which would be bitter if it did not come into being by the revelation of the Pleroma. Therefore it is not fitting to criticize the movement which is the Logos, but it is fitting that we should say about the movement of the Logos, that it is a cause of a system, which has been destined to come about (ibid. 76.30-77.11, p. 68).

This "destiny" foreshadows (or is reminiscent of) Plotinus' theory of emanations.

The rest of the system proceeds along familiar lines and we need not concern ourselves with it any further. One final point: With all of Plotinus' negativity towards the Gnostics, he nonetheless demonstrates a penetrating insight into the heart of the Valentinian teaching-- the origin and source of the darkness from within the Godhead: "so the responsibility goes back to the first principles." Plotinus writes:

> For the soul which declined saw, they say, and illuminated the darkness already in existence. Where, then, did the darkness come from? If they are going to say that the soul made it when it declined,

157

there was obviously nowhere for it to decline to, and the darkness itself was not responsible for the decline, but the soul's own nature. But this is the same as attributing the responsibility to pre-existing necessities; so the responsibility goes back to the first principles [i.e., belonging to the "higher world"] (*Enn.* II.9.12).

Chapter 6

THE ORIGIN AND NATURE OF THE WORLD

Platonism

In their views of the origin and nature of the world we find one of the crucial areas of difference between the Gnostics and, not only the Christian orthodoxy, but the world of late antiquity as well. (The nature of the world, of course, remains the principal area of agreement between the Gnostics and *A Course in Miracles*.) Bultmann has written:

> In Greek Gnosticism, it is true, the outward form of the Greek view of the universe is retained. It is still thought of as a harmonious structure, as unity of law and order. But it is just the cosmos so conceived which undergoes a radical depreciation. Its very law and order are now the source of its terror. This harmony is a prison. The stars, whose brilliant lustre and orderly movement were once contemplated as symbols of the divine nature, now become satanic powers, in whose prisons the sparks of light are bound. The separation between God and the world has become complete. God's transcendence is conceived in radical terms, and therefore eludes all definition. His transcendence is purely negative. He is *not* the world [the world being deprived of all divinity] (Bultmann, p. 167).

Since it is in the ambivalent view of the world that the Platonic tradition provides both the greatest influence on Gnostic thought as well as the greatest divergence, we begin this chapter by a full scale discussion of this tradition, beginning with Plato. We place special emphasis on Plotinus, whose passionate rage was ignited by the Gnostic teachings that "threatened" his students. Moreover, we shall find, surprisingly, that this Platonic influence was felt not only in the non-dualistic thinking, where one would expect to find it, but also in the dualism of Manicheism, which *psychologically* mirrors the Platonic ambivalence towards the world.

1. Plato

We begin with Plato's clear distinction between what is real and what is not (at least what is "never fully real"), the intelligible world of Ideas versus the shadowy world of materiality. (All quotes, unless otherwise noted, are from the *Timaeus*.)

159

> We must in my opinion begin by distinguishing between that which always is and never becomes from that which is always becoming but never is. The one is apprehensible by intelligence with the aid of reasoning, being eternally the same, the other is the object of opinion and irrational sensation, coming to be and ceasing to be, but never fully real (27d-28a).

But if not "fully real," where did the phenomenal world come from, and how and by whom was it made?

> To discover the maker and father of this universe is indeed a hard task, and having found him it would be impossible to tell everyone about him. Let us ... ask to which pattern did its constructor work ...? If the world is beautiful and its maker good, clearly he had his eye on the eternal.... for the world is the fairest of all things that have come into being and he is the best of causes. That being so, it must have been constructed on the pattern of what is apprehensible by reason and understanding and eternally unchanging; from which again it follows that the world is a likeness of something else (28c-29b).

In other words, the world we perceive is a reflection of the immaterial world we cannot perceive through our senses. We find this Platonic idea influencing the Hermetic-Gnostic text "Asclepius": "And the good world is an image of the Good One" (Ascl. VI.74.31, in *NHL*, p. 305). As to why the Demiurge ("the maker and father of the universe") would create such a likeness, Plato, like the Judaeo-Christian theologians, can provide no real reason other than adverting to the omnibenevolence of the deity:

> Let us therefore state the reason why the framer of this universe of change framed it at all. He was good, and what is good has no particle of envy in it; being therefore without envy he wished all things to be as like himself as possible. This is as valid a principle for the origin of the world of change as we shall discover from the wisdom of men, and we should accept it. God therefore, wishing that all things should be good, and so far as possible nothing be imperfect, and finding the visible universe in a state not of rest but of inharmonious and disorderly motion, reduced it to order from disorder, as he judged that order was in every way better. It is impossible for the best to produce anything but the highest (29e-30a).

Plato now challenges himself to account for the origin of the disorder, but for this challenge he has no real answer either, other than to describe the nature of the chaos and how evil and imperfection emerged from it. Plato introduces the word "necessity," which is basically equivalent to substanceless matter, having the unstable qualities of fire, water, earth, and air. Necessity was always there, and its origins cannot really be accounted for:

> It is not for us to describe the original principle or principles (call them what you will) of the universe, for the simple reason that it would be difficult to explain our views in the context of this discussion (48c).

Plato then discusses how Intelligence (the Demiurge) apprehended necessity, controlling it

> by persuading it for the most part to bring about the best result, and it was by this subordination of necessity to reasonable persuasion that the universe was originally constituted as it is (48a).

Thus, from this state of disorganization was brought about a state of "the greatest possible perfection."

Plato introduces the creative role of the soul. Created by the Demiurge, the soul is a subordinate group of gods who take over the task of creation. We see here, incidentally, the seeds for the teachings of the later Middle Platonists:

> He [the Demiurge] made the divine with his own hands, but he ordered his own children [the subordinate gods] to make the generation of mortals. They took over from him an immortal principle of soul, and, imitating him, encased it in a mortal physical globe, with the body as a whole for vehicle (69c).

The phenomenal world is thus seen by Plato as a living god:

> And so the most likely account must say that this world came to be in very truth, through god's providence, a living being with soul and intelligence. . . . For God's purpose was to use as his model the highest and most completely perfect of intelligible things, and so he created a single visible living being, containing within itself all living beings of the same natural order. . . . His creation . . . was a blessed god . . . . a visible god, supreme in greatness and excellence, beauty and perfection, a single, uniquely created heaven (30b; 30d; 34b; 92c).

Plato continues the cosmogony by discussing the creation of time in an evocative passage which, we shall see later, the Gnostics parodied, seeing time as but another of the Demiurge's (or the archons') tricks for trapping us in the physical world. Here, as is quite obvious, Plato's view differs markedly:

When the father who had begotten it perceived that the universe was alive and in motion, a shrine for the eternal gods, he was glad, and in his delight planned to make it still more like its pattern; and as this pattern is an eternal Living Being [i.e., the Ideas], he set out to make the universe resemble it in this way too as far as was possible. The nature of the Living Being was eternal, and it was not possible to bestow this attribute fully on the created universe; but he determined to make a moving image of eternity, and so when he ordered the heavens he made in that which we call time an eternal moving image of the eternity which remains for ever at one. For before the heavens came into being there were no days or nights or months or years, but he devised and brought them into being at the same time that the heavens were put together; for they are all parts of time, just as past and future are also forms of it.... As a result of this plan and purpose of god for the birth of time, the sun and moon and the five planets ... came into being to define and preserve the measures of time.... In this way and for this purpose the stars [elsewhere called "living beings divine and eternal" (40b)] which turn back in their course through the heavens were made, so that this world should in its imitation of the eternal nature resemble as closely as possible the perfect intelligible Living Creature (37c-e; 38c).

Plato, incidentally, was displeased with the etymological meaning of "planet," which is "wanderer," as it suggested an irrational and disordered movement, clearly antithetical to the divine order Plato apprehended as he gazed upwards at the heavens. In the *Epinomis* he writes:

For mankind it should have been proof that the stars and their whole procession have intelligence, that they act with unbroken uniformity, because their action carries out a plan resolved on from untold ages; they do not change their purpose confusedly, acting now thus, and again thus, and wandering from one orbit to another. Yet most of us have imagined the very opposite; because they act with uniformity and regularity, we fancy them to have no souls. Hence the mass has followed the leading of fools; it imagines that man is intelligent and alive because he is so mutable, but deity, because it keeps to the same orbits, is unintelligent. Yet man might have chosen the fairer, better, more welcome interpretation; he might have understood that that which eternally does the same acts, in uniform way and for the same reasons, is for that very reason to be deemed intelligent, and that this is the case with the stars. They are the fairest of all sights to the eye, and as they move through the figures of the fairest and most glorious of dances they accomplish their duty to all living creatures (*Epin.* 982d,e).

Plato also gives great detail on "how body and soul were created part by part by the agency and providence of the gods" (44c). We shall largely skip over these accounts now except to mention the gods' bestowal of the senses, that we may model ourselves after the ordered movement of the heavenly spheres, bringing our own disorder into harmony accordingly:

> ... the cause and purpose of god's invention and gift to us of sight was that we should see the revolutions of intelligence in the heavens and use their untroubled course to guide the troubled revolutions in our own understanding, which are akin to them, and so, by learning what they are and how to calculate them accurately according to their nature, correct the disorder of our own revolutions by the standard of the invariability of those of god. The same applies again to sound and hearing, which were given by the gods for the same end and purpose. Speech was directed to just this end ... and all audible musical sound is given us for the sake of harmony ... (47b,c).

Incidentally, Clement of Alexandria echoed Plato's benevolent understanding of the body's creation:

> Those who censure the creation and speak evil of the body, speak without reason, for they do not consider the structure of man is erect, and fitted for the contemplation of heaven, and that the organs of sensation contribute to the acquisition of knowledge, and that the members are formed for that which is good, not for pleasure. Hence the body becomes the habitation of the soul, which is most precious to God, and is thought worthy of the Holy Spirit by the sanctification of the soul and body, being perfected by the perfection of the Savior (in Mansel, p. 268).

In Part III, we shall contrast this benevolent view of the body with that of *A Course in Miracles*, where the body is also seen as fulfilling *its* maker's (i.e., the ego's) purpose: the hiding of reality.

2. Philo

As we have seen in Part I, Philo reconciled his Platonic philosophical background with his biblical heritage by imputing the cosmogonic principle to the Logos, which he described as God's "shadow":

> ... but God's shadow is His Word [i.e., Logos] which he made use of like an instrument, and so made the world. But this shadow, and what we may describe as the representation, is the archetype for further creations. For just as God is the Pattern of the Image, to which

163

the title of Shadow has just been given, even so the Image becomes the pattern of other beings, as the prophet [Moses] made clear at the very outset of the Law-giving by saying, "And God made the man after the Image of God" (Gn 1:27), implying that the Image had been made such as representing God, but that the man was made after the Image when it had acquired the force of a pattern (*Alleg. Interp.* III.96).

Thus we see the Platonic idea that the visible world was created based upon the pattern of the world of Ideas (the Logos), as Philo says elsewhere: creation "is a copy of the Divine image" (*On the Creation* 25). In explaining the Genesis account of God's creating the Ideas of heaven, earth, air, voice, water, mind, and light on the first day, followed on the succeeding days by the creation of the sensible world, Philo emphasizes that there were not six literal days. Creation was in reality instantaneous and outside of time: "For time there was not before there was a world" (ibid. 26). Moreover, the biblical passage is "quite foolish" if taken literally, for days are measured by the passage of the sun, which had not as yet been created. Thus it would be more correct

to say that the world was not made in time, but that time was formed by means of the world . . . (*Alleg. Interp.* I.2).

In another passage, from *On Providence* (1.7), Philo describes the timeless nature of creation:

God is continuously ordering matter by his thought. His thinking was not anterior to his creating and there never was a time when he did not create, the ideas themselves having been with him from the beginning. For God's will is not posterior to him, but is always with him, for natural motions never give out. Thus ever thinking he creates, and furnishes to sensible things the principle of their existence, so that both should exist together; the ever-creating Divine Mind and the sense-perceptible things to which beginning of being is given (*Philo of Alexandria*, p.15).

Obviously horrified at the implication of the biblical statement that God saw that what He created was good, Philo makes it clear that it is not matter itself which is good:

Now God praised not the material which He had used for His work, material soul-less, discordant and dissoluble, and indeed in itself perishable, irregular, unequal, but He praised the works of His own art, which were consummated through a single exercise of power equal and uniform, and through knowledge ever one and the same (*Who is the Heir?* 160).

It is indeed explicitly stated by Philo that God created the world out of a pre-existent matter, but it is exceedingly unclear whether that matter was itself, in Philo's view, a product of God's creative act. His descriptions of pre-existent matter appear to be almost deliberately vague. Clearly he was confronted by the same problem as was Plato, who also ambiguously explained how the copies of the eternal Ideas came into being. Moreover, the Athenian's promise to "follow this up some other time" (*Tim.* 50c), if fulfilled, is not extant. Regardless, the general tenor of the Platonic tradition is that the material world is only the shadow-image of what truly exists, and that "shadowy existence is a constant embarrassment that needs to be glossed over as inconspicuously as possible" (Winston, *Philo of Alexandria*, p. 11).

Winston has cogently summarized the Platonic dilemma as it confronted Philo:

> Furthermore, to attribute to Philo the view that God created pre-existent matter would be incongruous with his whole language of creation. First, if God created the copies of the four elements according to the pattern of the divine Forms, why should they be disordered? Second, how could God who, according to Philo, is never the source of evil, and is always introducing harmony and order, be the source of a pre-existent matter that is "contentious," "disordered," "dead," "chaotic," and "out of tune"? Moreover, the argument that God created the cosmos because he did not begrudge a share in his own excellence to an existence that in itself had nothing fair or lovely would completely miss its mark if this "unlovely existence" was itself created by God. Philo's assertion that God did not confer benefits on pre-existent matter in proportion to his own bounties, but rather in proportion to the capacities of the recipients, implies an inherent limitation in the nature of this matter. Why, then, should God have created copies of the Forms [Ideas] in the first place? If, as we have just seen, the copies are inherently disordered and disharmonious and can be rendered ordered and harmonious only up to a point, what reason could there be for the all-beneficient Deity to initiate the production of such limited phantoms, a "faulted reality" from a faultless one? . . . Logically, of course, God is, for Philo, indirectly the source of pre-existent matter, but Philo would have recoiled from ascribing it to the *creative* activity of God, just as he recoiled from ascribing the *shaping* of matter directly to God (Winston, *Philo of Alexandria*, pp. 11f).

It is thus obvious that Philo's purpose was to free God from any involvement and implication in creating the material world, which clearly was seen to be an inferior dimension of reality. Rather, the creative or demiurgic function was given to a lesser principle. This idea finds clear statement in the words of the Middle Platonist Albinus, speaking of Plato's statement that the material world has been generated:

> ...we must take this to mean not that there was a time when the world did not exist, but that the world is always becoming and reveals a more fundamental cause of its existence. And the Soul of the world, existing always, is not made by God, but ordered by him. *And God is said to make in this sense* ... that he awakens and turns the mind of the World-Soul to him ... so that she [the World-Soul] will contemplate his thoughts [the Forms-Ideas] and receive the Forms (quoted by O'Meara, "Gnosticism and the Making of the World," in Layton, p. 368).

Thus the world is fashioned by the World-Soul, not the highest God. We shall see presently how Plotinus extended this idea by hypothesizing the dynamic of emanation that originates with the ultimate One, and evolves downward through the Mind and Soul, giving rise ultimately to the material world.

3. Origen

Unlike Plotinus, whose thought in many ways he shares, and his fellow Christian Platonists, Origen sees the creation of the material world as serving a purely functional purpose, deliberately undertaken by God. For Plotinus, as we shall see, the phenomenal world was the inevitable (if not unfortunate) effect of the emanationist dynamic of the One and the Soul. For Augustine, whom we shall examine after Plotinus, the world was the creation of the good God. Origen, however, understands the world as created by the good God only as a necessary creation to help remedy the fall.

Once the soul "fell" it was immediately placed in a body, which mirrored the extent and character of the fall. The body, therefore, symbolizes the state of the fallen soul; the greater the fall from God, the "lower" the corporeal frame around the soul. This hierarchy ranges from the angels at the top, through human beings, animals, down to the demons. Consequently, every rational being was placed in a physical body that corresponded to the level of its own choice relative to its fall from God. The celestial bodies or angelic beings, for example, reflect those souls who did not fall far, while the "lower" animals encase those souls who fell quite a distance (all quotes in this section are from *On First Principles*):

> These beings, disturbed and drawn away from that state of goodness, and then tossed about by the diverse motions and desires of their

souls, have exchanged the one undivided goodness of their original nature for minds that vary in quality according to their different tendencies (II.1.1).

Origen thus does not see this hierarchy as fixed, but rather that the souls can move through the hierarchy, as a student progresses from grade to grade, until the journey back to God is completed. The body, therefore, is God's gift--although in the form of a punishment--to the soul, enabling it to make its journey of return. On the cosmic scale, then, the stars, sun, and planets become the setting in which such movement can occur. The body will last as long as the necessity for it remains.

Like his Middle Platonic predecessors, Origen does not see God the Father as creator. This function is reserved for the second person in the Trinity, the Johannine Word or Logos. The Word thus is the mediator between the spiritual and material worlds, in which latter the fallen souls can undo their fall. Christ the Word contains within Himself, therefore, the perfection of God as well as the souls striving to return to Him. The Word, insofar as it is the creative principle of the Godhead, can be equated with Plato's Demiurge and Plotinus' Mind; in its function as mediator with the fallen souls (the "rational beings") it is analogous to Plato's World Soul or Plotinus' Soul. We shall discuss the relationship between Christ the Word and Jesus in Chapter 9.

Origen's cosmogony thus contains both positive and negative elements. It begins with the separation; the "loss or fall, of those who live negligently" (I.4.1). These are the rational beings (minds or souls), created in God's image and likeness, "equal and alike" (ibid.), and yet possessing free will "either to make progress through the imitation of God or to deteriorate through negligence" (II.9.6):

> For the Creator granted to the minds created by him the power of free and voluntary movement, in order that the good that was in them might become their own, since it was preserved by their own free will; but sloth and weariness of taking trouble to preserve the good, coupled with disregard and neglect of better things, began the process of withdrawing from the good. Now to withdraw from the good is nothing else than to be immersed in evil; for it is certain that to be evil means to be lacking in good. . . . From this source . . . the Creator of all things obtained certain seeds and causes of variety and diversity, in order that, according to the diversity of . . . rational beings . . . he might create a world that was various and diverse (II.9.2).

St. Jerome has preserved Origen's teaching even more forcefully:

> I think we must believe that there is in the regions above a more divine dwelling-place and a true rest, where rational creatures used to live

before they descended to these lower regions and travelled from invisible to visible surroundings, and where, before they were cast down to the earth and forced to wear gross bodies, they enjoyed a primeval blessedness. And, so, God the Creator made for them bodies appropriate to their lowly stations, and fashioned this visible world, and sent into it ministers to work for the correction and salvation of those who had fallen (St. Jerome, quoted in *On First Principles*, p. 240, n.3).

These ministers include the planetary bodies, and so we can see that, by the world, Origen means the entire cosmos, and he describes in detail the ultimate variety of our physical world and all the creatures in it, the "earthly" and "supercelestial." This variety of course is due to the respective levels of declension of the fallen souls, and is not God's doing. Nonetheless, despite this variety, God "gathered the diversities of minds into the harmony of a single world" (II.9.6). In a passage influenced by Plato's theory of the World-Soul, Origen writes that similar to St. Paul's "one body" composed of "many members" and held together by one soul, so too we should

accept the opinion that the universe is . . . an immense, monstrous animal, held together by the power and reason of God as by one soul (II.1.3).

In commenting on John 17:24--"you loved me before the foundation of the world"--Origen states that the Greek word *katabole* for "foundation" was mistranslated. The Greek carries with it the connotation of "to cast downwards" (III.5.4), and Origen sees this as scriptural evidence for the descent from the perfect Heaven resulting in the imperfect physical world.

Again, the end product of this descent is the placing of souls into bodies. The mechanics of this process involve the mingling of these mental qualities with the God-created matter, which "is clearly seen to have an existence in its own right apart from these qualities" (II.1.4). Thus for Origen, similar to Plato and Philo, matter is simply there: abstract and amorphous, freely adapting to the qualities that have come to it. This mingling produces the diversity in bodies. Thus Origen forcefully argues the point, obviously with the Gnostics in mind, that God did create the physical world, although it would not have been needed had it not been for the fall of the rational beings. However, given the fall, the need for the world was present, and so God's creation was designed to help these souls return to their natural state by providing a classroom in which they could learn and ascend the scale of being. In fact, Origen explores the possibility of additional world-classrooms after this one, providing a process of instruction and rational training through which those who in this present life have devoted themselves to these pursuits and, being made purer in mind, have attained here and now to a capacity for divine wisdom, may advance to a richer understanding of truth (II.3.1).

Even hell is given a positive meaning, wherein its fires serve as a purifying agent. Origen's own words were censored by a benevolent translator seeking to preserve his already shaky Church status, but his original teaching is preserved by St. Jerome:

As for the fire of Gehenna and the torments, with which holy scripture threatens sinners, Origen does not make them consist in punishments, but in the conscience of sinners, when by the goodness and power of God the . . . . entire crop of our sins . . . and every shameful and impious act that we have done is represented in an image before our eyes, so that the mind, beholding its former acts of self-indulgence is punished by a burning conscience and stung by the pricks of remorse (St. Jerome, quoted in *On First Principles*, p. 142, n.3).

Likewise, all painful events in our lives are seen as God's means for purifying our mistakes, washing "away the ills of the soul" and helping us to return to Him. The various ills that befall us are not God's punishment--because His love is just and equal--but are the product of our own decisions. The world thus is generally seen by Origen to be positive, despite his personal abhorrence of the body to which we shall return in Chapter 7.

4. Plotinus

In discussing Plotinus we find perhaps the clearest expression of the paradox: the world as good *and* evil. Let us begin Plotinus' cosmogony by briefly reviewing the three hypostases we discussed in Part I. The *One* is the ultimate source, undifferentiated and unknowable, from which proceeds the *Mind* (sometimes translated as "Intelligence"-- some of the great Plotinian scholars have been French, and there is no French word for "mind"). It is within the Mind that the productive or creative ability rests, although the One is the source of it. Within the Mind is found all being (cf. Plato's Ideas), distinct yet totally unified. From the Mind comes the *Soul*, wherein distinct being is no longer unified. Through the process of emanation, being is ultimately dispersed into unformed matter, resulting in the material or sensible world.

Each Idea in the Mind has its reflection in the physical realm: "And in each and every thing there is some *one* to which you will trace it back," and beyond each *one* is Intellect, "the most beautiful of all; . . . this beautiful universe of ours is a shadow and image of it, . . . and it lives a blessed life." Beyond this is an even greater Being, the Absolute One (all quotations are from the *Enneads* unless otherwise noted):

> As certainly, one who looks up to the sky and sees the light of the stars thinks of their maker and seeks him, so the man who has contemplated the intelligible world and observed it closely and wondered at it must seek its maker, too, and enquire who it is who has brought into being something like this, and how, he who produced a son like Intellect, a beautiful boy filled full from himself (III.8.10f).

Unable to find help in his revered Plato, whose "explanation" as we have seen is far from rational, Plotinus resorted to descriptions himself, images that also conceal the reality behind their material referents and do not provide any more rationality as to *why*. Plotinus writes:

> Think of a spring which has no other origin, but gives the whole of itself to rivers, and is not used up by the rivers but remains itself at rest, but the rivers that rise from it, before each of them flows in a different direction, remain for a while all together, though each of them knows, in a way, the direction in which it is going to let its stream flow (III.8.10).

The spring represents the underlying, unmoving Principle.

> And individual things proceed from this principle while it remains within; they come from it as from a single root which remains static in itself, but they flower out into a divided multiplicity, each one bearing an image of that higher reality, but when they reach this lower world one comes to be in one place and one in another, and some are close to the root and others advance farther and split up to the point of becoming, so to speak, branches and twigs and fruits and leaves; . . . in the same way there must not be just souls alone either, without the manifestation of the things produced through them, if this is in every nature, to produce what comes after it and to unfold itself as a seed does, from a partless beginning which proceeds to the final stage perceived by the senses, with what comes before abiding for ever in its own proper dwelling-place, but, in a way, bringing to birth what comes after it from a power unspeakably great, all the power which was in those higher beings, which could not stand still as if it had drawn a line round itself in selfish jealousy, but had to go on for ever, until all things have reached the ultimate possible limit (impelled) by the power itself, which sends them out and cannot leave anything without a share of itself (III.3.7; IV.8.6).

All that Plotinus could do, again, was confine his soaring vision to descriptions that in turn bound him to the paradox we have already observed of having the gross material world ultimately be derived from the perfect undifferentiated One. The process is a continuously devolving one wherein the pure spirituality of the One is inexorably diluted and dissipated in its downward emanation, its spiritual power weakening until the dynamic reaches its bottom: effete matter. The process is non-reflective on the part of the One and Mind, unlike Plato's Demiurge-Craftsman who is depicted in the *Timaeus* as consciously deciding to form the material world, much as an Athenian artisan fashions his work. In summary, then, the intelligible world at best is the reflection of the divine beings found within the Mind; at worst, it is the corruption of the spirituality of these beings. It is this "best" and "worst" that we turn to now, highlighting again the paradox inherent in Plotinus' thought, as in fact in all Platonism.

The paradox is seen in the dual function that is assigned to the Soul, what Bréhier has termed "the organizing force of bodies" and "the seat of destiny." The first is part of the normal emanation proceeding from the One, abstract and neutral. The second is the Soul's fall by attaching itself through attraction and desire to the body. This unnatural state can only be corrected through escaping from the prison that is the body. Plotinus' challenge was to reconcile the natural process of emanation with the soul's prideful tendency towards evil that causes it to hurtle itself into the gross materiality (Homer's "what the gods hate," cited by Plotinus [V.1.2]), the cause of all misery.

It somehow appears that the Soul has done more than it was supposed to. If we look at the process sequentially, we can ascertain three aspects to the Soul: the soul's loftier third remains in its source, the Mind; the lower third is "reflected" in the matter, the end-product of the natural and inevitable emanation; and the middle third remains between the two. This middle is the crucial "seat of destiny," wherein the choice to "descend" into matter occurs as the soul is attracted, like Narcissus, to its *image* that is reflected in the material. As Bréhier emphasizes, it is our *attitude* towards this reflection that has become the problem, i.e., the part of the Soul with which we identify: either the true Self that remains with the Mind, or the image that is reflected in the material.

This then gives rise to the paradoxical attitude Plotinus has for the material world. Plotinus reveres, in the words of Bréhier,

> the beauty of the world, of Providence and to such an extent that one wonders how his praise, which seems to be made without any reservation, is compatible with his description of the world as the land of exile and the habitation of evil (Bréhier, p. 170).

Plotinus' reverence for the beauty of the cosmos comes from the beauty' of the Ideas of the Mind that he perceives within it. His despising the world comes from his apperception of the faulty manner in which these Ideas were received by matter, not to mention the veils of obscurity in which this beauty is cloaked. Thus on the one hand his vision of light returns him to the world of light, while on the other his experience of darkness cuts him off from his origin--the source of the emanation of the Ideas-- and he feels trapped in the prison-world of matter, as is the light in the darkness. This ambivalence is seen in the following passages:

> [The universe] exists of necessity and not as the result of any process of reasoning, but of a better nature naturally producing a likeness of itself; ... for it produced a whole, all beautiful and self-sufficient and friends with itself and with its parts, both the more important and the lesser, which are all equally well adapted to it. So he who blamed the whole because of the parts would be quite unreasonable in his blame; one must consider the parts in relation to the whole, to see if they are harmonious and in concord with it; and when one considers the whole one must not look at a few little parts. ... Since, then, what has come into being is the whole universe, if you contemplate this, you might hear it say, "A god made me, and I came from him perfect above all living things, and complete in myself and self-sufficient, lacking nothing, because all things are in me, plants and animals and the nature of all things that have come into being, and many gods, and populations of spirits, and good souls and men who are happy in their virtue. ... but up there [heaven] are all good souls, giving life to the stars and to the well-ordered everlasting circuit of the heaven, which in imitation of Intellect wisely circles round the same centre for ever; for it seeks nothing outside itself" (III.2.3).

Plotinus writes from direct personal experience:

> Often I have woken up out of the body to my self and have entered into myself, going out from all other things; I have seen a beauty wonderfully great and felt assurance that then most of all I belonged to the better part; I have actually lived the best life and come to identity with the divine; ... after that rest in the divine, when I have come down from Intellect to discursive reasoning, I am puzzled how I ever came down, and how my soul has come to be in the body when it is what it has shown itself to be by itself, even when it is in the body (IV.8.1).

In ruminating on his experience, Plotinus consults his "illustrious Plato," who said many fine things about the soul and about its coming (into this world) in his writings, so that we hope we can get something clear from him. What, then, does this philosopher say? He is obviously not saying the same thing everywhere, so that one can easily know what his intention is; but he everywhere speaks with contempt of the whole world of sense and disapproves of the soul's fellowship with body and says that soul is fettered and buried in it, and that "the esoteric saying is a great one," which asserts that the soul is "in custody." . . . And in the *Phaedrus* he makes "moulting" the cause of coming here. . . . And, though in all these passages he disapproves of the soul's coming to body, in the *Timaeus* when speaking about this All he praises the universe and calls it a blessed god, and says that the soul was given by the goodness of the Craftsman, so that this All might be intelligent, because it had to be intelligent, and this could not be without soul. The Soul of the All, then, was sent into it for this reason by the god, and the soul of each one of us was sent that the All might be perfect: since it was necessary that all the very same kinds of living things which were in the intelligible world should also exist in the world perceived by the senses (IV.8.1).

We now consider more specifically the nature of the creating Mind or Soul, Plato's Demiurge, and its relationship to matter. The emanation or radiation of the spiritual power has an existence almost independent of its source, the Soul, from which it proceeds. In other words, the Mind supplies the model to the Soul, which image the Soul extends into the matter. Thus matter, or the body, receives only an image or imitation of the reality--Plato's Idea--which *remains* in the Mind. As Plotinus wrote:

The divine matter when it receives that which defines it has a defined and intelligent life, but the matter of this world becomes something defined, but not alive or thinking, a decorated corpse. Shape here is only an image; so that which underlies it is also only an image. But There the shape is true shape, and what underlies it is true too (II.4.5).

The things which Intellect [Mind] gives to the soul are near to truth; but those which body receives are already images and imitations (V.9.3).

Thus, the Idea radiates to matter as a reflection on a mirror, but leaves no real trace in the matter itself, which,

is as if cast out and utterly separated, and unable to change itself, but always in the state it was from the beginning--and it was non-existent. It was not anything actually from the beginning, since it stood apart from all realities, and it did not become anything. . . . it

> is only left for it to be potentially a sort of weak and dim phantasm
> unable to receive a shape. So it is actually . . . a falsity . . . (II.5.5).

Matter thus is totally unchanged in its essence, immaterial and without substance, and one finds in Plotinus a consistent abhorrence to even the faintest suggestion that there is some solidity or reality to the material world, apart from the Soul's reflection of the divine Idea. Matter remains merely "a shadow, and upon what is itself a shadow, a picture and a seeming" (VI.3.8):

> Its product is a living being, but a very imperfect one, and one which
> finds its own life disgusting since it is the worst of living things, ill-
> conditioned and savage, made of inferior matter, a sort of sediment
> of the prior realities, bitter and embittering (II.3.17).

We are not far here, as we shall see in Chapter 7, from the Gnostic hatred and disgust of the body.

However, more than being a passive shadow, there are passages where Plotinus speaks of matter as the "Primal Evil" (I.8.14), and that it is the cause of evil for having seduced the Soul. Thus, while at times Plotinus writes of evil as being the inevitable and even natural end-product of the emanation of the spiritual power, what Bréhier termed the "inevitable accompaniment of the cosmic harmony," there are passages where matter appears almost as an absolute evil that is forever in opposition to the good:

> When we understand the cause of the fall of the soul more clearly, and
> as it ought to be understood, what we are looking for, the soul's
> weakness, will be obvious. . . . matter is there, and begs it and, we may
> say, bothers it and wants to come right inside. . . . Matter darkens the
> illumination, the light from that source, by mixture with itself, and
> weakens it. . . . This is the fall of the soul, to come in this way to matter
> and to become weak, because all its powers do not come into action;
> matter hinders them from coming by occupying the place which soul
> holds and producing a kind of cramped condition, and making evil
> what it has got hold of by a sort of theft--until soul manages to escape
> back to its higher state. So matter is the cause of the soul's weakness
> and vice: it is then itself evil before soul and is primary evil (I.8.14).

We thus almost seem to find ourselves in the Persian dualism that in the next century appeared as Manicheism.

We write "almost" Persian dualism, for Plotinus is equally emphatic in stating that in no way can the reality of the One be rendered impure by the darkness, in sharp distinction from the Manichean doctrine. In fact, as we have seen, it was Plotinus' uncompromising teaching of the impossible adulteration of the One that converted the young Augustine, trapped in the Manichean dualism of light and darkness by the sin and guilt in his own mind. There can be no conflict between the divine light and the darkness because only the light is real. We have already examined this notion of the non-beingness of evil in Chapter 5 (p. 147) where we saw that Plotinus does not really mean that evil does not exist, but rather that it is "something other than being," a realm of existence almost infinitely remote from Mind, which is nonetheless evil's ultimate source. Matter thus, as we have seen above, is spoken of as non-being, a phantasm, shadow, and a falsity.

The problem is that the soul, pure within itself, has mistaken image with reality, form for content. It has identified itself with the image held within the matter, forgetting its true identity with the reality that is still within the Mind. This constitutes the soul's defect or weakness, having been seduced by the false reality and withdrawing itself from the ground of its own reality. As the soul becomes entrapped in the materialistic world of the body it becomes increasingly separated from the Mind, whole and complete within itself. Thus, according to the British philosopher and classicist Armstrong:

> The root sin of the soul is self-isolation, by which it is imprisoned in body and cut off from its high destiny [i.e., contemplation of and return to the Universal Soul]. But the mere fact of being in body . . . does not imply imprisonment in body. That only comes if the soul surrenders to the body; it is the inward attitude which makes the difference (Armstrong, p. 192).

Still, Plotinus also shares the other side of the conflict, wherein matter can be seen positively as the means whereby the illumination of the Soul (and the One) is seen and remembered. Thus we see again the paradoxical dynamic of the soul having wandered from its Source, becoming trapped in matter, also returning to its Source through remembering its home: the faulty procession downward is almost simultaneously corrected by the return upward. This paradox within Plotinus' mind became expressed in a similar ambivalence in his philosophy, and so he somehow had to rationalize his appreciation of the wondrous nature of the cosmic world with his otherwise repugnant attitude toward the material body: Though the world is not perfect, who would want it so and lose creation's "intellectual variety"? His attempts seem a step more sophisticated than Plato's:

> No, but the rational forming principle makes all these things as their sovereign . . . and makes the things which are called bad according to reason, because it does not wish that all should be good, just like a

craftsman who does not make everything eyes in his picture; in the same way the formative principle did not make everything gods but some gods, some spirits (a nature of the second rank), then men and animals after them in order, not out of grudging meanness but by a reason containing all the rich variety of the intelligible world. But we are like people who know nothing about the art of painting and criticize the painter because the colours are not beautiful everywhere, though he has really distributed the appropriate colours to every place; ... or we are like someone who censures a play because all the characters in it are not heroes but there is a servant and a yokel who speaks in a vulgar way; but the play is not a good one if one expels the inferior characters, because they too help to complete it (III.2.11).

Even though we have yet to consider them in this chapter, we turn now to Plotinus' specific attack on the Gnostics, the only group he isolated with such criticism. On one level his anger seems to have been motivated by some members of his school adhering to the "arbitrary, tyrannical assertion" of this particular Gnostic school. On this issue Porphyry wrote:

There were in his time many Christians and others, and sectarians who had abandoned the old philosophy, men of the schools of Adelphius and Aculinus, who ... produced revelations by Zoroaster and Zostrianus and Nicotheus and Allogenes and Messus and other people of the kind [readers of the *Nag Hammadi Library* will recognize most of these names], deceived themselves and deceiving many, alleging that Plato had not penetrated to the depths of intelligible reality. Plotinus hence often attacked their position in his lectures, and wrote the treatise to which we have given the title "Against the Gnostics"; he left it to us to assess what he passed over. Amelius went to forty volumes in writing against the book of Zostrianus. I, Porphyry, wrote a considerable number of refutations of the book of Zoroaster, which I showed to be entirely spurious and modern, made up by the sectarians to convey the impression that the doctrines which they had chosen to hold in honour were those of the ancient Zoroaster (Porphyry, in *Plotinus*, p. 45).

Plotinus states that he is tempering his remarks out of

regard for some of our friends who happened upon this way of thinking before they became our friends, and, though I do not know how they manage it, continue in it. Yet they themselves do not shrink from saying what they say.... But we have addressed what we have said so far to our own intimate pupils, not to the Gnostics (for we could make no further progress towards convincing them), so that they may not be troubled by these latter, who do not bring forward proofs--how could they?--but make arbitrary, arrogant assertions.

Another style of writing would be appropriate to repel those who have the insolence to pull to pieces what godlike men of antiquity have said nobly and in accordance with the truth (II.9.10).

The rest of their teachings I leave to you to investigate by reading their books, and to observe throughout that the kind of philosophy which we pursue, besides all its other excellences, displays simplicity and straightforwardness of character along with clear thinking, and aims at dignity, not rash arrogance, and combines its confident boldness with reason and much safeguarding and caution and a great deal of circumspection: you are to use philosophy of this kind as a standard of comparison for the rest. But the system of the others (the Gnostics) is in every part constructed on entirely opposed principles—for I would not like to say more; this is the way in which it would be suitable for us to speak about them (II.9.14).

While it is unclear exactly against what Gnostic sect Plotinus is pointing his remarks, the following passage indicates at least that it was of Valentinian origin:

One point must be mentioned which surpasses all the rest of their doctrine in absurdity--if absurdity is what one ought to call it. For they say that Soul declined to what was below it, and with it some sort of "Wisdom," and then they tell us that the other souls came down too, and as members of Wisdom put on bodies. . . . But again they say that very being for the sake of which these souls came down did not come down itself, did not decline, so to put it, but only illumined the darkness, and so an image from it came into existence in matter. Then they form an image of the image somewhere here below . . . and produce what they call the Maker, and make him revolt from his mother and drag the universe which proceeds from him down to the ultimate limit of images. The man who wrote this just meant to be blasphemous! (II.9.10)

Plotinus' criticism of the Gnostics is basically on two points: their rejection of the divine nature of the cosmos, and their total absence of a belief in virtue. Here we shall discuss the metaphysics, leaving the ethical criticisms for Chapter 10. Plotinus finds it impossible to believe that any rational person could fail to perceive the inherent divinity of the cosmos, and finds this failure on the part of the Gnostics the most abhorrent trait of all. Though Plotinus himself was ambivalent about the base material result of the process of emanation, as we have seen, he nonetheless remained staunchly pro-cosmic and opposed to the distinctly anti-cosmic position of the Gnostics. He is especially concerned about protecting the integrity of his beloved Plato, as is seen in the following passage:

These are the terms of people inventing a new jargon to recommend their own school: they contrive this meretricious language as if they had no connection with the ancient Hellenic school, though the Hellenes knew all this and knew it clearly, and spoke without delusive pomposity of ascents from the cave and advancing gradually closer and closer to a truer vision. Generally speaking, some of these peoples' doctrines have been taken from Plato, but others, all the new ideas they have brought in to establish a philosophy of their own, are things they have found outside the truth. . . . And in general they falsify Plato's account of the manner of the making, and a great deal else, and degrade the great man's teachings as if they had understood the intelligible nature, but he and the other blessed philosophers had not. . . . If they wish to disagree on these points, there is no unfair hostility in saying to them that they should not recommend their own opinions to their audience by ridiculing and insulting the Greeks but that they should show the correctness on their own merits of all the points of doctrine which are peculiar to them and differ from the views of the Greeks, stating their real opinions courteously, as befits philosophers, and fairly on the points where they are opposed, looking to the truth and not hunting fame by censuring men who have been judged good from ancient times by men of worth and saying that they themselves are better than the Greeks (II.9.6).

One sees how the Gnostics

introduce all sorts of comings into being and passings away, and disapprove of this universe, and blame the soul for its association with the body, and censure the director of this universe, and identify its maker with the soul, and attribute to this universal soul the same affections as those which the souls in parts of the universe have. . . . For if it has come into life in such a way that its life is not a disjointed one--like the smaller things in it which in its fullness of life it produces continually night and day--but coherent and clear and great and everywhere life, manifesting infinite wisdom, how should one not call it a clear and noble image of the intelligible gods? If, being an image, it is not that intelligible world, this is precisely what is natural to it; if it was the intelligible world, it would not be an image of it. But it is false to say that the image is unlike the original; for nothing has been left out which it was possible for a fine natural image to have. . . . Now certainly the whole earth is full of living creatures and immortal beings, and everything up to the sky is full of them: why, then are not the stars, both those in the lower spheres and those in the highest, gods moving in order, circling in well-arranged beauty? Why should they not possess virtue? What hindrance prevents them from acquiring it? The causes are not present there which make people bad here below, and there is no badness of body, disturbed and disturbing (II.9.6,8).

Plotinus derides the Gnostic attempts to denigrate the cosmos, and speaks of their arrogance in believing that they are wiser than the divine cosmos:

> For who of those who are so mindlessly high-minded in looking down on it is as well ordered or has as intelligent a mind as the All? The comparison is ridiculous and very much out of place; anyone who made it except for the sake of argument would not be able to avoid impiety. It is not the part of an intelligent man even to enquire about this but of someone who is blind, utterly without perception or intelligence, and far from seeing the intelligible universe, since he does not even see this one here. For how could there be a musician who sees the melody in the intelligible world and will not be stirred when he hears the melody in sensible sounds? Or how could there be anyone skilled in geometry and numbers who will not be pleased when he sees right relation, proportion and order with his eyes? . . . will anyone be so sluggish in mind and so immovable that, when he sees all the beauties in the world of sense, all its good proportion and the mighty excellence of its order, and the splendour of form which is manifested in the stars, for all their remoteness, he will not thereupon think seized with reverence, "What wonders, and from what a source?" (II.9.16)

Plotinus, of course, could not argue with the Platonic influence, since he himself shared it. Yet, as discussed above, he does not include the "higher" visible world--the cosmos--in this category of being a hindrance to the Soul's ascent. He thus urges his Gnostic opponents to make the same distinction:

> Even if it occurred to them to hate the nature of body because they have heard Plato often reproaching the body for the kind of hindrances it puts in the way of the soul--and he said that all bodily nature was inferior--they should have stripped off this bodily nature in their thought and seen what remained. . . . For the beauties here exist because of the first beauties. If, then, these here do not exist, neither do those; so these are beautiful in their order after those. . . . Then one should be aware that there is not the same beauty in part and whole and in all individual things and the All: and then that there are such beauties in things perceived by the senses and in partial things (the beauties of spirits, for instance) that one admires their maker, and believes that they come from the higher world, and judging from them, says that the beauty there is overwhelming. . . . But what was there to hinder the All, which is beautiful, from being also beautiful within? . . . While we have bodies we must stay in our houses, which have been built for us by a good sister soul which has great power to work without any toil or trouble (II.9.17,18).

Yet, again, Plotinus is actually guilty of the same "sins" of which he accuses the Gnostics. On the one hand, Plotinus emphasizes that creation is timeless: the process of emanation or radiation is eternal. And so he is quite denigrating of the Gnostic denigrations of Plato's account of the soul's descent from eternity into the world of matter and time, as can be seen in this passage:

> But if they [the Gnostics] are going to assert that the soul made the world when it had, so to speak, "shed its wings" [from Plato], this does not happen to the Soul of the All; but if they are going to say that it made the world as the result of a moral failure, let them tell us the cause of the failure. But when did it fail? If it was from eternity, it abides in a state of failure according to their own account. If it began to fail, why did it not begin before? But we say that the making act of the soul is *not a declination but rather a non-declination* (II.9.4, my italics).

On the other hand Plotinus finds himself speaking of the cosmogonic event in temporal terms, and negative ones at that. Thus he ends up using the same type of mythological explanations he accuses the Gnostics of using, and cannot avoid seeing the soul's declination as a fall, a negative event that is an aberration from the eternal Divine:

> [Time] was at rest with eternity in real being; it was not yet time, but itself, too, kept quiet in that. But since there was a restlessly active nature which wanted to control itself and be on its own, and chose to seek for more than its present state, this moved, and time moved with it . . . and constructed time as an image of eternity. For because soul had an unquiet power, which wanted to keep on transferring what it saw there to something else, it did not want the whole to be present to it all together; and, as from a quiet seed the formative principle, unfolding itself, advances, as it thinks, to largeness, but does away with the largeness by division and, instead of keeping its unity in itself, *squanders* it outside itself and so goes forward to *a weaker extension*; in the same way Soul, making the world of sense in imitation of that other world, moving with a motion which is not that which exists There, but like it, and intending to be an image of it, first of all put itself into time, which it made *instead* of eternity . . . (III.7.11, my italics).

We are thus a far cry in Plotinus--not only in the Gnostics! --from Plato's account in the *Timaeus* of time being a moving image of eternity.

5. Traditional Christianity - St. Augustine

The traditional Christian view can be succinctly summed up in this passage from the Book of Revelation:

> You are our Lord and our God, you are worthy of glory and honor and power, because you made all the universe and it was only by your will that everything was made that exists (Rv 4:11).

Irenaeus, in the *Proof of the Apostolic Preaching*, wrote the following, obviously one of the foundations of the later Apostles' Creed:

> God is the eternal being, above all created things; all is set beneath him, and it is God who has created all. Of necessity the things created here below draw from some cause the principle of their existence, and the principle of all things is God. For he himself has been created by no one, but by him all has been created. So this is how the Christian teaching should be expressed: one God, the uncreated father, creator of the universe, above whom there is no other God, and beside whom there is no other God. One God, creator of the universe: this is the very first article of our faith (in Tresmontant, p. 42).

A century later, Clement of Alexandria wrote this criticism of the Greek philosophers for divinizing the cosmos. Thus, Clement was expressing the strict dualism that separated the creator God from His creation:

> Some have somehow gone so far wrong as to worship, not God, but a divine work, the sun, the moon, the whole choir of the stars: against all reason they think of them as gods (*Protrepticus* 4.63, in Tresmontant, p. 42).

Indeed, humanity was created to contemplate in wonder the splendor of the cosmos, but to worship it as a living god was a serious error:

> Let no one of you worship the sun, but let him turn his desire towards the sun's maker: let him not regard the world as divine, but seek the creator of the world (ibid.).

This core belief of the orthodox Church was clearly articulated in the thirteenth century by St. Thomas Aquinas, who extended the classical Greek formulations in a Trinitarian framework:

> ...creation is God's action by reason of his existence, which is his very nature.... God is the cause of things through his mind and will, like

an artist of works of art. An artist works through an idea conceived in his mind and through love in his will bent on something. In like manner God the Father wrought the creature through his Word, the Son, and through his Love, the Holy Ghost (*Sum. Theol.* 1a.45.6).

We may remark here that for the Platonists the Logos was of course impersonal, as were all the divine powers. To the Christian, however, the Logos was a specific person, a Divine Person, through whom not only was the world made, but without whom no one could attain God.

Returning to our own "cast of characters," we see that Augustine allows no purpose for the creation of the world other than it being the product of the omni-benevolent God. He writes in the *Enchiridion*:

By the Trinity, thus supremely and equally and unchangeably good, all things were created; and these are not supremely and equally and unchangeably good, but yet they are good, even taken separately. Taken as a whole, however, they are very good, because their ensemble constitutes the universe in all its wonderful order and beauty (*Ench.* 10, in Bourke, p. 65).

As Plato before him, Augustine sees the world of time representing the movement of eternity. From the *Literal Commentary on Genesis*:

Living, then, in immutable eternity, He has created all things together, and from them periods of time flow, places are filled, and the centuries unroll in the temporal and local motions of real things. Among these things, He has established some as spiritual and others as corporeal, giving form to the matter that He Himself created without form but capable of being formed-matter which was made by no other being but which did have a Maker. This matter preceded its formation, not in time but its origin.... With these points established, [it is evident that] God, the omnipotent and all-supporting, Who is unmoved in time or place and ever the same in the immutability of eternity, truth, and will, moves spiritual creation in the course of time, and also moves corporeal creation through both time and place (*Lit. Com. Gen.* VIII.20.39; 26.48, in Bourke, pp. 63-65).

In almost ecstatic terms, and in language reminiscent of his beloved Plotinus, Augustine cries out in awe-filled joy to the Creator of the world, whose wonders he sees as reflecting the wonder of Heaven (though previously quoted, the relevance of this passage warrants its repetition):

Some people read books in order to find God. Yet there is a great book, the very appearance of created things. Look above you; look below you! Note it; read it! God, whom you wish to find, never wrote that book with ink. Instead, He set before your eyes the things that

He had made. Can you ask for a louder voice than that? Why, heaven and earth cry out to you: "God made me!" (*Sermon*, quoted in Bourke, p. 123).

Whence and in what manner was it, if it was not from you, from whom are all things, in so far as they are? But so much more distant is anything from you, in so far as it is more unlike you, and this distance is not of place. Therefore, Lord ... you created something, and that something out of nothing. You made heaven and earth, not out of yourself, for then they would have been equal to your Only-begotten, and through this equal also to you. But in no way was it just that anything which was not of you should be equal to you. There was nothing beyond you from which you might make them, O God, one Trinity and trinal Unity. Therefore, you created heaven and earth out of nothing, a great thing and a little thing. For you are almighty and good, to make all things good, the great heaven and the little earth. You were, and there was naught else out of which you made heaven and earth: two beings, one near to you, the other near to nothingness, one to which you alone would be superior, the other to which nothing would be inferior (*Conf.* 7.7).

Yet Augustine could not deny the obvious imperfections in the world, and we shall return to his horror of the body in Chapter 7. However, some attention need be given here to his explanation for evil in the world of matter. Here we do not find any expression of disgust, but rather the glib dismissal of the problem by his famous formulation of evil being merely the absence of good:

And in the universe, even that which is called evil, when it is regulated and put in its own place, only enhances our admiration of the good; for we enjoy and value the good more when we compare it with the evil. For the Almighty God, who, as even the heathen acknowledge, has supreme power over all things, being Himself supremely good, would never permit the existence of anything evil among His works, if He were not so omnipotent and good that He can bring good even out of evil. For what is that which we call evil but the absence of good? ... what are called vices in the soul are nothing but privations of natural good. And when they are not transferred elsewhere: when they cease to exist in the healthy soul, they cannot exist anywhere else.

All things that exist, seeing that the Creator of them all is supremely good, are themselves good. But because they are not, like their Creator, supremely and unchangeably good, their good may be diminished and increased. But for good to be diminished is an evil, although, however much it may be diminished, it is necessary, if the being is to continue, that some good should remain to constitute the being. For however small or of whatever kind the being may be, the good which makes it a being cannot be destroyed without destroying the being itself (*Enchir.* 11,12, in Bourke, pp. 65f).

Duality

As in the previous chapters, we begin the presentation of the Gnostics by exploring the dualistic view. We first look at the Manichean cosmogony which paradoxically, given our preceding comments, is one of the very few Gnostic systems that places a positive value on the creation of the world, though not without great ambivalence. For this reason many scholars do not consider Manicheism to be a genuine Gnostic system. The cosmic world, albeit not its inhabitants, is seen as the work of God and therefore, as we shall see presently, the very structure of the world becomes part of the cosmic plan of redemption. Nonetheless, the soul is trapped in this alien world that is not its home. Fragments from a Manichean poem and psalm will serve as examples of the exiled state we shall explore more fully in Chapter 7.

> Born of light and of the gods
> I am in exile and cut off from them.
> The enemies who have covered me
> Have carried me off among the dead.
> May he be blessed and find deliverance
> Who will deliver my soul from anguish!
> I am a god, and born of gods,
> Shining, sparkling, luminous,
> Radiant, perfumed and beautiful,
> But henceforth reduced to suffering.
> (In Guitton, p. 65)

> O soul, whence art thou? Thou art from on high. Thou art a stranger to the world.... I looked forth in the whole world ... I found no harbor save thy [the Lord's] harbor (in Allberry, pp. 181,184).

We pick up the thread of the Manichean myth at the point where the light is trapped in the darkness, setting the stage for the liberation or separation of the light from the darkness. To achieve this end the physical world is created. There are in fact two levels of redemptive activity, with the world's creation being a necessary part of the second. At first, when the Primal Man realizes that he has been made captive to the powers of Darkness he cries out for help. The King of Light responds by creating the Friend of Lights, who in turn brings forth the Great Architect, who then brings forth the Living Spirit (the analog to the Persian Mithras). This Spirit has five Sons and they all descend together to the abyss of darkness. The Living Spirit calls to Primal Man who responds, and in their joining--Call and Answer--the entrapped light is liberated and ascends to the realm of Light. However, his soul is left behind--Primal Man's power, as it were--for these particles of light had become too commingled with the darkness to be extricated and redeemed.

Thus is the stage set for the second phase of redemption, the liberation of these particles of light. For this purpose the world was created. We shall return to this first stage of redemption in Chapter 8, when we consider this theme in its entirety. It was necessary to introduce it here in order to set the stage for the creation of the world, to which we now turn.

The first cosmogonic step has the Living Spirit separate out the light from the Darkness, which then necessitates the deliverance (literally) of the particles of light to the Great Light. It is accomplished in this way: The initial separation of the light from the Darkness weakens the archons (i.e., rulers and guardians) of Darkness sufficiently to allow the Spirit to use their "carcasses"--flesh and bones--to form the heaven and the earth, while the particles of liberated light become the sun, moon, and stars. As one of the Bema Psalms describes it:

> When the First Man had finished his war the Father sent his second son. He came and helped his brother out of the abyss; he established this whole world out of the mixture that took place of the Light and the Darkness. He spread out all the powers of the abyss to ten heavens and eight earths, he shut them up into this world once, he made it a prison too for all the powers of Darkness, it is also a place of purification for the soul that was swallowed in them. The sun and moon he founded, he set them on high, to purify the Soul. Daily they take up the refined part to the height, but the dregs however they erase . . . . they convey it above and below (in Allberry, pp. 10f).

Theodore bar Konai summarizes the same situation:

> The Mother of Life spread out the heavens from their skins; she made ten heavens, and she cast their bodies into the Land of Darkness. And they made eight earths and each of the five sons of the Living Spirit completed his work: It was the Adornment of the Light who seized the five Light Gods by their haunches, and the heavens were spread out beneath their haunches. It was the "Bearer" who down on one knee held up the earths. When the heavens and the earths had been created, the great King of Honor sat down in the center of the sky and watched over them all. Thereupon the Living Spirit disclosed to the sons of darkness his shapes, and from the light which had been swallowed up by them [i.e., the Demons], he purified the light, and made out of it the sun and moon and over a thousand stars. And he

formed the spheres which are there: wind, water and fire (Konai 11, in Haardt, p. 292).

Thus, the cosmos is fashioned from both light *and* darkness. The power of Darkness still remains, however, and has not lost its demonic attributes for, in the words of Jonas, "all the parts of nature that surround us come from the impure cadavers of the power of evil" (p. 224); and in a quote from a Manichean source: "the world is an embodiment of the Arch-Ahriman [the God of Darkness]" (Jonas, p. 224). This world, incidentally, also includes the planets, which remain under the rule of the archons.

Now enters another figure who is responsible for setting the cosmos into motion and delivering the light particles still "imprisoned, oppressed, sullied" (Jonas, p. 225):

> Thereupon the Mother of Life, Primal Man, and the Living Spirit raised their prayers and pleaded with the Father of Greatness. And the Father of Greatness heard them and in a third summons called forth the messenger. The messenger called forth the twelve Virgins in their garments, crowns and attributes [the twelve signs of the Zodiac]. . . . When the emissary came to these vessels [i.e., the sun and moon], he ordered the three servants to set the vessels in motion. He commanded the Great Architect to construct the New Earth and the three Spheres to raise themselves up (Konai 11, in Haardt, pp. 292f).

> This is the reason why the Cosmos came into existence and the sun and moon in it, which by their waxing and waning are forever separating the Divine Power from Hyle [Matter] and leading it up to God. . . . During the periods when the moon is waxing, it receives the power separated from Hyle and throughout the period becomes filled with it, but when it is full, it sends it up to the sun during its period of waning. The sun in turn sends it to God. When this has happened, it again receives an increase in Soul, which passes to it from the next full moon, takes it up, permits it in similar fashion to reach God, automatically, and consistently carries on this activity (Alexander of Lycopolis, in Haardt, p. 337).

This ingenious machinery of the Zodiac, portrayed as a cosmic ferris wheel, is now set into motion by the Messenger. The lower portion of the wheel descends to earth where it scoops up the particles of liberated light, bearing them aloft along the Milky Way until the wheel's circular motion reaches the moon, where the particles of light are deposited. The cycle takes twenty-eight days and the fullness of the moon signifies the completion of the cycle. The particles of light are then emptied from the moon to the sun, and eventually returned to the Great Light. The New Moon reflects the total emptying of the particles and the cycle resumes.

In order to hasten the liberation process of the light from the Darkness, the Messenger

> revealed his forms, the male and the female, and became visible to all the Archons, the children of the Darkness, the male and the female. And at the sight of the Messenger, who was beautiful in his forms, all the Archons became excited with lust for him, the male ones for his female appearance and the female ones for his male appearance. And in their concupiscence they began to release the Light of the Five Luminous Gods which they had devoured (Konai, in Jonas, pp. 225f).

The released light is quickly carried away by the wheel and eventually returned home. However, the Messenger's tactic is not without its negative consequences, for particles of darkness also escape and try to board the cosmic carriers. These particles consist of semen or aborted embryos, stimulated by the nakedness of the Messenger. Thwarted in their plan to remain with the light, these substances fall to the ground. As Rudolph states in his summary:

> The semen falls ... on dry land and brings forth the world of plants. ... The aborted embryos, too, fall upon the earth, become demons and devour the fruit of the plants, i.e. the seed of darkness mixed with light, fertilize themselves and thus produce the animal kingdom (Rudolph, p. 338).

Thus, as Jonas quotes from an ancient source: All plants,

> grains, herbs and all roots and trees [to which we can also add the animals] are creatures of the Darkness, not of God, and in these forms and kinds of things the Godhead [particles of light] is fettered (Jonas, p. 226).

There is a final strategy on the part of the Darkness to counter the plan of the Messenger: the creation of Adam and Eve. We defer discussion of this ploy until the following chapter.

In summary, then, in content somewhat parallel to Platonism, the Manicheans understood the greater cosmos to be divine, while the forms of life within the world were seen as the ugly products of sin, most specifically sexuality. We shall return to this aspect of the system in Chapter 10, when we consider its morality and guides for behavior.

Another example of this benign cosmogonic view is found in the *Poimandres*, which we have already considered. We quoted this text as stating that the elements of nature had arisen from the Will of God (here seen as feminine, incidentally). It is this Will who

> having received into herself the Word [Logos] and beheld the beau-

tiful [archetypal] Cosmos, imitated it, fashioning herself into a cosmos . . . according to her own elements and her progeny, i.e., the souls. But the divine Nous [the Mind of God], being androgynous, existing as Life and Light, brought forth by a word another Nous, the Demiurge, who as god over the fire and the breath fashioned seven Governors, who encompass with their circles the sensible world, and their government is called Heimarmene [Destiny] (in Jonas, pp. 149f).

Thus we see, in contradistinction from most of our other Gnostic sources, that there is no inference of evil to these Governors. To the contrary, as in Manicheism, the creation of the cosmos--patterned after an already existent (archetypal) cosmic principle--is accomplished for the purpose of liberating the divine principle that had fallen prisoner to the lower realms of a pre-cosmic Darkness.

The same doctrine is seen in "The Paraphrase of Shem," the Nag Hammadi text we considered in Chapters 4 and 5. The act of creation by Derdekeas is couched in strong sexual overtones, most of which we omit in this rendering, to be returned to in Chapter 7. Derdekeas' actions are necessitated by the entrapment of the light of spirit by the evil Darkness:

I went down to chaos to save the whole light from it . . . . I put on the beast [the body], and laid before her [Nature] a great request that heaven and earth might come into being in order that the whole light might rise up. For in no other way could the power of the Spirit be saved from bondage except that I appear to her in animal form. Therefore she was gracious to me as if I were her son.

And on account of my request, Nature arose since she possesses of the power of the Spirit and the Darkness and the fire. For she had taken off her forms. When she had cast it off, she blew upon the water. The heaven was created. And from the foam of the heaven the earth came into being. And at my wish it brought forth all kinds of food in accordance with the number of the beasts. And it brought forth dew from the winds on account of you (pl.) and those who will be begotten the second time upon the earth. For the earth possessed a power of chaotic fire. Therefore it brought forth every seed (Para. Shem VII.18.12; 19.26-20.1-20, in NHL, pp. 316f).

This view as we have seen, is a minority one within the Gnostic literature, where almost always the physical universe is seen right from the beginning as the product of an inferior (or fallen) principle, frequently identified with the Platonic Demiurge.

Finally, we consider the Mandean literature which combines differing aspects of cosmogony, reflecting an underlying ambivalence towards the world and its creator. As we have seen, the Mandeans posit coexistent states of light and darkness, and before there is a commingling of light and darkness, the world is created by Ptahil, the fourth and final emanation of light. In some of the Mandean accounts, Ptahil's act is actually prefaced by a gradual deflection from the King of Light. Thus we read the words of the third emanation, known as Abathur or B'haq-Ziwa:

> "I am the father of the uthras [divine beings]. . . . I shall call forth a world" . . . . He called Ptahil-Uthra, embraced him, and kissed him like a mighty one. He bestowed names on him . . . . called him, gave command, and spoke to him: "Arise, go, descend to the place where there are no skinas or worlds. Call forth and create a world for yourself, just like the sons of perfection, whom you saw. Set up and establish a world, establish a world for yourself and make uthras in it" (GR III.p.93, in F II, p. 171).

Nothing was said to Ptahil about the powers of Darkness, who were going about their own creation process. In one of the Mandean versions, Ruha, a fallen spirit of light, issues forth the Lord of Darkness, a monster dragon, who in turn creates his own world. He then is invited by Ruha into an incestuous union:

> "Arise, sleep with your mother, and you will be released from the chain which binds you . . . ." He slept with Ruha, and she conceived seven forms by the one act . . . . [She] brought forth the despicable ones. She gave birth to the Seven [Planets] . . . (ibid., 94, in F II, p. 172).

Ptahil then, without the authorization of the King of Light, merges with Ruha, prepares a "solidification," which then becomes established as the earthly world, called "Tibil":

> By my [Ptahil's] first cry I solidified the earth and spanned out the firmament in perfection. By my second cry I dispersed jordans and canals in it. By my third cry I called forth the fish of the sea and feathered birds of every type and variety . . . . By my fifth cry evil reptiles came into being. By my sixth cry the whole structure of darkness came into being . . . . When Ptahil said this, his house was taken away from him . . . . and he was put in grievous bonds. He was fastened by a chain until the disappearance of Tibil. Because he altered the pronouncement of his father (GR XV.13, in F II, p. 179).

Non-Duality

1. Non-Valentinian

There are several important Gnostic documents that reflect the non-dualistic view of the world. We have already touched upon this basic Gnostic stance, but we can now elaborate on its essential characteristics. As we have seen, what distinguishes a Gnostic position from any other is its distinctly anti-world view. Such feeling directly follows from the almost universal Gnostic belief that the physical world was not the creation of the one true God, but rather the result of an inferior principle. The themes we will consider here are the logical outgrowth of the original theory of separation from God that we considered in the preceding chapter. The culmination of this thought process is the Valentinian *gnosis*, which we shall consider after presenting other formulations that are similar to, but lack the uniqueness of, Valentinus' genius.

In general the Gnostics were most inventive in their attempts to explain the fall from the perfect unity of the Godhead. However, they hardly were able to explain it in any rational manner. Yet, they did recognize the impossibility of anything real or good existing outside the heavenly Pleroma. To Irenaeus and his fellow orthodox Christians this idea was anathema, for how else explain the "reality" of the physical world *except* for the creative efforts of God, "the Father of All"? As the Church Father writes in *Against the Heretics*:

> It is proper, then, that I should begin with the first and most important head, that is, God the Creator, who made the heaven and the earth, and all things that are therein . . . and to demonstrate that there is nothing either above Him or after Him; nor that, moved by any one else, but of His own free will, He created all things, since He is the only God, the only Lord, the only Creator, the only Father, alone containing all things, and far surpassing all things that they might exist (*Adv. haer.* II.1.1, in Layton, p. 156).

We begin with the parallel texts in the *Nag Hammadi Library* that we examined in the preceding chapter: "The Hypostasis of the Archons" and "On the Origin of the World." They date from the late-third or early-fourth centuries A.D., and are illustrative of a relatively late summary of Gnostic ideas. They show a strong Valentinian influence, yet without the sophistication we find in the original Valentinian teachings.

In "The Hypostasis of the Archons" we read of the Power that opposes and that separated from the Father of Truth. This Power exclaimed: "It is I who am God; there is none (apart from me)" (Hypos. Arch. II.86.30, in *NHL*, p. 153). These blasphemous thoughts became expelled and went to Chaos and the Abyss, his mother. She in turn

established each of his offspring in conformity with its power--after the pattern of the realms that are above, for by starting from the invisible world the visible world was invented (ibid., 87.8-11).

Later in the text we find a more explicit rendering of the creation myth. We pick up where we left off on page 156 above.

A veil exists between the World Above and the realms that are below and Shadow came into being beneath the veil; and that Shadow became Matter; and that Shadow was projected apart. And what she had created became a product in the Matter, like an aborted fetus. And it assumed a plastic form molded out of Shadow, and became an arrogant beast resembling a lion. It was androgynous, as I have already said because it was from Matter that it derived (ibid., 94.9-19, p. 158).

The beast is variously known as Samael, Sakla, and Yaldabaoth.

The narrative is expanded in the companion text "On the Origin of the World." We have already seen that the fall of Sophia led to the creation of the Darkness of Chaos. From within the darkness

a power appeared as ruler over the darkness. . . . Then the shadow perceived that there was one stronger than it. It was jealous, and when it became self-impregnated, it immediately bore envy. Since that day the origin of envy has appeared in all of the aeons and their worlds. But that envy was found to be a miscarriage without any spirit in it. It became like the shadows in a great watery substance. Then the bitter wrath which came into being from the shadow was cast into a region of Chaos. Since that day a watery substance has appeared. . . . Just as all the useless afterbirth of one who bears a little child falls, likewise the matter which came into being from the shadow was cast aside. . . . And when Pistis [Sophia] saw what came into being from her deficiency, she was disturbed. And the disturbance appeared as a fearful work (Orig. Wld. II.99.2-31, in *NHL*, pp. 162f).

Thus we see again the Gnostic idea that matter arises from a negative activity, the "folly of Sophia," as it is known in Valentinianism. And the cosmos, the object of great veneration by the world of antiquity, is reduced to nothing more than a "useless afterbirth," the product of the shadow and a parody of the world of light. Rudolph has pointed out the influence of the classical notion of creation occurring through the "shadow of God," a positive activity (*see* Philo), although here that notion, as is typical of Gnostic thought, is given a negative connotation.

We find a similar phenomenon in the next stage of creation, the emergence of the figure of world creator, frequently called the Demiurge, the name taken from the Platonic figure in the *Timaeus* who fashions the divine being of the universe. As we saw earlier, this figure is almost always denigrated by the Gnostics as the creator God of the Old Testament who has sought to imprison the true creations of light in his world of darkness. We continue the narrative from "On the Origin of the World":

> . . . a ruler first appeared out of the waters, lion-like in appearance, and androgynous, and having a great authority within himself, but not knowing whence he came into being. . . . When the ruler saw his greatness--and he saw only himself; he did not see another one except water and darkness--then he thought that he alone existed. His (thought was) made complete by means of the word, and it appeared as a spirit moving to and fro over the waters (ibid., 100.5; 100.29-101.2, p. 163).

The narrative proceeds with the creation of the world, paralleling the creation myth in Genesis. Influences of Greek mythology are also seen when the rulers or archons who are created by Yaldabaoth begin to fight among themselves, reminiscent of the clash of the titans. The conflict is never truly resolved, for it gives rise to all manner of demons which pollute the world:

> But these [demons] taught men many errors with magic and potions and idolatry, and shedding of blood, and altars, and temples, and sacrifices, and libations to all the demons of the earth, having as their co-worker Fate who came into being according to the agreement by the gods of injustice and justice. And thus when the world came to be in distraction, it wandered astray throughout all time . . . . [in] an ignorance and a stupor (ibid., 123.8-22, pp. 176f).

Thus we see in this parody of the Genesis creation myth and the resulting Judaeo-Christian religions a clear depiction of the Gnostic devaluation of this world.

Our final excerpt from this text completes the Gnostic denigration of creation in its "exposure" of the arrogance of the creator God of the Old Testament:

> But after the heavens and their powers and all of their government set themselves aright, the First Father [the Demiurge, Yaldabaoth] exalted himself, and was glorified by the whole army of angels. And all the gods and their angels gave him praise and glory. And he

rejoiced in his heart, and he boasted continually, saying to them, "I do not need anything." He said, "I am god and no other one exists except me." But when he said these things, he sinned against all of the immortal imperishable ones, and they protected him. Moreover, when Pistis saw the impiety of the chief ruler, she was angry. Without being seen, she said, "You err, Samael," i.e. "the blind god" (ibid., 103.1-13, p. 165).

We move next to "The Apocryphon of John." We saw in the previous chapter how Sophia failed in her desire to create like God, and her actions resulted in the creation of Yaltabaoth. He is called the first archon, and it is stated that he derived his power from his mother (i.e., Sophia), which he then sought to deny:

And he removed himself from her and moved away from the places in which he was born [i.e., in the mind of Sophia]. He became strong and created for himself other aeons with a flame of luminous fire which still exists now. And he joined with his madness which is in him and begot authorities for himself.... [The creation of the twelve authorities or archons is then described.] And when the light had mixed with the darkness, it caused the darkness to shine. And when the darkness had mixed with the light, it darkened the light and it became neither light nor dark, but it became weak.

Now the archon who is weak has three names. The first name is Yaltaba(oth), the second is Saklas [meaning "fool"], and the third is Samael. And he is impious in his madness which is in him. For he said, "I am God and there is no other God beside me," for he is ignorant of his strength, the place from which he had come.... And when he saw the creation which surrounds him and the multitude of the angels around him which had come forth from him, he said to them, "I am a jealous God and there is no other God beside me." But by announcing this he indicated to the angels who attended to him that there exists another God, for if there were no other one, of whom would he be jealous? Then the mother [Sophia] began to move to and fro. She became aware of the deficiency when the brightness of her light diminished. And she became dark because her consort had not agreed with her (ApocryJohn II.10.21-28; 11.10.22; 13.5-7, in *NHL*, pp. 104-106).

The remainder of the narrative will be discussed in the chapters to follow, when we discuss the repentance of Sophia and the plan of redemption.

"The Second Treatise of the Great Seth," a Nag Hammadi text, provides another example of the Gnostic denigration of the Old Testament God and his creation, and is an overt polemic against Church orthodoxy. The figure of Seth, incidentally, never appears, and is obviously meant to be a symbol of Jesus, the ostensible source of the revelation.

> 'For those . . . in the world had been prepared by the will of our sister Sophia--she who is a whore--because of the innocence which has not been uttered. And she did not ask anything from the All, nor from the greatness of the Assembly, nor from the Pleroma. Since she was first she came forth to prepare monads and places for the Son of Light, and the fellow workers which she took from the elements below to build bodily dwellings from them. But, having come into being in an empty glory, they ended in destruction in the dwellings in which they were, since they were prepared by Sophia (Gr. Seth VII.50.25-51.13, in *NHL*, p. 330).

After discussing the role of Jesus, the text proceeds to denigrate almost all the Old Testament figures--Adam, the patriarchs, Moses, David, Solomon, the prophets, even John the Baptist--by calling them laughingstocks.

> For the Archon was a laughingstock because he said, "I am God, and there is none greater than I. I alone am the Father, the Lord, and there is no other beside me." . . . As if he had become stronger than Jesus and my brothers! . . . Thus he was in an empty glory. And he does not agree with our Father (ibid., 64.18-33, pp. 335f).

As for the world,

> . . . the archons around Yaldabaoth were disobedient because of the Ennoia [Thought] who went down to him from her sister Sophia. They made for themselves a union with those who were with them in a mixture of a fiery cloud, which was their Envy, and the rest who were brought forth by their creatures, as if they had bruised the noble pleasure of the Assembly. And therefore they revealed a mixture of ignorance in a counterfeit of fire and earth and a murderer, since they are small and untaught, without knowledge . . . (ibid., 68.28-69.13, p. 337).

In "The Gospel of Thomas," sometimes mistakenly referred to as a Gnostic text, we find these two very Gnostic teachings: "A grapevine [the world] has been planted outside of the Father, but being unsound, it will be pulled up by its roots and destroyed" and "Whoever has come to understand the world has found only a corpse, and whoever has found a corpse is superior to the world" (GTh II.40.13; 42.30, in *NHL*, pp. 122,124). Further, we find this denigrating portrait of the Old Testament God in the "Acts of Thomas," as Thomas questions the serpent, the offspring of Ialdabaoth, as to his origin. The serpent answers:

> I am a reptile of reptile nature, the baleful son of a baleful father; I am

son of him who . . . sits upon the throne and has power over the creation which is under heaven. . . . I am he who entered through the fence into Paradise and said to Eve all the things my father charged me to say to her; I am he who kindled and inflamed Cain to slay his own brother. . . . I am he who hurled the angels down from above, and bound them in lusts for women, that earth-born children might come from them and I fulfill my will in them. . . . I am he who hardened Pharoah's heart . . . (ATh II.32, in *NTA* II, p. 460).

In "The Treatise on Resurrection," a Valentinian tract we shall discuss when we consider the resurrection of Jesus, we find this striking line, in the context of resurrection: "It [the resurrection] is no illusion, but it is truth. Indeed, it is more fitting to say that the world is an illusion. . . ." The author also quotes from an unidentified Gnostic text: "Strong is the system of the Pleroma; small is that which broke loose and became the world" (Treat. Res. I.48.12; 46.35, in *NHL*, pp. 52f).

"The First Apocalypse of James," still another example of the Gnostic denigration of the Judaeo-Christian tradition, presents Jesus saying to James: ". . . leave Jerusalem. For it is she who always gives the cup of bitterness to the sons of light. She is a dwelling place of a great number of archons" (1 ApocJs V.25.15, in *NHL*, p. 243). Jerusalem, being the place of Jesus' crucifixion, thus becomes a symbol for the sufferings of the material world.

Our final Gnostic text before turning to the Valentinian *gnosis* is "The Gospel of Philip," which most likely dates from the latter half of the third century. Though basically Valentinian in its character, it shares the hostile worldview that we find in many of the other Gnostic writings, but which is largely absent in the writings we can attribute either to Valentinus himself, or to disciples such as Ptolemaeus who immediately followed him, where the tone is more neutral. The following examples will be illustrative:

The world is a corpse-eater. All the things eaten in it themselves die also (GPh II.73.19, in *NHL*, p. 144).

And as soon as Christ went down into the water he came out laughing at everything of this world, not because he considers it a trifle, but because he is full of contempt for it. He who wants to enter the kingdom of heaven will attain it. If he despises everything of this world and scorns it as a trifle, he will come out laughing (ibid., 74.28-36, pp. 144f).

Now you who live together with the Son of God, love not the world, but love the Lord, in order that those you will bring forth may not resemble the world, but may resemble the Lord (ibid., 78.20-25, p. 147).

A more characteristic Valentinian statement from this text will provide a summarizing introduction to the Valentinian view:

> The world came about through a mistake. For he who created it wanted to create it imperishable and immortal. He fell short of attaining his desire. For the world never was imperishable, nor, for that matter, was he who made the world (ibid., 75.2-10, p. 145).

2. Valentinian

Our contemporary psychological age would certainly consider the Valentinian *gnosis* to be the most sophisticated of all the Gnostic theological systems. Church Father Tertullian claimed that Valentinus "found the seed of an older doctrine" (F I, p. 122, n.9), which some commentators have seen as the Ophites and/or the Barbelognostics, whose most representative and highly developed work, "The Apocryphon of John," we have already examined. Whatever the antecedents of certain ideas or forms of expression may have been, clearly Valentinus applied an originality if not genuine inspiration to these ideas, focusing the cosmic events of separation and world creation on a purely internal phenomenon. His psychological understanding, as we have seen, provides an ancient counterpart to the particular brand of modern Gnosticism we find in *A Course in Miracles*. Midst the Gnostic theater in which Valentinus found himself in the mid-second century A.D., this great teacher reinterpreted the role of Sophia, the central figure in the Gnostic cosmic drama, recasting her as the prototype for everyone who "wanders in the world uncertain, lonely, and in constant fear" (*A Course in Miracles*: text, p. 621).

As in the preceding chapter, we will present the Valentinian myth as it is found in Irenaeus, supplemented by other writings that are illustrative of the narrative. We left off our discussion in Chapter 5 with the production of Sophia's "folly"--called variously a "formless entity," "frail fruit," and an "abortion"--and the creation of Horos. As Cross and Limit, Horos has a dual function, to reiterate what we discussed above: Sophia is returned to the Pleroma which is restored to its fullness, at the same time the Pleroma is protected by the Limit excluding the "formless entity." Thus we have essentially two Sophias, upper and lower. It is the "lower Sophia," outside the Pleroma, that is our concern here, and which is the object of the Gnostic redemption.

> She [Sophia] was outside the light and the Pleroma and was without shape and form, like an abortion, since she comprehended nothing (*Adv. haer.* I.4.1, in F I, p. 133).

Alone with her unfulfilled passion, "violently excited" as it were by her unsuccessful attempt, Sophia

> fell into all sorts of suffering which has many forms and varieties: she experienced sorrow, because she had not comprehended; fear, lest life might abandon her, as light had done; and, in addition, perplexity: but all these (she suffered) in ignorance.... Moreover, there came upon her another disposition, namely, that of turning to him who gave her life.
> This, they say, was the formation and substance of the matter from which this universe came into being. From that returning of hers [i.e., repentance and subsequent grief] every soul in the world and that of the Demiurge had its origin: from her fear and sorrow, all the rest took its beginning ... (ibid., 4.1-2, p. 134).

This same passage is presented in Jonas, with a slightly different translation. The importance of this passage in the general argument of this book warrants its immediate repetition, along with Jonas' comments:

> The formless entity to which in her [Sophia's] striving for the impossible she gave birth is the objectivation of her own passion; and at the sight of it, and reflecting upon her fate, she is moved by varying emotions: grief, fear, bewilderment and shock, repentance. These emotions too become embodied in the formlessness, and their complete series, developed in ever-new variations by the individual thinkers, plays an important ontological role in the system: [quoting Irenaeus *Adv. haer*. I.2.3] "From here, from the ignorance, the grief, the fear and the shock, material substance took its first beginning." ... This substance ... is nothing else than a self-estranged and sunken form of the Spirit solidified from acts into habitual conditions and from inner process to outer fact (Jonas, pp. 183,187).

This movement from "inner process to outer fact" is, of course, the psychological dynamic of projection, here remarkably depicted in texts written almost eighteen centuries before Freud! Jonas adds that

> "matter" is the external, "oblivion" the internal aspect of the "deficiency" in which Error objectified itself. In the final product, the "deficiency" is the world as fashioned by Error in a "shape," in which the force of oblivion that lies at its root lives on (Jonas, p. 317n).

Moreover, we see that Sophia's "repentance" does not heal the split, but becomes in fact part of the projection into matter: believing that there was something to repent *for*, she ends up making the error real. We shall return to this important point in Part III.

Jonas comments further that we may see the centrality of Sophia's reactions for the Valentinian thought system by the many and varied accounts that are given throughout their writings, cutting across their many schools:

> The very fact that the correlation of emotions and elements is not fixed in detail but varies considerably from author to author, and probably even within the thought of one and the same author, illustrates how the subject was again and again pondered on (Jonas, p. 187).

Examining this process more closely, we find that there are actually three divisions, corresponding to the three divisions found in humanity which we shall consider in more detail in the following chapter. As we have already observed, the Valentinian systems show an impressive consistency in terms of their anthropology reflecting the basic ontology.

In Chapter 5 we saw that Sophia was restored to her perfection by Christ and the Holy Spirit, and that, in fact, Sophia became separated into an upper and a lower self. The lower Sophia is our current focus, and corresponds to the separated self, called the ego by *A Course in Miracles*; the upper Sophia is our true nature as spirit and light, called *pneuma* by the Gnostics, and Christ by the Course. This Self of course does not concern us here, for the *pneuma* plays no role in the fashioning of the world.

Jonas has pointed out that although ignorance is usually classified as one of the resulting emotions of Sophia's folly, along with grief, fear, and bewilderment, it actually is the reigning principle that is immanent in the other three, the condition out of which they arise. The Gnostic writers sought to have four emotions, from which to derive the traditional four elements of matter, and so ignorance was added on. However, the importance of ignorance as *the* problem as well as being the ultimate cause of the material world will become apparent when we consider the Gnostic theory of salvation in Chapter 8. Nonetheless, it is this combination of emotions that directly leads to the world of matter--earth, water, air, and fire--as is seen in this excerpt from Irenaeus:

> The corporeal elements of the universe sprang, as has been said before, from the terror and perplexity, as from a more permanent [the translator notes that the Greek reads "more ignoble"] source: earth, as a result of the state of terror; water, as a result of the agitation of fear; air, as a result of the congealing of sorrow. Fire is inherent in all of these elements as death and decay, just as they also teach that ignorance is hidden in the three passions (*Adv. haer.* I.5.4, in F I, p. 137).

The remaining emotion in the series is the conversion or turning back to God, what Hippolytus' account refers to as the supplication for ascent. It is this entreaty that ultimately leads to the psychical (or mental) element in people, which falls between matter and spirit, or what we may call the soul (to be distinguished from the spirit). The psychics, in the Valentinian system, are those who have the choice of turning upward to God or else falling deeper into the world of matter, and we shall consider them in more detail in the following chapter. At this point, however, we shall consider the dual manner in which the "conversion" operates. On the one hand, the soul may choose to reflect the spirit that is seen in the Savior, and it is this that leads to the presence of the spirit--or the pneumatic element--in this world. On the other hand, the soul may choose to identify with the materialization that gives rise to the material universe. This second aspect is the function of the Demiurge, the representative (symbol) of the process of taking the substances of the emotions and translating them into matter.

Two parallel accounts follow, which summarize this part of the process. The first is from Church Father Clement of Alexandria and is taken from his *Excerpta ex Theodoto*, a compilation of the writings of Theodotus as well as other Valentinians.

> Immediately therefore the Savior [Jesus] bestows on her [Sophia] the form according to knowledge and healing from her passions, showing to her the things in the Pleroma from the unbegotten Father as far as herself. He removed the passions from her who had suffered them and made her impassible [i.e., incapable of suffering], but having separated the passions from her, he kept them. And they were not dispersed, as in the case of the inner [the upper Sophia], but he made both them and those of the second disposition into substances. So by the appearance of the Savior, Sophia becomes passionless and what is outside [the Pleroma] is created. For "all things were made by him and without him was not anything made" (John 1:3) (*Excerpta* 45.1, in F I, pp. 146f).

This last quotation, incidentally, is an example of the kind of scripture citation of which the Gnostics were so characteristically fond--using the traditional Church texts to support their own arguments--and which so enraged the Church authorities. Clement continues:

> So, from incorporeal and contingent passion he first molded them [the passions] into a still incorporeal matter and then, in the same way, changed them into compounds and bodies--for it was not possible to turn the passions into substances all at once--and he created in the bodies a capability according to [their] nature (ibid., 46.1, p. 147).

A similar report is found in Irenaeus, and is quoted now as illustrative of the process similar to what is found in the gospels. As Foerster points out (F I, p. 146), one may find a similar relationship between Clement and Irenaeus as is seen between Luke and Matthew (one may add Mark as well), in the sense that these later documents used the same earlier source, but reinterpreted it through the particular lens of the evangelist or Church Father. Now, Irenaeus:

> When their mother had passed through all her suffering and had, with difficulty, emerged from it, she is said to have turned her attention to supplicating the light which had left her, that is, Christ. He had gone up into the Pleroma, and was naturally reluctant to descend a second time, and so he sent to her the Paraclete, that is, the Savior [again, Jesus], to whom in fact the Father gave all power and put all things under his authority, and the aeons too. . . . But he was sent to her along with the angels, who were his coevals. Achamoth [variant name for Sophia], they say, put a veil over her countenance out of reverence for him, but then, when she had seen him with all his fructifying power, she ran to him and received strength from his appearing. And he gave to her the formation that is in accordance with knowledge and healed her of her passions and separated them from her, but he still was concerned about them, because it was not possible for them to disappear, like those of the former [the upper Sophia], for they had already become fixed by habit and powerful. Therefore he separated them and made them solid and transformed them from an incorporeal passion into (an) incorporeal matter.

I interrupt this account to point out what appears to be another example of the strong Platonic influence in many of the Gnostic theories, to be discussed more fully later. The passage in question deals with the intermediate step between the "incorporeal passions" and the world of matter, what Clement and Irenaeus term "incorporeal matter." This intermediary is reminiscent, albeit in distorted fashion, of Plato's Ideas: the idealization of form that subsequently becomes manifest in the world of multiplicity, the material world of shadows and illusions. Plato himself gives no cosmological sequence to this, which remained the task of the Gnostic theorists. This Platonic borrowing renders more sensible the generally benevolent Valentinian attitude towards the Demiurge.

Returning to Irenaeus' narrative,

> Then he [Christ] implanted into them [Sophia's passions] an aptitude and nature such that they could come together into compounds and bodies, so that two substances might come into being, the one evil, resulting from the passions, the other passible, resulting from the conversion. In this way, they maintain, the Savior in effect created

all. But Achamoth, freed from her passions, received with joy her vision of the lights coming with him (that is, the angels with him), became pregnant, and ... gave birth to progeny after their image, a spiritual offspring which was formed after the likeness of the Savior's bodyguards.

These three substances underlie all else, in their opinion: one from the passion, and this was matter; a second from the conversion, and that was (the) psychic; and, thirdly, what she herself brought forth, and that was (the) spiritual (*Adv. haer.* I.4.5-5.1, in F I, p. 134f).

Again, in the next chapter we shall discuss the threefold nature of humanity that results from these three substances.

We turn our attention now to the role of the Demiurge in the creation of the world. It is in their respective cosmologies that we see most graphically depicted the difference between the Gnostics and the Church and, in fact, the difference between the Gnostics and *A Course in Miracles*. In the former comparison, the differences are specific to the actual metaphysical teachings themselves; i.e., regarding the role of God in creating the world. In the latter, despite a generally shared metaphysics, we find differences in the tone of the writing, reflecting differing attitudes towards the world and body: differences, as we shall see, every bit as important as those existing between the Gnostics and their adversaries in the orthodox Church.

As a result of her contact with the Savior Jesus, the lower Sophia or Achamoth forms the Demiurge, referred to as Ialdabaoth in other Gnostic sources. The Demiurge is known as the "king" of all that follows from his creation. The term "king" is not without its Gnostic irony, however, for unbeknownst to the Demiurge he merely carries out the desires of his mother Sophia who is the true creative agent. As we shall see, the Gnostics derived much satisfaction, not to mention polemic enjoyment, from reminding their Church readers of the Demiurge's "*conceit* and presumption in which he believes himself to be alone and declares himself to be the unique and highest God" (Jonas, p. 191).

What the Demiurge shapes has both spiritual and material fruits; the former is called the Right, the latter the Left, which includes the eventual creation of humanity. First on the Demiurge's agenda was to create the heavens, above which becomes his own home. As Irenaeus summarizes:

He ... prepared seven heavens above which the Demiurge [himself] was to dwell. And, for this reason, they name him Hebdomad, and the mother, Achamoth, Ogdoad: she thereby preserves the number of the original and primary Ogdoad of the Pleroma (*Adv. haer.* I.5.2, in F I, p. 136).

Topographically, then, we can understand that first there is the Pleroma, beneath which is the lower Sophia (Ogdoad, Achamoth, Mother) who awaits the consummation of her salvation. Beneath her is her son, the Demiurge (the Hebdomad), who resides in the "Place of the Middle," beneath whom is the material universe. It is interesting to note that one of the Hebrew synonyms for God, to avoid calling Him by name directly, is *Hamakom*, "The Place."

Clement's collection provides the reason for the "seven heavens." As we have already seen, the Gnostic writers were fond of citing scripture as justification for their own theologies, just as the New Testament authors repeatedly cited Old Testament sources for their own purposes. In Clement's version, some of the details differ but the basic substance remains the same:

> The first and universal Demiurge is the Savior [i.e., Jesus, by virtue of his having saved Sophia], but Sophia, as the second, "built herself a house and supported it with seven pillars" (Pr 9:1) (*Excerpta* 47.1, in F I, p. 147).

The narrative continues:

> And first of all things she put forth, as an image of the Father, the god [the Demiurge] through whom she made "the heaven and the earth" (Gn 1:1), that is, the heavenly and the earthly, the Right and the Left (ibid., 47.2).

Clement now provides one Gnostic version of the Genesis creation story, and not an altogether positive one, as its conclusion suggests:

> He [the Demiurge], being an image of the Father, becomes a father and brings forth first the psychic Christ, an image of the Son, then the archangels, as images of the aeons, then angels, as images of the archangels, all from the psychic, luminous substance [the Right], of which the prophetic word says, "And the spirit of God hovered over the waters" (Gn 1:2). Because the two substances made by him were combined he declares concerning the pure that it "hovered over," and concerning what was heavy, material, muddy, and dense, that it "lay underneath." That this also, in the beginning, was incorporeal he indicates by calling it "invisible," though it was invisible neither to man, who did not then exist, nor to God, for he in fact formed it; rather, he has somehow expressed in this way the fact that it was unformed, unshaped, and undesigned.
>
> The Demiurge separated the pure from the heavy, since he perceived the nature of both, and made light, that is, he let it appear and brought it to light and form, for the light of the sun and of the heaven was made much later. And of the material he made the one out of the

sorrow, creating substantially "the spiritual powers of wickedness" (Ep 6:12), with whom we have to struggle . . . he made from the fear, namely, the wild beasts, and another from the terror and perplexity, namely, the elements of the universe (ibid., 47.3-48.3, pp. 147f).

We find a similar expression of the deity's arrogance in this Mandean account of the King of Darkness' cry:

> "Is there any one who is stronger than I, whom all the worlds serve? If there is someone who is stronger than I, then let him come forward and fight with me, whose food is the mountains, in whose belly only its wrath is found. All the great ones and giants, together with their demons . . . they are all subservient to me . . . and prostrate themselves daily before me." . . . [Then] Ruha spoke to her son and instructed the King of Darkness: "There is someone who is greater than you, and whose power surpasses all your worlds. There is a world which is more extensive than yours, in which mighty ones dwell . . . .and their forms are more radiant than all the worlds" (GR III, in F II, pp. 205f).

Hippolytus' narrative continues with the account of the Demiurge's ignorance of the true creative agent:

> The Demiurge, they say, knows nothing whatsoever, but is, in their view, without understanding and silly, and he does not know what he is doing or bringing to pass. In him, who does not know what he is doing, Sophia was active and operative, and when she was active he believed that he was bringing about by himself the creation of the world. Therefore he began to say, "I am God, and apart from me there is no other" (Is 45:5) . . . .Foolishness . . . is the power of the Demiurge. For he was foolish and without understanding, and believed that he himself was creating the world, unaware that Sophia, the mother, the Ogdoad, was accomplishing everything for the creation of the world, without his knowledge (*Ref.* VI.33.1; 34.8, in F I, pp. 190,192).

Finally, we consider Irenaeus' account of the Demiurge's ignorance and arrogance which, again, allows us to see the Platonic influence:

> They say that the Demiurge believed that he had created all this of himself, but in fact he had made them because Achamoth prompted him. He made the heaven without knowing the heaven; he formed man without knowing him; he brought the earth to light without knowing it. And, in every case, they say, *he was ignorant of the idea of the things he made,* and even of his own mother, and imagined that he alone was all things (*Adv. haer.* I.5.3, in F I, p. 136, my italics).

As Jonas has pointed out (p. 191), this passage is a deliberate revision of Plato's Demiurge who is very much conscious of the ideas from which he creates the world.

Almost without exception, the Gnostics, including the Valentinians, equated the Demiurge or creator God with the God of the Old Testament and, as we have already seen, not in the kindliest of lights. However, of all the Gnostic schools it is the Valentinian which seems to have the most charitable view. Exceptions would be Clement's account, already quoted, and that of Hippolytus, as seen in the following reference to the Old Testament:

> All the prophets and the law spoke from the Demiurge, a silly god ... and they were foolish and knew nothing ....For none of the prophets ... said anything at all concerning the things of which we speak. For everything was unknown because it was spoken by the Demiurge alone (*Ref.* VI.35.1, in F I, p. 192).

The most benevolent view toward the creator God and the Old Testament is found in the "Letter to Flora" by the famous Valentinian disciple Ptolemaeus, whose teachings appear to be the basis for much of Irenaeus' criticisms. The letter was preserved in its entirety by the fourth-century Church Father Epiphanius, and its basic purpose was to instruct a certain lady who was obviously not yet a part of the Valentinian community. We shall return to this letter when we discuss the question of asceticism and libertinism in Chapter 10. Here, we comment on the specific view expressed about God in the two great ethical teachings of the Old and New Testaments: the Decalogue (the Ten Commandments) and the Sermon on the Mount.

Ptolemaeus' argument is that there are essentially three "Gods." The first is the true God, incorruptible and light; the third is the "adversary," or the Devil, whose nature is corruptible and darkness; the second God is the Old Testament creator God, who stands between these two extremes. Ptolemaeus discusses this in the context of the Law, where he says:

> For it is evident that this law was not ordained by the perfect God and Father ... because it is not only imperfect and in need of completion by another, [Jesus is meant here] but also contains commands which are not consonant with the nature and disposition of such a God. ... It is clear to you from what has been said that these people completely miss the truth. Each of the groups has experienced this in its own way: the one, because they do not know the God of righteousness [the Demiurge], and the other, because they do not know the Father of all whom alone the one [Jesus] who knew him revealed by his coming. It remains for us [the Valentinian Gnostics] who have been counted worthy of the knowledge of both of these to provide you with an accurate and clear account of the nature of the law and

of the law-giver by whom it was ordained. We shall draw the proofs of what we say from the words of our Savior [Jesus], for through these alone are we led without stumbling to the comprehension of that which is (*Panar.* XXXIII.3.4,7-8, in F I, pp. 155f).

Ptolemaeus develops his argument by references to the Sermon on the Mount and other New Testament passages, showing how Jesus has corrected the mistakes of the Old Testament. He does this, however, without the denigration of the biblical God that is found in most of the other Gnostic texts. He concludes his argument by summarizing his view about this "Middle" God:

There remains the question who this God is who ordained the law. But I think that I have shown you this as well in what has been already said, if you have listened carefully. For if this (law) was ordained neither by the perfect god himself, nor by the Devil . . . then the one who ordained the law must be other than these two. But in fact he is the Fashioner [Demiurge] and Maker of this entire universe and of what is in it. He is different from these two realities and since he stands in the midst between them, he rightly bears the name "Middle." And if the perfect God is good by his own nature . . . and if the one of the opposite nature is evil and wicked, characterized by injustice, then the one who is situated in the midst of the two and who is neither good nor evil and unjust, can be properly called just . . . . This God is inferior to the perfect God, and lower than his justice, since he is generated and not ungenerated . . . but he is greater and more powerful than the adversary, and is of a substance and of a nature other than the substance of either of these. The nature of the adversary is corruption and darkness, for he is material and multipartite. The nature of the ungenerated Father of All is incorruption and self-existence, simple, and homogeneous light (ibid., 7.1-7, p. 160).

It is clear from this how far removed this early Valentinian account is from the more general and characteristic Gnostic attitude. It serves to illustrate again how these second-century theologians never considered themselves to be anything other than Christians, part of the Church that traced its roots back to Jesus himself and the apostles. Finally, Ptolemaeus leaves for another time the explanation of how this "Middle" God evolved, the explanation of the separation we have made the burden of Chapter 5.

For the present do not let this trouble you as you desire to learn how from *one* beginning of all things, which is simple and, as we acknowledge and believe ungenerated, incorruptible, and good, there were constituted these natures, namely that of corruption [the Devil] and that of the Middle, which are of different substance, although it is the nature of the good to generate and produce things which are like itself and of the same substance (ibid., 7.8, p. 161).

Thus, we have seen that the Valentinian Demiurge, on one level at least, bears little resemblance to the demonic figure of Ialdabaoth of other Gnostic writers. To be sure, the basic teaching that the physical world is not the creation of the supreme transcendent God remains the same. Nonetheless, there is a decided shift in mood from the Ialdabaoth who seems no different from the Devil, and the Valentinian Demiurge who while perhaps foolish and beneath the supreme goodness of the true God, shares not in the evil nature of his non-Valentinian counterparts. An explanation, on one level at least, for this difference in mood can possibly be found in the aforementioned Platonic influence so prominent in Valentinus and his disciples. In addition to what we have already seen we can cite two more, one apparently from the pen of Valentinus himself. Let us begin with Irenaeus' report of the teaching of Marcus, a Valentinian who seemed to distinguish himself by his (at least according to Irenaeus) grandiose prophetic claims for himself, not to mention his preoccupation with numerical symbolism. The passage to follow is of interest in illustrating at least one divergence from other Valentinians, insofar as here the Demiurge does have awareness of the nature of the world above himself, even though he is unable to replicate it without serious distortion:

> In addition . . . the Demiurge wished to imitate the infinitude, the eternity, the limitlessness, and the timelessness of the Ogdoad above. But he could not express its permanence and eternity because he was the offspring of deficiency; consequently he spread out its eternity into long periods of time, seasons, and vast numbers of years, thinking to imitate its infinitude by means of the multitude of these times (*Adv. haer.* I.17.2, in F I, p. 213).

As Jonas has discussed (Jonas, p. 194), this passage is a parody on the more famous passage in Plato's *Timaeus* which describes in quite positive terms the creation of the world of time, resembling the eternal universe beyond the world of materiality: "a moving image of eternity." Marcus' description, placed side by side with Plato's, provides us with a compelling illustration of the strong polemic found in much of the Gnostic writings. Here, we can almost feel the rage grow within the Platonists as they read these words, a rage no doubt delighted in by their Gnostic counterparts. We have already discussed in this chapter the reaction of one such philosopher, the third-century Neoplatonist Plotinus.

In what is perhaps the closest we will ever come to Valentinus' own thought and expression, even if it is not his own work--"The Gospel of

Truth"--we find the following succinct statement of the aforementioned process:

> Ignorance of the Father brought about anguish and terror. And the anguish grew solid like a fog so that no one was able to see. For this reason error became powerful; it fashioned its own matter foolishly, not having known the truth (GT I.17.10-16, in *NHL*, p. 38).

Clement of Alexandria has preserved some precious few fragments, seemingly original to Valentinus himself. One of them offers another clear example of the free borrowing of which the Gnostics availed themselves of the words and thoughts of Plato:

> Concerning this god he [Valentinus] speaks as follows, in a rather obscure way, writing thus: "The world is as much inferior to the living aeon as the picture is inferior to the living figure. What then is the reason for the picture? It is the majesty of the living figure, which presents the example for the painter so that it may be honored through his name. For the form was not found to correspond to the actuality, but the name filled up what was lacking in the image. But the invisible power of God works for the authenticity of the image." Then Valentinus designates the creator of the world, in so far as he was called God and Father, as the likeness of the true God and as his herald, but Sophia as the painter whose work the likeness is, for the glorification of the invisible one . . . [Clement's excerpt breaks off here] (*Strom.* IV.13, in F I, p., 242).

Valentinus is identifying the aeon--representative of the Pleroma, created by the true God--with the living figure. Sophia is the painter who in her awe of God, the true Creator, attempts to replicate the heavenly majesty by fashioning the Demiurge. This Demiurge becomes the painter's picture, of obviously inferior quality. Nonetheless Valentinus does not denigrate the Demiurge, for the power of God has still worked through Sophia establishing "the authenticity of the image."

Fineman discusses this cosmogonic process:

> That Achamoth and a Demiurge, issue of Sophia's fall, proceed to repeat her initial mimesis, engendering the lower world through declensive reflections of her first substitution, illustrates the principle that, once set in motion, the free play of substitution goes on and on, imitating imitation, repeating repetition, in a series that traces the course of Gnostic desire directly back to the displacements and deferments initiated by the origin lost through the Name itself ("Gnosis and the Piety of Metaphor," in Layton, p. 304).

207

This echoes the description in *A Course in Miracles* of the process of substitution that followed the original substitution, to which we shall return in Chapter 13. Fineman's passage also mirrors the Course's understanding that our individual ego experiences in the world are ultimately derived from the ontological experience of separation and substitution.

The reader here is thus immediately thrown back into the world of Plato's thought which, in this context, we may summarize very briefly as reflecting three levels. The first and highest is the Good, symbolized in one of Plato's metaphors as the sun. This Good is the source of the Ideas, the idealizations of objects. The Good and the Ideas together constitute the level of perfect reality. Second, the manufactured objects of this world correspond, albeit in imperfect ways, to the perfect Idea. Finally, the artistic representations of these manufactured objects, referred to as shadows or illusions, are still further from the truth of the ideal.

A summarizing analogy for the theory of the Ideas is given by Plato near the end of the *Republic* (596c-602b), where he contrasts "god," the carpenter, and the painter in their respective makings of a bed. The analogy is the basis for Valentinus' image of the painter and the living figure. Plato portrays art here rather clearly as being but an imitation of a secondary reality, and thus it can tell us nothing about what is real. God created one bed-in-itself; the carpenter builds a particular bed, and more than one; and the artist makes a representation of the bed the carpenter made, which in turn is but a reflection of the real bed-in-itself:

> what he [the carpenter] produces is not the form of bed which according to us is what a bed really is, but a particular bed . . . .his product . . . *resembles* "what is" without *being* it. And anyone who says that the products of the carpenter or any other craftsman are ultimately real can hardly be telling the truth . . . .the bed the carpenter makes is a shadowy thing compared to reality . . . .there are three sorts of bed. The first exists in nature, and we would say . . . that it was made by god. No one else could have made it. . . . The second is made by the carpenter. . . . And the third by the painter. . . . the artist's representation stands at third remove from reality . . . . So the tragic poet, if his art is representation, is by nature at third remove from the throne of truth; and the same is true of all other representative artists (598b-e).

I interrupt Plato's argument to point to the borrowing of this idea by *A Course in Miracles*. In a passage from the manual, partly quoted earlier, we read the following statement regarding words, which were made by separated minds to keep them in the illusion of separation. . . . Let us not forget, however, that words are but symbols of symbols. They are thus twice removed from reality (manual, p. 51).

Being "twice removed" of course places words in the third position—"at third remove." We incidentally find the same idea expressed in Philo, where he writes in the context of the descent of the human race from the perfection of Adam:

I have observed the same thing happening in the case of sculpture and painting: the copies are inferior to the originals, and what is painted or molded from the copies still more so, owing to their long distance from the original . . . .As generation follows generation the powers and qualities of body and soul which men receive are feebler (*On the Creation* 141).

We return to Plato who continues by pointing out that the painter represents not the thing-itself (as it truly is as an Idea), but the thing that the craftsman makes, and not even as that thing is made, but as it *appears* to the painter. He now concludes his argument:

The art of representation is therefore a long way removed from truth, and it is able to reproduce everything because it has little grasp of anything, and that little is of a mere phenomenal appearance . . . . In all such cases . . . we should bear the following considerations in mind. When someone tells us that he has met someone who is a master of every craft and has a more exact understanding about all subjects than any individual expert, we must answer that he is a simple-minded fellow who seems to have been taken in by the work of a charlatan, whose apparent omniscience is due entirely to his own inability to distinguish knowledge, ignorance, and representation. . . . We may assume, then, that all the poets from Homer downwards have no grasp of truth but merely produce a superficial likeness of any subject they treat, including human excellence (*Rep.* 598b-d; 600e).

The Metaphysics of Time

Attitudes toward time, of course, correspond to attitudes toward the physical world. Time and space are, as *A Course in Miracles* states, but different forms of one illusion, i.e., the belief in separation (text, p. 519). From our previous examination of the cosmologies of Platonism, Christianity, and Gnosticism it will be clear how time is seen, at least in a general sense. Let us take each of these specifically in turn. The contours of this discussion are largely based on the fine paper "Gnosis and Time" by Henri-Charles Puech.

1. Platonism

The ancient Greeks conceived of time as mirroring the eternal Ideas. We have already quoted Plato's evocative phrase from the *Timaeus* that time was "the moving image of eternity." The religious inspiration for the Greeks, Plato being one of the clearest examples of this, was the ordered movement of the cosmos. For classical antiquity this great and living god that was the physical universe reflected the eternal and unchanging nature of the Supreme non-material principle, God or the Idea of the Good. Puech states:

> Time is perceived and considered in the light of a hierarchized vision of the universe, in which the inferior realities are only degraded and necessary reflections of the superior realities which give them being and life and govern their movements. Time is part of a cosmic order; on its own level it is an effect and an expression of that order. If it moves in a circle, it is because, in its own way, it imitates the cyclical course of the stars on which it depends. Its endlessness, its repetition of conjunctures, are, in a mobile form, images of the unchanging, perfect order of an eternal universe, eternally regulated by fixed laws, an order of which the heavens, with their uniform revolution of their luminaries, offer still more sublime images (Puech, pp. 43f).

In his reverence for the heavens (the cosmos) we find in Aristotle the same attitude we have already examined in Plato and Plotinus. For Aristotle, too, eternity is outside of time and the material universe:

> It is clear then that there is neither place, nor void, nor time, outside the heaven. Hence whatever is there, is of such a nature as not to occupy any place, nor does time age it; nor is there any change in any of the things which lie beyond the outermost motion; they continue through the entire duration unalterable and unmodified, living the best and most self-sufficient of lives (*On the Heavens* 279a18-22).

The Platonic or Greek notion of time is unique, however, for it is seen as circular: the events occurring now are the same as have already occurred in prior cycles, and will yet recur in future ones. In truth, then, for the ancient Greeks there is nothing new under the sun. All has been, is now, and will yet be again. There are thus, for example, alternating periods of an inspired Golden Age of happiness and the degenerative instability that followed, such as Plato experienced in the Athenian city-state which had murdered Socrates, an event which must therefore occur again and again throughout all of time. In the *Republic* Plato writes:

> It will be difficult to bring about any change for the worse in a state

210

so constituted; but since all created things must decay, even a social order of this kind cannot last for all time, but will decline. And its dissolution will be as follows. Not only for plants that grow in the earth, but for animals that live on it, there are seasons of fertility and infertility of both mind and body, seasons which come when their periodic motions come full circle, a period of longer duration for the long-lived, shorter for the short-lived (*Rep.* VIII.546a).

And in the *Statesman*:

There is an era in which God himself assists the universe on its way and guides it by imparting its rotation to it. There is also an era in which he releases his control. He does this when its circuits under his guidance have completed the due limit of the time thereto appointed. Thereafter it begins to revolve in the contrary sense under its own impulse-- for it is a living creature and has been endowed with reason by him who framed it in the beginning (*States.* 269c).

Regarding this cyclical nature of the world of time, in which all events simply recur and recur, Aristotle says, by way of an example: "as a movement can be one and the same again and again, so too can time, e.g., a year or a spring or an autumn" (*Physics* 220b12). The basic motion of time is circular, since only the circular is the motion of unchanging eternity, having no beginning nor end. Its origin is the prime mover, "indivisible and . . . without parts and without magnitude" (*Physics* 267b25), and so this unceasing circularity is the only true measure of time. We find an even stronger statement of time's circularity in this passage that was originally thought to be Aristotle's, but is now generally considered to be a product of his school:

How should one define the terms "before" and "after"? Should it be in the sense that the people of Troy are before us, and those previous to them before them and so on continuously? Or if it is true that the universe has a beginning, a middle and an end, and when a man grows old he reaches his limit and reverts again to the beginning, and those things which are nearer the beginning merit the term "before," what is there to prevent us from regarding ourselves as nearer the beginning? If that is true, then we should be "before." As therefore in the movement of the heavens and of each star there is a circle, what is there to prevent the birth and death of perishable things from being of this nature, so they are born and destroyed again? So they say that human affairs are a cycle (*Problems* XVII.3).

While the circularity of time was not an essential part of Plotinus' system, he did discuss it, as seen here:

> ... if one ranks the Good as a centre one would rank Intellect as an unmoved circle and Soul as a moving circle; but moving by aspiration (Enn. IV.4.16).

The soul continues to seek the Good, its source and its home. Its aspiration for the "unmoving circle" moves the heavenly spheres, and so we see that the dimension of time in the soul is mirrored in the cosmos.

Aristotle, incidentally, differed from Plato in his emphasis of the real nature of time from the point of view of the material world, studying what time does by observing its expression in the world. Plato's emphasis was on the metaphysical and spiritual qualities of time's relation to eternity, time being its moving image. Moreover, time helps the universe to become perfect like eternity, as the soul uses time as the means to recognize its innate perfection. Remembering Plotinus' system, we see that time is conceived as less than eternity, a diminution consisting of downward emanations that in essence are inferior and imperfect intermediaries between eternity and the phenomenal world. Nonetheless Plotinus, like his great predecessors, saw eternity reflected in the soul through its presence in the ordered movement of the cosmos.

The typical Greek response, as we have seen, was to venerate this ordered movement of the cosmos as a living god, an indication of the fundamental good of the world. In late antiquity, however, one finds interestingly enough the opposite reaction to the same perceived phenomenon: a depressed pessimism which saw no way of changing the inexorability of the cosmos nor its unceasing circularity, an anguished and hopeless weariness with it all. Marcus Aurelius, the second-century Stoic Roman Emperor gave articulate expression to this ennui in his *Meditations*:

> Consider in what condition both in body and soul a man should be when he is overtaken by death; and consider the shortness of life, the boundless abyss of time past and future, the feebleness of all matter. ... How small a part of boundless and unfathomable time is assigned to every man? for it is very soon swallowed up in the eternal. ... and on what a small clod of the whole earth you creep? Reflecting on all this consider nothing to be great, except to act as your nature leads you, and to endure that which the common nature brings (*Meditations* XII.7,32).

The cause of this resignation is the unending circularity of the world:

> ... all things from eternity are of like forms and come round in a circle. ... Everywhere up and down you will find the same things, with

which the old histories are filled, those of the middle ages and those
of our own day with which cities and houses are filled now. There
is nothing new; all things are both familiar and shortlived. . . .
everything which happens, always happened so and will happen so,
and now happens so everywhere . . . (ibid., II.14; VII.1; XII.26).

The ordered movement of the stars and planets is thus experienced
as a prison-house of monotony at best, and abject slavery at worst.
Unable to change what already is, however, these philosophers had no
recourse but to adopt a pessimistic resignation and acceptance. No
way out was seen. It remained for the Gnostics to rebel openly against
this planetary slavery by denying the divine origins of the cosmos
itself, thereby freeing the individual from its yoke.

2. Christianity

The Christian view of time is that it is linear, with a definite
beginning and end that has been, is, and will be under the control of
God the Creator and Final Judge. For the Christian, time from beginning to end is part of "salvation's history." It begins with the events
of creation narrated in Genesis, proceeds through Adam's fall from
perfection, on through the calls for salvation of the prophets which
foreshadow the manifestation of God in the person of His Son Jesus,
and then culminating finally in the Second Coming of Jesus to announce the Last Judgment and the end of the world. Thus from the
very beginning of original sin, all of time is oriented for the Christian
towards this saving event of God, which eschatologically ends time.

The world that God created is therefore real, and from time to time
has been thought of as the manifestation of God Himself. The progression through time is purposive, the past announcing and setting the
stage for the future; its purpose nothing less than the salvation of humanity, with the central focus of God's involvement and interventions
in the world being the saving of the total person--mind, body, and
spirit. The true center of history is the coming of Jesus in Palestine.
From this point all the past and future derive their meaning. It is a
unique event, happening once and for all, which gives significance to
history and to time. Thus Christianity grafted itself onto Judaism, seen
as the religion of the past yet also the means of unifying all history.
Though sorely tempted in its early years to establish itself as separate
from and in opposition to Judaism, the Church eventually opted to
retain Judaism and its biblical canon as its precursors. This established
links with the ancient past, and gave greater meaning and credence to
its own revelation.

To sum up, the Christians of the first centuries conceived of time as rectilinear, continuous, irreversible, and progressive; they saw in it a true, direct, and meaningful manifestation of God's will. In this organic whole each event--past, present, future--has its place and its meaning; each event forms a unity with those that preceded and with those that will follow. In time and by time, to employ the language of the period, there is accomplished a divine "disposition" or "dispensation," an *oikonomia*--a word which designates both the providential development of history according to the plans of God and, in a more restricted sense, the Incarnation, the central point in this development, through which all things are ordered and explained (Puech, p. 52).

Thus, the Greek circular view of time would make no sense, as Origen strongly argues:

> ...I do not know what proof they [the Greeks] can bring in support of this theory. For if it is said that there is to be a world similar in all respects to the present world, then it will happen that Adam and Eve will again do what they did before, there will be another flood, the same Moses will once more lead a people numbering six hundred thousand out of Egypt. Judas will also twice betray his Lord, Saul [Paul] will a second time keep the clothes of those who are stoning Stephen, and we shall say that every deed which has been done in this life must be done again. I do not think that this can be established by any reasoning, if souls are actuated by freedom of choice and maintain their progress or the reverse in accordance with the power of their own will. For souls are not driven on some revolving course which brings them into the same cycle again after many ages... (*First Princ.* II.3.4).

St. Augustine was the first Christian theologian to devote full energy and thought to the problem of time, seeking to understand it psychologically through his particular blend of Neoplatonic thought and Christian faith. Thus he enables us to compare and contrast the Neoplatonic and Christian positions. Augustine's eternity is changeless and antedates time, though not temporally of course. God does not exist in a temporal mode prior to the creation of the universe. Yet God in eternity *is* ontologically prior to time, insofar as He is its cause; without eternity there could be no time. God is eternal and, being perfect and immutable, has always existed. Yet this eternal God brought time into being with the creation:

> And if the sacred and infallible Scriptures say that in the beginning God created the heavens and the earth, in order that it may be understood that He had made nothing previously... then assuredly

the world was made, not in time, but simultaneously with time (*City of God* 11.6).

Time is, for Augustine, a psychological phenomenon occurring within the soul ("a stretching out of the soul"). This is in contrast to Plotinus who saw time metaphysically. In fact there is for Augustine no true past or future, but only the present which, as in Heraclitus, is in constant flux. Thus Augustine demonstrates the inherent transitoriness and instability of this world, for only in God is there permanence and unchanging truth.

For both Plotinus and St. Augustine, eternity precedes time and is not coeternal with it. Plotinus believed that time is necessary, following the principle of emanation, although, as we have seen, time is the product of an inherently inferior downward procession. It is thus implied in the very being of eternity. Not so with Augustine, for whom time is simply the creation of God, not necessary by virtue of eternity; thus the difference in emphasis in the two Neoplatonists: Plotinus is able to derive time from the understanding of eternity, while Augustine cannot do this in his system, but must rely instead upon the psychological examination of our experience of time, which becomes his datum for understanding. For Augustine the soul exists within the world of time, from which it must be saved through the Will of God. For Plotinus, on the other hand, the soul is not truly in time, though time exists within it; the soul, rather, is within the Mind that preceded it in the descent. As Callahan phrased it: "time [for Plotinus] is the life of soul as it passes from one state of actualization to another" (Callahan, p. 120).

3. Gnosticism

Though sharing some of the Hellenic and Christian understandings of time, as we have seen, the Gnostic view is essentially a negative one. Similar to their notion of the physical world, the Gnostics see time as an instrument of the archons or world-rulers to control and imprison the souls trapped here. Thus, rather than seeing time and the world as reflections of eternity (Platonism) or as an instrument of the divine Will (Christianity), and therefore worthy of awe and veneration, the Gnostics rebelled against what had become for them a symbol of the soul's imperfection that led to its imprisonment by the archons. Time, thus, is perceived as alien and evil; the home of a degrading slavery, a somnolent ignorance in sharp contrast to the heavenly state of eternity. Our current life is not our true one, and time, whose instants engender and destroy one another, in which each moment arises only to be engulfed in the next moment, in which all things appear, disappear, and reappear in a twinkling, without order, without aim or cessation or end--time contains within it a rhythm of death beneath an appearance of life (Puech, pp. 65f).

This constellation of attitudes towards time and the world can lead to pessimism unless a means is given for escaping from it. We are not too far here from the sentiments of Marcus Aurelius who, as we have seen, knew no way out except for acceptance and resignation for the good and divinely ordered cosmos. The Gnostics, on the other hand, saw time and the cosmos as evil antagonists to truth and reality, mutually exclusive of each other. As Puech succinctly states:

> The Greek says: "God *and* the world," linking the two terms indissolubly; the Gnostic says: "God *or* the world," dissociating the two terms, which for him represent two heterogeneous, independent, irreconcilable realities (Puech, p. 60).

The Gnostics accept the Platonic view that time and the world descended from eternity, but far from seeing such descent as a positive and inevitable expression of the divine, they see it rather as the product of the fall. Time is thus a horrifying condition to be negated, rebelled against, and finally transcended. As for the Gnostic position *vis à vis* the Christian, it takes the Christian divine linearity and breaks it through the intervention of a God who is totally alien to history and its rulers. This ends their rule of ignorance, substituting instead the saving *gnosis*. Thus, in relation to the Greek, the Gnostic position is anti-cosmic, while regarding the Christian, it is anti-historical.

With all the Gnostic vituperation against time, we find relatively little written about it from a philosophical point of view, as we have found in the Greek philosophers. The Gnostics concerned themselves mainly with their *experience* of horror of finding themselves in time, not with its origin. We may cite two exceptions, however. One is in "The Apocryphon of John," in a passage absent from the *Nag Hammadi Library*, but found in another version in a collection known as the Berlin Papyrus. Ialdabaoth, the leader of the archons and son of Sophia who casts him out, attempts to imitate the power of the aeons:

> Being ignorant, he did not know that she [Sophia] was wiser than he; he took counsel with his Powers; they engendered Destiny and bound the gods of the heavens, the angels, the demons, and men in measure, duration, and time, in order to subject them all to the chain of Destiny, which governs all--an evil, tortuous thought (Berlin Papyrus 8502, fol. 71, in Puech, p. 71).

216

Time, under the power of Ialdabaoth, thus becomes the distorted and evil imitation of eternity belonging to the aeons of the Pleroma. The purpose of this imitation is to enslave humanity and keep it *from* remembering its eternal home. We have already discussed the Gnostic denigration of Plato's "time is the moving image of eternity." From this image of time flowing smoothly from eternity, we are left with a fearful caricature of time masquerading as the truth. The second exception is in the more complete version of "Asclepius," also not found in the *Nag Hammadi Library:*

> For where things are discerned at intervals of time, there are falsehoods; and where things have an origin in time, there errors arise (Asclepius, 37, in Puech, p. 72n).

Salvation, or the way out of the prison of destiny, does not really occur in time, as in the Christian revelation, but is atemporal in its essence. It comes through a sudden shift from the horizontal plane to the vertical, of the sudden reception of the Gnostic revelation. For most Gnostics, salvation does not depend on any prior state, condition, or preparation, nor does it require any kind of divine intervention such as is seen in the incarnation of Jesus. The perfect one (i.e., the Gnostic) simply awakens to the treasure of the Self that was always there, and whose gold has never been sullied by the mud of this world. As we will see again in Chapter 9, salvation is acorporeal and the resurrection is purely of the mind or spirit, for which the body is totally irrelevant. Thus, while the Gnostic cannot deny the experience of time while in the body, its importance is minimized, if not outrightly denied. The historical life of Jesus is relegated almost to insignificance, while the Gnostic's experience of the Jesus living in the mind, the source of the *gnosis*, is of great importance.

In summary then, one can see, after Puech, that the Greek view of time is circular, the Christian's linear, while for the Gnostic it is a broken line, cut into by the revelation which lifts the trapped soul out of time entirely. Time and its figures are seen almost as mythological figures, relegated in importance to being mere symbols of a process occurring in a reality rooted in the Gnostic's present experience. It is this experience that alone can save; time may furnish the arena for salvation, but only to allow the soul to escape its evil clutches.

Chapter 7

THE NATURE OF HUMANITY:
SPIRIT, MIND (SOUL), BODY

The creation of homo sapiens is the culmination of the work of the Demiurge, just as it is in the more traditional cosmogonic and anthropogonic accounts. The same principles and dichotomies (or even trichotomies) we have seen on the macrocosmic level regarding the world appear in the microcosmic body. As has been stated, the Gnostics exhibit a consistency between their macrocosmic and microcosmic levels.

Foerster writes in his introduction to the collection of patristic writings on the Gnostics that "the totality of Gnosis can be comprehended in a single image....'gold in mud." The gold refers to our true identity, what we may call the spiritual Self and the Gnostics called the *pneuma*. "The mud is that of the world: it is first of all the body, which with its sensual desires drags man down and holds the 'I' [the Self] in thrall" (F I, p. 2).

It is this oppositional duality that mirrors the duality we considered earlier between God and the world. And so it must be, for the Sophia that separated herself from God began a long downward process that culminated in the emergence of the human being, set off from God by the body. Within the body, however, is found what some Gnostics termed the spark, which is actually part of the great light of God, "a portion of the divine substance from beyond which has fallen into the world" (Jonas, p. 44). In many of the texts we shall consider, it can be seen that the world rulers, derived from Ialdabaoth, made the body so as to imprison this spark. We shall expand on this motivation in Part III in our comparative discussion of the body's purpose.

Finally, there is the psychical,[8] which may be recalled from our discussion in the preceding chapter. This aspect of humanity, like the body, is part of the non-divine element and therefore must be saved. It is intermediate between the spirit and the flesh. The object of salvation, which is the subject of the following chapter, is to "rescue" the spirit that is imprisoned in the body. Its state is variously described as being numb, asleep, or intoxicated by the world. The consequences of this state are that humanity is ignorant of its true origins, and yet feels alienated in this world that is not its home.

Since almost all the Gnostic systems are in agreement as to the

---

8. I use this word instead of the simpler "psychic," to avoid confusion with the latter's contemporary trans-physical connotation.

219

general contours of the spirit-mind-body constellation, and, in fact, of the remaining parts of this story (the nature of salvation, the redeemer Jesus, and the practical implications), we shall dispense with our previous structure of duality vs. non-duality as we proceed with our analysis. The differences noted among the various schools cut across these lines, and so we shall consider these differences as we go along. This chapter has the following three sections: creation, the spirit-mind-body configuration, and the states of alienation, sleep, and drunkenness.

Creation of Humanity: Gnosticism

We have in our possession two extensive treatments of the creation myth: "On the Origin of the World" and "The Apocryphon of John," which we considered in previous chapters. We begin this section with an examination of these, along with the parallel Nag Hammadi tractate, "The Hypostasis of the Archons." These Gnostic texts are based upon the Genesis story, though of course with the characteristic Gnostic reinterpretations. The basic components of the Gnostic myth are that Adam is made by Ialdabaoth in collaboration with the other rulers, which include the seven planets; however, he is made without life. Ialdabaoth (also called the Demiurge or First Father) and the seven correspond, of course, to the Lord God and His host of the Genesis narrative. The *pneuma,* or divine spirit, is surreptitiously given to Adam by Sophia (actually his grandmother), which in effect places him higher than his father, Ialdabaoth, and sets the stage for his subsequent redemption. It is this divine spark that has "fallen asleep." Adam therefore is seen to have two natures--his body given by the archons, and his spirit (referred to as Light-Adam), ultimately derived from God himself. Adam's importance for the Gnostics lay of course in his being the symbolic expression of the existential state in which all people find themselves, conscious of this "sleeping" state or not. We thus all share the need to awaken to our true identity, recognizing the inherent valuelessness of the body and of its creator, and thwarting the plan of the "archons" to keep us asleep. In Part II-B we shall present *A Course in Miracles'* version of the ego's plan (the Course's psychological counterpart to the mythological archons) to protect itself by keeping the Son of Light (or God) asleep. Here in the Gnostic literature we see the plan expressed in a more primitive form than in the more sophisticated Course, yet the underlying content of obscuring humanity's spiritual identity remains the same. We pick up the narrative in "On the Origin of the World," at the point where the archons conceive the plan to make a man (Adam) to ensure their own survival:

220

> ... if you desire that he [the Light-Adam] be not able to destroy our
> work, come, let us create a man [Adam] from the earth according to
> the image of our body and according to the likeness of that one, in
> order that he may serve us so that whenever that one sees his likeness
> he may become enamored of it. Then he will no longer ruin our work,
> but we shall make those who will be begotten from the light servants
> to ourselves (Orig. Wld. II.112.32-113.5, in *NHL*, p. 170).

The Demiurge summons the seven archons (corresponding to the
seven planets) and orders them to proceed with the plan:

> Then each one of them cast his seed on the midst of the navel of the
> earth. Since that day, the seven rulers have formed the man: his body
> is like their body, his likeness is like the man [the Light-Adam] who
> appeared to them. His molded body came into being according to a
> portion of each one of them. . . . He became a living man, and he who
> is the father was called "Adam," according to the name of the one
> who was before him (ibid., 114.27-115.2, pp. 171f).

The parallel with, and therefore denigration of, the Old Testament
God is apparent here in the deliberate use of the Genesis language: "in
the likeness of God," and the plural form of the Hebrew word for God,
"Elohim." Without a soul Adam was left for forty days by First Father
who feared his son, lest he discover the true nature of the plot. On this
final day Sophia Zoe gave him her breath, and so he began to move,
although he still could not rise. This frightened the archons who
questioned the breath. Assured that it could not escape its imprisonment in Adam's body and that Adam still could not arise, they "rested
themselves from their troubles," and so "they called that day 'the
rest'" (ibid., 115.25, p. 172), the Gnostic equivalent of the Sabbath.

We proceed next to the awakening of Adam. After Sophia sent her
daughter Zoe (life), also called Eve, to enliven Adam by bestowing the
light-spirit on him, he rises, opens his eyes, and exclaims: "You will be
called 'the mother of the living' because you are the one who gave me
life" (ibid., 116.20, p. 172). Intrigue follows upon intrigue as the
archons attempt to counteract this "invasion" from the light. Part of
their plan is to conceal from Adam Eve's true origin:

> But let us not tell Adam that she is not derived from us, but let us bring
> a stupor upon him, and let us teach him in his sleep as though she
> came into being from his rib so that the woman will serve and he will
> rule over her (ibid., 116.20, p. 173).

The archons also plan sexually to defile her, thereby entrapping her in
the body and preventing her return to the light. Eve counters by
entering the tree of knowledge, leaving her mere earthly body with

Adam. The rulers thus "cast their seed upon her," resulting in the birth of "Adam's children."

In "The Hypostasis of the Archons," a sister text to "On the Origin of the World," the same event is described this way:

> And when they [the Authorities or Archons] saw his [Adam] female counterpart . . . they became agitated with great agitation; and they became enamored of her. They said to one another, "Come, let us sow our seed in her," and they pursued her. And she laughed at them for their witlessness and their blindness; and in their clutches, she became a tree, and left before them her shadowy reflection resembling herself; and they defiled it foully.--And they defiled the form that she had stamped in her likeness, so that by the form they had modeled, together with their own image, they made themselves liable to condemnation (Hypos. Arch. II.89.18-30, in *NHL*, pp. 155f).

Fearful that Adam may learn the truth from the spiritual Eve in the tree of knowledge, a possibility the archons somehow learn about, they plot further: "Then the seven took counsel . . . ." Their plot, so familiar to our Western world, is taken from the third chapter of Genesis, the story of the fall. In the Gnostic version, however, the serpent (here called the beast, subsequently called the instructor by Eve) is "the one who is wiser than all of them." Therefore, Adam's and Eve's partaking of the tree's fruit is the dawning of wisdom: "Then their mind opened. For when they ate, the light of knowledge shone for them" (Orig. Wld. II.119.12, in *NHL*, p. 174).

The rulers now retaliate by sending in an earthquake, from which Adam and Eve seek to hide. Confronted finally, Adam and Eve "confess" their sin, and the rulers realize the great threat now upon them. They devise a test for Adam, asking him if he knows the names of the animals, an ingenious Gnostic refashioning of the story of the naming of the animals:

> When he [Adam] saw them, he named their creatures. They were troubled because Adam had sobered from every ignorance (ibid., 120.23, p. 175).

The rulers had no recourse, now that Adam had become aware of the light of knowledge, but to banish him and Eve from Eden, as is recounted in the dramatic close to Chapter 3 in Genesis.

Thus Adam and Eve reflect the essential Gnostic duality of all humanity--spirit and flesh--setting the stage for the redemptive activity of awakening the sleeping light through the acquisition of knowledge, the subject matter of Chapter 8. Let us turn now to our second creation myth, found in "The Apocryphon of John."

While some details differ, we find here a similar account as in "The Origin of the World." We begin with the fear of the chief archon, Yaltabaoth, as he is made to recognize that there is one greater than he:

And the ... chief archon trembled, and the foundations of the abyss shook. And of the waters which are above matter, the underside was illuminated by the appearance of his image which had been revealed .... And he said to the authorities [archons] which attend to him, "Come, let us create a man according to the image of God and according to our likeness, that his image may become a light for us." And they created by means of each other's powers in correspondence with the indications which were given. And each authority supplied a characteristic by means of the form of the image which he had seen in its psychic form. He [the chief archon] created a being according to the likeness of the first, perfect Man. And they said, "Let us call him Adam, that his name may become a power of light for us" (Apocry-John II.14.25-30; 15.1-13, in *NHL*, pp. 106f).

What of course we see here is what centuries later Voltaire would give sharp expression to: "God created man in his own image; and then man returned the compliment." This idea finds numerous parallels in other Gnostic texts, as for example in the Valentinian "Gospel of Philip:"

God created man. But now men create God. That is the way it is in the world--men make gods and worship their creation. It would be fitting for the gods to worship men! (GPh II.71.35-72.3, in *NHL*, p. 143).

And in the Hermetic tract "Asclepius" we read:

Just as God has willed that the inner man be created according to his image, in the very same way man on earth creates gods according to his likeness (Ascl. VI.69.22, in *NHL*, p. 302).

The seven powers (planets) then begin the process of creation, described in minute detail by our text--each step along the way having a corresponding name--until the creation is complete and Yaltabaoth believes that his power is safely protected.

In what amounts to a mythological chess game, the powers of light now make their counter move. The mother (Sophia) petitions the "Mother-Father of the all who is most merciful" for help to regain the power she had lost to her son (Yaltabaoth). Her plea is not in vain and is met with a clever plan of divine deception. This incongruity is quite familiar in the Gnostic literature, and not without its antecedents in the classical Greek gods' very human ego activities. Angels of light convince Yaltabaoth to

> bring forth the power of the mother. . . . "Blow into his [Adam] face something of your spirit and his body will arise." And he blew into his face the spirit which is the power of his mother [Sophia]; he did not know this, for he exists in ignorance. And the power of the mother went out of Yaltabaoth into the psychic soul [of Adam] which they had fashioned after the image of the One who exists from the beginning. The body moved and gained strength, and it was luminous (ApocryJohn II.19.22-35, in *NHL*, p. 109).

The archons now become jealous that Adam's intelligence is greater than theirs, he now having the light, and so they sought to throw him "into the lowest region of all matter." The true God counters by sending to Adam a helper, "luminous Epinoia," also called Life (Zoe). She

> assists the whole creature by toiling with him and by restoring him to his fullness and by teaching him about the descent of his seed and by teaching him about the way of ascent, which is the way he came down. And the luminous Epinoia was hidden in Adam in order that the archons might not know her, but that the Epinoia might be a correction of the deficiency of the mother (ibid., 20.19, p. 110).

Thus we see the sum and substance of the Gnostic teaching of the fall and redemption through the Gnostic revelation.

The chess game continues, and the archons' gambit is to bury the light within Adam, enshrouding it by creating the body:

> . . . the whole array of archons and angels . . . brought him [Adam] into the shadow of death in order that they might form him again from earth and water and fire and the spirit which originates in matter, which is the ignorance of darkness and desire, and their opposing spirit which is the tomb of newly-formed body with which the robbers had clothed the man, the bond of forgetfulness; and he became a mortal man (ibid., 20.35-21.13, p. 110).

This, of course, is the Genesis creation story of Adam, here deliberately brought about by the evil powers to defend against the light of truth that shines in all humanity: "This [mortal man] is the first one who came down and the first separation. But the Epinoia of the light which was in him, she is the one who will awaken his thinking" (ibid., 21.14-15).

The archons continue by placing this Adam in paradise, whose luxury, however, is "deception and their trees are godlessness and their fruit is deadly poison and their promise is death." However, the rulers attempt to shield the tree of knowledge of good and evil from Adam. Moreover, here, as opposed to other Gnostic texts, the serpent is evil, an extension of the archons: "The serpent taught them to eat from wickedness, begetting, lust, (and) the destruction, that he might be useful to him" (ibid., 22.12, p. 111).

Yaltabaoth now puts Adam to sleep as further defense against the light, and attempts to extract this light from him by creating Eve out of his rib:

> And he made another creature in the form of a woman according to the likeness of the Epinoia which had appeared to him. And he brought the part which he had taken from the power of the man into the female creature (ibid., 22.34).

But the plan backfires, for as soon as Adam sees the earthly Eve by his side the luminous Epinoia within

> lifted the veil which lay over his mind [just placed there by the chief archon]. And he became sober from the drunkedness of darkness. And he recognized his counter-image (ibid., 23.6-9).

It is at this point that our text brings in the eating from the tree of knowledge, now revealed to Adam and Eve by the Epinoia in the form of an eagle, that she

> might teach and awaken them out of the depth of sleep. For they were both in a fallen state and they recognized their nakedness. The Epinoia appeared to them as a light and she awakened their thinking (ibid., 23.30-35, pp. 111f).

Enraged, Yaltabaoth banishes Adam and Eve from paradise midst much cursing. The remaining stages of the narrative--the chief archon's vengeance and the counter ploys of the spirit--we will pass over quickly. The chief archon seduces the pure maiden he notices standing beside Adam, and the two sons that follow are called Eloim and Yave, Old Testament names denoting God, who then become Cain and Abel. They rule over the body that is called a tomb. From Yaltabaoth's act sexual intercourse becomes an integral part of the evil, physical world, further evidence of the strong anti-corporeal and anti-sexual tone that runs through many of the Gnostic traditions. The Flood is one of the more destructive aspects of the archons' plan, though it is partially thwarted by Noah who is forewarned by the beings of light.

We move now from these anthropogonic myths, all found in the *Nag Hammadi Library*, to the Valentinian, Manichean, and Mandean versions. In the preceding chapter we considered the Valentinian view of creation. Let us continue our examination of Irenaeus' reporting of Ptolemaeus, the prominent Valentinian teacher, from that point in the narrative after the Demiurge had formed the world:

> When he [the Demiurge] had formed the world, he made the choic [fleshly] man, not out of this present dry land, but out of the invisible substance, the liquid and flowing part of matter, and into him he breathed the psychic man, and this is he who came into being "after the image and likeness" (Gn 1:26): "after the image" refers to the material which is similar to God but not of the same substance: and "after the likeness" is the psychic man, and therefore his substance is also called the "spirit of life" (Gn 2:7), for it derives from a spiritual emanation. Finally, they say, there was put on him the coat of skin by which is meant according to them the flesh that is subject to sense-perception.
>
> But the offspring of their mother, Achamoth . . . was inserted secretly into him [the Demiurge] without his knowing it, in order that through him it might be sown in the soul which derives from him and in the material body, and, having been born and increased there, might be prepared to receive the perfect Logos. . . . Thus they [the Valentinians] have their soul from the Demiurge the body from the dust, flesh from matter, and the spiritual man from the mother Achamoth.
>
> There are then three substances: the material, which they also call "left," must of necessity they say perish . . . the psychic, which they also term "right," stands midway between the spiritual and the material and consequently passes to whichever side it is inclined; the spiritual was sent forth in order that after being linked with the psychic it might be shaped and trained with it in conduct . . . (*Adv. haer.* I.5.5-6, in F I, pp. 137f).

From these three substances Ptolemaeus then deduces three types of men, to which we will return in the next chapter when we discuss salvation:

> They assume three types of men; the spiritual, the choic, and the psychic, corresponding to Cain, Abel, and Seth [Seth, as we have seen, is the epitome of the spiritual man for the Gnostics, their ideal], in order that they may represent by these the three natures, not with reference to an individual but with reference to kinds of men (F I, p. 141).

We have seen that the earlier Basilides similarly has three classes of humanity, relating to the extent to which people have yielded to the seductions of the body and the world: the highest class returns directly to Heaven, the middle eventually returns, while the third remains in the physical world below. Basilides, however, as Stead points out, does not deny even this group some benefits, though they must remain beyond Heaven (Layton, p. 93).

We turn next to the creation myth of Mani. In the previous chapter we left our narrative at the point when the Darkness launched its final strategy to entrap the Light: the creation of Adam and Eve in imitation of the divine forms it has already seen. Jonas dramatically summarizes the motivation of the King of Darkness:

> Anticipating the eventual loss of all Light through the continual separating effect of the heavenly revolutions [the cosmic ferris wheel we observed in the previous chapter]; seized by the ambition to create out of himself something equal to that vision; reckoning by this means to devise the safest prison for the alien force; and finally, wishing to have in his world a substitute for the otherwise unattainable divine figure, over which to rule and through which to be sometimes freed from the odious company of his kind, the King of Darkness produces Adam and Eve in the image of the glorious form, and pours into them all the Light left at his disposal (Jonas, pp. 226f).

This process, in characteristic Manichean style, is filled with rather gruesome and sexual details involving demonic intercourse and infanticide through devouring. Setting these aside, however, we observe the common Gnostic theme of the inferior principle (whether the Darkness, Sophia, or the Demiurge) creating the human being in the image of God, the end product being a gross distortion--the body--of the purity of the divine spirit. As Jonas exclaims: "This is what has become of the Biblical idea of man's being created in the image of God!" (Jonas, p. 227).

The body is correspondingly seen as the work of the devil, literally, which leads to the extreme hostility towards the body, especially sex, and the almost total asceticism for which Manicheism is known. It is the most extreme form of a principle we have seen at work in most of the Gnostic systems, yet nowhere with the intensity we find in the Manichean texts. Jonas comments: "In the context of this theoretical underpinning [the general Gnostic view], the dwelling on the especially repulsive details of man's begetting by the demons merely adds an element of the nauseous to an otherwise 'rationally' supported enmity" (Jonas, pp. 227f).

Thus, for Mani, humanity mirrors the dualism of the world: light and darkness; spirit and flesh; good and evil. The particles of light-spirit are trapped in dark-body, kept there by the desires of the flesh that entrap still further. This of course is the King's purpose for creating Eve: "To her they [the demons of darkness] imparted of their concupiscence in order to seduce Adam" (Jonas, p. 228). The awakening of Adam's lust has a twofold purpose: First, it roots him still further in the flesh, wallowing in what the Manicheans regarded as its filth; second, through reproduction, the Darkness' plan to disperse the light is given greater advancement. More and more particles of light become trapped in the body, thereby multiplying the needs and efforts of the powers of light to recover them.

To Mani, therefore, the struggle becomes centered on the Darkness' continuing attempts to seduce men through women, and the Light's awakening them before the allurement of the flesh becomes too strong. Rudolph summarizes the situation in this way:

> ... man is the central subject of world events. His soul, as part of the light [i.e., of God], is the element to be saved, and the saving element is the "spirit" that was granted to him by revelation or knowledge. The body is the dark, evil, component of man, which in death returns to its origin, the darkness, in order to let the soul ascend, in its liberated state, to its state of origin. But the soul that remains unawakened is reborn on earth unto a new life (Rudolph, p. 338).

Finally, we consider the creation myth of the Mandeans and, although clothed in the unique Mandean style, we shall find many of the same ideas we have already seen. We begin with the inability on the part of the creating principle to enliven Adam,

> They [Ptahil and the planets] created Adam and laid him down but there was no soul in him. . . . They appealed to the ether wind, that it might hollow out his bones . . . that marrow be formed in them, that he might become strong and stand on his feet. . . . (GR III.p101, in F II, p. 187).

On it goes, as the rulers appeal to other elements in nature until

> the Planets gave utterance and spoke to Ptahil: "Grant us, that we may cast into him some of the spirit which you brought with you from the father's house." All the planets exerted themselves, and the lord of the world [Ptahil] exerted himself. Despite their exertions, they could not set him on his feet (ibid., p. 188).

At this point in the narrative there are many and conflicting versions, but in general they all reflect the influence of what is called the Anthropos myth. In one version, Ptahil finally appeals to the "father of the uthras" who sends the great Mana (the great Adam) who eventually enters the body of Adam:

> While Ptahil lifted Adam up it was I [Manda dHaiye] who raised up his bones. While he laid his hands on him, it was I who made him

breathe the breath of life. His body filled with marrow, and the radiance of the Life spoke in him (GR III.p.102, in F II, pp. 189f).

One thing leads to another and it then becomes the turn of the evil forces to counter:

> When Ruha [the evil mother] and the planets heard of this, they all sat down and lamented. . . . They rose up to forge evil plans and said: "We shall capture Adam and seize him. . . . and detain him with us in the world." And they said: "When he speaks with a soft voice, *we* shall speak with the voice of rebellion. When he eats and drinks, *we* shall seize the world. *We* shall entrap the world and produce all kinds of forms in it. . . . we shall seize and lay hold of his [Adam] heart. We shall capture him with horns and flutes so that he cannot escape from us" (GR III.pp.104-105, in F II, p. 193).

The "gentle" uthras respond by creating Eve and, in contrast with many of the other Gnostic systems, she is a force of light. In fact, the Mandeans trace their ancestry to the union of this heavenly couple:

> May the Family of Life be multiplied, and by them may the world be roused. . . . [and] the Life will be grateful to them. . . . will release them and make them rise up from this world of evil (ibid., p.107, p. 196).

To summarize, this part of the Gnostic myth depicts all humanity as composed of three parts--spirit, soul (mind), and body. Spirit is created from spirit, its ultimate origin being God; while both the soul and body are the product of the inferior principle, the cosmic power. The body is made in the image of the Light-Adam or Primal Man, which is animated (enlivened) by the psychical forces, also derived from the cosmic power. The spirit, which has fallen into the world, is entrapped there by the body, created by the world rulers for just this purpose. This physical and psychical prison that houses the spirit consists of seven components that derive from the seven planetary spheres that enclose the world of matter and keep it imprisoned. After an examination of the Platonic tradition which, as we have seen, was an important source of the Gnostic tripartite view, we will return to a more detailed examination of these three components.

Spirit, Mind (Soul), Body: Platonism

1. Plato

Plato's tripartite view of the soul has had great influence throughout Western intellectual history, not the least of which has been its influence on Freud's tripartite psyche.[9] The soul is discussed in the *Republic*, but in the *Timaeus* we find a more complete treatment, including specific discussion of the physical location of these three parts, which detail need not concern us long here.

The divine reason makes its home in the head, and is kept apart by the neck from the mortal emotion and appetite, localized in the lower portions of the body. The seat of the emotions is found in the heart and breast (the higher and lower emotions are also divided by the anatomy), while the base appetites (food, sex, etc.) are found in the belly, genitalia, etc. There they are secured like "a wild beast," or a "savage, many-headed monster," and kept quite separate from the higher functioning of reason:

> And they [the lower gods] put it in this position in order that it . . . be as far as possible from the seat of deliberation . . . so leaving the highest part of us to deliberate quietly about the welfare of each and all . . . (*Tim.* 70e).

The lower part is described as rebellious, needing to be placed under the firm guidance of reason, with the help of the higher emotions. Plato immortalized this struggle in the *Phaedrus* with his analogy of the charioteer (reason) and his good (emotion) and bad (appetites) horses:

> Let it [the soul] be likened to the union of powers in a team of winged steeds and their winged charioteer. . . . With us men . . . it is a pair of steeds that the charioteer controls; moreover one of them is noble and good, and of good stock, while the other has the opposite character, and his stock is opposite. Hence the task of our charioteer is difficult and troublesome. . . . He that is on the more honorable side is upright and clean-limbed, carrying his neck high, with something of a hooked nose; in color he is white, with black eyes; a lover of glory, but with temperance and modesty; one that consorts with genuine renown, and needs no whip, being driven by the word of command alone. The other is crooked of frame, a massive jumble of a creature, with thick short neck, snub nose, black skin, and gray eyes; hot-blooded, consorting with wantonness and vainglory; shaggy of ear, deaf, and hard to control with whip and goad (*Phaedrus* 246a; 253d-e).

The goal of reason is the integration of the soul's duality, inspiring one to lift higher and higher until the vision of the Good is achieved, as we shall see in Chapter 9 with the Allegory of the Cave. In the *Republic*

---

9. For a fuller discussion of the similarities between Freud's psychology and Plato's, see *Plato*, William and Mabel Sahakian, pp. 38-59.

Plato likens the body to the encrustations that formed around the sea-God Glaucas:

> But if we want to see it [the soul] as it really is, we should look at it, not as we do now, when it is deformed by its association with the body and other evils, but in the pure state which reason reveals to us. We shall then find that it is a thing of far greater beauty.... and its original nature is as difficult to see as his [Glaucas] was after long immersion had broken and worn away and deformed his limbs, and covered him with shells and seaweed and rock, till he looked more like a monster than what he really was. That is the sort of state we see the soul reduced to by countless evils.... Think how its [the soul's] kinship with the divine and immortal and eternal makes it long to associate with them and apprehend them; think what it might become if it followed this impulse wholeheartedly and was lifted by it out of the sea in which it is now submerged, and if it shed all the rocks and shells which, because it feeds on the earthly things that men think bring happiness, encrust it in wild and earthy profusion. Then one really could see its true nature ... (*Rep.* 611c-612a).

Yet we have already seen in Chapter 6 a contrasting benevolent attitude, where Plato views the body as created by the "providence of the gods" to be the vehicle for apprehending the majesty of the heavens. We shall return to this Platonic paradox in this and subsequent chapters.

2. Philo

In Philo we also find three classifications of people: earth-born, heaven-born, and God-born:

> The earth-born are those who take the pleasures of the body for their quarry, who make it their practice to indulge in them and enjoy them and provide the means by which each of them may be promoted. The heaven-born are the votaries of the arts and of knowledge, the lovers of learning. For the heavenly element in us is the mind.... And it is the mind which pursues the learning of the schools and the other arts ... and trains and drills itself solid in the contemplation of what is intelligible by mind. But the men of god are priests and prophets who have refused to accept membership in the commonwealth of the world and to become citizens therein, but have risen wholly above the sphere to sense-perception and have been translated into the world of the intelligible and dwell there registered as freemen of the commonwealth of Ideas, which are imperishable and incorporeal (*On the Giants* 60f).

Thus, the earth-born are descended souls who have already fallen and become stuck to the world, the "men of God" have not really fallen at all, and the heaven-born must nourish and reinforce their desire to return to God. Incidentally, Dillon has commented that Philo appears to have been the first to suggest that there may be souls in bodies for reasons other than the fall, a notion that was certainly picked up by the Gnostics with their doctrine of the pneumatics (in Layton, p. 363). According to Philo, the men of God, the wise, are those who

> are never colonists leaving heaven for a new home. Their way is to visit earthly nature as men who travel abroad to see and learn. So when they have stayed awhile in their bodies, and beheld through them all that sense and mortality has to show, they make their way back to the place from which they set out at the first. To them the heavenly region, where their citizenship lies, is their native land; the earthly region in which they became sojourners is a foreign country (*The Confusion of Tongues* 77f).

Elsewhere, Philo comments that when the other souls have descended into bodies they are as if fallen into a stream,

> sometimes...caught in the swirl of its rushing torrent and swallowed up. . . . [These souls] have held no count of wisdom. They have abandoned themselves to the unstable things of chance, none of which has aught to do with our noblest part, the soul or mind, but all are related to that dead thing which was our birth-fellow, the body, or to objects more lifeless still, glory, wealth, offices, and honors, and all other illusions which like images or pictures are created through the deceit of false opinion by those who have never gazed upon true beauty (*On the Giants* 13,15).

Later in the same text Philo writes of these unfortunate souls who are bound by ignorance, whose

> chief cause . . . is the flesh, and the tie which binds us so closely to the flesh. . . . [in which] the divine spirit cannot abide. . . . Nothing thwarts its [wisdom's] growth so much as our fleshly nature. For on it ignorance and scorn of learning rest. . . . [And] those which bear the burden of the flesh, oppressed by the grievous load, cannot look up to the heavens as they revolve, but with necks bowed downwards are constrained to stand rooted to the ground like four-footed beasts (ibid., 29-31f).

These then are doomed forever to the lower regions of the body, which Philo considers, as do many other Platonists, to be a corpse: "that dwelling-place of endless calamities" (*The Confusion of Tongues*

177). A century later Marcus Aurelius echoed a similar sentiment when he wrote in his personal journal of the "rottenness of the matter which is the foundation of everything! water, dust, bones, filth. . . . [the body being] a dead thing" (*Meditations* IX.36; X.33).

Simply by being created in this body is proof of sin to Philo. Moses' offering of the calf to bring about forgiveness of the people's sins shows that

> sin is congenital to every created being, even the best, just because they are created, and this sin requires prayers and sacrifices to propitiate the Deity, lest His wrath be roused and visited among them (*Moses* II.147).

In an allegorical interpretation of God's slaying of Er, Judah's first-born (Gn 38:7), Philo writes:

> For He is well aware that the body, our "leathern" bulk ["leathern" is the meaning of "Er"],[10] is wicked and a plotter against the soul, and is even a corpse and a dead thing. For . . . each of us [is] nothing but corpse-bearers, the soul raising up and carrying without toil the body which of itself is a corpse. . . . For when the mind soars aloft and is being initiated in the mysteries of the Lord, it judges the body to be wicked and hostile; but when it has abandoned the investigation of things divine, it deems it friendly to itself, its kinsman and brother. The proof of this is that it takes refuge in what is dear to the body (*Alleg. Interp.* III.69,71f).

Yet as in all Platonists, before and after, we find in Philo great ambivalence towards the body, despicable on the one hand and yet to be honored as God's creation on the other. In the same passage on the killing of Er, Philo interjects that the body that was slain by God was yet the body he made: "But from the beginning he (God) made the body a corpse" (*Alleg. Interp.* 70, in Baer's translation, p. 93, n.1). Moreover, just as God slew Er without reason, so has He "conceived a hatred for pleasure and the body without giving reasons" (*Alleg. Interp.* III.77). The nature of Adam, the first man, shares this ambivalence for he was made

> excellent in each part of his being, in both soul and body. . . . the Creator excelled . . . in skill to bring it about that each of the bodily parts should have in itself individually its due proportions, and

---

10. Philo was indulging in allegorical license here by changing the Hebrew vowel "e" to "o" to accommodate his own interpretation: *Er* means "watcher"; *Or* means "skin" connoting "leathern," *see* 2 K 1:8; Mt 3:4.

should also be fitted with the most perfect accuracy for the part it was to take in the whole. ... And we may guess that the sovereignty with which that first man was invested was a most lofty one, seeing that God had fashioned him with the utmost care and deemed him worthy of the second place making him His own viceroy and lord of all others (*On the Creation* 136,138,148).

And yet we see that Philo in the same set of passages really means that perfection is found in the soul and not the body:

That in soul also he was most excellent is manifest; for the Creator ... employed for its making no pattern taken from among created things, but solely ... His own Word. ... It is on this account that he says that man was made a likeness and imitation of the Word, when the Divine Breath was breathed into his face. ... Every man, in respect of his mind, is allied to the divine Reason, having come into being as a copy or fragment or ray of that blessed nature, but in the structure of his body he is allied to all the world (ibid., 139,146).

Furthermore, the soul placed in the created body must change, unlike God:

Now every created thing must necessarily undergo change, for this is its property, even as unchangeableness is the property of God. ... since no created thing is constant, and things mortal are necessarily liable to changes and reverses, it could not but be that the first man too should experience some ill fortune (*Alleg. Interp.* II.33; *On the Creation* 151).

Thus Philo sees the body as a wicked tempter that we would do much better without, though cannot deny is present. We must therefore be continually on guard to resist the temptations and seductions of bodily pleasure, to which we return in Chapter 10.

3. Origen

To Origen the body is the visible expression of the soul's fall, the "grosser bodies" that are the lowest rung on the ladder of descent. In this powerful passage we see the influence of Plato's *Phaedrus* in Origen's description of the downward transmigration of souls:

But by some inclination towards evil these souls lose their wings and come into bodies, first of men; then through their association with the irrational passions, after the allotted span of human life they are changed into beasts; from which they sink to the level of insensate nature. Thus that which is by nature fine and mobile, namely the soul, first becomes heavy and weighed down, and because of its wickedness comes to dwell in a human body; after that, when the faculty of reason is extinguished, it lives the life of an irrational animal; and finally even the gracious gift of sensation is withdrawn and it changes into the insensate life of a plant (*First Princ.* I.8.4).

Our true nature thus is the same as God's, pure incorporeal spirit, and our fall from this nature must ultimately lead to the return to it. St. Jerome was horrified by this teaching, but fortunately left it extant (after Origen's translator Rufinus had omitted it) for the modern reader to judge its worth:

> That all rational natures, that is, the Father, the Son and the Holy Spirit, all angels . . . and other powers, and even man himself in virtue of the soul's dignity, are of one substance. For . . . [this] rational nature [is in] the "inner man," who was made in the image and likeness of God. From which the conclusion is drawn that God and all these creatures are in some way of one substance (ibid., p. 326, n.1).

Origen also spoke of humanity having a "kind of blood-relationship with God" (ibid., IV.4.10), and in *An Exhortation to Martyrdom* Origen speaks of the soul's rational nature having "a certain kinship with God" (*Martyrdom* XLVII). Thus Origen asks immediately afterwards:

> . . . why do we hang back and hesitate to put off the perishable body, the earthly tent that hinders us, weighs down the soul and burdens the thoughtful mind? (ibid.)

And in his *Homily XXVII on "Numbers"*:

> . . . the soul so grows that when it has ceased being driven by the troubles of the flesh, it has completed visions and gains perfect understanding of things . . . (*Homily* XXVII.12).

The body, then, is anything but holy or divine:

> . . . we must know that . . . [Christ] . . . affectionately loves nothing earthly, nothing material, nothing corruptible. For it is against its nature to love anything corruptible affectionately, since it is itself the source of incorruption (*Prologue*, in *Origen* trans. Greer, p. 226).

Nonetheless, the body for Origen remains the vehicle whereby souls can restore themselves to their natural non-corporeal state:

> . . . a rational mind . . . by advancing from things visible to things

> invisible, may attain to an increasingly perfect understanding. For it
> has been placed in a body, and of necessity advances from things of
> sense, which are bodily, to things beyond sense perception, which are
> incorporeal and intellectual. . . . and when their restoration is
> perfectly accomplished these bodies are dissolved into nothing (*First
> Princ.* IV.4.10,8).

We shall return to this final stage of the soul's ascent in Chapter 8.

We now will see how Plotinus mirrors the same attitude as did
Origin, wherein the body is seen both as the negative expression of the
soul's fall from God, and the positive expression of its return to Him.

4. Plotinus

The non-Christian Plotinus is far more expressive of the body's
negative effects on the soul than his Christian Neoplatonic counterpart:

> . . . the human soul . . . is said to suffer all kinds of evils and to be in
> misery because it comes to exist among stupidities and desires and
> fears and all other evils, in that the body is its chain and tomb and the
> universe its cave and dens. . . . Here the "moulting," as it is called,
> happens to it, and the being in the fetters of the body, since it has
> missed the immunity which it had when it was with the universal
> soul directing the better part [of the universe]; it was altogether better
> for it before when it was running upwards; it is fallen, therefore, and
> is caught, and is engaged with its fetter, and acts by sense because its
> new beginning prevents it from acting by intellect, and it is said to be
> buried and in a cave (*Enn.* IV.8.3,4).

The "lower" faculties of the incarnate soul are but distortions of the
Soul's true and eternal nature. It is in the Soul's union with the body,
what Bréhier termed a "dangerous and unstable alliance," that problems arise that cloud the remembrance of the Soul's divine origins.

In passages remarkable for their parallels to *A Course in Miracles'*
descriptions of special relationships, we find further evidence of
Plotinus' penetrating insight into the distortions that follow the Soul's
identification with the body:

> This universe . . . is not truly one; for it is many and divided into a
> multiplicity, and one part stands away from another and is alien to
> it, and there is not only friendship but also enmity because of the
> separation, and in their deficiency one part is of necessity at war with
> another. For the part is not self-sufficient, but in being preserved is
> at war with the other by which it is preserved. . . . The attacks of living

beings on each other, and their destruction of each other, are necessary. . . . and men must fall sick if they have bodies (*Enn.* III.2.2,4,5).

So therefore when we look outside that on which we depend we do
not know that we are one, like faces which are many on the outside
but have one head inside. But if someone is able to turn around,
. . . he will see God and himself and the All; at first he will not see as
the All [i.e., as a whole] but then, when he has nowhere to set himself
and limit himself and determine how far he himself goes, he will stop
marking himself off from all being and will come to all the All [i.e.,
as a unity]. . . . as long as it is in that which has the impression
perceived by the senses, the lover is not yet in love; but when from
that he himself generates in himself an impression not perceptible by
the senses in his partless soul, then love springs up. But he seeks to
see the beloved that he may water him when he is withering. But if
he should come to understand that one must change to that which is
more formless, he would desire that; for his experience from the
beginning was love of a great light from a dim glimmer (*Enn.* VI.5.7;
7.33).

5. St. Augustine

In St. Augustine we find our by now familiar tripartite view of
humanity. In a letter to Coelestinus he wrote:

There is a nature which is susceptible of change with respect to both
place and time, namely the corporeal. There is another nature which
is in no way susceptible of change with respect to place, but only with
respect to time, namely the spiritual. And there is a third Nature
which can be changed neither in respect to place nor in respect to
time: that is, God (in Bourke, p. 45).

In the following passages we find, as with Plotinus, evidence of the
powerfully ambivalent attitude towards the world and the body. We
have already seen Augustine articulating the Platonic view of the divine cosmos. Here, in a passage from the *City of God* we find it again,
along with the notion of the upright physical structure of the human
body reflecting God's specific intention, a belief Augustine shared
with Plotinus and Clement as we saw in Chapter 6.

Moreover, even in the body, though it dies like that of the beasts and
is in many ways weaker than theirs, what goodness of God, what
providence of the great Creator, is apparent! The organs of sense and
the rest of the members, are not they so placed, the appearance, and
form, and stature of the body as a whole, is it not so fashioned, as to
indicate that it was made for the service of a reasonable soul? Man

has not been created stooping towards the earth, like the irrational animals; but his bodily form, erect and looking heavenwards, admonishes him to mind the things that are above. Then the marvelous nimbleness which has been given to the tongue and the hands, fitting them to speak, and write, and execute so many duties, and practice so many arts, does it not prove the excellence of the soul for which such an assistant was provided? And even apart from its adaptation to the work required of it, there is such a symmetry in its various parts, and so beautiful a proportion maintained, that one is at a loss to decide whether, in creating the body, greater regard was paid to utility or to beauty. Assuredly no part of the body has been created for the sake of utility which does not also contribute something to its beauty (*City of God* 22.22).

And yet elsewhere in the *City of God* and the *Confessions* we read exactly the opposite. Listen to the ardent seeker after God bemoaning the awesome burden of his own body:

I marveled that now I loved you [God], and not a phantom in your stead. Yet I was not steadfast in enjoyment of my God: I was borne up to you by your beauty, but soon I was borne down from you by my own weight, and with groaning, I plunged into the midst of those lower things. This weight was carnal custom.... "For the corruptible body is a load upon the soul, and the earthly habitation presses down upon the mind that muses upon many things" (*Conf.* 7.17.23).

And then we read this searing, all-inclusive condemnation of physical existence in this world. We have room only for excerpts from this three-page diatribe:

That the whole human race has been condemned in its first origin, this life itself, if life it is to be called, bears witness by the host of cruel ills with which it is filled. Is not this proved by the profound and dreadful ignorance which produces all the errors that enfold the children of Adam, and from which no man can be delivered without toil, pain, and fear? Is it not proved by his love of so many vain and hurtful things, which produces gnawing cares . . . wars . . . perfidy . . . it is shameful so much as to mention; sacrileges, heresies . . . and whatever similar wickedness has found its way into the lives of men. . . . [they spring from] that root of error and misplaced love which is born with every son of Adam . . . . who can conceive the number and severity of the punishments which afflict the human race--pains which are not only the accompaniment of the wickedness of godless men, but are a part of the human condition and the common misery . . . . For at their hands we suffer robbery . . . torture, mutilation . . . the violation of chastity to satisfy the lust of the oppressor, and many other dreadful evils. What numberless casualties threaten our bodies

from without--extremes of heat and cold, storms . . . earthquakes
. . . countless poisons . . . What disasters are suffered by those who
travel by land or sea! . . . As to bodily diseases, they are so numerous
that they cannot all be contained even in medical books. And in very
many, or almost all of them, the cures and remedies are themselves
tortures. . . . Has not the madness of thirst driven men to drink human
urine, and even their own? Has not hunger driven men to eat human
flesh, and that the flesh not of bodies found dead but of bodies slain
for the purpose? Have not the fierce pangs of famine driven mothers
to eat their own children, incredibly savage as it seems? (*City of God*
22.21-22)

On and on this Platonist goes, decrying "the miseries of this life . . . this
hell on earth." One can only wonder, echoing the lines from Blake as
we ponder this last passage: did he who wrote the encomium of God's
created world also write thee?

Spirit, Mind (Soul), Body: Gnosticism

Discussion of the Gnostic tripartite view of homo sapiens follows
logically from our discussion of the Gnostic creation myth. To summarize briefly again, part of the divine substance--*pneuma* or spirit--has
found itself in this world through some sort of declination; second,
there is the psychical, or what we may term the mind or soul, which is
the part of nature that can choose; finally there is the body or *hyle*
(matter), which is doomed to corruption, the "living" symbol of the
creator god, the inferior principle that is a poor imitation of the true
God. The spirit is the equivalent to what *A Course in Miracles* calls the
Christ or our true Self. It has many synonyms in the Gnostic literature,
including the Mandean Mana, the Manichean luminous or living self,
the Naassene Man or Adam, the Primal Man or Anthropos, and the
spark or seed of light. In Pauline theology spirit is the counterpart to
the inner or new man. Jonas has pointed out the interesting fact that
Paul does not use the Greek word "psyche" for this spiritual principle,
as had been the practice since Plato. Rather, like the Gnostics who
came after him, he juxtaposes the psychic man (sometimes translated
as "natural") with the pneumatic.

We begin by examining some of the texts that set forth this trinity.
First, "The Apocryphon of James":

For without the soul [mind] the body does not sin, just as the soul is
not saved without the spirit. But if the soul is saved when it is without
evil, and the spirit is also saved, then the body becomes free from sin.
For it is the spirit that quickens the soul, but the body that kills it; that

239

is, it is it [the soul] which kills itself. Verily I [Jesus] say unto you, he [God] will not forgive the soul the sin by any means, nor the flesh the guilt; for none of those who have worn the flesh will be saved. For do you think that many have found the kingdom of heaven? (Apocryjs I.12.1-15, in *NHL*, p. 34)

From "The Tripartite Tractate":

The first man is a mixed formation, and a mixed creation, and a deposit of those of the left and those of the right, and a spiritual word whose attention is divided between each of the two substances from which he takes his being (Tri. Tract. I.106.18-25, in *NHL*, p. 83).

In the hermetic "Poimandres" we also find reference to the twofold origin of man.

That is why man, unlike all the living things on earth, is twofold: mortal because of the body, immortal because of the essential Man (*Corp. Herm*. I.15, in F I, p. 331).

The component that receives the most extensive treatment by far, however, is the body, the object of such great derision by the Gnostics. This strong emphasis placed on the body in the Gnostic literature reflects the importance and psychological reality that was given to it. In this section we present the evidence; the significance of this emphasis will be discussed in Part III.

The Gnostic literature is replete with descriptions of the body, most of which are very negative. The ethical and behavioral implications of this denigration will be discussed in Chapter 10. For now we shall content ourselves with examining this anti-corporeal stance.

As we have already observed, Marcion sees homo sapiens, the product of the creator of the world, as a despicable creature, impotent and helpless. Of the sexual reproductive act, which was a bestial activity to many Gnostics, Marcion has this to say:

In the womb a foetus coagulates out of horrible materials of generation, is nourished for nine months by the same filth, comes to light through the genitals, and is fed and raised by a buffoonish process (in Nigg, p. 62).

And the final proof for Marcion of the meaninglessness of human life is the grave. Nigg has summarized Marcion's sentiments as being that all creation is but "a miserable tragicomedy for which only its creator can be blamed" (Nigg, p. 62).

In "The Acts of John" the apostle chastises the painter Lycomedes for his portraits: "You have drawn a dead likeness of what is dead" (AJ 29, in *NTA* II, p. 221); while in the Manichean "Psalms to Jesus" we read:

> The enemy of my soul is the world, its riches and its deceit. All life hates godliness: what am I doing in the place of my enemies? . . . in the flesh of death that burns . . . (CCLXI, in Allberry, p. 75).

> I have not mingled with the intercourse of the flesh, for it is a thing that perishes (CCLXVIII, in Allberry, p. 86).

> O Christ whom I have loved, belonging unto thee, I fell into the snares of the body of death. The trappers that set traps for me brought me beneath their nets, they excluded me from the air of the freedom of the beautiful birds (CCLXXI, in Allberry, p. 89).

In the "Psalms of Heracleides" the human bodies are referred to as the "Abortions, the Sons of Matter" (CCLXXXV, in Allberry, p. 108). And Augustine writes of his erstwhile associates:

> They ascribe the origin of sin not to free will but to the substance of the enemy race. This, in their doctrine, is mingled with man and all flesh is not the work of God, but of the evil spirit, which derives from the contrary principle and is eternal, together with God (*de haer.* in Haardt, p. 348).

Turning now to the Nag Hammadi texts we find these statements in "The Gospel of Thomas," reminiscent of the "gold in mud" metaphor:

> If the flesh came into being because of spirit, it is a wonder. But if spirit came into being because of the body, it is a wonder of wonders. Indeed, I [Jesus] am amazed at how this great wealth has made its home in this poverty. . . . Wretched is the body that is dependent upon a body, and wretched is the soul that is dependent on these two (GTh II.38.31-39.1; 48.5, in *NHL*, pp. 121,127).

Similarly, the Valentinian "Gospel of Philip":

> No one will hide a large valuable object in something large, but many a time one has tossed countless thousands into a thing worth a penny. Compare the soul. It is a precious thing and it came to be in a contemptible body. . . . In this world those who put on garments are better than the garments. In the kingdom of heaven the garments are better than those who have put them on (GPh II.56.21-26; 57.20, in *NHL*, pp. 134f).

In this fragment preserved by Clement of Alexandria we find a purportedly authentic statement by Valentinus himself:

> For many [evil] spirits dwell in it [the heart] and do not permit it to be pure; each of them brings to fruition its own works, and they treat it abusively by means of unseemly desires. To me it seems that the heart suffers in much the same way as an inn: for it [an inn] has holes and trenches dug in it and is often filled with filth by men who live licentiously and have no regard for the place because it belongs to another. Likewise, the heart, so long as it is not cared for is unclean and the abode of many demons (*Strom*. II.20.4-6, in F I, pp. 241f).

The Ophites, more primitive forerunners to Valentinus, made this statement:

> Adam and Eve previously had light, clear and as it were spiritual bodies, just as they had been created. But when they came here [the world] they turned into something more opaque and thick and sluggish. The soul, too, became lax and limp, since they had from the creator only a breath of the world; so much so that Prunicos [meaning the Lewd, an early version of the female Sophia] pitied them and restored to them a whiff of sweetness of the trace of light. Through this they came to recollect who they themselves were, and they knew that they were naked and had material bodies; and they knew that they were burdened with death. They became patient, knowing that the body is their garment only for a time (*Adv. haer.* I.30.9, in F I, p. 90).

The same hostility towards the body is seen in the Mandean literature where the uthras, simple beings of light, take the pure soul, the "treasure of Life," and

> they put it in filth and clothe it in the colors of the flesh . . . . with a perishable garment . . . . and bring about imperfection and deficiency in it (GR III.p.96, in F II, p. 202).

The body is described as

> a rapacious sea, which robs and devours sheep [i.e., the soul]. It is a dragon, a wicked son of man who has seven heads [corresponding to the seven planets] . . . . he has neither understanding nor heart (GR III.9, in F II, pp. 223f).

And in a lament by Adam:

> Alas, alas, that my brothers beguiled me, removed me from their

midst, and brought, cast and hurled me into a stinking body, to the destructive lions, the rebellious, unruly lions. They led me and hurled me to the dragon, who surrounds the whole world. They brought, cast and hurled me among the evil planets, who daily provoke uproar (GL I.2, in F II, p. 224).

While these excerpts have been rather clear in their expression of the Gnostic abhorrence of the body, perhaps nowhere is this hatred of the Gnostics more dramatically seen than in their attitudes toward sexuality: the almost incarnate expression of evil. We have already seen some evidence of this, especially in the Manichean cosmology, and will return to this in Chapter 10. In the present chapter we shall illustrate this attitude with several examples from the *Nag Hammadi Library*. First we will consider "The Exegesis of the Soul," which reflects a strong Platonic influence, including the hostility towards the body and sexuality. Here, we read of the fall of the soul into the body in sexual terms:

As long as she [the soul] was alone with the Father, she was virgin and in form androgynous. But when she fell down into a body and came to this life, then she fell into the hands of many robbers. And the wanton creatures passed her from one to another.... Some made use of her by force, while others did so by seducing her with a gift. In short, they defiled her.... And in her body she prostituted herself and gave herself to one and all, considering each one she was about to embrace to be her husband. When she had given herself to wanton, unfaithful adulterers, so that they might make use of her, then she sighed deeply and repented. But even when she turns her face from those adulterers, she runs to others and they compel her to live with them and render service to them upon their bed, as if they were her masters. Out of shame she no longer dares to leave them, whereas they deceive her for a long time, pretending to be faithful, true husbands, as if they greatly respected her. And after all this they abandon her and go. . . . And her offspring by the adulterers are dumb, blind, and sickly. They are feeble-minded (Exeg. Soul II.127.22-128.25; in *NHL*, p. 181).

The anonymous Gnostic author of this treatise quotes Old and New Testament sources as expressions of this vice of prostitution, and concludes:

As long as the soul keeps running about everywhere copulating with whomever she meets and defiling herself, she exists suffering her just deserts (ibid., 131.13, in *NHL*, pp. 181,183).

From the strongly ascetic "Book of Thomas the Contender," aimed

243

in part against the orthodox Church that was seen in the Thomas tradition as not being ascetic enough, we find the following excerpts denigrating the body. As in many of these Gnostic texts the speaker is the risen Jesus, bestowing his revelation on the Gnostic apostle, here his "twin brother" Thomas.

> The Savior said, "All bodies of men and beasts are begotten irrational [sexual intercourse is meant]. Surely it is evident in the way.... these visible bodies eat of creatures similar to them with the result that the bodies change.... just as the body of the beasts perishes, so also will these formations perish. Do they not derive from intercourse like that of the beasts? If the body too derives from intercourse, how will it beget anything different from beasts? So, therefore, you are babes until you become perfect.... for just as beasts devour one another so also men . . . devour one another" (Th Cont. II.138.40-139.12; 141.27, in *NHL*, pp. 189, 191).

And finally, in words and tone reminiscent of Chapter 23 in Matthew, we have Jesus of this tradition cursing those who put their faith in the body. We present excerpts from this diatribe:

> Woe to you who hope in the flesh and in the prison that will perish! How long will you be oblivious?... Your hope is set upon the world and your god is this life! You are corrupting your souls!
>
> Woe to you for the fire that burns in you, for it is insatiable!.... You darkened your hearts and surrendered your thoughts to folly, and you filled your thoughts with the smoke of the fire that is in you! And your light has hidden in the cloud of darkness and the garment that is put upon you, you pursued deceitfully and you were seized by the hope that does not exist.... Woe to you who love intimacy with womankind and polluted intercourse with it!
>
> And woe to you because of the powers of your body, for those will afflict you! (Ibid., 143.10-144.12, p. 193)

We find a similar description of the fate of the soul fallen into the debauched life of the flesh in "Authoritative Teaching," a Gnostic text that does not seem to reflect any specific Jewish or Christian influences:

> ... In this very way, when the spiritual soul was cast into the body, it became a brother to lust, and hatred, and envy, and a material soul. So therefore the body came from lust, and lust came from material substance. For this reason the soul became a brother to them.... That one then will fall into drinking much wine in debauchery. . . . Therefore she does not remember her brothers and her father, for pleasure and sweet profits deceive her.... For if a thought of lust en-

ters into a virgin man, he has . . . been contaminated. . . . Our soul indeed is ill, because she dwells in a house of poverty [the body], while matter strikes blows at her eyes, wishing to make her blind (Auth. Teach. VI.23.12-25.9; 27.25-30, in *NHL*, pp. 279-80).

The text continues with a most telling description of what it means to be in a body in this world. The image used is that of a fisherman (the devil) laying the bait of the flesh with which to catch the fish--the soul trapped in the body:

> For this reason, then, we do not sleep, nor do we forget the nets that are spread out in hiding, lying in wait for us to catch us . . . . And we will be taken down into the dragnet, and we will not be able to come up from it because the waters are high over us . . . submerging our hearts down in the filthy mud. And we will not be able to escape from them. For man-eaters will seize us and swallow us, rejoicing like a fisherman casting a hook into the water . . . . In this very way we exist in this world, like fish . . . . For he places many foods before our eyes, things which belong to this world . . . . Now all such things the adversary prepares beautifully and spreads out before the body, wishing to make the mind of the soul incline her towards one of them and overwhelm her, like a hook drawing her by force in ignorance, deceiving her until she conceives evil, and bears fruit of matter, and conducts herself in uncleanness, pursuing many desires, covetousnesses, while fleshly pleasure draws her in ignorance (ibid., 29.2-31.24, p. 281).

Finally, from the non-Christian "Paraphrase of Shem" we find these strong sexual statements. In the preceding chapter we discussed the creation myth found here, but omitted these sexual images which we present now.

> And when her [Nature] forms returned, they rubbed their tongue(s) with each other; they copulated; they begot winds and demons and the power which is from the fire and the Darkness and the Spirit. But the form which remained alone cast the beast from herself. She did not have intercourse, but she was the one who rubbed herself alone. And she brought forth a wind which possessed a power from the fire and the Darkness and the Spirit.
>
> And in order that the demons also might become free from the power which they possessed through the impure intercourse, a womb was with the winds resembling water. And an unclean penis was with the demons in accordance with the example of the Darkness, and in the way he rubbed with the womb from the beginning. And after the forms of Nature had been together, they separated from each other. . . . But the winds, which are demons from water and fire and darkness and light, had intercourse unto perdition. And through

this intercourse the winds received in their womb foam from the penis of the demons. They conceived a power in their vagina. From the breathing the wombs of the winds girded each other until the times of the birth came. . . . They gave birth to all kinds of unchastity (Par. Shem VII.21.23-23.30, *NHL*, p. 318).

Alienation, Sleep, and Drunkenness

This final section describes the state of being in this world of the body: a state of alienation from the soul's true home in which the soul is described as either being asleep or drunk. Many moving passages are found in the Gnostic literature. We begin with the theme of alienation.

The Gnostics recognize that this world is not their home, for the material universe is totally alien to the spiritual world which is their origin. As Jonas summarizes the situation: the world

> is just as incomprehensible to the alien that comes to dwell here, and like a foreign land where it is far from home. Then it suffers the lot of the stranger who is lonely, unprotected, uncomprehended, and uncomprehending in a situation full of danger. Anguish and home-sickness are a part of the stranger's lot. The stranger who does not know the ways of the foreign land wanders about lost; if he learns its ways too well, he forgets that he is a stranger and gets lost in a differ-ent sense by succumbing to the lure of the alien world and becoming estranged from his own origin. Then he has become a "son of the house." This too is part of the alien's fate. In his alienation from himself the distress has gone, but this very fact is the culmination of the stranger's tragedy (Jonas, pp. 49f).

The most radical of all the Gnostic treatments of this theme is found in Marcion's system, where it receives an interesting twist, which we have already examined. It is radical because the alienation of human-ity is not from this world, but from God. Humanity *is* at home here because

> man in his *complete* constitution like all nature is a creature of the world-god and prior to the advent of Christ his rightful and unre-stricted property, body and soul alike. "Naturally," therefore, no part of him is alien in the world, while the Good God is alien in the absolute sense to him as to everything created (Jonas, p. 138, my italics).

Returning to the mainstream Gnostic tradition we find that concomi-tant to this state of alienation are the themes of the sleeping and intoxicated soul, numbed into forgetfulness by its fall. We shall see presently how this state is the result of an active plan on the part of the world to keep the entrapped soul a prisoner. Upon the awakening of the soul and removal from the world of matter, the powers of the world are diminished. We shall explore these in the context of the following excerpts.

We begin with one of the most famous Gnostic myths, "The Hymn of the Pearl" which, as we have seen, tells the tale of a prince sent down to Egypt to retrieve the missing pearl from the clutches of the devouring dragon. The alienation of this celestial sojourner in the land of matter is expressed thus:

> And I was alone and foreign in appearance, and I looked strange even to my own [household companions]. . . . I put on their [Egyptian] clothes, so that I might not appear foreign, as one from abroad.

While there, however, the prince's identity is discovered:

> But I do not know how they discovered that I was not from their land. But they cunningly devised a trap for me, and I tasted their food. I ceased to know that I was a king's son, and I served their king. I forgot the pearl for which my parents had sent me, and under the weight of their food I sank into deep sleep (ATh 109, in F I, p. 356).

The fate of the prince mirrors that of the pearl itself which has become trapped in the world of matter: the one guarded by the dragon, symbol of the evil world of matter, the other weighted down by the food of the world (matter) and fallen into a sleep of forgetfulness. This is the result of the active intervention on the part of the world and its evil, dark powers. A Manichean fragment offers the following parallel passage:

> [Ahriman, King of Darkness] captured the fair Soul and fettered it within the impurity. Since he had made it blind and deaf, it was unconscious and confused, so that (at first) it did not know its true origin (in Jonas, p. 69).

From this Manichean psalm we find a poetic expression of the soul's existential condition of finding itself caught in the body:

> Since I went forth into the darkness I was given a water to drink . . . I bear up beneath a burden which is not my own. I am in the midst of my enemies, the beasts surrounding me; the burden which I bear is of the powers and principalities. They burned in their wrath, they rose up against me. . . . Matter and her sons divided me up amongst

them, they burnt me in their fire, they gave me a bitter likeness. The strangers with whom I mixed, me they know not; they tasted my sweetness, they desired to keep me with them. I was life to them, but they were death to me; I bore up beneath them, they wore me as a garment upon them (in Jonas, p. 229).

The richest segment of the Gnostic corpus in terms of expressing the Gnostic awareness of the existential predicament of alienation is found in the Mandeans, and we cite several examples of their horror and pain of being removed from their spiritual home:

I (the soul) will speak to the uthras, my brothers: . . . "What sin have I committed among you, that you beguiled me and have removed me from your midst? You have taken me prisoner from my dwelling" (GL III.1 in F II, p. 222).

The Mandeans compiled a book of funeral dirges, from which the following are examples of the plaintive cry of the entrapped spiritual substance (the mana):

A mana I am of the Great Life: who has made me dwell in the Tibil [the world of matter]? . . . Who has cast me into the bodily trunk, with no hands or feet? . . . and knows not how it should walk. It lies there and crawls, and has no strength. Why did they call me from my place and bring me hither and cast me into the trunk? My feet are feet of radiance, now they must serve the trunk for walking . . . . Who cast me to the misery of the angels, to the hideous ones, whose smell is odious and whose form is hideous and unsightly? How shall I grow up in their midst, for their dwellings are unsightly to me? How shall I put on their garment and live where they live? (GL sect. 1; GL II.7, in F II, pp. 253,256)

In these next two excerpts we see the plotting of the world (the "wicked") to keep the being of light (perhaps the Mandean Savior Manda dHaiye) prisoner:

Let us unleash lust upon him . . . . and detain him with us in the world! He shall go astray and his heart shall take fright, and he shall forget what his lord charged him. He shall forget the calm, and revolt shall dwell in him. He shall forget the gentle path and he shall follow at our heels with sinners (GR XVI.8, in F II, p. 226).

Elsewhere the Mandean texts speak of the plan of the evil Ruha and the planets:

"Arise, let us make a drinking-feast. Let us practise the mysteries of love and seduce the whole world! . . . The call of Life we will silence, we will cast strife into the house, which shall not be settled in all eternity. We will kill the Stranger." . . . They took the head of the tribe and practised on him the mystery of love and of lust, through which all the worlds are inflamed. They practised on him seduction, by which all the worlds are seduced. They practised on him the mystery of drunkenness, by which all the worlds are made drunken (in Jonas, p. 72).

And in a passage reminiscent of "The Hymn of the Pearl" we read of the alien nature of the spiritual one thrown into the evil world of matter:

A poor one am I from the Fruit [the Pleroma], a removed one am I, who is from afar. . . . They brought me from the dwelling of the good ones. . . . Yea, they installed me in the abode of the wicked, which is completely full of malice . . . . and full of consuming fire. I did not wish it and do not wish to dwell in the worthless place. . . . By my illumination and my praise have I kept myself a stranger from the world. I have stood among them [the wicked], like a child who has no father. . . . I hear the voice of the Seven [the planets], who whisper to each other and say: "Where does this alien Man come from, whose speech is not like our speech?" I did not listen to their talk, and they were filled with evil rage against me (ML Oxf. I.56, in F II, pp. 243f).

The "Pistis Sophia" is a relatively late Gnostic document-- dating from at least the third century--that was discovered in the middle of the nineteenth century. For many years it remained one of the few primary sources of Gnostic material. Since the discovery of the Nag Hammadi library, the inferior quality of the "Pistis" has become even clearer relative to the higher level of the "Sophia" branch of Gnostic thought we have seen in the work of the Valentinians. In this excerpt we hear the lamentations of the fallen Sophia:

Deliver me, O Light, for evil thoughts have entered into me. . . . I went, and found myself in the darkness which is in the chaos beneath, and I was powerless to hasten away and to return to my place, for I was afflicted by all the Emanations of the Authades (the Arrogant One) (in Jonas, p. 68).

The Nag Hammadi texts present several clear examples of these themes of alienation, sleep, and drunkenness. We begin with "The Apocryphon of James," where the risen though angry Lord says:

You have received mercy . . . . Do you not, then, desire to be filled? And your heart is drunken; do you not, then, desire to be sober?

249

Therefore be ashamed! . . . O you pretenders to the truth; O you falsifiers of knowledge; O you sinners against the Spirit: can you still bear to listen when it behooved you to speak from the first? Can you still bear to sleep, when it behooved you to be awake from the first, so that the kingdom of heaven might receive you? Verily I say unto you, it is easier for a pure one to fall into defilement, and for a man of light to fall into darkness, than for you to reign or not reign (ApocryJs I. 3.8-11; 9.25-10.5, in *NHL*, pp. 30,33).

"The Hypostasis of the Archons" continues the now familiar Gnostic theme of the sleep of ignorance:

The Rulers took counsel with one another and said, "Come, let us cause a deep sleep to fall upon Adam." And he slept. --Now the deep sleep that they "caused to fall upon him, and he slept" is Ignorance (Hypos. Arch. II.89.2, in *NHL*, p. 154).

In "Authoritative Teaching" we find the following comparison between the Gnostic, who knows this world is not his own, and the unknowing ones:

We [the Gnostics] have nothing in this world, lest the authority of the world that has come into being should detain us in the worlds that are in the heavens, those in which universal death exists . . . . we are ashamed of the worlds, though we take no interest in them when they malign us. And we ignore them when they curse us. When they cast shame in our face, look at them and do not speak . . . . Our soul is indeed ill, because she dwells in a house of poverty, which matter strikes blows at her eyes, wishing to make her blind (Auth. Teach. VI.26.26-27.29, in *NHL*, p. 280).

"The Concept of Our Great Power" is a very late Christian Gnostic document, dating from the latter part of the fourth century. We find here the typical Gnostic exhortation to awaken from the dreams of this world:

Yet you are sleeping, dreaming dreams. Wake up and return, taste and eat the true food! Hand out the word and the water of life! Cease from the evil lusts and desires . . . (Conc. Great Power VI.39.33-40.7, in *NHL*, p. 286).

"The Teachings of Silvanus" is considered by some scholars to be the only true non-Gnostic text in the Nag Hammadi library, as it does not share many of the core teachings found in other Gnostic writings, as well as generally remaining within the orthodox doctrine. This belief is not shared by all scholars, however, for the text does extol the salvific role of knowledge from within. Its emphasis on reason as integrating mind, body, and soul is also reflective of the Hellenistic influence, especially of the Middle Platonism of the second century, while its extolling wisdom expresses the influence of the Jewish Wisdom heritage. It is probably dated from the turn of the third century, and the teacher Silvanus is most likely either the New Testament figure who was Peter's associate (1 P 5:12) or Paul's companion (2 Th 1:1). This passage could be taken from almost any Gnostic text.

> My son, listen to my teaching which is good and useful, and end the sleep which weighs heavy upon you. Depart from the forgetfulness which fills you with darkness . . . . Christ came in order to give you this gift. Why do you pursue the darkness though the light is at your disposal? . . . Wisdom summons you, yet you desire folly. Not by your own desire do you do these things, but it is the animal nature within you that does them.
> Wisdom summons you in her goodness, saying, "Come to me, all of you, O foolish ones, that you may receive a gift, the understanding which is good and excellent. I am giving to you a high-priestly garment which is woven from every kind of wisdom." What else is evil death except ignorance? What else is evil darkness except familiarity with forgetfulness? . . . clothe yourself with wisdom like a robe, put knowledge upon you like a crown, and be seated upon a throne of perception. . . . O soul, persistent one, be sober and shake off your drunkenness, which is the work of ignorance. . . . If you do not know yourself, you will not be able to know all of these [the heavenly host] (Silv. VII.88.22-89.24; 94.19; 117.2, in *NHL*, pp. 349-51,360).

We conclude this section by considering the Valentinian treatise, "The Gospel of Truth." Our first excerpt reiterates for us the theme of drunkenness, here having been overcome by the Gnostic:

> Each one's name comes to him. He who is to have knowledge in this manner knows where he comes from and where he is going. He knows as one who having become drunk has turned away from his drunkenness and having returned to himself, has set right what are his own. He has brought many back from error (GT I.22.12-21, in *NHL*, p. 40).

In emphasizing the illusory nature of our dreams, despite their seeming reality, this final passage is remarkable for its parallels with *A Course in Miracles*. In Part III we shall discuss the meaning of this passage as well as its parallels with the Course.

> Thus they were ignorant of the Father, he being the one whom they did not see. Since it was terror and disturbance and instability and

doubt and division, there were many illusions at work by means of these, and there were empty fictions, as if they were sunk in sleep and found themselves in disturbing dreams. Either there is a place to which they are fleeing, or without strength they come from having chased after others, or they are involved in striking blows, or they are receiving blows themselves. . . . Again, sometimes it is as if people were murdering them, though there is no one even pursuing them, or they themselves are killing their neighbors, for they have been stained with their blood. When those who are going through all these things wake up, they see nothing, they who were in the midst of all these disturbances, for they are nothing. Such is the way of those who have cast ignorance aside from them like sleep, not esteeming it as anything, nor do they esteem its works as solid things either, but they leave them behind like a dream in the night (ibid., 28.32-30.3, p. 43).

There is also a striking parallel in this passage to the dream metaphor in the *Timaeus*, where Plato writes about space:

. . . we look at it indeed in a kind of dream and say that everything that exists must be somewhere and occupy some space, and that what is nowhere in heaven or earth is nothing at all. And because of this dream state we are not awake to the distinctions we have drawn and others akin to them, and fail to state the truth about the true and unsleeping reality (*Tim.* 52b,c).

Chapter 8

THE MEANING OF SALVATION

Introduction

In this chapter we shall be discussing the principles of salvation, reserving for Chapter 10 the more specific applications of these principles to religious and ethical practice. The way that a problem (i.e., separation) is understood points the way to its solution (i.e., salvation). While the Gnostic teachings on the separation and salvation are clear and straightforward, as are their Platonic and Christian counterparts, we yet find inconsistencies in the logic that leads from one to the other. These inconsistencies have given rise to the God-world paradox that is one of the principal themes of this book, and we continue to explore this paradox in the present chapter.

For the traditional Christian the problem of the world is sin, traced back symbolically (at least for the non-fundamentalist Christian) to the disobedience of Adam. Redemption, or salvation from sin, is understood through forgiveness, mediated by the death and resurrection of Jesus. The savior Jesus, God's only Son, is sent into this world for the specific purpose of redeeming it through his suffering death. Thus are the people vicariously offered salvation by the blood sacrifice that is God's plan of atonement:

> Yes, God loved the world so much that he gave his only Son, so that everyone who believes in him may not be lost but may have eternal life. For God sent his Son into the world not to condemn the world, but so that through him the world might be saved (Jn 3:16f).

Salvation thus consists in confessing one's faith in the Risen Lord, and keeping his commandments as understood and carried out by his true Church.

For the Neoplatonic Augustine, the soul is the "middle-man" between the Divine Intelligible world and the visible world of the body; yet again, the soul cannot become free of its fallenness in the body without the grace of God. Thus, near the close of that diatribe against the world we excerpted from the *City of God* in Chapter 7, we find these words:

> From this hell upon earth there is no escape, save through the grace of the Savior Christ, our God and Lord. The very name Jesus shows this, for it means Savior; and He saves us especially from passing out

of this life into a more wretched and eternal state, which is rather a death than a life (*City of God* 22.22).

And in his famous and very moving prayer from the *Confessions*, Augustine's soul sings:

> Late have I loved Thee, O Beauty so ancient and so new, late have I loved Thee! And behold, thou wert within and I was without. I was looking for Thee out there, and I threw myself, deformed as I was, upon these well-formed things which Thou hast made. Thou wert with me, yet I was not with Thee. These things held me far away from Thee, things which would have not existed had they not been in Thee. Thou didst call and cry out and burst in upon my deafness; Thou didst shine forth and glow and drive away by blindness; Thou didst send forth Thy fragrance, and I drew in my breath and now I pant for Thee; I have tasted, and now I hunger and thirst; Thou didst touch me, and I was inflamed with desire for Thy peace (*Conf.* 10.27).

In distinction from the Gnostics, as we shall see presently, this traditional Christian notion of salvation does not logically follow from its view of sin, for Adam's choice to disobey God is never truly undone: Humanity's salvation requires the direct if not magical intervention of God, freely given as an expression of His grace, *independent* of the original source of the problem in Adam's mind, where his wrong choice was made. In its purest form, on the other hand, we can see the Gnostic notion of salvation to be the direct counterthrust to the problem. The Christian notion of sin is replaced by ignorance, elevated to an existential condition, and thus is undone through *gnosis*, or knowledge. The Gnostic understanding of salvation received its classic statement in the Valentinian formula, twice repeated in "The Gospel of Truth":

> Since the deficiency came into being because the Father was *not known*, therefore when the Father *is known*, from that moment on the deficiency will no longer exist (GT I.24.28-32, in *NHL*, p. 41, my italics).

The text explains further:

> As with the ignorance of a person, when he comes to have knowledge his ignorance vanishes of itself, as the darkness vanishes when light appears, so also the deficiency vanishes in the perfection (ibid., 24.32-25.2).

We shall return to this statement when we discuss the Valentinian redemption in more depth.

In one way at least, the more orthodox Christian Gnostics, especially those who are within the Platonic tradition, integrated their Platonism with the Christian revelation (as did Philo with the Jewish). The non-Christian Platonists held that the knowledge of the Divine was attainable through human effort, directed by reason and a life of virtue, whereas the Christians believed that the vision of God could come only through God's grace, given through His Son and acquired through the study of His holy Word, the Bible. Moreover, it was considered heretical by later Church Councils to believe that one could attain such a state on one's own (the Pelagian error). The Gnostic view of salvation integrated both of these by holding to the Platonic tradition, yet also insisting on the need for a genuine *gnosis* (revelation).

Jean Guitton, a contemporary French Catholic writer, has presented the general Gnostic view of redemption, as if spoken by a Gnostic:

> That salvation toward which I am tending, which ordinary Christians imagine to be far off, uncertain, elusive, and depending on merit, is not outside of me but within me. I need not run the risk of losing it, because I have it. All I need do is to become aware of this eternal fact. Instead of the effort of hoping for salvation, I now shall take my rest in recalling its possession. Instead of the effort of faith, I now have a clear *knowledge, gnosis* (Guitton, p. 56).

Bultmann summarizes the Gnostic process of redemption as freeing

> man from his prison by freeing him from himself .... redemption must be an absolutely eschatological event, a breach, a dissolution or separation of the real Self from the body and the soul. It can only be realized mythologically as the separation of the constituent elements in the human personality which ensues upon death. On leaving the body and soul, the real Self, the pre-existent spark of light, ascends to its home, the heavenly world of light. Both the real Self and its redemption are objects of faith. Such redemption can only be secured by the preaching of a word which comes as a message from the other world, by a message brought by the emissary from the world of light. In the last resort, this is the only way in which the transcendent can become a present experience. ... This faith in the reality of the calling which comes to the individual through the medium of the tradition is thus the true Gnostic existence. It is belief in a message which combines cosmological information with a summons to repentance or a call to awake and detach oneself from this world. It is a faith which at the same time includes the hope of an eschatological deliverance and the ascent of the soul (Bultmann, p. 168).

Clearly, for the Gnostic, the problem is seen within the mind, the seat of ignorance, which is where the correction must occur. The world, the epiphenomenon of the mind's error, must automatically disappear when this error is corrected through knowledge. Salvation, however, is not that clear-cut when we consider the full extent of the Gnostic corpus. After a discussion of Gnostic salvation we will in turn discuss the ascent of the soul, eschatology, and the Platonic understanding of redemption.

Gnosticism

We begin by discussing the nature of salvation for the Manicheans, which shares much in common with other Gnostic traditions, especially regarding the role of the Messenger of Light sent to redeem the fallen particles of light. We actually saw the beginning of the redemptive process in Chapter 6 when we considered the origin of the world which, for Mani, was part of the plan to redeem the particles of light trapped in the forms of the darkness. As in other Gnostic systems, the "plot" of the story consists of moves and countermoves, necessitating the events that comprise what we call our history, not to mention prehistory. We left off our narrative in the preceding chapter with the Darkness' brilliant foil to the plan of the Light to free the entrapped light particles and deliver them to the Sun. The creation of Adam and Eve and the introduction of sex as means to keep the light imprisoned in the body set the stage for the conflict that now exists from the beginning of history until the final victory. The battlefield is now Adam, where the forces of Darkness and Light vie for his soul.

Horrified by the defilement of the light-soul of Adam through the seduction by Eve, the angels appeal to the Living Spirit. This Being is part of a chain whose preceding links were the Great Architect and the second-creation Friend of Light, called forth by God to help in the battle against the Darkness. The Living Spirit is thus asked to send someone to awaken Adam from his sleep of death and deliver him from the dark forces of evil. This divine Messenger is known as the Luminous Jesus, distinguished from the historical figure who comes later. The Luminous Jesus is a more specific expression or emanation of the Messenger of Light mentioned earlier. This latter's mission was to the trapped Light; the former is sent to the first man. We quote from the account of Theodore bar Konai, the eighth-century heresiologist:

> Jesus the Luminous approached the innocent Adam. He awakened him from the sleep of death, so that he might be delivered from the many demons.... And Adam examined himself and discovered who he was. Jesus showed him the Father on high and his own Self [that of Jesus] cast into all things, to the teeth of panthers and elephants,

devoured by them that devour, consumed by them that consume, eaten by the dogs, mingled and bound in all that is, imprisoned in the stench of darkness. He raised him up and made him eat of the tree of life (in Jonas, pp. 86f).

The Manichean psalms are replete with ecstatic expressions of gratitude to the Luminous Jesus, an important part of the Manichean liturgical life. We cite only two of these:

Let us bless our Lord Jesus who has sent to us the Spirit of Truth [the Paraclete; i.e., Mani]. He came and separated us from the Error of the world, he brought us a mirror, we looked, we saw the Universe in it (CCXXIII, in Allberry, p. 9).

Come, my Lord Jesus, the Savior of souls, who hast saved me from the drunkenness and Error of the world. Thou art the Paraclete whom I have loved since my youth: thy Light shines forth in me like the lamp of light: thou hast driven away from me the oblivion of Error: thou hast taught me to bless God and his Lights (CCXLVIII, in Allberry, p. 56).

Thus, it is this Jesus who counsels Adam in the Garden of Eden to eat of the tree of knowledge, a reversal of the Genesis story we have referred to before, and which blasphemy clearly had the desired effect of outraging the Church. This passage in addition reflects the important tenet of the Manichean creed known as the *Jesus patibilis*, or the suffering Jesus. This doctrine remains one of the most original of Mani's teachings and, as we shall see in Chapter 10, had tremendous consequences for the life of the individual Manichee. Jesus not only is the divine Messenger from whom comes all subsequent revelations, he is also the symbol of all the particles of light that have been trapped in the dark world of matter and thus suffer until their deliverance. We shall return to this theme also in Chapter 9 when we consider the "Redeemed Redeemer." This Jesus of the Light is the Self "cast into all things," and who

hangs from every tree . . . is served up bound in every dish . . . every day is born, suffers and dies (in Jonas, p. 229).

The suffering Jesus--light trapped in matter--is found throughout creation, but special emphasis is placed by the Manicheans on the passive world of the vegetables. Jonas quotes from an early source:

What is "the soul that is slaughtered, by being killed, oppressed, murdered in the enemy"?--What has been called the "slaughtered,

257

killed, oppressed, murdered soul" is the (life) force of the fruits, the cucumbers and seeds, which are beaten, plucked, torn to pieces, and give nourishment to the worlds of flesh. Also the wood, when drying up, and the garment, when getting old, will die: they too are a part of the total "murdered, slaughtered soul" (in Jonas, p. 229).

This dual function of the Luminous Jesus--the Redeemer coming into the world and the one to be redeemed from within the world--is poetically expressed in this Manichean psalm--reminiscent of the Hymn of Jesus from "The Acts of John"--the first half of which we cited in the preceding chapter:

> I am in everything, I bear the skies, I am the foundation, I support the earths, I am the Light that shines forth, that gives joy to the souls. I am the life of the world: I am the milk that is in all trees: I am the sweet water that is beneath the sons of Matter ... I bore these things until I had fulfilled the will of my Father; the First Man is my father whose will I have carried out. Lo, the Darkness I have subdued; lo, the fire of the fountains I have extinguished it, as the Sphere turns hurrying round, as the sun receives the refined part of life (CCXLVI, in Allberry, pp. 54f).

The Luminous Jesus fulfills his function, part of which includes warning the First Man of the seductive advances of Eve. Adam heeds the warning for a while, but eventually succumbs to the attraction of the flesh as the demons come to the "rescue." Their sexual union begins the process of reproduction and history begins. The Darkness seemingly has won, having succeeded in scattering and burying the particles of light in the myriad bodies of the world.

However, the Light counters with its final move, the introduction of the great prophets who speak the message of the Luminous Jesus in the religious language of the time period:

> From aeon to aeon the apostles of God did not cease to bring here the Wisdom and the Works. Thus in one age their coming was into the countries of India through the apostle that was the Buddha; in another age, into the land of Persia through Zoroaster; in another, into the land of the West through Jesus. After that, in this last age, this revelation came down and this prophethood arrived through myself, Mani, the apostle of the true God, into the land of Babel (in Jonas, p. 230).

It is clear from other of Mani's writings that he considered himself not only as an equal to the historical Jesus, but even greater since his message was universal and was the final chapter in salvation's plan. He saw himself as the culmination and consummation of the one true Messenger who from the beginning of the world, altering his forms with his names, courses through the Aeon [world] until he shall have reached his time and, anointed by God's mercy for his labor, attained to eternal rest (in Jonas, p. 230).

Augustine quotes from what might be Mani's own words, and then makes this summarizing statement:

These are the words of salvation from the eternal and living source. Whoever hears them and at first believes, then follows their teachings, shall never be subject to death but shall enjoy eternal and glorious life. For he shall verily be considered blessed who has been instructed in this divine knowledge, and thereby saved, shall dwell in eternal life (*Contra. epist. fund.*, in Haardt, p. 296).

From *The Living Gospel*, claimed to be the work of Mani himself, only brief fragments are extant. As has been discussed in Part I, it is difficult to deduce the contents and structure of the entire work. The surviving text praises the Luminous Jesus and his emissary, Mani:

Praised is . . . the dear son of Love, the life-giver Jesus, the chief of all these gifts. Praised is . . . the Virgin of Light, the chief of all excellences. Praised is . . . the holy religion through the power of the Father, through the blessing of the Mother and through the goodness of the Son (Jesus). Salvation and blessing upon the sons of salvation and upon the speakers and hearers of the renowned word! Praise and glory be to the Father and to the Son and to the elect Breath, the Holy Spirit . . . .I, Mani, the emissary of [the Luminous] Jesus the friend, in the love of the Father, of God the renowned . . . (in *NTA* I, p. 359).

The final stage of redemption is the appearance of the Great Thought, which closes the reign of Darkness and history. We shall return to this stage later in this chapter when we discuss eschatology.

We turn now to Marcion. We have briefly discussed his doctrine of salvation in Chapter 6, but it now warrants our fuller attention. Marcion's thesis is that humanity is *totally* alien from God, and thus salvation does not consist, as it does for almost every other Gnostic, of a *gnosis* which causes the sleeping *pneuma* to awaken and remember its home. Humanity's home *is* this world. And thus it is saved from this world by a "grace freely given" by the alien and true God who purchases us from the creator God through the death of Jesus on the cross. Here, Marcion cites Ga 3:13: "Christ redeemed us from the curse of the Law by being cursed for our sake . . . ." As Jonas summarizes:

The purchase price was Christ's blood, which was given not for the remission of sins or the cleansing of mankind from guilt or as a vicarious atonement fulfilling the Law--not, in brief, for any reconciliation of mankind with God--but for the cancellation of the creator's claim to his property (Jonas, p. 139).

Marcion's radical view--so radical, as we have seen, that for many scholars it places him outside the Gnostic category--led to an interesting interpretation of redemption. What Jesus effected through his death had no bearing on this world at all, since he came at the request of the acosmic Deity who has *absolutely* nothing to do with this world. Its effect and purpose is only regarding the *future* state of the soul. Through faith in the redemptive work of Jesus, one can achieve the peace of anticipating this future salvation, but this does not change the existential condition of being in this world. Nor does it change the course of world history. As a result, we find paradoxically (a word often used to describe the Marcion system) that this great Gnostic teacher is in agreement with the prevailing Jewish belief that the expected Messiah--son of the "Most High," the earthly God--was still to come to establish his kingdom on earth. However, since this figure has only to do with the creator God, his messianic activity is totally irrelevant to the redemptive work of Jesus, which is not of this world and which in fact awaits the end of this world.

The true and Good God therefore has no relation to the cosmos, and does not intervene in its workings at all. Marcion, in his biblical canon, struck out all references to God's caring for His children, such as is found, for example, in the Sermon on the Mount where Jesus teaches about God's providential care in the analogies about the birds in the air and the lilies in the field. God's *only* act is to send Jesus. As Tertullian quotes Marcion, cited in Jonas:

> Man, this *work of the creator-god*, that better God [i.e., Jesus] chose to love, and for his sake he labored to descend from the third heaven into these miserable elements, and on his account he even was crucified in this puny cell of the creator [i.e., the body] (*Contra Marc.* [= *Adv. Marc.*] I.14, in Jonas, p. 143).

We can see also how this idea affects the traditional Christian view of sin. Since the Good God has no connection with humanity, and never has had any, there could never have been a sin against Him. God's relationship to us has no past. Original sin thus has no meaning for Marcion, and any idea of reconciliation or divine forgiveness must also be meaningless, as indeed are related concepts such as atonement, fear of God's wrath and judgment, and God's mercy in the face of our sins against Him. Nonetheless, there is a kind of mysterious mercy that is inherent in Marcion's system. Jonas describes it as

... the paradox of a grace given inscrutably, unsolicited, with no antecedents to prompt and to prepare it, an irreducible mystery of divine goodness as such (Jonas, p. 144).

Despite the absence of any divine intervention in this world, which must continue on the inexorable path begun by its creator, the ones who are filled with faith in the redemptive activity of Jesus express this future anticipation by a life of increased detachment (read: asceticism) from the just and creator God who made this world. (As with our treatment of Manicheism, we shall return to this aspect of Marcion's theology in Chapter 10.) This faith in a future redemption from the world of matter reflects a decision made by each person whether to heed the call of the Redeemer or to remain bound to the voice of the creator of this world. We quote now from Irenaeus' presentation of Marcion's explanation for why the "good people" of the Old Testament were not saved by Jesus when he descended to the underworld, while the "bad people" were. Here we see that Irenaeus has joined the world of polemic that Marcion (along with many Gnostics) undoubtedly enjoyed playing in. We can almost feel the perverse pleasure the Gnostics must have derived from "egging" their opponents on by deliberately making statements the orthodox Church could not have avoided seeing as blasphemous. Jonas describes the following explanation of Marcion (found in Irenaeus) as being "original if somewhat facetious" (Jonas, p. 140n), to which we should certainly add the word provocative:

He [Marcion] says that there will be salvation only for souls which have learned his doctrine; the body, doubtless because it was taken from the earth ... cannot participate in salvation. To this blasphemy against God he adds the following story, truly assuming the role of the devil and saying everything contrary to the truth. When the Lord descended to Hades, Cain and those like him, the Sodomites, the Egyptians, and those like them, and in general all the peoples who have walked in every compound of wickedness, were saved by him; they ran to him and were taken up into his kingdom. But Abel, Enoch, Noah, and the rest of the righteous, and the patriarchs related to Abraham, along with all the prophets and those who pleased God, did not participate in salvation. (The serpent who was in Marcion proclaimed this!) For since they knew ... that their God was always testing them, and suspected that he was testing them then, they did not run to Jesus nor did they believe his proclamation; and therefore ... their souls remained in Hades ... (*Adv. haer.* I.27.3, in Grant, p. 46).

As the knowledge of truth has no transformative power here, Marcion's notions of redemption cannot be truly classified as Gnostic.

The soul is not changed; the spirit or *pneuma* is not awakened or re-leased. All that has occurred is a "legal transaction" involving the true God and the demiurgic creator, and the purchased souls have now been saved by their belief and faith in the efficacy of the divine deal.

We now consider "The Gospel of Truth," which understanding of salvation provides us with perhaps the clearest and most sophisticated Gnostic teaching. As the Gospel's understanding directly follows its notion of the problem we have considered in Chapter 5, much of what we say here is a repetition. The plight from which we must be saved is the ignorance of who we truly are and who created us. The basic "formula" is repeated twice, evidence of the importance it held in the Valentinian school. Here is its first appearance, near the beginning of the gospel:

> Oblivion did not come into existence under the Father. . . . But what comes into existence in him is knowledge, which appeared in order that oblivion might vanish and the Father might be known. *Since oblivion came into existence because the Father was not known, then if the Father comes to be known, oblivion will not exist from that moment on* (GT I.18.1-11, in *NHL*, p. 38, my italics).

Authority for this statement comes from Jesus himself:

> This is the gospel of the one who is searched for, which was revealed to those who are perfect through the mercies of the Father—the hidden mystery, Jesus, the Christ (ibid., 18.11-16, in *NHL*, p. 38).

Its second appearance, virtually unchanged except "deficiency" replaces "oblivion," reads:

> *Since the deficiency came into being because the Father was not known, therefore when the Father is known, from that moment on the deficiency will no longer exist.* As with the ignorance of a person, when he comes to have knowledge his ignorance vanishes of itself, as the darkness vanishes when light appears, so also deficiency vanishes in the perfection (ibid., 24.28-25.2, in *NHL*, p. 41, my italics).

There is, interestingly enough, a third mention of this formula in the literature, this time in Irenaeus. The immediate context is discussion of the Valentinian dismissal of sacraments as unnecessary for salvation:

> . . . one ought not to celebrate the mystery of the ineffable and invisible power by means of visible and corruptible created things, the inconceivable and incorporeal by means of what is sensually tangible and

corporeal. The perfect redemption is said to be the knowledge of the ineffable "Greatness." *From ignorance both deficiency and passion derived: through "knowledge" will the entire substance derived from ignorance be destroyed.* Therefore, this "knowledge" is redemption of the inner man. And this is not corporeal, since the body perishes, nor psychic, because the soul also derives from the deficiency and is like a habitation of the spirit: the redemption must therefore be spiritual. The inner, spiritual man is redeemed through knowledge: sufficient for them is the knowledge of all things, and this is the true redemption (*Adv. haer.* I.21.4, in F I, p. 220, my italics).

"Deficiency" is used here as well, so that we may conclude that for the Valentinians the concepts of deficiency and oblivion were identical. Jonas has pointed out an important addition in the citation of Irenaeus. Not only does the formula here state that ignorance is the cause of the deficiency, which will be undone by knowledge, but it adds the phrase "the entire substance" (Jonas translates the Greek as "the whole system") as having come from ignorance. This "substance" (or "system") refers to the entire cosmos. As Jonas summarizes:

> . . . the "system" in question is nothing less than this world, the cosmos, the whole realm of matter in all its elements, fire, air, water, earth, which only seem to be substances in their own right but are in truth by-products and expressions of spiritual [i.e., psychological] processes or states (Jonas, p. 312).

Furthermore, it is clear from the entire Valentinian system that Irenaeus presents, that ignorance, deficiency, and passion are ontological states, not mere psychological dynamics. To emphasize this, Jonas writes them with capital letters:

> . . . the Ignorance and Passion here named are not ordinary ignorance and ordinary passion as in us, but Ignorance and Passion writ large, on a metaphysical scale and at the origin of things: that far from being mere abstracts they denote concrete events and entities of the cosmogonic myth: that the subjective states they apparently name, being those of divine powers, have objective efficacy, and an efficacy on the scale of the inner life whereof they are states--the inner life of divinity--and therefore can be the ground of such substantive, total realities as cosmos and matter (Jonas, pp. 312f).

This Valentinian teaching is more than abstract philosophical speculation, for it reflects here in this second-century Gnostic tractate the same profundity we find eighteen centuries later in *A Course in Miracles*, integrating metaphysics with our personal experience in the ego's world and salvation from it. The ontological state of separation is fully present within the mind of each of us, just as our individual spiritual identity is part of the oneness of Christ. Thus, the salvation of the one is at the same time the salvation of the One, or better, its awakening. We quote "The Gospel of Truth" again, from the paragraph containing the second mention of the formula. The emphasis in this passage suddenly shifts from the macrocosmic view of salvation of the universal Sonship--i.e., the fate of the aeons still within the realm of the spirit or the Pleroma: " . . . through the mercies of the Father the aeons may know him . . . "--to the microcosmic salvation of the individual: "It is within Unity that each one will attain himself." It is the same shift we see occurring in the Course, reflecting the inherent atemporal, though still illusory, relationship between the One and the many, the universal and individual, the inner and outer:

> The Father reveals his bosom [the Holy Spirit] . . . . so that through the mercies of the Father the aeons may know him and cease laboring in search of the Father . . . . So from that moment on the form is not apparent, but it will vanish in the fusion of Unity, for now their works lie scattered. In time Unity will perfect the spaces [i.e., the gaps between the separated individuals]. It is within Unity that each one will attain himself [Jonas translates thus: "through Unity shall each one of us receive himself back"]; within knowledge he will purify himself from multiplicity into Unity, consuming matter within himself like fire, and darkness by light, death by life (GT I.25.2-19, in *NHL*, p. 41).

As Jonas summarizes:

> . . . the human-individual event of pneumatic [i.e., spiritual] *knowledge* is the inverse equivalent of the pre-cosmic universal event of divine *ignorance*, and in its redeeming effect of the same ontological order; and that thus the actualization of knowledge in the person is at the same time an act in the general ground of being (Jonas, pp. 318f).

Jonas has made the interesting observation that "The Gospel of Truth" is basically an elliptical summary--"a mere condensed repetition of well-known doctrine" (p. 316)--that presumes a prior acquaintance with, and understanding of Valentinianism by the reader. One coming to Gnosticism for the first time through this tractate would be totally lost. Key terms such as "Error," "Anguish," "Deficiency," etc., are merely presented without explanation. It is only through reading the far more extensive Valentinian treatment in Irenaeus or Hippolytus, not to mention a familiarity with the general tenor of second-century Gnostic thought, that a contemporary reader could make sense of this otherwise strange language. The extensive mythological system found in these other Valentinian accounts, replete with a full cast of characters, provides the explanatory background to the otherwise enigmatic "Gospel of Truth." We quote this summary from Jonas:

> For the speculative passages of the GT ["The Gospel of Truth"] are not merely an abridgment or summary of some fuller version: they point up, in their symbolic contraction, the essence of the doctrine, stripped of its vast mythological accessories and reduced to its philosophical core. Thus, as the GT can only be read with the help of the circumstantial myth, so the myth receives back from such reading a transparency as to its basic spiritual meaning which the density of its sensuous and necessarily equivocal imagery somehow disguises. In this role the GT acts like a pneumatic transcription of the symbolic myth. And what is truly inestimable: since its discovery we have it on their own authority *what* the Valentinians themselves considered as the heart of their doctrine: and that the heart of that heart was the proposition expressed in the "formula" (Jonas, pp. 317f).

Interestingly enough, this ignorance (deficiency)-knowledge "formula," which was obviously important to the Valentinians by virtue of its repetition in "The Gospel of Truth," seems to have been "stuck in" by Irenaeus who, it seemed, did not appreciate its importance. It is found near the end of his lengthy report on Valentinianism, and among tangential information. It is like a shining jewel discovered midst ordinary baubles.

We find another statement in the tractate that nicely summarizes the ontological situation of the deficiency and its undoing. Most interesting is the use of "forgiveness," a word not commonly found in the Gnostic literature:

> For this reason incorruptibility breathed forth; it pursued the one who had sinned in order that he might rest. For forgiveness is what remains for the light in the deficiency, the word of the pleroma. For the physician runs to the place where a sickness is because that is his will that is in him. He who has a deficiency, then, does not hide it, because one has what the other lacks. So with the pleroma, which has no deficiency; it fills up his deficiency--it is that which he provided for filling up what he lacks, in order that therefore he might receive the grace (GT I.35.24-36.2, in *NHL*, p. 45f).

This teaching is parallel to *A Course in Miracles*, where it is taught that God placed the remedy (the Holy Spirit's Atonement) in the place (the mind) wherein the sickness (the belief in separation) is found.

The Ascent of the Soul

For the Gnostic, the ultimate release from the prison of the body and the material world, set up by the experience of *gnosis* in his or her lifetime, came at the moment of death, when

> [the Gnostic] encounters the everlasting, reawakening fact of release from the fetters of the body, and is able to set out on the way to his true home (Rudolph, p. 171).

This setting out is frequently known as the ascent of the soul. In many ways it can be seen as the retracing of the steps of the fall from the Pleroma, in the end restoring the soul to the integrity it had at the beginning. The Gnostic eschatological emphasis is alternately on the individual and the collective. In this section we shall address the fate of the individual soul. Later in the chapter we shall examine the Gnostic view of the end of the world.

The Gnostic ascent, while treated mythologically *quasi* literally, is in fact a depiction of an inward, psychological process; not that any given Gnostic writer believed that necessarily, but our more psychologically sophisticated age would recognize this process. Jung, for example, has written about the medieval alchemists who sought to turn base metal into gold, spending a lifetime in the attempt to extract the quintessence ("fifth essence") from matter. These men, he described, were really projecting their own internal spiritual journey onto the alchemical process. Likewise one can denote in the music of Beethoven all the stages of the spiritual journey. Some commentators have spoken of three stages in his music, which roughly correspond to the three stages many see as comprising the spiritual path: awakening, illumination, union. The soul's ascent, returning to its origin and Source, is likewise treated spiritually in Plotinus, for example, as we shall see below. Jonas has described this evolutionary spiritual process:

> Historically there is an even more far-reaching aspect to the ascent doctrines than their literal meaning. In a later stage of "gnostic" development (though no longer passing under the name of Gnosticism) the external topology of the ascent through the spheres, with the successive divesting of the soul of its worldly envelopments and the regaining of its original acosmic nature, could be "internalized" and find its analogues in a psychological technique of inner transformations by which the self, *while still in the body*, might attain the Absolute as an immanent, if temporary, condition: an ascending scale of mental states replaces the stations of the mythical itinerary: the dynamics of progressive spiritual self-transformation, the spatial thrust through the heavenly spheres. Thus could transcendence itself be turned into immanence, the whole process become spiritualized

and put within the power and the orbit of the subject. With this trans-position of a mythological scheme into the inwardness of this person, with the translation of its objective stages into subjective phases of self-performable experience whose culmination has the form of ec-stasis, gnostic myth has passed into mysticism . . . and in this new medium it lives on long after the disappearance of the original mythological beliefs (Jonas, pp. 165f).

In the third-century Sethian document "The Three Steles of Seth" it is written: "The way of ascent is the way of descent" (3 St. Seth VII.127.20, in *NHL*, p. 367), paralleling the Plotinian formulation. We recall from our discussions of the creation of the world that the descent followed a logical path, involving the creation of the various archons in whose image the world was formed by the Demiurge. It is thus these rulers that the soul must get past in order to return to its starting point. And it is not an easy task. We have already seen that the archons--the mythological rulers of darkness, here anthropomorphized--have very strong interest in maintaining the soul a prisoner, thereby helping to perpetuate the material world and their own existence. It is as preparation for this journey that the full significance of the experience of *gnosis*, not to mention correlative aspects such as ritual, ethical, and instructional teachings, can be more properly understood and appre-ciated. The Gnostic treatment of the ascent, therefore, is filled with accounts of danger, frequently surmounted by recourse to magic formulas, incantations, and elaborate ceremonies at the time of death. Again, these accounts are merely externalizations of the internal process of confronting the guilt and fear within the mind. This will be discussed more fully in Part III. There are illustrative examples from many traditions, and we shall present some of them now, beginning with the *Poimandres* from the *Corpus Hermeticum*.

The process begins with the dissolution of the material body and, as the soul ascends through each circle (corresponding to the seven planets), another part of its accretion returns to its source, what Jonas has termed "a series of progressive subtractions which leaves the 'naked' true self" (Jonas, p. 166).

First, at the dissolution of the material body you surrender the body to change, and the form you have disappears, and you surrender your character to the demon as ineffectual. . . . And so he [the soul] then goes upwards through the Harmony, and to the first circle he gives the capacity to grow or to diminish, to the second his evil machinations, guile, unexercised, to the third the deceit of lust, unexercised, to the fourth the ostentation of command not exploited, and to the fifth impious boldness and the rashness of audacity, to the sixth the evil urges for riches, unexercised, and to the seventh circle the lurking lie. And then, freed of all the activities of the Harmony, he reaches the nature of the Ogdoad with his own power, and with those who are there he praises the Father. Those who are present rejoice together that this one has come, and becoming like those with him he hears also certain powers above the nature of the Ogdoad praising God with a sweet sound. And then in order they go up to the Father, change themselves into powers and having become powers they come to be in God. This is the good end of those who have obtained knowledge, to become God (*Corp. Herm.* I.24-26, in F I, pp. 333f).

In "The Gospel of Mary," which was part of the "Berlin Codex" purchased in Egypt at the close of the nineteenth century, we find a graphic description of the soul's ascent after death. Unfortunately, the beginning description--some four pages--is missing from the manuscript. The theme of the Gospel is the revelation to Mary Magdalene from Jesus, explaining the soul's confrontation with the hypostasized "seven powers of wrath":

> They ask the soul, "Whence do you come, slayer of men, or where are you going, conqueror of space?" The soul answered and said, "What binds me has been slain, and what turns me about has been overcome, and my desire has been ended, and ignorance has died. In a world I was released from a world ... and from the fetter of oblivion which is transient. From this time on will I attain to the rest of the time ... of the aeon, in silence" (GM BG 7.16-13-17.7, in *NHL*, p. 473).

To the Mandeans belong the richest collection of excerpts relating to the soul's ascent, since this aspect was the predominant element in the Mandean doctrine of redemption. Supported by the prayers and rituals of the surviving Mandean community, the soul makes its way, guided by its "helper." The soul's ascent is greatly facilitated by its past life of good works, which seem in Mandean mythology to have almost become hypostasized entities. It is an arduous and dangerous path:

> When spirit and soul came forth from the body, from the garb of blood and flesh, from the boiling cauldron, from the glowing oven, from the tombs, the rocky places, and pitfalls, this soul hastened away and came upon a watchhouse, where instruments of torture, torment, and affliction are deposited and where sinful souls are judged with unjust judgement. ... As it stood there, this soul trembled and shook, and its whole form trembled in its raiments, and it cried to the great and sublime Life ... (GL I.4, in F II, pp. 246f).

One hymn traces the treacherous ascent through the seven planets, and we excerpt it here:

> My soul yearned in me for the Life .... and I set my course for the

Place of Life. I flew and went on, until I arrived at the First [of the planets]. The slaves of the First came forth to meet me . . . : "Friend, whence have you come and where are you going?" "I come from the Tibil [earth], from the house which the planets built."

The planet tries to tempt him to stay, but to no avail. The hymn continues through the remaining six planets,

until I arrived at the House of Life . . . . the Life came forth to meet me . . . . he clothed me with radiance and brought light and covered me with it. He reckoned me with his number, and indeed: the good ones came forth from its midst: "Among the lamps of light shall your lamps be drawn aloft and shine there" (GL III.51, in F II, pp. 251f).

The ascent is thus the return to the world of Light from which the soul fell. Unlike other Gnostic systems, notably the Valentinian schools, this system has the fall occurring through no fault of the soul. For the journey it receives the assistance it needs from its "helper" or "planter." In one text, the helper states:

You belong to me here; I shall take you out of the world and cause you to ascend . . . and shall leave all behind . . . . You are my counterpart, I shall . . . keep you safe in my garment . . . . which the Great Life gave to me, and in the pure fragrance which is entrusted to me. This garment in which you lived I shall cast at the head of its maker, for the men who made it shall disappear and perish (GL II.5, in F II, pp. 255f).

These words are addressed to the mana in the soul, the particle of light that is divine, and thus the helper is the counterpart to the Messenger of Light who comes at the moment of death to assist the soul on its journey. In another context we may think of the Messenger as being the spiritual Self of the soul that has been trapped in the body. This notion carries with it some profound metaphysical implications, as we shall see later when we consider "The Hymn of the Pearl."

The soul must escape the clutches of the dark and evil forces which are like an iron wall encircling the world, not to mention the "super-terrestrial penal stations" which detain and punish those who have sinned. The soul could not overcome these obstacles and successfully complete its journey without the helper, sent to it by the Light:

If you, soul, hear what I say to you and do not act contrary to my word, a bridge shall be thrown across that great sea for you. . . . I shall guide you past the watch-house, at which the rebels stand. I shall guide you past the flames of fire the smoke of which rises up and reaches the firmament. I shall guide you past the double pits which

Ruha has dug on the way. Over that high mountain I shall smooth out a path for you. In this wall, this wall of iron [another source adds: "which encircles the world like a wreath"], I shall hack a breach for you. I shall hold you with all my strength and take you with me to the Place of Light (GL III.25, in F II, pp. 268f).[11]

Church Father Epiphanius quotes from the "heresy of the Archontics" in a passage that expresses a similar theme. We find here as well the reason behind the archons' refusal to let the ascending soul pass:

And they say that the soul is food for the authorities and powers [the archons], without which they cannot live, since it derives from the dew which comes from above and gives them strength. And when it acquires knowledge . . . it ascends from heaven to heaven and speaks its defense before each power and so attains to the higher power, the Mother and to the Father of all, from whom it has come down into this world (*Panar.* XL.2.7-8, in F I, p. 297).

Epiphanius also reports a Gnostic sect whose libertinism (*see* Chapter 10, pp. 365-70) served the purpose of eluding the evil archons whose moral code served as a prison to those souls adhering to it.

In the following passage from this heresiologist, we also find the characteristic Gnostic denigration of the Old Testament deity, here identified, as in other Gnostic systems, with the chief Archon called Sabaoth.

And some say that Sabaoth has the face of an ass, others, that of a swine; for this reason . . . he commanded the Jews not to eat swine. And he is the maker of heaven and earth and of the heavens after him and of his own angels. And the soul as it leaves this world passes by these Archons but cannot pass through unless it is in full possession of this knowledge, or rather condemnation, and being carried past escapes the hands of the Archons and the authorities (ibid., XXVI.10.6-7, pp. 322f).

We find a graphic account of a soul's ascent in the Nag Hammadi "Apocalypse of Paul," where the protagonist-soul is St. Paul's. The biblical basis for this text is Paul's famous "out of body" experience recounted in 2 Corinthians 12:1-4. The text seems to date from the second century and to reflect strong Jewish apocalyptic influences, not to mention Gnostic ones. The setting is Paul's meeting a heavenly child who is the source of the revelation:

---

11. For a more extensive expression of the soul's journey through the various watch-houses of judgment, *see* F II, pp. 247-50.

"Let your mind awaken, Paul, and see that this mountain upon which you are standing is the mountain of Jericho, so that you may know the hidden things in those that are visible . . . ." Then the Holy Spirit who was speaking with him caught him up high to the third heaven, and he passed beyond to the fourth heaven . . . .I saw the angels resembling gods, the angels bringing a soul out of the land of the dead. They placed it at the gate of the fourth heaven. And the angels were whipping it (ApocPaul V.19.10-20.12, in *NHL*, p. 240).

Under the guide of the Spirit, Paul continues through the various gates of judgment until he reaches the seventh heaven.

. . . and I saw an old man [the Old Testament creator God--the Demiurge] . . . whose garment was white. . . . The old man spoke, saying to me, "Where are you going, Paul, O blessed one and the one who was set apart from his mother's womb?" . . . And I replied . . . "I am going to the place from which I came." . . . The old man replied to me, saying, "How will you be able to get away from me? Look and see the principalities and authorities." The Spirit spoke, saying, "Give him the sign that you have, and he will open for you." And then I gave him the sign. He turned his face downwards to his creation and to those who are his own authorities.

And then the seventh heaven opened and we went up to the Ogdoad [the eighth heaven]. And I saw the twelve apostles. They greeted me, and we went up to the ninth heaven. I greeted all those who were in the ninth heaven, and we went up to the tenth heaven. And I greeted my fellow spirits (ibid., 22.25-24.8, p. 241).

In "The Hymn of the Pearl" we see how differently the motif of the Messenger is treated, combined with the important idea of the re-deemed redeemer. In Chapter 7 we left our princely hero drugged asleep by the food of the Egyptians. His state is noticed by his parents in the East who decide to send help via a letter (i.e., the Messenger). This letter is yet another example of the Call from the world of Light. The letter symbolism is found also in another Gnostic document, "The Odes of Solomon," dating from roughly the same time period: the late second century. Like the Hymn, the Odes provide an important example of the close connection that existed between the Gnostic world and the traditional Church. We quote from one stanza of the twenty-third Ode:

And His thought was like a letter;
His will descended from on high, and it was sent like
an arrow which is violently shot from the bow:
And many hands rushed to the letter to seize it and to
take and read it:

> And it escaped their fingers and they were affrighted
> at it and at the seal that was upon it.
> Because it was not permitted to them to loose its seal:
> for the power that was over the seal was greater than
> they. (*Eden*, pp. 131f)

Returning to the Hymn, this is the content of the letter:

> From the father, the king of kings, and the mother who possesses the
> East, and the brother who is the second beside us, to our son in Egypt,
> greetings. Get up and sober up out of your sleep, and listen to the
> words of this letter. Remember that you are a king's son. You have
> come under a servile yoke. Think of your suit shot with gold; think
> of the pearl on account of which you were sent to Egypt, so that your
> name may be mentioned in the book of the valiant, and you may be
> an heir with your brother in our kingdom (ATh 110, in F I, p. 357).

To guard against interception by the wicked, the letter flew to the
prince in the form of an eagle, "the king of all birds," calling the
sleeping soul to awaken. The passage has many Gnostic counterparts,
many of which we shall consider elsewhere, but one from the "Acts of
John" can be cited here. John is exhorting Lycomedes, whose faith has
been weakened by his paralytic wife: "You too must wake up and
open your soul. Cast off this heavy sleep of yours!" (AJ 21, in *NTA* II,
p. 217). One non-Gnostic citation may be mentioned here as well. It is
what amounts almost to a formula of awakening from the sleep of
forgetfulness or death, found in deutero-Paul's letter to the Ephesians
where it is quoted anonymously: "Wake up from your sleep, rise from
the dead, and Christ will shine on you" (Ep 5:14).

We find in the letter sent to the prince the curious fact that the letter--
in the role of the messenger or savior--duplicates the role of the Prince,
who was himself the messenger. He is the savior of the lost pearl (also
asleep within the prison of the world, as the clam is the prison of the
pearl within it, sunken and buried at the bottom of the sea). We shall
return to this paradox presently when the hero returns home.

When it landed by the sleeping prince's side the letter "became
entirely speech" and wakens him:

> And at the sound and sight of it I started up from sleep, took it, kissed
> it tenderly, and read. And it had written in it just what was written
> down in my heart. And immediately I remembered that I was a son
> of kings, and my freedom longed for its kind. And I remembered also
> the pearl for which I had been dispatched to Egypt (ATh 111, in F I,
> p. 357).

The narrative moves quickly now; within two quick sentences the prince disposes of the dragon, regains the pearl, and begins his journey home:

> I began to charm the terrible dragon with spells and put him to sleep by uttering the name of my father, the names of our second [son] and of my mother, the queen of the East. I stole the pearl, took it away, and . . . [began the return] to my parents (ibid.).

The charms and spells, barely mentioned here, are given much more elaboration in other texts, depicting the soul's overcoming of the powers of darkness. The soul's power is inherent in what it is; i.e., light can always shine away darkness, if the light is allowed to be what it is. Recalling one's true identity (awakening to the call of truth) is a psychological experience which is here mythologically depicted. Stated another way, the Light is literally poison to the Darkness (as darkness disappears when in the presence of light), just as the darkness can be a poison to the light, acting as a soporific and agent of amnesia. We have already seen, for example, that the prince fell into a deep sleep when he tasted the Egyptians' food, and that the Manichean Primal Man--a being of Light--gave himself and his five Sons as a sacrifice to the devouring Darkness, thereby poisoning him.

This sacrifice of the savior-figure, giving himself to the power of darkness in order to vanquish it--is a soteriological theme common to most mythologies, and obviously it found its way into the mythology of the early Church wherein Jesus descended into the bowels of hell to free the trapped souls and defeat the evil powers. The connection between the Christian borrowing of this motif with older, less sophisticated forms is seen when we consider again "The Odes of Solomon," from the forty-second:

> Sheol [hell] saw me and was made miserable:
> Death cast me up and many along with me.
> I had gall and bitterness, and I went down with him to
> the utmost of his depth:
> And the feet and the head he let go, for they were not
> able to endure my face. (*Eden*, p. 140)

In the Mandeans we find another and more primitive rendering of this same mythological idea. Hibil, the savior-god, describes his rather harrowing descent into the hell. Here, interestingly enough, the descent occurs *before* the creation of the world; the theme of sacrificial redemption of the savior, however, remains clear. Hibil confronts Krun, lord of the underworld, who speaks to the Messenger of Light:

> "Be off with you before I swallow you!" When he thus spoke to me,

273

> I Hibil-Ziwa stood fast girt about with the array of swords, sabres, spears, knives, and blades, and I said to him: "Swallow me!" Then he said: "Now I will swallow you," and he swallowed me up to the middle. Then he spewed me up and brought me forth. He spat venom from his mouth: his intestines, liver, and kidneys were cut off. He cried: "What shall I do to the man who came to me, whom the Life sent?" Then he spoke and addressed me: "You are giants and we are weaklings, you are gods and we are men, you are mighty and we are puny" (GR V.1, in F II, p. 216).

Returning again to our prince, he continues his journey home:

> ... at once I directed my course towards the light of the homeland in the East. And I found on the way [the letter] that had roused me. And this, just as it had by its sound raised me up when I slept, also showed the way by the light [shining] from it ... (ATh 111, in F I, p. 357).

We find the same ideas expressed in the thirty-eighth Ode of Solomon where, however, the letter as the hero's guide is replaced by Truth:

> I went up to the light of truth as if into a chariot:
> And the Truth took me and led me: and carried me across
>   pits and gulleys; and from the rocks and the waves it
>   preserved me:
> And it became to me a haven of Salvation: and set me on
>   the arms of immortal life. (*Eden*, p. 137)

We have seen in the Mandean literature how the Life greets the returning soul (mana), and now we find another Mandean description of the soul's return, even using the word "pearl" at one point:

> Go, soul, in victory to the place from which you were transplanted. ... The soul has loosened its chain and broken its fetters. It shed its bodily coat, then it turned about, saw it, and shuddered. The call of the soul is the call of life which departs from the body of refuse [the stinking body]. ... Come in peace, you pure pearl, who were brought from the Treasure of Life. ... The soul flies and proceeds thither, until it reached the gate of the House of Life. ... the escort comes to meet it. He bears ... a garment in both his arms. "Bestir yourself, soul, put on your garment. ... Rise up, go to the skina. ... The Life stretched out his hand, and joined in communion with it, just as the elect join in communion in the Place of Light" (GL III.5,6, in F II, pp. 262f).

This meeting of the returning soul with its Self finds perhaps its finest and most profound expression in "The Hymn of the Pearl," where the Prince's Self is symbolized by his garment, which he puts on when he returns to Heaven. This interesting detail, as well as illustrating an important Gnostic theme, has important implications for this study. It parallels the central teaching of *A Course in Miracles* that the seemingly fragmented parts of the Sonship re-unite, thus returning to their awareness the inherent unity of Christ. The Course reinterprets the traditional Christian concept of the Second Coming to denote this process. We quote from the final portion of the Hymn now, and will return to it in Part III.

> My parents sent me by their treasurers my shining suit and my long robe. And I did not remember any more my brightness. For when I was still a child and quite young I had left it behind in my father's palaces. And suddenly I saw the suit which resembled me as it were in a mirror, and I spied my whole self in it, and I knew and saw myself through it; for we were partially separated from each other, though we were from the same, and again we are one through one form. ... they [the royal treasurers] gave me precious things, the gorgeous suit which had been skillfully worked in bright colors with gold and precious stones and pearls of brilliant hues.... And the image of the king of kings was fully present through the whole suit.... I heard it speak: "I am the property of him who is bravest of all men, for whose sake I was engraved by the father himself." And I myself noticed my stature, which increased in accordance with its impulse. It made haste, straining towards him who should take it from his hand. And love roused me to rush to meet him and receive it. And I reached out, adorned myself with the beauty of its colors, and drew my brilliant garment entirely over me.
>
> But when I had put it on I was lifted up to the gate of acknowledgment and worship. And I bowed my head and acknowledged the radiance of the father who had sent this to me; for I had done what had been commanded, and he likewise, what he had promised. And in the gates of the palace I mingled with those of his dominion.... And he promised me that I would also be sent with him to the gates of the king, so that with my gifts and my pearl I might together with him appear before the king (ATh 112-113, in F I, pp. 357f).

In a Mandean text we read: "I go to meet my image and my image comes to meet me: it caresses and embraces me as if I were returning from captivity" (quoted in Jonas, p. 122).

Jonas has traced this doctrine of the Self reuniting with its split-off self to Zoroastrian times, where the Avesta, part of the Zoroastrian canon, states that the departed soul of a believer is confronted by the Self ("religious conscience"), who responds to its question of her identity:

> I am, O youth of good thoughts, good words, good deeds, good conscience, none other than thine own personal conscience.... Thou

hast loved me . . . in this sublimity, goodness, beauty . . . in which I
now appear unto thee (quoted in Jonas, p. 122).

We have already seen the Persian influence on Manicheism, and it is
present here as well. The Manichean soul returns to its home after
death and is met by a garment, among other things, and "the virgin
like unto the soul of the truthful one" (quoted by Jonas, p. 122). In the
language of *A Course in Miracles* the joining of the soul with its Self
corresponds to the return of the self to the home it never truly left; the
union of what never was truly separated. One also finds a similar idea
in the Course when it describes the creations of Christ--part of the Self--
rushing to meet the returning self (text, p. 76).

This reunion of self with Self is the culmination of salvation, presup-
posing the idea that what has to be saved, or better, corrected, is this
splitting off, or separation. In many Gnostic texts, as we shall presently
see, there is a double or twin brother in heaven who awaits the return
of the one who has been dispatched to earth in the role of savior. In one
Mandean text it is stated of the savior who descends that "his image is
kept safe in its place [i.e., above]" (in Jonas, p. 122). In what Jonas has
referred to as the reversal of the situation in Oscar Wilde's *The Picture
of Dorian Gray*, the Self that has remained grows, is made perfect and
full as the self completes its tasks below.

In the Hymn there is a brother to the prince who remains with his
parents, and who is to claim joint inheritance of the King's house--
"with your brother, our second, become an heir in our kingdom" (ATh
108, in F I, p. 356). Interestingly enough the brother is no longer
mentioned upon the prince's return. As Jonas has discussed, this is
because his identity has become fused with the garment, with which
the prince himself becomes one.

One of the common Gnostic terms is "rest," which signifies the end
of the ascent. It is a term found frequently in *A Course in Miracles* as
well, as we shall see in Chapter 15. The "rest" is the goal of every
Gnostic's journey, the yearned-for end of the stressful sojourn in the
wretched body. In the vision of the Last Judgment in "The Concept of
Our Great Power" we read:

Then the souls will appear, who are holy through the light of the
Power, who is exalted above all powers....And they all have become
as reflections in his light. They all have shone, and they have found
rest in his rest (Conc. Great Power VI.47.9-26, in *NHL*, p. 289).

In the "Acts of Thomas" the apostle exclaims: "Behold, I become
carefree and unpained, dwelling in rest!" and he exhorts some of the
faithful: "Be thou their rest in a land of the weary" (ATh 142,156, in
NTA II, pp. 518,525). And finally in "The Gospel of the Hebrews" we

read of the baptism of Jesus in the Jordan, where the Holy Spirit rests upon him and the Lord hears:

> My Son, in all the prophets was I waiting for thee that thou shouldest come and I might rest in thee. For thou art my rest... (GH Fragment 2, in *NTA* I, p. 164).

The "rest" has a different meaning from that found in the Bible, for here it has an eschatological connotation; i.e., the final union of the Spirit of God with Jesus. Thus the coming of Christ in Jesus, "resting upon him," ushers in the End Times. The "rest" is the end-product of salvation, as seen in the continuation of this quotation from the Gospel:

> He that seeks will not rest until he finds; and he that has found shall marvel; and he that has marvelled shall reign; and he that has reigned shall rest (ibid., Frag. 4b).

We turn our attention now to the End Times, the collective conclusion of the journey.

Eschatology: Gnosticism

Eschatology during the early Christian period is a subject properly deserving book-length treatment, since its influences trace back to the Old Testament and inter-testamental periods. We concern ourselves here only with the specific Gnostic elements as they emerged in the early Christian centuries.

As is the case with the general apocalyptic literature, we find in Gnostic eschatology the strong influence of Persian dualism. The Gnostic contrasts the divine spiritual world of the Pleroma with the material world of the present age. The former is eternal and becomes realized as the latter disappears. Thus no hope is possible within the current world, which is the home of the demonic elements that seek to keep us from God. Unlike the traditional Jewish vision of the End, the late-biblical, post-biblical, and Gnostic apocalyptic eschatologies do not convert or transform the current age into a "New Jerusalem": The world's moral regeneration cannot be healed or fulfilled; only destroyed in the final conflagration. Thus, as we have already seen, the Gnostic is no longer concerned with history, let alone God's activity in it, for the only importance is the truth of eternity and its immanent realization in the Gnostic.

First we consider the "Megale Apophasis" ("Great Proclamation"), dating from the second century and attributed to Simon Magus. It is known only by the excerpts found in Hippolytus, which we summarize here. Within every person, the "Megale" teaches, is found a "potential" divine power which is infinite. It is "him that stands, took his stand, and will stand." The author equates it with the spirit of God that hovered over the deep at the creation of the world in Genesis, and is analogous to the Middle Platonic Logos that created the world. It is

> the spirit who contains all things in himself, the image of the infinite power ... an image of an incorruptible form, which alone gives order to all things (*Ref.* VI.14.4, in F I, p. 255).

It is this power that, if it is not fully actualized at death, becomes like a tree bearing no fruit and which is then cut down and burned in the fire:

> ... if he remain only as a potentiality ... and be not fully formed, then he disappears and is lost ... and just as if it never existed, it perishes with the man at his death .... [and] will perish with the world (ibid., 12.4, p. 254).

If, however, it is realized and fully formed, it

> comes into being from an indivisible point ... then what is little will become great; but this great thing will become the infinite and unalterable Aeon, which no longer enters into becoming. ... [Like] perfect fruit fully formed ... resembling the unoriginate and infinite power (ibid., 14.6, 16.5, pp. 256, 258).

This "blessed and incorruptible being" is within all of us, yet must be developed in the course of one's life. It is the spark of light we have seen described in other Gnostic systems.

We turn now to the Nag Hammadi texts to see how these authors view the nature of the soul's final redemption. As a general statement to introduce this section we begin with the Valentinian "Tripartite Tractate," which discusses the commonly expressed Gnostic theme of the redemption of the three types of people: spiritual, psychic, and material. The spiritual obviously need no salvation; the material are beyond redemption; while the psychic become the focus of redemptive efforts. We find here, of course, the inevitable ego projection of its own internal split onto the world: the good are rewarded, the bad are punished. Be it ever thus.

> The spiritual race will receive complete salvation in every way. The material will receive destruction in every way, just as one who resists him. The psychic race, since it is in the middle when it is brought forth and also when it is established, is double in its determination for both

278

good and evil.... Those... who are from the thought of lust for power ... they will receive their end suddenly. Those who will be brought forth from the lust for power... they will receive the reward for their humility, which is to remain forever. Those, however, who are proud because of the desire for ambition, and who love temporary glory. .. they will receive judgment for their ignorance and their senselessness... they will be judged for their wickedness.... the perfect man received knowledge immediately so as to return in haste to his unitary state, to the place from which he came.... [The psychics], however, needed a place of instruction... until all the members of the body of the church are in a single place and receive the restoration at one time, when they have been manifested as the sound body--the restoration is the Pleroma.... [coming] at the end, after the Totality reveals what it is ... (Tri. Tract. I.119.16-24; 120.15-121.10; 123.4-30, in *NHL*, pp. 89-91).

In "The Apocryphon of John," that important text considered earlier, we find a similar description of groups:

And I said to the savior, "Lord, will all the souls then be brought safely into the pure light?" He answered and said to me, "Great things have arisen in your mind, for it is difficult to explain them to others except to those who are from the immovable race. Those on whom the Spirit of life will descend and with whom he will be with the power, they will be saved and become perfect and be worthy of the greatnesses and be purified in that place from all wickedness and the involvements in evil ...." I said to him, "Lord, the souls of those who did not do these works, but on whom the power and Spirit of life descended, will they be rejected?" He answered and said to me, "If the Spirit descended upon them, they will in any case be saved and they will change for the better.... no one can lead it astray with words of evil. But those on whom the opposing spirit descends are drawn by him and they go astray" (ApocryJohn II.25.16-28; 26.7-23, in *NHL*, p. 113).

The Savior is then asked where the souls go of those who are saved and those who are yet to be saved:

The soul in which the power will become superior to the despicable ["counterfeit" in other translations] spirit... she is taken up to the rest of the aeons.... [Those in whom] the despicable spirit has gained strength ... [are cast] down into forgetfulness. And after she comes out of the body, she is handed over to the authorities... they bind her with chains and cast her into prison... until she is liberated from the forgetfulness and acquires knowledge (ibid., 26.26-32; 26.36-27.10).

As for those "who have turned away, where will their souls go?"

To that place where the angels of poverty go they will be taken, the place where there is no repentance. And they will be kept for the day on which those who have blasphemed the spirit will be tortured, and they will be punished with eternal punishment (ibid., 27.24-30, p. 114, in *NHL*, pp. 112-14).

The third-century Valentinian "Gospel of Philip" compares undoing the source of wickedness with ending a tree's life by exposing its root, teaching that it is only by exposing the root of wickedness (i.e., ignorance) that it will disappear:

For so long as the root of wickedness is hidden, it is strong. But when it is recognized it is dissolved. When it is revealed it perishes (GPh II.83.8-10, in *NHL*, p. 149).

On a psychological level we understand this to mean that the problem is not the root itself, but the concealment of it. When we undo the repression and expose the problem to the light of truth it simply disappears. As *A Course in Miracles* advocates, we bring the darkness to the light, illusions to the truth. The Gnostic would bring the ignorance to knowledge:

Jesus pulled out the root of the whole place, while others did it only partially. As for ourselves, let each one of us dig down after the root of evil which is within one, and let one pluck it out of one's heart from the root. It will be plucked out if we recognize it. But if we are ignorant of it, it takes root in us and produces its fruit in our heart. It masters us. We are its slaves. It takes us captive, to make us do what we do not want; and what we do want we do not do [*see* Romans 7:18-23]. *It is powerful because we have not recognized it.* While it exists it is active. Ignorance is the mother of all evil. Ignorance will eventuate in death, because those that come from ignorance neither were nor are nor shall be. But those who are in the truth will be perfect when all the truth is revealed. For truth is like ignorance: while it is hidden it rests in itself, but when it is revealed and is recognized, it is praised inasmuch as it is stronger than ignorance and error. It gives freedom. ... Ignorance is a slave. Knowledge is freedom ... (ibid., 83.16-84.11, pp. 149f, my italics).

"On the Origin of the World" provides this eschatological vision:

Before the consummation of the aeon [world], the whole place will be shaken by a great thunder. Then the rulers will lament, crying out on account of their death [as will angels, demons and other men]. ... Its kings will be drunk from the flaming sword and they will make war against one another, so that the earth will be drunk from the blood which is poured out (Orig. Wld. II.125.32-126.9, in *NHL*, p. 178).

The great cosmic disruption continues, in typical fashion, with the darkening of the sun and moon, the upheavals of the seas, stars, etc. Sophia then

> puts on a senseless wrath ... [and] will drive out the gods of Chaos whom she had created together with the First Father [Ialdabaoth]. She will cast them down to the abyss. They will be wiped out by their own injustice (ibid., 125.19-24).

The angry and obviously insane Demiurge first destroys the gods, and then himself:

> ... their heavens will fall upon one another and their powers will burn.... And his [the First Father's] heaven will fall and it will split in two.... They will fall down to the abyss and the abyss will be over-thrown (ibid., 126.29-35, p. 179).

The darkness of the deficiency is now totally undone:

> The light will cover the darkness, and it will wipe it out. It will become like one which had not come into being. And the work which the darkness followed will be dissolved. And the deficiency will be plucked out at its root and thrown down to the darkness. And the light will withdraw up to its root. And the glory of the unbegotten will appear, and it will fill all of the aeons, when the prophetic utterance and the report of those who are kings are revealed and are fulfilled by those who are called perfect [i.e., the Gnostics] (ibid., 126.35-127.10).

There remains, however, a form of divine justice: each one must reap the fruits of his or her own choices:

> Those who were not perfected in the unbegotten Father will receive their glories ... in the kingdoms of immortals. But they will not ever enter the kingless realm.
> For it is necessary that every one enter the place from whence he came. For each one by his deed and his knowledge will reveal his nature (ibid., 127.10-17).

The Hermetic "Asclepius" consists of a dialogue between the mystagogue (spiritual master) Hermes Trismegistus and his disciple Asclepius. It is a mixed document, yet shows decidedly Gnostic characteristics in the salvific power granted to knowledge and, as we see here, in its views on death. It vividly depicts the punishment of those who remain rooted in ignorance and evil.

And this is death: the dissolution of the body and the destruction of the sensation of the body. And it is not necessary to be afraid of this. ...Now, when the soul comes forth from the body, it is necessary that it meet . . . [a great] demon [i.e., a judge appointed by God]. Immediately he (the demon) will surround this one, and he will examine him in regard to the character that he has developed in his life. . . . [If the soul] brought his life into evil deeds, he grasps him ...and throws him down so that he is suspended between heaven and earth and is punished with a great punishment. And he will be deprived of his hope . . . put in the places of the demons, which are filled with pain, and which are always filled with blood and slaughter. And ...[his] food is weeping, mourning, and groaning ...(Ascl. VI.76.13-17; 76.28-77.10; 78.26-31, in *NHL*, pp. 305-307).

In the Manichean eschatology, when the great cosmic fire has purged all the good souls and their light is purified of the darkness, the remaining unpurified light together with the darkness are assembled into what is called the "mass" or "lump." This heap of darkness is sealed forever and can nevermore be a threat to the Kingdom of Light, invading it as occurred at the Beginning. These recalcitrant souls, assigned to "this terrible 'mass' of darkness," now must pay the price of

> their own misdeeds, because they made no effort to understand these teachings concerning the future, and when they were granted time to do so, distanced themselves from it (Evodius, *de fide contra Manichaeos*, in Haardt, p. 301).

These souls are inherently good, but were unable to "be cleansed of their contact with the vile nature" (Augustine, *de haer*. 46.6, in Haardt, p. 349).

In the *Kephalaia*, Mani speaks of this End time in three stages, where the fallen souls and demons of the dark receive three hard blows. In the first of these the Darkness is defeated by the Living Soul and separated from the Land of Darkness. Next comes the "great Fire" where the Darkness is "dissolved and melted away ... destroyed and annihilated." Finally the male and female members of the Darkness are separated out, one chained to the mass, the other cast into the grave:

> In this manner the Enemy shall be bound, in heavy and painful bondage, from which there is no way out, ever, but they have succeeded in binding him and have bound him in eternity, they have succeeded in separating him off and have separated him off for eternity (*Kephalaia* 41, in Haardt, p. 326).

Thus the world of matter (the *Hyle*) is consumed, leaving only the now protected Kingdom of Light and the eternally chained Darkness. Augustine has described this same Manichean process, allowing us to see even more clearly how the mass came to symbolize the projection of unconscious guilt.

[They say that] the substance of evil shall be separated from us and imprisoned in a lump when the end of the world has come following the universal fire, and it shall live as in an eternal prison (Augustine, *de haer.* 46, in Haardt, p. 349).

In the Mandean literature we find ample examples of the Last Judgment, in which the good are rewarded and the evil are destroyed in horror. In one powerful passage, Manda dHaiye addresses a soul who has obviously been led astray by fascination with worldly treasures, contaminated by the evil of the world:

O soul! When I cried to you, you gave me no answer, now, when you cry, who shall give you an answer? Because you loved gold and silver, you will be locked up in the innermost Sheol. Because you loved dreams and phantoms, you will sink into the cauldron, as it seethes (GL III.57, in F II, p. 272).

The soul, however, is given a second chance, but if it fails, its "eyes will not see the light."

The body, as we have seen, is hated and despised by the Mandeans, and any attraction to it is sufficient to condemn the soul forever. At Adam's death the Messenger comes by his bed and awakens him from his sleep:

Arise... throw off this stinking body, the clay coat in which you lived. Cast off the bodily coat, the rotting body ... and smite the Seven and the Twelve, the men who created it, on the head. ... Set your course to the Place of Light, the place where you once lived. ... In the House of Life there is no body, and the body does not ascend to the House of Life (GL I.2,12 in F II, p. 274).

Having left the body, the soul then ascends, a process we have already considered. The end of the world is then described in this way:

Then all generations will come to an end, and all creatures will pass away. All fountains and oceans will dry up, and canals and rivers will run dry. The mountains and hills will split asunder, fall, and cave in. ... The Tibil [the earth] will be destroyed for ever, and the works of the House will be razed to the ground. The wheels of heaven will fall into disorder, the chains of the dark, unlit earth will be torn apart.

283

When ... the spirit of the Seven meets its end, the form of the Twelve will be ruined, which persecuted this family of life. ... Then Yosamin, Abathur, and Ptahil [three fallen beings of light] come and see this world. Groaning seizes their heart, and they strike themselves on their breast. They behold the container of souls, which lies completely degraded on the ground. On that great day of judgment sentence will be pronounced on [them]. Then Hibil-Ziwa [the Redeemer] comes and lifts them from this world (GR XV.3, in F II, pp. 274-76).

The soul is thus returned to its world of Light.

Eschatology: Traditional Christianity and Origen

The traditional Christian eschatology is remarkably similar to the Gnostic. As it is generally more than familiar to most readers it will not be discussed at length. Its general theme is the reward of the just in heaven and the corresponding punishment of the wicked in hell, and its most famous expression is the parable of "The Last Judgment" in Matthew 25:

When the Son of Man comes in his glory ... he will take his seat on his throne of glory. All the nations will be assembled before him and he will separate men one from another as the shepherd separates sheep from goats. He will place the sheep on his right hand and the goats on his left. Then the King will say to those on his right hand, "Come, you whom my Father has blessed, take for your heritage the kingdom prepared for you since the foundation of the world ...." Next he will say to those on his left hand, "Go away from me, with your curse upon you, to the eternal fire prepared for the devil and his angels ...." And they will go away to eternal punishment, and the virtuous to eternal life (Mt 25:31-46).

In sharp contrast to this harshness is Origen's totally benign view. We have already seen that while Origen does speak of a Last Judgment, his concept has no place for a final condemnation or conflagration in which the evil sinners are destroyed. Rather the End is the culmination of the soul's education, its final graduation as it were. It is the return of the wandering souls to their original status as rational beings, but on a higher level so that a future fall is impossible. There are passages in Origen that suggest that at this End, God remains the teacher and the rational beings continue to learn. This learning appears commensurate with the degree to which each being had fallen at the Beginning. However, there is no question at this point of a failure to learn. In a sense, there can be only an ongoing perfectibility of perfection, in which the concept of a permanent hell does not exist.

Thus what appears to the world as retribution or punishment is really to Origen educational. Regardless of how low a soul may have fallen, there is always the potential (and ultimately the inevitability) of returning. There is no limit on the power of God's love to recall His creations, in the words of St. Paul that Origen was fond of quoting: "So that God may be all in all" (1 Co 15:28). Thus, in principle, the devil, the fallen angel, will also return to the unity and perfection of Heaven, along with all rational beings. St. Paul's "destruction" of the last enemy (death or the devil) is understood by Origen not as a material destruction, but rather as the undoing of the *purpose* for which the material was wrongly used:

> ...not that its substance which was made by God shall perish, but that the hostile purpose and will which proceeded not from God but from itself will come to an end. It will be destroyed, therefore, not in the sense of ceasing to exist, but of being no longer an enemy and no longer death (*First Princ.* III.6.5).

One could well imagine that this was a teaching upon which the orthodox Church did not look kindly. St. Jerome sarcastically states that Origen taught

> after many ages and the one restoration of all things Gabriel will be in the same state as the devil, Paul as Caiaphas and virgins as prostitutes (St. Jerome in *First Princ.* p. 57, n.1).

The Second Council of Constantinople, convened by the emperor Justinian in the sixth century to combat heresies, issued the following anathemas (literally: curses; i.e., a series of heretical charges) which clearly point to Origen:

> That the heavenly powers and all men and the devil and spiritual hosts of wickedness are as unchangeably united to the Word of God as the Mind itself which is by them called Christ. . . . That all rational creatures will form one unity, hypostases and numbers alike being destroyed when bodies are destroyed. . . . That the life of spirits will be the same as it formerly was, when they had not yet descended or fallen, so that the beginning is the same as the end, and the end is the measure of the beginning (in *First Princ.*, p. 250, n.3).

Bodies as we know them will fall away gradually as the ascent progresses, until they become totally spiritualized in a process Origen can only speculate about. As negative as he feels about the body, and despite his assertion elsewhere that rational beings are incorporeal in their pre-fall essence, Origen still cannot conceive

> how beings so numerous and mighty can exist and live their life without bodies; since we believe that to exist without material substance and apart from any association with a bodily element is a thing that belongs only to the nature of ... the Father, the Son and the Holy Spirit. Perhaps ... in the end every bodily substance will be so pure and refined that we must think of it as being like the ether, as it were of a heavenly purity and clearness (ibid., I.6.4).

Origen of course is referring to St. Paul's spiritual body (1 Co 15:44). It is in effect the same body as before, but

> having cast off the weaknesses of its present existence . . . [and] transformed into a thing of glory . . . with the result that what was a vessel of dishonor shall itself be purified and become a vessel of honor and a habitation of blessedness (*First Princ.*, III.6.6).

Origen had no illusions about the great span of time in which such return would occur. Thus he posited successive worlds (preceding as well as following our own) in the manner of grades in a school, in which the souls could achieve their education and ultimately "graduate." The end of the world, therefore, far from being the final judgment foreseen in the twenty-fifth chapter of Matthew, marked for Origen the consummation of the ascent of the soul, the time

> when every soul shall be visited with the penalties due for its sins. . . . when everyone shall pay what he owes. . . . even his [God's] enemies being conquered and subdued. . . . It is the same subjection by which we too desire to be subjected to him, and by which the apostles and all the saints who have followed Christ were subject to him. . . . [And] so from one beginning arise many differences and varieties, which in their turn are restored, through God's goodness, through their subjection to Christ and their unity with the Holy Spirit, to one end, which is like the beginning (ibid., I.6.1,2).

The "outer darkness" spoken of in Jesus' warning about the Jews (Mt 8:12) is also given a more benevolent, if not partially Gnostic interpretation, focusing on the psychological rather than material reality. It is

> not to be understood as a place with a murky atmosphere and no light at all, but rather as a description of those who through their immersion in the darkness of deep ignorance have become separated from every gleam of reason and intelligence (ibid., II.10.3).

Thus these ignorant ones would take on heavier and murkier garments, reflecting the "gloom of ignorance," until they complete their learning in other worlds. Once again, Origen explicitly denies an everlasting punishment:

> There is a resurrection of the dead, and there is punishment, but not everlasting. For when the body is punished the soul is gradually purified, and so is restored to its ancient rank.... For all wicked men, and for demons, too, punishment has an end, and both ... shall be restored to their former rank (ibid., II.10.3).

Evil is banished, for all that remains is God and thoughts that are like God:

> The mind will no longer be conscious of anything besides...God, but will think God and see God and hold God and God will be the mode and measure of its every movement; and in this way God will be all to it. For there will no longer be any contrast of good and evil, since evil nowhere exists.... all consciousness of evil has departed and given place to what is sincere and pure ... (ibid., II.6.3).

Spiritual Specialness: Gnosticism

It is obvious from the foregoing material that Gnostic and orthodox Christians alike, whether implicit or explicit, shared the belief that their group was ontologically better than others. Indeed, there can be no more insidious nor contradictory characteristic of religious groups than the belief that they are somehow "special"--i.e., better, holier, more beloved of God than other groups. The paradox of such belief in a movement that purports to be rooted in God and His revelation is obvious, when one recalls the unity that *is* the condition of the creation of Christ. It is but another example of what *A Course in Miracles* refers to as the attempt to reconcile the irreconcilable, and unite mutually exclusive ideas.

If one can point to a common element in all religious forms and institutions that has contributed to their descent from an authentic spirituality, it would be this belief in specialness. In our Western tradition we see it from the beginning, and it has continued to the present day. In this next section, we shall primarily consider its expression in Gnosticism, reserving for Part III a discussion of the spiritual specialness arising within students of *A Course in Miracles*. We begin, however, with the first-century Christian teaching and, as this cannot be understood apart from its historical roots, we make brief mention of Judaism, where the concept of the "chosen people" finds a prominent place.

While it is true that this notion of "chosenness" can be interpreted in ways other than the obvious, it nonetheless remains as a concept of separation that is based upon a spiritual arrogance that places oneself and one's group somehow closer to the Creator than others, a conclusion reached only by interpretations of data mediated through the narrow eyes (and mind) of one's personal and special universe. This "chosenness" was taken over by Christianity, which unabashedly saw itself as the heir to the throne of the beloved people, the throne vacated by the recalcitrant Jews. St. Paul provided the foundation for this belief in his famous image of the olive tree and its branches, written to the Romans:

> . . . have the Jews fallen for ever, or have they just stumbled? Obviously they have not fallen for ever: their fall, though, has saved the pagans in a way the Jews may now well emulate. . . . all the branches are holy if the root is holy. No doubt some of the branches [the Jews] have been cut off, and, like shoots of wild olive you [non-Jewish Roman Christians] have been grafted among the rest to share with them the rich sap provided by the olive tree itself . . . (Rm 11:11,16f).

They--first the Jews who accepted Jesus as the promised Messiah, joined later with the Gentiles--were now God's chosen, witnessed to by their confession of faith in the risen Lord Jesus. This group, as we have seen, became more rigorously (if not rigidly) defined as the decades and centuries passed, and emerged as a narrowing exclusive Church which self-righteously proclaimed itself as the true heir to Jesus and the apostles. A small hierarchy defined this Church and became the arbiter of those who belonged within its special circle and those who did not. Moreover, without this Church, the hierarchy claimed, salvation was impossible.

The Gnostic Christians were excluded from this circle and so, in true ego fashion, set up their own criteria for membership in the eschatological circles of the saved and the damned. This membership, considered previously, was born out of the Gnostics' own sense of spiritual specialness. They believed that they were the special recipients of *gnosis*, which set them apart from the rest of humanity who clearly were not as privileged. In the Christian forms of Gnosticism, our principal interest in this book, this specialness obviously was meant, at least in part, as a defensive position against the specialness of the more orthodox Church. Thus in many of the following excerpts we find the Gnostics proclaiming themselves to be chosen by God, as opposed to the orthodox, to fulfill the special mission of bringing the light of truth to the world of darkness.

"The Apocryphon of James" is a revelation dialogue between the resurrected Jesus and James and Peter. It was probably composed in the third century or slightly earlier. As in all such texts, including some of the later books of the New Testament, the authors seek to derive legitimacy from identification with the apostles. Furthermore, the recipients of the document are singled out as having been specially chosen. Thus, we find this statement:

> Since you asked that I [James] send you a secret book [apocryphon] which was revealed to me and Peter by the Lord, I could not turn you away or gainsay you; but I . . . sent it to you, and you alone. But since you are a minister of the salvation of the saints . . . take care not to rehearse this text to many--this that the Savior did not wish to tell to all of us, his twelve disciples (ApocryJs I.1.9-25, in *NHL*, p. 30).

The tractate closes after the ascension of Jesus in a "chariot of spirit." James and Peter, the chosen disciples, experience the beatific vision and are called back by the other disciples, who wish to know the content of the revelation from the Master:

> He has ascended, and he has given us [James and Peter] a pledge and promised life to us all and revealed to us children who are to come after us . . . as we would be saved for their sakes (ibid., I.15.35-16.1, p. 36).

In order to appease the "resentment" of the other disciples, James sends them out to different cities, while he reserves Jerusalem for himself:

> And I pray that the beginning may come from you [the readers of this text], for thus I shall be capable of salvation, since they will be enlightened through me, by my faith (ibid., I.16.12-16).

In "The Gospel of Truth" we find the theme of Gnostic specialness in the context of what seems to be a doctrine of predestination:

> Since the perfection of the all is in the Father and it is necessary for the all to ascend to him and for each one to receive what are his own, he enrolled them in advance, having prepared them to give to those who came forth from him.
> Those whose name he knew in advance were called at the end, so that one who has knowledge is the one whose name the Father has uttered. For he whose name has not been spoken is ignorant. . . . Therefore, if one has knowledge, he is from above. If he is called, he hears, he answers, and he turns to him who is calling him, and ascends to him. . . . Having knowledge, he does the will of the one who called him, he wishes to be pleasing to him, he receives rest (GT I.21.8-22.12, in *NHL*, p. 40).

These Valentinian Gnostics are thus urged to

> speak of the truth with those who search for it, and of knowledge to those who have committed sin in their error. Make firm the foot of those who have stumbled and stretch out your hands to those who are ill.... For you are the understanding that is drawn forth. If strength acts thus, it becomes even stronger. Be concerned with yourselves; do not be concerned with other things which you have rejected from yourselves.... Do not strengthen those who are obstacles to you who are collapsing as though you were a support for them. For the unjust one is someone to treat ill rather than the just one.... So you, do the will of the Father, for you are from him (ibid., I.32.35-33.32, pp. 44f).

The Gnostic recipients of the revelations of "The Hypostasis of the Archons" are told that they are protected from the evil power of the "Authorities" (i.e., the archons):

> You, together with your offspring, are from the Primeval Father; from Above, out of the imperishable Light, their souls are come. Thus the Authorities cannot approach them because of the Spirit of Truth present within them; and all who have become acquainted with this Way exist deathless in the midst of dying Mankind (Hypos. Arch. II.96.19-27, in *NHL*, p. 159).

The parallel document, "On the Origin of the World," reveals the same:

> Since the immortal Father knows that a deficiency came into being in the aeons and their worlds out of the truth, therefore when he desired to bring to naught the rulers of destruction by means of their molded bodies, he sent your likenesses, i.e. the blessed little guileless spirits, down to the world of destruction (Orig. Wld. II.124.5-10, in *NHL*, p. 177).

These "guileless spirits"--i.e., the Gnostics--have as their function to "reveal the pattern of indestructibility for a condemnation of the rulers and their powers" (ibid., 124.19-21).

In another tradition, the apostle Thomas is the chosen one by the risen Lord, whose words are recorded by the apostle Matthew, written down as he "was walking, listening to them [Jesus and Thomas] speak with one another."

> Now, since it has been said that you [Thomas] are my twin and true companion, examine yourself that you may understand who you are, in what way you exist, and how you will come to be. Since you are called my brother, it is not fitting that you be ignorant of yourself. And I know that you have understood, because you had already

understood that I am the knowledge of the truth. So while you accompany me, although you are uncomprehending, you have in fact already come to know, and you will be called "the one who knows himself" (Th Cont. II.138.7-16, in *NHL*, p. 189).

To "know oneself" of course means to know one's spiritual self as opposed to the physical. Indeed, as we have seen before, the Thomas tradition is a strongly ascetic one. Thomas responds by asking Jesus to explain to him about the "hidden things," for these truths are "difficult to perform before men." The tractate essentially consists of the teachings given to Thomas that he may share them with the ignorant world. But just as the canonical gospels say of their teachings, the Gnostics believe that the world will not understand their truth, hearing the words as "ridiculous and contemptible." Of these unbelievers the Savior speaks these words of harsh and prophetic judgment:

> I tell you that he who will listen to your word and turn away his face . . . he will be handed over to the Ruler above . . . and he will turn that one around and cast him from heaven down to the abyss, and he will be imprisoned in a narrow dark place. . . . [pursued by] fiery scourges that cast a shower of sparks . . . (ibid., 142.27-143.1, p. 192).

In the Christianized "Sophia of Jesus Christ" we read of the immortal nature of the Gnostics, whose true home is in the Father, unsullied by the grossness of the sexual world of the body:

> Now as for you, whatever is fitting for you to know . . . will be given to them—whoever has been begotten not by the sowing of the unclean rubbing but by the First who was sent, for he is an immortal in the midst of mortal men (Sophia III.93.16-24, in *NHL*, p. 209).

And these immortal ones are to

> shine in the light more than these [the unknowing ones]. . . . [They are to] tread upon their graves, humiliate their malicious intent, and break their yoke, and arouse my own [Jesus']. I have given you authority over all things as sons of light, so that you might tread upon their power with your feet (ibid., 114.7-8; 119.7, pp. 224,228).

Part of the specialness of the Gnostics--especially for the disciples of Jesus--was manifest in their suffering as their Lord suffered. Thus the tradition of martyrdom was not the exclusive domain of the orthodox, as we have already seen. The special holiness of the Gnostics, bestowed upon them by the world of the Pleroma, is also expressed to the Sethian Gnostics in the non-Christian "Apocalypse of Adam." Here Adam reveals to his son Seth what had been revealed to him about his own downfall, how he fell under the power of the creator-god who, among other things, tried to destroy the world with the Great Flood. However,

> those who reflect upon the knowledge of the eternal God in their hearts will not perish (ApocAdam V.76.21-22, in *NHL*, p. 260).

Moreover,

> the generation without a [worldly] king over it says that God chose him from all the aeons. He caused a knowledge of the undefiled one of truth to come to be in him. He said, "Out of a foreign air, from a great aeon, the great illuminator came forth. And he made the generation of those men whom he had chosen for himself shine, so that they should shine upon the whole aeon" (ibid., 82.19-83.3, p. 263).

Meanwhile, the unknowing ones

> will cry out with a great voice, saying, "Blessed is the soul of those men because they have known God with a knowledge of the truth! They shall live forever, because they have not been corrupted by their desire ... they have stood in his presence in a knowledge of God like light that has come forth from fire and blood" (ibid., 83.9-23).

They continue berating themselves, and then are answered by a voice:

> And your thought is not like that of those men [the Gnostics] whom you persecute. ... Their fruit does not wither. But they will be known up to the great aeons, because the words they have kept, of the God of the aeons, were not committed to the book, nor were they written. But angelic beings will bring them, whom all the generations of men will not know (ibid., 84.23-85.9, pp. 263f).

In "The Apocalypse of Peter" the apostle is told by the Savior, "sitting in the temple":

> ... from you I have established a base for the remnant whom I have summoned to knowledge (ApocPt VII.71. 19-21, in *NHL*, p. 340).

The revelation continues with the message of martyrdom that is the fate of the Gnostic disciples of Jesus. Thus the Gnostic Peter is urged:

> Be strong, for you are the one to whom these mysteries have been given, to know them through revelation. ... These things, then, which you saw you shall present to those of another race who are not of this

age. For there will be . . . honor . . . only in those who were chosen from an immortal substance. . . . therefore, be courageous and do not fear at all. For I shall be with you in order that none of your enemies may prevail over you (ibid., 82.18-20; 83.15-24; 84.6-10, pp. 344f).

Derdekeas, the Gnostic redeemer of "The Paraphrase of Shem," says to Shem (Seth), the father of this Gnostic tradition:

You are blessed, Shem, for your race has been protected from the dark wind. . . . O Shem, no one who wears the body will be able to complete these things. But through remembrance he will be able to grasp them. . . . They have been revealed to your race. . . . For none will be able to open the forms of the door except the mind alone who was entrusted with their likeness. . . . they will bear witness to the universal testimony; they will strip off the burden of Darkness; they will put on the Word of the Light. . . . For every power of light and fire will be completed by me because of you. For without you they will not be revealed until you speak them openly (Para. Shem VII.34.16-32; 42.18-31; 48.32-49.2, in *NHL*, pp. 323,326,328).

Part of the Church Fathers' denunciations of the Gnostics centered on this self-perception of specialness. In the group Hippolytus called the Docetists we find similar sentiments. Speaking of the thirty forms put on by Jesus after his resurrection, corresponding to the thirty aeons in the Valentinian Pleroma, Hippolytus presents the Docetists' claims that only they can know the *full* Savior:

But from each of the thirty Aeons all the forms are held fast here below as souls, and each of them possesses a nature so as to know Jesus who is according to their nature. . . . Now those who derive from their nature from the places below cannot see the forms of the Savior that are above them, but those who derive from above . . . these men understand Jesus the Savior not in part but in full, and they alone are the perfect ones from above: but all the rest understand him only in part (*Ref.* VIII.10.9-11, in F I, pp. 311f).

Of Carpocrates and his disciples, Irenaeus, certainly not an objective witness, writes:

They say that the soul of Jesus was lawfully nurtured in the traditions of the Jews, but despised them and thereby obtained powers by which he vanquished the passions which attach to men for punishment. The soul which like the soul of Jesus is able to despise the creator archons likewise receives power to do the same things. Hence they have come to such presumption that some say they are like Jesus, and actually affirm that they are even stronger than he, and some declare that they are superior to his disciples, like Peter and Paul and

the other Apostles; they are in no way inferior to Jesus himself . . .
(*Adv. haer.* I.25.1, in F I, p. 36).

According to Irenaeus, the "Valentinians" claimed to be perfect:

> . . . it is impossible that the spiritual--and by that they mean them-
> selves--should succumb to decay, regardless of what kind of actions
> it performs. . . . For it is not conduct that leads to the Pleroma, but the
> seed, sent forth from there in an immature state, but brought to
> perfection here (ibid., I.1.6.2, p. 139).

These perfect ones, of course, favorably compare themselves to the rest
of humanity who either remain forever outside of salvation, or else,
like the bishops of the Church, must labor to attain it. Against the
disciples of the Valentinian Marcus, who also passed themselves off as
perfect, Irenaeus levels the following charge, part of which was
already quoted in Chapter 3:

> . . . as if none could equal the extent of their knowledge, not even if
> you were to mention Paul or Peter, or any other of the apostles. They
> claim that they have more knowledge than all others, and that they
> alone have attained the greatness of the knowledge of the ineffable
> power. They claim that they are in the heights beyond every power.
> . . . [and] claim that they are unassailable by and invisible to the judge
> (ibid., 13.6, p. 202).

The Gnostics recorded in Clement's aforementioned *Excerpta ex
Theodoto* considered themselves to be the true Church, a chosen race
whose superior seeds have an "affinity with the light" that was
brought forth by the Christ in the person of Jesus. They were thus
purified by him as together they entered into the Pleroma: "Consequently, it is rightly said of the Church that it was chosen before the
foundation of the world" (*Excerpta* I.41.2, in F I, p. 229).

In "The Kerygmata Petrou" we find this specialness expressed in the
context of the lineage of the "true prophet," which begins with Adam
and continues through Moses to Jesus. This holy figure is properly
Gnostic and is described as the one

> [who] brings knowledge in place of error. . . . by knowledge [he] slays
> ignorance, cutting and separating the living from the dead (Ker. Pet.
> H XI.19.2, in *NTA* II, p. 116).

This specialness is first and foremost sexist. The prophet, always male,
is juxtaposed with his false counterpart, usually portrayed as female
and beginning of course with Eve:

If any one denies that the man (Adam) who came from the hands of the Creator . . . possessed the great and holy Spirit of divine fore-knowledge, but acknowledges that another did this who was begot-ten of impure seed [Eve], how does he not commit a grievous sin? . . . There are two kinds of prophecy, the one is male. . . . the other is found amongst those who are born of women. Proclaiming what pertains to the present world, female prophecy desires to be consid-ered male. On this account she steals the seed of the male, envelops them with her own seed of the flesh and lets them . . . come forth as her own creations (ibid., III.17.1; 23.1-3, pp. 115, 117).

And on and on the diatribe against women continues. However, the specialness also includes Peter and his disciples, set off against Paul who is seen as the representative of the female prophet. The author (Peter) sets forth his theory of syzygies, wherein God assembled his creation in pairs, with the weaker (feminine) coming first and the stronger (male) second. Citing as examples Cain and Abel, Ishmael and Isaac, Esau and Jacob, Aaron and Moses, the author comes down to Paul and Peter:

. . . there came as the first the one who was among those that are born of women [Paul], and after that there appeared the one who was among the sons of men. He who follows this order can discern by whom Simon [Paul], who as the first came before me [Peter] to the Gentiles, was sent forth, and to whom I belong who appeared later than he did and came in upon him as light upon darkness, as knowl-edge upon ignorance, as healing upon sickness (ibid., II.17.2-3, p. 122).

Of himself, the chosen apostle, Peter says:

[I] am his [Jesus'] confidant . . . a firm rock, the foundation stone of the church. . . . I proclaim what I have heard in my own person from the Lord. . . . God . . . revealed Christ to me . . . [and] called me blessed on account of the revelation (ibid., XVII.19.4-6, p. 123).

In the "Acts of John" Jesus speaks of his chosen (Gnostic) race, compared to the inferior nature of the non-believers:

The multitude around the Cross . . . is the inferior nature. . . . But when human nature is taken up, and the race that comes to me and obeys my voice, then he who now hears me shall be united with this race and shall no longer be what he now is, but shall be above them as I am now . . . . Therefore ignore the many and despise those who are outside the mystery . . . (AJ 100, in *NTA* II, pp. 233f).

Some Gnostic groups had hierarchies themselves, notably the

Manichean Church. Augustine refers to the Elect who considered themselves to be "holier ... and more splendid than that of their congregations" (Haardt, pp. 342f). Needless to say the Manicheans in general considered themselves superior to all other groups.

Finally we consider Plotinus' criticism of the Gnostics' "spiritual specialness." He addresses the Gnostics who manage to talk themselves and others into believing that they are better than all other people, if not the gods (the greater cosmos), themselves, and their creator, "the blessed Soul":

> But stupid men believe this sort of talk as soon as they hear "you shall be better than all, not only men, but gods"--for there is a great deal of arrogance among men--and the man who was once meek and modest, an ordinary private person, if he hears "you are the son of God, and the others whom you used to admire are not, nor the beings they venerate according to the tradition received from their fathers; but you are better than the heaven without having taken any trouble to become so"--then are other people really going to join in the chorus? It is just as if, in a great crowd of people who did not know how to count, someone who did not know how to count heard that he was a thousand cubits tall; what would happen if he thought he was a thousand cubits, and heard that the others were five cubits? He would only imagine that the "thousand" was a big number (*Enn.* II.9.9).

Platonism

We turn now to the Platonic view that salvation or redemption (words the non-Christian philosophers would never use) consists merely in remembering the truth that is already present in us. In this section we shall specifically discuss Plato, Origen, and Plotinus. (Augustine's views, already considered, tend more towards orthodoxy--certainly more than the near-heretic Origen--for to him salvation without Jesus is unthinkable. This of course was his principal criticism of his much-admired though pagan Plotinus, who omits mention of Jesus entirely.) If our problem is the forgetting of truth, covered over by the attraction to the corporeal, then, for the Platonist, the remembering comes by dislodging our attention, orienting it more towards the sublimity of the light and truth of the Intelligible world beyond the world of the senses.

1. Plato

The Allegory of the Cave in the *Republic* (VII 514-520) is one of the most famous of all passages in Plato, indeed in all philosophy. Students of *A Course in Miracles* will recognize allusions to the Cave Allegory on pages 401 and 492 (and indirectly p. 559) in the text. The allegory specifically deals with the theme that preoccupied Plato all of his life: the relationship between appearance and reality.

Simplifying Plato's description, the setting is a cave with prisoners fastened with chains, facing an interior wall:

> In this chamber are men who have been prisoners there since they were children, their legs and necks being so fastened that they can only look straight ahead of them and cannot turn their heads.

In back of them is the entrance to the cave, and behind this is a road along which passes the normal stream of everyday commerce. Behind the road is a burning fire, whose light shines into the cave, casting shadows of the passing traffic of the road onto the interior wall directly in front of the chained prisoners. Finally, still farther behind the fire shines the sun, the ultimate source of light. The prisoners, unable to see behind them to the reality of the figures passing along the road, see only their shadows, believing them to be what is real:

> Do you think our prisoners could see anything of themselves or their fellows except the shadows thrown by the fire on the wall of the cave opposite them? ... And would they see anything more of the objects carried along the road? ... Then if they were able to talk to each other, would they not assume that the shadows they saw were the real things? ... And if the wall of their prison opposite them reflected sound, don't you think that they would suppose, whenever one of the passers-by on the road spoke, that the voice belonged to the shadow passing before them? ... And so in every way they would believe that the shadows of the objects we mentioned were the whole truth?

At some point one of the prisoners is freed (he later becomes the philosopher-king) and walks toward the mouth of the cave and the fire. He begins to realize that what he and the others have been knowing as reality is merely an illusion of reality:

> ... what he used to see was so much empty nonsense and that he was now nearer reality and seeing more correctly, because he was turned towards objects that were more real ....

The freed prisoner continues on into the sunlight, with his eyes at first hurting from the glare. Eventually he is able to gaze more and more fixedly on the upper world outside the cave:

> First, he would find it easiest to look at shadows, next at the

reflections of men and other objects in water, and later on at the objects themselves. After that he would find it easier to observe the heavenly bodies and the sky itself at night, and to look at the light of the moon and stars rather than at the sun and its light by day .... The thing he would be able to do last would be to look directly at the sun itself, and gaze at it without using reflections in water or any other medium, but as it is in itself .... Later on he would come to the conclusion that it is the sun that produces the changing seasons and years and controls everything in the visible world, and is in a sense responsible for everything that he and his fellow-prisoners used to see.

Feeling sorry for his fellow-prisoners, the enlightened man would return to the cave to share his newly acquired knowledge. However, he would "make a fool of himself," as his eyes would now have to readjust to the cave's world of darkness and shadows. And so the prisoners would say that

his visit to the upper world had ruined his sight, and that the ascent was not worth even attempting. And if anyone tried to release them and lead them up, they would kill him if they could lay hands on him.

Clearly the model for this freed prisoner who attains the knowledge of the Good is Socrates, who was indeed killed by the Athenians because he tried to awaken in them the truth of the difference between appearance and reality. Later, Plato continues, with Socrates obviously in mind:

Nor will you think it strange that anyone who descends from contemplation of the divine to human life and its ills should blunder and make a fool of himself, if while still blinded and unaccustomed to the surrounding darkness, he's forcibly put on trial in the law-courts or elsewhere about the shadows of justice . . . and made to dispute about the notions of them held by men who have never seen justice itself.

Plato now interprets the metaphor for us, referring back to what he had written about the sun:

The realm revealed by sight corresponds to the prison, and the light of the fire in the prison to the power of the sun. And you won't go wrong if you connect the ascent into the upper world and the sight of the objects there with the upward progress of the mind into the intelligible region. ... the final thing to be perceived in the intelligible region, and perceived only with difficulty, is the form of the good; once seen, it is inferred to be responsible for whatever is right and valuable in anything, producing in the visible region light and the source of light, and being in the intelligible region itself controlling source of truth and intelligence. And anyone who is going to act rationally either in public or private life must have sight of it.

Earlier Plato writes that

> though the sun is not itself sight, it is the cause of sight and is seen by the sight it causes. . . . that is what I called the child of the good . . . [which] has begotten it in its own likeness, and it bears the same relation to sight and visible objects in the visible realm that the good bears to intelligence and intelligible objects in the intelligible realms.

He continues by drawing an analogy to seeing dimly at night without sunlight, and trying to understand without benefit of the reality of the Good:

> When the mind's eye is fixed on objects illuminated by truth and reality, it understands and knows them, and its possession of intelligence is evident; but when it is fixed on the twilight world of change and decay, it can only form opinions, its vision is confused and its opinions shifting, and it seems to lack intelligence (VI 508b-d).

Paralleling the Allegory of the Cave to the bed analogy we discussed in Chapter 6, we find that the bed-in-itself corresponds to the world of Ideas, the object of all knowledge; the bed made by the carpenter represents the figures of the world walking along the road outside the cave; while the copies of the bed by the painter correspond to the shadows seen by the prisoners on the wall.

The task of the freed prisoner, now the philosopher-king, is to educate his fellow prisoners. This of course was the purpose of Plato's Academy, and the principal message of the *Republic*: how to develop an educational and training program for the philosopher-kings, including helping them to recognize their responsibilities to return to the lower world to teach the others:

> Then our job as lawgivers is to compel the best minds to attain what we have called the highest form of knowledge, and to ascend to the vision of the good as we have described, and when they have achieved this and see well enough, prevent them behaving as they are now allowed to. . . . [i.e.,] Remaining in the upper world, and refusing to return again to the prisoners in the cave below and share their labors and rewards, whether trivial or serious.

The philosopher-kings will be told:

> You must therefore each descend in turn and live with your fellows

in the cave and get used to seeing in the dark; once you get used to it
you will see a thousand times better than they do and will distinguish
the various shadows, and know what they are shadows of, because
you have seen the truth about things admirable and just and good.

In an earlier passage Plato speaks about these philosopher-kings--
the truly wise--who as "saviors of our society" (VI 502d) no longer
value the *appearance* of the Good, but the Good itself; the reality
illuminated by the truth and not the shadows:

> One trait in the philosopher's character we can assume is his love of
> any branch of learning that reveals eternal reality, the realm unaf-
> fected by the vicissitudes of change and decay. . . . our true lover of
> knowledge naturally strives for reality, and will not rest content with
> each set of particulars which opinion takes for reality, but soars with
> undimmed and unwearied passion till he grasps the nature of each
> thing as it is [i.e., the Ideas], with the mental faculty . . . only released
> from travail when it has thus attained knowledge and true life and
> fulfillment. . . . His eyes are turned to contemplate fixed and
> immutable realities, a realm where there is no injustice done or
> suffered, but all is reason and order, and which is the model which
> he imitates and to which he assimilates himself as far as he can. . . .
> So the philosopher whose dealings are with the divine order himself
> acquires the characteristics of order and divinity so far as a man may
> (VI 485b; 490b; 500c-d).

Plato contrasts the popular theory that education consists in putting
into the mind knowledge that was not previously there, with his own
theory which teaches that knowledge

> is a capacity which is innate in each man's mind . . . [which] must be
> turned away from the world of change until its eye can bear to look
> straight at reality, and at the brightest of all realities which is what we
> call the good (VII 518c).

The name given by Plato to the process of such education, is "dialec-
tic," whose goal is to attain the vision of the Good, symbolized in the
Cave Allegory by the final ability to gaze directly at the sun. It can be
characterized by

> the progress of sight from shadows to the real creatures themselves
> and then to the stars themselves, and finally to the sun itself. So when
> one tries to get at what each thing is in itself by the exercise of dialec-
> tic, relying on reason without any aid from the senses, and refuses to
> give up until one has grasped by pure thought what the good is in
> itself, one is at the summit of the intellectual realm, as the man who
> looked at the sun was of the visual realm (532a,b).

This process of attaining the vision and experience of the truth is individualized and occurs internally; it cannot be "put in" from outside. The purpose of any external program, such as the Republic, is to provide structure and guidance that facilitates the individual's interior journey.

Returning to the tripartite mind discussed in the previous chapter, we see that "salvation" for Plato rests with the soul. As he writes in the *Timaeus*:

> We should think of the most authoritative part of our soul as a guardian spirit given by god, living in the summit of the body, which can properly be said to lift us from the earth towards our home in heaven.... and our divine part attaches us by the head to heaven, like a plant by its roots, and keeps our body upright. If therefore a man's attention is centered on appetite and ambition, all his thoughts are bound to be mortal.... But a man who has given his heart to learning and true wisdom ... is surely bound ... to have immortal and divine thoughts, and cannot fail to achieve immortality as fully as is permitted to human nature.

To maintain such balance it is thus imperative that people align themselves with the harmony of the cosmos through education and contemplation:

> And the motions that are akin to the divine in us are the thoughts and revolutions of the universe. We should each therefore attend to these motions and by learning about the harmonious circuits of the universe repair the damage done at birth [when the soul forgot its heavenly home] to the circuits in our head, and so restore understanding and what is understood to their original likeness to each other. When that is done we shall have achieved the goal set us by the gods, the life that is best for this present time and for all time to come (*Tim.* 90a-d).

2. Origen

Origen, too, emphasizes the process within the mind, writing of two motivating forces present in the rational being or soul. The first is the soul's free choice that led to its fall from spirit and continually choosing to identify with the lower or physical self; the second is the soul's capacity to choose freely the return to God and the awareness of its true spiritual identity. This "second" freedom unites with the Will of God that continually calls the fallen soul back to it. It was this emphasis on the soul's need and ability to choose God that led to the later development of the Pelagian heresy, so opposed by Augustine, that taught that

301

salvation came from humanity's choice and not God, who was essentially unnecessary to the process.

However, Origen is equally emphatic on the role that God plays in His call, teaching that God's providence is the means by which every fallen soul eventually will return. Redemption thus becomes the framework through which the soul's mistakes are eventually corrected, according to the time span that *it* decides for itself. The fall and its consequences, freely chosen by the soul, become the classroom that the Divine Teacher uses to bring about salvation. We shall see in Part II-B the similarities between Origen's theory and *A Course in Miracles*. Origen states in various places:

> But it [what our soul has received] becomes evident through temptations, so that we no longer escape the knowledge of what we are like. . . . we give thanks for the good things that have been made evident to us through temptations. . . . For when we have accomplished all we can by ourselves, God will fulfill what is lacking because of human weakness (*On Prayer* XXIX.17.19).

> For in no other way can the soul reach the perfection of knowledge except by being inspired with the truth of the divine wisdom (*First Princ.* IV.2.8).

> Why is it that however great the progresses made by the soul nonetheless temptations are not taken away from it? Here it becomes clear that temptations are brought to it as a kind of protection and defense. . . . Temptation . . . is a kind of strength and defense for the soul (*Homily*, in *Origen*, pp. 263,265).

Trials or temptations for Origen, therefore, are given by God, not as punishment, but rather as means to return to Him.

Origen always returns to the basic premise, the very foundation of his teaching, that the substance of the soul shares in the incorruptibility and immortality of the Divine Trinity:

> . . . it follows logically and of necessity that every existence which has a share in that eternal nature must itself also remain forever incorruptible and eternal, in order that the eternity of the divine goodness may be revealed in this additional fact, that they who obtain its blessings are eternal too (*First Princ.* IV.4.9).

Nonetheless, each soul has the freedom to choose to have its vision of this divine goodness obscured or heightened, though it

> always possesses within some seeds . . . of restoration and recall to a better state, which become operative whenever the inner man, who

is also termed the rational man, is recalled into the image and likeness of God who created him (ibid.).

These "marks of the divine image" are obviously not perceived through the corruptible body, but rather through the "prudence of his mind" along with all its virtues. This perception is a gradual one, accomplished little by little as the soul grows in virtue and is weaned from the corporeal until its return to its original state.

In summary, therefore, though we may choose to hurt ourselves, God, for Origen, uses such painful circumstances of sin to lead us back to Him. In this respect, our freedom and God's loving providence combine to effect our salvation. Our bodies, the repository of sin and distress, are, according to Origen, the result of our fall and serve to hide the divine splendor from us. Yet this same body becomes God's vehicle for leading us through the darkness back to Him. God's unshaking love makes such return inevitable in the end, even though the choice remains our own as to how quickly this return occurs.

3. Plotinus

Plotinus' notion of redemption is implicit in his teachings on the fall and the making of the world, as we have already seen in Chapter 6 as well as in our discussion of Origen. If the problem is that the soul has by its own choice become enmeshed in the world of materiality, then it is redeemed by reversing its decision and, in effect, climbing up the ladder its fall led it down. It is this change, brought about through the cultivation of reason and conscious detachment from the body, that constitutes the soul's redemption. It is not brought about by any agents--divine or otherwise--that are outside the soul, but rather simply by the efforts of the soul itself. In a context alien to Plotinus' thought we may say that the One knows absolutely nothing of the fate of the soul. Yet, it is the memory of its divine nature that impels the soul upward to its source. It is not so much an active call, such as Origen seems to conceptualize it, but rather the ongoing presence that serves to remind the fallen soul and thus "call" it back to Itself.

This divine Self is immanent in the soul, while at the same time transcendent in the sense of having been its source. Thus, as Bréhier has cogently discussed, the transcendent One or Platonic Good remains the source and standard by which all else is evaluated. On the other hand it also becomes the object of the soul's yearning to return. The former is akin to rationalism, the other to ecstasy:

> Let us clearly contrast the two points of view. Platonic rationalism is the affirmation of the transcendence of the One, the universal meas-

ure of things, which, consequently, is unlike them. The theory of ecstasy is the affirmation of the immanence of Soul and Intelligence in the One. The Platonic doctrine affirms a bond of external dependence between the One and the many. The One is external to the many as the unit of measure is to the things measured. This transcendence alone guarantees the trustworthy operation of reason. The immanence of things within the One, on the other hand, abolishes these boundaries (Bréhier, p. 159).

It does this by absorbing the lower into the higher, the immanent in the transcendent, in what is the ecstatic obliteration of the subject-object duality. Plotinus writes:

> ...one of us, being unable to see himself, when he is possessed by that god brings his contemplation to the point of vision, and presents himself to his own mind and looks at a beautified image of himself; but then he dismisses the image, beautiful though it is, and comes to unity with himself, and, making no more separation, is one and all together with that god silently present, and is with him as much as he wants to be and can be. But if he returns again to being two, while he remains pure he stays close to the god, so as to be present to him again in that other way if he turns again to him. In this turning he has the advantage that to begin with he sees himself, while he is different from the god; then he hastens inward and has everything, and leaves perception behind in his fear of being different, and is one in that higher world; and if he wants to see by being different, he puts himself outside (*Enn.* V.8.11).

The spiritual novice should not abandon the use of divine images, yet should recognize that it is the unity of subject and object that is the ultimate goal; thus, he is no longer the seer, but the seen:

> How then can anyone be in beauty without seeing it? If he sees it as something different, he is not yet in beauty, but he is in it most perfectly when he becomes it. If therefore sight is of something external we must not have sight, or only that which is identical with its object. This is a sort of intimate understanding and perception of a self which is careful not to depart from itself by wanting to perceive too much (*Enn.* V.8.11).

Thus we find in Plotinus that yearning for the experience of unity with the One:

> ...all men are naturally and spontaneously moved to speak of the god who is in each one of us one and the same.... they would come to rest in this way somehow supporting themselves on what is one and the same, and they would not wish to be cut away from this

unity. And this is the firmest principle of all, which our souls cry out.
... that principle ... that all things desire the good ... would be true
if all things press on to the one and are one, and their desire is of this.
... For this is the good to this one nature, belonging to itself and being
itself: but this is being one. It is in this sense that the good is rightly
said to be our own; therefore one must not seek it outside. For where
could it be if it had fallen outside being? Or how could one discover
it in non-being? But it is obvious that it is in being, since it is not non-
being. . . . We have not, then, departed from being, but are in it, nor
has it departed from us: so all things are one (*Enn.* VI.5.1).

Redemption for Plotinus therefore lies in the ecstatic unfolding of the
unity of Being that is already present, brought about by the meditative
and ascetic practice which we shall explore in Chapter 10.

I do not mean in . . . beings of the sense-world—for these three are
separate . . . but in . . . beings outside the realm of sense-perception;
. . . so the corresponding realities in man are said to be "outside," as
Plato speaks of the "inner man" (*Enn.* V.1.10).

Plotinus makes it very clear that he is not talking about a spatial or
material principle, but one totally immaterial, the source of which is
God. Thus the self is transformed from within, turning inward unto
itself to be revealed as itself: one with the One.

Denial of this unity within and unity among all created beings leads
to the forms of disorder and conflict in the world, while acceptance of
unity restores the natural order and escape from the world. It is this
acceptance which is the path of the sage, as we have already seen and
will examine in more detail in Chapter 10: the path of redemption that
liberates the soul from the entrapments of this world; the natural
return that corrects the unnatural fall. Awakening to one's true self is
thus the task and challenge of every person; it remains that individual's responsibility and is not to be shouldered by anyone else.

Chapter 9

THE REDEEMER - JESUS

The preceding chapter clearly showed the important role played by the figure of the redeemer in the process of salvation, and, indeed, this redeemer figure cannot easily be separated from the Gnostic and Christian plans of redemption. However, particularly when we compare these Gnostic and Christian plans, it is helpful to discuss more specifically in a separate chapter the nature of the redeemer.

Even to raise the issue of a Gnostic redeemer is somewhat paradoxical, given the emphasis the Gnostics placed on self-knowledge. The Delphic "Know Thyself" was an important Gnostic ideal. However, many of the texts emphasize the impossibility of the sleeping soul to awaken without outside help. We have already considered the emphasis placed upon the call to awaken, which presupposes an awakener--the bearer of the call. In addition to awakening the soul, the redeemer also serves in many Gnostic traditions to teach the ways of liberation from the world. As Rudolph comments:

> One may call them just as well revealers or emissaries or messengers, who at the command of the supreme God impart the saving message of the redeeming knowledge (Rudolph, p. 119).

Thus we have the important emphasis on the *gnosis* or revelation as the source of this redeeming knowledge. We have also seen in some of the Gnostic myths that the redeemer assists the soul in its ascent after death.

Contrary to what some scholars have asserted about the Christianized Gnostic idea of a redeemer--i.e., that there is no genuine, autonomous Gnostic redeemer figure--one can see how the Gnostic need for a redeemer is an inherent part of its world view:

> The gnostic view of the world simply demands a revelation which comes from outside the cosmos and displays the possibility of deliverance; for of himself man cannot escape from his prison in which according to this religion he is shut up (Rudolph, p. 119).

The figure of Jesus is but one of many figures and, as we shall see presently, the Gnostics were hardly in agreement as to the person of Jesus and the means of the salvation he offered to the world. The range is from the near-orthodox view of some of the Valentinians to the docetic view that Jesus never truly existed as a physical person.

There is further the important Gnostic notion of the "redeemed redeemer," which we introduced earlier in the discussion of "The Hymn of the Pearl" where the returning prince is identified with the pearl and the garment. We shall resume our study of this notion in a separate section of this chapter.

Non-Christian Redeemers

Let us begin with examples of the redeemer from non-Christian sources, including the Mandeans, the Sethian Gnostics, and the Manicheans. In the Mandean literature we find no examples of an historical redeemer. Redemption is accomplished through messengers of light who are essentially mythological figures. In the case of the most important of these--Manda dHaiye--the redeemer is a mythic personification of the redemption through knowledge. His name means literally the knowledge of life. There are certain Mandean texts where the mythological redeemer appears in an historical setting; namely in Jerusalem where Jesus is accused of being a prophet of lies, as opposed to John the Baptist, the true prophet. This sole example reflects the strong anti-Christian attitude of the Mandeans. Other aspects of this literature, however, do suggest that the messenger of life returns from time to time to re-present the original revelation that was made to Adam. We find an example of this in the following hymn:

> Who saw Manda dHaiye, when he went and came into the world?
> . . . He discoursed and his voice was lovely. . . . he demolished the world and forsook it. . . . and Ruha thus sits there in mourning. . . . and the Seven [the ruling planets] sit there in dismay. They weep and prolong their lamentation, because their mysteries have been disclosed.
> . . . [and] they will die on the great last day (ML Oxf. I.14, in F II, p. 237).

The following excerpts--in the "I am" formula--from various Mandean texts reflect how the messenger of light is seen. It is interesting to note the strong Christian parallels in many of these statements:

> I am a shepherd, who loves his sheep, I protect the sheep and the lambs. . . . I carry them and give them water to drink. . . . A fisherman am I of the Great Life . . . . a messenger whom the Life sent. He said to me: "Go and catch fish . . . ." The Treasure am I . . . the Treasure of the Mighty Life . . . . I became a crown to the king of glory . . . . I became the illuminator of the worlds of Light. . . . I became a king to the Nasoreans, who received praise and stability through my name. . . . and by my name they ascend to the Place of Light. . . . and Manda

dHaiye was established in their hearts. Whoever puts me on ... as a garment, he loves neither wife nor child, gold nor silver ... I speak to them: "The vine which bears fruit ascends, the vine which bears nothing is cut off here from the light. ... I am a gentle vine .... I was planted from the glorious root and the Great Life was my planter. He called me forth, established and commissioned me, he prepared me by his word and gave me helpers" (Jb. 11; 36-37; 57-59; GR XV.2, in F II, pp. 232-34).

The *Nag Hammadi Library* has provided us with several examples that point up the rich variation in the Gnostic literature on the theme of the redeemer. The definite non-Christian (if not even pre-Christian) character seen here denies the allegations of earlier scholars that the Gnostic redeemer was merely a derivative concept based upon the Christian understanding of revelation. Rather, we can see the free borrowing of Old Testament figures such as Adam, Eve, their children Abel and Seth, and even the three anonymous men (angels) who visited Abraham. In "The Paraphrase of Shem," the redeemer figure is Derdekeas (whose name is probably derived from the Aramaic word for child). We have already met Hermes Trismegistus in the *Poimandres*, Zostrianos who is obviously patterned after Zoroaster, and the Mandean figure of Manda dHaiye. We also find redemptive functions associated with abstract entities such as Wisdom (Sophia), Understanding (Nous), Thought (Ennoia), etc. To be sure, there is a great emphasis in the Gnostic literature on the role of Jesus, as we shall see, but the Christocentric view of Gnostic redemption clearly does not do justice to the rich traditions from which the Gnostics so freely borrowed.

We have two examples of the Sethian brand of Gnosticism in the *Nag Hammadi Library*. In "The Apocalypse of Adam" we possess an extraordinary document that perhaps dates from as early as the first century. The strong influence of the Jewish apocalyptic that comes from that period is clear, as is the definite absence of any Christian themes. The basic substance of this text is the revelation that Adam received from the three heavenly visitors we recognize from the story of Abraham:

Arise, Adam, from the sleep of death, and hear about ... the seed of that man [Seth] to whom life has come, who came from you and from Eve, your wife (ApocAdam V.64.1-5, in *NHL*, p. 257).

Despite the fall which enslaved him and Eve to the creator God, Adam is nonetheless able to transmit the content of what had been revealed to him to his son Seth:

> . . . the vigor of our eternal knowledge was destroyed in us, and weakness pursued us. Therefore the days of our life became few. For I knew that I had come under the authority of death.
> Now then, my son Seth, I will reveal to you the things which those men whom I saw before me at first revealed to me (ibid., 64.5-15).

We skip over the contents of the revelation that deal with the attempt of the Demiurge Sakla to punish the world, first through the great Flood, and then by fire and brimstone (shades of Sodom and Gomorrah), and the salvation of the proto-Gnostics in defiance of Sakla's efforts. Finally, there is the coming of the "illuminator of knowledge," by whom is meant Seth. He

> will pass by in great glory, in order to leave something of the seed of Noah and the sons of Ham and Japheth. . . . And he will redeem their souls from the day of death (ibid., 76.10-18, p. 260).

The creator God is obviously distressed and attempts in vain to destroy him. The angels and powers of this world ask about his origins, and there follows a description of thirteen kingdoms, each having its own account of the illuminator's origin. These are rather varied and reflect many different traditions. The second kingdom, for example, states that the illuminator

> came from a great prophet. And a bird came, took the child who was born and brought him onto a high mountain. And he was nourished by the bird of heaven (ibid., 78.7-14, pp. 260f).

The third relates a virgin birth and a casting out of the city where he and his mother are brought to the desert. The fifth teaches he came from a drop from heaven, thrown into the sea, while the seventh continues the saga of the drop of water, now brought by dragons to a cave where he grows. The accounts are not without their sexual elements: the ninth describes one of the Muses going by herself to a high mountain, fulfilling her desire alone and becoming pregnant from this desire; the tenth conceives the illuminator from the desire of the god for a "cloud of desire," begetting the child in his hand; and the eleventh narrates an incestuous beginning of the illuminator, born of the union of father and daughter. While on one level these narratives suggest alternative explanations of the birth of the redeemer, on another they reflect a linear view of the ongoing revelation of the redeemer throughout history. He makes his appearance in many forms, and these culminate in the fourteenth and final one which tells the tale of the "kingless race":

But the generation without a king over it says that God chose him [the illuminator] from all the aeons. He caused a knowledge of the undefiled one of truth to come to be in him. He said, "Out of a foreign air, from a great aeon, the great illuminator came forth. And he made the generation of those men whom he had chosen for himself shine, so that they should shine upon the whole aeon" (ibid., 82.19-83.4, p. 263).

This is the time now, and the tractate urges those non-Gnostics who have condemned the "chosen race" to repent:

And your thought is not like that of those men whom you persecute ....Their fruit does not wither....they will be on a high mountain, upon a rock of truth. Therefore they will be named "The Words of Imperishability and Truth." ...This is the hidden knowledge of Adam, which he gave to Seth, which is the holy baptism of those who know the eternal knowledge through those born of the word and the imperishable illuminators, who came from the holy seed . . . [i.e., Seth] (ibid., 84.24-85.1; 10-30, pp. 263f).

The second of the Nag Hammadi texts from the Sethian tradition is "The Gospel of the Egyptians," which picks up as it were where "The Apocalypse of Adam" leaves off, and traces the work of Seth on earth, as he protects his race of Gnostics. The text begins with the usual Gnostic ontology, followed by the separation, making of the world, and the arrogance of the Demiurge Sakla. At this point

the great Seth [the son of Adamas, the primal, pre-separation Anthropos] saw the activity of the devil, and his many guises, and his schemes which will come upon his incorruptible, immovable race. ...Then...[he]...gave praise to the great, uncallable, virginal Spirit ...and the whole Pleroma.... And he asked for guards over his seed [the Gnostics].
Then there came forth from the great aeons four hundred ethereal angels...to guard the great, incorruptible race, its fruit, and the great men of the great Seth . . . (GEgypt III.61.16-62.19, in *NHL*, p. 202f).

Seth is then sent to this plane from the Pleroma, and assumes the body of Jesus, passes through the lower worlds, and is baptized

through a Logos-begotten body which the great Seth prepared for himself, secretly through the virgin, in order that the saints may be begotten by the holy Spirit . . . (ibid., 63.10-15, p. 203).

"The Paraphrase of Shem" has many elements in common with the Sethian Gnosticism already considered. Derdekeas, as we saw in earlier chapters, is the son of the Light who gives his revelation to Shem (Seth) who is "from an unmixed power . . . the first being upon the earth" (Para. Shem VII.1.17-22, in *NHL*, p. 309). Derdekeas speaks:

> It is I who opened the eternal gates which were shut from the beginning. . . . I granted perception to those who perceive. I disclosed to them all the thoughts and the teaching of the righteous ones. . . . But when I had endured the wrath of the world, I was victorious. There was not one of them who knew me. The gates of fire and endless smoke opened against me. All the winds rose up against me. . . . For this is my appearance: for when I have completed the times which are assigned to me upon the earth, then I will cast from me my garment of fire. And my unequalled garment will come forth upon me . . . (ibid., 36.2-19; 38.29-40, pp. 323-25).

Shem in turn must, in true Gnostic fashion, bring this revelation to the world: "For without you they [the power of light and fire] will not be revealed until you speak them openly" (ibid., 49.1-3, p. 328).

Another Nag Hammadi tractate that appears to have been secondarily Christianized, and which also reflects (if not actually belongs to) the Sethian brand of Gnosticism, is the "Trimorphic Protennoia." Its teaching is similar to "The Apocryphon of John" and dates from approximately the same late-second-century period. The heavenly redeemer is Protennoia, the First Thought of God, and her descent comes in three forms (trimorphic): "She is called by three names, although she exists alone" (Tri. Prot. XIII.35.6-7, in *NHL*, p. 462). We shall skip over the first two--Father or Voice, Mother or Sound--and quote only from the third: the Son or Word. The parallels with the accounts of Jesus in the New Testament are obvious, especially with the Logos of the Prologue to John's gospel, and are probably not found in the original version which is no longer extant:

> I am the Word who dwells in ineffable Silence. I dwell in undefiled Light and a Thought revealed itself perceptibly through the great Sound of the Mother. . . . The third time I revealed myself to them in their tents as the Word and I revealed myself in the likeness of their shape. . . . I dwell within all the Sovereignties and Powers and within the Angels and in every movement that exists in all matter. And I hid myself within them until I revealed myself to my brethren. And none of them [the Powers] knew me, although it is I who work in them. . . . they are ignorant, not knowing their root, the place in which they grew. . . . I came down to the world of mortals on account of the Spirit that remains in that which descended and came forth from the guileless Sophia. . . . As for me, I put on Jesus. I bore him from the cursed wood, and established him in the dwelling places of his Father. And those who watch over their dwelling places did not recognize me (ibid., 46.5-10; 47.14-17; 50.12-17, pp. 468-70).

Our last example of a non-Christian redeemer is Mani, who, as we have seen, identified himself as a redeemer and prophet, with a role superior even to that of Jesus, since the Persian considered himself to be the last and the greatest. In the following excerpts from the psalms we see this virtual identification in role of Jesus and Mani. The term "Paraclete" in Manicheism, incidentally, was reserved solely for its founder.

> Light resplendent . . . thou art come; we call unto thee, the children of the Paraclete, our Lord Mani. . . . I bless thee, O glorious seat, the sight of the Wisdom; we worship the sign of thy greatness and thy mysteries ineffable. Thou art the blessed Root. . . . Thou art the manifestation of the victory of the Light . . . . Thou art he that waits for Christ [the Luminous Jesus], that he may judge the sinners through thee; today also through thee the Mind puts to shame the Sects of Error. . . . Thou art he that crushes evil, setting a garland upon godliness; thou art he that cleanses the Light from the Darkness; thou art he that gives rest unto the souls of men. Thou art the honor that is honored before all the apostles; thou art the throne of the judges of godliness that separate the two natures (CCXXX, in Allberry, p. 26).

> Come to me, O living Christ; come to me, O Light of day. The evil body of the Enemy I have cast away from me, the abode of Darkness that is full of fear. . . . O compassionate, O Paraclete, I call up to thee, that thou wouldst turn unto me in the hour of dread (CCXLVII, in Allberry, p. 55).

> I am like a sheep seeking for its pastor; lo, my true shepherd I have found, he has brought me to my fold again. . . . I was heading for shipwreck before I found the ship of Truth; a divine tacking was Jesus who helped me (CCLIII, in Allberry, p. 63).

> Taste and know that the Lord is sweet. Christ is the word of Truth: he that hears it shall live. I tasted a sweet taste, I found nothing sweeter than the word of Truth. . . . Put in me a holy heart, my God: let an upright Spirit be new within me. The holy heart is Christ: if he rises in us, we also shall rise in him. . . . If we believe in him, we shall pass beyond death and come to life (fragmentary unnumbered psalms, in Allberry, pp. 158f).

The Redeemed Redeemer

One of the frequently cited characteristics of Gnosticism is the notion of the "redeemed redeemer." Though not foreign to some Gnostic traditions, it actually finds its most complete expression in Manicheism. In the pages that follow we shall examine this theme in more

313

depth, drawing upon these other traditions in addition to the Manichean. The classic statement of the Gnostic redeemer myth is from
Bultmann, here summarized by Yamauchi:

> 1) In the cosmic drama . . . [the] Primal Man of Light falls and is torn
> to pieces by demonic powers. These particles are encapsulated as the
> sparks of light in the "pneumatics" of mankind.
> 2) The demons try to stupefy the "pneumatics" by sleep and forget-
> fulness so they will forget their divine origin.
> 3) The transcendent Deity sends another Being of Light, the "Re-
> deemer," who descends the demonic spheres, assuming the decep-
> tive garments of a bodily exterior to escape the notice of the demons.
> 4) The Redeemer is sent to awaken the "pneumatics" to the truth of
> their heavenly origins and gives them the necessary "gnosis" or
> "knowledge" to serve as passwords for their heavenly re-ascent.
> 5) The Redeemer himself re-ascends, defeating the demonic powers,
> and thereby makes a way for the spirits that will follow him.
> 6) Cosmic redemption is achieved when the souls of men are col-
> lected and gathered upward. In this process the Redeemer is himself
> redeemed, i.e. the Primal Man who fell in the beginning is reconsti-
> tuted (Yamauchi, pp. 29f).

We begin with the interesting Gnostic theme of the redeemer coming
to gather his scattered self together. This theme, which has important
antecedents, is a variant of the notion of the "redeemed redeemer."
Epiphanius has preserved for us a passage from "The Gospel of
Philip" which is not contained in the tractate of the same name found
in the *Nag Hammadi Library*. Scholars are yet unsure if the same gospel
is meant or, if so, it is the same version. Perhaps both gospels are
variants of an earlier text. Epiphanius quotes the Lord's revelation to
Philip, who is told

> what the soul must say as it ascends into heaven, and how it must
> answer each of the higher powers; "I have known myself . . . and I
> have collected myself from every side; I have sowed no children for
> the Archon, but I have uprooted his roots and I have collected the
> members that were scattered, and I know who thou art. For I . . . am
> one of those from on high;" and so it [Philip's gospel] says, it is
> allowed to go. But . . . if it is found to have begotten a son, it is held
> fast here below until it can recover its own children and restore them
> to itself (*Panar.* XXVI.13.1, in F I, pp. 324f).

In addition to the familiar Gnostic themes of the ascent--the passwords
to elude the hostile archons as the soul makes its way back to the
eternal world above--we find in this passage the clear statement of the
soul's gathering to itself its own self, re-uniting the scattered particles

(elsewhere: of light) of the soul's self that had been dispersed in the lower world of matter. Thus the soul is its own redeeming agent, and escapes imprisonment by the archons through this process of re-collection from the flesh. Nothing then is left of the soul in the world below ("I have sowed no children for the Archon"). As we have already seen in the Manichean literature, the plan of the Darkness is to trap the light by dispersing it through the world of the body by sexual reproduction. It is thus understandable why the Manicheans utilized this gospel so heavily.

We find many other references to this theme in the Gnostic literature. For example, Epiphanius cites the Phibionites, a docetic and libertine source similar to the Barbelognostics, Ophites, and followers of Basilides:

> But if . . . a man attains this knowledge and collects himself from the world through the periods and the flowing-out of desire, he is no longer held fast in this world, but passes beyond the aforesaid Archons (*Panar.* XXVI.10.9, in F I, p. 323).

In the "Acts of Andrew," the apostle addresses Maximilla, one of his converted women:

> Well done, O nature, you who are saved despite your weakness and though you did not hide yourself.
> Well done, O soul, you who have cried aloud what you have suffered and are returning to yourself.
> Well done, O man, you who are learning what is not yours and desiring what is yours (AA CV 6, in *NTA* II, p. 411).

A woman beseeches the apostle in the "Acts of Thomas" to help rid her of demon possession, so that she "may be free and . . . gathered together into my original nature, and receive the gift that has been given to my kindred" (ATh Aa.II.2.42, in *NTA* II, p. 467). The demon is expunged, after which Thomas invokes Jesus, he "who dost gather all his nature into one place" (ibid., 2.48, p. 469).

Most interestingly, as Puech points out (*NTA* I, p. 275), these Gnostic expressions of gathering oneself back to oneself have pronounced Platonic and Neoplatonic antecedents, illustrating again the Platonic-Gnostic connections. In these antecedents, of course, the context is more philosophical and directly spiritual in its expression than the more mythological forms found in the Gnostic literature. In the *Phaedo*, Socrates discusses the end of his journey and the attainment of

> the object to which all our efforts have been directed during my past life. So this journey which is now ordained for me carries a happy prospect for any other man also who believes that his mind has been

prepared by purification. . . . [which] consists in separating the soul as much as possible from the body, and accustoming it to withdraw from all contact with the body and concentrate itself by itself, and to have its dwelling . . . alone by itself, freed from the shackles of the body. . . . philosophy takes over the soul in this [imprisoned] condition and by gentle persuasion tries to set it free. . . . and encourages it to collect and concentrate itself by itself (*Phaedo* 67b-d; 83a).

Plotinus discusses the Soul's fall into the clutches of the body and its purification of this alien material substance, reminding us of the "gold in mud" metaphor cited in earlier chapters.

In the same way the soul too, when it is separated from the lusts which it has through the body with which it consorted too much, and freed from its other affections, purged of what it gets from being embodied, when it abides alone has put away all the ugliness which came from the other nature (*Enn.* I.6.5).

Plotinus' student Porphyry, borrowing from his teacher, writes in a letter to a pupil:

If thou study to ascend into thyself, gathering from the body all thy scattered members which have been scattered into a multitude from the unity which up to a point held sway . . . (in *NTA* I, p. 275).

As saw in our discussion of Mani's system, the Son of Man--the being sent from Heaven to rescue the trapped particles of light-- becomes trapped himself and also needs redeeming. Thus he leaves part of himself--particles of light--below in the darkness and returns to the realm of Light. What has remained behind becomes part of the "soul of light" that has become scattered throughout the world. Thus, the redeemer must return to gather back together the scattered particles of light (including his own!), restoring the original unity of the light. This idea is obviously blasphemous to the orthodox Christian notion that Jesus was perfect, before, during, and after his earthly sojourn, having come solely for the redemption of the world. Several other Gnostic texts contain the same idea of Jesus' own redemption. In "The Gospel of Philip" we read:

Jesus revealed himself at the Jordan: it was the fullness of the kingdom of heaven. He who was begotten before everything was begotten anew. He who was once anointed was anointed anew. He who was redeemed in turn redeemed others (GPh II.70.34-71.3, in *NHL*, p. 142).

In a remarkable passage, "The Tripartite Tractate" states of Jesus, as well as all heavenly beings:

Not only do humans need redemption but also the angels, too, need redemption along with the image and the rest of the Pleromas of the aeons and the wondrous powers of illumination. So that we might not be in doubt in regard to the others, even the Son himself, who has the position of redeemer of the Totality, needed redemption as well— he who had become man--when he gave himself for each thing which we need, we in the flesh, who are his Church. Now when he first received redemption from the Logos who had descended upon him, all the rest received redemption from him, namely those who had taken him to themselves (Tri. Tract. I.124.25-125.10, in *NHL*, p. 92).

In the excerpts from the Valentinian Theodotus, we are told that

"Redemption" was necessary even for Jesus, in order that he might not be detained by the Ennoia of the deficiency in which he was placed, though conducted thereto through Sophia . . . (*Excerpta* 22.7, in F I, p. 225).

The apocryphal "Acts of John" contains a hymn sung by Jesus with his disciples before he is delivered up to the "lawless Jews" for the crucifixion he never really undergoes. Part of the hymn includes the following:

And why we give thanks, I tell you:
I will be saved, and I will save. Amen.
I will be loosed, and I will loose. Amen.
. . . .
I will be united, and I will unite. Amen.
(AJ 95.4,5,20, in *NTA* II, pp. 228f)

Similarly in "The Odes of Solomon" we find the redeemer Jesus first being redeemed:

Ask, and abound and abide in the love of the Lord.
And yet beloved ones in the Beloved: those who are kept, in Him that liveth:
And they that are saved in Him that was saved.

After Jesus is saved, he in turn saves his own people:

And I imparted my knowledge without grudging.
. . . .
And I sowed my fruits in hearts, and transformed them into myself:
and they received my blessing and lived;
And they were gathered to me and were saved; because they were to me as my own members and I was their head. (In *Eden*, pp. 124,129)

We have already examined "The Hymn of the Pearl" where the prince is both the savior and the saved. In fact, one can especially recognize in this lovely Gnostic story the underlying psychological dynamic that both the redeemer and the redeemed are one. Through the fall or separation from God they have been split off (as the Course would say, mind from Mind), and thus it is the burden of the spiritual path to reunite what had been separated (the derivation of the word "religion," of course, is to "bind again"). As Jesus is quoted in "The Second Treatise of the Great Seth":

> ... I ["that perfect Blessed One of the eternal and incomprehensible Father and the infinite light"] came to my own and united them with myself. There is no need for many words, for our Ennoia was with their Ennoia (Gr. Seth VII.59.9-14, in *NHL*, p. 333).

And again from "The Gospel of Philip":

> Because of this [the separation] Christ came to repair the separation which was from the beginning and again unite the two, and to give life to those who died as a result of the separation and unite them (GPh II.70.12-18, in *NHL*, p. 142).

"The Gospel of Eve," an apocryphal gospel dating from perhaps as early as the second century, is not really related to a gospel story of Jesus but rather has Eve in the role of Gnostic revealer of the truth. Only one brief fragment remains, from which it is impossible to tell for certain the characters in the dialogue, although Jesus is a likely candidate for the tall man, as Eve is for the recipient of the *gnosis*:

> I stood upon a high mountain and saw a tall man .... Then he spoke to me and said: I am thou and thou art I, and where thou art there am I, and I am sown in all things; and whence thou wilt, thou gatherest me, but when thou gatherest me, then gatherest thou thyself (GEve in *NTA* I, p. 241).

This typical Gnostic passage can be understood as referring to the integral oneness of life. The "gathering" reflects the re-uniting of the spiritual substance that had been dispersed in the world of materiality. Thus the gathering One is essentially gathering himself: the light that had been split off, fragmented, and imprisoned in the body.

Jesus

We turn now to the specific Christian Gnostic notions of the redeemer. We will organize this section under three categories: 1) the splitting off of the historical Jesus from the mythological Christ; 2) the resurrection; and 3) non-docetism and docetism, the latter teaching that Jesus' earthly existence was illusory, being basically a "phantom."

1. History vs. Mythology

We have already seen how the process of redemption has two essential components: the primal revelation with its strong mythological emphasis, and the ongoing revelation which takes us into the world of history, albeit not always without mythic or symbolic traits associated with the "historic" revelation. Students of the New Testament are familiar with this dual aspect in the figure of Jesus. The Prologue to John's gospel is perhaps the most famous example of the cosmic Christ, pre-existent to the creation of the world. The hymn in Philippians (2:6-11) also falls into this category. In these hymns we see Jesus not only as the Son of God, but as the pre-existent Son who is with God from all eternity and shares the function of creating: "He was with God in the beginning. Through him all things came to be, not one thing had its being but through him" (Jn 1:2f). In the Johannine Christology especially, we see the cosmic Christ as the foundation for the saving work of the historically incarnate Jesus.

The bringing of the mythic redeemer into contemporary history has been seen already in the Mandean literature, not to mention those early "heretics," Simon Magus and Menander, who set themselves up as divine redeemers. By and large, however, the Gnostic authors do not concern themselves with the historical Jesus, focusing more on the mythic Christ or revelatory Jesus who dispenses *gnosis* to the enlightened Gnostic. While one can denote in the evolving Church a similar duality (see John's Prologue), the orthodox never indulged their mythological fantasies anywhere near their Gnostic counterparts.

The primal Christ is also seen in a Manichean psalm quoted in Chapter 8, page 258. That psalm is indicative of the typical Gnostic view of the cosmic Christ, de-emphasizing the historical Jesus of Nazareth. Even when the historical Jesus is the revealer, as he frequently is, the overriding emphasis is on the nature of his revelation with personal references almost always confined to his crucifixion and resurrection, just as we also find, incidentally, in Jesus' references to himself in *A Course in Miracles*. For insight into some of the political influences and ramifications of this position the reader may consult Pagels' *The Gnostic Gospels*. The Nag Hammadi texts provide ample evidence for this type of revelation. For the most part they are directed to the elect of the disciples--John, Thomas, Peter, and James. Some examples follow.

"The Apocryphon of James" is a dialogue between the risen Jesus, and James and Peter, and actually is a Gnostic denigration of Peter with James elevated to a superior position. In addition to the usual Gnostic teachings on awakening from the sleep of drunkenness, the evils of the flesh, etc., Jesus exhorts his followers to remember him:

> Scorn death, therefore, and take thought for life! Remember my cross and my death, and you will live! . . . Verily I say unto you, none will be saved unless they believe in my cross. . . . And I have commanded you [James] to follow me, and I have taught you what to say before the archons. Observe that I have descended and have spoken and undergone tribulation and carried off my crown after saving you (plural). For I came down to dwell with you so that you in turn might dwell with me (ApocryJs I. 5.31-36; 6.1-5; 8.33-9.1-5, in *NHL*, pp. 31, 33).

Continuing for the moment this theme of Jesus' coming down from Heaven to save us, we note Church Father Hippolytus' reporting of a Naassene psalm. He introduces it this way: "They have strung together this psalm, through which they suppose they are celebrating all the mysteries of their error." The beginning of the psalm relates the fate of the soul trapped in the body: "without escape the wretched soul enters a labyrinth of evils in its wanderings." Jesus observes the soul's suffering and says:

> Father, behold:
> Pursued by evils here upon the earth
> There roams the work of thine own breath;
> It seeks to escape the bitter chaos
> · But knows not how it shall win through.
> Therefore send me, Father;
> Bearing the seals I will descend,
> I will pass through all the Aeons,
> I will disclose all mysteries,
> I will show the forms of the gods
> And the hidden things òf the holy way,
> Awaking knowledge, I will impart.
> (*Ref.* V.10.1, in F I, p. 282)

These Naassene sentiments are similar in tone, if not content, to a Romance of the sixteenth-century St. John of the Cross. In this great mystic's poem, Jesus is in Heaven with God, who tells His Son that the time has come to "ransom the bride serving under the hard yoke," who differs from the Son by virtue of living in the flesh. Jesus replies:

My will is Yours,
The son replied,
And My glory is
That Your will be Mine

. . . .

I will go and tell the world,
Spreading the word
Of Your beauty and sweetness
And of Your sovereignty.

I will go seek My bride
And take upon Myself
Her weariness and labors
In which she suffers so;

And that she may have life
I will die for her,
And, lifting her out of that deep,
I will restore her to You.
(*St. John of the Cross*, p. 731)

Hippolytus also discusses a group he calls the "Docetists," which appears to be a separate group from those Gnostics who have expressed docetic ideas. The theme of Christ descending and taking on the body of the virgin-born Jesus we have already seen, yet Hippolytus' Docetists have the union occurring at birth, and not at the baptism in the river Jordan.

That only-begotten Son . . . willed to come down and save them. And knowing that not even the Aeons can endure to behold in its entirety the fullness of all the Aeons. . . . he contracted himself like a lightning-flash in a minute body. . . . So . . . the eternal only-begotten Son . . . came into this world, being so great as we have said, invisible, unknowable, without honor, without credit . . . in order that he should clothe himself with outer darkness—meaning the flesh. . . . and when . . . [he] was born, then he who came from on high clothed himself with it, and did everything as it is described in the Gospels. . . . so that when the Archon condemned his own creation to death, to the Cross, that soul which had been trained within the body should put off the body and nail it to the Cross, and through it should triumph over authorities and powers . . . (*Ref.* VIII.10.3-7, in F I, pp. 310f).

We return to the *Nag Hammadi Library*. "The Gospel of Thomas," as we have seen, is perhaps the best known of these texts, and bears many resemblances to the sayings in the synoptic gospels, in addition to reflecting many Gnostic ideas. The "Gospel" consists of "secret sayings which the living Jesus spoke and which Didymos Judas Thomas wrote down." Of himself Jesus says:

> It is I who am the light which is above them all. It is I whom am the All. From Me did the All come forth, and unto Me did the All extend. Split a piece of wood, and I am there. Lift up the stone, and you will find Me there (GTh II.46.23-29, in *NHL*, p. 126).

In the Christianized "Sophia of Jesus Christ," delivered by Jesus, we read:

> But I taught you about Immortal Man, and I loosed the bonds of the robbers from him. I broke the gates of the pitiless ones before their faces. I humiliated their malicious intent. They all were shamed and rose from their ignorance. Because of this, then, I came here, so that they might be joined with that spirit and breath, and might from two become one . . . and go up to the one who is from the beginning . . . (Sophia BG 121.13-III.117.1-6, in *NHL*, pp. 226f).

"The Letter of Peter to Philip" is, except for the opening paragraph, not a letter at all but another revelation discourse from Jesus, "an illuminator in the darkness." He appears to the apostles as a voice speaking out of a great light. He answers the standard questions about the Pleroma and the "deficiency of the Aeons," and says of himself:

> Next concerning the Pleroma, it is I. And I was sent down in the body because of the seed which had fallen away. And I came down to their dead product. But they did not recognize me; they were thinking of me that I was a mortal man (Pt Ph VIII.136.16-23, in *NHL*, p. 396).

As we have seen, the Nag Hammadi text "Melchizedek" is a Gnostic revelation given to the Old Testament high priest, which prophecies the coming of Jesus and does so in a distinctly anti-docetic fashion, as is seen in the following:

> They will come in his name, and they will say of him that he is unbegotten though he has been begotten, that he does not eat even though he eats, that he does not drink even though he drinks, that he is uncircumcised though he has been circumcised, that he is unfleshly though he has come in flesh, that he did not come to suffering though he came to suffering, that he did not rise from the dead though he arose from the dead (Mel. IX.5.1-12, in *NHL*, p. 400).

We find many of the aforementioned themes, including the anti-docetic one, in "The Gospel of Truth," which in tone and statement sounds in many places like the orthodox view:

This is the gospel of the one who is searched for, which was revealed to those who are perfect through the mercies of the Father--the hidden mystery, Jesus, the Christ. Through it he enlightened those who were in darkness. Out of oblivion he enlightened them, he showed them a way. And the way is the truth which he taught them.

For this reason error grew angry at him, persecuted him, was distressed at him, and was brought to naught. He was nailed to a tree; he became a fruit of the knowledge of the Father, which did not, however, become destructive because it was eaten, but to those who ate it it gave cause to become glad in the discovery ... (GT I.18.11-30, in *NHL*, p. 38).

Before continuing, we note here the clear parallels of the above with Jesus' own words in *A Course in Miracles*, describing the world's reaction to his message of guiltlessness and truth. We shall return to these in Chapter 16.

... he was nailed to a tree; he published the edict of the Father on the cross. O such great teaching! He draws himself down to death though life eternal clothes him. Having stripped himself of the perishable rags, he put on imperishability, which no one can possibly take away from him. Having entered the empty spaces of terrors, he passed through those who were stripped naked by oblivion, being knowledge and perfection, proclaiming the things that are in the heart of the Father in order to teach those who will receive teaching. ... For when they had seen him and had heard him, he granted them to taste him and to smell him and to touch the beloved Son. ... For he came by means of fleshly appearance while nothing blocked his course because it was incorruptibility and irresistibility. .... Light spoke through his mouth, and his voice gave birth to life. He gave them thought and understanding and mercy and salvation and the powerful spirit from the infiniteness and the gentleness of the Father. He made punishments and tortures cease, for it was they which were leading astray from his face some who were in need of mercy, in error and in bonds; and with power he destroyed them and confounded them with knowledge. He became a way for those who were lost and knowledge for those who were ignorant, a discovery for those who were searching, and a support for those who were wavering, immaculateness for those who were defiled (GT I.20.25-21.2; 31.13-36, in *NHL*, p. 44).

Few traditional Christians would take exception to these words, despite their Gnostic flavor.

We find another traditional view of Jesus in "The Treatise on Resurrection," which we shall return to when we consider the Gnostic views of resurrection. Here at the beginning of the treatise we find a passage whose content could easily have come from Paul:

How did the Lord make use of things while he existed in flesh and after he had revealed himself as Son of God? He lived in this place where you remain, speaking about the Law of Nature—but I call it "Death"! Now the Son of God . . . was Son of Man. He embraced them both, possessing the humanity and the divinity, so that on the one hand he might vanquish death through his being Son of God, and that on the other through the Son of Man the restoration to the Pleroma might occur; because he was originally from above, a seed of the Truth, before this structure of the cosmos had come into being (Treat. Res. I.44.13-37, in *NHL*, p. 51).

Finally, "The Tripartite Tractate" says this of a Jesus incapable of suffering, yet otherwise spoken of in traditional terms:

And there is one who is greater than they, who was appointed since they have need of him, begotten by the spiritual Logos along with them as one who needs the exalted one, begotten in hope and expectation in accord with the thought which is the seed of salvation . . . . but he alone is the one of whom it is worthy to speak . . . the one eternally, an unbegotten, impassible Logos who came into being in flesh . . . . he appeared being exalted, because he had let himself be conceived without sin, stain, and defilement . . . . The Savior was a bodily image of the unitary one. He is the Totality in bodily form. Therefore he preserved the form of indivisibility, from which comes impassibility. (Tri. Tr. I.111.23-30; 113.31-38; 115.15-18; 116.28-34, in *NHL*, pp. 85-88).

2. Resurrection

A key point of contention between the Gnostics and the orthodox Church was their respective understandings of the resurrection of Jesus. Briefly stated here, the orthodox position was that the resurrection was a *physical* event seen with one's naked eye. Quite different from this was the Gnostic understanding that the resurrection was a spiritual event, apprehended through the *mind*, and thus was not restricted to the fifty-day period between the crucifixion and ascension as is related in the New Testament literature. The Gnostics taught that the resurrection was an experience available to all, especially to the "elect" able to receive it. Removed from its literal physical interpretation, Jesus' resurrection, according to the Gnostics, occurred *before* his crucifixion; in other words, his spiritual awakening preceded his death on the cross.

As Pagels has pointed out, much of the Gnostic literature begins with the resurrection of Jesus and moves forward from there, in contradistinction to the canonical gospels, which begin either with Jesus' earthly and cosmic birth (Matthew, Luke, and John) or with the beginning of his ministry (Mark). This highlights the importance for the Gnostic of the *experience* of Jesus, rather than his life or its historical witnesses. Pagels discusses at great length the political implications of this distinction in the battle over who represented the true Church; the interested reader may consult *The Gnostic Gospels*.

That this controversy was already raging in full form at the turn of the century is seen in the reference in 2 Timothy, quoted before in Part I:

> Talk of this kind [pointless philosophical discussions] corrodes like gangrene, as in the case of Hymenaeus and Philetus, the men who have gone right away from the truth and claim that the resurrection has already taken place. Some people's faith cannot stand up to them (2 Tm 2:18).

Referring to this citation, Hippolytus wrote:

> This Nicholas [considered by the Church to be one of the ancestors of this heresy] . . . impelled by an alien (diabolical) spirit, was the first to affirm that the resurrection has already come, meaning by "resurrection" the fact that we believe in Christ and receive baptism, but he denied the resurrection of the flesh. And at his instigation several men founded sects. These included above all the so-called Gnostics, to whom belonged Hymenaeus and Philetus combatted by the Apostle (in Puech, p. 81).

Regarding Menander, another Gnostic ancestor, Irenaeus wrote:

> His [Simon Magus'] successor was Menander, a Samaritan by race, who himself attained to the highest point of magic. . . . His disciples received resurrection through baptism into him, and they can no longer die, but remain without growing old and immortal (*Adv. haer.* I.23.5, in F I, p. 33).

Similarly, Tertullian wrote:

> But the insane opinion of the Samaritan heretic Menander is also rejected, who will have it that death has not only nothing to do with his disciples, but in fact never reaches them. He pretends to have received such a commission from the secret power of One above, that all who partake of his baptism become immortal, incorruptible, and instantaneously invested with resurrection-life (in Puech, p. 81).

Let us now look at the specific Gnostic teachings. We begin with

"The Treatise on Resurrection," written by an anonymous teacher to a certain Rheginos in the late second century. The tract is interesting in its combining a clear Gnostic (mostly Valentinian) point of view with, in many respects, an almost traditional Pauline one. Nonetheless, it is noteworthy that the teaching here is very similar to that of Hymenaeus and Philetus cited in 2 Timothy. The treatise is in response to the pupil's questions about the meaning of death and resurrection. This meaning is understood by very few, for others (the orthodox) are reluctant to learn the truth, believing they already have it. The first statement of this truth comes right out of the Pauline tradition:

> The Savior swallowed up death . . . for he put aside the world which is perishing. He transformed himself into an imperishable Aeon and raised himself up, having swallowed the visible by the invisible, and he gave us the way of our immortality. Then, indeed, as the Apostle said (Rm 8:17, Ep 2:5f): "We suffered with him, and we arose with him, and we went to heaven with him." Now if we are manifest in this world wearing him, we are that one's beams, and we are embraced by him until our setting, that is to say, our death in this life. We are drawn to heaven by him, like beams by the sun, not being restrained by anything. This is the spiritual resurrection which swallows up the psychic in the same way as the fleshly (Treat. Res. I.45.14.46.2, in *NHL*, p. 51).

However, the strong Gnostic teaching becomes apparent as the Treatise continues:

> The thought of those who are saved shall not perish. The mind of those who have known him shall not perish. Therefore, we are elected to salvation and redemption since we are predestined from the beginning not to fall into the foolishness of those who are without knowledge, but we shall enter into the wisdom of those who have known the Truth . . . . What, then, is the resurrection? . . . It is no illusion, but it is truth. Indeed, it is more fitting to say that the world is an illusion, rather than the resurrection which has come into being through our Lord the Savior, Jesus Christ . . . . the resurrection . . . is the revelation of what is, and the transformation of things and a transition into newness. For imperishability descends upon the perishable; the light flows down upon the darkness, swallowing it up; and the Pleroma fills up the deficiency. These are the symbols and the images of the resurrection. This is what makes the good.
> Therefore, do not think in part, O Rheginos, nor live in conformity with this flesh for the sake of unanimity, but flee from the divisions and the fetters, and already you have the resurrection. For if he who will die knows about himself that he will die . . . why not consider yourself as risen and already brought to this? (Ibid., 46.22-33; 48.2-49.25, pp. 52f)

The aforementioned "Gospel of Mary" was found in the early part of this century, and is reproduced in the English publication of the *Nag Hammadi Library*. The emphasis here is placed not on the physical perception of Jesus' resurrection, but on the interior vision. The "Gnostic" Mary explains to the "orthodox" Peter:

> I saw the Lord in a vision and I said to him, "Lord, I saw you today in a vision.... does he who sees the vision see it through the soul or through the spirit?" The Savior answered and said, "He does not see through the soul nor through the spirit, but the mind which is between the two--that is what sees the vision..." (GM BG 1.10.10-24, in *NHL*, p. 472).

We will return to the Gnostic visionary experiences in Part III when we consider the important issue of hearing the Voice of the Holy Spirit.

"The Gospel of Philip" has particular importance for our discussion on the sacraments in the following chapter. Yet, this third-century Valentinian tract also contains some important statements concerning the Gnostic view of resurrection, as seen here:

> Those who say that the Lord died first and then rose up are in error, for he rose up first and then died.... Those who say they will die first and then rise are in error. If they do not first receive the resurrection while they live, when they die they will receive nothing (GPh II.56.15-19; 73.1-5, in *NHL*, pp. 134,144).

The "Acts of Thomas" contains a lovely parable of the soul's journey. Thomas rides on a talking colt who carries him to the "rest." On arriving at the gates to this city the colt drops dead at the apostle's feet and Thomas refuses to resurrect him:

> I could indeed raise it up through the name of Jesus Christ. But this is not expedient at all. For he who gave it speech that it might speak was able also to make it not die. But I do not raise it up, not because I am not able but because this is what is useful and helpful for it (ATh Aa II.2.41, in *NTA* II, p. 466).

The colt symbolizes the body, whose only function is to carry the soul to its heavenly rest. Having served that function, and having no inherent worth, it is simply laid aside (buried). Its resurrection therefore would make no sense and is not "useful and helpful."

Finally we consider "The Testimony of Truth," that Gnostic polemic against the orthodox Church as well as numerous Gnostic groups. The text is fragmentary, yet is intact enough in these sections to present a coherent statement that the resurrection is self-knowledge:

And some say, "On the last day we will certainly arise in the resurrection." But they do not know what they are saying, for the last day is when those belonging to Christ.... those who have knowledge ... the resurrection ... come to know the Son of Man, that is, he has come to know himself. This is the perfect life, that man know himself by means of the All.

Do not expect, therefore, the carnal resurrection, which is destruction, and they are not stripped of it [the flesh] who err in expecting a resurrection that is empty. They do not know the power of God, nor do they understand the interpretation of the scriptures on account of their double-mindedness (Test. Truth IX.34.26-35.5; 36.21-37.10, in *NHL*, pp. 408f).

3. Non-Docetism and Docetism

One of the most widely known forms of Gnosticism is docetism, the belief that Jesus did not really live in the flesh but merely *appeared* to do so. "Appear" is the root meaning of "docetism," the Greek word for "appearance" being *dokein*. It is a mistake, however, to believe that all Gnostics were adherents to this view, a mistake not even some scholars have avoided. We begin our discussion by citing some examples of non-docetic Gnostics who emphasize the *real* sufferings undergone by Jesus.

"The Tripartite Tractate" speaks of Jesus as the "one who will be begotten and who will suffer" (Tri. Tract. I.113.32-35, in *NHL*, p. 86f):

He it was who is our Savior in willing compassion, who is that which they [humanity] were. So, for their sake he became manifest in an involuntary suffering. They became flesh and soul--that is, eternally—which things hold them, and in corruptibility they die. ... Not only did he take upon himself the death of those whom he thought to save, but also he accepted their smallness to which they had descended, when they had fasted in body and soul. He did so because he had let himself be conceived and born as an infant, in body and soul (ibid., 114.31-115.3-12, p. 87).

Another strong witness to certain Gnostic groups believing in a suffering Jesus is found in "The Letter of Peter to Philip." After the revelation to the apostles was completed, they

gave thanks to the Lord with every blessing. And they returned to Jerusalem. And while coming up they spoke with each other on the road concerning the light [Jesus] which had come. And a remark was made concerning the Lord. It was said, "If he, our Lord, suffered, then how much must we suffer?"

Peter answered, saying, "He suffered because of us, and it is necessary for us too to suffer because of our smallness."
Then a voice came to them, saying, "I have told you many times, it is necessary for you to suffer. It is necessary that they bring you to synagogues and governors, so that you shall suffer" (Pt Ph VIII.138.7-28, in *NHL*, p. 397).

"The Interpretation of Knowledge" originally was most likely a homily delivered to a church community torn apart by jealousy and judgment. The audience is exhorted to be like Jesus, who emulated the true Father who is beyond judgment and hatred, as opposed to the jealous Demiurge or false father. In this context the writer says of Jesus:

And he was crucified and he died—not his own death, for he did not deserve to be killed because of the Church of mortals. They removed him so that they might keep him in the Church. And he answered her with humiliations, since in this way he bore the suffering which he had suffered.... And through him who was disgraced we receive the forgiveness of sins. And through the one who was disgraced and the one who was redeemed we receive grace (Interp. Kn. XI.30.38; 12.25-30, in *NHL*, pp. 429,431).

We have already quoted from "The Gospel of Truth" and so will simply highlight the relevant passages:

For this reason [salvation] the merciful one, the faithful one, Jesus, was patient in accepting sufferings until he took that book ["the living book of the living" that is part of the Father's mind], since he knows that his death is life for many .... For this reason Jesus appeared; he put on that book.. (GT I.20.10-15; 23-25, in *NHL*, p. 39).

It is clear from this why Valentinus considered himself to be part of the apostolic Church. One could not ask for a more fervent "confession of faith" in the suffering Lord who died for the salvation of the world. This, despite the more docetic comment later in the text:

For he came by means of fleshly appearance while nothing blocked his course because it was incorruptibility and irresistibility (ibid., 31.4-9, p. 43).

It is also clear that suffering does not have the role in Valentinus we find in the orthodox position. There suffering is in itself redemptive, as we have seen. Here the suffering is, in Jonas' words, a "stratagem" designed to divert the attention of the archons as Christ leaves the body of Jesus *before* his death (Jonas p. 195). Thus Christ is able to return to the Pleroma, a theme spelled out more clearly in other Valentinian texts. The real suffering is Sophia's, before the making of the world, and this is the true Valentinian emphasis.

We turn now to the docetic references among the Gnostics, beginning with Marcion who professed an extreme form of this belief. We have already seen the tremendous revulsion this second-century teacher felt for the body and the material world, the creations of the inferior God of the Old Testament. Thus Jesus, God's true Son, could have nothing whatsoever to do with such tainted flesh that was born of the antipathy to the true Father. In fact, Marcion's Jesus was not even born in this world through a woman's body. He suddenly appears, sent to earth from the heavenly realm having gone through none of the human developmental stages. Tertullian cites Marcion's interpretation of the gospel statement "Who is my mother?" (Mt 12:48)[12] as illustrative of this fact. We find a similar expression in Manicheism, where the notion that Jesus was born of a woman was repugnant:

> If Christ was conceived in a woman's womb he cannot be divine: the whole structure of his royal origin is brought tumbling to the ground in ruins by any that shall say he was born in a woman's womb (Allberry, p. 121n).

Thus, not even the doctrine of the Virgin Birth, avoiding the taint of any involvement with sexuality, was enough for the extreme anti-corporeal Manicheans.

We have already seen that Marcion recognized only an edited version of Luke's gospel as canonical. In his treatment of the beginning of Jesus' earthly "life" we see an example of this in his omissions, transposition, and interpolation of the word "God" for "Jesus," and his rendering of Luke 3:1 and 4:31. The original reads:

> In the fifteenth year of Tiberius Caesar's reign . . . the word of God came to John son of Zechariah . . . . He [Jesus] went down to Capernaum, a town in Galilee, and taught them on the sabbath.

Marcion's version reads:

> In the fifteenth year of Tiberius Caesar's reign God went down to Capernaum, a town in Galilee, and taught them on the sabbath (in Mansel, p. 215).

The seeming death of Jesus is brought about by the hatred of the

---

12. *See also* "The Gospel of the Ebionites," p. 337 below.

demiurgic God of the Old Testament, who jealously observed this Son of the good God, whose power and glory were manifest in this world. It was this heavenly power that represented the end of the Old Testament's law and the power of its God. As this God witnessed his subjects being attracted to Jesus, according to Marcion, he aroused the wrath of the Jews, his sons, against this divine intruder. The Jews, faithful to their creator, persecute and eventually murder Jesus who then descends to hell. It goes without saying that Marcion denies the physical resurrection of this illusory yet nonetheless abhorrent body.

However, as commented earlier, Marcion does not deny the prophecies of the Old Testament prophets, nor the Messianic expectations of the Jews, since these have nothing to do with the coming of Jesus, but rather with the advent of the earthly ruler, the son of the Demiurge. This messianic figure will come only for the restoration and salvation of the already dispersed Jews. Jesus on the other hand was sent by his Father for the redemption of the whole world, at least for those who believe in him and reject the Old Testament Jewish God.

Returning to the Manicheans, Augustine describes their docetism:

> They assert ... that Christ was the one called by our Scriptures the Serpent, and they assure us that they have been given insight into this in order to open the eyes of knowledge and to distinguish between Good and Evil. Christ came in the latter days to save souls, not bodies. He did not really exist in the flesh, but in mockery of the human senses proferred the simulated appearance of fleshly form, and thereby also produced the illusion not only of death, but also of resurrection (Augustine *de haer.* 46.5, in Haardt, p. 347).

In the Nag Hammadi sources we find many expressions of docetism. One of the major themes of "The First Apocalypse of James" is the so-called suffering of Jesus. The Lord appears to the concerned James who says:

> "Rabbi, I have found you! I have heard of your sufferings, which you endured. And I have been much distressed. ... I was wishing that I would not see this people. They must be judged for these things that they have done ...." The Lord said, "James, do not be concerned for me or for this people. I am he who was within me. Never have I suffered in any way, nor have I been distressed. And this people has done me no harm" (1 ApocJs V.31.5-23, in *NHL*, p. 245).

"The Second Treatise of the Great Seth" is an overtly polemic attack on the orthodox Church. It focuses heavily on the Gnostic interpretation of the crucifixion as against the orthodox view, and holds to the "laughing Jesus" docetic portrait found in Basilides. The revealer is Jesus himself and he states:

> I visited a bodily dwelling. I cast out the one who was in it first, and I went in. And the whole multitude of the archons became troubled. And all the matter of the archons as well as all the begotten powers of the earth were shaken when it saw the likeness of the Image, since it was mixed. And I am the one who was in it, not resembling him who was in it first. For he was an earthly man, but I, I am from above the heavens . . . . I am a stranger to the regions below (Gr. Seth VII.51.20-11, in *NHL*, pp. 330f).

The archons plot against Jesus, but to no avail:

> I did not succumb to them as they had planned. But I was not afflicted at all. Those who were there punished me. *And I did not die in reality but in appearance,* lest I be put to shame by them because these are my kinsfolk. . . . I was about to succumb to fear, and I suffered according to their sight and thought, in order that they may never find any word to speak about them. For my death which they think happened, happened to them in their error and blindness, since they nailed their man [Simon of Cyrene] unto their death. For their Ennoias did not see me, for they were deaf and blind. But in doing these things, they condemn themselves. Yes, they saw me; they punished me. It was another, their father, who drank the gall and the vinegar; it was not I. They struck me with the reed; it was another, Simon, who bore the cross on his shoulder. It was another upon whom they placed the crown of thorns. But I was rejoicing in the height over all the wealth of the archons and the offspring of their error, of their empty glory. And I was laughing at their ignorance . . . . I am Jesus Christ . . . who is exalted above the heavens . . . . I alone am the friend of Sophia. I have been in the bosom of the father from the beginning, in the place of the sons of the truth, and the Greatness (ibid., 55.14-56.20; 69.21-23; 70.4-9; pp. 337f, my italics).

"The Apocalypse of Peter," probably belonging to the third century A.D., is another Gnostic treatise attacking the orthodox Church. Parallels are drawn between the persecution of Jesus and the persecution of the Gnostics at the hands of the Church authorities. Near the end of his revelation to Peter, Jesus exhorts his apostle to be brave. Peter then sees Jesus

> seemingly being seized by them. And I said, "What do I see, O Lord, that it is you yourself whom they take, and that you are grasping me? Or who is this one, glad and laughing on the tree? And is it another one whose feet and hands they are striking?"
> The Savior said to me, "He whom you saw on the tree, glad and laughing, this is the living Jesus. But this one into whose hands and feet they drive the nails is his fleshly part, which is the substitute being put to shame, the one who came into being in his likeness. But look at him and me" (ApocPt VIII.15-25, in *NHL*, p. 344).

We see expressed in these passages the prominent Gnostic view that the power of Christ descended upon the earthly Jesus at the moment of his baptism, and left his body just before the crucifixion. Thus all redemptive meaning is removed from the cross, as Jesus the Christ never suffered. Rather, the world's redemption is accomplished by virtue of the Call Jesus brings from above, as well as his being the model for the "distinction of kinds," separating out the true from the false, the formless from the form, the divinity from the corporeal (*see* Basilides below, p. 335). In Chapter 5, page 155, we quoted from the "Acts of John," concerning the ontological separating out by the cross of the fixed from the unstable. We continue that passage now:

> ... nor am I the man who is on the Cross. ... I was taken to be that I am not, I who am not what for many others I was .... I have suffered none of those things which they will say of me .... You hear that I suffered, yet I suffered not ... and that I was pierced, yet I was not wounded; that I was hanged, yet I was not hanged; that blood flowed from me, yet it did not flow (AJ 99, in *NTA* II, p. 233).

The disciple John, recipient of this revelation, then describes his reactions to the people:

> ... he was taken up, without any of the multitude seeing him. And going down I laughed at them all, since he had told me what they had said about him; and I held this one thing fast in my mind, that the Lord had performed everything as a symbol and a dispensation for the conversion and salvation of man (ibid., 102, pp. 234f).

We turn now to the Gnostic witnesses as described by the Church Fathers. Of the infamous (to the Church Fathers) Cerinthus, a contemporary of John, Irenaeus writes:

> Jesus, he suggested, was not born of a virgin, for that seemed to him impossible, but was the son of Joseph and Mary, just like the rest of men, but far beyond them in justice and prudence and wisdom. After his baptism Christ descended upon him in the form of a dove, from the power that is over all things, and then he proclaimed the unknown Father and accomplished miracles. But at the end Christ separated again from Jesus, and Jesus suffered and was raised again, but Christ remained impassible, since he was pneumatic [i.e., of the spirit] (*Adv. haer.* I.26.1, in F I, p. 36).

Carpocrates' span of activity was the early decades of the second century, and Irenaeus continues:

> Carpocrates and his disciples say that ... Jesus was born of Joseph

and like the rest of men, but he was distinct from the rest in that, since his soul was strong and pure, it remembered what it had seen in the regions of the unbegotten God: and for this reason power was sent down to him that he might escape the world-creators by it. It passed through them all and was set free in all, and ascended up to him, and likewise the souls which embraced the like (ibid., I.25.1, p. 36).

Saturninus was probably a contemporary of Basilides, and Irenaeus reports:

The Savior he [Saturninus] assumed to be unbegotten, incorporeal, and without form, but appeared in semblance as a man. The God of the Jews, he says, was one of the angels; and because all the archons wanted to destroy the Father, Christ came for the destruction of the God of the Jews and the salvation of those who believe in him; these are they who have the spark of life in them (ibid., I.24.2, p. 41).

We saw in Chapter 1 that the Church Fathers presented two different versions of Basilides' theory, and this difference is most manifest in their understanding of Jesus' suffering and death. We first quote Irenaeus, writing about the docetic Basilides:

The unoriginate and ineffable Father, seeing their disastrous plight, sent his first-born Nous--he is the one who is called the Christ--to liberate those who believe in him . . . . he appeared on earth as a man and performed miracles. For the same reason also he did not suffer, but a certain Simon of Cyrene was compelled to carry his cross for him; and this Simon was transformed by him [Jesus] so that he was thought to be Jesus himself, and was crucified through ignorance and error. Jesus, however, took on the form of Simon, and stood by laughing at them. For since he was an incorporeal power and the Nous of the unborn Father, he was transformed in whatever way he pleased, and in this way he ascended to him who had sent him, laughing at them . . . .Therefore those who know these things have been set free from the rulers who made the world. It is not right to confess him who was crucified but him who came in the form of a man . . . . Thus . . . if anyone confesses the crucified, he is still a slave, and under the power of those who made the bodies; he who denies him has been set free from them, and knows the saving dispensation made by the unoriginate Father (ibid., I.24.6, pp. 60f).

In the version of Hippolytus, we find quite a different view of Jesus' suffering, paralleling other Gnostic systems; namely, that Jesus' sufferings were real and served to separate out his spirit from his body, and so make the distinction for all people. As different as these two versions are, they nonetheless agree in differing from the orthodox

Christian understanding that Jesus' sufferings were redemptive, atoning for the sins of the world.

> When the birth . . . had taken place, all that concerns the Savior happened in a similar way to what is written in the gospels. These things happened, says he, so that Jesus might become the first-fruits of the "distinction of kinds" among what was confused [form and formlessness] . . . . There suffered, therefore, that bodily part of him which derived from the formlessness, and it returned to the formlessness. There rose up that psychic part of him . . . . He bore aloft what was from the boundary Spirit, and it stayed in the boundary Spirit. . . . the suffering of Jesus took place with no other object than the distinction into kinds of what had been confused. For he [Basilides] says the whole Sonship which was left behind in the formlessness to give and receive benefit must be distinguished into kinds in the very way in which Jesus also was distinguished into kinds (*Ref.* VII.27.8-12, in F I, pp. 73f).

We turn now to the Ophites, a Gnostic group we spoke of earlier. In their understanding, Jesus is the product of Sophia's pleas for help in releasing the power of light that is trapped in the body. Christ (Sophia's brother) thus descends through the spheres until he enters the body of Jesus at his baptism (a theme we have already seen), and then leaves before his death after preaching the "unknown God." Jesus then rises in his psychic body, not the physical body that was believed by the orthodox to have risen. The risen Christ takes with him the trapped particles of light that are released from those (the Ophites) who receive the secret Gnostic revelation. It is interesting to note not only the strong Valentinian influence, but the fidelity in many places to the biblical tradition, not to mention the parallel with this Manichean teaching:

> Christ . . . is the Nous. He came once from the Upper Region, liberated the major share of this [trapped Divine] power for God, and when at last he was crucified, he thereby established the Gnosis that in this way the Divine Power is also imprisoned in Hyle [Matter] and crucified in it (in Haardt, pp. 338f).

The Ophites:

> Since she [Sophia] had herself no respite either in heaven or in earth, in her grief she summoned her mother [First Woman] to her aid . . . who took pity at the repentance of her daughter, and . . . Christ was sent . . . . out and descended to his sister . . . . When Sophia who is below knew that her brother was coming down to her, she both announced his coming through John, and prepared a baptism of

repentance, and prepared in advance Jesus, so that when he came down Christ would find a clean vessel, and so that... a woman might receive annunciation from Christ. . . . And Jesus, being born from a virgin . . . was wiser and purer and more just than all men. Bound up with Sophia, Christ descended, and so Jesus Christ came to be.

Many of his disciples, they say, did not know the descent of Christ upon him, but when Christ descended on him, then he began to perform acts of power, to heal, and to proclaim the unknown Father, and to confess himself openly as son of the First Man. At this the rulers [archons] and the fathers became angry with Jesus and arranged for him to be killed. While he was being led to it, Christ himself and Sophia went off, they say, to the Imperishable Aeon, but Jesus was crucified. Christ did not forget him, but sent a certain power down into him, which raised him in the body. This body was of soul and spirit [the psychic body of the Valentinians]; for what was worldly he left in the world. When the disciples saw that he had risen, they did not know him; they did not even know Christ himself, through whom he rose from the dead. They [the Ophites] say that the greatest error which arose among his disciples was that they thought he had risen in a worldly body, and did not know that "flesh and blood do not possess the kingdom of God" (1 Co 15:50) (*Adv. haer.* I.30.12-13, in F I, pp. 92f).

We examine now the Valentinian system of Ptolemaeus as given by the Church Father Clement of Alexandria, closely parallel to the account given by Irenaeus. It is also most likely one of the prototypes for the Ophite speculation seen above. We pick up the story with the descent into Jesus:

> But when he came to the "place," Jesus found, ready to be put on, the Christ who had been foretold, whom the prophets and the law had proclaimed, who was the image of the Savior. But this psychic Christ whom he put on was invisible. Therefore it was necessary that he who was to come into the world, that he might be seen and touched, and be active in affairs there, should also wear a body perceptible to the senses. A body was therefore woven for him out of invisible, psychic substance, and, by the power of a divine preparation, it came into the world of sense.... That he himself was other than that which he assumed is made clear from what he confesses . . . .

Here Clement cites various scriptural passages in support of the Valentinian assertion that Jesus and Christ are not the same; i.e., the Jesus who suffers and the Christ who departs before the crucifixion. We continue after these citations:

> He died, when the Spirit which had come upon him in Jordan departed from him; not that it might exist separately, but rather it

withdrew in order that death might operate. For how would the body have died, if life had been present in him? Death would then in fact have had dominion over the Savior, which is absurd. But death was outwitted by craftiness. For when the body died and when death had taken hold of it, the Savior sent forth the ray of power which had come upon him and destroyed death, and he raised the mortal body after he had scattered the passions. The psychic element is raised again in this way and is saved. The spiritual [obviously referring to the Gnostics] who have believed obtain a higher salvation, receiving the souls as wedding garments (*Excerpta* 59.1-61.1; 61.6-8, in F I, pp. 151f).

The narrative here concludes similarly to the Ophite text above with the "fullness of joy and peace" that characterizes the end of the world and the consummation of the "eternal marriage of the union."

"The Gospel of the Ebionites," which dates from the first half of the second century, also attests to the docetic Jesus: Jesus was not born of a virgin, for his divinity does not rest with a divine begetting, but rather with the bestowal by the Holy Spirit when he was baptized. This bestowal is the union of Jesus with the divine Christ. Fragments of this text are found in the writings of the Church Father Epiphanius:

And as he came up from the water, the heavens were opened and he saw the Holy Spirit in the form of a dove that descended and entered into him.... Moreover they [the Ebionites] deny that he was a man, evidently on the ground of the word which the Savior spoke...: Who is my mother and who are by brethren? (*Haer.* 30.13,7f; 14.5, in *NTA* I, pp. 157f)

Elsewhere Epiphanius supplies another passage which expresses this docetic belief that Jesus was not really born:

... this Christ is the one who descended and showed men this knowledge, whom they also call Jesus. And he was not born from Mary, but was manifested through Mary. And he has not assumed flesh, unless it be a mere appearance (*Panar.* XXVI.10.4-5, in F I, p. 322).

In the very few fragments that the Fathers purport to be Valentinus' own words, we have but one, cited by Clement, in which this great teacher speaks of Jesus. The fragment is of particular note because of its agreement with Hippolytus' report that the Valentinians believed that Jesus' body was spiritual. As we see here, Jesus could not digest nor eliminate what he ate.

In the letter to Agathopus Valentinus says: "While enduring

everything he was continent. Jesus realized divinity: he ate and drank in a special way, without evacuating the food. So great was his power of continence that the food was not corrupted in him, for he did not possess corruptibility . . ." (*Strom.* III.7, in F I, p. 242).

Returning to the "Acts of John" we find several strong docetic passages. In one group, Jesus' appearance is continually changing: to James he is first like a child and then a young man, while to John, a handsome man and later a bald-headed man with a thick flowing beard. John never sees Jesus with his eyes closed, and his breast sometimes is soft and smooth, other times is hard as a rock.

> I will tell you another glory, brethren; sometimes when I meant to touch him I encountered a material, solid body; but at other times again when I felt him, his substance was immaterial and incorporeal, and as if it did not exist at all.... And I often wished, as I walked with him, to see his footprint in the earth, whether it appeared--for I saw him raising himself from the earth--and I never saw it (AJ 93, in *NTA* II, p. 227).

On Mount Tabor, John sees Jesus

> not dressed in clothes at all, but stripped of those [that] we [usually] saw [upon him], and not like a man at all (ibid., 90, p. 226).

One of the more popular gospel literary genres was the infancy gospels, all of which reflected at least a tendency to docetism, where the young Jesus is portrayed as being a super-human miracle worker, in the words of Cullmann, a "playful divine boy" (*NTA* I, p. 391).

In "The Infancy Story of Thomas," possibly dating from the end of the second century, Jesus is also seen as a youthful Gnostic revealer. Here, as a five-year-old, he speaks to his teacher Zacchaeus and to his father Joseph:

> ...I am apart from you, though I dwell among you. Honor in the flesh I have not.... For when thou wast born, I was.... And as for the cross of which thou hast spoken, he shall bear it, whose it is. For when I am greatly exalted, I shall lay aside whatever mixture I have of your race (in *NTA* I, p. 399).

In an untitled infancy gospel, the midwife to Jesus' birth states:

> And I stood there stupefied.... For I was looking upon the intense brightness of the light which was born. But the light itself ... became like a child, and in a moment became a child as children are customarily born. And I ... took him up in my hands ... and was seized with

terror because he had no weight like other children who are born. And I looked at him and there was no defilement in him, but he was in all his body shining as in the dew of the most high God, light to carry, radiant to behold. And . . . I wondered greatly because he did not cry as new-born babes are accustomed to cry . . . (in *NTA* I, p. 414).

Origen - Platonism

Of all the Christian writers--Gnostic and orthodox alike--considered in this book, Origen alone adopts a position in regard to Jesus that approximates *A Course in Miracles*, clearly subordinating him to God the Father. We briefly touched upon this "Subordinationism" in Chapter 2, but shall explore it more fully here and take it up again in Part III.

According to Origen, Jesus was eternally begotten or generated from God, but Origen cites Paul's "first-born of all creation" (Col 1:15) in maintaining that Jesus was still a creature, thus emphasizing that he is secondary or subordinate to his Creator. The soul of Jesus, then, like those of all other rational beings, was pre-existent. However, when in that original instant the other souls began to fall away from God through their own negligence and sloth, Jesus remained constant in his remembrance of his Creator. He is thus among that group (if not the first member of that group as suggested elsewhere by Origen) of "others . . . [who fell] so little from their original state that they appear to have lost scarcely anything" (*First Princ.*, p. 249, n.1). Sin never tainted Jesus' soul and he retained the innocence of his creation, having, in the words of Isaiah 7:15f, chosen good and refused evil. This innocence of Christ was so close to him that, in time, it became indissolubly linked with his soul, and Jesus and Christ became one. It was this united soul that entered this world as the flesh of the Virgin Mary:

> It is therefore right that this soul [i.e., Jesus'], either because it was wholly in the Son of God, or because it received the Son of God wholly into itself, should itself be called, along with that flesh which it has taken, the Son of God and the power of God, Christ and the wisdom of God; and on the other hand that the Son of God, "through whom all things were created," should be termed Jesus and the Son of man . . . . Moreover what could more appropriately be "one spirit" with God than this soul, which joined itself so firmly in love to God as to be worthy of being called "one spirit" with him? . . . it was the perfection of his love and the sincerity of his true affection which gained for him this inseparable unity with God . . . . As a reward for its love . . . it is anointed with the "oil of gladness," that is the soul with the word of God is made Christ (*First Princ.* II.6.3,4).

Origen is aware of the difficulty of his teaching, especially in view of his assertions that "among all rational creatures there is none which is not capable of both good and evil" (ibid., I.8.3). However, this is not to assert that every soul has chosen evil, nor for that matter, that every soul has chosen good. Thus, though

> it cannot be doubted that the nature of his [Jesus] soul was the same as that of all souls . . . . this soul which belongs to Christ so chose to love righteousness as to cling to it unchangeably and inseparably in accordance with the immensity of its love; the result being that by firmness of purpose, immensity of affection and an inextinguishable warmth of love all susceptibility to change or alteration was destroyed, and what formerly depended upon the will was by the influence of long custom changed into nature. Thus we must believe that there did exist in Christ a human and rational soul, and yet not suppose that it had any susceptibility to or possibility of sin (ibid., II.6.5).

Origen's Christology was of course subject to condemnation by the Church Council convened by Justinian, and is condemned in words it can be assumed are drawn from the Alexandrian's own:

> . . . the race of daemons appears two-fold, being composed of human souls and of higher spirits that have fallen to this condition, and that out of all the original unity of rational beings one mind remained steadfast in the divine love and contemplation, and that he, having become Christ and king of all rational beings, created all bodily nature, both heaven and earth and the things that are between them (ibid., II.8.3).

For Origen, then, Jesus becomes a model for us all to choose the good and refuse evil:

> . . . so, too, should each one of us, after a fall or transgression, cleanse himself from stains by the example set before him, and taking a leader for the journey proceed along the steep path of virtue, that so perchance by this means we may as far as is possible become, through our imitation of him, partakers of the divine nature (ibid., IV.4.4).

In this sense then, of Jesus being a "non-cosmic" teacher, Origen is closer to the Platonic tradition then the Christian. We have already discussed the role of the philosopher-king in Plato's system and seen its important place in the plan of the Republic. This person obviously is not a redemptive figure, but merely one whose example and teaching leads the pupil higher and higher on the path of reason to the apperception of the Good. Plotinus, however, does not even go that far. One finds in his philosophical system the almost total absence of a savior-teacher, let alone a mediator figure, who brings people closer to God. Rather, it is through the contemplative efforts of the individual soul that the ascent back to the One is accomplished. All this is brought about without any effort at all on the part of the One or any of the divine beings or Ideas. They simply *are*. This position differs, for example, from that of the religious Philo, who posited an intermediate figure-- the Logos--guiding people back to the Good, supplemented by the prayers and devotions that emphasize our gratitude to this Divine Being, without whom our goal could never be attained. We shall return to this theme in Chapter 10.

Chapter 10

PRACTICAL IMPLICATIONS

Now that we have considered the various Gnostic theories the crucial question remains: What does all this mean in terms of living in this world? "By their fruits you shall know them" remains a critical criterion in evaluating any system, philosophic, psychological, or religious. What is within our minds--our belief system--will inevitably have behavioral expression, and it is by these expressions--the fruits of our belief system--that we can often more properly evaluate and understand these beliefs. I do not speak here of the forms of our behavior as such, but rather their underlying motivation and the meaning given to them. In this chapter, then, we shall examine the practical implications of the Gnostic, Christian, and Platonic systems for living in this world of the flesh.

We begin with the Gnostics who, though denying reality to this world and not according it any importance, nonetheless had some serious things to say about living here. We shall divide this part of the chapter into two essential parts: religious practice, including teachings regarding ritual and sacrament; and the ethical and moral implications for living in the world: libertinism, asceticism, and moderateness.

Gnosticism: Religious Practice

The great Gnostic schools of the second century were basically that: philosophical schools, not religious or cultic communities. As we have seen, by virtue of their very theologies these Gnostic schools eschewed organizations and institutionalization of their teachings. Nonetheless in some Gnostic groups, at least according to the Church Fathers, there was a strong tendency towards being a cultic community. An example of a Gnostic cult is found in Irenaeus' description of the Carpocratians:

> Some of them mark their own disciples by branding them on the back of the right ear-lobe.... They call themselves gnostics. They have also images, some painted, some too made of other material, and say they are the form of Christ made by Pilate in that time when Jesus was with men. These they crown, and they set them forth with the images of the philosophers of the world, Pythagoras, Plato, Aristotle, and the rest; and their other observance concerning them they carry out like the heathen (*Adv. haer.* I.25.6, in F I, p. 38).

And Epiphanius attests to the following:

> And if a visitor comes to them who holds the same opinion, there is
> a sign in use among them, the men for the women and the women for
> the men; when they stretch out their hand, by way of a greeting of
> course, they make a tickling stroke beneath the palm of the hand,
> indicating by this means that the new arrival belongs to their cult
> (*Panar*. XXVI.4.1, in F I, p. 318).

It was the general Gnostic tendency to see as anathema all church-related activities--rituals, sacraments, cultic communities--yet there were at the same time many groups that did emphasize certain sacraments and rituals, looking very much like the orthodox Church in some cases as we shall see, though clearly with very different understandings of these rituals. One of the most important references for these Gnostic practices is "The Gospel of Philip," which discusses five sacramental ceremonies: baptism, anointing, Eucharist, redemption, and the bridal chamber. We shall use these five as the basis for our discussion of Gnostic sacramentology. Obviously these Gnostic groups did not escape recourse to magical interventions as means to effect salvation and avoid entrapment by the archons of the world. In general these rituals are in the minority, probably due in part to the attempt of these dissident sects to differentiate themselves from the orthodox. The major exceptions are with the non-Christian Mandeans and the Valentinians who, as we have seen, did not see themselves as separate from the Great Church. We begin with the rites and rituals surrounding water: baptism and lustrations (washings).

1. Baptism

As the Mandeans trace their beginnings to John the Baptist, the "messenger of the King of Light," it is not surprising to see the important role that baptism plays in their religious life:

> Let the Jordan flow [symbol of the baptismal waters] and baptize
> ... your souls with the living baptism, which I have brought you from
> the World of Light. .... Every person who is marked with the "Sign
> of Life" and over whom the name of the King of Light is pronounced,
> and every person who is firm and steadfast in baptism ... will not be
> impeded by anyone on his way to the place of light (GR I.123-24, in
> F II, p. 277).

"The Gospel of Philip" describes baptism in a uniquely powerful manner, yet nonetheless sounds very orthodox in its understanding of the meaning of this sacramental ritual:

344

The living water is a body. It is necessary that we put on the living man. Therefore, when he is about to go down into the water, he unclothes himself, in order that he may put on the living man ... (GPh II.75.21-25, in *NHL*, p. 145).

In Greek the words for "to baptize" and "to dye" are similar (*baptizein* and *baptein*), and this leads the author of our text to write:

God is a dyer. As the good dyes, which are called "true," dissolve with the things dyed in them, so it is with those whom God has dyed. Since his dyes are immortal, they are immortal by means of his colors. Now God dips what he dips in water (ibid., 61.12-21, p. 137).

Characteristic of the Gnostic understanding of baptism was the total absence of its power to forgive sins, which the Gnostics felt was a demeaning of the ritual. Baptism had far greater importance as a rite of admission to the Gnostic awareness of immortality, part of the initiation into the realm of knowledge. Irenaeus explains this Gnostic view:

They affirm that it is necessary for those who have attained to perfect knowledge, that they may be regenerated into the power which is above all. Otherwise, it is impossible to enter into the Pleroma, for it is this redemption which leads them down into the profundities of Bythos [i.e., the abyss wherein dwells the divine Source]. For the baptism of (that is, instituted by) the visible Jesus took place for the remission of sins, but the redemption by the Christ who descended upon him for perfection. They allege that the former is psychic and the latter spiritual (*Adv. haer.* I.21.2, in F I, p. 218).

Baptism thus is seen as bestowing upon the Gnostic, in the words of Rudolph "the spirit of immortality, redemption and resurrection" (Rudolph, p. 227). Hippolytus quotes the Naassenes:

For the promise of the washing in baptism is, they say, nothing less than the introduction into unfading enjoyment of him who in their fashion is washed in living water and anointed with unutterable anointing (*Ref.* V.7.19, in F I, p. 267).

The Sethians, Hippolytus writes, cite the parallels drawn between the baptism of Jesus and what is required of everyone who desires initiation into the Gnostic mysteries:

But ... it is not enough that the perfect man, the Word, entered a virgin's womb and "loosed the pangs" that were in that darkness; but after he entered into the foul mysteries of the womb he washed himself and drank the cup of living, springing water, which everyone must needs drink who is to put off the form of the servant and put on the heavenly apparel (*Ref.* V.19.20-21, in F I, p. 303).

In "The Gospel of the Egyptians," part of the Nag Hammadi library, we find the following prayer involving sacraments focusing on baptism and leading to eternal life. We see here recourse to strange sounds and syllables, seemingly expressive of the specific mysteries of this Gnostic (Sethian) school:

> Ie ieus eo ou eo oua! Really truly, O Yesseus Mazareus Yessedekeus, O living water, O child of the child, O glorious name, really truly, aion o on, iiii eeee eeee oooo uuuu oooo aaaa.... This great name of thine is upon me, O self-begotten Perfect one, who art not outside me.... Now that I have known thee, I have mixed myself with the immutable. I have armed myself with an armor of light; I have become light.... Therefore the incense of life is in me. I mixed it with water after the model of all archons, in order that I may live with thee in the peace of the saints, thou who existeth really truly for ever (GEgypt III.66.8-68.1, in *NHL*, pp. 204f).

In "The Kerygmata Petrou," discussed above, there is an extensive discussion about the doctrine of baptism:

> And do not believe that you will ever have hope if you remain unbaptized even if you are more pious than all the pious have been hitherto.... when you are born again for God of water, then through fear you get rid of your first birth which came of lust (Ker. Pet. H XI.25.1; 26.1, in *NTA* II, p. 124).

Such baptismal purification, however, cannot be truly efficacious unless it is accompanied by the good works associated with a life of ascetic purity:

> Therefore cleanse your hearts from wickedness by heavenly thoughts ... and wash your bodies with water (ibid., 28.2, p. 125).

The "Acts of Thomas" provides many examples of the use of sacraments to seal the initiation into the Christian family brought about by the apostle Thomas. Central to these acts are the rituals of anointing by oil and the Eucharist, which we shall discuss below. Characteristically reduced in importance is the role of water-baptism. Where mention is made it is clear that we have instances of "Catholicizing," wherein a later Catholic editor appended his own interpretation. Two such examples follow. In the Tenth Act, Thomas teaches about baptism:

This baptism is forgiveness of sins. It brings to new birth a light that is shed around. It brings to new birth the new man, raises up the new man in three-fold manner, and is partaker in forgiveness of sins (ATh 132, in *NTA*, II, p. 512).

In the Thirteenth Act, Thomas seals a conversion in these words: "And when he had anointed them he led them down to the water in the name of the Father and of the Son and of the Holy Spirit" (ibid., 157, p. 526).

2. Anointing

By far the most important of the Gnostic rituals was the sacrament of anointing, including the sealing of the initiate--before or at death--to ensure safe passage through the realms of the archons. There are obvious magical overtones in all recourse to rites and sacraments, whether in orthodox or heterodox circles, and these are seen particularly in the rituals associated with anointing. Here, as in baptism, anointing plays a relatively insignificant role in most Gnostic systems. Yet in certain sects, again principally within the Valentinian circle, we see its importance.

The anointing was performed with oil (rarely in conjunction with water), and one of its purposes for the Gnostics was to act as a seal to protect the person from foreign, not to mention demonic, influence. However, its principal purpose was to transmit to the Gnostic the immortality that was their promise as redemption for the original fall.

In "The Gospel of Philip" we find the connection of this "magical" oil with the olive tree, called the tree of life, which also served as the source of the wood on which Jesus was crucified:

> Philip the apostle said, "Joseph the carpenter planted a garden because he needed wood for his trade. It was he who made the cross from the trees which he planted. His own offspring hung on that which he planted. His offspring was Jesus and the planting was the cross." But the tree of life is in the middle of the garden. However, it is from the olive tree that we get the chrism [oil], and from the chrism, the resurrection (GPh II.73.8-19, in *NHL*, p. 144).

The prominence of the anointing is seen in a later passage from "The Gospel of Philip:"

> The chrism is superior to baptism, for it is from the word "chrism" that we have been called "Christians," certainly not because of the word "baptism." And it is because of the chrism that "the Christ" has his name. For the Father anointed the Son, and the Son anointed the apostles, and the apostles anointed us [the Gnostics]. He who has

been anointed possesses everything. He possesses the resurrection, the light, the cross, the Holy Spirit (ibid., 74.12-22).

Irenaeus cites the followers of Marcus similarly:

But some say that it is superfluous to bring people to the water [baptism], but they mix oil and water together and pour it on the heads to be initiated . . . : this is regarded as being the redemption. They also anoint with balsam (*Adv. haer.* I.21.4, in F I, pp. 219f).

Irenaeus then continues by contrasting this position with others who obviously do not take kindly to the more magical view of redemption:

But others reject all this and say that one ought not to celebrate the mystery of the ineffable and invisible power by means of visible and corruptible created things, the inconceivable and incorporeal by means of what is sensually tangible and corporeal. The perfect redemption is said to be the knowledge of the ineffable "Greatness" . . . (ibid., F I, p. 220).

We find in "The Acts of Thomas" clear expression of the importance the sacrament held in this Gnostic group. We shall cite two examples: Thomas expels a demon from a woman, who exclaims to him:

"Apostle of the Most High, give me the seal, that that enemy may not return to me again!" Then he made her come near to him, and laying his hands upon her sealed her in the name of the Father and of the Son and of the Holy Spirit. And many others also were sealed with her (ATh 48, in *NTA*, II, p. 470).

In his final act before his martyrdom, Thomas converts Vazan, son of the king, and anoints him with words which also reflect the association of the oil with the power of the olive tree:

O fruit fairer than the other fruits, with which no other can be compared at all . . . power of the tree which if men put on they conquer their adversaries. . . . Jesus, let thy victorious power come, and let it settle in this oil as then it settled in the wood that is its kin . . . and they who crucified thee did not endure its word; let the gift also come by which, breathing upon thine enemies, thou didst make them draw back and fall headlong, and let it dwell in this oil, over which we name thy holy name! (Ibid., 157, p. 525)

As has been mentioned, the Gnostic sacrament for the dying was of great importance in certain sects as the means by which the departed soul could safely make the ascent to the Pleroma, unimpeded by the hostile archons who sought to enslave it. Sometimes the soul is rendered invisible and thus escapes notice by the hostile archons. We shall see later in Gnostic libertinism that another means for evading capture by the archons, whose hold is mediated by justice--i.e., adherence to the world's morality--was to flout all the moral laws. By the use of certain formulas and passwords the soul becomes unchained by the powers of the world, and is restored to the wholeness of the Pleroma. Several Gnostic groups practiced such rituals, or "masses for the dead." Irenaeus provides us with a clear statement of this, attributed to the Valentinians:

> Still others there are who redeem the dying up to the point of their departure by pouring on their heads oil and water . . . in order that they may become unassailable by and invisible to the powers and authorities, and that their inner man may ascend above the realm of the invisible, whilst their body remains behind in the created world, and their soul is delivered to the Demiurge (*Adv. haer.* I.21.5, in F I, p. 220).

As we saw in Chapter 8, Irenaeus continues by citing the invocations the soul is to perform as it makes its ascent.

Parenthetic to our discussion of anointing as preparation for the ascent, we may note here a moving example of the Gnostic petition at death. It is the prayer of Thomas at his martyrdom:

> My Lord and my God . . . be thou with all who serve thee, and lead me today, since I come to thee! Let none take my soul, which I have committed unto thee. Let not the tax-collectors see me, and let not the exactors lay false charge against me! Let not the serpent see me, and let not the children of the dragon hiss me! Behold, Lord, I have fulfilled thy work and accomplished thy command. I have become a slave; therefore today do I receive freedom (ATh 167, in *NTA*, II, p. 529).

The Mandeans offer by far the most elaborate ritual or mass for the dead, called "masiqta" meaning "ascent." We already have seen examples of the prayers and rituals for the ascent in Chapter 8. The entire ritual includes anointings with oil, washings from the Jordan, ceremonial meals, and of course prayers and recitations. All these serve the purpose variously of accompanying and nourishing the soul on its forty-five day journey through purgatory to the light; a journey which for the Mandeans was fraught with danger and thus necessitated the safeguards of the rituals. Interestingly enough the Mandeans' graves were unmarked, for they believed that they only contained the transitory body; the essence of the individual returned to the realm of light. In the following excerpt, we find instructions for the living:

> When a soul is set free and leaves the body, do not weep or lament for it.... Anyone who weeps for a soul, the seas and river-courses will cut him off from the realm of light. Whoever rends his clothes for it, he will when he ascends have a blemish in his garment.... When a soul in your midst departs, let the people hear hymns and recitations and instruct them, so that their heart be not ruined (GR II.1, in F II, p. 282).

The following Mandean hymn was meant for the placing of a sealed flask of oil with the dead. It is referred to as a letter (cf. "The Hymn of the Pearl"), and serves to protect the soul as it travels past the "watch-houses" to its home in the light:

> It is a sealed letter which leaves the world. A letter written with kusta [Life] and sealed with the seal of the Mighty. Perfect men wrote it and believing men gave it their guarantee. They hung it about the soul's neck and dispatched it to the gate of life. The soul in her wisdom impressed her nail on the letter [the plug that seals the bottle] (ML Qol 73, in F II, p. 285).

3. Eucharist

The Eucharistic sacrament, or "sacred meal," is described in some of the texts we have already examined. However, it is even less frequently found in Gnostic texts than references to baptism or anointing. There is, nonetheless, a non-Christian reference in "The Prayer of Thanksgiving," a Hermetic text found in the *Nag Hammadi Library*. At the close of the prayer it is stated:

> When they had said these things in prayer, they embraced each other and they went to eat their holy food, which has no blood in it (Thanks. VI.65.2-8, in *NHL*, p. 299).

We also find the ritual of a meal in the Mandean literature, as we have just seen in the description of their ritual for the dead. It was part of the Sunday worship which included baptism and anointing.

The traditional Christian Eucharistic usage of bread and wine is retained in "The Gospel of Philip," yet with a characteristically Gnostic understanding:

> So it is also with the bread and the cup and the oil, even though there is another one superior to these.... The cup of prayer contains wine and water, since it is appointed as the type of the blood for which thanks is given. And it is full of the Holy Spirit, and it belongs to the wholly perfect man. When we drink this, we shall receive for

ourselves the perfect man (GPh II.74.36-75.1; 75.14-21, in *NHL*, p. 145).

The Gnostic interpretation of the Eucharistic union as a prototype of the re-union with the "angel image" or the heavenly aeons is expressed here:

> He [Jesus] said on that day in the Thanksgiving [i.e., the Eucharist], "You who have joined the perfect, the light, with the Holy Spirit, unite the angels with us also, the images" (ibid., 58.10-14, p. 135).

This meaning of the reuniting with the aeons is clarified in the *preceding* page:

> Because of this he [Jesus] said, "He who shall eat my flesh and drink my blood has not life in him." What is it? His flesh is the word, and his blood is the Holy Spirit. He who has received these has food and he has drink and clothing (ibid., 57.2-9).

In the Valentinian cosmology "word" and "Holy Spirit" are among the pairs of aeons.

Thus, at least in the Valentinian system expressed in "The Gospel of Philip," the components of the Eucharist are representative, not of the body and blood of Jesus, but of the heavenly Pleroma and the guarantor of the perfection and eternal life that is the Gnostic goal. This shift in meaning follows from the docetic Gnostic strain that taught, as we have seen, that the body of Jesus was illusory. Thus it would make no sense to establish a cult meal around what is *not* real, and so the focus becomes the reality of the spirit rejoined to the Pleroma.

A quite different interpretation, and much more traditional in its non-docetic nature, is found in this Eucharistic blessing by Thomas in the aforementioned "Acts." It illustrates again that the so-called Gnostic-Orthodox dichotomy was not as clear-cut as is frequently understood, for here in this text we find a blending of Gnostic ideas within a more traditional framework.

> Thy holy body which was crucified for us we eat, and thy blood which was poured out for us for salvation we drink. Let thy body, then, become for us salvation, and thy blood for remission of sins! (ATh 158, in *NTA* II, p. 526)

One of the most interesting reports we have of a Gnostic interpretation of a traditional sacrament comes from Irenaeus. It deals with the Valentinian Marcus, here exposed as a charlatan who uses the Eucharist as a means to further his seduction of women. The reliability of the

351

report of course is questionable, though it cannot be definitely dis-
proven. Nonetheless, Irenaeus' treatment is of importance for at least
expressing the ideas of the orthodox Church. The accuracy of its reporting should at least be considered, however, given the frequent
reports in our own time of sexual exploitation of devotees on the part
of spiritual leaders or gurus.

> There is another of those among them who prides himself on being
> an improver of his master's [Valentinus] teaching. His name is
> Marcus, and he is knowledgeable in magical deceit, by means of
> which he has led astray many men and not a few women and has
> induced them to turn to him as to one possessed of great skill and who
> has received a great power from the invisible and ineffable regions,
> an actual precursor of the Antichrist.... Over a cup mixed with wine
> he pretends to pray and, whilst greatly prolonging the invocation, he
> contrives that it should appear purple and red so that Grace [one of
> the Gnostic aeons], who belongs to the company of those who are
> superior to all things, may seem to be dropping her blood into that
> cup by means of his invocation, and that those present should fer-
> vently desire to taste of that cup in order that the Grace called hither
> by that magician may let her blood flow into them. Again he gives
> to women cups already mixed and full, and bids them offer thanks
> in his presence. When this is done, he produces another cup much
> larger than the one over which the deluded woman has given thanks,
> and he then pours from the smaller one over which she has given
> thanks into the one which he has brought forward--which was much
> larger--and at the same time he speaks as follows: "May 'Grace' who
> is before all things, who is beyond thought and description, fill thine
> inner man and multiply in thee her knowledge, sowing the mustard
> seed in good soil." By saying such things and by making the
> wretched woman deranged, he appears as a wonder-worker, when
> the larger cup is filled from the smaller one to such an extent that it
> actually overflows. By doing other things like this he has deceived
> many and drawn them into following him (*Adv. haer.* I.13.1-2, in F I,
> pp. 200f).

4. Redemption

The sacrament mentioned in "The Gospel of Philip" as "redemption" has no specific referents, but seems to have been used rather to
designate the physical or ritualistic expression of the abstract *gnosis*
that was received. Psychologically of course, we can recognize in this
the almost universal need to rely on external recognitions and safeguards to buttress our weakened faith and trust in the spiritual reality
we are so fearful of. As one German commentator, H. G. Gaffron, observed:

The intellectual act seemed too intangible, and perhaps not certain enough. What was substantial, the action, the sign, the words and formulas, they provided a more positive guarantee of salvation (in Rudolph, p. 243).

Thus we find the same need as that which motivated the orthodox Church in its development of rituals and sacraments.

5. The Bridal Chamber

The bridal chamber has important mystical connotations, as is seen in its appropriation by some of the greatest Christian mystics who, reminiscent of the sexual imagery of the biblical Song of Songs, wrote of the spiritual marriage. By shifting the symbolism of the bridal chamber, yet retaining its spiritual content of joining, we emerge with the "holy relationship" of *A Course in Miracles*, which we consider in Part II-B.

The meaning of the bridal chamber rests in the Gnostic understanding of the fall, i.e., the splitting off of part of the Godhead from itself. This has been symbolized by the mythology of Sophia, most clearly elaborated in the Valentinian brand of Gnosticism. The Gnostic goal is thus the reuniting of these divine elements, restoring unity to the Pleroma. This reunion is the meaning of the sacred wedding, and is reminiscent of the self's gathering unto itself that we discussed in "The Redeemed Redeemer" in the previous chapter. Several Gnostic texts provide examples of this sacrament, and we begin with "The Gospel of Philip:"

> When Eve was still in Adam death did not exist. When she was separated from him death came into being. If he again becomes complete and attains his former self, death will be no more (GPh II. 68.22-27, in *NHL*, p. 141).

Three buildings are then described--the Holy, the Holy of the Holy, and the Holy of the Holies--representing, respectively, the sacraments of baptism, redemption, and the bridal chamber:

> But the bridal chamber is in that which is superior to it and the others, because you will not find anything like it . . . . If the woman had not separated from the man, she would not die with the man. His separation became the beginning of death. Because of this Christ came to repair the separation which was from the beginning and again unite the two, and to give life to those who died as a result of the separation and unite them. But the woman is united to her husband in the bridal chamber. Indeed those who have united in the

353

bridal chamber will no longer be separated. Thus Eve separated from Adam because she was never united with him in the bridal chamber (ibid., 69.27-30; 70.9-23, p. 142).

In discussing the Valentinian system of Theodotus, the Church Father Clement writes of the "Lord's Day":

Then comes the wedding-feast, common to all the saved, until all become equal and mutually recognize one another.
The pneumatics [Gnostics] then lay aside the souls and, at the same time as the mother receives her bridegroom, each of them too receives his bridegroom, the angels [i.e., symbolic of the reuniting of the soul with the Pleroma]; then they enter the bridal chamber within Horos [i.e., one of the aeons: Limit] and attain to the vision of the Father, and become intellectual aeons, entering into the intelligible and eternal marriage of the union [syzygy].
The "ruler of the feast," the best man of the wedding, the "friend of the bridegroom," stands outside before the bride-chamber and greatly rejoices on hearing the voice of the bridegroom. This is the fullness of joy and of repose (*Excerpta* 63.1-2; 64.1, in F I, pp. 152f).

Of the Marcosians Irenaeus writes, continuing from the excerpts quoted above:

Some of them prepare a bridal chamber and perform a mystic rite, with certain invocations, for those who are being consecrated, and they claim that what they are effecting is a spiritual marriage, after the image of the conjunctions [syzygies] above (*Adv. haer*. I.21.3, in F I, p. 219).
It is clearly recognizable that he [Marcus] has a demon too residing in him, by means of which he appears to be able to prophesy and to enable the women whom he counts worthy to be partakers of his Grace to prophesy as well. ... saying, "I desire to make thee a partaker of my Grace, since the Father of all doth continually behold thy angel before his face. The place of thy greatness is ever in us; we must come together. First receive from me and through me Grace. Adorn thyself as a bride who expects her bridegroom, that thou mayest be what I am, and I what thou art. Receive in thy bride-chamber the seed of light. Receive from me the bridegroom, and give him a place, and have a place in him." ... She tries to repay him, not only with the gift of her possessions ... but also by physical intercourse, prepared as she is to be united with him in everything in order that she, with him, may enter into the One (ibid., 13.3, pp. 201f).

This report of Irenaeus is the lone reference of this type, and actually is inconsistent with the basic Valentinian and Gnostic understanding of the non-corporeal and non-sexual aspects of this spiritual marriage.

The metaphor is of an earthly marriage, yet it is firmly contrasted with the "defilement" of the sexual union. Thus we read in "The Gospel of Philip" that the "undefiled marriage"

> is not fleshly but pure. It belongs not to desire but to the will. It belongs not to the darkness or the night but to the day and the light. If a marriage is open to the public, it has become prostitution, and the bride plays the harlot not only when she is impregnated by another man but even if she slips out of her bedroom and is seen . . . . Bridegrooms and brides belong to the bridal chamber. No one shall be able to see the bridegroom with the bride unless one become one (GPh II.82.6-27, in *NHL*, p. 149).

Also expressive of this spiritual understanding of the conjugal union is the inscription found on a third-century tombstone in Rome. It speaks of a Gnostic woman, Flavia Sophe:

> You, who did yearn for the paternal light, Sister, spouse, my Sophe, anointed in the baths of Christ with everlasting, holy oil, hasten to gaze at the divine features of the aeons . . . ; you entered the bridal chamber and deathless ascended to the bosom of the Father (in Rudolph, p. 212).

It is interesting to note the importance that is placed in "The Gospel of Philip" on the need for the ceremony of the bridal chamber for the earthly fulfillment of what will come later. Thus, the celestial consummation of the union is dependent on the earthly sacrament, reflecting to us again the strange compromises of true spirituality with magic that the Gnostics, as well as the orthodox Church, fell into. This principle of the connection between the use of symbols in this world ("types and images") and the realization attained in the next world ("truth") is clearly enunciated in this passage:

> Truth did not come into the world naked, but it came in types and images. One will not receive truth in any other way. There is a rebirth and an image of rebirth. It is certainly necessary that they should be born again through the image. What is the resurrection? The image must rise again through the image. The bridegroom and the image must enter through the image into the truth: this is the restoration (GPh II.67.9-19, in *NHL*, p. 140).

While the process expressed here of working with symbols ("types and images") is essential for one's salvation (*see* workbook lesson 184 in the Course), the Gnostics fell into the trap of making the error real-- treating the symbols as reality--that we shall return to in Part III.

Speaking specifically now of the sacrament of the bridal chamber, the text reads:

> The powers [that would entrap the soul] do not see those who are clothed in the perfect light, and consequently are not able to detain them. One will clothe himself in this light sacramentally in the union .... If anyone becomes a son of the bridal chamber, he will receive the light. If anyone does not receive it while he is in these places [i.e., in this world], he will not be able to receive it in the other place [i.e., the world after death] (ibid., 70.5-10; 86.4-8, pp. 142,151).

Our final example comes from the "Acts of Thomas," where in his first act on his journey the apostle finds himself at a wedding. This serves as the setting wherein he sings the famous Wedding Hymn. This song, filled with rich imagery, describes the wedding of the virgin of light and the heavenly bridegroom, (a symbol found in Manicheism as well). The wedding also represents the redemption of the bride, who here is symbolic of the fallen Sophia we are already familiar with in the Valentinians. The hymn is presented here in abbreviated prose form:

> The maiden is the daughter of light.... Radiant with shining beauty .... Truth rests upon her head .... Thirty and two [the Valentinian aeons] are they that sing her praises .... Her fingers open the gates of the city. Her chamber is full of light.... [Her groomsmen] gaze and look toward the bridegroom, that by the sight of him they may be enlightened; and for ever shall they be with him in that eternal joy, and they shall be at that marriage ... and they shall glorify the Father of all ... and were enlightened by the vision of their Lord, which ambrosial food they received, which has no deficiency at all ... (ATh 6-7, in NTA II, pp. 445f).

The wedding continues after the hymn, and when the bride and groom retire to the wedding chamber it is Jesus they find there, in the image of Thomas. He instructs them in the difference between the celestial and earthly marriage:

> ... know this, that if you abandon this filthy intercourse you become holy temples, pure and free from afflictions and pains both manifest and hidden, and you will not be girt about with cares for life and for children, the end of which is destruction.... But if you obey, and keep your souls pure unto God, you shall have living children whom these hurts do not touch ... waiting to receive that incorruptible and true marriage as befitting for you, and in it you shall be groomsmen entering into that bridal chamber which is full of immortality and light (ibid., 12, p. 449).

The couple hears and believes, and refrains from the "filthy passion." In the morning, visited by her parents the king and queen, the bride teaches the Gnostic message:

...I have set at naught this man, and this marriage which passes away from before my eyes...because I am bound in another marriage. And that I have no intercourse with a short-lived husband, the end of which is remorse and bitterness of soul, is because I am yoked with the true man (ibid., 14, p. 450).

6. Rituals

In his diatribe against the Gnostics, which we first considered in Chapter 6, Plotinus at one point accuses his adversaries of not being specific about *how* one returns to God. He begins this passage by attacking the Gnostics for not emphasizing the pursuit of virtue, a cardinal sin for any Platonist.

This, too, is evidence of their indifference to virtue, that they have never made any treatise about virtue, but have altogether left out the treatment of these subjects; they do not tell us what kind of thing virtue is, nor how many parts it has, nor about all the many noble studies of the subject to be found in the treatises of the ancients, nor from what virtue results and how it is to be attained, nor how the soul is tended, nor how it is purified. For it does no good at all to say "Look to God," unless one also teaches how one is to look. . . . but God, if you talk about him without true virtue, is only a name (*Enn.* II.9.15).

Indeed, Plotinus was basically correct. Most Gnostic texts are vague, and more than likely deliberately so. The Gnostics characteristically prevented their instructions from becoming institutionalized and ritualized, and much preferred highly individualized instruction under the direction of advanced teachers. Therefore, what seems to us as a fuzzy "come-on," was really a theory of spiritual attainment inherent in the whole Gnostic thought system. The Gnostics obviously took their spiritual path seriously, and had little tolerance (at least in the higher Gnostic schools) for the superficialized spirituality often found in large communities. They knew that true spiritual progress could only be attained through the individual direction of a spiritual adept. This has always been the Eastern way, as seen in some of the higher Buddhist and Hindu schools of learning, for example.

Nonetheless, there are some texts in the *Nag Hammadi Library* that do supply descriptions of spiritual disciplines. We shall discuss two of these, both of which exhibit definite Neoplatonic influences. "The Discourse on the Eighth and Ninth" is also part of the Hermetic tradition, and probably dates from the mid-second century. It is a dialogue between the now familiar mystagogue Hermes Trismegistus and one of his initiates. The "Eighth and Ninth" refers to two of the spheres surrounding the earth. The first seven consist of the sun, moon, and planets, all aspects of the lower world which serve to imprison human life. The eighth and ninth mark the beginning of the divine realms, and thus become the goal of the departed soul after it makes the sometimes harrowing ascent through the first seven. A tenth sphere--the home of God Himself--is implied here, though not directly expressed as it was in St. Paul's ascent, discussed earlier. The passage through the spheres also represents the process of spiritual growth, as is seen in this tractate. The dialogue begins with the disciple recalling to Hermes' mind his promise:

> O my father, yesterday you promised me that you would bring my mind into the eighth and afterwards you would bring me into the ninth. You said that this is the order of the tradition (Disc. Eighth Ninth VI.52.3-7, in *NHL*, p. 292).

Hermes explains the need to study the sacred texts:

> Your part, then, is to understand; my own is to be able to deliver the discourse from the fountain which flows to me (ibid., 55.19-22, p. 294).

Thus it is the responsibility of the student to accept what the teacher offers. The teacher supplies the truth; the student must let it in. Hermes then calls upon his disciple to pray with him to the Father, the "perfect, the invisible God to whom one speaks in silence," after which there is an uttering of a series of obviously sacred sounds:

> Zoxathazo a oo ee ooo eee oooo ee oooooo ooooo oooooo uuuuuu ooooooooooooooo Zozazoth [printed here without accents] (ibid., 56.17-22).

From here on, the reader without personal experience will remain in the dark regarding these higher realms:

> Lord, grant us a wisdom from thy power that reaches us, so that we may describe to ourselves the vision of the eighth and the ninth. . . . Allow us through the spirit to see the form of the image that has no deficiency, and receive the reflection of the pleroma from us through our praise . . . . Let us embrace each other affectionately, O my son. Rejoice over this! . . . I am mind and I see another mind, the one that moves the soul! I see the one that moves me from pure forgetfulness. . . . Language is not able to reveal this. For the entire eighth, O my son, and the souls that are in it, and the angels, sing a hymn in silence. And I, Mind, understand (ibid., 56.22-25; 57.5-9; 57.26-58.22, pp. 294-95).

The student requests not to be deprived of the celestial vision, and Hermes places this responsibility back on him:

> Return to praising, O my son, and sing while you are silent. Ask what you want in silence (ibid., 59.19-22, p. 295).

The student does what he is told, and ecstatically exclaims:

> Father Trismegistus! What shall I say? We have received this light. And I myself see this same vision in you. And I see the eighth and the souls that are in it and the angels singing a hymn to the ninth and its powers. And I see him who has the power of them all, creating those that are in the spirit (ibid., 59.24-60.1).

Hermes instructs him to remain silent "in a reverent posture," and simply to continue to sing a hymn to the father

> until the day to quit the body . . . . What is proper is your praise that you will sing to God so that it might be written in this imperishable book (ibid., 60.5-16, p. 296).

"Allogenes" is a third-century text also with Neoplatonic themes, and is most likely the text that Porphyry states was known by Plotinus. It, too, is a revelation discourse, the Gnostic revealer being called Allogenes which literally means stranger or one of another race. It was a common term for semi-divine teachers in Gnostic writings from this period, and Allogenes is often equated with the Sethians. The receiver of Allogenes' revelations is his son, Messos. The tractate is in two parts. The first half consists of the revelations of the female Goddess Youel to Allogenes, reminiscent of the Barbelognosis we have seen previously. This is followed by an account of the ascent of Allogenes, culminating in the revelation of the "Unknown One." This places "Allogenes" in the apophatic tradition we have already discussed in relation to works such as "The Apocryphon of John." The reader's mind must thus move beyond the philosophical language of this process to the actual experience and practice that is only hinted at in the tractate.

Allogenes shares with Messos his own process of spiritual attainment, telling him his reactions in the presence of Youel's revelations:

> . . . and I escaped and I was very disturbed and I turned to myself. Having seen the light that surrounded me and the Good that was in me, I became divine.
>
> And the one pertaining to all glories, Youel, anointed me again and she gave power to me. She said, "Since your instruction has become complete and you have known the Good that is within you, hear concerning the Triple Power those things that you will guard in great

silence and great mystery, because they are not spoken to anyone except those who are worthy" (Allog. XI.52.7-23, in *NHL*, p. 446).

The revelation continues and, as we saw in "The Discourse on the Eighth and Ninth," contains also a "silent" sound: "zza zza zza." Pagels has suggested that perhaps this represents a kind of meditative technique consisting of the intonations of sound, not too different from certain Eastern and contemporary practice (Pagels, p. 166). She also comments on the possibility of the following passage being part of a ritual, completing one stage of the spiritual initiation wherein the spiritual initiate listens to the recitation on the part of the adepts.

> Now after I heard these things, I saw the glories of the perfect individuals and the all-perfect ones who exist together.... And then I prayed that the revelation might occur to me. And then the one pertaining to all the glories, Youel, said to me, "O Allogenes.... If you seek with a perfect seeking, then you will know the God that is in you; then you will know yourself as well, as one who exists with the God who truly pre-exists. After a hundred years there shall come to you a revelation of That One...." I prepared myself therein.... When I was taken by the eternal Light out of the garment [i.e., body: an "out of body experience"] that was upon me, and taken up to a holy place whose likeness can not be revealed in the world, then by means of a great blessedness I saw all those about whom I had heard.... "O Allogenes, behold your blessedness in the manner that exists in the silence, wherein you know yourself as you are, and, seeking yourself, ascend to the Vitality that you will see moving.... And when you receive a revelation of him by means of a primary revelation of the Unknown One--the One whom if you should know him, be ignorant of him.... Do not know him, for it is impossible...." And I ascended to the Vitality.... And I saw an eternal ... undivided motion that pertains to all the formless powers, one which is unlimited by limitation.... And when I was confirmed in these matters, the powers of the Luminaries said to me, "Cease hindering the inactivity that exists in you by seeking incomprehensible matters; rather hear about him in accordance with the capability provided by a primary revelation... " (Disc. Eighth Ninth VI.55.12-15; 55.31-56.23; 57.29; 58.26-37; 59.9-60.28; 61.22-31, in *NHL*, pp. 446-50).

The revelation then proceeds in the "negative theology" so characteristic of the apophatic Gnostic and orthodox traditions.

Pagels quotes the arch heresy-hunter Tertullian's complaint against this form of initiation (Tertullian refers specifically to the Valentinian), which he derogatorily compares to the great Mystery schools of antiquity:

> [They] first beset all access to their group with tormenting conditions;

and they require a long initiation before they enroll their members, even instruction for five years for their adept students, so that they may educate their opinions by this suspension of full knowledge, and, apparently, raise the value of their mysteries in proportion to the longing for them which they have created. Then follows the duty of silence . . . (Tertullian *Adversus Valentinianos* 1, in Pagels, p. 169).

Even in the Gnostic text we have considered we find a lack of specific instructions, but what we see certainly does suggest the ritualistic spiritual discipline that was present in many of the Gnostic sects. However, these chants, instructions, and meditative practices were kept hidden, to be revealed only to those judged worthy of receiving them, and thereby able to reach the Gnostic goal of Self-knowledge that leads to the knowledge of God Himself. In "Allogenes" this knowledge of the divine is a negative one, since the true God is unknown. However, the Gnostic initiate can be prepared to receive "in accordance with the capability provided by a primary revelation."

Gnosticism: Ethics - Morality

Metaphysical principles inevitably entail practical implications, though we shall see how the same principles can be interpreted quite differently. From the basic Gnostic teaching that the true God did not create the material world, which rather was the work of an inferior principle, the Gnostics deduced three different ethical positions: libertinism, asceticism, and moderateness. As we have seen, the basic Gnostic stance is one of total alienation from the physical and social world. The ego-bodily self is totally ignored, for the object of salvation is the spark of spiritual light that is trapped. Thus there is no concern for one's individual existence in a world that is inherently hostile and evil. Whether one flouts the authority of the cosmic rulers through libertinism or ascetic detachment, the result is the same: total denigration of the cosmos on all levels. We shall consider each of these in turn.

1. Libertinism

The libertine position directly follows from the Gnostic belief that God did not create this world. Therefore our attachment to any aspect of this world is part of the archons' plan to enslave us here. The basic argument of the Gnostic libertines thus ran as follows: Enslavement by the archons--the ruling powers of the world--occurs through adherence to their moral laws. As Jonas has summarized this mentality:

> For what is the law . . . but the means of regularizing and thus
> stabilizing the implication of man in the business of the world and
> worldly concerns; of setting by its rules the seal of seriousness, of
> praise and blame, reward and punishment, on his utter involvement;
> of making his very will a compliant party to the compulsory system,
> which thereby will function all the more smoothly and inextricably
> (Jonas, p. 272).

Therefore, the way to become free of such imprisonment is for the enlightened Gnostic--the pneumatic--to flout these laws, thereby demonstrating his freedom from the evil archons. Certain Gnostic systems held that if any moral law remained unbroken during a given lifetime, the individual was then impelled to reincarnate until the list was completed. The punishments that accrue to such a defiance can affect only the body and psyche, but hardly the spirit which alone is real and true. One finds a modern expression of this attitude in Mathieu the protagonist in Sartre's *Age of Reason*. This existential hero, sitting in a restaurant, exemplifies his defiance of the world by calmly sticking a knife into his outstretched palm, affirming his freedom from any social or physical concern. Conventional morality is no longer binding on this now free man.

It seems quite apparent that this approach was in the clear minority among Gnostics. Not one instance of libertinism, for example, can be found in the Nag Hammadi library (although of course these texts were collected by monks hardly likely to be attracted to libertine material), nor in any of the other Gnostic finds of the last two centuries. In fact, almost all of our information about this Gnostic morality (or amorality) is from the Church Fathers, whose predilection for exaggeration has already been noted. Nowhere is this exaggeration more clearly exemplified than in the area of morality, where the Fathers no doubt reveled in presenting what they believed to be the gross excesses of Gnostic cultic and orgiastic immorality. In one instance, however, quoted below, Irenaeus does question whether these principles were ever put into practice. Let us examine the heresiologists' writings, if not evidence for the Gnostic immorality, at least then for the excesses of the Fathers in attempting to corrupt the teachings and practices of their opponents.

We begin with Irenaeus' treatment of Simon Magus. While there is no evidence that Simon himself engaged in any licentious behavior--in fact, "The Testimony of Truth" in the *Nag Hammadi Library* speaks thus: "For the Simonians take wives and beget children" (Test. Tr. IX.58.1-3, in *NHL*, p. 413)--Irenaeus claims that Simon's teachings lead to this:

> . . . those who have their hope in him [Simon] . . . trouble themselves

no further .... For through his grace are men saved, and not through righteous works. Nor are works just by nature, but by convention, as the angels who made the world ordained, in order to enslave men by such precepts. Hence he promised that the world will be dissolved, and those who are his liberated from the dominion of those who made the world.

Therefore their mystery priests live licentiously .... They practice ... love potions and erotic magic; ... and from them the falsely so-called Gnosis took its beginnings ... (*Adv. haer.* I.23.3, in F I, p. 31).

And Hippolytus adds:

These became imitators of error and of Simon Magus and do the same things, saying that one must engage in intercourse without consideration, affirming: "All earth is earth, and it makes no difference where a man sows, if only he sows." Indeed, they count themselves blessed because of this union, and say that this is perfect love and the holy of holies (*Ref.* VI.19.5, in F I, p. 31).

Of Carpocrates and his disciples Irenaeus writes:

They practice ... evil things, saying that they already have the power to prevail over the archons and creators of this world.... They say that conduct is good and evil only in the opinion of men. And after the transmigrations the souls must have been in every kind of life and every kind of deed .... [so] when they depart (from the body) they are deficient in nothing .... So long must a man continue to be reincarnated, until he has been in absolutely every action in the world. When no more is lacking, then his soul, set free, goes to that God who is above the creator angels, and so it is saved .... Now if these things are done among them which are godless and unrighteous and forbidden, I could not believe. But in their writings it is so written ... (*Adv. haer.* I.25.3,4-5, in F I, pp. 37f).

The Cainites, according to Irenaeus, believed as did the Carpocratians:

... they say they cannot be saved in any other way, except they pass through all things, just as Carpocrates also said. And at every sinful and base action an angel is present and instills in him who ventures the deed audacity and impurity; what it is in act they say in the angel's name: "O thou angel, I make use of thy work; ..." And this is the perfect "knowledge," to enter without fear into such operations, which it is not lawful even to name (ibid., I.31.2).

Clement describes the Entychites, followers of Simon Magus, as exemplifying the same philosophy of rebellion against the ruling power of the world--the creator God of the Old Testament:

> ...some others ... say that God is by nature the Father of us all, and everything that he has made is good. But one of his creatures [the creator God] sowed tares by creating the nature of evil, with which he has entangled us all and made us oppose the Father. For this reason we also oppose him in order to avenge the Father by resisting the will of this second power. So since he has said "Thou shalt not commit adultery," let us commit adultery, they say, in order to nullify his commandment (*Strom.* III.4, in F I, pp. 314f).

Basilides, as we shall see, adopted a moderate if not ascetic moral stance, but some of his disciples evidently, at least as exemplified in this quote from Clement, drew other conclusions from their master's teachings:

> I [Clement] have quoted these words [from a more moderate position] to refute these Basilideans who do not live rightly, whether on the grounds that they have the right even to sin because of their perfection, or that they will in any case be saved by nature even if they sin now, because of their inborn state of election. For the progenitors of their doctrine do not even permit the very things they do (ibid., III.1.3, p. 80).

The notion that those Gnostics who were perfect need not be concerned with morality finds restatement in Irenaeus' presentation of the Valentinians. These "perfect" are contrasted with the "psychics," who require the conventional morality until they are freed through *gnosis*. According to Irenaeus the adherents to this school included the orthodox Church in this category, which is corroborated in some of the Nag Hammadi texts. This Gnostic put-down of opponents is obvious, and parallels the orthodox position that these unredeemable heretics belong in hell.

> The psychic men ... are strengthened by works and mere faith, and do not have perfect knowledge; and these, they teach are we of the Church. Therefore they affirm that for us good conduct is necessary--for otherwise it would not be possible to be saved--but they themselves, in their opinion, will be for ever and entirely saved, not by means of conduct, but because they are spiritual by nature. ... Just as gold, when placed in mud, does not lose its beauty but retains its own nature, since the mud is unable to harm the gold, so they say that they themselves cannot suffer any injury or lose their spiritual substance, whatever material actions they may engage in.
> For this reason the most perfect among them freely practice everything that is forbidden. ... And some, who are immoderately given over to the desires of the flesh, say that they are repaying to the flesh

what belongs to the flesh, and to the spirit what belongs to the spirit. And some of them secretly seduce women. . . . Others again who initially made an impressive pretense of loving with women as with sisters were convicted in course of time, when the "sister" became pregnant by the "brother." And while they carry on many other foul and impious practices they slander us, who through fear of God guard ourselves against sins even of thought and word, saying we are simple-minded and know nothing; while they give themselves a superior dignity and call themselves "perfect" and "an elect seed" . . . [possessing a grace] which has come down from above with them from the unutterable and unnameable Conjunction [syzygy]; and for this reason it will be increased for them. Therefore they must always in every possible way practice the mystery of Conjunction [i.e., the Bridal Chamber sacrament] (*Adv. haer.* I.6.2,3, in F I, pp. 138f,313f).

This excerpt from Irenaeus on the immorality of the Valentinians appears discrepant from his earlier treatment of this great Gnostic teacher, not to mention from descriptions taken from other Fathers. Either Irenaeus is speaking of an isolated Valentinian sect ("the most perfect among them") or of other Gnostic groups. His description of the sexual exploitation found in the "mystery of Conjunction" is directly reminiscent of his description of the Valentinian Marcus. Therefore, perhaps this is the group he has in mind. If so, Marcus' form of Valentinianism (excessive numerology, etc.) is far removed from the higher form of metaphysical speculation of Valentinus himself that we find, for example, in the insightful vision of "The Gospel of Truth."

We commented earlier on the notorious unreliability of Epiphanius, the fourth-century bishop who was perhaps the most viciously vindictive of the Church Fathers in his pursuit of the Gnostics. We must therefore take Epiphanius' reports of the Gnostics' libertine practices with more than a grain of salt. Nonetheless, the rather strange and outright pornographic practices he reports do have a sound, if not perverse, theoretical basis in a metaphysics that strongly resembles the teachings of Mani surrounding the seeds of light that are trapped in matter--plants, animals, homo sapiens. These seeds, when released, must be collected and returned to God (through ingestion; this was *not* the Manichean practice, however: *see below*, pp. 381f) and not allowed to escape out into the world where they run the risk of being imprisoned once more. Epiphanius writes:

And the power which resides in the periods and in the semen, they say, is the soul, which we collect and eat. And whatever we eat, be it meat, vegetables, bread, or anything else, we are doing a kindness to created things, in that we collect the soul from all things and transmit it with ourselves to the heavenly world. For this reason they take meat of every kind, saying that it is in order that we may show mercy

> to our race. And they say that it is the same soul which is implanted in living creatures—beasts, fishes, serpents, and men, as well as in plants, trees, and fruits (*Panar.* XXVI.9.4, in F I, p. 321).

The extreme literalness of these understandings inevitably led Epiphanius' Gnostics to "rescue" the seeds of light in semen and menstrual blood by ingesting them in rites. Reminiscent of Jewish lore, the belief according to these Gnostic groups was that semen contained the seed of life (light), as did menstrual blood. We shall see evidence indicating that these rites actually existed, at least in some groups; but there can be no question that the Church Father embellished his account of these rituals to prove the "bestiality" of these heretics. One finds, incidentally, similar descriptions in Augustine's reporting of the Manicheans:

> ... their Elect are forced to consume a Eucharist, so to speak, sprayed with human semen, so that by it, as by the other food which they consume, the divine substance may be purified (Augustine *de haer.* 46.2, in Haardt, p. 344).

We shall devote more space to Epiphanius' descriptions than their worth deserves, for they are instructive not only as examples of the exaggerated anti-Gnostic polemic of the heresiologists, but also for their value as extreme examples of the mistake of confusing form with content. This is a mistake, as we have already seen, far from peculiar to the Gnostics. It is found to be just as prevalent in the formulations and practices of the orthodox Church, not to mention in these early years of *A Course in Miracles*. It is sound pedagogy to teach with extreme examples, and Epiphanius' are as extreme as can be found. Some of these examples follow (all quotes are taken from Epiphanius' *Panarion* in F I, pp. 316-25):

> ... the advocates of Gnosis falsely so called have begun their evil growth upon the world .... For each of these has contrived his own sect to suit his own passions and has devised thousands of ways of evil .... [Some] honour a certain Prunicus [Sophia] and ... when they indulge their passions have recourse to a myth to give this pretext of their shameful deeds; they say, "We are collecting the power of Prunicus from bodies by their fluids"--which means the semen and the periods (XXV.2.1; 3.2).

Epiphanius proceeds now to the rites of this collection, the first of which is a love-feast in which all the women are shared:

> When they have had intercourse out of the passion of fornication, then, holding up their own blasphemy before heaven, the woman and the man take the man's emission in their own hands, and stand

there looking up towards heaven. And while they have uncleanness in their hands they profess to pray . . . offering to the natural Father of the Universe that which is in their hands, and saying, "We offer thee this gift, the body of Christ." And so they eat it, partaking of their own shame and saying, "This is the body of Christ, and this is the Passover; hence our bodies are given over to passion and compelled to confess the passion of Christ." Similarly with the woman's emission at her period; they collect the menstrual blood which is unclean, take it and eat it together, and say "This is the blood of Christ" (XXVI.4.5-8).

These bizarre descriptions were not unusual during this period, where charges and counter-charges flew back and forth midst different religious groups, including various Gnostic and other heretical groups (e.g., the Montanists), the orthodox Church, and the Jews. These accusations not only included the strange rites described by Epiphanius, but various kinds of fornications and ritual infanticides and cannibalisms. These reports have even extended into the modern era. Chadwick reports that the nineteenth-century French priest Boullan encouraged women to speed themselves along the spiritual path by having sexual relations with him. He also evidently practiced, similar to Epiphanius' group, a Eucharistic rite mixed with semen and menstrual blood (in Layton, p. 5).

Like the later Manicheans, the Gnostic group of which Epiphanius writes opposed the bearing of children not only on ascetic grounds, but because the newborn child carried with it the seed of light, "protected" from collection and redemption. Thus Epiphanius:

And while they have intercourse with each other they forbid the bearing of children. For this shameful conduct is pursued by them not for the bearing of children but for the sake of pleasure . . . . They have their pleasure, and take for themselves their seed which is unclean, not implanting it for the bearing of children, but themselves eating the shameful thing. But if one of them mistakenly implants the natural emission and the woman becomes pregnant, attend to the further outrage that these men perform. They extract the embryo when they can lay hands on it and take this aborted infant and smash it with a pestle in a mortar, and when they have mixed in honey and pepper and other condiments and spices to prevent them from vomiting, then they all assemble, every member of this troop of swine and dogs, and each one with his fingers takes a piece of the mangled child. And so when they have finished their feast of human flesh, they pray to God and say, "We have not been deceived by the Archon of lust, but we have retrieved our brother's transgression." And this they consider the perfect Passover (XXVI.5.2-6).

Epiphanius is far from finished, and continues by describing one sect which attempts to return to the innocence of Adam by praying naked:

> And they have other outrageous practices. When they are excited to madness they moisten their own hands with the shamefulness of their own emissions and get up and with their own hands thus polluted they pray with their whole bodies naked, as if by such a practice they could gain free access to God .... And they curse the man who fasts, saying that it is wrong to fast; for fasting belongs to this Archon who made the world.... and they are not ashamed to say that our Savior and Lord Jesus Christ himself revealed this shameful practice. For ... they pretend that he gave her [Mary Magdalene] a revelation; that he took her to the mountain and prayed and took out a woman from his side and began to have intercourse with her, and so took up his emission and showed it to her say, saying. "We must do this, that we may live" (XXVI.5.7-8; 8.1-3).

The idea of nakedness reflecting the return to the freedom and innocence of Adam was also found in the "Adamites," a medieval Gnostic group (Rudolph, p. 257).

One of the common Church complaints against the Gnostics was the free use they made of scripture to suit their own purposes. As we have already seen, the more polemic of the Gnostic groups never tired of making the most outlandish interpretations of what was considered to be sacred texts. Likewise, Epiphanius complains:

> They use the Old and the New Testament, but they reject Him who has spoken in the Old Testament. And when they find any saying whose sense can be contrary to them, they say that this was spoken by the spirit of this world. But if any text can be adapted to make a pattern for their lust ... they alter it according to their lust and say that it was spoken by the spirit of truth .... And the text, "When ye see the Son of Man going up where he was before" (Jn 6:62) means the emission which is taken up to the place from which it came, and the saying, "Unless ye eat my flesh and drink my blood" (Jn 6:53) ... they quote this as if the saying referred to indecency, this being the reason why they were overcome and "went backward" (Jn 6:66); for, he says, they were not yet established in the Pleroma. And when David says, "He shall be as a tree that is planted by the springs of the waters, which shall give forth its fruit in due season" (Ps 1:3), he refers, he says, to the male member. "By the water-springs" and "which shall give forth its fruit" refers, he says, to the emission with its pleasure; and "his leaf shall not fall," because, he says, we do not allow it to drop upon the ground, but eat it ourselves (XXVI.6.1-3; 8.3-7).

And on and on.

The prophet Elijah (Elias), venerated by the Church, was hardly exempt from re-evaluation:

And such are their fantasies and romances that they even dare to insult the holy Elias and say that when he was taken up into heaven he was cast down again into the world. For there came a female demon . . . and seized him and said to him, "Where are you going? For I have children of yours, and you cannot ascend and leave your children here." And Elias . . . replied, "How did you get children of mine, when I lived in purity?" It answered him . . . "Why, when you were dreaming dreams and often discharged an emission of the body, it was I who received the seed from you and bore you sons" (XXVI.13.4-5).

The Gnostic group Epiphanius identifies in much of his diatribe is the Phibionites, and in this excerpt he specifies further sexual immoralities in the name of Gnostic aspirations. They

offer the shameful sacrifices of their immorality . . . to 365 names which they themselves invented, belonging supposedly to Archons [the Basilidean system is the referent]; and they delude their wretched womenfolk, saying, "Be one with me, that I may present you to the Archon"; and at each [sexual] union they pronounce the outlandish name of one of their inventions [i.e., one of the 365 Archons], and make as if to pray, saying "To thee . . . I present my offering, that thou mayest present it to . . . [another Archon]." And at the next union he pretends to present her likewise to another (XXVI.9.6-7).

They go through the 365 names with 365 different women, in an ascending and then descending series, totaling 730 in all:

So when he arrives at the enormous total of 730 falls, that is of immoral unions and of names that they have invented, then the man in question dares to say, "I am Christ, for I have descended from above through the names of the 365 Archons" (XXVI.9.9).

Epiphanius exhausts the sexual repertoire, including masturbation and homosexuality, in his catalogue:

Some of them do not consort with women but corrupt themselves with their own hands, and they take their own corruption in their hands and so eat it, using a falsified proof-text, namely, "These hands were sufficient, not only for me but for those with me" (Ac 20:34), and again: "Working with your own hands, so that you may have something to share with those who have nothing" (Ep 4:28) . . . . For those who corrupt themselves with their own hands, and not only they, but also those who consort with women, since they are not satiated with their promiscuous intercourse with women, are inflamed towards one another, men with men . . . . For there is no satisfying their licentiousness, but the more infamous a man is in his conduct among them, the more he is honored among them (XXVI.11.1-9).

As was stated above, we possess no original texts to substantiate Epiphanius' charges. Yet interestingly enough there comes a repudiation of such libertine practices from a Gnostic source dating from the third or fourth centuries, the "Pistis Sophia." There we find a curse in the name of Jesus on those "who take male semen and female menstrual blood and make it into a lentil dish and eat it" (quoted in Rudolph, p. 250). This is quite reminiscent of the Phibionite rite described above.

2. Asceticism

The writings of the Church Fathers to the contrary, the overwhelming evidence that we possess points to a governing Gnostic practice being an ascetic morality that deviated from the orthodox position. We shall see below that almost as predominant, at least in the second century, was a moderate position that one generally finds in the New Testament as well as in the early Church. Later in this chapter we shall discuss the paradoxical phenomenon of the orthodox Church adopting the Gnostic form of asceticism as its own, eventually leading to the development of the monastic spirituality that was to become such an important part of Christian spirituality from the fourth and fifth centuries onward to the present day. We have already observed the inaccuracy of the older notion that in the early centuries of Christianity, especially in the second, there was a marked distinction between the heterodox and orthodox. The great Gnostic teachers--Basilides, Marcion, and Valentinus--very much saw themselves as Christians, part of the tradition that dated from Jesus and the apostles. The boundaries between these two groups were fluid, and the situation did not begin to change until the fierce opposition of Irenaeus in the latter decades of the second century spawned the heresiological tradition taken up by opponents even more fierce in their response.

It is clear that the Fathers were ambivalent about the Gnostic ascetic stance, since it did find favorable response with them. Thus, we find these heresiologists questioning the sincerity of the Gnostic position. Epiphanius says of the Archontics:

> And some of them have polluted their bodies by licentiousness, but others pretend to an affected abstinence and deceive the simpler sort of men by making a show of withdrawal from the world in imitation of the monks (*Panar.* XL.2.4, in F I, p. 297).

While Irenaeus states of the followers of Saturninus:

> Marriage and procreation, he [Saturninus] says, are of Satan. Many of his followers abstain also from animal food, and through this feigned continence they lead many astray (*Adv. haer.* I.24.2, in F I, p. 41).

The basic premise of asceticism--Gnostic or otherwise--is that the body is evil ("the world, the flesh, and the devil"), and involvement with it leads to participating in that evil, what many Gnostics described as entrapment. While the orthodox Church accepted this practice as its own, it certainly did not accept the radical acosmic premise that underlay the Gnostic asceticism: Since the physical universe was not only *not* created by the true God, but was the product of an inferior and sometimes evil deity, it was mandatory if Gnostics were to return to the Pleroma that they avoid any involvement with the world and the body. The flesh was a trap that kept the soul imprisoned in darkness, apart from the light. The Gnostic stance thus was a violent protest against the evil intentions of the world ruler, and as the decades wore on, this stance became more and more extreme. Its culmination came in the moral teachings of Mani in the third century. Having discussed the Gnostic view of the body, we turn now to the specific behavioral implications of this view, beginning with the writings of the Church Fathers. The predominant focus, not surprisingly, is sex and food.

Epiphanius writes of Severus, the third-century follower of Marcion, who taught that the Devil was the son of the chief ruler, called either Ialdabaoth or Sabaoth. From him came the vine:

> And the grapes of the vine are like ... drops of poison. ... Wine ... confuses the mind of man ... [leading] to the enchantment of sexual pleasure ... [and] frenzy. Or again it instills wrath. ... Hence such people abstain completely from wine.
> They say that woman also is a work of Satan. ... Hence those who consort in marriage fulfill the work of Satan. Even in regard to man, half is of God and half of the Devil. From the navel upwards ... he is the creation of the power of God; from the navel down he is the creature of the evil power. Hence ... everything relating to pleasure and passion and desire originates from the navel and below (*Panar.* XLV.1.3; 2.1-3, in F I, pp. 46f).

Clement writes of the Basilideans' interpretation of Matthew 19:10-12, where Jesus speaks of becoming eunuchs for the kingdom of heaven:

They explain the saying like this: "Some have from birth a natural aversion from woman; these do well to follow this natural bent of theirs by not marrying. These are... the eunuchs from birth. Those who are such by necessity are those theatrical ascetics who weigh on the other side the good repute that they want to have, and master themselves. These become eunuchs by necessity and not by rational reflection. But those who have made themselves eunuchs for the sake of the eternal kingdom arrive at this determination... because of the things that arise from marriage; they dread the bother that goes with providing the necessities of life" (*Strom.* III.1.1, in F I, p. 79).

In commenting on Paul's teaching that if unable to control one's sexual urges a man should marry--"It is better to be married than to be tortured" (1 Co 7:9)--Clement quotes Basilides' son Isidore as teaching that one should

endure... a quarrelsome wife, so that you may not be dragged away from God's grace, and when you have slaked the fire of passion through satisfaction you may pray with good conscience (*Strom.* III.1.2, in F I, p. 79).

Hippolytus writes of the Naassenes, the worshippers of the serpent (Naas), and their interpretation of the teaching from the Sermon on the Mount not to "give dogs what is holy... [and not to] throw your pearls in front of pigs" (Mt 7:6):

... for they say that this is pigs' and dogs' business, the intercourse of women with men (*Ref.* V.8.32, in F I, p. 276).

And later:

For these men have nothing to offer [to the Great Mother] beyond what is done there, except that they are not castrated, they only perform the functions of those who are castrated. For they urge most severely and carefully that one should abstain, as those men do, from intercourse with women; their behavior otherwise... is like that of the castrated (ibid., 9.10, p. 280).

Clement has preserved for us excerpts from an interesting book written in the second century by Epiphanes, the son of Carpocrates whose teachings we have already examined. According to Clement, Epiphanes died at the age of seventeen and was worshipped as a god in Cephallenia (his mother's birthplace) where a temple was built to commemorate him. His book, "On Righteousness," provides an interesting contrast with his father's libertine teachings, at least in those aspects dealing with worldly attachments. His tract is actually a

Gnostic form of communism, and can be seen to reflect the effect of Plato's *Republic* since Clement mentions that Epiphanes was taught Plato by Carpocrates. New Testament influences are clear as well.

> The righteousness of God is a communion with equality. For ... God has poured forth from above equally upon the earth for all who can see, but they all see in common, for he makes no distinction of rich or poor, people or ruler, foolish and wise, female and male, free and slave ... The sun causes common food to grow up for all creatures, and the common righteousness is given to all equally. . . . . For righteousness among them [members of the animal kingdom] is shown to be community. . . . But the laws ... since they could not restrain men's incapacity to learn, taught them to transgress. For the private property of the laws cut up and nibbled away the fellowship of the divine law . . . . "mine" and "thine" were introduced through the laws, and that people would no longer enjoy in community the fruits either of the earth or of possessions, or even of marriage (*Strom.* III.2.6.1-4; 7.2-3, in F I, pp. 38f).

We thus find interesting foundations for the later development of monasticism: a spiritual communism in which one finds the total absence of private ownership, out of fear of the monks' developing attachments to worldly goods. We shall presently see continuation of this ethic in some of the Nag Hammadi texts and the Apocrypha.

The logical libertine culmination of Epiphanes' arguments (and his book is very logical) when applied to the sphere of morality is obvious, and of course this was Clement's principal purpose in presenting it:

> In that God made all things in common for man, and brought together the female with the male in common and united all the animals likewise, he declared righteousness to be fellowship with equality.
>
> But those thus born rejected the fellowship which had brought about their birth, and say: "Who marries one, let him have her," when they could all share in common, as the rest of the animals show . . . . Hence the words of the lawgiver [the Old Testament God] "You shall not covet" must be understood as laughable, and yet more laughable is it to say "what is your neighbor's." For the very one who gave the desire as embracing the things of birth commands that it be taken away, though he takes it away from no animal. But that he said "your neighbor's wife" is even more laughable, since he compels what was common possession to become private property (ibid., 8.1-2; 9.3, p. 40).

It is interesting to note the relative paucity of ascetic material from the Church Fathers' denunciations of the Gnostics, juxtaposed with the weight placed on the libertine excerpts, at the same time comparing the total absence of libertine material from the Nag Hammadi texts, with their numerous ascetic teachings. We also find numerous teachings on asceticism in the apocryphal Acts of the Apostles. These documents exhibit definite Gnostic tendencies if not outright teachings, especially regarding a strong asceticism. Clearly, celibacy was a primary concern and focal point for these Gnostics who believed that sexual abstinence was at the core of Jesus' teachings.

In fragments from the "Acts of John" the disciple uses his presence at a wedding to preach chastity:

> Children, while your flesh is still clean and you have a body that is still untouched, and you are not caught in corruption nor soiled by Satan . . . know now more fully the mystery of conjugal union: it is the device of the serpent . . . an injury to the seed . . . a shedding of blood, a passion in the mind, a falling from reason . . . an union with bitterness . . . a fetter of darkness, an intoxication . . . that separates from the Lord, the beginning of disobedience, the end and death of life. Hearing this, my children, bind yourselves . . . in an indivisible, true and holy matrimony, waiting for the . . . true bridegroom from heaven, even Christ, who is a bridegroom for ever (NTA II, pp. 209f).

John's final prayer is:

> Lord, who hast kept me from my infancy until this time untouched by woman, who hast separated my body from them, so that it was offensive to me even to see a woman (NTA II, p. 209).

The "Acts of Peter" also contains strong teachings on celibacy and the horrors of sexuality as an impediment to salvation. In one episode Peter, while staying in Rome, converts the four concubines of the prefect Agrippa to chastity, as well as many other wives. The husband of one of them, Albinus, complained bitterly to an already furious Agrippa:

> "Either you must get me satisfaction from Peter, who caused my wife's separation, or I shall do so myself"; and Agrippa said that he had been treated in the same way by him . . . . and Albinus said to him, "Why then do you delay . . . ? Let us find him and execute him as a trouble-maker, so that we may recover our wives, and in order to give satisfaction to those who cannot execute him, who have themselves been deprived of their wives by him" (APt 34, in NTA II, p. 317).

Peter is then apprehended and martyred in an edifying death, crucified upside down with these final words upon his lips:

> . . . withdraw your souls from every outward sense and from all that appears but is not truly real; close these eyes of yours, close your ears,

withdraw from actions that are outwardly seen; and you shall know the facts about Christ and the whole secret of salvation (ibid., 37, p. 319).

Like the "Acts of Peter," the "Acts of Andrew" cannot truly be said to be Gnostic, although it shares the same encratism (extreme asceticism) as do its Gnostic neighbors. The "Acts of Andrew" also exhibits definite Platonic influences--pro-cosmic and yet urging the return to the One by turning away from the illusory and shadowy world of multiplicity. We find here a story similar to Peter's. This time the victimized husband is the judge Aegeates and the wife Maxmilla. He vows vengeance on the apostle, who continues to urge the chaste life on Maxmilla:

> I know ... that you are moved to resist the whole allurement of sexual intercourse, because you wish to be separated from a polluted and foul way of life. . . . And I rightly see in you Eve repenting and in myself Adam being converted: for what she suffered in ignorance you are now bringing to a happy conclusion because you are converted: and what the mind suffered which was brought down with her and was estranged from itself, I put right with you who know that you yourself are being drawn upon. For you yourself who did not suffer the same things have healed her affliction; and I by taking refuge with God have perfected his [Adam's] imperfection: and where she disobeyed, you have been obedient ... (AA 5, in *NTA* II, p. 410).

Speaking more generally, Andrew gives the philosophical foundation for his asceticism:

> If, O man, you understand all these things in yourself, namely that you are immaterial, holy, light, akin to the unbegotten, intellectual, heavenly, translucent, pure, superior to the flesh, superior to the world . . . to authorities, over whom you really are, if you perceive yourself in your condition, then take knowledge in what you are superior (ibid., 6, p. 411).

Later he exhorts the faithful to remember that

> they live in transient evils while they enjoy their harmful delusions. From which things I always exhorted you to keep clear and to press towards the things that are permanent and to take flight from all that is transient. . . . no one of you stands firm. . . . because the soul is untrained and has gone astray in "nature" (ibid., 15, p. 414).

Andrew too is crucified, and during his martyrdom he is yet able to deliver a final exhortation:

> Pay heed to us who hang here for the Lord's sake and soon forsake this body; renounce every worldly desire . . . . yet we have not persuaded our own to flee from the love of earthly things! But they are still bound to them and abide in them and do not wish to leave them . . . . How long will you be taken up with earthly and temporal things? How long will you fail to understand what is higher than yourselves and not press forward to lay hold of what is there? Leave me now to be put to death in the manner you see. . . . For there has been allotted me this destiny: to depart out of the body and to live with the Lord, with whom I am even being crucified (ibid., Narr. 32,33, p. 421).

The "Acts of Thomas" is most definitely Gnostic and contains, as seen above, "The Hymn of the Pearl." In one scene Thomas prays to Jesus, emphasizing his ascetic life:

> Look upon us, because for thy sake we have left our homes and our fathers' goods . . . . that we may behold thy Father and be satisfied with his divine nourishment. . . . for thy sake we have left our bodily consorts and our earthly fruits . . . (ATh 61, p. 476).

Thomas then exhorts the crowd:

> Abstain then first from adultery, for of all evils this is the beginning . . . and from all disgraceful deeds, especially those of the body, and from the horrid intercourse and couch of uncleanness, whose outcome is eternal condemnation. For this impurity is the mother-city of all evils (ibid., 84, pp. 487f).

Of his own life Thomas boasts to his Lord:

> Thou art he who made himself known to me . . . and I withheld myself from woman, that what thou dost require might not be found in defilement . . . .But I believed thy revelation and remained in the poverty of the world. . . . I have fulfilled thy work and accomplished thy command; and I have become poor and needy and a stranger and a slave, despised and a prisoner and hungry and thirsty and naked and weary (ibid., 145, p. 519).

From "The Pseudo-Clementines," a group of writings originally attributed to St. Clement of Rome--being the supposed history of his life and family--but dated as late as the first half of the third century, we find this strong and damning indictment of adultery:

> They [the elders] should urge on to marriage not only the young people but also those who are older, in order that lust may not flare up and infect the church with unchastity and adultery. For God hates the committing of adultery more than any other sin. . . . To urge the

brethren to morality is love's highest service, for it is the saving of the soul, whereas the nourishing of the body is only refreshment (Pseudo-Clementines 68.1-4, in *NTA* II, pp. 555f).

We have already seen the marked ascetic tone of the group of writings attributed to Thomas, most especially regarding sexual passions. In "The Book of Thomas the Contender" Jesus teaches his "twin:"

> O bitterness of the fire that burns in the bodies of men and in their marrow ... and making their minds drunk and their souls deranged and moving them within males and females.... Therefore it is said, "Everyone who seeks the truth from true wisdom will make himself wings so as to fly, fleeing the lust that scorches the spirits of men" (Th Cont. II.139.32-140.3, in *NHL*, p. 190).

In "The Dialogue of the Savior" Matthew asks his Lord:

> "I wish to see that place of life, that place in which there is no evil, but rather it is the pure light."
> The Lord said, "Brother Matthew, you cannot see it, as long you wear the flesh." ...
> Judas [i.e., Thomas] said, " .... When we pray, how should we pray?"
> The Lord said, "Pray in the place where there is no woman" (Dial. Savior III.144.14-15, in *NHL*, p. 237).

Not surprisingly, as "The Dialogue of the Savior" shares many parallels with the earlier "Gospel of Thomas," this final misogynist statement is reminiscent of the end of the Gospel:

> Simon Peter said to them, "Let Mary [Magdalene] leave us, for women are not worthy of Life."
> Jesus said, "I shall myself lead her in order to make her male, so that she too may become a living spirit resembling you males. For every woman who will make herself male will enter the Kingdom of Heaven" (GTh II.51.18-26, in *NHL*, p. 130).

"The Acts of Peter and the Twelve Apostles" is, strictly speaking, not a Gnostic document. Its appearance in the monastic library unearthed at Nag Hammadi, reflects, however, the fluid boundaries that existed between the orthodox and heterodox that can be observed even as late as the fourth century. This text could well have been written in the second century, and its emphasis on poverty and criticisms of the rich are familiar ground for the orthodox. Interestingly enough, its ascetic teachings on doing without possessions are placed within a framework of symbolism more reminiscent of Gnosticism: strangers in an alien world, the hidden pearl, and the garment of the world. The speaker is Lithargoel, later revealed to be Jesus:

> No man is able to go on that road [to the city, i.e., the rest], except one who has forsaken everything that he has and has fasted daily from stage to stage. For many are the robbers and wild beasts on that road. The one who carries bread with him on the road, the black dogs kill because of the bread. The one who carries a costly garment of the world with him, the robbers kill because of the garment (APt 12 VI.5.21-6.1, in *NHL*, p. 267).

Though exhibiting many Valentinian elements, "The Testimony of Truth" presents a far more ascetic teaching than what we find in the Valentinian school (*see* next section). The author, probably living in the third century, is emphatic in seeing the total renunciation of the world and all sexual passions as the only means of salvation. The Old Testament Law is seen as the path of darkness, a position similar to the strong anti-Judaism found in many Gnostic texts:

> For no one who is under the Law will be able to look up to the truth, for they will not be able to serve two masters.... The Law commands one to take a husband or to take a wife, and to beget, to multiply like the sand of the sea. But passion which is a delight to them constrains the souls of those who are begotten in this place.... in order that the Law might be fulfilled through them. And they show that they are assisting the world; and they turn away from the light, who are unable to pass by the archon of darkness until they pay the last penny.
> But the Son of Man came forth from Imperishability.... He came to the world by the Jordan river.... and John bore witness to the descent of Jesus.... he knew that the dominion of carnal procreation had come to an end. The Jordan river is the power of the body, that is, the senses of pleasures. The water of the Jordan is the desire for sexual intercourse. John is the archon of the womb (Test. Tr. IX.29.22-31.5, in *NHL*, p. 407).

"The Testimony of Truth" is more than simply an anti-Jewish tract, however, for as we have seen in earlier chapters it is quite vehement in its denunciation of the orthodox Church. Here, we cite its attack on the Church's emphasis on sacraments, especially baptism, as the way of salvation:

> Some enter the faith by receiving a baptism, on the ground that they have it as a hope of salvation, which they call "the seal." They do not know that the fathers of the world [archons] are manifest to that place. . . . But the baptism of truth is something else; it is by renunciation of the world that it is found (ibid., 69.7-24, p. 414).

378

The Hermetic literature offers one source of non-Christian Gnostic thought, and here we include a quotation on the world's entrapment of the soul through sex:

> The spiritual man shall recognize himself as immortal, and love as the cause of death. . . . He who has cherished the body issued from the error of love, he remains in the darkness erring, suffering in his sense the dispensations of death (in Jonas, pp. 72f).

A specific expression of asceticism was martyrdom, if not theologically, then certainly psychologically in its emphasis on bodily punishment. Clearly, identifying with the sufferings of Jesus was central to the orthodox Church's understanding of the gospel, as we saw in Part I, for such suffering was seen as the ultimate expression of the disciples' love for their Lord. Suffering, therefore, whether in the form of the ascetic turning away from the pleasures of the world, or actively seeking to suffer and die in the name of Jesus, was all seen as the Will of God. Many Gnostics, too, emphasized martyrdom as being part of salvation. Since they were the targets of the Church Fathers, it logically follows, as it did for the orthodox who were attacked by the synagogue and the Romans, that they would lift the experience of a suffering victimhood to a spiritual ideal. The *Nag Hammadi Library* offers several examples of this, most prominent of which is "The First Apocalypse of James."

In this revelation to James, Jesus extols the life of suffering in his name and for his love:

> Fear not, James. You too will they seize . . . .thus you will undergo these sufferings. But do not be sad. For the flesh is weak. It will receive what has been ordained for it. But as for you, do not be timid or afraid (1 ApocJs V.25.13,14; 32.17-22, in *NHL*, pp. 243,246).

James weeps at these words, but Jesus continues:

> James, behold, I shall reveal to you your redemption. When you are seized, and you undergo these sufferings, a multitude will arm themselves against you that they may seize you (ibid., 32.29-33.5, p. 246).

The revelation continues with the ascent of James' soul, and instructions as to becoming free of the "detainers."

While "The First Apocalypse of James" treats the predictions of James' sufferings and martyrdom, "The Second Apocalypse of James" actually describes these events. James appears before the unpersuaded crowd, who cry out against him:

> "Come, let us stone the Just One [James]. . . . let us kill this man, that he may be taken from our midst.". . . And they . . . found him standing beside the columns of the temple. . . . They seized him and struck him as they dragged him upon the ground. They stretched him out, and placed a stone on his abdomen. They all placed their feet on him, saying, "You have erred!"
> Again they raised him up, since he was alive, and made him dig a hole. They made him stand in it. After having covered him up to his abdomen, they stoned him in this manner (2 ApocJs V.61.13-62.12, in *NHL*, pp. 254f).

In "The Letter of Peter to Philip" Peter teaches the other apostles that it was not necessary that Jesus suffer for his own salvation, for he was divine, but that it *is* necessary that his followers do:

> Our illuminator, Jesus, came down and was crucified . . . . and he was buried in a tomb. And he rose from the dead. My brothers, Jesus is a stranger to this suffering. But we are the ones who have suffered at the transgression of the mother [Sophia] (Pt Ph VIII.139.15-23, in *NHL*, p. 397).

We have already considered the theology of Marcion, the influential Gnostic teacher of the second century. His norms for behavior and ethical (moral) imperatives logically if not severely follow from his teaching. Recalling what we discussed before, we can see that Marcion's morality is based on a strict acosmic dualism, in which the true God is totally separate and indifferent to the physical world, which is under the law of its creator, the Demiurge. As was observed with other Gnostic theorists, Marcion also emphasized the necessity of not being beholden to *any* of the laws of the world, and of not being bound to *any* aspect of this world. Thus, Marcion advocated the bare minimum of involvement in the world of matter, thereby reducing its hold over us:

> By way of opposition to the Demiurge, Marcion rejects the use of the things of this world. . . . [He] believes that he vexes the Demiurge by abstaining from what he made or instituted (in Jonas, p. 144).

Jonas has observed that this extreme ascetic morality was not "a matter . . . of ethics but of metaphysical alignment" (Jonas, p. 144); i.e., the Gnostics aligning themselves with the reality of God, as opposed to the tyranny of the Demiurge and his world. The major expression of this asceticism, not surprisingly again, was in the areas of sex and food. Of sexual intercourse Marcion taught, according to Clement:

> Not wishing to help replenish the world made by the Demiurge, the Marcionites decreed abstention from matrimony, defying their crea-

tor and hastening to the Good One who has called them and who
... is God in a different sense: wherefore, wishing to leave nothing
of their own down here, they turn abstemious not from a moral
principle but from hostility to their maker and unwillingness to use
his creation (*Strom.* III.4.25, in Jonas, pp. 144f).

The principal Marcionite argument against sex therefore is not the act itself, but its result of reproduction. Celibacy becomes the attempt to foil the Demiurge's plan of capturing the separated souls of light from their Source, imprisoning them still further in the material world of darkness. In terms of food, abstaining as much as possible was

for the sake of destroying and contemning and abominating the
works of the creator (Jerome *Adv. Jovinian* II.16, in Jonas, p. 144).

Jonas concludes his discussion of Marcion:

Thus Marcion's asceticism, unlike that of the Essene or later of
Christian monasticism, was not conceived to further the sanctifica-
tion of human existence, but was essentially negative in conception
and part of the gnostic revolt against the cosmos (Jonas, p. 145).

We are thus very far from the point of view that asceticism was a positive activity mandated by God, as maintained by the orthodox Church. Rather, it is here reflective of that extreme negative reaction to the nature of this world and its creator. Hardly ordered by the good God, who remains totally indifferent to what occurs in this world, total abstention nonetheless becomes the only sane Gnostic reaction to the existential situation here, and thus the means to become free of it.

While Marcion gave the most complete statement of the behavioral implications of the Gnostic world-view that existed to his time, it remained for Mani in the third century to give this ascetic position its consummate expression. A quotation from Mani himself serves as a fine summarizing introduction to a discussion of Manichean morality:

Since the ruin of the Hyle [the world of matter] is decreed by God, one
should abstain from all ensouled things and eat only vegetables and
whatever else is non-sentient, and abstain from marriage, the de-
lights of love and the begetting of children, so that the divine Power
may not through the succession of generations remain longer in the
Hyle (in Jonas, p. 231).

What was implied in Marcion's system is here clearly spelled out in Mani's. The trapped particles of light in matter must not only not be harmed, but also must not be ingested. This attitude, incidentally, is in clear contrast with the libertine sects that are witnessed to by the heresiologists. Those Gnostics, according to the Church Fathers, believed that it was *by* ingesting the divine element in semen and menses that they could be returned to God. For Mani, it was just such incorporation (though without the scatological elements reported by the Church Fathers) that imprisoned, preventing the "cosmic ferris wheel" from collecting the light particles from the world. In addition, Mani advocated a rigorous poverty as part of the continuing process of separating from the world's material darkness.

These premises, taken to their ultimate, result in the most extreme asceticism ever imagined and a justification for the ultimate quietism. If particles of light are trapped all over and everywhere, any movement can trample underfoot the divine, including breathing which engulfs such particles. The light so contained is described as the "slaughtered, killed, oppressed, murdered soul" (Rudolph, p. 341), and the reader may recall our discussion from Chapter 8 on *Jesus patibilis*, the archetypal symbol for these suffering particles. Thus one finds a strange form of compassion inherent in Mani' system. Nonetheless, this "compassion" for the light particles has resulted in what Jonas refers to as "the most exaggerated idea of sin that has ever been conceived" (Jonas, p. 232). He cites some of Mani's teachings:

> When someone walks on the ground he injures the earth [i.e., more accurately, the Light mixed in with it]; he who moves his hand injures the air, for this is the soul of men and beasts. . . . It behooves man that he look down at the ground when walking on his way, lest he tread under his foot the cross of the Light and destroy the plants (*Kephalaia* 208.7, in Jonas, p. 232).

Interestingly enough, this latter directive found its way into Christian monasticism in the teaching of "custody of the eyes." This aspect of the monastic life emphasized the temptation of the world, and in a more extreme form, as in the writings of St. Bernard of Clairvaux, would have monks walking with their eyes cast down lest the beauties of nature tempt them to forget the inner world of God.

Augustine further describes the extreme asceticism of the Manichees:

> Nevertheless they eat no meat, since the divine substance has fled from dead or slain creatures. What remains, after the death of an animal, is of such quantity and quality that it is no longer worthy of being purified in the body of one of the elect.
> They do not even eat eggs, since these too died when they were broken, and no dead bodies must be eaten, and the only part of flesh that is living is what can be trapped in meal so that it does not die. Nor do they use milk as food, though it is milked or sucked from the body

of the living animal. . . . They assume that plants and trees are in this way living, that the life which is in them feels and suffers when they are injured; and none of them could tear off or pluck anything of these without causing pain. They even consider it wrong, therefore, to cleanse a field of thorns. As a result they foolishly charge agriculture, the most innocent of all skills as a still greater murderer. . . . And when they copulate, they should avoid conception and procreation, so that the divine substance entering them through food and drink may not be fettered in fleshly bonds in succeeding generations. They believe that souls obtain entry to all flesh, and through food and drink. This is no doubt why they condemn marriage, and prevent it as far as they can . . . (Augustine *de haer.* 46.3-4, in Haardt, pp. 345-47).

In the Manichean Psalms we read:

Let us give ourselves to him and he is able to guide us.
Guide my eyes that they look no evil look.
Guide my ears that they hear not a . . . word.
Guide my nostrils that they smell not the stink of lust.
Guide my mouth that it utter no slander.
Guide for me my hands that they serve not Satan.
Guide for me my heart that it do no evil at all.
Guide for me my Spirit in the midst of the stormy sea.
. . . .
Guide my feet that they walk not in the way of Error.
(Unnumbered fragment, in Allberry, p. 150).

Sin therefore is unavoidable in this world of bodies, and emphasizes still further the evil designs of the Prince of Darkness in making humanity. This belief led to the elaborate Manichean manual of confession, from which we now quote. The manual begins by describing the fate of the Five Gods who suffered the fate of being trapped in this world:

Because they fought for a while with the Devil, were injured as a result and mingled with the Dark, they are now on this earth.

Thus they are subject to the almost infinite variety of sins, for which the Manichean auditors must beg forgiveness:

My God! Should we ever in any way have injured or shattered the Five Gods, through Imprudence or evil wickedness; should we have caused them the fourteen-type Wounds, should we have destroyed Life with the ten snake-headed fingers and the thirty-two teeth, in order to take it into us as food and drink, and if we thereby should have hurt and tormented the Five Gods in any way; should we ever have offended in any way against the dry and against the damp Earth, against the fivefold Living Being, against the fivefold Plants and Trees, we now beg, My God, Forgiveness for our Sins.

The manual continues by enumerating sins against the members of the Elect, all members of the human race, and the entire animal kingdom. And finally, these ten sins:

1) should we have in any way lied or in any way borne false witness; 2) . . . have been witness to a lie; 3) . . . have calumnied a sinless man; 4) . . . have practiced magic; 5) and should we thereby have slain manifold living beings; 6) . . . in commerce have practised deception; 7) . . . have used up property entrusted to us by an absent person; 8) . . . have done anything to displease the Sun- and the Moon-God; 9) . . . have committed an offense with the first Body and with this Body, and have sinned with them, by making a living as a male paramour; 10) . . . have caused harm to so many creatures, My God, we now pray, therefore, for Forgiveness for these ten types of sin (in Haardt, pp. 327-29).

This extreme emphasis on sin, incidentally, found its way into the confessions and theology of St. Augustine. Though abandoning the theology of his former compatriots, Augustine apparently never lost the guilt that underlay such teachings.

When one entered the Manichean community the powers of Darkness were banished, but this did not rule out the falling to temptation, especially when, as we have seen, any bodily activity was considered a form of sin. This led to the Manichean emphasis on confession as enabling the sin to be undone by a simple willingness to repent.

Parallel to the standard Gnostic triad of *pneumatic, psychic,* and *hylic,* the Manicheans had a triad of the Elect, Soldiers, and sinners. The ideal of extreme asceticism was only for those few spiritually advanced--the Elect, also called the Perfect, Righteous, or True--who could maintain such standards. It was incumbent upon them to maintain a strict schedule of prayer, Manichean scriptural readings, and fasting. One hundred fast days per year were required, thirty of which were consecutive. Central to each day was "the table," a meal that the elect took in common, and which consisted of those vegetables, fruits, and bread that had "a high content of light" and thus were considered sacred. This included cucumbers, melons, and wheat bread. By their consumption of this food the Elect would deliver the light from the bondage of matter through a process of purification. St. Augustine, reflecting back on the Manicheans he knew, sarcastically relates how an Elect

breathes out of it angels, yea, there shall burst forth particles of divinity, at every moan or groan in his prayer, which particles of the most high and true God had remained bound in that fig, unless they had been set at liberty by the teeth or belly of some "Elect" saint (*Conf.* 3.10, in Rudolph, pp. 341f).

The Elect also were to dedicate themselves to studying and copying religious writings as their principal activity, and their reputation here for excellence both in writing materials as well as artistry has far exceeded the content of what they were copying. Rudolph quotes one Arab author (al-Jahiz) as saying:

> When the Manicheans expend effort on the production of their holy writings, it is like the Christians doing the same for the churches (in Rudolph, p. 340).

Clearly, the Elect on their own could never manage to run a community. It was the function of the second group, the Soldiers (also referred to as Hearers) to assume the responsibility for the practical details and exigencies of daily life. The sins that they would amass by virtue of their worldly involvement would be promptly forgiven by the Elect. Quite obviously the Soldiers were second-class citizens of the community who could never achieve salvation in this lifetime, which was only possible if they would be reborn as a member of the Elect, or as a plant with a high degree of light:

> they must return again and again into the "world and its terrors . . . until [their] light and . . . spirit shall be freed and after long wandering back and forth [they attain] to the assembly of the Elect" (in Jonas, p. 233).

Material wealth of course was denied to the Elect, but not to this second group, who were allowed to amass large amounts of wealth to form the economic foundation for the community. In addition, their responsibilities included observing basic commandments of renunciation of sins, including sexual infidelity, lying, killing of animals, and doubts of the Manichean faith.

The third group comprised the sinners who, it goes without saying, were confined to the power of the Darkness and eternal damnation in hell:

> Hail to all those who escape the end of the Sinners and Deniers and avoid the ruin which confronts them in concealment for all eternity! (From *Kephalaia*, in Haardt, p. 327)

Manicheism also strongly emphasized martyrdom, Mani's eventual fate, as seen in his own words:

Endure persecutions and temptations, which will come to ye, fortify yourselves in these commandments which I gave unto ye, that ye may escape that second death and these bonds, in which there is no hope of life, and that ye may avoid the evil end of the Deniers and Blasphemers who have seen the Truth with their own eyes and have turned away from it. They shall come unto the Place of Punishment at which there is no day of life. For the shining Light shall hide from them, and from that hour onward they shall not see it (ibid., p. 326).

3. Moderateness

For the more moderate Gnostic view of morality we find our greatest examples in the Mandean community and Valentinian schools--though not necessarily as related by the heresiologists who, as we have seen, almost always chose to highlight if not exaggerate the dramatic and grossly deviant.

Our only specific example of Valentinian ethics, from which it is possible to derive some implications, is the "Letter of Ptolemaeus to Flora," preserved for us by Epiphanius. We discussed this letter in Chapter 6 (pp. 204f), where we considered its view of the "three Gods." As we saw then, this Valentinian teacher is instructing a hitherto uninitiated lady as prelude for the higher teachings which will follow later. The letter is instructive for us as it illustrates clearly the importance for the Valentinians of the Ten Commandments (with some reservations) and the Sermon on the Mount as ethical guides. It is thus an interesting document, illustrating once again how close the Gnostic schools could be to the orthodox Church in many important areas. While teaching that the "perfect God and Father" did not create this world, this school did not hold that the world was evil or the work of the devil. Rather, as mentioned earlier, it was seen as coming from a "God who is just and hates evil." Let us look specifically at the Ten Commandments.

The Law--i.e., the body of laws found in the five books of Moses--has three parts: that given by the Middle or Just God--good but imperfect; that containing the additions made by Moses himself as adaptations to the need of the people; and those commandments introduced by the "elders of the people" who came after Moses.

The law given by this God of Justice is itself divided into three parts: that which is to be fulfilled (the Ten Commandments) by Jesus because, while not evil, the legislation was not perfect; that which is evil and unjust (e.g., an eye for an eye), and so was destroyed by Jesus; and that which is to be understood symbolically (such as fasting and circumcision): The first part is fulfilled as is stated in the Sermon on the Mount, as is the second abrogated there as well (e.g., turning the other cheek).

386

It is the third part of the laws given by the Just God with which we are particularly concerned and now address.

Ptolemaeus is in essence here talking about form and content, teaching Flora that the content or meaning of the various Jewish rituals was true, while the form of any particular one was no longer needed. One example is fasting, the spiritual meaning of which is the "abstinence from all that is evil." Because of Jesus the truth (content) has come, and so the commandment to abstain from food (form) is obsolete. However, interesting to note, Ptolemaeus does not consider obedience to the commandment to be evil, for it is still practiced within his circle. Let him speak for himself:

> But the part which is exemplary [symbolic] . . . I mean what is laid down about offerings, circumcision, Sabbath, fasting, Passover, unleavened bread, and other such matters. All these are images and symbols and they were changed when the truth appeared. As far as their phenomenal appearance and literal fulfilment are concerned, they were destroyed; but as far as spiritual meaning is concerned, they were restored; the names remained the same, but the content changed. For the Savior. . . .wants us to be engaged not in physical fasting, but in spiritual fasting, which amounts to abstinence from all that is evil. External, physical fasting is observed even among our followers, for it can be of some benefit to the soul, if it is engaged on reasonably. . . .At the same time we fast as a way of remembering the true fast, in order that those who are not yet able to keep that fast may have a reminder of it from the physical fast (*Panar.* XXXIII.5.8-14, in F I, pp. 156-59).

Thus we find in this Letter a prominent example of how the Gnostic metaphysics, here the Valentinian form, can be adapted to meet the ethical and practical needs of the community and specific individuals.

In quite a different vein we also find a moderate position in "Asclepius," a Hermetic text in the *Nag Hammadi Library*. We have already considered this document, but its discussion of sex in a positive light is relevant here. The treatise begins with the Revealer Hermes Trismegistus instructing his initiate Asclepius on the similarities between the "mystery" (of spiritual union) and the experience of sexual intercourse, certainly a curious positive comparison to find in the Nag Hammadi collection, another argument for not truly seeing this text as purely Gnostic. It serves as another example of the thin line that sometimes served to separate Gnosticism from other contemporary systems of thought, not always Christian. Hermes says:

> And if you wish to see the reality of this mystery then you should see the wonderful representation of the intercourse that takes place between the male and the female. For when the semen reaches the

387

climax, it leaps forth. In that moment the female receives the strength
of the male; the male for his part receives the strength of the female
. . . (Ascl. VI.15-25, in *NHL*, p. 300).

Our final example of a moderate ethical position among the Gnostics
is the Mandeans, an interesting amalgam of heterodox Jewry and
Gnosticism. As Rudolph has summarized the situation:

> One may indeed say that here gnosis has been grafted on to an old
> branch of the cultic community of unorthodox Jewry, but from this
> an authentic and even typical Mandean-Nasorean product has been
> created (in F II, pp. 139f).

Much closer to the Old Testament ethic as its norm, the Mandean
literature contains no real ascetic nor libertine morality, but rather a
focus on living a "good" and "just" life, devotion to good works,
dispensing alms to the poor, etc. Nonetheless, the Gnostic anti-cosmic
bias is unmistakably present. Thus, at times the Mandean literature on
morality is almost indistinguishable from the biblical soil from which
it grew, while at others it fits comfortably into a Gnostic context.
Moreover, as we have seen, emphasis on rites of baptism, washings,
etc., as mandatory for salvation, co-equal with the role of knowledge,
distinguishes the Mandean way of life.

The more traditional Judaeo-Christian moral precepts clearly prevail, and can be seen in the following examples:

> Perfect and faithful: do not deviate from your words and love not lies
> and falsehood. Love not gold and silver and the possessions of this
> world, for this world will come to nothing and perish, and its
> possessions and its works will be abandoned. Do not worship Satan,
> the idols, the images, the error, and the confusion of this world . . . .
> Do not put your trust in the kings, rulers, and rebels of this world, nor
> in military forces, arms conflict, and the hosts which they assemble
> (GR I.95f, in F II, pp. 289f).

The following excerpt is reminiscent of the teaching of Ptolemaeus to
Flora:

> I say to you, my chosen . . . . Fast the great fast, which is not a fasting
> from the eating and drinking of the world. Fast with your eyes from
> immodest winking, and do not see or practice evil . . . . Fast with your
> mouths from wanton lies and do not love falsehood and deceit. Fast
> with your hearts from wicked thoughts . . . . with your hands from
> committing murder and do not commit robbery. Fast with your body
> from the married woman who does not belong to you (GR I.110-16,
> in F II, p. 290).

In what follows, we find the same ethic and behavioral norm so characteristic of Old Testament thinking, taken over in the New Testament most clearly in the Sermon on the Mount and the parable of the Last Judgment in Matthew:

> If you see a prisoner who is believing and true, then pay the necessary ransom and release him. Do not however simply release the soul with gold and silver, but also with . . . faith, and pure words of the mouth release the soul from darkness to light, from error to truth . . . from unbelief to belief in your lord. . . . Give alms to the poor and be a guide to the blind. And when you give alms, my chosen, do not give ostentatiously. . . . When you see anyone who is hungry, then satisfy his hunger. When you see anyone who is thirsty, then give him to drink. When you see anyone naked, then give him clothes and coverings for his nakedness. For whoever gives, receives, and whoever makes loans, is repaid. Whoever gives alms will find abundant alms as his support. Whoever clothes the naked with raiment, will find clothes and covering for his nakedness. Whoever releases a prisoner, will find a Messenger of Life advancing to meet him. . . . Give bread, water, and shelter to poor and persecuted people who suffer persecution. (GR I.103-105; 138, in F II, p. 291).

Regarding sexuality and worldly pleasures:

> Take a wife and found a family, so that the world may multiply through you . . . . Do not commit adultery or fornicate, do not sing or dance . . . . and do not neglect the night prayer. Love not treacherous spirits and seductive courtesans . . . . Drink not and do not become intoxicated, and do not forget the lord in your thoughts (GR I.92,146; GR XVI.2, in F II, pp. 292f).

In the following excerpt we find a teaching very reminiscent of the Old Testament--that we love our brothers, but not our enemies:

> Love and support one another, as the eyes take care for the feet. Love and support one another, and you shall cross the great Ocean of Suf [the Red Sea: Mandean symbol for the dividing line between this world and the next; i.e., death]. For brothers of flesh come to nothing, but brothers of kusta [truth] are established (in the realm of light) (GR I,128, in F II, pp. 291f).

Finally, we look at some Mandean passages that are more frankly Gnostic in their anti-cosmic attitude:

> Do not put your trust in the beauty of bodies, which soon pass into corruption . . . for everything that is born, dies, and everything that is made with the hands, passes into corruption. The whole world

comes to an end, and idolatry comes to nothing.... Do not praise the
Seven and the Twelve, the ringleaders [archons] of the world, who
travel day and night, those who seduce the family of souls, who were
transplanted here from the House of Life. Do not praise the sun and
the moon, the luminaries of this world, for this radiance does not belong to them: it was only given to them in order to illuminate the dark
abode. They are the angels of the perishable house.... Adam, look
upon the world, which is a completely unreal thing.... in which you
can put no trust.... I wander about searching after my soul, which
is worth ages and worlds to me. I went and found my soul—what are
all the worlds to me? (GR XVI.2,5, in F II, pp. 289f,293f)

Platonism

The Platonic ethic of living a virtuous life in pursuit of truth has been
discussed in the preceding chapters, and so will not be dealt with in
depth here. The exception is Plotinus who, as we shall see presently,
addresses the subject of morality specifically in the context of the
Gnostic position, and we will close the chapter with Plotinus' moving
description of the culmination of the spiritual life, doubtless drawn
from his own experience.

1. Plato

In Chapter 7 we discussed Plato's notions of the body and the
tripartite mind. We specifically referred to his telling image in the
Phaedo of the charioteer (reason) reining in the recalcitrant forces of the
emotions and appetites (body). It is especially important to recall that
for Plato the body is seen as the agent and cause of moral evil in the
world, with the soul being the innocent victim of the body's grossly
material and evil qualities. Plato saw the problem as resting in the
failure of society to educate people properly in the use of reason and
cultivation of virtue:

> ...no one wishes to be bad, but a bad man is bad because of some flaw
> in his physical make-up and failure in his education, neither of which
> he likes or chooses.... The responsibility lies with the parents rather
> than the offspring, and with those who educate rather than their
> pupils; but we must all try with all our might by education, by
> practice and by study to avoid evil and grasp its contrary (*Tim.* 86e-
> 87b).

We saw in Chapter 8 that the practice of virtue is Plato's version of salvation, and leads him to describe the various ethical and educational practices that foster the development of reason in attaining knowledge of the Good. This is the goal of justice, summarized in this way in the *Republic*:

> Justice['s] . . . real concern is not with external actions, but with a man's inward self, his true concern and interest. The just man will not allow the three elements which make up his inward self to trespass on each other's functions or interfere with each other, but, by keeping all three in tune . . . will in the truest sense set his house to rights, attain self-mastery and order, and live on good terms with himself. When he has bound these elements into a disciplined and harmonious whole, and so become fully one instead of many, he will be ready for action of any kind . . . (*Rep.* IV.443c-e).

The emphasis, judged by this passage, is placed by Plato on the *process* of attaining inner harmony, not the action itself.

2. Philo

We find in Philo a more subtle expression of the Platonic paradox with which we are now more than familiar. Clearly negative in his estimation of the body, he nonetheless does not attack the body with the repulsion we find in most other Platonists, and emphatically repudiates a life of physical austerity or neglect. He writes:

> If then thou observest anyone not taking food or drink when he should, or refusing to use the bath and oil . . . or sleeping on the ground, and occupying wretched lodgings, and then on the strength of all this fancying that he is practicing self-control, take pity on his mistake, and show him the true method of self-control; for all these practices of his are fruitless and wearisome labors, prostrating soul and body by starving and in other ways maltreating them. A man may submit . . . to purifications befouling his understanding while cleansing his body; he may, having more money than he knows what to do with, found a temple, providing all its furniture on a scale of lavish magnificence; . . . yet shall he not be inscribed on the roll of the pious. No, for this man . . . has gone astray from the road that accords with piety, deeming it to be ritual instead of holiness, and offering gifts to Him who cannot be bribed and will not accept such things . . . who welcomes genuine worship of every kind, but abhors all counterfeit approaches. Genuine worship is that of a soul bringing simple reality as its only sacrifice; all that is mere display, fed by lavish expenditure on externals, is counterfeit (*The Worse Attacks the Better* 19-21).

Not only is an error made in this ritualistic approach but, on a more directly practical level, opposing the flesh through ascetic practices merely compounds the problem, as we see in this passage, filled with psychological wisdom:

> ... for in this way you will rouse your adversary's spirit and stimulate a more dangerous foe to the contest against you (*On Flight and Finding* 25).

In other words, you merely intensify the fear by reinforcing the fact that there is an "enemy" outside you that needs to be defeated before it defeats you. Beginning with fear, the ascetic attack upon the flesh ends with fear, completing the vicious circle that Philo intuitively sensed. Thus, he urged a more moderate approach to the physical and social world:

> Begin then by getting some exercise and practice in the business of life both private and public; and when by means of the sister virtues, household-management and statesmanship, you have become masters in each domain, enter now, as more than qualified to do so, on your migration to a different and more excellent way of life. For the practical comes before the contemplative life; it is a sort of prelude to a more advanced contest; and it is well to have fought it out first (*ibid.*, 36).

Such involvement even includes indulging in life's physical pleasures, if done with self-control, for

> the countenance of wisdom is not scowling and severe, contracted by deep thought and depression of spirit, but on the contrary cheerful and tranquil, full of joy and gladness (*Noah's Work as a Planter* 167).

Thus it is not the world that is good or bad, but the use that we make of it:

> We have to say . . . that sense-perception comes under the head neither of bad nor of good things, but is an intermediate thing common to a wise man and a fool, and when it finds itself in a fool it proves bad, when in a sensible man, good (*Alleg. Interp.* III.67).

It is our attitude towards the physical world and its gifts that is the problem, not the physical gifts themselves, for they are nothing. Philo illustrates this point by his allegorical interpretation of one of the Old Testament's strictures against incest: "A man shall not go near to any that is akin to his flesh to uncover their shame" (Lv 18:6). Philo explains this passage as a command to spurn the flesh: "Let not our appetites . . . be whetted and incited towards anything that is dear to the flesh" (*On the Giants* 35). However, Philo quickly points out that he is speaking of the *attraction* to the things of the flesh:

> The meaning of these words it would be well to explain. Men have often possessed an unlimited profusion of wealth, without engaging in lucrative trade, and others have not pursued glory and yet been held worthy to receive civic eulogies and honors. . . . Let all such learn to "go near" with deliberate purpose to any of these gifts, that is, not to regard them with admiration or undue satisfaction, judging that each of them is not only no true blessing, but actually a grievous evil. . . . For it is the lovers of these things in each case who make the "approach." . . . They have abandoned the better to the worse, the soul to the soulless. The sane man brings the dazzling and coveted gifts of fortune in subjection to the mind as to a captain. It they come to him, he accepts them to use them for improvement of life, but if they remain afar off, he does not go to them, judging that without them happiness might still be quite possible (*On the Giants* 36-38).

Philo thus cautions not to make the mistake of embracing the body as a source of pleasure. The body is, as it were, a necessary evil in our experience in this world, and pleasure thus is a

> serpent . . . bad of itself; and therefore it is not found at all in a good man, the bad man getting all the harm of it by himself. . . . Just as joy, being a good condition of soul, deserves prayer, so pleasure, the passion *par excellence* [its "starting-point and foundation"], deserves cursing. . . . beyond all the wild beasts (*Alleg. Interp.* III.68,107,113).

In *The Sacrifices of Cain and Abel* he writes even more strongly denouncing the pleasures of the body (21-32), leading the reader to expect the same stirring exhortations to the ascetic life we have found in many of the Gnostics:

> So Pleasure comes languishing in the guise of a harlot or courtesan. Her gait has the looseness which her extravagant wantonness and luxury has bred; the lascivious roll of her eyes is a bait to entice the souls of the young; her look speaks of boldness and shamelessness; her neck is held high; she assumes a stature which Nature has not given her; she grins and giggles . . . (21).

For page after page Philo continues with this portrait of physical pleasure, culminating in a list of almost 150 adjectives that describe the one who becomes a "pleasure-lover." Yet unexpectedly, as we have already discussed, Philo is an ethical moderate, for he recognizes that pleasure, as a by-product of this physical participation is not to be avoided, but it must never be allowed to distract one from the true purpose here: the practice and attainment of virtue, the goal of becoming Plato's philosopher-king. And here Philo's Platonic heritage comes to the fore, as we saw in Chapter 7, wherein he sees the body as a corpse, "that dwelling place of endless calamities" (*On the Confusion of Tongues* 177). The body thus is merely a means that we discard when the goal of reaching God has been attained. It is the philosopher-kings who have attained this goal, they who walk the fine middle line of working within the physical framework without becoming enticed in the corporeal snare:

> Now some of the souls have descended into bodies, but others have never deigned to be brought into union with any of the parts of earth. They are consecrated and devoted to the service of the Father and Creator whose wont it is to employ them as ministers and helpers, to have charge and care of mortal man. . . . [they] have risen to the surface and then soared upwards back to the place from whence they came. These . . . are the souls of those who have given themselves to genuine philosophy, who from first to last study to die to the life in the body, that a higher existence immortal and incorporeal in the presence of Him who is Himself immortal and uncreated, may be their portion (*On the Giants* 12-14).

Elsewhere, Philo states that these souls,

> free from flesh and body spend their days in the theater of the universe and with a joy that none can hinder see and hear things divine, which they have desired with love insatiable (ibid. 31).

3. Origen

Despite his strongly mystical and ascetical bent, Origen nonetheless upholds the Church's belief in sacraments, seeing them as the framework within which the non-ritual spiritual practices are carried out. Thus in his writings, one finds references to the sacraments of penance, baptism, and the Eucharist. Martyrdom, as we have seen, especially finds favor, for to shed blood purifies and cleanses the Church, as is stated in this passage from *An Exhortation to Martyrdom*:

> At any rate, clearly "the cup of salvation" in Psalms is the death of the martyrs. . . . Therefore, death comes to us as "precious" if we are God's saints and worthy of dying not the common death, if I may call it that, but a special kind of death, Christian, religious, and holy.
> Let us also remember the sins we have committed, and that it is

impossible to receive forgiveness of sins apart from baptism ... and that the baptism of martyrdom has been given to us (*Martyrdom* XIV).

As previously discussed, Origen sees the physical world as the effect of the fall of the rational beings, coming into existence as God's means of allowing the fallen soul to return to its true state. The body thus is indeed a prison, being the antithesis of our reality, yet it is one used by God as the means of returning to Him. Origen discusses this in some detail in *On Prayer*:

> ... the soul always preserves free choice; and on its own responsibility it either comes to be in nobler things, advancing step by step to the summit of goods, or descends from failing to pay attention in diverse motions to one flood or another of evil (*On Prayer* XXIX.13).

In many cases God allows, as it were, the evil or diseased condition to remain because of its potential for helping the soul to freely choose other than sin. Too precipitous a healing would simply set up a repeat of the problem, as long as the soul does not choose otherwise. Thus, the purpose of God

> is that they may become satiated by long exposure to evil, and by being filled with the sin they desire may so perceive the harm they have taken. Then they hate what they previously welcomed; and since they have been healed more firmly, they are able to profit from the health of their souls, which is theirs by the healing (ibid.).

In choosing the lusts of the body, people have forsaken God:

> For they have lowered to a body without soul or sense the name of Him who gives to all sentient and rational beings not only the power of sentience, but also of sensing rationally, and to some even the power of sensing and thinking perfectly and virtuously (ibid., 15).

Yet in the midst of this "fire and prison" they are not really punished, but rather

> they gain a beneficence for cleansing them of the evils in their error. This is accompanied by saving pains that follow those who love pleasure. And so they are freed from all the filth and blood by which they had been so stained and defiled that they could not even think of being saved from their own destruction.... For God does not wish that the good should belong to anyone by necessity but willingly, since there are perhaps some who by their long association with evil will come by toil and pain to understand its ugliness and will turn away from it as something falsely supposed beautiful (ibid.).

Thus God does not drag us away from our bodies, but waits for *us* to make the inevitable choice of drawing the soul away from the "lowly body." God cannot be known as long as we cling to the corporeal, and so Origen, good Platonist that he is, urges the cultivation of reason, wisdom, and virtue:

> ... the perfect establishment of His kingdom is not possible unless there also comes the perfection of knowledge, of wisdom, and, probably, of the other virtues. ... the kingdom of sin cannot coexist with the kingdom of God. If, therefore, we wish to be ruled by God, let not sin rule in any way in our bodies; and let us not obey its commands, when it summons our soul to the works of the flesh and to what is alien to God. Rather, let us put to death the members that are on earth; and let us bring forth the fruits of the Spirit (ibid., XXV.3).

Elsewhere Origen discusses the "food" of contemplation which nourishes the soul's pursuit of virtue and God:

> ... this food must be understood to be the contemplation and understanding of God, and its measures to be those that are appropriate and suitable to this nature which has been made and created. These measures will rightly be observed by every one of those who are beginning to "see God," that is, to understand him through "purity of heart" (*First Princ.* II.11.7).

4. St. Augustine

We depart here from our usual chronological sequence in presenting St. Augustine after Origen and before Plotinus. For Augustine, as we have seen, the body is far less than the soul; in fact, it is the soul's master, enslaving and keeping it from God:

> And therefore the soul, being turned from its Lord to its slave, necessarily weakens; and again, being turned from its slave to its Lord, necessarily progresses and gives to this same slave a most easy life and therefore a life very little toilsome and troublesome. ... nothing keeps us farther from the truth than a life given over to the pleasures of the flesh and a mind crowded with the deceiving impressions of sensible objects, impressions which arise from the sensible world, are transmitted by the body, and give rise to the most varied beliefs and errors. We must try, therefore, to achieve perfect mental health, that we may attain to the vision of the immutable pattern of things, to the beauty which is always constant with itself and everywhere the same, beauty never distorted by changes of place or time, but standing out one and the same under all circumstances. ... It is given only to the rational and intelligent souls among all these

creatures to enjoy the contemplation of his eternal nature, to be moved and adorned by it, and to be able to merit eternal life (*On Music* VI.5.13; *The True Religion*, 3.3, in Bourke, pp. 46-48).

Thus Augustine follows in Plato's footsteps by advocating the contemplation of the Divine through detaching from the distractions of the lesser physical world. This process, however, in marked contrast to Plato, Plotinus, and the pagan Platonists in general, cannot be achieved without the grace of God. In his elaboration of the role of grace in salvation, Augustine achieved perhaps his most lasting position in the Church, the Doctor of Grace, as mentioned earlier. Augustine developed his teachings on grace by opposing Pelagius, who emphasized that for salvation, grace, though helpful, was not necessary; it was sufficient for people to exercise their own free will on behalf of heaven. On the other hand, Augustine taught:

The grace of God through Jesus Christ our Lord must be understood as that by which *alone* men are delivered from evil, and *without which* they do absolutely no good thing, whether in thought, or will and affection, or in deed . . . (*On Admonition and Grace* 3.3, in Bourke, p. 176, my italics).

5. Plotinus

Plotinus, in distinction from Augustine, taught that it made no sense to think of God as being in a place different and separate from our own existence. The Good already is present within our minds, and thus all its attainment requires is a change in our minds or attitudes. Hence, as we have seen, there is no place in Plotinus' system for the traditional religious practices. God, or the One, is absolutely impersonal and simply shines like an eternal light. It is this unceasing radiance that constitutes the Call, not an anthropomorphically personal deity. He cites Plato as his authority here:

Plato says the One is not outside anything, but is in company with all without their knowing. For they run away outside it, or rather outside themselves. They cannot then catch the one they have run away from, nor seek for another when they have lost themselves. A child, certainly, who is outside himself in madness will not know his father; but he who has learnt to know himself will know from whence he comes (*Enn.* VI.9.7).

Likewise, Plotinus saw no need for rituals. He faulted the particular Gnostic sect that was the object of his diatribe for its use of certain liturgical prayers or formulas:

> But they themselves most of all impair the inviolate purity of the higher powers in another way too. For when they write magic chants, intending to address them to those powers, not only to the soul but to those above it as well, what are they doing except making the powers obey the word and follow the lead of people who say spells and charms and conjurations, any one of us who is well skilled in the art of saying precisely the right things in the right way, songs and cries and aspirated and hissing sounds and everything else which their writings say has magic power in the higher world? But even if they do not want to say this, how are the incorporeal beings affected by sounds? So by the sort of statements with which they give an appearance of majesty to their own words, they, without realising it, take away the majesty of the higher powers (*Enn.* II.9.14).

Plotinus encourages none of these prayerful or ritualistic practices, emphasizing almost exclusively the inner concentration on the divine that is basically abstract, a process lacking the qualities of personal relationship that are so characteristic of most forms of Western spirituality. In one remarkable section, however, Plotinus does speak of praying to the sun, stars, etc., who are spoken of anthropomorphically as hearing and remembering our prayers:

> For it is obvious that if when we pray they act, and do not do it at once, but afterwards, and very often after a long delay, they have memory of the prayers which mortals offer to them (*Enn.* IV.4.30).

But it is clear that Plotinus is speaking not of a magical intervention of a celestial being, but rather of the individual's self-orienting with the unity of the divine universe:

> We must, then, take a general view of all actions and experiences which occur in the whole universe: ... some of the natural ones are effects of the All on its parts. ... By the acts of the whole universe I mean those which the whole heavenly circuit does to itself and its parts—for as it moves it disposes both itself and its parts in a certain way--both those within the circuit itself and all the effects which it produces on the things on earth. ... this All is a "single living being which encompasses all the living beings that are within it"; it has one soul which extends to all its parts, in so far as each individual thing is a part of it; and each thing in the perceptible All is a part of it, and completely a part of it as regards its body; and in so far as it participates in the soul of the All, it is to this extent a part of it in this way too (*Enn.* IV.4.31,32).

Plotinus continues by drawing the analogy between the human body and the universe, aspects seemingly separate yet working harmoniously or disharmoniously among each other, each part affecting all others.

Plotinus' spirituality therefore is utterly solitary. He does not advocate "good works," since this would be emphasizing the wrong reality. Rather, by knowing our spiritual selves we know all selves--we know God--and thus we feel one with all creation. At that point, clearly, "good works" involving others is inevitable, as was the case in Plotinus' own life. In addition, mere intellectual pursuits are insufficient if not combined with the attitudinal shift discussed above. The pursuit of reason is the means towards such a shift, but not the end itself. Greek that he is, Plotinus advocates a life of restraint--moderation in all things--rather than the so-called freedom that comes from the libertinism practiced by certain sects, Gnostic and otherwise. Freedom lies in contemplation, not action, and the foundation for this is virtue. The world may impress upon this freedom, yet can virtue rise above such seeming constraint, valuing only its "high aim":

> . . . in practical actions self-determination and being in our own power is not referred to practice and outward activity but to the inner activity of virtue itself, that is, its thought and contemplation (*Enn.* VI.8.6).

What we term freedom is really the experience of consciousness actualizing itself, emerging from the contrast of what we truly are with what we believe we are; of true with apparent reality. Action which comes from such contrast merely drives us still further from our true self. Passivity, however, is not the ideal, but rather an action that comes from contemplation; activity is not evil, but rather a shadow of the reality shown to us by contemplation.

Another of Plotinus' major criticisms of the Gnostics involved their lack of morality; specifically, the total disregard in the particular Gnostic sect he is criticizing of the Greek ideal of virtue. Plotinus, and correctly so, traces this absence of virtue to the total rejection of the cosmos. We have observed in Plato and Plotinus the great importance placed on the cultivation of virtue as the means whereby individuals could ascend from the shadows of this world to the vision of the highest realm, the world of Ideas, the Good. This ideal had no place in many Gnostic sects, as we have seen--though this by no means included all of them--and Plotinus is quite emphatic in his denunciation of this position:

> But there is one point which we must be particularly careful not to let escape us, and that is what these arguments do to the souls of those who hear them and are persuaded by them to despise the universe and the beings in it. . . . this doctrine censures the lord of providence

and providence itself still more crudely, and despises all the laws of this world and the virtue whose winning extends back through all time, and makes self-control here something to laugh at, that nothing noble may be seen existing here below.... for nothing here is of value for them, but something else is, which they will go after one day. Yet those who already have the *gnosis* should start going after it here and now, and in their pursuit should first of all set right their conduct here below, as they come from a divine nature; for that nature is aware of nobility and despises the pleasure of the body. But those who have no share of virtue would not be moved at all towards that higher world (*Enn.* II.9.15).

The remainder of this passage on the absence of virtue in the Gnostics was quoted earlier in this chapter, p. 357.

Plotinus later discusses the importance of souls living in bodies

in such a way that they are very close to the dwelling of the soul of the All in the universal body. This means no clashing with, nor yielding to the pleasures or sights which hurl themselves upon us from outside, and not being disturbed by any hardship. The soul of the universe is not troubled; it has nothing that it can be troubled by. We, while we are here, can already repel the strokes of fortune by virtue, and make some of them become less by greatness of mind and others not even troubles because of our strength. As we draw near to the completely untroubled state we can imitate the soul of the universe and of the stars, and, coming to a closeness of resemblance to them hasten on to the same goal and have the same objects of contemplation, being ourselves, too, well prepared for them by nature and training (but they have their contemplation from the beginning) (*Enn.* II.9.18).

Plotinus concludes his defense of the cosmos and, in fact, his chapter against the Gnostics, with the following interesting argument, comparing the Gnostics with his own school. It is interesting to note that Plotinus characterizes his view of living in the body as belonging to one who "does not revile," which certainly does not fit with his comments about the body elsewhere in the *Enneads*, nor with his strong ascetic personal life.

But perhaps they will assert that those arguments of theirs make men fly from the body since they hate it from a distance, but ours hold the soul down to it. This would be like two people living in the same fine house, one of whom reviles the structure and the builder, but stays there none the less, while the other does not revile, but says the builder has built it with the utmost skill, and waits for the time to come in which he will go away, when he will not need a house any longer: the first might think he was wiser and readier to depart because he knows how to say that the walls are built of soulless stones and timber and are far inferior to the true dwelling-place, not knowing that he is only distinguished by not bearing what he must--unless he affirms that he is discontented while having a secret affection for the beauty of the stones (*Enn.* II.9.18).

Elsewhere he writes that the

exhortation to separate ourselves is not meant in a spatial sense--this (higher part) of soul is naturally separated--but refers to our not inclining to the body, and to our not having mental images, and our alienation from the body--if by any chance one could make the re-maining form of soul ascend, and take along with us to the heights that of it which is established here below, which alone is the crafts-man and modeller of the body and is actively concerned with it (*Enn.* V.1.10).

Our destiny, therefore, does not lie in what we do, but rather in the rational knowledge or apperception of truth, of our real self. And, again, this knowledge of our self is the knowledge of the divine, awareness of which comes without an intermediary, whether divine or community. It comes without a divine summons, but simply by the individual's pursuit of the spiritual life. This pursuit unites the soul directly with God: the goal of the true philosopher. The soul finds the One within itself, and is merged with it. The goal for Plotinus, therefore, is the mystical state in which all distinctions are gone, when the Love of the universe is finally known without impediment. Near the end of the *Enneads* we find perhaps Plotinus' clearest statement of this vision, made possible by the inner ordering, the "preparation," of the soul through contemplation and asceticism:

But when the soul has good fortune with it, and it comes to it, or rather, being there already, appears, when that soul turns away from the things that are there, and has prepared by making itself as beautiful as possible and has come to likeness (the preparation and the adornment are clearly understood, I think, by those who are preparing themselves) and it sees it in itself suddenly appearing (for there is nothing between, nor are there still two but both are one; nor could you still make a distinction while it is present; lovers and their beloveds here below imitate this in their will to be united), it does not still perceive its body, that it is in it, and does not speak of itself as anything else, not man, or living thing, or being, or all (for the contemplation of these would be somehow disturbing), and it has no time for them nor wants them. . . . and in its happiness is not cheated in thinking that it is happy; and it does not say it is happy when the body tickles it, but when it has become that which it was before, when it is fortunate. But it says it in contempt of all the other things in which it delighted before, offices or powers or riches or beauties or sciences, and it would not have spoken if it had not met better things than these; it is not afraid, either, that anything may happen to it, since it does not even see it while it is with that; but if all the other things about it perished, it would even be pleased, that it might be alone with this; so great a degree of happiness has it reached (*Enn.* VI.7.34).

The non-rational One thus is beyond reason, which nonetheless remains the essential means for its attainment. However, "the end of the journey" is ultimately reached through the transcendence of reason and the duality of the world, to the sublime vision of the "solitary":

When therefore the seer sees himself, then when he sees, he will see himself as like this, or rather he will be in union with himself as like this and will be aware of himself as like this since he has become single and simple. But perhaps one should not say "will see", but "was seen", if one must speak of these as two, the seer and the seen, and not both as one--a bold statement. So then the seer does not see and does not distinguish and does not imagine two, but it is as if he had become someone else and he is not himself and does not count as his own there, but has come to belong to that and so is one, having joined, as it were, centre to centre. For here too when the centres have come together they are one, but there is duality when they are separate. This also is how we now speak of "another". For this reason the vision is hard to put into words. For how could one announce that as another when he did not see, there when he had the vision, another, but one with himself? . . . he was as if carried away or possessed by a god, in a quiet solitude and a state of calm, not turning away anywhere in his being and not busy about himself, altogether at rest and having become a kind of rest. . . . But if it runs the opposite way, it will arrive, not at something else but at itself, and in this way since it is not in something else it will not be in nothing, but in itself; but when it is in itself alone and not in being, it is in that; for one becomes, not substance, but "beyond substance" by this converse. If then one sees that oneself has become this, one has oneself as a likeness of that, and if one goes on from oneself, as image to original, one has reached "the end of the journey". . . . This is the life of gods and of godlike and blessed men, deliverance from the things of this world, a life which takes no delight in the things of this world, escape in solitude to the solitary (*Enn.* VI.9.10,11).

And so does the *Enneads* end.

PART II-B

THE BASIC MYTH:

A COURSE IN MIRACLES

INTRODUCTION TO PART II-B

Now that we have presented the Gnostic, Platonic, and traditional Christian views of the seven stages of our myth, we shall continue with *A Course in Miracles*. Before proceeding with a summary of the myth, by way of introducing the fuller treatment given below, brief comment need be made on some of the striking similarities between a number of the key ideas discussed in Part II-A and what we shall now consider in the Course. These will be returned to later in the chapters to come as well.

The rather startling insight of the Valentinian form of Gnosticism was the recognition of the *psychological* aspects of the separation. While practically every Gnostic system taught that the true God did not participate in the making of the cosmos (even where, as in Manicheism, God does participate in it, the physical world is nonetheless never considered as good), none spoke of the dream nature of the world except for the Valentinians. Though generally couched in mythological language (except for the de-mythologized "Gospel of Truth"), the Valentinian conception of the separation and the subsequent making of the material universe was that they were internal processes, i.e., they occurred within the *mind*. We have already expressed the view, to be returned to again, that the full implications of this understanding were not to be realized until *A Course in Miracles* blended non-dualistic metaphysics with twentieth-century psychology. Nonetheless, we can still stand in awe before the Valentinian understanding of "Sophia's folly."

We might also point out that the Gnostic understanding of the Pleroma parallels in many ways the Plotinian One and Mind, and the nature of God and Christ as seen by the Course. In all three systems we find the concept of a totally unified and undifferentiated Source extending itself in non-material creation. This creation by the Mind of God consists of, for want of a better term, divine Thoughts (in Gnosticism, aeons or glories; in Plotinus, divine Ideas or beings; in the Course, Christ and His creations) sharing in the perfection of their Creator, though somehow distinct from Him since they are the created, He the Creator.

We can also note again the crucial difference between Gnosticism and *A Course in Miracles*; namely, the behavioral or practical implications of their shared metaphysics. Though both systems recognize the impossibility of the perfect non-material God creating an imperfect material world, the Gnostics nonetheless make the world *psychologically* real by seeing it as an evil prison from which one had to escape. The Course, as we shall discuss in depth below, avoids that trap by shift-

405

ing the imprisonment to the mind; salvation thus comes from changing our thinking, and does not involve the world at all.

We turn now to a brief summary of the Course's version of our myth, reminding the reader that the presentation of *A Course in Miracles* is generally more psychological, in contrast to the philosophical and theological language we have been considering heretofore:

1) God is defined as spirit--formless, changeless, perfect, and eternal-- as is the Christ whom God created one with Him. Their unity, Father and Son, *is* Heaven.

2) The separation resulted from God's Son *believing* that he could be separated from his Creator. God answered the Son's (or ego's) thought of separation by creating the Holy Spirit, the presence of God's love in our minds that undoes the "tiny, mad idea." However, the Son listens to the voice of the ego instead and takes the thought of separation seriously. The Son's belief that the separation has actually occurred translates as sin, which leads to guilt, and subsequent fear of God's retaliation which requires defense. These beliefs constitute the psychological foundation of the ego's thought system.

3) The ego concludes its answer to the Holy Spirit by projecting the thought of separation out of the mind, thereby protecting itself from love. This projection gives rise to the material world--cosmos and body--as a defense in which the ego hides its guilt and fear of God's avenging wrath.

4) The true essence of God's creation is spirit, equated with the Mind of Christ that has never left its Source. This identity is hidden from our awareness by the ego, which cloaks itself in a body. Thus, the traditional triadic view that homo sapiens consists of mind-body-spirit is not valid according to *A Course in Miracles*: body and spirit are mutually exclusive states and cannot coexist as shared realities, for God did not create the body. The word "mind," here, can be equated with "ego" or even "soul," similar to its frequent usage in contemporary metaphysical thought to denote the idea of an "entity."

5) Salvation is defined as correction, or Atonement, which undoes the belief in the reality of the separation. In other words, we learn to listen to the Holy Spirit, no longer taking the separation or the resulting world seriously ("remembering to laugh"). This learning is accomplished through the miracle, whose principle is forgiveness.

6) Jesus is the name of the one who first completed his own Atonement

path, transcending the ego belief in separation and remembering his true identity as part of Christ. Thus he becomes the manifestation of the Holy Spirit (the Atonement principle) and our world's greatest symbol of forgiveness. In establishing this example Jesus is able to help all his brothers and sisters accept his teaching lesson.

7) The plan of the Atonement calls for each separated Son of God to learn the single lesson of undoing guilt and separation through very specific forgiveness lessons that appear in personal relationships. Thus, though the phenomenal world is seen as inherently illusory, it serves a very important function in the Holy Spirit's plan of correcting our misperceptions, since errors can only be corrected on the level on which they are manifested and experienced. The Course fosters an *a*morality, emphasizing that it is not our behavior that is important, but rather the purpose that our minds impute to our behavior. In other words, it is the content (purpose) that is essential, not the form (behavior). Religious sacraments and rituals thus are not essential to reach God.

Chapter 11

THE NATURE OF GOD AND HIS HEAVEN:
The Pre-Separation State

The metaphysics of *A Course in Miracles* is non-dualistic which, as discussed in Chapter 4, expresses *one* pre-existent state, that of God. Moreover, the Course belongs within the same "Syrian-Egyptian" school of Gnosticism that Hans Jonas defined. This brand of non-dualism held that only God is truth, and therefore we can extrapolate that only God is real. To the Gnostic non-dualist, the imperfection of separation that arises (the Course would say *appeared* to arise), is present *within* the Godhead itself (i.e., is not due to an external force). As we have briefly noted in earlier chapters, the Course's insistence on the illusory, dreamlike nature of this imperfect thought was prefigured in the work of Valentinus and his school. We shall explore the Course's metaphysical treatment of the illusory world in the following three chapters.

Earlier we discussed the apophatic tradition, which emphasizes that God is beyond all human attempts to define or classify Him. His nature remains forever ineffable and unknowable in this material world, beyond our power of comprehension and expression which are inherently limited by the physical and psychological dimensions of our ego self. At home within that tradition, *A Course in Miracles* does not define our Source, but rather simply designates God as the First Cause, the Creator of all life. In light of the Gnostic effusions we explored earlier, how refreshing then is this simple apophatic statement from *A Course in Miracles*: "We say 'God is,' and then we cease to speak, for in that knowledge words are meaningless" (workbook, p. 315). The Course teaches that before the beginning of time there is only God. God *is*, and the nature of His Self is spirit, whose characteristics include being formless, changeless, limitless, perfect, and eternal. To go beyond these few words would be futile, an example of what the Course calls "senseless musings."

According to *A Course in Miracles*, the basic dynamic of spirit is extension, wherein God is continually expressing His being in creation. In the Course, the words "extension" and "projection" reflect the identical dynamic--the proceeding outward of what is within the mind. "Extension," as we shall see, is reserved for the "movement" or "outflow" of spirit, while "projection" is almost always utilized for the ego. In fact, in the first mention of this dynamic, the Course speaks of projection as being the "inappropriate use of extension" (text, p. 14); thus we can likewise speak of extension as being the "appropriate" use of projection. It is interesting to note that the Greek word used in the Gnostic writings to denote this process of spirit's extension is *probole*, which literally means "projection." However, the Greek word is almost always translated as "emanating," the counterpart to the Course's "extension." As we have seen, "emanating" is a word common to Platonism and Gnosticism.

It should also be stated that while we are using words and concepts-- e.g., "extension"--that have temporal and spatial connotations, the dynamics they reflect totally transcend time and space. Thus in our popular speech "extension" connotes someone or something extending itself across time and space. We who are bound by our own conceptual limitations must use words--"symbols of symbols"--that share these limitations. Therefore we should keep in mind that these concepts point to a state of reality that is *beyond* concepts entirely. The Course reiterates:

> There is no need to further clarify what no one in the world can understand. . . . for those in time can speak of things beyond. . . . Yet what meaning can the words convey to those who count the hours still, and rise and work and go to sleep by them? (workbook, p. 316)

Thus, spirit's basic function is extension:

> Being *must* be extended. . . . Spirit yearns to share its being as its Creator did. Created by sharing, its will is to create. . . . to extend His [God's] Being.
> The extension of God's Being is spirit's only function. Its fullness cannot be contained, any more than can the fullness of its Creator. Fullness is extension (text, pp. 122f).

The extension of God--His creation--is Christ, defined in *A Course in Miracles* as God's one Son. Paradoxically, in many places the Course speaks of God's Sons or the collective Sonship. For example:

> It should especially be noted that God has only *one* Son. If all His creations are His Sons, every one must be an integral part of the whole Sonship. The Sonship in its oneness transcends the sum of its parts (text, p. 29).

Similarly, the Course talks about the Great Rays (not Ray), which are the extensions of the light of God, similar to the rays of light that emanate from the sun. Although conceptually no separated or frag- mented mind can understand this, we may yet state that Christ consists of infinite Rays (Sons of God), all perfectly united and indivis- ible; however, we clearly are not speaking here of personal individu- ality as we experience it in the world.

It should be especially noted--to be returned to in Chapter 16--that, in distinction from traditional Christianity and all the Christian Gnostics, Christ is not to be exclusively identified with Jesus, who is understood in the Course as being part of Christ, as we all are. In the light of St. Paul's teaching in Galatians, Jesus was seen as the only Son of God, while we remained adopted sons, second class citizens as it were: "But when the appointed time came, God sent his Son . . . to redeem the subjects of the Law and to enable us to be adopted as sons" (Ga 4:4f). In *A Course in Miracles*, however, Jesus states that he has nothing that we cannot attain, and that he is not "in any way separate or different" from us except in the world of time (text, p. 5). What distinguishes Jesus from the rest of the Sonship is that he was the first to have transcended the split mind and remember his Source, recalling his true Identity as Christ. As the Course says of him:

> The name of *Jesus* is the name of one who was a man but saw the face of Christ [the Course's symbol of total forgiveness] in all his brothers and remembered God. So he became identified with *Christ*, a man no longer, but at one with God. . . . Is he the Christ? O yes, along with you (manual, p. 83). [13]

As an extension of His Father or Source, then, Christ shares in the attributes of His Creator. He, too, is spirit--formless, changeless, limitless, perfect, and eternal. In addition, Christ shares His Father's attribute of extending or creating. As God extended His Self, creating Christ, so too does Christ extend His Self. These extensions of Christ are what the Course refers to as creations, and have their counterpart in the "glories" that appear in certain Gnostic texts (*see* Chapter 4). "Creations" is a term that appears throughout the material, even though, for the reasons just discussed, they can never really be explained. Thus, for example, the Course states:

> As God's creative Thought proceeds from Him to you, so must your creative thought proceed from you to your creations. . . . He created the Sonship and you increase it. . . . Your creations belong in you, as you belong in God. You are part of God, as your sons are part of His Sons (text, p. 104).

Together with Christ, these creations make up what Christianity has termed the Second Person of the Trinity and, again, what the Gnostics refer to as the Pleroma. In distinction from its philosophical forefathers, however, *A Course in Miracles* avoids the excessive mytholo-

---

13. For further discussion of the Course's Christology, see *Forgiveness and Jesus*, pp. 317-20.

gizing about the nature of the Pleroma--God and the nature and number of the aeons--that is so prevalent in Gnostic teachings, and which is also found in Plato and his school. The Course simply presents God and His creation as a given, emphasizing, as we have seen already, that it is impossible to understand what is beyond the capability of the separated mind, which made the body and brain to *prevent* understanding. Our psychologically more sophisticated age is better able to tolerate such an intellectual position than were the two-millennia-older philosophers.

A *Course in Miracles* teaches that "Ideas leave not their source" (text, p. 515), a principle that is crucial for understanding its theoretical system. As the workbook states:

> The emphasis this course has placed on that idea is due to its centrality in our attempts to change your mind about yourself. It [this principle] is the reason you can heal. It is the cause of healing. It is why you cannot die. Its truth established you as one with God (workbook, p. 311).

In looking at the process of creation or extension we can imagine God to be a Mind which had a Thought, called Christ. Christ, then, can be defined as an Idea in the Mind of God. Therefore, if ideas leave not their source, then the Idea that is Christ can never leave *its* Source, nor can Christ's creations leave theirs:

> God created His Sons by extending His Thought, and retaining the extensions of His Thought in His Mind. All His Thoughts are thus perfectly united within themselves and with each other (text, p. 90).

> Christ is God's Son as He created Him.... He is the Thought Which still abides within the Mind that is His Source. He has not left His holy home, nor lost the innocence in which He was created. He abides unchanged forever in the Mind of God (workbook, p. 421).

This undivided unity of God and Christ, and Christ and His creations, constitutes the state of Heaven. Returning to our image of the sun and its rays, God is the sun, and Christ and His creations are the emanating rays. Yet they are not separate from their Source. Similarly, a wave in the ocean cannot be understood or known separate from the water that is its source. In the following chapter we shall consider in more detail this important principle of the indivisibility of idea and source.

Interestingly enough, the Course uses the word "knowledge" (*gnosis* in Greek) as a synonym for the state of Heaven. This meaning obviously falls within the Gnostic tradition, for it is independent of the more common usage which implies a subject-object duality: a body of information to be "known" and one who "knows" it. Knowledge is the non-dualistic and abstract state that is beyond perception, and is thus "changeless, certain, pure and wholly understandable" (manual, p. 82). Further, unlike perception

> There is nothing partial about knowledge. Every aspect is whole, and therefore no aspect is separate. You are an aspect of knowledge, being in the Mind of God, Who knows you. . . . Perception, at its loftiest, is never complete (text, pp. 240f).

Within Heaven, therefore, there is no differentiation, contrast, or variation. It is not a place:

> It is merely an awareness of perfect oneness, and the knowledge that there is nothing else; nothing outside this oneness, and nothing else within (text, p. 359).

However, though God and Christ share in spirit's function of creating and are totally one, there is one essential difference: God created Christ; Christ did not create God. Though we are *like* God, creating as He does, we are *not* God. As the Course emphasizes:

> . . . in creation you are not in a reciprocal relation to God, since He created you but you did not create Him. I have already told you that only in this respect your creative power differs from His. Even in this world there is a parallel. Parents give birth to children, but children do not give birth to parents. They do, however, give birth to their children, and thus give birth as their parents do (text, p. 104).

The Course explains further:

> If you created God and He created you, the Kingdom could not increase through its own creative thought. Creation would therefore be limited, and you would not be co-creators with God. . . . Only in this way can all creative power extend outward. God's accomplishments are not yours, but yours are like His (text, p. 104).

In summary, then, God is Father-Creator, and Christ is Son-created; joined as one, united in the perfect love and peace of Heaven as expressed in this lovely passage:

> There is a place in you which time has left, and echoes of eternity are heard. There is a resting place so still no sound except a hymn to Heaven rises up to gladden God the Father and the Son. Where both abide are They remembered, both. And where They are is Heaven and is peace (text, p. 570).

Chapter 12

THE SEPARATION FROM GOD

We come now to *A Course in Miracles'* depiction of the central philosophical problem that we have been exploring: the coming into existence of imperfection. The Course does not speculate about *how* or *why* this imperfection arose, agonizing over it as did Plotinus, for example, although it does address the issue, as we shall see below. The Course simply teaches that into the heavenly world of perfect creation it *appeared* as though the impossible occurred. At some point, that the Course teaches never really happened, the thought of separation arose within the mind of God's Son; into the perfect unity of Heaven there entered this one insane thought wherein God's Son decided to be different from his Father, and to establish a will and self independent of Him:

> Into eternity, where all is one, there crept a tiny, mad idea, at which the Son of God remembered not to laugh (text, p. 544).

This "tiny, mad idea" is the thought of separation.

The fundamental unreality of this thought is what marks the uniqueness of *A Course in Miracles'* contribution to the problem of the God-world paradox and its resolution. From this basic premise it draws out, in rigorous logic, a thought system that embraces *every* aspect of our physical universe--from its inception to our everyday individual experience--explaining how the initial illusory thought of separation fragmented into an illusory world that "has never left its source." The Course's approach to understanding the separation is what provides its power in correcting the error that gave rise to the world as we know and experience it. In other words, the basic unreality of the thought of separation carries with it the seeds of salvation from this thought. The chapters to come will explore this in more depth. Let us continue now with this "tiny, mad idea."

As we have seen, God has but one Son, and when the thought of separation seemed to arise, it did so in the mind of this one Son. Thus, we may also say that in the original separation there was but one thought. The process of fragmentation into many different egos had not yet taken place. Building on the image used in the previous chapter of the sun and its emanating rays, we may think of this thought appearing somewhere within the rays, and laser-beaming throughout, as a colored dye that is dropped into a solution of water quickly spreads throughout the solution.

Inherent in this thought of separation is the wish to be God, to be self-created instead of God-created; the wish to create on one's own, as did Sophia in the Valentinian myth. As the Course states:

> God is not the author of fear. You are. You have chosen to create unlike Him, and have therefore made fear for yourself (text, pp. 49f).

Staying for the moment within the Valentinian parallels, we may note the Course's occasional use of the word "ignorance"--central to Valentinus' system--to denote the state of the Son's mind when he chose to separate himself from knowledge. In the following passages, especially, one can note the strong similarity between "The Gospel of Truth" and the Course in describing the power of knowledge to dispel ignorance:

> The journey that we undertake together is the exchange of dark for light, of ignorance for understanding. Nothing you understand is fearful. It is only in darkness and in ignorance that you perceive the frightening (text, pp. 264f).

> What do you want? Light or darkness, knowledge or ignorance are yours, but not both. . . . *As darkness disappears in light, so ignorance fades away when knowledge dawns.* . . . To God, unknowing is impossible. It is therefore not a point of view at all, but merely a belief in something that does not exist. It is only this belief that the unknowing have, and by it they are wrong about themselves. They have defined them-selves as they were not created (text, pp. 266f, my italics).

When the Course speaks of the guardians of darkness (elsewhere sentinels), as in the following passage, it refers to the same dynamics of the ego's defensive system the Gnostics personified as archons:

> Would you continue to give imagined power to these strange ideas of safety? They are neither safe nor unsafe. They do not protect; neither do they attack. They do nothing at all, being nothing at all. As guardians of darkness and of ignorance look to them only for fear (text, p. 265).

The ego therefore is the thought of separation we made real, so horrifying to our minds that we believe in the need for these strange and insane defenses: ignorant guardians of darkness. The ego is the belief that we not only have separated from God, but are our own creator, thus destroying the true Creator and usurping His role on the throne of Heaven. Yet it is essential to bear in mind that the ego is nothing more than this belief system of separation, having no reality outside of the mind that thought it. It is not anything real, but simply a *thought* or *belief* of what is "real." As the Course defines it:

> What is the *ego*? But a dream of what you really are. A thought you are apart from your Creator and a wish to be what He created not. It is a thing of madness, not reality at all. A name for namelessness is all it is. . . . nothing but an ancient thought that what is made has immortality (manual, p. 77).

There remains, however, the most basic question anyone could ask at this point, and one which we raised at the beginning of the book: how could such a thought of self-creation, independent of the Father-Creator, ever possibly have arisen? how could the perfect, awake Son of God have fallen into a sleep of imperfection? how, in fact, could the separation have occurred at all? in Valentinian terms, how could the aeon Sophia have possibly fallen into error? Unless my memory fails me, my wife Gloria and I--together or separately--have not conducted a class or workshop on the Course where someone has not asked this question. The question, moreover, is hardly new. We have seen it expressed in Plotinus, as well as being a concern for all Platonists in one way or another. In the non-Christian Gnostic text "Zostrianos" the protagonist asks:

> Now concerning Existence: How do those who exist, who are from the aeon of those who exist, come from an invisible spirit and from the undivided self-begotten? . . . What is the place of that one there? What is his origin? . . . How has Existence which does not exist appeared in an existing power?
> I [Zostrianos] was pondering these matters in order to understand them. I kept bringing them up daily to the god of my fathers according to the custom of my race. . . (Zostr. VIII.2.24-3.16, in *NHL*, pp. 369f).

However, this god, as well as other celestial revelatory beings mentioned in the treatise, does not provide a real answer. In the Mandean literature the question is also posed, again without answer:

> Since you, Life, were there, how did darkness come into being there? . . . how did imperfection and deficiency come into being? (GR III.p.73, in F II, p. 164)

While these are perfectly logical questions to ask, they are nonetheless spurious ones, as *A Course in Miracles* points out. In fact, the Course addresses the issue in two places. The text states, "It is reasonable to ask how the mind could ever have made the ego," and then provides a very practical explanation:

417

> There is, however, no point in giving an answer in terms of the past because the past does not matter, and history would not exist if the same errors were not being repeated in the present (text, p. 51).

In other words, why should we persist in wondering how the ego occurred in the past, when we are still choosing it in the present? Near the end of the manual for teachers is found a more penetrating answer to the ego's question of its own origins:

> The ego will demand many answers that this course does not give. It does not recognize as questions the mere form of a question to which an answer is impossible. The ego may ask, "How did the impossible occur?", "To what did the impossible happen?", and may ask this in many forms. Yet there is no answer; only an experience. Seek only this, and do not let theology delay you (manual, p. 73).

And later:

> Who asks you to define the ego and explain how it arose can be but he who thinks it real, and seeks by definition to ensure that its illusive nature is concealed behind the words that seem to make it so.
> There is no definition for a lie that serves to make it true (manual, p. 77).

Restated, the Course's argument is that once we ask how the impossible (the ego) happened, we are really affirming that the ego *did* happen. Otherwise we could not ask the question. Thus we are making a statement, not really asking a question at all. It must, then, be only the ego that could pose such a question-statement. This statement then leads to the crux of the God-world paradox, for it makes both aspects equally real: the true Creator God as well as the illusory ego and its miscreated world. By denying the reality of the world (once seen as a miscreated dream), the paradox disappears since what does not exist cannot be held antithetical to what does:

> The opposite of love is fear, but what is all-encompassing can have no opposite (text, intro.).

Thus, the issue of *how* the thought of separation arose (and later, *how* the separated world arose as a defense against God) is itself unresolvable and beyond comprehension or belief; as mentioned above, the ego is unable to understand a reality beyond itself. Thus, no non-dualistic metaphysical system provides an answer to this pseudo-question: even to attempt an answer is to give the ego a reality it does not have. The best approach to this problem, I believe, comes from an Eastern source, which has the guru respond to his disciple's question in this way: "When you are caught in a burning building, you do not worry about how the fire began; you simply get out as quickly as possible." Since one of the Course's claims for itself is that it will save us time, this seems to be the most practical and helpful response to this question. More important than the question and answer themselves are the implications of the basic premise: If the thought of separation is real, then the separated world must be real as well; if illusory, then too must the world be illusory. We shall return to this essential point in Chapter 17, and again in Part III.

We move on now to the next stage of our story: God's "response" to the "tiny, mad idea." In the instant that the thought of separation entered into the mind of God's Son, giving birth to the ego, in that same instant God gave an Answer. As the Course states, using the metaphor of sleep: "... He [God] thought, 'My children sleep and must be awakened'" (text, p. 96). If the sleep or dream of separation is seen as the ego's answer to creation--the state of being awake in God--then God's Answer to the ego was the creation of the Holy Spirit. The separation took place in the mind, where the dream is, and so God placed His Answer where it was needed: in the mind. Since the core of the ego's thought is that it has separated itself from God, the creation of the Holy Spirit undoes this error. Therefore, the Holy Spirit is defined as "the communication link between God . . . and His separated Sons" (text, p. 88). Through Him we remain connected with our Creator, thus undoing the ego's fundamental premise that we have ruptured this connection. This correction is what the Course refers to as the Atonement, as is seen in this summarizing statement:

> [The Holy Spirit] is the Call to return with which God blessed the minds of His separated Sons. . . . [He] is God's Answer to the separation; the means by which the Atonement heals. . . . The principle of Atonement and the separation began at the same time. When the ego was made, God placed in the mind the call to joy (text, p. 69).

On a more sophisticated level we can understand the Holy Spirit to be the memory of God's perfect love that "came" with the Son when he fell asleep. In this sense then the Holy Spirit is not really a person, but an ongoing presence that lies within each seemingly fragmented mind; a distant memory of our Source that continually "calls" out to us, like a forgotten song:

> . . . an ancient state not quite forgotten; dim, perhaps, and yet not altogether unfamiliar, like a song whose name is long forgotten, and the circumstances in which you heard completely unremembered.

Not the whole song has stayed with you, but just a little wisp of melody, attached not to a person or a place or anything particular. But you remember, from just this little part, how lovely was the song, how wonderful the setting where you heard it, and how you love those who were there and listened with you.

The notes are . . . a soft reminder of what would make you weep if you remembered how dear it was to you (text, p. 416).

The Holy Spirit's "Voice" is this song, but in truth it is abstract and formless, and therefore does not "say" (or "sing") anything--"This form [as God's Voice] is not His reality, which God alone knows . . ." (manual, p. 85). His song has only one note, as did the protagonist of "Johnny One Note," a song popular in an earlier generation. However, the Holy Spirit's perfect love assumes the form that is needed, taking on the words that the ego's questions demand. The contours of the Holy Spirit's presence are therefore the ego's thoughts, but filled with love instead of fear. The Course explains, that when all these thoughts are gone,

and no trace remains of dreams of spite in which you dance to death's thin melody. . . . the Voice is gone, no longer to take form but to return to the eternal Formlessness of God (manual, p. 86).

This understanding of the Holy Spirit helps resolve a problem that has plagued many a thoughtful student of *A Course in Miracles*: How could God have given an Answer to a problem that the Course states clearly does not exist, and that God does not even know about: "Spirit in its knowledge is unaware of the ego. It does not attack; it merely cannot conceive of it at all" (text, p. 53). And yet the Course says elsewhere: "There was a need He did not understand, to which He gave an Answer" (workbook, p. 309). Once again, we can see the Course using language metaphorically, words that are not to be taken as literal truth. This is why we have spoken of the Course's mythology, however psychologically sophisticated its form. God does not think, weep, nor give answers, any more than He makes things happen in the world, heal physical illness, nor end human suffering. These are metaphoric expressions Jesus (himself a symbol) uses in the Course to express the love of God that cannot be expressed except through such literary and anthropomorphic devices. As he says to us: "You cannot even think of God without a body, or in some form you think you recognize" (text, p. 364).

Therefore, strictly speaking, God did not give an Answer--the Holy Spirit--to the birth of the thought of separation; rather, His "Answer" is simply His own unchanging and eternal love that forever shines in our split minds, as does a beacon of light shine out into the darkness.

God's love does not do anything; it simply *is*: an ongoing state of love's presence which we call the Holy Spirit. We shall return to the Holy Spirit and the principles of salvation in Chapters 15 and 17, and, in Chapter 19, to the Course's use of metaphorical language.

Thus, when the error of separation seemed to occur it was corrected. As the Course explains, in the context of sickness:

> Yet separation is but empty space, enclosing nothing, doing nothing, and as unsubstantial as the empty place between the ripples that a ship has made in passing by. And covered just as fast, as water rushes in to close the gap, and as the waves in joining cover it. Where is the gap between the waves when they have joined, and covered up the space which seemed to keep them separate for a little while? (text, p. 554)

In that same instant that the thought-that-never-was seemed to be, in that same instant it was undone:

> The tiny instant you would keep and make eternal, passed away in Heaven too soon for anything to notice it had come. What disappeared too quickly to affect the simple knowledge of the Son of God can hardly still be there, for you to choose to be your teacher (text, p. 512).

Nonetheless, within his dream the Son is yet able to choose this thought system of separation as his teacher.

The ego now counterattacks, seeing the Holy Spirit as a threat to its existence, which of course He is. To more fully explore the nature of the Son's mind at this point, I too shall resort to a myth or story, based upon the more abstract dynamics that are found in the Course.[14]

The situation as it now stands in our story is that the mind of the Son of God has become a battlefield, in which two mortal enemies are pitted one against the other. At least this is the perception of the "tiny, mad idea" (the ego) that now appears to have an existence all its own. The battlefield of the mind that appears to have been split off from its Source has, in effect, three components: the thought of separation (the "tiny, mad idea" that has conceived of itself as separate and independent from its Creator and Source); the thought of perfect love (the Holy Spirit) that was carried along with the thought of separation as a memory of what truly is, and that dispels what is not; and the component of the mind that must choose between these two thoughts. The reader may recall the Platonic and Gnostic tripartite mind dis-

---

14. For a fuller exposition of this myth, in different form, see *Awaken from the Dream*, pp. 21-41.

cussed in Chapters 7 and 8, and see that we are not too far here from these earlier, relatively unsophisticated formulations.

From the standpoint of perfect love nothing has happened. That is the meaning of the memory: nothing has happened because nothing *could* happen. God's Son remains as he was created, for, love being forever invulnerable, how could what is of God separate from Itself? The evident impossibility of God's and Christ's vulnerability renders as non-existent the situation of separation, continued belief in which is simply silly. And yet to call the ego silly is anathema to its thought that something *has* happened; namely, the Son of God has indeed become separate and independent. To this thought, therefore, the presence of the Holy Spirit in the Son's mind is a great danger, bitterly to be defended against if the tiny, mad idea is to survive:

> The Holy Spirit . . . seems to be attacking your fortress, for you would shut out God, and He does not will to be excluded.
> You have built your whole insane belief system because you think you would be helpless in God's Presence, and you would save yourself from His Love because you think it would crush you into nothingness (text, p. 226).

If the Son listens to and accepts the Voice of love--remembering to laugh at the silliness of the thought that a part of God could actually be separate from Him--then he will awaken from the dream of separation that then disappears back into its own illusion.

It is thus incumbent upon the ego to convince the Son to believe its story of separation, rather than the Holy Spirit's story of non-separation. Thus the ego conceives a plan to accomplish its goal of silencing the Holy Spirit's Voice of love, telling the Son to look at where it finds itself, split off and separate from God, and recognize what it has done. "You," the ego tells the Son, "by refusing to accept as sufficient His gifts to you, have committed a sin against your Father and Creator. You," the ego continues, "decided that perfection and everything as Christ was not enough, and that there had to be something more: 'freedom' to choose to be other than God." It is this illusory exercise of choice in the name of "freedom" that the ego terms sin. The Course describes this belief:

> . . . that what God created can be changed by your own mind. . . . that what is perfect can be rendered imperfect or lacking. . . . that you can distort the creations of God, including yourself. . . . that you can create yourself, and that the direction of your own creation is up to you.
> These related distortions represent a picture of what actually occurred in the separation, or the "detour into fear" (text, p. 14).

The Son, in a manner reminiscent of the anguish of the Valentinian Sophia, now gazes with disgust at the *sin* the ego has convinced him he has committed. And this is the beginning of *guilt*: the horror of believing that a terrible sin has been committed against God, a sin so heinous that it can never be forgiven or undone. The Son is overwhelmed with the enormity of these thoughts of sin and guilt, and is further instructed by the ego to be on guard, for this sinned-against God wants nothing less than murderous vengeance against His sinning Son. Moreover, the ego counsels the Son, the so-called loving presence of the Holy Spirit in the mind is hardly that at all. The Holy Spirit, rather, is the Voice of hatred, vengeance, and jealousy that the Father has sent to the Son to bring His words of wrath and to carry out His punishment. Incidentally, while a loving God is not a major theme found in the Gnostic literature, we do find a relatively rare passage that speaks of a non-vengeful Creator. It comes in the "Acts of John," where the apostle speaks of the loving God who does not punish nor seek retribution, for

> we have done much ill and nothing well towards him, [yet he] has given us not retribution but repentance; and although we knew not his name, he did not forsake but forgave us; and though we blasphemed, he did not punish but pitied us; and though we disbelieved, he bore no grudge; and though we persecuted his brethren, he made no such return, but moved us to repentance and restraint of wickedness and so called us to himself ... (AJ 81, in *NTA* II, pp. 251f).

Fear now grips the Son's mind for he sees no way out, and the truly loving Voice of the Holy Spirit has been drowned out and, in effect, silenced. Guilt and fear become the reigning principles of his mind, for love and truth have been distorted into their opposite.

The Course summarizes this situation in powerful passages from its three books. First, in the context of magic thoughts (which include all post-separation ego thoughts), the manual states:

> A magic thought ... acknowledges a separation from God. It states ... that the mind which believes it has a separate will that can oppose the Will of God, also believes it can succeed. That this can hardly be a fact is obvious. Yet that it can be believed as fact is equally obvious. And herein lies the birthplace of guilt. Who usurps the place of God and takes it for himself now has a deadly "enemy." And he must stand alone in his protection, and make himself a shield to keep him safe from fury that can never be abated, and vengeance that can never be satisfied. ... An angry father pursues his guilty son. Kill or be killed, for here alone is choice. Beyond this there is none, for what was done cannot be done without. The stain of blood can never be removed ... (manual, p. 43).

From the text:

> Think what this seems to do to the relationship between the Father
> and the Son. Now it appears that they can never be one again. For
> one must always be condemned, and by the other. Now are they
> different, and enemies. And their relationship is one of opposition.
> ...And fear of God and of each other now appears as sensible, made
> real by what the Son of God has done both to himself and his Creator
> (text, p. 456).

And from the workbook:

> The ego is idolatry; the sign of limited and separated self....It is the
> "will" that sees the Will of God as enemy, and takes a form in which
> it is denied. The ego is the "proof" that strength is weak and love is
> fearful, life is really death, and what opposes God alone is true.
> The ego is insane. In fear it stands beyond the Everywhere, apart
> from All, in separation from the Infinite. In its insanity it thinks it has
> become a victor over God Himself. And in its terrible autonomy it
> "sees" the Will of God has been destroyed (workbook, p. 457).

In the text, the ego is also equated with the anti-Christ, an idol that
serves to replace God:

> This is the anti-Christ; the strange idea there is a power past omnipo-
> tence, a place beyond the infinite, a time transcending the eternal
> (text, p. 576).

The thought of separation has now reached its full potential in the
constellation of sin, guilt, and fear within the Son's mind. These have
been elevated to the level of reality, while truth, love, and peace have
disappeared behind the clouds of illusion. The Voice of reason and
sanity, speaking of the impossibility of the ego's lies, is no longer
heard, for the Son only listens to the ego's voice, which seems effectively to have counterattacked the Holy Spirit's correction (the Atonement). The psychological states of sin, guilt, and fear thus represent
the ego's pleroma, effectively paralyzing the Son and leaving his mind
helpless in its war with God, with no seeming way out of the dilemma.
The stage is now set for the ego's ingenious solution: the making of the
world. This solution belongs to the following chapter.

Chapter 13

THE ORIGIN AND NATURE OF THE WORLD

To recap the situation we left at the end of Chapter 12, confronted with its own imminent demise by God's Answer to the separation--the presence of perfect love in the Son's mind--the ego sets upon *its* plan to save itself. If it is to continue to exist, the ego must somehow deal with its perceived threat of the Holy Spirit, whose love signals its own immediate dissolution. We have already seen that the beginning stages of the ego's plan were to convince the sleeping Son of God that his dream of sin, guilt, and fear was real; a reality so compelling that he was in immediate danger of destruction in the "war" against God. The ego, however, "comes to the rescue" of the Son.

While the ego is the epitome of arrogance, believing it can supplant God, its arrogance does not extend to the belief that it can actually defeat God's Answer and drown out the Voice of love in the separated mind, the ego's home. Realizing its powerlessness against this presence--which it can never remove--the ego's only recourse is to separate itself from the Holy Spirit. Thus the ego tells the Son that, although he cannot defeat the Holy Spirit, he *can* escape from Him by removing himself from God's Answer, a psychological process we call projection. It should be stated, before we proceed further, that although we speak of the ego as if it functioned autonomously, having an existence independent from the Son, in reality of course the ego is ourselves, or at least what we experience to be ourselves. As Jesus states:

> I have spoken of the ego as if it were a separate thing, acting on its own. This was necessary to persuade you that you cannot dismiss it lightly, and must realize how much of your thinking is ego-directed. ... The ego is nothing more than a part of your belief about yourself (text, p. 61).

We have observed before that the basic dynamic of spirit is extension. This reflects the fundamental law of mind that "Thoughts begin in the mind of the thinker, from which they reach outward. This is as true of God's Thinking as it is of yours" (text, p. 90). What is within the mind *must* "reach outward." When the Mind is God's or Christ's, this dynamic is called extension and, as was already emphasized, this "reaching outwards" has no spatial or temporal dimensions. When, however, the mind is the separated or split mind of the ego, the dynamic is called projection, and here we do find ourselves existing in the world of time and space. Thus the Course teaches: spirit extends (or creates), while the ego projects (or makes): "You make by projection, but God creates by extension" (text, p. 179).

Therefore, this idea of separation is projected from the mind of the ego in the attempt to escape and hide from the Holy Spirit. We observed that in creation (or extension), what God extended became like Him, sharing His attributes. The same principle holds in projection: what the ego projects shares in its attributes. Thus the projection of the thought of separation--born in guilt--gives rise to a world of separation--based on guilt:

> That was the first projection of error [the separation] outward. The world arose to hide it, and became the screen on which it was projected and drawn between you and the truth (text, p. 348).

The world then is *nothing but* this thought in the mind projected outward. By the term "world," incidentally, the Course means the entire phenomenal universe, encompassing not only our individual physical lives and all life on earth, but the solar system and every system and galaxy beyond our own. In a poignantly poetic passage near the end of the text, we read:

> What *seems* eternal all will have an end. The stars will disappear, and night and day will be no more. All things that come and go, the tides, the seasons and the lives of men; all things that change with time and bloom and fade will not return. Where time has set an end is not where the eternal is (text, p. 572).

This is echoed in the manual:

> The world you see is an illusion of a world. God did not create it, for what He creates must be eternal as Himself. Yet there is nothing in the world you see that will endure forever. Some things will last in time a little while longer than others. But the time will come when all things visible will have an end (manual, p. 81).

If one imagines a funnel, the thought of separation lies at the narrow end with the rest of the funnel comprising the physical world. Regardless of the seeming magnitude of the larger portion of the funnel, the two ends remain the same: Ideas leave not their source. The world is the idea of separation given form, and has not truly left its source in the mind. Idea and source, effect and cause, can never be separated in truth, though our minds have the power to believe that they can, and indeed have been. Thus, paralleling the conclusions of contemporary quantum physicists, the Course teaches that the inner and outer are one; what appears to be outside is really one with what is inside. As Krishnamurti consistently taught: The observer and the observed are one. The Course states:

> The world is false perception. It is born of error, and it has not left its source. It will remain no longer than the thought that gave it birth is cherished (workbook, p. 403).

This principle of the unity of idea and source, effect and cause, is seen also in certain Gnostic systems, where the evil and imprisoning attributes of the mother Sophia are manifest in her son Ialdabaoth, and therefore also are manifest in the world he (mis)creates.

As the basic thought of separation is illusory--since the unity of Heaven can never be anything other than what it is--all that follows from this single belief must share in its same illusory nature. Any aspect of the funnel is as unreal as any other. Thus, the seeming magnitude of the error or misbelief is irrelevant: A monster in a dream is as illusory as an ant in the same dream; one times zero is the same as a thousand times zero--an illusion is an illusion is an illusion. As the Course says:

> Is it harder to dispel the belief of the insane in a larger hallucination as opposed to a smaller one? Will he agree more quickly to the unreality of a louder voice he hears than to that of a softer one? ... And do the number of pitchforks the devils he sees carrying affect their credibility in his perception? His mind has categorized them all as real, and so they are all real to him. When he realizes they are all illusions they will disappear (manual, pp. 23f).

Yet this illusory situation is not what *appears* to be the case, for it is the purpose of the ego to confuse us about the unity that is our true reality, and of which reality the Holy Spirit in our minds is continually reminding us. Therefore, once the initial projection of separation occurred, it continued to occur. Projected from the mind, the thought of separation now separated over and over again, resulting in a physical world of separation. We observe this process in the biological phenomenon of mitosis, where the fertilized egg in the mother's womb divides and subdivides: one becoming two, then four, eight, sixteen, thirty-two, etc. This development of the physical organism reflects the birth of the physical world. The Course discusses this original substitution of the ego for God, fear for love:

> You who believe that God is fear made but one substitution. It has taken many forms, because it was the substitution of illusion for truth; of fragmentation for wholeness. It has become so splintered

> and subdivided and divided again, over and over, that it is now almost impossible to perceive it once was one, and still is what it was (text, p. 347).

What is "almost impossible," of course, *is* the ego's purpose. Through this projection of itself, the ego has constructed a massive smokescreen within which it can hide. It has diverted our attention from our minds, which is where the true problem is, not to mention its Solution, and caused us to see our problems outside ourselves, where they are *not*.

A final step is now required if the ego's plan is to work: Once the ego has erected a cosmos to distract us from the spiritual world, it must ensure that we will fall into the trap of believing that truth is illusion, and illusion truth. We are once again reminded of the parallels between *A Course in Miracles* and many of the Gnostic systems. In this discussion of the ego's plot against the Holy Spirit, the reader can recall the plot of the archons and the Manichean Darkness to entrap the particles of light. While the form certainly differs between these two basic systems, the content is startlingly similar.

We return to the Course. What ensures the success of the ego's deception, reinforcing belief in the false reality it has made, is the body, which witnesses to the seeming reality of the external world. It teaches us, as does Newtonian physics, that the physical universe is independent and separate from our minds (ideas *leave* their source), and that observers can look at the seeming physical reality outside them and study, measure, quantify, manipulate, predict, and control it. What we forget, however, is that the body is as much a part of the physical world as is the world itself. Thus the body is the crowning achievement in the ego's plan. Convincing us that our physical identities are real, the ego works through the body, bringing back witnesses to the split mind that convince it of what it has *already* determined to be reality:

> This body, purposeless within itself, holds all your memories and all your hopes. You use its eyes to see, its ears to hear, and let it tell you what it feels. *It does not know.* It tells you but the names you gave to it to use, when you call forth the witnesses to its reality (text, p. 538).

The circularity of this process never dawns on our minds, and the ego seems to be forever "safe" from the Holy Spirit. As the Course asks, speaking of the stranger that is our false identity:

> Ask not this transient stranger, "What am I?" He is the only thing in all the universe that does not know. Yet it is he you ask, and it is to his answer that you would adjust. This one wild thought, fierce in its arrogance, and yet so tiny and so meaningless it slips unnoticed

through the universe of truth, becomes your guide. To it you turn to ask the meaning of the universe. And of the one blind thing in all the seeing universe of truth you ask, "How shall I look upon the Son of God?" (text, p. 401)

Thus we continuously ask the body, which was made to keep reality away from us, to tell us what reality is. The body, if one can pardon the pun, becomes the embodiment of the ego, and thus can be understood, as with the world, to be the thought of separation given form. Yet still we ask the ego-body to tell us what truth is, which can only be known through the spirit and thus never understood within an ego framework. And so the ego has been seemingly successful in hiding the Son from his true Self:

> The world began with one strange lesson, powerful enough to render God forgotten, and His Son an alien to himself, in exile from the home where God Himself established him (text, p. 601).

Following the principle of the unity of idea and source, we have already seen that God and His Son, sharing the same being and nature, must share the same attributes, as must the ego and *its* "son" (the world). One of the essential elements in the ego's system is that its thought of separation constitutes an attack on God. The Son tells his Creator, in effect: "What you have created is not good enough. I want something other than what You have given me. Thus I shall make a will, self, and world that will substitute for the Will, Self, and Heaven You created." The ego thus kicks God off the throne as Creator, usurping His role and sitting in His place. Clearly the ego's "action" has no reality and exists only within the dream of God's separated Son; this is why the Course teaches that ultimately there is no sin. Yet this seeming attack does have reality for the Son within his dream, and a reality with far reaching consequences within the illusion, as we shall soon see. The Course states: "Everyone is free to refuse to accept his inheritance, but he is not free to establish what his inheritance is" (text, p. 44).

Therefore, the world of separation shares with the thought of separation its basic attribute of attack. The Course teaches that "The world was made as an attack on God" (workbook, p. 403), and elsewhere:

> If the cause of the world you see is attack thoughts. . . . [there] is no point in trying to change the world. It is incapable of change because it is merely an effect. . . . Each of your perceptions of "external reality" is a pictorial representation of your own attack thoughts. One can well ask if this can be called seeing. Is not fantasy a better

word for such a process, and hallucination a more appropriate term for the result? (workbook, p. 34)

We can further understand why the Course teaches that the world was made as an attack on God by examining the ego's world, which is the exact opposite of God's Heaven: formless, changeless, perfect, limitless, united, and eternal. The phenomenal universe is a place of form where everything is continuously changing and in a state of flux (cf. Heraclitus' famous teaching); it is obviously far from perfect, and consists of boundary markers we call bodies which set off everything from everything else, limiting our communication with each other; and finally it is a place where all who enter come to die. As the Course states, seeming to share the Gnostic anti-cosmic spirit:

> The world you see is the delusional system of those made mad by guilt. Look carefully at this world, and you will realize that this is so. For this world is the symbol of punishment, and all the laws that seem to govern it are the laws of death. Children are born into it through pain and in pain. Their growth is attended by suffering, and they learn of sorrow and separation and death. Their minds seem to be trapped in their brain, and its powers to decline if their bodies are hurt. They seem to love, yet they desert and are deserted. They appear to lose what they love, perhaps the most insane belief of all. And their bodies wither and gasp and are laid in the ground, and are no more. Not one of them but has thought that God is cruel.
> If this were the real world, God *would* be cruel (text, p. 220).

Earlier in the text we are asked about this world:

> Consider the kingdom you have made and judge its worth fairly. Is it worthy to be a home for a child of God? Does it protect his peace and shine love upon him? Does it keep his heart untouched by fear, and allow him to give always, without any sense of loss? Does it teach him that this giving is his joy, and that God Himself thanks him for his giving? This is the only environment in which you can be happy. You cannot make it, any more than you can make yourself. It has been created for you, as you were created for it (text, p. 126).

A *Course in Miracles* is unequivocal on this point that God did not create the physical world. No compromise is possible here without rendering ineffectual the Course's entire thought system. The uncompromising position the Course takes towards the integrity of its teaching in general is reflected in the following statement:

> This course will be believed entirely or not at all. For it is wholly true or wholly false, and cannot be but partially believed. And you will

either escape from misery entirely or not at all. Reason will tell you that there is no middle ground where you can pause uncertainly, waiting to choose between the joy of Heaven and the misery of hell. Until you choose Heaven, you *are* in hell and misery (text, p. 440).

Thus we can understand the tremendous investment the ego has (and therefore all of us who believe we are the separated self called the ego) in maintaining the belief in the world's reality. If the world of the body were real--as a source of pleasure or pain--then the ego thought that gave rise to it must be real as well. And if the ego is real, God cannot be, for mutually exclusive states cannot coexist. As the Course teaches, using the example of pain:

> Pain is a sign illusions reign in place of truth. It demonstrates God is denied, confused with fear, perceived as mad, and seen as traitor to Himself. If God is real, there is no pain. If pain is real, there is no God, for vengeance is not part of love. And fear, denying love and using pain to prove that God is dead, has shown that death is victor over life. The body is the Son of God, corruptible in death, as mortal as the Father he has slain (workbook, p. 351).

To summarize up to this point: God created His Son Christ like Himself, and their perfect unity is Heaven. When the thought of separation entered into the Son's mind, this unity appeared to be shattered. This misthought was corrected by God, who "gave" His Answer to the problem, which Answer is the Holy Spirit, the memory of God's love in the split mind. The ego then "retaliated" by 1) convincing the Son of the reality of the sin-guilt-fear constellation, which 2) required the Son's defense against a wrathful God, necessitating the projection of the thought of separation beyond itself, thus 3) making a world of separation in which the ego could hide. This one projection would be the equivalent of the "Big Bang" understood by many scientists to have begun the cosmos. The physical world, and even more specifically the body, thus becomes the home of the ego, which can hide in the place whose very nature excludes God, perceived as a mortal enemy.

Now the ego's plot begins to thicken. Once it projected its thought, thereby giving rise to a physical world, the ego repressed its motivation so that the true cause of the world--the ego's purpose in protecting itself against the Holy Spirit in the Son's mind--would remain unconscious and hidden, beyond all correction. As a result of this "forgetting," it appeared as if the world were external to, and independent of the mind. The cause and effect connection was broken, and the truth of the world's origin hidden behind the screen of its seeming material solidity. The ego's triumvirate of sin, guilt, and fear now continues to reinforce our belief in the reality of the physical universe that is the ego's fortress against God. *A Course in Miracles* summarizes this dynamic in a powerful passage that describes the ego's purpose for this world and the body. It is difficult reading, made more so by the Course's use of pronouns. I have thus added the appropriate nouns in brackets:

> The circle of fear lies just below the level the body sees, and seems to be the whole foundation on which the world is based. Here are all the illusions, all the twisted thoughts, all the insane attacks, the fury, the vengeance and betrayal that were made to keep the guilt in place, so that the world could rise from it [guilt] and keep it [guilt] hidden. Its [Guilt's] shadow rises to the surface, enough to hold its [guilt's] most external manifestations in darkness, and to bring despair and loneliness to it [shadow, i.e., world] and keep it [shadow, i.e., world] joyless. Yet its [guilt's] intensity is veiled by its [guilt's] heavy coverings [body], and kept apart from what [body] was made to keep it [guilt] hidden. The body cannot see this [guilt], for the body arose from this [guilt] for its [guilt's] protection, which [guilt's protection] depends on keeping it [guilt] not seen. The body's eyes will never look on it [guilt]. Yet they will see what it [guilt] dictates (text, pp. 367f).

In a parallel passage earlier in the chapter, partially cited above, we read:

> The world arose to hide it [the original error], and became the screen on which it [the thought of separation] was projected and drawn between you and the truth. For truth extends inward, where the idea of loss is meaningless and only increase is conceivable. Do you really think it strange that a world in which everything is backwards and upside down [a reference to the upside-down retinal image] arose from this projection of error? For truth brought to this could only remain within in quiet, and take no part in all the mad projection by which this world was made. Call it not sin but madness, for such it was and so it still remains. Invest it not with guilt, for guilt implies it was accomplished in reality. And above all, *be not afraid of it* (text, p. 348).

Recalling to mind this "smokescreen effect," we also read in the Course this clear either-or statement, whose meaning the ego uses to prevent, seemingly forever, the Son's remembrance of his Source and true home:

> The world can add nothing to the power and the glory of God and His holy Sons, but it can blind the Sons to the Father if they behold it.

You cannot behold the world and know God. Only one is true (text, p. 138).

Thus, the ego appears to have triumphed over God, for what began as an insignificant idea has now assumed almost monstrous proportions within the Son's mind, wherein it has become

a serious idea, and possible of both accomplishment [the separation] and real effects [the world] (text, p. 544).

One of the ego's strongest allies in its tactical war against God, carried out in the theater of the Son's mind, is time. As it is beyond the scope of this book to treat this subject in depth, we shall confine this discussion of time to a few pages.[15]

Like the ancient Greeks, the Course asserts that all has already happened; however, where the Greeks perceived time as proceeding linearly or sequentially within a large cyclic framework, the Course teaches that all has already happened *in one instant*, non-linearly. So where the Greeks perceived time cyclically, the Christians linearly, *A Course in Miracles* sees time holographically; namely, that all of time can be found within that original ontological instant.

As we saw in Chapter 7, one's concept of time depends directly upon one's understanding of the nature of the world. While not sharing the Gnostic fear and hatred of time, the Course nonetheless shares the Gnostic view of time's role when it describes the ego's plan to convince the Son of God *not* to remember his spiritual identity, which returning to his abstract, timeless mind would surely accomplish. Thus time becomes part of the ego's cosmic trap, a magician's plan to trick us into believing that reality is what appearances tell us it is. We have seen that in the same instant that the ego had its birth, the Holy Spirit was created as the Answer, and so the error or misthought was corrected and undone. In other words, time was over the instant that it seemed to begin:

The instant the idea of separation entered the mind of God's Son, in that same instant was God's Answer given. In time this happened very long ago. In reality it never happened at all (manual, p. 4).

In that one instant, therefore, the entire ego thought system appeared. To complete its purpose of confounding the sleeping Son, this one vertical instant is, as it were, pressed down by the ego and flattened horizontally into the dimension we experience as time. Included in

---

15. See *A Vast Illusion: Time According to* A Course in Miracles for a fuller presentation of the concept of time in the Course.

this instant, however, are not only the ego's thoughts of sin, guilt, and fear, but the Holy Spirit's thoughts of unity, forgiveness, and love. Both are fully present in every aspect of the fragmented mind. Thus it seems that we are living in time, and making real choices within time; in fact, however, *all* has already occurred. Our only choice, therefore, is which fragmentary aspect of the mind we wish to experience: the Holy Spirit or the ego, love or fear.

Imagine the sleeping Son sitting in front of a television screen, with a VCR perched on top. On either side of the set are two almost infinitely large libraries of video tapes, filled with different aspects of fear and love respectively. The Son, asleep *outside of time*, chooses which video tape he will experience, which dream he will have. Once making that choice, it seems to him that he is actually experiencing that video drama, when in truth he is merely re-experiencing what has *already* happened:

> For we but see the journey from the point at which it ended, looking back on it, imagining we make it once again; reviewing mentally what has gone by (workbook, p. 291).

And as the manual says:

> The world of time is the world of illusion. What happened long ago seems to be happening now. Choices made long since appear to be open; yet to be made. What has been learned and understood and long ago passed by is looked upon as a new thought, a fresh idea, a different approach. Because your will is free you can accept what has already happened at any time you choose, and only then will you realize that it was always there. As the course emphasizes, you are not free to choose the curriculum, or even the form in which you will learn it. You are free, however, to decide when you want to learn it. And as you accept it, it is already learned.
>
> Time really, then, goes backward to an instant so ancient that it is beyond all memory, and past even the possibility of remembering. Yet because it is an instant that is relived again and again and still again, it seems to be now (manual, p. 4).

Included in the Holy Spirit's library is a video tape in which the Son finally gives Him his undivided attention and accepts the truth, rejecting the ego's illusion. This is the tape that reflects the acceptance of the Atonement that ushers in the "real world," the Course's symbol of total forgiveness and the denial of the ego's separation. The experience viewed on this tape also has already happened. Salvation requires only our acceptance of its truth:

The revelation that the Father and the Son are one will come in time to every mind. Yet is that time determined by the mind itself, not taught.

The time is set already. It appears to be quite arbitrary. Yet there is no step along the road that anyone takes but by chance. It has already been taken by him, although he has not yet embarked on it. For time but seems to go in one direction. We but undertake a journey that is over. Yet it seems to have a future still unknown to us.

Time is a trick, a sleight of hand, a vast illusion in which figures come and go as if by magic. Yet there is a plan behind appearances that does not change. The script is written. When experience will come to end your doubting has been set (workbook, p. 291).

Yet the problem remains that, having believed the ego's story about the need to protect ourselves against God's love, we also believe that time and space are very present to us, and can "protect" us from "the revelation that the Father and the Son are one." Thus the Holy Spirit patiently climbs up with us the ladder of time that separation led us down (text, p. 553). Or to use another metaphor:

To you who still believe you live in time and know not it is gone, the Holy Spirit still guides you through the infinitely small and senseless maze you still perceive in time, though it has long since gone (text, p. 511).

We but sleep and dream of time, yet all the while our true Self remains awake in God:

When the mind elects to be what it is not, and to assume an alien power which it does not have, a foreign state it cannot enter, or a false condition not within its Source, it merely seems to go to sleep a while. It dreams of time; an interval in which what seems to happen never has occurred, the changes wrought are substanceless, and all events are nowhere. When the mind awakes, it but continues as it always was (workbook, p. 312).

The Gnostics spoke of the archons (the world-rulers) employing time to trap us here and keep us from eternity. If we strip away the anthropomorphic mythology we are not too far removed from *A Course in Miracles'* teachings. The Course, however, adds the psychological dimension to the ego's use of time. Time is what roots us in the seeming reality of the sin-guilt-fear foundation, which is the bedrock of the ego's existence. The ego repeatedly tells us that we have sinned in the *past*, should experience guilt in the *present*, and fear the *future* punishment that is our just deserts. Thus does time become a prison in which we remain forever trapped by a vicious thought system that offers no way out except suffering and death, the ultimate punishment for our sins:

> How bleak and despairing is the ego's use of time! And how terrifying! For underneath its fanatical insistence that the past and future be the same is hidden a far more insidious threat to peace. The ego does not advertise its final threat, for it would have its worshippers still believe that it can offer them escape. But the belief in guilt must lead to the belief in hell, and always does. The only way in which the ego allows the fear of hell to be experienced is to bring hell here, but always as a foretaste of the future (text, p. 281).

And thus in the world in which we find ourselves (to be explored more fully in the next chapter), we simply relive again and again the original instant when we believed we separated, and believed the ego's tale of sin and punishment:

> Yet in each unforgiving act or thought, in every judgment and in all belief in sin, is that one instant still called back, as if it could be made again in time. You keep an ancient memory before your eyes. . . .
> Each day, and every minute in each day, and every instant that each minute holds, you but relive the single instant when the time of terror took the place of love. And so you die each day to live again, until you cross the gap between the past and present, which is not a gap at all. Such is each life; a seeming interval from birth to death and on to life again, a repetition of an instant gone by long ago that cannot be relived. And all of time is but the mad belief that what is over is still here and now (text, pp. 512f).

In this sense, then, time *is* cyclical insofar as, listening to the ego, we continually relive that ancient moment of terror. Over and over we replay the same drama of sin, guilt, and fear of punishment. On a still deeper level of understanding, hinted at infrequently in the Course, this cosmic drama of time is actually continually occurring. Time's dimension is not horizontal at all, but vertical. Each of the components of time exists, *now*, layered in our minds to confuse us. The bottom or innermost layer is the ontological separation that passes up through the almost infinite number of filters we identify as individual existences and experiences. Thus, that "time of terror" is not really being *re*lived, as if there were a past experience to be relived, but is actually *being* lived, as long as we continue to believe the ego's story. In this sense, then, we do not go back to that instant, we go down to it.

And yet, again, there are other dramas also waiting in our minds to be replayed or re-experienced; these are in the Holy Spirit's "videotape library," His corrections for the ego's teachings:

God gave His Teacher to replace the one you made, not to conflict with it. And what He would replace has been replaced. Time lasted but an instant in your mind, with no effect upon eternity. And so is all time passed, and everything exactly as it was before the way to nothingness was made. The tiny tick of time in which the first mistake was made, and all of them within that one mistake, held also the Correction for that one, and all of them that came within the first. And in that tiny instant time was gone, for that was all it ever was. What God gave answer to is answered and is gone (text, p. 511).

It is at this point of experiencing a choice between these two dramas that we begin to shift from the more abstract metaphysics of the "one Christ/one ego" level of discourse, to the more individualized structure of this ego as it becomes reflected in the consciousness of each of us who walks this earth. Thus, where the ego made the world to achieve its purpose of perpetuating the illusion of sin, guilt, and fear, establishing separation as real and attack as salvation, the Holy Spirit reinterprets the world as the classroom in which we learn a different lesson. That lesson learned, the world serves no more purpose and "spins into nothingness from where it came" (manual, p. 81). In the next chapter, after considering more specifically the nature of our individual experience, we shall explore the Holy Spirit's use of the world, and then again in Chapter 17.

Chapter 14

THE NATURE OF HUMANITY:
SPIRIT, MIND (SOUL), BODY

The Course's view of the spirit-mind-body triad is decidedly different from the previous views we have discussed, and it logically follows from its basic metaphysics. *Spirit* is the only part of our identity that is real, being what God created. In this sense we can equate spirit with Mind. The split *mind*, however, is illusory, and becomes, in Bréhier's term to denote Plotinus' soul, the seat of destiny. The mind's primary defense is the *body*, made to protect the separation thought against spirit's truth. Before we discuss the mind and body in detail, however, we shall review the basic dynamics of the ego and its unholy trinity of sin, guilt, and fear. These dynamics have been described in depth in *Forgiveness and Jesus*, and so will be reviewed only briefly here. However, they will become the basis for the later discussion of the essential differences between the Gnostic beliefs and practices, and the Course. This sin-guilt-fear constellation is the means whereby the ego roots us in this world. In Chapters 12 and 13 we discussed the tripartite ego mind on a metaphysical level, specifically relating to our beliefs about God our Creator, and His presence (the Holy Spirit) in our split minds. Now we shift the dynamics to what we experience as our individual mind or self, which but reflects the ontological foundation of our distorted relationship with God.

Sin refers to our belief in the reality of the separation, and this mistaken thought is reflected in one of the original Hebrew definitions of sin as "missing the mark." From our belief in sin arises the experience we call *guilt*, which encompasses all our negative beliefs and experiences about ourselves, both conscious and unconscious. Once we feel guilty, we must also *fear* the punishment we believe must be forthcoming and which is justified by our sinfulness. As the ultimate object of our sin is God, since we believe we have attacked Him, the ultimate object of our fear must be God as well, since we must believe that He is justified in attacking us in return. The strange and paradoxical belief of many religions that a loving God punishes has its root in this insane thought. Moreover, this fear of God is so overwhelming that we would do anything to avoid getting too close to it, which confronting our guilt would certainly bring about. Thus, we find ourselves in the uncomfortable position of making guilt real, becoming afraid of it, and then requiring a massive defense to protect ourselves from that fear. The Course explains:

> How can this unfair battle [between ourselves and God] be re-
> solved? Its ending is inevitable for its outcome must be death. . . .
> Forget the battle. Accept it as a fact, and then forget it. Do not
> remember the impossible odds against you. Do not remember the
> immensity of the "enemy," and do not think about your frailty in
> comparison. Accept your separation, but do not remember how it
> came about. Believe that you have won it, but do not retain the
> slightest memory of Who your great "opponent" really is (manual,
> p. 43).

A key element in this defense is the belief that the world of the body is
real, for the body provides seeming witness to the reality of our sin, for
which defense is needed. Moreover, this witness to our sin becomes
the very place we seek to hide from the great Punisher. The biblical tale
of Adam and Eve similarly describes how these prototypes for our
separated egos sought to hide from God among the trees of the garden
in fear of His expected vengeful wrath.

Since the body is the tangible expression of the ego, serving thus to
make the sin of separation real, it must inevitably become sin's symbol.
On the deepest level, therefore, any ego involvement in body thoughts
or activities must remind us of our perceived terrible sinfulness. The
Course calls such thoughts "magic," and summarizes this dynamic in
a powerful passage that describes the ego's use of such symbolism to
reinforce the terror that sustains the ego's existence:

> But what will now be your reaction to all magic thoughts? They can
> but reawaken sleeping guilt, which you have hidden but have not let
> go. Each one says clearly to your frightened mind, "You have
> usurped the place of God. Think not He has forgotten." Here we
> have the fear of God most starkly represented. For in that thought has
> guilt already raised madness to the throne of God Himself (manual,
> p. 43).

This same principle, in addition, underlies the almost universal
phenomenon of associating sexuality with sin (or, as in some religious
or secular belief systems, holiness; this inversion follows the ego
dynamic of reaction formation, whereby our conscious thoughts or
behavior become the opposite of the unconscious thought). The Adam
and Eve story graphically expresses this association, for the two
sinners' first act after eating the forbidden fruit was to cover their
nakedness. Thus we see the immediate projection of their guilt over
the sin of turning against God--a thought in their minds--onto their
bodies, and very specifically onto their sexual organs, which now
become the "source" of their shame. Interestingly enough, the Dutch
word for pubic hairs means "shame hairs." Since the Bible, at least in

part, came through the unconscious egos of the people of that time, we can understand this association by examining the specific purpose sex has had for the ego. Sex is the means of physical reproduction, which we arrogantly believe is the source of life. This expresses the basic ego belief that we--our ego (bodily) selves--are the creators. Sex, then, becomes the manifest symbol of our "original sin" of having usurped God's role of Creator, displacing Him on His throne. It is no wonder, then, that there is so much guilt associated with sexuality, and that for so many religions and spiritualities, including the classical ones discussed in this book, sex has been seen as anti-spiritual, if not the concrete expression of sin. As mentioned earlier, St. Augustine identified original sin with concupiscence, setting the tone for Christians for centuries to come. We shall return to this idea in Chapter 17.

Since all guilt and fear rest on the prior belief that we have sinned, or that the separation from God has actually occurred, any experience of guilt and fear must automatically reinforce the belief that the world of separation is real as well. It is this guilt and fear that roots us in this world, not only making the world real in our perception, but setting up a vicious circle in which we feel caught without seeming escape. It was this entrapment in an alien world that the Gnostics experienced in a particularly painful way, as we have seen. *A Course in Miracles* too expresses this alienation of our self from Self, though without the Gnostic belief in entrapment. Many passages in the Course, however, are reminiscent of the anguished cries of the Gnostics who found themselves to be "strangers in a strange land." The words "alien," "stranger," and "homeless," for example, recur frequently, as can be seen in these representative passages:

> God is not a stranger to His Sons, and His Sons are not strangers to each other. . . . There are no strangers in God's creation (text, pp. 36f).

> God's Son is indeed in need of comfort. . . . The Kingdom is his, and yet he wanders homeless. At home in God he is lonely, and amid all his brothers he is friendless (text, p. 184).

> You *will* undertake a journey because you are not at home in this world (text, p. 208).

> Nothing at all has happened but that you have put yourself to sleep, and dreamed a dream in which you were an alien to yourself. . . (text, p. 551).

One entire workbook lesson--"I am at home. Fear is the stranger here"--treats this theme of alienation and estrangement in a world not our home. Excerpts follow:

Fear is a stranger to the ways of love. Identify with fear, and you will be a stranger to yourself. And thus you are unknown to you. What is your Self remains an alien to the part of you which thinks that it is real, but different from yourself. . . . There is a stranger [fear] in our midst, who comes from an idea so foreign to the truth he speaks a different language. . . . Stranger yet, he does not recognize to whom he comes, and yet maintains his home belongs to him, while he is alien now who is at home. . . . Who is the stranger? Is it fear or you that is unsuited to the home which God provided for His Son? . . . Who fears has but denied himself and said, "I am the stranger here. And so I leave my home to one more like me than myself, and give him all I thought belonged to me." Now is he exiled of necessity, not knowing who he is, uncertain of all things but this; that he is not himself, and that his home has been denied to him.

What does he search for now? What can he find? A stranger to himself can find no home wherever he may look, for he has made return impossible (workbook, p. 295).

Life in this illusory and insane world is powerfully portrayed in this passage from a later workbook lesson, depicting how the world is experienced by one who believes it real:

Here is the only home he thinks he knows. Here is the only safety he believes that he can find. Without the world he made is he an outcast; homeless and afraid. He does not realize that it is here he is afraid indeed, and homeless, too; an outcast wandering so far from home, so long away, he does not realize he has forgotten where he came from, where he goes, and even who he really is. . . . He wanders on, aware of the futility he sees about him everywhere, perceiving how his little lot but dwindles, as he goes ahead to nowhere. Still he wanders on in misery and poverty, alone. . . . He seems a sorry figure; weary, worn, in threadbare clothing, and with feet that bleed a little from the rocky road he walks. No one but has identified with him, for everyone who comes here has pursued the path he follows, and has felt defeat and hopelessness as he is feeling them (workbook, p. 308).

A most beautiful lesson--"I will be still an instant and go home"-- expresses still again the haunting anguish of our being in a world that is not our home, desperately seeking to recall our true home:

This world you seem to live in is not home to you. And somewhere in your mind you know that this is true. A memory of home keeps haunting you, as if there were a place that called you to return, although you do not recognize the voice, nor what it is the voice reminds you of. Yet still you feel an alien here, from somewhere all unknown. Nothing so definite that you could say with certainty you are an exile here. . . . No one but knows whereof we speak. . . . We speak today for everyone who walks this world, for he is not at home. He goes uncertainly about in endless search, seeking in darkness what he cannot find; not recognizing what it is he seeks. A thousand homes he makes, yet none contents his restless mind. He does not understand he builds in vain. The home he seeks can not be made by him. There is no substitute for Heaven. All he ever made was hell (workbook, p. 331).

And finally, these excerpts from lessons "There is no peace except the peace of God" and "The peace of God is shining in me now":

Come home. You have not found your happiness in foreign places and in alien forms that have no meaning to you, though you sought to make them meaningful. This world is not where you belong. You are a stranger here. But it is given you to find the means whereby the world no longer seems to be a prison house or jail for anyone (workbook, p. 374).

Light is not of the world, yet you who bear the light in you are alien here as well. The light came with you from your native home, and stayed with you because it is your own. It is the only thing you bring with you from Him Who is your Source. It shines in you because it lights your home, and leads you back to where it came from and you are at home (workbook, p. 347).

Another metaphor used by the Course to depict life in this alien world is sleep, a metaphor not unfamiliar to the Gnostic literature. An even more widely used metaphor is the dream, which embraces both the nightmare illusions of the ego, and the happy ones of the Holy Spirit. These latter express our forgiveness, which ultimately enables us to waken from the world of dreams entirely. The state of sleep is usually contrasted with the state of being awake, the condition of life in Heaven. Some examples:

Your will is still in you because God placed it in your mind, and although you can keep it asleep you cannot obliterate it. . . . Rest does not come from sleeping but from waking. The Holy Spirit is the call to awaken and be glad. The world is very tired, because it is the idea of weariness. Our [Jesus' and our] task is the joyous one of waking it to the Call for God (text, pp. 69,71).

You have chosen a sleep in which you have had bad dreams, but the sleep is not real and God calls you to awake. There will be nothing left of your dream when you hear Him, because you will awaken. . . . God's extending outward, though not His completeness, is blocked when the Sonship does not communicate with Him as one.

So He thought, "My children sleep and must be awakened" (text, pp. 94,96).

You are at home in God, dreaming of exile but perfectly capable of awakening to reality.... You do not remember being awake (text, p. 169).

You who have spent your life in bringing truth to illusion, reality to fantasy, have walked the way of dreams. For you have gone from waking to sleeping, and on and on to a yet deeper sleep. Each dream has led to other dreams, and every fantasy that seemed to bring a light into the darkness but made the darkness deeper. Your goal was darkness, in which no ray of light could enter (text, p. 352).

The mind can think it sleeps, but that is all. It cannot change what is its waking state. It cannot make a body, nor abide within a body. ... What seems to die is but the sign of mind asleep.... What seems to be the opposite of life is merely sleeping (workbook, pp. 311f).

Within the ego's world of alienation there *is* no escape for, as we have seen, imprisonment is the purpose of the world. As long as we believe that our problems are in the physical world, we will seek for solutions there as well. The "solutions" the ego offers--all different forms of what the Course calls special relationships--are merely subtle ways of reinforcing the problem, for they continue to teach us to look at the world as real and separate from its internal cause. As the Course explains, the ego's maxim is: Seek but do not find (text, p. 318). Thus we can better appreciate the importance of our earlier discussions in Part II-A on the origin--within or with-out the Godhead--of the dark thought of separation. The way we define the problem dictates where we look for its solution. Defining a problem externally inevitably means we must seek to solve it externally, through what *A Course in Miracles* refers to as magic. Salvation thus can never be found by looking outside (magic), but only by looking within (miracle)--in our minds--where the problem is. This inner search is, of course, the very thing the ego does not want. A definition of golf from an anonymous source provides a humorous description of the inherent silliness of the ego's thought system: "an ineffectual attempt to drive an uncontrollable sphere into an inaccessible hole, with an instrument ill adapted to the purpose." Thus the so-called problems of the world and their solution are simple, once we redefine them: the one problem of the world is our belief in it, i.e., in the reality of the separation; the one solution to the problem is accepting the Atonement, i.e., changing our minds. We return to this in Chapter 17.

An extensive discussion of special relationships--the ego's primary weapon against God--is beyond the immediate scope of this book.[16] However, some comments need be made as the concept specifically interfaces with our basic theme. The function of all relationships from the ego's point of view is to fulfill its primary purpose of keeping separation and guilt real in our minds, and thereby banishing God and the Holy Spirit. Special relationships thus begin with the ego's teaching that there is something missing in us, which lack is the direct product of sin and is known as the scarcity principle. The experience of guilt attests to our recognition that there is something radically wrong with us, a gnawing sense of emptiness that can never be alleviated. What is lacking of course is Christ, the spiritual Identity that unifies us with God, and that the ego tells us is gone forever; in other words, our sin has actually occurred with real effects, and thus this lack is real and can never be undone. We shall return to this presently.

The original special relationship, therefore, is with our Creator. We demanded His special love so that we would not have to face the guilt over our separation from Him. We bargained with God, hoping that He (really our image of Him) would accept our offer of suffering and sacrifice as payment back for our sin against Him. When God does not accept our bargain--again, all this occurs only within our minds--our guilt begins to overwhelm us, leading to our terror of His vengeful wrath. This terror in turn results in the defense of projection: It is not we who rejected God; He rejected us. Thus are we now justified in turning to others for the love that He denied us, and in that decision are all our special relationships born:

> It is in the special relationship, born of the hidden wish for special love from God, that the ego's hatred triumphs. For the special relationship is the renunciation of the Love of God, and the attempt to secure for the self the specialness that He denied (text, pp. 317f).

This denial of the Love who created us and who we are as Christ ("Love created me like Itself" [workbook, p. 112]), is the underlying foundation for all that follows. Just as the ego originally counseled the sleeping Son to escape from the pain of his guilt by projection, so too does it counsel us here, in our seeming individual existence, to escape from the pain caused by this inner emptiness by seeking outside ourselves for relief. This external search has two basic forms, what the Course terms special hate and special love relationships.

In our hate relationships we seek respite from pain by projecting the cause of our emptiness and loneliness onto others, saying in effect: I am

---

16. The interested reader may consult *Forgiveness and Jesus*, pp. 32-50, and *Awaken from the Dream*, pp. 89-101.

unhappy (in pain, etc.) because of what you have done (or failed to do); I am the innocent victim and you the victimizer, and so I am justified in my anger and in blaming you for my suffering:

> The ego's plan for salvation centers around holding grievances. It maintains that, if someone else spoke or acted differently, if some external circumstance or event were changed, you would be saved. Thus, the source of salvation is constantly perceived as outside yourself. Each grievance you hold is a declaration, and an assertion in which you believe, that says, "If this were different, I would be saved." The change of mind necessary for salvation is thus demanded of everyone and everything except yourself (workbook, p. 120).

For the ego thought system to survive, therefore, it is mandatory that there be an enemy perceived outside of our minds, for this "protects" the Son from ever consulting the true source of his distress: the decision he made to listen to the voice of sin, guilt, and fear, rather than the Voice of love. Once the true "enemy" is recognized, the Son's attention is directed back to his mind, where the healing presence of the Holy Spirit is found. And so the ego continually counsels us to seek for those "special" people, objects, thought systems, and external forces to hate, attack, and overcome. Thus, a perception of a we-they world is built up, solidified through our justified anger:

> Anger always involves projection of separation, which must ultimately be accepted as one's own responsibility, rather than being blamed on others. Anger cannot occur unless you believe that you have been attacked, that your attack is justified in return, and that you are in no way responsible for it (text, p. 84).

It should be emphasized here that this principle of unjustified anger does not condone the anger or attacks of others. It simply deals with our own reaction to these magic thoughts in others. The projected hatred observed in the world is the responsibility of those separated minds, as it is ours when we project.

An historical example of the special hate object is the Jew, and we find this projection not only within the orthodox Church, as we have already seen, but in the Gnostic community as well. The Gnostic "Acts of John," for example, refers to the "lawless Jews, whose lawgiver is the lawless serpent," and has Jesus state: "I am your God, not the god of the traitor [the Old Testament God]" (AJ 94; 96.44, in *NTA* II, pp. 227,231). In the anti-Gnostic "Gospel of Peter," which dates from the mid-second century, there is exhibited definite anti-Jewish traits, where all the guilt for the death of Jesus is placed upon their heads:

And then the Jews drew the nails from the hands of the Lord and laid · him on the earth. . . . And the Jews rejoiced and gave his body to Joseph that he might bury it. . . . Then the Jews and the elders and the priests, perceiving what great evil they had done to themselves, began to lament . . . (GPt 6.21,23; 7.25, in *NTA* I, p. 185).

In the same Petrine tradition is "The Kerygmata Petrou," discussed earlier, which comes from a Jewish-Christian-Gnostic milieu and shares the anti-Jewish sentiment common to that environment, especially exhibiting great antipathy to the Old Testament. A distinction is made between Moses and the prophets, the latter being those

> who wrote the law, since they did not foresee its destruction, are convicted of ignorance and were not [really] prophets (Ker. Pet., in *NTA* II, p. 118)

"The Testimony of Truth" echoes this anti-Old Testament feeling as well:

> Others have demons dwelling with them as did David the king. He is the one who laid the foundation of Jerusalem; and his son Solomon, whom he begat in adultery, is the one who built Jerusalem by means of the demons, because he received their powers (Test. Tr. IX.70.1-10, in *NHL*, p. 415).

Special love relationships follow the same dynamic pattern we find in hate relationships, but with the opposite form. Now the ego counsels us not to project our guilt and self-hatred onto others directly, but rather to cannibalize what is outside of us, wresting it from another (or the world) and incorporating it within ourselves to fill the gaping hole of nothingness the ego has convinced us is our reality. Thus the orienting premise of the ego is the aforementioned scarcity principle: that we are missing something within, a lack that has its origin in the separation from God:

> While lack does not exist in the creation of God, it is very apparent in what you have made. It is, in fact, the essential difference between them. Lack implies that you would be better off in a state somehow different from the one you are in. Until the "separation," which is the meaning of the "fall," nothing was lacking. There were no needs at all. Needs arise only when you deprive yourself. . . . [The] sense of separation would never have arisen if you had not distorted your perception of truth, and had thus perceived yourself as lacking (text, p. 11).

These "special" people, therefore, are loved for what they can do for us, and not for who they are as Christ:

> The "better" self the ego seeks is always one that is more special. And whoever seems to possess a special self is "loved" for what can be taken from him (text, p. 318).

Stated another way, people and things outside of us fulfill the special needs we believe we have, which are nothing more than specific forms of the underlying abstract belief in the reality of our own guilt and scarcity. The primary motivation in all special relationships, then, is the belief that by "joining" with another in love (affection, approval, etc.) we are completing the inherent incompletion within ourselves:

> No one who comes here but must still have hope, some lingering illusion, or some dream that there is something outside of himself that will bring happiness and peace to him. If everything is in him this cannot be so. And therefore by his coming, he denies the truth about himself, and seeks for something more than everything, as if a part of it were separated off and found where all the rest of it is not. This is the purpose he bestows upon the body; that it seek for what he lacks, and give him what would make himself complete. And thus he wanders aimlessly about, in search of something that he cannot find, believing that he is what he is not (text, p. 573).

When these needs are met by this special person, we are in love, which is merely another term for dependency. And where "both partners see this special self in each other, the ego sees a 'union made in Heaven'" (text, p. 318). When, however, these needs are not met as we have established them, then our love quickly turns to hate, and we are right back into blaming someone or something outside ourselves for our distress.

The core of all special relationships is the bargain. It does not matter, incidentally, whether or not my special love partner is aware of this bartering insanity: I am acting it out for both of us in my own mind. Returning to our non-dualistic metaphysics for the moment, since in truth nothing exists outside the mind, there is no person out there anyway. Just as in a sleeping dream, where all the characters in our dreams are but projections of our own minds, so too in our waking dreams. Thus again, my relationship with you (from *my* point of view) exists only in my mind: You are not really there at all. The drama of bargaining, then, takes this form: I am in desperate need of completion, which only you (my chosen special love partner) can provide for me. However, since I am so wretched, there is no way you will let me have what I need (which is really a part of your self) without receiving something of value in return. However, I have nothing of value to give you (since I have already decided that I am guilty and worthless). And so I must deceive you into believing that I am indeed giving you something of value in return for the great value that you are giving me. Of this, then, is the ego's kingdom of heaven: a veritable hell built on lies and deceit, on theft and cannibalistic rape. It is a state of mind that begins with guilt, and must end with guilt over the continuing attack that *is* the ego's distorted version of salvation and Heaven:

> Most curious of all is the concept of the self which the ego fosters in the special relationship. This "self" seeks the relationship to make itself complete. Yet when it finds the special relationship in which it thinks it can accomplish this it gives itself away, and tries to "trade" itself for the self of another. . . . Each partner tries to sacrifice the self he does not want for one he thinks he would prefer. And he feels guilty for the "sin" of taking, and of giving nothing of value in return. How much value can he place upon a self that he would give away to get a "better" one? . . . Through the death of your self you think you can attack another self, and snatch it from the other to replace the self that you despise (text, pp. 318f).

The murderous insanity of the ego's thought system is forever hidden from our sight by the special relationship, and we can never look beyond its blood-drenched glitter to what it truly is:

> To know reality is not to see the ego and its thoughts, its works, its acts, its laws and its beliefs, its dreams, its hopes, its plans for its salvation, and the cost belief in it entails. In suffering, the price for faith in it is so immense that crucifixion of the Son of God is offered daily at its darkened shrine, and blood must flow before the altar where its sickly followers prepare to die (workbook, p. 457).

In the section entitled "The Two Pictures" (text, p. 333), the Course contrasts the special and holy relationship, using the image of a picture and its frame. The ego's frame, heavily laden with seeming jewels, conceals the picture of death it presents to us as its gift; the Holy Spirit's picture, on the other hand, is lightly framed so that its inner light can be clearly visible as it leads us into itself, and then beyond to God.

Such a turnabout from special love to special hate is inevitable for several reasons: first, no one person or thing has the capacity to be there always and in all ways for us; second, the ego's goal, as the Course tells us, is murder, and so our special love partners are "set up" by the ego eventually to fail and thus become scapegoats for our justified wrath; finally, since it is our guilt that has made this special love relationship necessary as a defense, the love object must become a symbol of the guilt that is the relationship's purpose. Thus, while consciously we are aware only of love and gratitude for the beloved who has enabled us to deny our pain under the cover of specialness, unconsciously our thoughts continually move from the beloved to what he/she/it symbolizes: our guilt. And since it is our guilt we hate more than anything else in the world, we must also come to hate the one who symbolizes it for us. This hatred, therefore, is always present, even when we are protesting our love the most strongly. It is only a matter of time until the storm of hate breaks through the barricades of special love and reveals itself for what it always was.

The battleground of specialness is the body, since hatred demands a specific object:

> Hate is specific. There must be a thing to be attacked. An enemy must be perceived in such a form he can be touched and seen and heard, and ultimately killed (workbook, p. 298).

Thus *A Course in Miracles* unequivocally asserts that God's creative principle had nothing at all to do with the separated mind or body. Nonetheless, the Course does not attack the body nor speak of it in derogatory tones, although in some passages it does reflect *our* denigration of our alien home. In one such passage the Course addresses us:

> Condemn him [the Son of God] not by seeing him within the rotting prison [the body] where he sees himself (text, p. 505).

And earlier:

> And you want your Father, not a little mound of clay [the body], to be your home (text, p. 385).

And still earlier:

> The body is a tiny fence around a little part [the ego] of a glorious and complete idea. It draws a circle, infinitely small, around a very little segment of Heaven, splintered from the whole, proclaiming that within it is your kingdom, where God can enter not (text, p. 364).

To be sure, however, the Course does poke gentle fun at our world's worship of the body, as seen in this characteristic passage:

> The body is the central figure in the dreaming of the world. There is no dream without it, nor does it exist without the dream in which it acts as if it were a person to be seen and be believed. It takes the central place in every dream, which tells the story of how it was made

by other bodies, born into the world outside the body, lives a little while and dies, to be united in the dust with other bodies dying like itself. In the brief time allotted it to live, it seeks for other bodies as its friends and enemies. Its safety is its main concern. Its comfort is its guiding rule. It tries to look for pleasure, and avoid the things that would be hurtful. Above all, it tries to teach itself its pains and joys are different and can be told apart.

The dreaming of the world takes many forms, because the body seeks in many ways to prove it is autonomous and real. It puts things on itself that it has bought with little metal discs or paper strips the world proclaims as valuable and real. It works to get them, doing senseless things, and tosses them away for senseless things it does not need and does not even want. It hires other bodies, that they may protect it and collect more senseless things that it can call its own. It looks about for special bodies that can share its dream. Sometimes it dreams it is a conqueror of bodies weaker than itself. But in some phases of the dream, it is the slave of bodies that would hurt and torture it (text, p. 543).

Yet nowhere does *A Course in Miracles* fall into the trap of making the body real by seeing it as the enemy to be overcome. As the Course writes of the process of transcending the limitations of the body's laws:

> There is no violence at all in this escape. The body is not attacked, but simply properly perceived. . . . Not through destruction, not through a breaking out, but merely by a quiet melting in (text, pp. 361f).

Being nothing, the body does not live nor die. Thus the Course asks, referring to the body:

> Can you paint rosy lips upon a skeleton, dress it in loveliness, pet it and pamper it, and make it live? And can you be content with an illusion that you are living?
> There is no life outside of Heaven. Where God created life, there life must be. In any state apart from Heaven life is illusion. At best it seems like life; at worst, like death (text, p. 459).

Later, the Course emphasizes the utter neutrality of the body which, like a wooden marionette, has no life but simply carries out the wishes of the mind that is its master:

> Who punishes the body is insane. For here the little gap is seen, and yet it is not here. It has not judged itself, nor made itself to be what it is not. It does not seek to make of pain a joy and look for lasting pleasure in the dust. It does not tell you what its purpose is and cannot understand what it is for. It does not victimize, because it has no will, no preferences and no doubts. It does not wonder what it is.

And so it has no need to be competitive. It can be victimized, but cannot feel itself as victim. It accepts no role, but does what it is told, without attack.

It is . . . a thing that cannot see . . . [and] cannot hear. . . . it has no feeling. It behaves in ways you want, but never makes the choice. It is not born and does not die. It can but follow aimlessly the path on which it has been set. . . . It takes no sides and judges not the road it travels (text, pp. 559f).

Thus the body is not the enemy at all, but a silly construct of the ego to convince us that the impossible--the separation from God--has occurred. The Holy Spirit, as we shall explore in Chapters 15 and 17, uses the body as His classroom so that we may learn, finally, His lesson of salvation. This attitude towards the illusory body distinguishes the Course from the other thought systems we have been considering, and we shall return to this in Part III.

Let us now reconsider the spirit-mind-body triad, so that we may better understand the nature and purpose of each of them. We begin with spirit.

As we have seen, spirit is the Self that God created. It is equated with Christ, created in the "image and likeness" of God. Similar to the Gnostic *pneuma*, this Self is totally other-worldly and thus has no referent in this world. Spirit is not part of humanity, but rather is "in spite" of it. What we call humanity (the ego-body) was made to defend *against* spirit. An unpublished modern haiku by Patrick Lysons poetically summarizes the ego's use of the body:

> This bodily prejudice
> buries
>
> Itself in lies
> carries
>
> Its needs crazily
> Needing
>
> To justify, justify
> countermeasures
>
> Against my simple
> Miracle

As we have discussed, when the mind appeared to separate from its Source, thereby becoming split, the ego was born. Thus we now speak of two minds: Mind--one with God; and mind--split off from Him. This latter mind is what emerges as the ego, the separated and illusory self. In the words of Plotinus, this self is non-being. *A Course in Miracles* in fact distinguishes between being, which refers only to spirit, and existence, which is the realm of the separated mind, or non-being. The first part of this passage was partially quoted earlier when we noted the similarity between the Course and Basilides:

> Existence as well as being rest on communication. Existence, however, is specific in how, what and with whom communication is judged to be worth undertaking. Being is completely without these distinctions. It is a state in which the mind is in communication with everything that is real. . . . This is your reality. Do not desecrate it or recoil from it. It is your real home, your real temple and your real Self.
>
> God, Who encompasses all being, created beings who have everything individually. . . . Remember that in the Kingdom there is no difference between *having* and *being*, as there is in existence. . . . *Being* alone lives in the Kingdom, where everything lives in God . . . (text, pp. 64,94).

We are therefore tripartite, though in a manner different from what we have considered: mind and body belong to the unreal world of existence (non-being); spirit alone is being, and therefore real. *A Course in Miracles* is thus on one level uninterested in the body, which is merely an epiphenomenon of the separated mind, having no existence outside our thoughts. On this level the Course's exclusive focus is the mind: the seat of the problem as well as the answer. "Mind," incidentally, can be roughly equated with one popular understanding of the soul, wherein the soul is the part of our self that journeys back to God. In this context, then, "soul" should not be equated with spirit, that "being of God . . . is eternal and was never born" (manual, p. 75).

Therefore, the term "spirit" really does not belong in any discussion of a physical being, let alone homo sapiens. Spirit in fact is exactly what is *not* found in a physical organism for, again, the body--the embodiment of the thought of separation--was specifically made to exclude the spiritual Self. The traditional human trichotomy now becomes, for the Course, a dichotomy of mind and body. Within the mind, however, we can discern three parts, as was described in Chapter 12. Once the mind (written in lower case to distinguish it from the Mind of Christ, the home of spirit) split off from God and seemed to exist on its own, there were within itself, as we have seen, two "voices." One speaks for the reality of the separation; this is the voice of the ego that teaches sin, guilt, fear, and the need for defense. The other speaks for the unreality of the separation; this is the Voice of the Holy Spirit, whose teaching is forgiveness and defenselessness. A third part of the mind is the decision maker, which must choose between these two voices. In fact this is the *only* choice truly available to us:

> In this world the only remaining freedom is the freedom of choice;
> always between two choices or two voices (manual, p. 75).

The ego's voice apparently wins out, at least in our experience, because we believe we are here in the illusory world we call reality. To summarize a process discussed earlier, the ego convinces the Son to decide for *it* instead of for God. Believing the tale of his own sin, the Son seeks to hide from God's wrath and makes a body as a cloak, hoping against hope that God has forgotten: "Projecting your 'forgetting' onto Him, it seems to you He has forgotten too" (manual, p. 43). And so we walk this earth, terrified in our deepest consciousness that God will one day find us out. We continually use the body--ours and others'--as the means of distracting our thoughts from the awful "truth" the ego has made real. Once we have accepted the ego's miserable image of ourselves, the ego in turn "mercifully" represses it for us. The Course has powerfully summarized this notion of the self the ego has told us we must never look at:

> You think you are the home of evil, darkness and sin. You think if anyone could see the truth about you he would be repelled, recoiling from you as if from a poisonous snake. You think if what is true about you were revealed to you, you would be struck with horror so intense that you would rush to death by your own hand, living on after seeing this being impossible.
> These are beliefs so firmly fixed that it is difficult to help you see that they are based on nothing (workbook, p. 159).

The body, then, becomes a powerful instrument in the hands of the ego, serving its purpose very well. The point is essential and bears restating: The body is literally nothing, and therefore deserves neither praise nor condemnation. It is never the problem, which remains only in the mind, where the belief in sin is held in place by our guilt, the fearful presence of which necessitates the body as a defense. The body therefore is neutral, simply assuming the role that has been assigned to it.

However, the Holy Spirit also has a use for the body: as an instrument of communication. In a series of parallel passages, the Course emphasizes the holy use of the body as an instrument of salvation by the Teachers of God.[17] Perhaps the most moving of these is the passage where Jesus speaks as the manifestation of the Teacher:

> For this alone I need; that you will hear the words I speak, and give

---

17. *See* my *Glossary-Index for* A Course in Miracles, p. 31, for a list of these references.

them to the world. You are my voice, my eyes, my feet, my hands through which I save the world (workbook, p. 322).

Used by the ego to attack God and exclude Christ from our minds, the body for the Holy Spirit becomes the means to correct the Son's mistakes in having chosen the wrong guide. In a passage already quoted, we find this teaching succinctly summarized:

> The body was not made by love. Yet love does not condemn it and can use it lovingly, respecting what the Son of God has made and using it to save him from illusions (text, p. 359).

In the following chapter we shall discuss more specifically how the Holy Spirit uses the body (and our special relationships) to undo the ego's thought system.

In summary, then, we can see how *A Course in Miracles* differs radically from all the other systems we have explored: *spirit* plays no part at all in our human experience; the *mind* is split between the ego and the Holy Spirit, a split not too dissimilar from what is found in the other traditions we have considered; and the *body* is seen as illusory, ontologically the product of our guilt and fear, yet nonetheless neutral in terms of how it is used. It is its use that gives the body all the meaning it has for us, for being nothing, it is neither good nor evil. Thus, seeing the body as inherently one or the other fulfills the ego's purpose by ascribing to the illusory body a reality it does not have.

Chapter 15

THE MEANING OF SALVATION

Within *A Course in Miracles'* system, salvation is the correction of the misbelief in separation. It is equated with the process of Atonement, which undoes the error through a change in thinking, not through penance or sacrifice of the body, as has been traditionally taught. The instrument of salvation is forgiveness, the correction for our misperceptions of others: where previously we had judged someone as being our enemy, the agent or cause of our distress, now that same individual is seen as our friend. As one workbook lesson instructs:

> Today's idea ["Give me your blessing, holy Son of God"] is your safe escape from anger and from fear. Be sure you use it instantly, should you be tempted to attack a brother and perceive in him the symbol of your fear. And you will see him suddenly transformed from enemy to savior; from the devil into Christ (workbook, p. 299).

The Course teaches that we forgive each other for what we have *not* done, not for what we think has been done. This means that the reason we are upset is not because of another's actions, but always because of how we have *perceived* another's actions. Seeming attacks are corrected in our perception so that they now are seen as calls for help or for love. Thus, *A Course in Miracles* is teaching another way of seeing the world. This vision does not deny the outward actions or behavior our sensory organs report to us, but merely reinterprets what we have seen or, more properly, what we believed we have seen. As the Course points out: perception is an interpretation, not a fact. It is

> a continual process of accepting and rejecting, organizing and reorganizing, shifting and changing. Evaluation is an essential part of perception, because judgments are necessary in order to select (text, p. 41).

Crucial to the Course's understanding of salvation is that it is not "the world, the flesh, and the devil" from which one needs to be saved, for that is not the problem. Rather, the problem is the underlying thought system of separation--the way we think--that brought about the world, the flesh, and the devil. It is this "way of thinking" that we may more properly call the devil, it being nothing more than our belief that it is possible to have a force that opposes God, and that can succeed. As the Course states: "The mind can make the belief in separation very real and very fearful, and this belief *is* the 'devil'" (text, p. 45).

Therefore, if the problem is belief in separation, the solution can *only* be union. Forgiveness thus refers to the process of joining with another person (in a holy relationship) who heretofore had been seen as separate from us (in a special relationship). By joining with another we correct our ego's belief that attack is salvation. In this attack is the birthplace of guilt, the true "creator" of this world. God created Christ--our true Self--as one with Him, and therefore the continual joining with others, step by step corrects the thought system that had been erected to take the place of the unity of Heaven. The Course says of this gradual process:

> The Holy Spirit takes you gently by the hand, and retraces with you your mad journey outside yourself, leading you gently back to the truth and safety within (text, p. 348).

Referring back to our mythic story, salvation very simply consists of the process whereby the Son changes his mind and listens to the Holy Spirit, correcting his original mistake of choosing to believe the ego's tale of sin-guilt-fear which, as we have seen, set into motion the strategic defense leading to the cosmic drama of the making of the material universe. Thus the Son is "saved" from his wrong choice by *his* changing his mind. What is central here is that the instrument of salvation is the Son himself, not an external agent such as God or one of His representatives: Salvation does not come to us from the outside, but from a decision to accept the Holy Spirit's Atonement, thus undoing our previous decision to deny His truth. In this sense, then, the Course is similar to the emphasis placed on virtue by the Greek philosophers we have considered, not to mention also being similar to the Pelagian heresy.

A Course in Miracles however, also makes it very clear that such a retraining cannot come from the ego, but only from the *internal* presence of the Holy Spirit who yet remains *outside* the ego thought system. Salvation is thus a collaborative venture between the Son and the Holy Spirit, just as the Son had heretofore joined with the ego:

> ... you and your adviser must agree on what you want before it can occur. It is but this agreement that permits all things to happen. Nothing can be caused without some form of union, be it a dream of judgment or the Voice for God (text, p. 584).

This joining together of what the Son had originally decided should be kept separate (his mind from the truth), becomes reflected on the bodily level of experience when we join with those from whom we had decided we should be kept separate. Separation was the ontological choice that led to the separated mind and eventually to the separated world. Thus it is this mistaken choice that must be corrected. It appears as if the correction occurs on the level of our relationships with each other here in this physical world. But in truth the correction has *already* occurred on the mind level; stated even more clearly, the correction *is* already happening, since past and future are simply fabrications made up by the ego to deceive us.

One of the major forms of correcting this time distortion is to help change the Son's mind about his perception of God. We recall that the ego had convinced the sleeping Son that God was angry, hellbent on punishing him for his sins against Him. This nicely, from the ego's point of view, removed any possibility of help the Son might accept from his Creator:

> God ... must accept his Son's belief in what he is, and hate him for it.
> See how the fear of God is reinforced by this. ... Now it becomes impossible to turn to Him for help in misery. For now He has become the "enemy" Who caused it, to Whom appeal is useless. ... now is conflict made inevitable, beyond the help of God. For now salvation must remain impossible, because the savior has become the enemy.
> There can be no release and no escape. Atonement thus becomes a myth, and vengeance, not forgiveness, is the Will of God. From where all this begins, there is no sight of help that can succeed. Only destruction can be the outcome. And God Himself seems to be siding with it, to overcome His Son (text, p. 456).

We thus begin the process of salvation by questioning the voice of the ego, realizing that its teachings make no sense and contradict what must be the truth. Now we begin to realize that the Voice of the Holy Spirit does make sense, and it is in our best interests to listen to His teachings of forgiveness.

We have thus far discussed salvation more on the metaphysical or ontological level, as a correction of the Son's mind in terms of making a different choice. However, one of the unique aspects of *A Course in Miracles* is its integration of the metaphysical with the practical. Its principal focus on the level of practice is on learning the lesson of how to join with those specific persons we have formerly chosen to keep separate, whether in the form of special hate or special love relationships. This forgiveness of others (and ultimately ourselves) constitutes the Course's process of salvation. It is beyond the scope of this book to discuss this process at any length, since our major theme is the attitude towards the world and body, and how this attitude leads to the general theory of salvation. Yet a brief review of the principle of forgiveness exemplifies not only the Course's attitude towards the body, but towards salvation as well.

As was explained above, the correction for the mistake that led us to believe we are in this world in the first place must occur in the mind, because that is where the mistake occurs. The mind, not the body, is the active element in the dream of the separated world, and so it would make no sense to correct an error where it is not; yet of course the ego continually tries to convince us to do just that. Forgiveness essentially reverses the steps that the ego had the Son take in that original instant, an instant, as we have seen, that we relive over and over and over again. Let us retrace those steps now, so that we may understand forgiveness' correction.

As we recall, the ego begins by convincing the Son of the reality of its triad of sin, guilt, and fear, culminating in his believing that the sinned-against-God seeks to punish him, and that the Holy Spirit--the Voice of God's love in the Son's mind--is not to be trusted and must be denied and escaped *from*. The ego has effectively convinced the Son to deny his role in instigating God's "wrath": namely, that he attacked God first; it is *his* sin. Projecting his sin onto God, the Son now believes that God is attacking him, and unfairly so. Thus, the sin and guilt first have been denied and then projected. The next step projects the thought of separation from the mind, making (miscreating) a physical world and a body with which to experience the world as separate from, and independent of the mind that made it. The ego recognizes that if the Son remembered that *he* made the world, he would also realize it was illusory and designed to hide from him his sin and guilt, not to mention the presence of love in his mind that would undo the sin through forgiveness of what never was. In other words, the Son would simply awaken from the bad dream of separation.

Because of the efficacy of denial and projection, the world of time and space appears on the level of our individual experience to be external to our minds, and quite real. Thus we inevitably experience ourselves as victims of forces beyond our control. The daily experiences--physical and psychological--from birth to death, all conspire under the ego's guidance to convince us of the reality of the world and of our helpless place within it. This belief is the "face of innocence" powerfully described by the Course, a face

> often wet with tears at the injustices the world accords to those who would be generous and good. This aspect [of our self concept] never makes the first attack. But every day a hundred little things make small assaults upon its innocence, provoking it to irritation, and at last to open insult and abuse (text, p. 610).

This then is the ego's plan for its own salvation: denying its part in the making of the world and body, and then projecting the responsibility for it onto the world and body. Now it appears that what we have in fact done to the world is being done to us:

> The world but demonstrates an ancient truth; you will believe that others do to you exactly what you think you did to them. But once deluded into blaming them you will not see the cause of what they do, because you *want* the guilt to rest on them (text, p. 545).

Of course what has been "saved" is the ego, while the mind of the Son of God remains in seeming chains, imprisoned by powers he believes he can do nothing about.

True salvation now begins where the ego left off, and goes the other way. As the Course says:

> The world is full of miracles. They stand in shining silence next to every dream of pain and suffering, of sin and guilt. They are the dream's alternative, the choice to be the dreamer, rather than deny the active role in making up the dream. They are the glad effects of taking back the consequence of sickness to its cause. The body is released because the mind acknowledges "this is not done to me, but *I* am doing this." And thus the mind is free to make another choice instead. Beginning here, salvation will proceed to change the course of every step in the descent to separation, until all the steps have been retraced, the ladder gone, and all the dreaming of the world undone (text, p. 553).

Forgiveness, through the mind's correction called the miracle, thus consists of undoing the ego's principles of denial and projection, reversing the direction the mind had taken when it followed the ego's counsel. Forgiveness as the instrument of salvation can be summarized as a three-step process. (Although it is helpful to consider the process as consisting of three steps, we must remember that they are of course not sequential at all, for time is not linear.) The first step consists in realizing that the cause of our personal world of suffering and pain, of victim and victimization, is not in what appears to be external, but rather is within our own minds. Since the external world is nothing more than a portrait of what is in the mind--a dream not different in dynamic from the sleeping dream wherein nothing "real" is going on--anything that occurs in our lives has been dreamt by us, *literally*:

> The secret of salvation is but this: That you are doing this unto yourself. No matter what the form of the attack, this still is true. Whoever takes the role of enemy and of attacker, still is this the truth. Whatever seems to be the cause of any pain and suffering you feel, this is still true. For you could not react at all to figures in a dream you

knew that you were dreaming. Let them be as hateful and as vicious as they may, they could have no effect on you unless you failed to recognize it is your dream.

This single lesson learned will set you free from suffering, whatever form it takes. The Holy Spirit will repeat this one inclusive lesson of deliverance until it has been learned. . . . He would teach you but the single cause of all of them [forms of sorrow and pain], no matter what their form. And you will understand the miracles reflect the simple statement, "*I* have done this thing, and it is this I would undo" (text, pp. 545f).

Thus the first step in this process is returning the problem to the Son's mind, where it was before the ego removed it through projection; the cause has been returned to its rightful place:

This is the separation's final step, with which salvation, which proceeds to go the other way, begins. This final step is an effect of what has gone before, appearing as a cause. The miracle is the first step in giving back to cause [the mind] the function of causation, not effect. For this confusion has produced the dream, and while it lasts will wakening be feared. Nor will the call to wakening be heard, because it seems to be the call to fear (text, p. 552).

Seen in this light, our projections become a gift because we see in others what is within our own minds. There is no one really outside us, except whom we have put there in our dream. The hatred that the ego hid can now be looked at, and a different choice can at last be made.

The stage is set for the second step. Now that the cause has been returned to the Son's mind, we are returned to that part of our story *before* the Son believed the ego's tale. Thus, the Son is given another chance to choose between the two voices. This is what is meant by the Course's repeated request that we choose again, as we see in this passage at the end of the text:

In every difficulty, all distress, and each perplexity Christ calls to you and gently says, "My brother, choose again" (text, p. 620).

The Son has returned to "the scene of the crime" of his mistake, and now can change his mind. Where before he chose to believe the ego contention that he was the "home of evil, darkness and of sin," that he was the agent of sin and deserving of all the pain his guilt and fear brought to him, now he can hear a different Voice speak of God's true judgment of him:

"You are still My holy Son, forever innocent, forever loving and forever loved, as limitless as your Creator, and completely changeless and forever pure. Therefore awaken and return to Me. I am your Father and you are My Son" (workbook, p. 445).

With this choice to awaken from the ego's dream of guilt and terror, the Son's eyes slowly open, in the third step, to the wonderful truth God's Voice speaks to him. The memory of God's unchanging love begins to dawn within his mind, and he remembers the home with God that he never truly left.

To restate the steps of forgiveness, the first questions the validity of the ego's tale of victim and victimizer: we are subject to forces outside us and beyond our control. It brings the problem of sin and guilt back to our minds where it truly belongs, not in someone or something else. It is thus the undoing of projection, the ego's plan of defense against God's seeming wrath. The second step is now made possible by the first step's allowing the Son to reconsider his original decision to listen to the ego. The basis of the problem was the Son's belief that he was sinful and guilty. Now that belief can be looked at again, this time *with* the Holy Spirit, and our (really the ego's) investment in it withdrawn. Once this choice has been made and our decision changed, the guilt disappears, since it was held in place only by our belief in it:

> When you accept a miracle, you do not add your dream of fear to one that is already being dreamed. Without support, the dream will fade away without effects. For it is your support that strengthens it (text, p. 553).

> [The world] will remain no longer than the thought that gave it birth is cherished. When the thought of separation has been changed to one of true forgiveness, will the world be seen in quite another light; and one which leads to truth, where all the world must disappear and all its errors vanish (workbook, p. 403).

What remains then is the love of God that was always there. The third step, therefore, is really not a step at all. It is the natural and inevitable result of the acceptance (the first two steps) of the Holy Spirit's correction that *has already been accomplished.* That is why the Course teaches that the first two steps are *our* responsibility, and the third is not:

> ... you are not trapped in the world you see, because its cause can be changed. This change requires, first, that the cause be identified and then let go [second], so that it can be replaced [third]. The first two steps in this process require your cooperation. The final one does not (workbook, p. 34).

The three steps are summarized in another fashion in workbook lesson 196, "It can be but myself I crucify." Here we are asked to recognize again that our pain comes from within ourselves, and not from outside. This process is not without its terror, for bringing the guilt back within our minds is to confront directly the ego's story of God's furious wrath waiting impatiently in our minds for our return. Thus this process is placed within the larger metaphysical context we have been considering. I have added the numbered steps in brackets:

> [1] To question it [the belief that our salvation is won through attack] at all, its form must first be changed at least as much as will permit fear of retaliation to abate, and the responsibility returned to some extent to you.... Until this shift has been accomplished, you can not perceive that it is but your thoughts that bring you fear, and your deliverance depends on you. . . . For once you understand it is impossible that you be hurt except by your own thoughts, the fear of God must disappear. You cannot then believe that fear is caused without. And God, Whom you had thought to banish, can be welcomed back within the holy mind He never left.
>
> Salvation's song can certainly be heard in the idea we practice for today. If it can but be you you crucify, you did not hurt the world, and need not fear its vengeance and pursuit. Nor need you hide in terror from the deadly fear of God projection hides behind.... [2] There is an instant in which terror seems to grip your mind so wholly that escape appears quite hopeless. When you realize, once and for all, that it is you you fear, the mind perceives itself as split. And this had been concealed while you believed attack could be directed outward, and returned from outside to within. It seemed to be an enemy outside you had to fear. . . . Now, for an instant, is a murderer perceived within you, eager for your death, intent on plotting punishment for you until the time when it can kill at last. [3] Yet in this instant is the time as well in which salvation comes. For fear of God has disappeared. And you can call on Him to save you from illusions by His Love, calling Him Father and yourself His Son (workbook, p. 365).[18]

Salvation, as observed earlier, is basically accomplished by our own work, done in union with the Holy Spirit. However, the Holy Spirit is not conceived of as an external agent, magically sent by God to undo our fear and solve our problems. As Jesus states near the beginning of the text, addressing the traditional view of his "doing it for us":

> Fear cannot be controlled by me, but it can be self-controlled. Fear prevents me from giving you my control. . . . The correction of fear

---

18. For further discussion of the three steps of forgiveness, see *Forgiveness and Jesus*, pp. 56-63.

is your responsibility. When you ask for release from fear, you are implying that it is not. You should ask, instead, for help in the conditions that have brought the fear about. These conditions always entail a willingness to be separate. At that level you *can* help it (text, p. 25).

Jesus thus can help us in making another choice, but he cannot make that choice for us.

As we have seen, the Holy Spirit is actually the abstract and formless memory of God's perfect love "buried" within the Son's split mind. That love is seemingly lost forever, but in reality is always present, simply awaiting our return. The continual "call" to us of love's presence provides the means by which we return to it:

> Our Love awaits us as we go to Him, and walks beside us showing us the way. He fails in nothing. He the end we seek, and He the means by which we go to Him (workbook, p. 440).

Like a lighthouse, the Holy Spirit casts His beam into the guilt-darkened waters of our mind, as a mark of safety and direction for all those lost in the ego's sea. Gently, His love reminds us of the truth of our unity with God, and heals us of all thoughts of fragmentation. The workbook states:

> The Thought of peace was given to God's Son the instant that his mind had thought of war. There was no need for such a Thought before, for peace was given without opposite, and merely was. But when the mind is split there is a need of healing. So the Thought that has the power to heal the split became a part of every fragment of the mind that still was one, but failed to recognize its oneness. Now it did not know itself, and thought its own Identity was lost (workbook, p. 397).

To summarize, the process of salvation in *A Course in Miracles* is internal, because there is in truth no external theater in which to act. Salvation *appears* to be something we *do* (in the body), but it is in truth a process of *un*doing (in the mind), as is seen in these three quotations:

> Forgiveness ... is still, and quietly does nothing. ... It merely looks, and waits, and judges not ... (workbook, p. 391).

> Salvation is undoing in the sense that it does nothing, failing to support the world of dreams and malice. Thus it lets illusions go. By not supporting them, it merely lets them quietly go down to dust... (workbook, p. 397).

> A miracle is a correction. It does not create, nor really change at all. It merely looks on devastation, and reminds the mind that what it sees is false. It undoes error. . . . [and] paves the way for the return of timelessness and love's awakening (workbook, p. 463).

The process of salvation returns the mind to the point at which the original choice was made, and enables it to choose again. The Son's choice to hear the ego instead of the Holy Spirit is not past but *ongoing*, continually reflected in what appears to be our present choices. Recall that there is no time and so all is happening *now*. A decision to forgive an enemy is simply the outer expression of an inner shift in which the Son uses time--originally made by the ego to attack God--to allow his fear of God's wrath to dissipate. Each time we choose to forgive on this illusory physical plane, we express the choice to accept at last the salvation that is the principle of the Atonement.

Before proceeding to the figure of the redeemer, the subject of the next chapter, additional mention should be made of some of the parallels of the Course's language with Gnosticism. In the previous chapter we cited the metaphor of sleep. It would logically follow therefore that the correction or salvation from sleep would be awakening. Of the many references to our awakening, I quote the beginning of Chapter 17 in the text:

> The betrayal of the Son of God lies only in illusions, and all his "sins" are but his own imagining. His reality is forever sinless. He need not be forgiven but awakened. In his dreams he has betrayed himself, his brothers and his God. Yet what is done in dreams has not been really done. . . . Only in waking is the full release from them . . . (text, p. 327).

In Chapter 11 we discussed the Course's use of the word *knowledge* as synonymous with Heaven, paralleling the Gnostic usage. This awakening to knowledge is the ultimate goal of the spiritual journey, yet the Course emphasizes that *its* goal is the correction of the original error, the step immediately preceding the awakening:

> This course will lead to knowledge, but knowledge itself is still beyond the scope of our curriculum. Nor is there any need for us to try to speak of what must forever lie beyond words. . . . Where learning ends there God begins, for learning ends before Him Who is complete where He begins, and where there *is* no end. It is not for us to dwell on what cannot be attained. There is too much to learn. The readiness for knowledge still must be attained (text, p. 369).

> Your chosen home is on the other side, beyond the veil. It has been carefully prepared for you, and it is ready to receive you now. . . .

466

Your home has called to you since time began, nor have you ever failed entirely to hear. . . . In you the knowledge lies, ready to be unveiled and freed from all the terror that kept it hidden (text, p. 398).

Another prominent Gnostic theme, as seen in Part II-A, is *rest*, used synonymously with Heaven and attained by the reception of the saving *gnosis*. *A Course in Miracles* uses the term similarly, as seen in the following examples:

Rest in His Love and protect your rest by loving (text, p. 119).

Your relationship is now a temple of healing; a place where all the weary ones can come and rest. Here is the rest that waits for all, after the journey. And it is brought nearer to all by your relationship (text, p. 378).

For the whole new world rests in the hands of every two who enter here to rest. And as they rest, the face of Christ shines on them and they remember the laws of God, forgetting all the rest and yearning only to have His laws perfectly fulfilled in them and all their brothers. Think you when this has been achieved that you will rest without them? (text, p. 404)

The most extensive use of the rest imagery comes in workbook lesson 109, "I rest in God," and we close this chapter with excerpts from this beautiful lesson:

"I rest in God." This thought will bring to you the rest and quiet, peace and stillness, and the safety and the happiness you seek. . . . This thought has power to wake the sleeping truth in you, whose vision sees beyond appearances to that same truth in everyone and everything there is. . . . This is the day of peace. You rest in God, and while the world is torn by winds of hate your rest remains completely undisturbed. Yours is the rest of truth. . . . You call to all to join you in your rest, and they will hear and come to you because you rest in God. . . . In timelessness you rest, while time goes by without its touch upon you, for your rest can never change in any way at all. . . . You rest within the peace of God today, and call upon your brothers from your rest to draw them to their rest, along with you. . . . We rest together here, for thus our rest is made complete. . . . We give to those unborn and those passed by, to every Thought of God, and to the Mind in which these Thoughts were born and where they rest. And we remind them of their resting place each time we tell ourselves, "I rest in God" (workbook pp. 193f).

Chapter 16

THE REDEEMER - JESUS

The words "redeemer" or "savior" are used in different ways in *A Course in Miracles*, so we begin by exploring these usages before specifically discussing the person of Jesus. We have seen how redemption ultimately is our responsibility, for we must change our minds which had originally chosen wrongly. We ultimately then are our own redeemer or savior, for salvation cannot come from anywhere but ourselves. On another level, however, since the ego has convinced us to deny the problem of guilt from which we need to be saved, we *cannot* save ourselves because we do not recognize the problem that has been hidden through the dynamic of repression. Therefore, we need the help of those who appear to be outside ourselves to mirror to us what is really inside our own minds.

We have already discussed that our unconscious guilt has been projected onto others, thus allowing the Holy Spirit the opportunity to point out to us that the sin we are accusing another of is really *nothing more* than the sin we have successfully screened from our awareness. In this sense, then, other people become our saviors, for we see in them what needs to be forgiven in ourselves. Without their presence in our lives (however illusory that presence ultimately is), we would never have this opportunity of being saved from our belief in guilt. This is why the Course so frequently uses the word "savior" to denote this other person, our special love or hate partner:

> Within the darkness see the savior *from* the dark, and understand
> your brother as his Father's Mind shows him to you. He will step
> forth from darkness as you look on him, and you will see the dark no
> more. . . . His sinlessness but pictures yours (text, p. 486).

We can see then that at one important level the savior is not a supernatural being, but simply some aspect of our own minds (whether perceived in one's own body or in another's). Recall yet again that in truth there is no person outside us. What appears to be a person to whom we are relating in specialness is simply a projection of the part of our minds we wish to split off and deny in ourselves. Within this dream of a relationship, however, we are nonetheless able to perceive that person as not separate from us; this reflects the deeper thought that we are not separate from our Self. The relationship (and therefore the persons in the relationship) thus serves as the savior *from* (or correction *for*) this thought of separation of which we are no longer conscious.

However, the "person" of the Holy Spirit in the Course is also accorded an essential part in the process of salvation. We have discussed already how the Holy Spirit is not really a *person*, as the term is usually defined. Rather, the Holy Spirit is the pure and abstract Thought of love that is always present in our separated minds. Yet, as we have observed, *A Course in Miracles* has been written at a level that we can understand and use. To quote from the Course in another context:

> This does not necessarily mean that this is the highest level of communication of which he [the receiver of the Atonement] is capable. It does mean, however, that it is the highest level of communication of which he is capable *now*. The whole aim of the miracle is to raise the level of communication, not to lower it by increasing fear (text, pp. 20f).

Therefore, similar to what we have seen in other contexts in the Course, the Holy Spirit is spoken of *as if* He were a Person: loving, guiding, and teaching us in the form of a Voice in our minds. This is necessary for us who have been brought up to believe in God as an anthropocentric being, with all the attributes of our ideal of the perfect Father. So too with the Holy Spirit. The Course, coming to us on the ego level at which we function, uses the language and conceptual framework belonging to that level. However, when one carefully examines the metaphysical basis for its teachings, as we have been doing throughout this book, one can recognize the metaphoric nature of the Course's presentation. We shall return to this theme in Chapter 19, which deals with the mistakes that have already arisen regarding the Course, both in conceptual understanding and practical application.

Thus, speaking on the level on which the Course *is* written, we may say that the Holy Spirit is our savior, for this Thought of perfect love is what saves us from the ego's belief that our sin of separation from God is truly irreparable, love having been forever banished from our minds. The Holy Spirit is the experienced evidence that this has not occurred, and represents what the Course, again, refers to as the principle of the Atonement. However, His help is not magically dispensed to us; rather His Voice is continually urging us to make another choice, for He does not and cannot make the choice for us. His is the Voice that speaks to us of truth, gently explaining--in the face of the ego's loud and recurring voice of sin, guilt, and fear--that the separation never occurred. Thus, for example, the Holy Spirit's gentleness does not "fight back":

> The Voice of the Holy Spirit does not command, because it is

incapable of arrogance. It does not demand, because it does not seek control. It does not overcome, because it does not attack. It merely reminds. It is compelling only because of what it reminds you *of*. It brings to your mind the other way, remaining quiet even in the midst of the turmoil you may make. The Voice for God is always quiet, because it speaks of peace (text, p. 70).

In this sense the Holy Spirit is a "passive" presence in our minds because, as there is nothing that has to be done, He does not actively do anything. Salvation is achieved simply by the quiet recognition or remembrance that there is nothing from which we have to be saved. Nothing has happened. At one point the Course says of its means of attaining the goal of peace:

... when the goal is finally achieved ... it always comes with just one happy realization; *"I need do nothing"* (text, p. 363).

In the context of healing, the Course teaches:

To them [those who believe they are sick] God's teachers come, to represent another choice which they had forgotten. The simple presence of a teacher of God is a reminder. ... As God's messengers, His teachers are the symbols of salvation. ... They stand for the Alternative. With God's Word in their minds they come in benediction, not to heal the sick but to remind them of the remedy God has already given them. It is not their hands that heal. It is not their voice that speaks the Word of God. They merely give what has been given them. ... And they remind him [their sick brother] that he did not make himself, and must remain as God created him (manual, p. 18).

This, then, is the principle of the Holy Spirit, and we are asked as His messengers in the world to be this simple reminder for others. We shall return to this theme at the end of this chapter, and again in more depth in the following chapter when we discuss what it means to be a teacher of God.

To summarize, then, the Holy Spirit is our savior by representing the Atonement principle. His presence of love in our minds is the proof that the separation from love could not have occurred. We thus become a savior to each other by demonstrating this principle of total forgiveness: There is nothing to forgive because nothing happened. It is only the ego's tale that speaks of "something" happening, what it calls sin. The Holy Spirit's gentle Voice speaks only of the love of Heaven that could never be shattered by the sin that would render the Son homeless. Our one responsibility then is to accept the truth about who we are. It is this the Course refers to in its reiteration of our "sole responsibility," which receives its first statement in this form:

471

> The sole responsibility of the miracle worker is to accept the Atonement for himself (text, p. 22, italics omitted).

However, *A Course in Miracles* also explains that the separated world needed a concrete manifestation of this principle, for while the Atonement came into existence with the creation of the Holy Spirit (text, p. 68), some figure within the Son's dream had to represent it for us:

> The Atonement *principle* was in effect long before the Atonement began. The principle was love and the Atonement was an *act* of love. Acts were not necessary before the separation, because belief in space and time did not exist. It was only after the separation that the Atonement and the conditions necessary for its fulfillment were planned (text, p. 16).

The life of Jesus was this "act of love," for he was the "thought" within the separated mind that first remembered its relationship with God and Identity as Christ (along with the rest of the Sonship). He has been "placed" by the Holy Spirit as head of the overall plan, in charge of the Sonship and the Atonement. We may note at this point that all the Course's statements about Jesus come directly in the first person (i.e., Jesus himself being the speaker), except for three sections in the manual for teachers where Jesus is spoken about in the third person, as in the following quote:

> [The Holy Spirit] has established Jesus as the leader in carrying out His plan [of the Atonement] since he was the first to complete his own part perfectly. . . . The Atonement principle was given to the Holy Spirit long before Jesus set it in motion (manual, p. 85).

To continue this idea, we find elsewhere in the Course Jesus saying:

> I am in charge of the process of Atonement, which I undertook to begin. . . . I am the Atonement (text, pp. 6f).

Incidentally, the Course is here clearly speaking metaphorically, as if the Holy Spirit were the Commander-in-Chief of the troops, appointing Jesus to be His General. In reality of course this "appointment" occurred on quite a different level, since there is no time and all of what we know of time is happening in this one instant, *now*. The one we call Jesus is also existing within that instant. Moreover, as already discussed, there is no world at all, only outpictures of thoughts which are all present simultaneously: "There is no world! This is the central thought the course attempts to teach" (workbook, p. 237).

Jesus thus, as the thought of perfect love, is the light of that love shining throughout the mind of the Sonship, bearing a message different from the world's manifestations of the ego's voice. The Voice of the Holy Spirit that ontologically spoke to the Son is now given a specific name and form: Jesus, who walked the land of Palestine almost two thousand years ago. To say any more is to inhabit the world of myth: God *sending* His Son into the world, Jesus *choosing* the crucifixion as a means of teaching the invulnerability of love, or any of the countless theories about him--all miss the point if taken *literally*, in reality, for they speak of Jesus as if he actually lived in a world of time and space. He did not truly live, we do not truly live, because individual existence is part of the ego's magic show. *Within* such a magical world the various myths about Jesus play an important role, and the Course's version, by virtue of the consistency of its message, comes closest to the meaning of the truth reflected in that life we identify as Jesus. On this level, then, Jesus too is our savior, because he lived out before our dreaming eyes the principle of the Atonement. We return to this point later in the chapter.

We now begin our discussion of Jesus with the origin of *A Course in Miracles* itself. As was mentioned in the Preface, it was Jesus' voice which was "heard" by the scribe Helen Schucman, dictating the Course to her over a seven-year period. Again, much of the material is written in the first person and, whether or not a reader accepts Jesus as the source, it is clear that that is how the Course presents itself, not to mention it being an important part of Helen's own experience. Controversy about Jesus as the source of the material is ultimately meaningless because, in the end, as we have just seen, we are merely speaking of a symbol, just as our individual identities are symbols; he being a symbol of love and, for the most part, our personalities being symbols of guilt and fear.

We thus find the same issue present with the figure of Jesus as we found with the Holy Spirit, for the Course basically presents Jesus within the framework of the two-thousand-year tradition. Many passages specifically address the crucifixion and resurrection, or refer to words Jesus supposedly "said" as reported in the four gospels, correcting what from the perspective of the Course are serious misunderstandings of the original message he presented to the world. Therefore, because it meets our need on this level of Christian symbolism, it is important to work with the Course at the level on which it is written, just as the Course itself chooses to remain within its own context: ". . . we will not go beyond the names the course itself employs" (manual, p. 83). To skip over such a need and solution will simply perpetuate the problem through denial, not solve it. However, on the metaphysical level it is nonetheless important that we remain consistent, recognizing that Jesus too is a symbol. We shall have more to say regarding this issue in Part III when we compare the Course with Platonism, Christianity, and Gnosticism. Ultimately it makes no difference whether one believes in this or any other specific expression of the thought of Atonement. What *does* matter, however, is the acceptance of this thought in whatever form one *can* accept. The "universal course" the Course refers to in the manual, already quoted in the Preface, is the remembering of perfect love. Jesus represents a specific expression of this love, and *A Course in Miracles* represents a still more specific expression of his teaching.

Throughout the Course, Jesus speaks of himself as being no different from all of us, except in time. He is basically presented as having separated with the rest of the Sonship--the Son's mind being unified-- but the first to have awakened from the dream of separation by remembering his Identity as Christ. In other words, he has already completed the Atonement path that all of us must complete in time. There has been a continual unofficial discussion within some of the traditional Churches as to when in his life Jesus actually knew who he was (the Christ). Similarly, a student of *A Course in Miracles* may wonder when in his Palestinian incarnation, or "earlier," did Jesus "remember to laugh" and awaken from the dream. The discussion of course is intrinsically meaningless, because there is no time in which to remember, and we are simply talking about different aspects of the one illusion of time's linearity. From our previous discussion of time, all we can truly say is that Jesus represents the fragment of the Son's mind that listened to the Holy Spirit and "remembered to laugh." That fragment's life as Jesus reflects the *ongoing* choice to deny the reality of the ego's story, joining instead with the presence of love that awakens us from the dream. Thus the Course would take strong exception to the Church doctrine of the Incarnation, wherein the perfect God sends His perfect Son into the world, through the virgin birth. Regarding this teaching, referring to the famous prologue to John's gospel, the Course states:

> The Bible says, "The word (or thought) was made flesh." Strictly speaking this is impossible, since it seems to involve the translation of one order of reality into another. Different orders of reality merely appear to exist.... Thought cannot be made into flesh except by belief, since thought is not physical. Yet thought is communication, for which the body *can* be used. This is the only natural use to which it can be put. To use the body unnaturally is to lose sight of the Holy Spirit's purpose, and thus to confuse the goal of His curriculum (text, p. 141).

Jesus is therefore not the exclusive Christ of traditional Christianity, but a part of that one Self of which we all are a part; he, however, to

474

state it once again, is the name given to that fragment of the whole who first remembered who he was. The Course states:

> The name of *Jesus* is the name of one who was a man but saw the face of Christ [the symbol of forgiveness] in all his brothers and remembered God. So he became identified with Christ, a man no longer, but at one with God. . . . In his complete identification with the Christ—the perfect Son of God . . . Jesus became what all of you must be. He led the way for you to follow him. He leads you back to God because he saw the road before him, and he followed it. . . . Is he the Christ? O yes, along with you (manual, p. 83).

Jesus consistently teaches in the Course that he is no different from us in reality, but in the illusory and symbolic world of time he can be our teacher and guide if we so allow him. He is our

> elder brother . . . entitled to respect for his greater experience, and obedience for his greater wisdom. He is also entitled to love because he is a brother, and to devotion if he is devoted. It is only my devotion that entitles me to yours. There is nothing about me that you cannot attain. I have nothing that does not come from God. The difference between us now is that I have nothing else. . . . I bridge the distance [between ourselves and God] as an elder brother to you on the one hand, and as a Son of God on the other (text, p. 5).

In this sense, then, Jesus is unlike us in having no ego thoughts of separation--guilt, fear, or attack--to cloud his mind of the clear light of Christ. He is a pure manifestation of this clarity, for only the love of Christ is present in his mind. Therefore, while Jesus walked this illusory earth Christ's love was the only source of his actions. That is why he is described as being the manifestation of the Holy Spirit (manual, p. 85). Jesus thus reflects into the separated mind--of which he too is a part--this living witness to the love of God that we have never left. He, like the Holy Spirit, is the link back to God: the way, the truth, and the life that is described in the Bible. Therefore:

> It means that in remembering Jesus you are remembering God. The whole relationship of the Son to the Father lies in him. His part in the Sonship is also yours, and his completed learning guarantees your own success. . . . The Name of Jesus Christ as such is but a symbol. But it stands for love that is not of this world. . . . It becomes the shining symbol for the Word of God, so close to what it stands for that the little space between the two is lost, the moment that the Name is called to mind. . . . Jesus has led the way. . . . in his eyes your loveliness is so complete and flawless that he sees in it an image of his Father. . . . [He is] one who laid all limits by, and went beyond the farthest reach of

learning. He will take you with him, for he did not go alone.... Jesus has come to answer yours [need]. In him you find God's Answer. Do you, then, teach with him, for he is with you; he is always here (manual, pp. 55f).

When we examine the life and teachings of Jesus as understood through the Course, we can see how he specifically addressed the problem of the separation and resultant guilt, and provided its solution. In my earlier book I discussed the misunderstandings of his message, and how these evolved into a theology of suffering, sacrifice, and guilt, which only served to reinforce the very mistake that was Jesus' purpose to correct. In his words and actions he demonstrated that the phenomenal world, along with all its consequences, was inherently illusory and not at all what it seemed. His total forgiveness was the conclusive witness to the causelessness of the world of sin. Undoing sin's effects he demonstrated sin could not be a cause, and therefore could not exist. Thus were all sins forgiven, and the ego's fundamental premise along with it.[19] In other words, Jesus is the name we give to that part of the Sonship who knew the separation was illusory, thus manifesting the Atonement principle: the total unreality of separation and guilt. The realization of this truth is the end product of forgiveness, symbolized in the Course by seeing the "face of Christ" in another.

To state the meaning of Jesus' life another way, and as has been discussed elsewhere,[20] Jesus exemplified the principle of the Atonement by directly refuting the ego's original tale to the Son of sin, guilt, and fear, and the need for projection and attack as defense against God's wrath. Within the dream, the memory of God's love the Course calls the Holy Spirit extended into the Son's mind as an ongoing correction for the ego's thoughts. The crucifixion and resurrection of Jesus thus became this behavioral correction: the symbolic form in which the Holy Spirit's thought manifested itself in the dream as the undoing of the Son's belief that the love of God could be destroyed.

Recall still again the ego's story: The Son sins against his Father, for which he feels guilty and then fearful of the Father's retaliatory punishment. To escape this vengeance, the Son makes a world and flees into the body. However, not fully believing in the efficacy of the body as a defense, he then seeks to punish his body through sacrificial suffering as proof to God of his contrition, thereby hoping to ward off

---

19. For a more extensive discussion of the principle of cause and effect, and its connection with the redeeming role of Jesus in the Holy Spirit's plan of salvation, see *Forgiveness and Jesus*, pp. 64-70; 208-33.

20. See *Awaken from the Dream*, pp. 129-33.

the punishment of Heaven. Thus the ego's plan for salvation is this life of punishment and pain to appease the wrath of God, whose vengeance is justified by our original sin against Him. A world of attack and defense, of suffering and sacrifice, is the expression of this plan, all of which is symbolized in the Course by the term "crucifixion." Finally, the ego convinces us that we, and not others, are justified in seeing ourselves as victims. We are innocent for *we* have suffered, not by our own choices but by the actions of others. The ultimate paradigm for the victimizer, of course, is God, for within the ego's insanity He is perceived as the great enemy who has caused our distress. This thought system is the foundation for the making and sustaining of the world; and each who seems to inhabit a body here, separate from all other bodies, carries within the fragmented mind this microcosm of a thought system.

As we have seen, however, along with this thought system is its correction, which Jesus manifested in his death and resurrection. Of his crucifixion, Jesus says in the Course:

> The crucifixion is nothing more than an extreme example. . . . [Its] real meaning . . . lies in the *apparent* intensity of the assault of some of the Sons of God upon another. This, of course, is impossible, and must be fully understood *as* impossible. . . . The message the crucifixion was intended to teach was that it is not necessary to perceive any form of assault in persecution, because you cannot *be* persecuted. . . . I have made it perfectly clear that I am like you and you are like me. . . . You are free to perceive yourself as persecuted if you choose. When you do choose to react that way, however, you might remember that I was persecuted as the world judges, and did not share this evaluation for myself. . . . I therefore offered a different interpretation of attack, and one which I want to share with you. . . . I elected, for your sake and mine, to demonstrate that the most outrageous assault, as judged by the ego, does not matter. As the world judges these things, but not as God knows them, I was betrayed, abandoned, beaten, torn, and finally killed. . . . My one lesson, which I must teach as I learned it, is that no perception that is out of accord with the judgment of the Holy Spirit can be justified. I undertook to show this was true in an extreme case, merely because it would serve as a good teaching aid to those whose temptation to give in to anger and assault would not be so extreme. . . . The message of the crucifixion is perfectly clear: *"Teach only love, for that is what you are"* (text, pp. 84-87).

Jesus' crucifixion, therefore, became the world's greatest manifestation of the Holy Spirit's Atonement principle: the invulnerability of God's love. For what, then, must the world's reaction be when confronted by this perfect manifestation of God's love? Recall the

Allegory of the Cave, and Plato's similar question concerning the freed prisoner's return to the dark cave with his message of light and truth. And so Jesus, himself such a messenger, states of himself in the Course:

> Many thought I was attacking them, even though it was apparent I was not. . . . What you must recognize is that when you do not share a thought system, you are weakening it. Those who believe in it therefore perceive this as an attack on them. This is because everyone identifies himself with his thought system, and every thought system centers on what you believe you are (text, p. 98).

The outcome thus was inevitable, given the ego's attraction to the dynamics of guilt and fear:

> To the ego, *the guiltless are guilty.* Those who do not attack are its "enemies" . . . . When it was confronted with the real guiltlessness of God's Son it did attempt to kill him [Jesus], and the reason it gave was that guiltlessness is blasphemous to God (text, p. 224).

Jesus' perfect defenselessness undid the root of the ego's thought system by showing that attack has no meaning. If attack had no power to destroy God's love, as manifested in Jesus, then the Son's seeming attack on God in the separation also had no effect. As he wrote in the Course at Christmas time:

> The Prince of Peace was born to re-establish the condition of love by teaching that communication remains unbroken even if the body is destroyed. . . . The lesson I was born to teach, and still would teach to all my brothers, is that sacrifice is nowhere and love is everywhere (text, pp. 305f).

The lie the ego tells the Son thus has been exposed to the light of truth, in which it must disappear.

Jesus, to state the point still another way, was simply the Voice of the Holy Spirit given form, so it could be heard. This is the meaning of the Course's statement, based upon the verses of the Acts of the Apostles (1:8f).

> Jesus is the manifestation of the *Holy Spirit,* Whom he called down upon the earth after he ascended into Heaven. . . . He [the Holy Spirit] was "called down upon the earth" in the sense that it was now possible to accept Him and to hear His Voice (manual, p. 85).

This brings us to the heart of the matter: the resurrection. Strictly speaking of course, there can be no physical resurrection. If the body is illusory, then obviously it does not live. We have already discussed in Chapter 14 how the body is nothing more than a puppet, whose strings are pulled by the mind. Thus the body not only does not live, but it obviously also cannot die. On the physical plane, life must automatically presuppose death. The body is the expression in form of the thought of separation, of sin, guilt, and fear. Since God and spirit alone are life, anything separate from God must be its opposite and therefore lifeless, as we also saw in Chapter 14. Therefore, if the body does not live, it cannot die, and quite obviously then, it cannot come back to life or resurrect. The very term makes no sense.

Restating the issue, it is not the body that is the problem, but the mind that has *conceived* the body in the first place, and then made the body to be the locus of sin and thus the object of salvation. The Son has again fallen into the ego trap of being distracted from where the problem truly is, as well as the corresponding solution. Resurrection thus has meaning only within the mind that has believed that it is capable of dying. If crucifixion is the tale of guilt, attack, and death the Son believed in, then resurrection is the change of mind that accepts the Holy Spirit's truth instead. It is the remembrance in the Son's mind of the love that was always there:

> Very simply, the resurrection is the overcoming or surmounting of death. It is a reawakening or a rebirth; a change of mind about the meaning of the world. It is the acceptance of the Holy Spirit's interpretation of the world's purpose; the acceptance of the Atonement for oneself. . . . the single desire of the Son for the Father (manual, p. 65).

> Your resurrection is your reawakening. I am the model for rebirth, but rebirth itself is merely the dawning on your mind of what is already in it. God placed it there Himself, and so it is true forever. I believed in it, and therefore accepted it as true for me (text, p. 86).

Thus as the Gnostics taught almost two thousand years earlier, the Course would have us learn that the resurrection of Jesus occurred *before* the crucifixion. It was Jesus' "remembering to laugh" at the silliness of the ego's tale that enabled him to be the defenseless manifestation of the Holy Spirit's truth, not making real the error of believing in separation and attack. It is this defenselessness in the face of apparent attack--the basis for forgiveness--that was his ultimate message to the world. It is the lived message that allows the Son's fragmented mind to begin the process of remembering its Identity as the wholeness of Christ. As Jesus asks of us:

> Teach not that I died in vain. Teach rather that I did not die by demonstrating that I live in you (text, p. 193).

We demonstrate Jesus' resurrection by exemplifying its principle of total forgiveness. Thus is the world truly redeemed from the thought system that never was, as we remember at last the love that we truly are. Jesus symbolizes this love for us in our separated mind, and *our* resurrection is simply awakening to the truth of the Atonement that has always been present.

Chapter 17

PRACTICAL IMPLICATIONS

One of the unique qualities of *A Course in Miracles* is its strict consistency, from the underlying non-dualistic metaphysical principles to its discussion of our experience in the physical world. This consistency is the reflection of the logic on which the Course builds its theory, summed up succinctly in the introduction to the text, a passage quoted earlier:

> Nothing real can be threatened.
> Nothing unreal exists.
> Herein lies the peace of God.
> (text, intro.)

God and Christ alone are real, and therefore cannot be threatened by the "tiny, mad idea" of separation that is not of God, and so cannot be real and does not exist. *Any* and *every* problem thus must also be non-existent, since a problem in the presence of God is inconceivable: "There is no time, no place, no state where God is absent" (text, p. 563). The true "problem," then, must lie in the *belief* that there is a problem. In other words, the problem is the way that I am *perceiving* an apparent problem in the world (which includes my personal physical and/or psychological world). The direct implication of this principle for the solution to our perceived problems is the subject of this chapter.

We begin by returning to the story that the ego told the Son, restating it in terms relevant to this discussion. The ego convinced the Son that he was in a problematic situation, and a serious one at that. This problem the ego called sin, which was projected on to God, so that His avenging wrath now became the problem requiring immediate solution or defense. As *A Course in Miracles* would have us understand, all defenses are forms of magic, being the ego's attempts to provide a solution to a problem that simply does not exist. From that moment on, the ego's strategy became to perpetuate the illusion in the Son's mind of real problems that required real solutions. However, the ego did not want the Son to know that his only problem was *believing* in a non-existent situation; his mistaken way of looking at the "tiny, mad idea." Thus, taken in by the ego, the Son is continually convinced that his problem is outside his mind, in the body--whether his or someone else's is irrelevant. Once believing that his problems are in the world (made real by the ego thought system), the Son must also believe it is in the world of form and behavior that solutions (or salvation) are to be found.

481

This chapter is organized around the two classes of solutions that religions or spiritualities have typically advocated as salvation: the practice of sacraments and rituals, and ethical norms. The underlying premise in all solutions, stated or unstated, is that God is angry and must be appeased before His wrath destroys us. Thus in one sense, *all* religious practices and rituals are magical attempts to strike a bargain with God. They are statements that if we offer to God our suffering, sorrow, and sacrifice, He will forgive and love us. Thus the underlying *content* behind the *form* of religious devotion is this bargain or sacrifice, which serves only to convince us that the problem of separation is real (otherwise there would be no need for the bargain). Likewise with systems of morality, which attempt to govern our problematic behavior so that the underlying thought of separation in the mind is left untouched and unhealed.

Religious Practice

Many passages in the Course are subtly aimed at the sacraments and teachings found in the Roman Catholic Church, and illustrate this confusion of form with content that had turned a message of love into one of special love: the triumph of form over content. It is certainly true that since the Second Vatican Council, convened by Pope John XXIII in 1962, major changes have occurred within the Church regarding the practice surrounding some of these sacraments. Nonetheless, the basic premises underlying them have not been seriously questioned, certainly not in official channels. We now examine these references in the Course which are aimed at the official Church dogmas and teachings.

1. Eucharist

The most important sacrament to the Roman Catholic of course is the Eucharist, which is the heart of the celebration of Mass. It refers specifically to that part of the ritual when the priest consecrates the bread and wine on the altar. These are transubstantiated into the literal body and blood of Jesus, constituting the *Real Presence* of the risen Lord referred to as the Blessed Sacrament. This "Presence" is then ingested by those properly prepared for the sacred ritual, thereby achieving communion with Jesus' body. On another level, the Mass re-enacts the sacrifice and death of Jesus which gave salvation to the world, atoning for the world's sin by repaying the Father through the crucified Lord's blood. Thus the Eucharist is frequently referred to as the Holy Sacrifice of the Mass: daily is Jesus sacrificed at the altar, vicariously bringing salvation to the faithful. One product of the Protestant Reformation, incidentally, was the reinterpretation of the Mass into a *symbolic* re-enactment of the crucifixion and joining with Jesus; a shift which brings the ritual more in harmony with the principles of the Course by shifting the emphasis from the *form* to the *content* of joining in communion with Jesus.

While *A Course in Miracles* was being taken down by Helen Schucman, Jesus frequently expanded on some of the teachings that would be personally meaningful and helpful to her and William Thetford. Because many of these comments were meant for them alone, and not for the general readership, they were removed before publication. These included some specific references to Catholicism, for since her early childhood Helen had been an ambivalent observer of the Roman Catholic Church, and at different times in her life a regular attender (though not participant) at Mass. She never believed or subscribed to the teachings of the Church, yet found herself strangely fascinated by its rituals and often drawn to them.[21] Jesus made several comments to her bearing on the particular sacrament of the Eucharist, and these are quoted now, appearing for the first time in print:

> The idea of cannibalism in connection with the [Blessed] Sacrament is a reflection of a distorted view of sharing. I told you before that the word "thirst" in connection with the Spirit was used in the Bible because of limited understanding of those to whom I spoke. I also told you not to use it.

> I do not want to share my body in communion because this is to share nothing. Would I try to share an illusion with the most holy children of a most holy Father? But I do want to share my mind with you. ... Yet would I offer you my body, you whom I love, knowing its littleness? Or would I teach that bodies cannot keep us apart? Mine was of no greater value than yours. ... Communion comes with peace, and peace must transcend the body.

Many passages in the Course also reflect this association of the Mass with sacrifice and reification of the body. Perhaps the strongest are those dealing with special relationships, which glorify form at the expense of content. The language here is deliberately reminiscent of the Church ritual, for the heart of the special relationship is the secret wish to kill God so that the ego may live. It is this secret wish that also lies within the specific form of the special relationship expressed in the

---

21. For a fuller discussion of Helen and her religious experiences, *see* my *Absence from Felicity*.

sacrifice of the Mass. I might mention here that participation in the sacraments, or any formal means of worship or ritual, is directly antithetical to the study and practice of the Course--*if one believes that the form of the ritual is salvific*--for by affirming that spirit can exist in form, one makes real the error of believing in the reality of the world. Several passages in the Course reflect, directly or indirectly, this mistake of ritualization, and we shall return to these in a separate section below. The mistake is more usually spoken of in the Course as the confusion of form with content, most clearly seen in the discussion of special love relationships, where the content of hate and guilt is concealed behind the form of love. These passages, as seen in some representative examples, clearly demonstrate the Course's writing on different levels, so that those with eyes to see and ears to hear may understand:

> Knowing His Son as he is, you realize that the Atonement, not sacrifice, is the only appropriate gift for God's altar, where nothing except perfection belongs (text, p. 34).

> Suffering and sacrifice are the gifts with which the ego would "bless" all unions. And those who are united at its altar accept suffering and sacrifice as the price of union.... The central theme in its litany to sacrifice is that God must die so you can live. And it is this theme that is acted out in the special relationship. Through the death of your self you think you can attack another self, and snatch it from the other to replace the self that you despise.... You think it safer to endow the little self you made with power you wrested from truth, triumphing over it and leaving it helpless. See how exactly is this ritual enacted in the special relationship. An altar is erected in between two separate people, on which each seeks to kill his self, and on his body raise another self to take its power from his death. Over and over and over this ritual is enacted. And it is never completed, nor ever will be completed. The ritual of completion cannot complete, for life arises not from death, nor Heaven from hell.... The special relationship is a ritual of form, aimed at raising the form to take the place of God at the expense of content. There is no meaning in the form, and there will never be. The special relationship must be recognized for what it is; a senseless ritual in which strength is extracted from the death of God, and invested in His killer as the sign that form has triumphed over content, and love has lost its meaning (text, pp. 296,319f).

By its very nature, the special relationship altar of the Mass must exclude those that are not confessed believers in Jesus, which fact belies the seeming love of Jesus' "sacrifice" that in truth would only unify. This exclusion exposes the ego's avenging desire to separate, and therefore kill, that *is* the content underlying the form of the ritual, as the above passage describes. The distorted communion of the body obviously denies the true communion with the love in Jesus' *mind* that comes by joining with others in the forgiveness found in the holy relationship. This true joining is expressed in the following passage:

> Love, too, would set a feast before you, on a table covered with a spotless cloth. . . . This is a feast that honors your holy relationship, and at which *everyone* is welcomed as an honored guest. And in a holy instant grace is said by everyone together, as they join in gentleness before the table of communion. And I [Jesus] will join you there, as long ago I promised and promise still. For in your new relationship am I made welcome. And where I am made welcome, there I am. . . . Salvation is looked upon as a way by which the Son of God was killed instead of you. Yet no one can die for anyone, and death does not atone for sin. . . . Communion . . . goes beyond guilt, because it goes beyond the body (text, pp. 383f, my italics).

2. Martyrdom

Though not a sacrament, the practice and tradition of martyrdom has always been central to orthodox Christian teaching, being the ideal way of identifying with the sacrificial suffering and death of Jesus that is commemorated in the Mass. We have already explored the Church's position *vis à vis* the Gnostics who, for the most part, downplayed the historical life of Jesus, and therefore felt martyrdom missed the whole point and was essentially irrelevant. *A Course in Miracles* makes several direct references to this tradition. Early in the text, in the context of his crucifixion and not seeing God's children as sinners deserving of punishment, Jesus says: "I do not call for martyrs but for teachers" (text, p. 88). Later he states: "I have emphasized many times that the Holy Spirit will never call upon you to sacrifice anything"; the attitude of the martyr of course is that "God demands sacrifice. . . . [and] is crucifying him" (text, p. 150).

In back of this strange belief that suffering is salvation lies the unconscious desire to blame others for the suffering that can come only from our own decisions. Two sections especially treat this powerful theme, "The Picture of Crucifixion" and "Self Concept versus Self." We present brief excerpts from these, illustrating this choice for martyrdom as a means of punishing another, thereby escaping our own condemnation and reinforcing the ego's defensive system of denial and projection. Our suffering body thus accuses another and becomes "martyred to his guilt":

> . . . every pain you suffer do you see as proof that he [your brother]

485

is guilty of attack. . . . Wish not to make yourself a living symbol of his guilt, for you will not escape the death you made for him. . . . Whenever you consent to suffer pain, to be deprived, unfairly treated or in need of anything, you but accuse your brother of attack upon God's Son. You hold a picture of your crucifixion before his eyes, that he may see his sins are writ in Heaven in your blood and death, and go before him, closing off the gate and damning him to hell. . . . A sick and suffering you but represents your brother's guilt; the witness that you send lest he forget the injuries he gave, from which you swear he never will escape. This sick and sorry picture *you* accept, if only it can serve to punish him (text, pp. 525f).

We then adopt a "face of innocence," wherein we escape our own responsibility for hatred, blaming others for having forced us to become angry. We discussed this in Chapter 15, and amplify on it now:

This aspect [of our self concept] can grow angry, for the world is wicked and unable to provide the love and shelter innocence deserves. . . . The face of innocence the concept of the self so proudly wears can tolerate attack in self-defense, for is it not a well-known fact the world deals harshly with defenseless innocence?

But beneath this face lies another, which holds the betrayal that is the true source of our guilt: our secret wish to attack others through our martyrdom as a means of escaping responsibility for our pain, and ultimately for our separation from God:

Beneath the face of innocence there is a lesson that the concept of the self was made to teach. It is a lesson in a terrible displacement [i.e., projection], and a fear so devastating that the face that smiles above it must forever look away, lest it perceive the treachery it hides. The lesson teaches this: "I am the thing you made of me, and as you look on me, you stand condemned because of what I am." . . . If you can be hurt by anything, you see a picture of your secret wishes. . . . And in your suffering of any kind you see your own concealed desire to kill (text, pp. 610-13).

In "The Song of Prayer," companion pamphlet to the Course, we also read of

those who seek the role of martyr at another's hand. Here must the aim be clearly seen, for this may pass as meekness and as charity instead of cruelty. Is it not kind to be accepting of another's spite, and not respond except with silence and a gentle smile? Behold, how good are you who bear with patience and with saintliness the anger and the hurt another gives, and do not show the bitter pain you feel.

... [This face of innocence] shows the face of suffering and pain, in silent proof of guilt and of the ravages of sin ("The Song of Prayer," p. 12).

Martyrdom, thus, far from being a witness (the etymological root of "martyr") to forgiveness and love, has in fact witnessed to the hatred of the ego. It has "given up" nothing, but rather has unconsciously reinforced the ego's defensive system against the very love it seeks to emulate. One is reminded of William Thackeray's apothegm in *The History of Henry Esmond*: "'Tis not the dying for a faith that's so hard ...every man of every nation has done that--'tis the living up to it that's difficult."

3. Holy Structures

Logically following from the Roman Catholic Church's confusion of form with content, as seen in its sacraments and rituals, is the tremendous emphasis traditionally placed by all Christian Churches on "holy" structures such as churches, altars, shrines, etc. The notion that the Bible is God's *only* book also falls into this category of worshipping a *form* of truth at the expense of *content*. As we saw in the exclusive practice of Communion, we can also recognize love's distortions in the contradictions found in the Bible itself, not to mention in the centuries of bloodshed committed in the name of God, venerated through His "Holy Word" which had to be affirmed lest He or His self-appointed defenders would wreak punishment on all non-believers. The reader may recall the discussion in Chapter 3 of justification for such unchristian actions based on the Johannine writings.

One of the key scriptural passages repeatedly cited by Christians to substantiate this deification of the ego's world is St. Paul's reference to the body as the temple of the Holy Spirit (1 Co 6:19). Referring to this famous teaching, the Course states in the context of the "distorted belief that the body can be used as a means for attaining 'atonement'":

Perceiving the body as a temple is only the first step in correcting this distortion, because it alters only part of it. It *does* recognize that Atonement in physical terms is impossible. The next step, however, is to realize that a temple is not a structure at all. Its true holiness lies at the inner altar around which the structure is built. The emphasis on beautiful structures is a sign of the fear of Atonement, and an unwillingness to reach the altar itself. The real beauty of the temple cannot be seen with the physical eye.... For perfect effectiveness the Atonement belongs at the center of the inner altar, where it undoes the separation and restores the wholeness of the mind (text, p. 18).

The Course later deepens this teaching by denoting the temple of the Holy Spirit as the holy relationship. We may note here another example of the Course's references to the sacraments of the Catholic Church. The recurrent word "mystery" in the following passage is a clear reference to Church usage, and we also find a subtle reference to the Blessed Sacrament--the *body* of Christ--kept locked in a tabernacle and worshipped and "perceived in awe and held in reverence":

> Love has no darkened temples where mysteries are kept obscure and hidden from the sun. . . . The Holy Spirit's temple is not a body, but a relationship. The body is an isolated speck of darkness; a hidden secret room, a tiny spot of senseless mystery, a meaningless enclosure carefully protected, yet hiding nothing. . . . Here it [the unholy relationship] is "safe," for here love cannot enter. The Holy Spirit does not build His temples where love can never be. Would He Who sees the face of Christ choose as His home the only place in all the universe where it can not be seen?
>
> You cannot make the body the Holy Spirit's temple, and it will never be the seat of love. It is the home of the idolater, and of love's condemnation. For here is love made fearful and hope abandoned. Even the idols that are worshipped here are shrouded in mystery, and kept apart from those who worship them. This is the temple dedicated to no relationships. . . . Here is the "mystery" of separation perceived in awe and held in reverence. What God would have *not* be is here kept "safe" from Him (text, p. 407).

An altar therefore is defined, not by its form but by its content: "Altars are beliefs" (text, p. 102), and earlier:

> The Voice for God comes from your own altars to Him. These altars are not things; they are devotions. Yet you have other devotions now [i.e., to the ego]. Your divided devotion has given you the two voices, and you must choose at which altar you want to serve (text, p. 70).

A church too is redefined in the Course in terms of its purpose, having nothing at all to do with a formal structure. The context of this passage is Jesus' gospel words to Peter that the *apostle* will be the rock on which he shall build his church (Mt 16:18):

> . . . it is still on them [my brothers] that I must build my church. There is no choice in this, because only you can be the foundation of God's church. A church is where an altar is, and the presence of the altar is what makes the church holy. A church that does not inspire love has a hidden altar that is not serving the purpose for which God intended it. I must found His church on you, because those who accept me as a model are literally my disciples (text, p. 86).

In contrast, the ego's church is founded upon sin, and the existence of the traditional Christian churches would be inconceivable without it. As the Course states:

> There is no stone in all the ego's embattled citadel more heavily defended than the idea that sin is real; the natural expression of what the Son of God has made himself to be, and what he is. . . . Sin is but error in a special form the ego venerates. It would preserve all errors and make them sins. For here is its own stability, its heavy anchor in the shifting world it made; the rock on which its church is built, and where its worshippers are bound to bodies, believing the body's freedom is their own (text, pp. 376,442).

We shall expand on this error of making sin real in Part III.

Finally, we cite one of the poems Helen Schucman had taken down, "Dedication for an Altar," which nicely expresses the true nature of a temple (church) and its altar:

> Temples are where God's holy altars are,
> And He has placed an altar in each Son
> Whom He created. Let us worship here
> In thankfulness that what He gives to one
> He gives to all, and never takes away.
> For what He wills has been forever done.
>
> Temples are where a brother comes to pray
> And rest a while. Whoever he may be,
> He brings with him a lighted lamp to show
> My Savior's [Christ's] face is there for me to see
> Upon the altar, and remember God.
> My brother, come and worship here with me [Jesus].
> (*The Gifts of God*, p. 93)

4. Penance

Another Catholic sacrament that *A Course in Miracles* discusses, albeit in veiled terms, is Penance (also known as the Sacrament of Reconciliation, and popularly referred to as Confession). The Course's criticisms are essentially two-fold: The first is that the attitude towards forgiveness is based upon the reality of sin, therefore requiring atonement and penance. This is the mistake the Course refers to as "making the error real," and leads to what is called in "The Song of Prayer" forgiveness-to-destroy. Second, the practice of the sacrament is based upon the power of the priest to administer the forgiveness of Heaven, as if: 1) there were indeed something to forgive; and 2) that the priest possessed some special power not given to anyone else. While clearly it is not the Church alone that has misunderstood forgiveness, the Course frequently utilizes Church language to make its more general point because of Christianity's tremendous influence in Western civilization. It is patently clear how the institutionalization of a theology of "forgiveness-to-destroy" justified countless wars that affected the course of Western history. We begin with a discussion of the traditional distortions of forgiveness:

> No gift of Heaven has been more misunderstood than has forgiveness. It has, in fact, become a scourge; a curse where it was meant to bless, a cruel mockery of grace, a parody upon the holy peace of God. ... Forgiveness-to-destroy ... suit[s] the purpose of the world far better than its true objective, and the honest means by which this goal is reached. Forgiveness-to-destroy will overlook no sin, no crime, no guilt that it can seek and find and "love." Dear to its heart is error, and mistakes loom large and grow and swell within its sight. It carefully picks out all evil things, and overlooks the loving as a plague ... ("The Song of Prayer," p. 9).

Forgiveness-to-destroy makes error real by asserting that the sin of separation against God has actually been accomplished. This is certainly not unfamiliar to us, for we recall the ego's original tale to the Son, the opposite to what the Holy Spirit's presence represented. As *A Course in Miracles* teaches:

> To sin would be to violate reality, and to succeed. Sin is the proclamation that attack is real and guilt is justified. It assumes the Son of God is guilty, and has thus succeeded in losing his innocence and making himself what God created not. Thus is creation seen as not eternal, and the Will of God open to opposition and defeat. Sin is the grand illusion underlying all the ego's grandiosity. ... Any attempt to reinterpret sin as error is always indefensible to the ego. The idea of sin is wholly sacrosanct to its thought system, and quite unapproachable except with reverence and awe. It is the most "holy" concept in the ego's system; lovely and powerful, wholly true, and necessarily protected with every defense at its disposal. For here lies its "best" defense, which all the others serve (text, p. 375).

Common to all forms of false forgiveness is the perception that separation is truth and that the unity of Christ is illusory. From such an unhealed mind, only attack can result, regardless of the form of forgiveness that is adopted:

> The unhealed cannot pardon. For they are the witnesses that pardon is unfair. They would retain the consequences of the guilt they

overlook. Yet no one can forgive a sin that he believes is real. And what has consequences must be real, because what it has done is there to see. Forgiveness is not pity, which but seeks to pardon what it thinks to be the truth. Good cannot *be* returned for evil, for forgiveness does not first establish sin and then forgive it. Who can say and mean, "My brother, you have injured me, and yet, because I am the better of the two, I pardon you my hurt." His pardon and your hurt cannot exist together. One denies the other and must make it false (text, p. 528).

True forgiveness (pardon) on the other hand does not ask us

> to offer pardon where attack is due, and would be justified. For that would mean that you forgive a sin by overlooking what is really there. . . . You do not forgive the unforgivable, nor overlook a real attack that calls for punishment. Salvation does not lie in being asked to make unnatural responses which are inappropriate to what is real. Instead, it merely asks that you respond appropriately to what is not real by not perceiving what has not occurred. . . . Unjustified forgiveness is attack. And this is all the world can ever give. It pardons "sinners" sometimes, but remains aware that they have sinned. And so they do not merit the forgiveness that it gives.
> This is the false forgiveness which the world employs to keep the sense of sin alive (text, pp. 593f).

The ego's purpose of keeping sin real, and thus forever uncorrectable, is the premise underlying the Church position on the Sacrament of Penance. It is a practice that clearly serves the ego's defensive system. Sin can be punished or atoned for, yes, but this simply reinforces the guilt that something sinful has indeed been accomplished; and so the vicious cycle of sin, guilt, fear, and punishment remains inviolate. From this belief in the reality of sin, seen as outside the mind and therefore incapable of correction *by* the mind, results the inevitable "correction" which must then be seen as coming from the outside:

> The belief in sin is necessarily based on the firm conviction that. . . . the mind is guilty, and will forever so remain unless a mind not part of it can give it absolution (text, p. 374).

Forgiveness-to-destroy comes in many forms, and the one most relevant to our discussion is a person assuming the role of forgiver; this specialness of the forgiver in its Church form is the priest who grants absolution, the

> "better" person [who] deigns to stoop to save a "baser" one from what he truly is. Forgiveness here rests on an attitude of gracious

491

> lordliness so far from love that arrogance could never be dislodged.
> Who can forgive and yet despise? And who can tell another he is
> steeped in sin, and yet perceive him as the Son of God ("The Song of
> Prayer," pp. 11f).

"Psychotherapy," the second companion pamphlet to *A Course in Miracles*, reiterates the point in the context of the psychotherapist who must avoid the temptation of specialness, and instead truly join with the patient:

> For this, one thing and one thing only is required: The therapist in
> no way confuses himself with God. All "unhealed healers" make this
> fundamental confusion in one form or another, because they must
> regard themselves as self-created rather than God-created. ... he [the
> therapist] thought he was in charge of the therapeutic process, and
> was therefore responsible for its outcome. ... To understand there is
> no order of difficulty in healing, he must also recognize the equality
> of himself and the patient. There is no halfway point in this. Either
> they are equal or not ("Psychotherapy," pp. 14,20).

Clearly, however, one need not be a priest or therapist to demonstrate the arrogance of practicing forgiveness-to-destroy. The integrity of the ego's thought system rests on our all continuing to forgive the sin that really happened, regardless of our personal roles.

5. Prayer

Another important religious practice that has formed the heart of the Judaeo-Christian tradition is prayer. Here too we see that prayer in the usual sense--importuning God (or His representatives) to somehow make things come out all right--simply is another form of making the error real. This prayer is based on the assumption that there is a *real* problem *here*, that needs correction or "fixing" *here*. One does not need a doctorate in psychology to recognize that almost all prayer, directly or indirectly, is based upon an image of an anthropomorphic God who will magically meet our needs (grant requests to punish enemies, avert disasters, heal illness, bring material gains, etc.)--in other words, serving the role of the ideal parent none of us ever had. In this sense, certainly, Freud was correct in recognizing that our belief in God was a projection of our experience of our own parents--positively or negatively. Incidentally, while Freud was correct in terms of the ego's distortions of God, he missed the mark entirely by generalizing these distortions to *all* experiences of God. In truth, of course, our experiences of our parents, not to mention all relationships, are projections of our own deeply repressed experience of God.

A Course in Miracles' view of prayer logically follows from its metaphysical foundation. If there is no world outside of our collective mind, and no problem other than the *belief* that there is a problem, then prayer in the traditional sense is irrelevant. Why pray for something or for the amelioration of a condition that is inherently illusory? Our prayer, then, should be only for help in accepting the truth that is *already* there. In this sense, then, prayer is no different from forgiveness or the miracle, for they all reflect the process of undoing the ego thought system that never was, leaving to be itself the love of God that has always been. Prayer, therefore, is not *asking* for things or special favors. Rather it is an *attitude* of forgiveness, asking the Holy Spirit's help in joining with another in a holy relationship and correcting the special relationship that is the home of the ego's guilt.

The best account of the Course's view on prayer is found in "The Song of Prayer," where it is described as a ladder, the top rung being the true meaning of prayer--union with God:

> ... the single voice Creator and creation share; the song the Son sings to the Father, Who returns the thanks it offers Him unto the Son. ... The love they share is what all prayer will be throughout eternity ... ("The Song of Prayer," p. 1).

At the bottom of the ladder prayer "takes the form that best will suit your need," for the ladder reflects the *process* of prayer, "a way offered by the Holy Spirit to reach God." It is

> the means by which God's Son leaves separate goals and separate interests by, and turns in holy gladness to the truth of union in his Father and himself ("The Song of Prayer," p. 1).

Taking into consideration our discussion of the Holy Spirit in earlier chapters, we can better understand the meaning of certain passages in the Course that speak of the Holy Spirit's answering all of our needs:

> What could you not accept, if you but knew that everything that happens, all events, past, present and to come, are gently planned by One Whose only purpose is your good? Perhaps you have misunderstood His plan, for He would never offer pain to you. But your defenses did not let you see His loving blessing shine in every step you ever took (workbook, p. 247).

> The Holy Spirit will answer every specific problem as long as you believe that problems are specific. His answer is both many and one, as long as you believe that the One is many (text, p. 196).

And in this passage, derived in part from the famous passage in Isaiah 40:3, the Course states:

> Once you accept His plan as the one function that you would fulfill, there will be nothing else the Holy Spirit will not arrange for you without your effort. He will go before you making straight your path, and leaving in your way no stones to trip on, and no obstacles to bar your way. Nothing you need will be denied you. Not one seeming difficulty but will melt away before you reach it. You need take thought for nothing, careless of everything except the only purpose that you would fulfill. As that was given you, so will its fulfillment be. God's guarantee will hold against all obstacles, for it rests on certainty and not contingency. It rests on *you*. And what can be more certain than a Son of God? (text, p. 404)

A surface reading of such passages certainly leaves the impression of a personal God, or His Spirit, who magically fulfills our special needs, a "Sugar Daddy" whose love for us is measured by His beneficence. Clearly this is not the Course's teaching, as its metaphysical premise is that God does not even know about the dream. The workbook clearly states, for example:

> Think not He [God] hears the little prayers of those who call on Him with names of idols cherished by the world. They cannot reach Him thus. He cannot hear requests that He be not Himself, or that His Son receive another name than His. . . . Sit silently, and let His Name become the all-encompassing idea that holds your mind completely. Let all thoughts be still except this one. . . . Turn to the Name of God for your release, and it is given you. No prayer but this is necessary, for it holds them all within it. Words are insignificant, and all requests unneeded when God's Son calls on his Father's Name . . . (workbook, p. 335).

Thus, the above passages on the Holy Spirit's activity in our lives reflect, as we discussed in Chapter 12, the *experience* within our split minds of the abstract presence of God's love. The Holy Spirit's "plan" is the undoing, through His ongoing presence, of the ego's script of fear and pain. Our minds which are rooted in the ego's plan thus interpret *our* change of mind as being done for us by the Holy Spirit. Likewise, "God's guarantee . . . against all obstacles" reflects the care-free peace that inevitably follows the undoing of guilt by accepting "His plan." With guilt gone, the demand for punishment goes as well. Thus all seemingly outer events are perceived, following the Holy Spirit's judgment, as either expressions of love or calls for love (text, pp. 200-202,273), and God's certainty of us as His Son becomes our own as well.

Prayer, then, is content, not form--the content of love, our only purpose:

> Strictly speaking, words play no part at all in healing. The motivating factor is prayer, or asking. What you ask for you receive. But this refers to the prayer of the heart, not to the words you use in praying. ...God does not understand words, for they were made by separated minds to keep them in the illusion of separation. Words can be helpful, particularly for the beginner, in helping concentration and facilitating the exclusion, or at least the control, of extraneous thoughts (manual, p. 51).

In other words, prayer is for *our* benefit, not God's. As the Course states, regarding praising God:

> The Bible repeatedly states that you should praise God. This hardly means that you should tell Him how wonderful He is. He has no ego with which to accept such praise, and no perception with which to judge it (text, p. 64).

What we ask for, however, we *do* receive, but not from God. It is the power of our minds that gives us what our minds request: love or fear, peace or conflict, God or the ego:

> The prayer of the heart does not really ask for concrete things. It always requests some kind of experience, the specific things asked for being the bringers of the desired experience in the opinion of the asker.... The prayer for things of this world will bring experiences of this world. If the prayer of the heart asks for this, this will be given because this will be received. It is impossible that the prayer of the heart remain unanswered in the perception of the one who asks.... The power of his decision offers it to him as he requests. Herein lie hell and Heaven. The sleeping Son of God has but this power left to him (manual, p. 51).

Thus, in the original instant, the Son prayed for release from the presence of love in his mind, and the world was made by this mind in answer to his request for protection from God. He need only change his request, and the love already present in his mind will be experienced by him as well. This then is the only meaningful prayer, as we shall see presently.

Yet while we believe we are really here in this dream state of a world, there certainly appear to be needs that have to be met, and decisions that need be made. "The Song of Prayer" addresses this:

> You have been told [i.e., in the Course] to ask the Holy Spirit for the

495

answer to any specific problem, and that you will receive a specific answer if such is your need.... There are decisions to make here, and they must be made whether they be illusions or not. You cannot be asked to accept answers which are beyond the level of need that you can recognize. Therefore, it is not the form of the question that matters, nor how it is asked. The form of the answer, if given by God, will suit your need as you see it. This is merely an echo of the reply of His Voice. The real sound is always a song of thanksgiving and of love.

You cannot, then, ask for the echo. It is the song that is the gift. Along with it come the overtones, the harmonics, the echoes, but these are secondary. In true prayer you hear only the song. All the rest is merely added. You have sought first the Kingdom of Heaven, and all else has indeed been given you ("The Song of Prayer," p. 2).

The echoes, overtones, and harmonics correspond to the needs we believe we have, and our requests for help that are "answered" by the Holy Spirit. However, "these are secondary"; what is primary is the song: the Holy Spirit's presence of love that, being abstract, is beyond all needs:

The secret of true prayer is to forget the things you think you need. To ask for the specific is much the same as to look on sin and then forgive it. Also in the same way, in prayer you overlook your specific needs as you see them, and let them go into God's hands. There they become your gifts to Him, for they tell Him that you would have no gods before Him; no Love but His. What could His answer be but your remembrance of Him? Can this be traded for a bit of trifling advice about a problem of an instant's duration? God answers only for eternity. But still all little answers are contained in this ("The Song of Prayer," p. 2).

The question might be raised, then, as to why *A Course in Miracles* uses this language--i.e., that the Holy Spirit will meet our needs--if it means something else. The answer lies in the idea mentioned earlier, that the Course meets the needs of its readers on the level they can accept and understand, since its focus and purpose is always on the practical:

You have surely begun to realize that this is a very practical course, and one that means exactly what it says.... This is not a course in the play of ideas, but in their practical application. . . . The course is always practical.... and it is the practical with which this course is most concerned (text, pp. 147,196; manual, pp. 38,68).

Given this emphasis, it would certainly make no sense to present metaphysical truths that cannot be implemented. Speaking of the

Oneness of Christ that teaches us within our separated minds, the Course states:

> Yet must It use the language that this mind can understand, in the condition in which it thinks it is. And It must use all learning to transfer illusions to the truth, taking all false ideas of what you are, and leading you beyond them to the truth that *is* beyond them (text, p. 484).

Thus *A Course in Miracles* comes on two levels, as observed earlier in the book. It is in their integration that the Course's true power and scope can in time be realized by the student. This double level is evident in this passage dealing with time which, as previously pointed out, is clearly taught by the Course to be illusory: linearity merely being a magic trick or ploy on the part of the ego to convince the Son of the reality of the separation and the physical world. Yet the Course speaks a great deal about the need to save time, to forgive the past and, in this lovely workbook lesson, to "place the future in the Hands of God." Logically, of course, it makes no sense to trust a non-existent future to a timeless God. And so the workbook states:

> God holds your future as He holds your past and present. They are one to Him, and so they should be one to you. *Yet in this world, the temporal progression still seems real. And so you are not asked to understand the lack of sequence really found in time.* You are but asked to let the future go, and place it in God's Hands. And you will see by your experience that you have laid the past and present in His Hands as well, because the past will punish you no more, and future dread will now be meaningless (workbook, p. 360, my italics).

In other words, time is unreal, there being in God only the eternal present. However, since all of us in this world must believe in it otherwise we would not be here,[22] it would not be particularly helpful to demand that we practice a principle that is beyond our ability to understand. Therefore, the Course begins where we are, believing in the ego tale of past sin demanding God's punishment, making our future dread a justified reality. This workbook lesson, then, particularly addresses the Son's mind that believes it would be foolish to trust a God who will inevitably, so the ego counsels, destroy us. The terror would be too great. Thus the lesson here is that it *is* safe to trust God with our future, for the ego's story of sin, guilt, and fear is untrue. By

---

22. The only exception would be the very isolated examples of truly enlightened beings, whom the East calls avatars or bodhisattvas, and the Course, "Teachers of teachers" (manual, p. 61). These, however, are "so rare" that it is hardly necessary to discuss them here.

our learning this lesson of trusting our future to God (Level II), we will come eventually to learn that all of time is one, and thus we are gently led back to the timeless God we now can trust and love (Level I). This gentle process of correcting our errors through intermediate steps is what makes *A Course in Miracles* unique in the history of non-dualistic spiritualities. Its correction for the ego's story is not real, yet this correction does not oppose reality. It merely gently undoes the ego's voice, allowing the Son to hear the only Voice in this world that can lead him beyond it:

> So fearful is the dream, so seeming real, he [the Son of God] could not waken to reality without the sweat of terror and a scream of mortal fear, unless a gentler dream preceded his awaking, and allowed his calmer mind to welcome, not to fear, the Voice That calls with love to waken him. God willed he waken gently and with joy, and gave him means to waken without fear (text, p. 542).

This means is forgiveness which, the Course emphasizes, *is* illusory, as shown in the following passages:

> Illusion makes illusion. Except one. Forgiveness is illusion that is answer to the rest.
> Forgiveness sweeps all other dreams away, and though it is itself a dream, it breeds no others.... this is where illusions end. Forgiveness is the end of dreams, because it is a dream of waking. It is not itself the truth. Yet does it point to where the truth must be, and gives direction with the certainty of God Himself. It is a dream in which the Son of God awakens to his Self and to his Father, knowing They are one (workbook, p. 369).

> Forgiveness might be called a kind of happy fiction; a way in which the unknowing can bridge the gap between their perception and the truth. They cannot go directly from perception to knowledge because they do not think it is their will to do so. This makes God appear to be an enemy instead of what He really is. And it is just this insane perception that makes them unwilling merely to rise up and to return to Him in peace.
> And so they need an illusion of help because they are helpless; a Thought of peace because they are in conflict (manual, p. 79).

Therefore, it appears in our experience here that the Holy Spirit meets our specific needs on the level of form, seemingly justifying a life of praying to Him for help. In reality, as mentioned, the Holy Spirit is pure content, without form. Yet that content of God's love, automatically as it were, is present in our minds along with the ego's content of fear, and adapts itself to the needs arising from that fear. To quote again:

> God knows what His Son needs before he asks. He is not at all concerned with form, but having given the content it is His Will that it be understood. And that suffices. The form adapts itself to need; the content is unchanging, as eternal as its Creator (manual, p. 79).

The mind of God's Son is one, both in Heaven as Christ and on earth as the ego, and so the thoughts of love and fear coexist in each fragment of this ego mind. We are free to choose which thought we identify with: When we choose the thought of love we experience it as the Holy Spirit's intervention on our behalf; when we choose the thought of fear we experience it as an outside force's intervention against us. The former has given rise to centuries of belief in a magical God, while the latter has resulted in the corresponding belief in a devil or evil forces. Both are opposite forms of the same error, denying the power of our minds to choose. We believe that we are the recipients of God's grace or the devil's curse, both external to our minds. The language of the Course mirrors that tradition in the figures of the Holy Spirit and the ego, yet brings them back *within* our minds, repeatedly emphasizing the importance of our power to choose.

To summarize the ladder of prayer, then, the top rung is true prayer, the song of Heaven flowing endlessly between Father and Son. On this level "there is nothing to ask because there is nothing left to want" ("The Song of Prayer," p. 2). However, this is not the level of the world's experience, and so the Course presents prayer as a process, beginning on the ladder's bottom rung. Thus the pure content of prayer, like the Holy Spirit's love, becomes adapted to our needs as we perceive them:

> Prayer has no beginning and no end. It is a part of life. But it does change in form, and grow with learning until it reaches its formless state, and fuses into total communication with God. In its asking form it need not, and often does not, make appeal to God, or even involve belief in Him. At these levels prayer is merely wanting, out of a sense of scarcity and lack.
>
> These forms of prayer, or asking-out-of-need, always involve feelings of weakness and inadequacy, and could never be made by a Son of God who knows Who he is. No one, then, who is sure of his Identity could pray in these forms. Yet it is also true that no one who is uncertain of his Identity can avoid praying in this way.... It is also possible to reach a higher form of asking-out-of-need, for in this world prayer is reparative, and so it must entail levels of learning. Here, the asking may be addressed to God in honest belief, though not yet with understanding. A vague and usually unstable sense of identification has generally been reached, but tends to be blurred by a deep-rooted sense of sin. It is possible at this level to continue to ask for things of this world in various forms, and it is also possible to ask

for gifts such as honesty or goodness, and particularly for forgiveness for the many sources of guilt that inevitably underlie any prayer of need. Without guilt there is no scarcity. The sinless have no needs ("The Song of Prayer," p. 3).

Praying out of need, therefore, is really praying to the ego, for we have substituted its voice for God's. The ego's original story to the Son is one of scarcity and deprivation, necessitating his seeking outside his mind for protection from the wrathful God, fulfillment of imaginary needs, and salvation from the pain of guilt. Such prayer merely reinforces the "truth" of the ego's words to the Son, especially when these prayers appear to be answered:

> It is not easy to realize that prayers for things, for status, for human love, for external "gifts" of any kind, are always made to set up jailers and to hide from guilt. These things are used for goals that substitute for God, and therefore distort the purpose of prayer. The desire for them *is* the prayer. One need not ask explicitly. The goal of God is lost in the quest for lesser goals of any kind, and prayer becomes requests for enemies. The power of prayer [i.e., of the mind] can be quite clearly recognized even in this. No one who wants an enemy will fail to find one. But just as surely will he lose the only true goal that is given him. Think of the cost, and understand it well. All other goals are at the cost of God ("The Song of Prayer," p. 6).

Thus, our asking for help on one level reinforces the belief that we are sinful, guilty, and lacking in what we need. On another level, however, sincerely asking God's help facilitates the process whereby we learn that the Holy Spirit's Voice speaks truth, while the ego's tale is false. This undoes the ego's basic assertion that the presence of the Holy Spirit in our minds is a grave danger to us, and so He should not be trusted and must be avoided at all costs. Thus we are asked to trust this presence of love who wants only to help us. That is why *A Course in Miracles*, true to its practical emphasis, speaks of asking the Holy Spirit's help. This asking is the bottom rung of the ladder, where we believe we are. And of such asking and learning is the Kingdom of Heaven on earth, at least the beginning of the attainment of the Kingdom. Prayer, then, is like forgiveness:

> Prayer in its earlier forms is an illusion, because there is no need for a ladder to reach what one has never left. Yet prayer is part of forgiveness as long as forgiveness, itself an illusion, remains unattained. Prayer is tied up with learning until the goal of learning has been reached. . . . The stages necessary to its attainment, however, need to be understood . . . ("The Song of Prayer," p. 4).

The text states:

> Prayer is a way of asking for something. It is the medium of miracles. But the only meaningful prayer is for forgiveness, because those who have been forgiven have everything. Once forgiveness has been accepted, prayer in the usual sense becomes utterly meaningless. The prayer for forgiveness is nothing more than a request that you may be able to recognize what you already have (text, p. 40).

In other words, one cannot pray for something that is not there. One can only legitimately pray to remember or to accept the truth that is already within, to "Ask ... to receive what is already given; to accept what is already there" ("The Song of Prayer," p. 1). We pray for help to forgive (undo) the illusion that there was ever anything but the perfect unity of God and Christ.

Forgiveness, as we have seen, is a process, and its stages, which constitute the ladder of prayer, need not detain us too long here. True to the Course's emphasis on the healing of relationships the rungs of the ladder represent different aspects of our attitudes toward others. It begins with the "curious contradiction" of praying for one's enemies, which clearly makes the idea of victim and victimizer real. We proceed up the ladder by recognizing that

> prayer is always for yourself. . . . Why, then should you pray for others at all? . . . [which] rightly understood, becomes a means for lifting your projections of guilt from your brother, and enabling you to recognize it is not he who is hurting you ("The Song of Prayer," p. 5).

Thus, forgiveness switches the ego's purpose for relationships and the world in general. Made to be the object of guilt's projection and thus a smokescreen in back of which the ego hides, the world now becomes the means whereby these projections are returned to our minds where we can then make another choice:

> The purpose of the world you see is to obscure your function of forgiveness, and provide you with a justification for forgetting it. It is the temptation to abandon God and His Son by taking on a physical appearance. It is this the body's eyes look upon.
> Nothing the body's eyes seem to see can be anything but a form of temptation, since this was the purpose of the body itself. Yet we have learned that the Holy Spirit has another use for all the illusions you have made, and therefore He sees another purpose in them. To the Holy Spirit, the world is a place where you learn to forgive yourself what you think of as your sins. In this perception, the physical

> appearance of temptation becomes the spiritual recognition of salvation (workbook, p. 105).

> Here [forgiveness] is the only purpose that gives this world, and the long journey through this world, whatever meaning lies in them. Beyond this, they are meaningless (text, p. 395).

Next follows praying *with* others, recognizing that we--our brothers, sisters, and ourselves--share a common goal. This stage is reflected in the Course's central emphasis on joining with another in forgiveness. "The Answer to Prayer" in the text specifically addresses this meaning of prayer:

> Everyone who ever tried to use prayer to ask for something has experienced what appears to be failure. This is not only true in connection with specific things that might be harmful, but also in connection with requests that are strictly in line with this course (text, p. 152).

This is the case because we often are not in touch with the deep level of fear present in our minds that caused our need for defense, either in the form of pain (special hate relationships with others or our own bodies) or pleasure (special love relationships), both of which would mask the anxiety of our fear. Thus in these cases we are not really asking that God help free us from our fear, but rather unconsciously asking that God reinforce our magical defenses *against* our fear. The Course states:

> The Bible emphasizes that all prayer is answered, and this is indeed true. The very fact that the Holy Spirit has been asked for anything will ensure a response. Yet it is equally certain that no response given by Him will be one that would increase fear (text, pp. 152f).

Thus the answers to our requests for help are "waiting" for us until the instant we truly desire them. What facilitates our desire for God is having the "little willingness" to begin the process of changing our perceptions of those we have judged to be outside us, forgetting that they, like us, are a part of Christ. Our distrust of them mirrors our distrust of God, and ultimately our distrust of our minds that we believe originally chose to attack God and His Son. Therefore, the Course tells us:

> If you would know your prayers are answered, never doubt a Son of God. Do not question him and do not confound him, for your faith in him is your faith in yourself. If you would know God and His

502

Answer [the Holy Spirit], believe in me [Jesus] whose faith in you cannot be shaken. Can you ask of the Holy Spirit truly, and doubt your brother? Believe his words are true because of the truth that is in him. You will unite with the truth in him, and his words will *be* true.... Your brother may not know who he is, but there is a light in his mind that does know. This light can shine into yours, giving truth to his words and making you able to hear them. His words are the Holy Spirit's answer to you. Is your faith in him strong enough to let you hear?... If you would hear me, hear my brothers in whom God's Voice speaks. The answer to all prayers lies in them. You will be answered as you hear the answer in everyone. Do not listen to anything else or you will not hear truly.... Hear only God's Answer in His Sons, and you are answered (text, pp. 153f).

This, of course, does not mean that we should trust our brother's ego; "frightened people can be vicious," the Course reminds us (text, p. 33), and we are certainly not asked to deny the sometimes vicious forms of people's calls for help. However, we are asked, when in the presence of such expressions of fear, to look beyond them to the love of God that is truly being called for--to have faith that even in the midst of the ego's dark camouflage, the light of Christ remains undimmed.

In summary, then, true prayer is merely the Son's changing his mind about the ego's story of separation and attack. In the holy instant, the Holy Spirit's Voice is seen as speaking the only truth: the truth of a union--Father and Son--that has never been broken, and that is now reflected in our experience as union between the seemingly separated fragments of the Sonship. By choosing to join with one I have excluded from my mind, I am indeed "listening" to the Holy Spirit's Voice and rejoining with my Self and with my Creator. By learning how not to doubt (i.e., how to forgive) the Son of God I had perceived as treacherous, I am learning how not to doubt the Son of God I am, the Son of love who has never left his Source. This learning is the process of climbing up the ladder separation had led me down. The final rung, after which the ladder disappears, is remembering that our brothers and sisters are part of us; we are one mind, one Christ: "Prayer has become what it was meant to be, for you have recognized the Christ in you" ("The Song of Prayer," p. 8).

6. Rituals

Finally, we more specifically consider rituals as they are discussed in the Course, especially in the workbook which, given its structured exercises, *could* easily lend itself to ritual. Yet, it clearly cautions against such practices:

... these exercises should not become ritualistic.... Learning will not be hampered when you miss a practice period because it is impossible at the appointed time. Nor is it necessary that you make excessive efforts to be sure that you catch up in terms of numbers. Rituals are not our aim, and would defeat our goal (workbook, pp. 3,197).

However, in order to accomplish the Course's purpose of retraining our minds, some structure is obviously necessary:

An untrained mind can accomplish nothing. It is the purpose of this workbook to train your mind to think along the lines the text sets forth (workbook, p. 1).

Such structure is particularly important in the early stages of one's growth, and it is obviously between the individual and the Holy Spirit to determine the parameters of "early." The students uncertain of their spiritual progress

are not yet ready for such lack of structuring on their own part. What must they do to learn to give the day to God? There are some general rules which do apply, although each one must use them as best he can in his own way. Routines as such are dangerous, because they easily become gods in their own right, threatening the very goals for which they were set up (manual, p. 38).

Jesus addresses these uncertain students in lesson 95 of the workbook, explaining the purpose behind the more structured lessons at this stage of the training:

It is difficult at this point not to allow your mind to wander, if it undertakes extended practice. You have surely realized this by now. You have seen the extent of your lack of mental discipline, and of your need for mind training. It is necessary that you be aware of this, for it is indeed a hindrance to your advance.... In addition to recognizing your difficulties with sustained attention, you must also have noticed that, unless you are reminded of your purpose frequently, you tend to forget about it for long periods of time. . . . Structure, then, is necessary for you at this time, planned to include frequent reminders of your goal and regular attempts to reach it. Regularity in terms of time is not the ideal requirement for the most beneficial form of practice in salvation. It is advantageous, however, for those whose motivation is inconsistent, and who remain heavily defended against learning (workbook, pp. 164f).

However, anyone familiar with spiritual practice can easily recognize the two-edged-sword aspect to this kind of structure, especially in the context of the Course where the authority for the practice is no less a figure than Jesus. The "danger" to this kind of instruction comes when people forget structured times, as they almost all inevitably do, and feel guilty over failing to be properly mindful of God. Thus, this gentle advice follows:

> Do not, however, use your lapses from this schedule as an excuse not to return to it again as soon as you can. There may well be a temptation to regard the day as lost because you have already failed to do what is required. This should, however, merely be recognized as what it is; a refusal to let your mistake be corrected, and an unwillingness to try again.
> The Holy Spirit is not delayed in His teaching by your mistakes. He can be held back only by your unwillingness to let them go (workbook, p. 165).

In other words, the problem would not be the mistake of forgetting a practice period, but taking the mistake seriously and feeling guilty. This is no different, then, from saying that the problem was not the "tiny, mad idea" of separation, but rather remembering not to laugh and taking the separation thought seriously, calling it a sin; that is, listening to the ego's interpretation rather than the Holy Spirit's.

> Let us therefore be determined, particularly for the next week or so, to be willing to forgive ourselves for our lapses in diligence, and our failures to follow the instructions for practicing the day's idea. This tolerance for weakness will enable us to overlook it, rather than give it power to delay our learning. If we give it power to do this, we are regarding it as strength, and are confusing strength with weakness (workbook, p. 165).

Not only, of course, would our guilt be giving an ego thought a strength it does not have, it would be giving it a reality it does not have as well. Again, it is one thing to make a mistake, it is quite another to give it power by labeling it a sin which demands our guilt and punishment as retribution. Thus, Jesus' instructions here can be taken as symbolic of how we should look at the original separation. Recall again how all experiences are occurring simultaneously: Since there is no hierarchy of illusions, feeling guilty over a missed practice period is no different from feeling guilty over separating from God: a "small" illusion is no different from a "large" one. Moreover, ideas leave not their source, and the idea of feeling guilty over anything has its source in the guilt over the separation from God. Therefore, learning to forgive ourselves for our "failure" against God over a missed practice period is, at the same time, forgiving ourselves for our "failure" against Him in the separation. Thus Jesus tells us:

> When you fail to comply with the requirements of this course, you have merely made a mistake. This calls for correction, and for nothing else. To allow a mistake to continue is to make additional mistakes, based on the first and reinforcing it. It is this process that must be laid aside, for it is but another way in which you would defend illusions against the truth.
> Let all these errors go by recognizing them for what they are. They are attempts to keep you unaware you are one Self, united with your Creator, at one with every aspect of creation, and limitless in power and in peace. This is the truth, and nothing else is true (workbook, p. 165).

The ease with which spiritual devotees can slip into the worship of rituals is illustrated by this story from the East. A certain guru gathered his disciples together every morning at the ashram for meditation. A cat belonging to the community liked to join in as well, to the distraction of the others. Thus the guru asked that before morning meditation the cat be tied to a post so as not to disturb the meditators. Time passed and the guru died, as evidently did the cat. The community meanwhile continued its meditative practices; however, the older members recalled that the revered guru had asked that before the meditation the cat be tied to a post. Therefore, the members of the community searched for a cat to be tied to a post, so that the guru's instructions could be followed. Obviously the very practical content of the guru's original purpose was swallowed up by the form.

The power of our belief in establishing the sacredness of rituals or objects was also described by Krishnamurti in the following instruction on how to render an object holy:

> Take a piece of stick, put it on the mantelpiece and every day put a flower in front of it . . . and repeat some words--"Coca-cola," "Amen," "Om," it doesn't matter what word--any word you like. . . . If you do it, after a month you will see how holy it has become. You have identified yourself with that stick, with that piece of stone or with that piece of idea, and you have made it into something sacred, holy. But it is not. You have given it a sense of holiness out of your fear . . . giving yourself over, surrendering yourself to something, which you consider holy. The image in the temple is no more holy than a piece of rock by the roadside (*The Awakening of Intelligence*, pp. 214f).

Clearly, in this example, the focus once again has shifted from the content to the form, thereby rendering the activity meaningless and deceptively holy. All the while, the ego thought system in the devotee's mind remains unchanged, impervious to the "threat" of truth's content which has been successfully walled in by the worship of form.

Ethics-Morality

Serious students of *A Course in Miracles* recognize forgiveness as the principle that guides their behavior in their daily lives, and as the principle underlying the moral stance of the Course. Strictly speaking, all morality is of the ego, since it is based upon certain prescribed standards of behavior or conduct. Just as "a universal theology is impossible" (manual, p. 73), so too is a universal morality, as values differ from one culture to the next, and change within individual cultures over time. This relative nature of morality is proof that it cannot be of God, in whom only the changeless and universal reality of truth can exist. Therefore it is more appropriate to speak of the *a*morality (or new morality) of *A Course in Miracles*. We have already seen how the Course's treatment of forgiveness (content) differs radically from the conventional one, and therefore so must its understanding of ethical behavior (form). In this section we begin to explore the differences between the Course and other spiritualities regarding the issue of morality. The discussion will be concluded in Part III.

Through our forgiveness of all people we have seen as either special hate objects--those we treat as scapegoats for our own sins--or special love objects--those we see as our saviors and on whom we feel dependent for our own salvation, peace, and happiness--we find the Course's central norm for all behavior. Jesus has become the model and symbol for this forgiveness, continually reminding us to think of his lesson whenever we are tempted to make our own (or others') suffering and pain the condemning effect of someone else's sin. We are to see our one function here as demonstrating that our sins against each other have had no effect, and therefore do not exist. Thus does forgiveness heal. Once our minds are cleared of the investment in maintaining the ego's thought system, we are free to be guided by the gentle Voice of the Holy Spirit's love. It is this freedom from the tyranny of the ego's voice that allows all our behavior to be "moral" and loving. As St. Augustine taught, love and do what you will: When love is in our minds, all our thoughts and therefore actions will be loving. Forgiveness is thus the great moral and ethical principle we follow, for it removes all the barriers to the awareness and extension of love.

One of the Course's most important sections is "The Laws of Chaos," and after these five laws of the ego are described we read:

"No law of chaos could compel belief but for the emphasis on form and disregard of content" (text, p. 458). This emphasis on form is the essential ingredient in the ego's "smokescreen" plan, for it continually reinforces the belief that reality is external, of the body, and therefore unlike God. On one level, then, any ego involvement or investment with the body must lead to futility, since it is involvement with an inherent illusion. Yet, because we have made this illusion real for ourselves, as we have seen, we must begin where we believe we are. Through the process of forgiveness, we correct our misperceptions one by one until we have at last retraced our steps back to the original misperception--the separation from God and from our true Identity as Christ.

Thus, *A Course in Miracles* teaches that it *is* important how we live in this world, however illusory in nature it is. It describes how the Holy Spirit joins in our misbeliefs, correcting the interpretations of separation we have made to His interpretations of joining (forgiveness). The Course emphasizes, again, that forgiveness too is an illusion, for it corrects a mistake that is not there. Unlike the illusions of the world, however, forgiveness does not breed further ones, but leads us beyond them all to the truth of God.

Since we have already chosen to be here, it is necessary to live in the world of illusion, but with a changed perception. The world now takes on a mighty purpose--that of teaching us that there is no world. From being a place of hell, the world is converted into a classroom of joy, for what can be a more joyous lesson than learning that the pain and misery we thought was real was nothing but a bad dream? Now the dream is happy. Into this "dry and dusty world, where starved and thirsty creatures come to die," there is hope:

> Now the world is green. And everywhere the signs of life spring up, to show that what is born can never die, for what has life has immortality (workbook, p. 463).

In an important passage in workbook lesson 184, partially quoted in the Preface, the Course discusses the Holy Spirit's use of the illusory names and symbols of the world:

> It would indeed be strange if you were asked to go beyond all symbols of the world, forgetting them forever; yet were asked to take a teaching function. You have need to use the symbols of the world a while. But be you not deceived by them as well. They do not stand for anything at all, and in your practicing it is this thought that will release you from them. They become but means by which you can communicate in ways the world can understand, but which you recognize is not the unity where true communication can be found.

> Thus what you need are intervals each day in which the learning of the world becomes a transitory phase; a prison house from which you go into the sunlight and forget the darkness. Here you understand the Word, the Name Which God has given you.... And then step back to darkness, not because you think it real, but only to proclaim its unreality in terms which still have meaning in the world that darkness rules.
>
> Use all the little names and symbols which delineate the world of darkness. Yet accept them not as your reality. The Holy Spirit uses all of them.... Use all the names the world bestows on them but for convenience, yet do not forget they share the Name of God along with you (workbook, p. 337).

Thus we are urged, again echoing the words of John's gospel, to be in the world, yet knowing we are not of it. "The Special Function" is one of the key sections in the text that bears on this issue of reinterpreting the forms or symbols of the world, providing perhaps the clearest statements in the Course in this regard. The context is the special relationship that, as we have seen, is the ego's most powerful weapon in its war against God. In this sense, then, specialness becomes a symbol of the entire physical world, which the ego made as an attack on God's love. It is no surprise then that we find such ambivalence--special love and hate--in our physical experience here. Yet because we believe this love-hate world is our reality, symbolized again by our special relationships, it is within this belief system that the correction must be made: "In crucifixion is redemption laid" (text, p. 518), the Course teaches. Let us therefore consider this section, finding here the perfect blend of metaphysical truth with gentle and loving correction.

"The Special Function" begins with a restatement of the Holy Spirit's message to the sleeping Son, urging him to look on his sin with forgiving eyes, washed with the grace of God:

> The grace of God rests gently on forgiving eyes, and everything they look on speaks of Him to the beholder. He can see no evil; nothing in the world to fear, and no one who is different from himself.... He would no more condemn himself for his mistakes than damn another. He is not an arbiter of vengeance, nor a punisher of sin.... And being in accord with what God wills, he has the power to heal and bless all those he looks on with the grace of God upon his sight (text, p. 492).

Of course, the Son can be free from the role of avenger only because his Father is, since what is true of one must be true of the other. The Holy Spirit's loving message to the Son was not only about God, but about himself as well.

The Son, however, does not believe this, setting into motion the insane drama of specialness, which began with his original special relationship with God (as was seen in Chapter 14). Thus was a world of specialness made, a world of hatred and murder. It is this world that becomes the Holy Spirit's classroom, inspiring an attitude of gratitude and appreciation, in contrast to the bitter resentment and despair that usually characterizes our experience here, and which is described in so many moving passages in the Gnostic literature. ,

The Voice of love in our minds continually provides the correction for the ego's voice of hate. Again, as we have seen, the Holy Spirit does not really do anything; He simply *is*, and this presence of pure, abstract love is transformed into the correction of forgiveness when confronted by the ego's unforgiveness. Special relationships, when brought to forgiveness, become transformed into holy relationships. Both are equally illusory, based as they are upon separation, yet when brought together they dissolve together, leaving only the memory of love in the Son's holy mind, its altar cleansed. As the manual states:

> This is the shift that true perception brings: What was projected out is seen within, and there forgiveness lets it disappear. For there the altar to the Son is set, and there his Father is remembered. Here are all illusions brought to truth and laid upon the altar.... seen within your mind, guilt and forgiveness for an instant lie together, side by side, upon one altar. There at last are sickness and its single remedy joined in one healing brightness. God has come to claim His Own. Forgiveness is complete.... Gone is perception, false and true alike. Gone is forgiveness, for its task is done. And gone are bodies in the blazing light upon the altar to the Son of God (manual, p. 82).

When the world of the special relationship gives way to the holy relationship, it becomes

> the Holy Spirit's kind perception of specialness; His use of what you made, to heal instead of harm. To each He gives a special function in salvation he alone can fill; a part for only him.... Here, where the laws of God do not prevail in perfect form, can he yet do *one* perfect thing and make *one* perfect choice. And by this act of special faithfulness to one perceived as other than himself, he learns the gift was given to himself, and so they must be one. Forgiveness is the only function meaningful in time. It is the means the Holy Spirit uses to translate specialness from sin into salvation.... The specialness he chose to hurt himself did God appoint to be the means for his salvation, from the very instant that the choice was made. His special sin was made his special grace. His special hate became his special love.... The Son of God can make no choice the Holy Spirit cannot employ on his behalf, and not against himself. Only in darkness does your specialness appear to be attack. In light, you see it as your special function in the

plan to save the Son of God from all attack, and let him understand that he is safe, as he has always been, and will remain in time and in eternity alike. This is the function given each of you for one another. Take it gently, then, from one another's hand, and let salvation be perfectly fulfilled in both of you. Do this *one* thing, that everything be given you (text, pp. 493f).

This different attitude towards the world--that it is neither to be avoided nor sought after--leads to an *amorality*, as discussed at the beginning of this section. Our function in the world is therefore not to feed the hungry, free the oppressed, or serve any other social cause. How can we serve a world that is not there? Since there is no body, no world, no problem, any moral position or stance would be falling into the same trap we have described throughout the book. There can be no *right* behavior, because in truth there is *no* body that can behave. How then could we properly judge any behavior? The focus, as we have continually seen, is on the thoughts that lead to the behavior, and it is these thoughts that must be changed, not the behavior. There is an interesting parallel in the Gnostic "Acts of John," where the same principle is underscored. The scene is a bizarre one, as is often the case in these legendary Acts. John comes upon a young man who has killed his father for objecting to the son's sexual affair with a married woman. John resurrects the father, causing such contrition in the young man that the son quickly cuts off his own genitals with a sickle and presents them to his lover, exclaiming: "There you have the ... cause of all this." The young man proudly reports to John what he has done, but is quickly reproved by the apostle:

the one [the devil] who tempted you to kill your father and commit adultery with another man's wife, he has also made you take off the unruly members *as if* this were a virtuous act. But you should not have destroyed the place of your temptation, *but the thought which showed its temper through those members*; for it is not those organs which are harmful to man, *but the unseen springs through which every shameful emotion is stirred up and comes to light* (AJ 54, in *NTA* II, p. 241, my italics).

These "unseen springs" are the belief in separation and resultant guilt (the content), which manifest in behavior (the form) designed to witness to the reality of these thoughts, thereby reinforcing them.

On the level of the mind, therefore, one can indeed speak of "right" or "wrong": a "right" thought (what the Course calls right-minded thinking) is forgiveness or joining; a "wrong" thought (wrong-minded thinking) is guilt and separation. These, however, are not moral judgments, but simply judgments based on their effect: A thought of forgiveness leads to peace as inevitably as does a thought of guilt lead to pain.

The Course emphasis is thus always on the level of the mind, where the problem and solution lie, and not the illusory world. It is the *purpose* of our actions that give them their meaning or value. A powerful example of this teaching is found in the *Bhagavad Gita,* one of the pearls of Hindu scripture. The setting is a battlefield, where the warrior Arjuna dialogues with Lord Krishna. Arjuna asks whether doing battle is defensible, and Krishna's answer constitutes the heart of the Gita. Speaking within the non-dualistic framework with which we are familiar, Krishna asks how Arjuna could kill someone who is already dead, for how can the immortal die (students of *A Course in Miracles* will recognize this line cited on page 375 in the text). If it is Arjuna's dharma (his life's path) to be a warrior, Krishna explains, then he must be the best warrior he can; not because the battlefield is holy, but because it is the stage on which he has chosen to learn a spiritual lesson. As with the Course, the Gita is clearly not for the spiritually immature who seek to use spiritual teachings to justify ego motivations (Chapter 19 discusses this issue in greater depth). Thus the Gita is not condoning killing; rather the purpose of its teaching is to shift our perspective of the world that we may better understand the difference between truth and illusion. It is within this same context that the Course states:

> Therefore, seek not to change the world, but choose to change your mind about the world (text, p. 415).

Further, we are urged:

> To learn this course requires willingness to question every value that you hold. Not one can be kept hidden and obscure but it will jeopardize your learning (text, p. 464).

All our values, therefore, need to be questioned in light of the metaphysical principles of truth and illusion, helping us to understand and experience the causal relationship between mind and body.

It would thus be a misreading of *A Course in Miracles* to believe that it advocates a life of careless disregard for others; however, the basis for its caring is not that a hostile action is wrong, but rather that the wish to hurt another will only bring the aggressor pain and guilt. The distinction here is crucial. Remember our metaphysical foundation: there is literally nothing and no one that exists outside our minds. In this sense, then, the Course could be seen as adopting a moderate position between asceticism and libertinism. However, again, its reasons would differ from the moderate stances we have discussed.

The Course's "ethical" teaching is not based on behavioral consequences, because any extreme position, for example, must dogmatically hold that a specific form of behavior is salvific. Stated another way, the Course would echo Hamlet's famous line: ". . . for there is nothing either good or bad, but thinking makes it so" (II,ii,255-257).

In Part III we shall explore in more depth some of the common errors students of *A Course in Miracles* have made in seeking to apply its teachings to specific experiences and problems in the world. Suffice it to say for now, an ego identification with any cause, movement, or concern in the world--personal or international--can only be due to this confusion of form and content, illusion and truth. Once again, the Son would have fallen for the ego's lies about what is real and what is not, where the problem is and its solution as well. It certainly does not appear to be the case that our concern for the welfare of human beings, or members of the animal and vegetable kingdoms, not to mention the planet and universe, is an ego ploy. And yet what else could it be when our concern is rooted in the premise that there is danger, hurt, pain, or suffering? No compromise is possible in this regard without falling into the same trap that ensnared Plato and the Platonists, as well as the Gnostics and orthodox Christians we have considered.

The Course can appear insensitive at first when we are told that it does not recognize as problems the very concerns that people have held from the beginning of time: sickness, poverty, starvation, death, etc. It is here that we observe the power and cleverness of the ego system. Once deluded into believing the phenomenal world is real, one must inevitably make physical and/or psychological suffering real as well. However, because we believe our bodies are the locus of our experience, *A Course in Miracles* does not ask us to deny our bodily experiences in this world, or the experiences of others. Such denial merely serves the ego by having made something terrible appear to be real and external to our minds, thereby protecting the thought of guilt that *is* the only problem. As the Course teaches in an important passage that highlights its gentle practicality, even within the context of an uncompromising non-dualism:

> The body is merely part of your experience in the physical world. Its abilities can be and frequently are overevaluated. However, it is almost impossible to deny its existence in this world. Those who do so are engaging in a particularly unworthy form of denial. The term "unworthy" here implies only that it is not necessary to protect the mind by denying the unmindful. If one denies this unfortunate aspect of the mind's power, one is also denying the power itself (text, p. 20).

Thus we are asked to respect the power of our minds to make illusions, so that over time we can use this power to change our minds about truth and illusion. Later in the text Jesus says to us:

> I will love you and honor you and maintain complete respect for what you have made, but I will not uphold it unless it is true (text, p. 56).

However, we are asked not to take the world so seriously, as we find in an incisive passage dealing with the dreamlike nature of the world we caused, a world whose origin lay in believing the ego's story when "the Son of God remembered not to laugh" (text, p. 544). The *cause* of the world's suffering rests not with the physical forms of suffering, which are merely effects. The cause rather lies with our having been fooled by the ego in the first place. Here, then, we are asked to bring our minds back to the point at which we listened to the wrong voice, and to choose again. Specifically, we understand this request to be the Course's guide for all behavior, for we are asked to bring to the Holy Spirit every pain and concern, and together with Him laugh at the silliness of it all:

> It is not easy to perceive the jest when all around you do your eyes behold its heavy consequences, but without their trifling cause. Without the cause do its effects seem serious and sad indeed. Yet they but follow. And it is their cause that follows nothing and is but a jest.
> In gentle laughter does the Holy Spirit perceive the cause, and looks not to effects. How else could He correct your error, who have overlooked the cause entirely? He bids you bring each terrible effect to Him that you may look together on its foolish cause and laugh with him a while. *You* judge effects, but *He* has judged their cause. And by His judgment are effects removed. Perhaps you come in tears. But hear Him say, "My brother, holy Son of God, behold your idle dream, in which this could occur." And you will leave the holy instant with your laughter and your brother's joined with His (text, p. 545).

The same theme is reiterated in a passage from the workbook which, if taken out of context, seems harsh and unfeeling indeed. Properly understood, however, in the context of our discussion of reality and illusion, the passage expresses the theme of salvation from all forms of suffering and distress. The immediate context is sacrifice as the underlying dynamic of all problems:

> Never forget you give but to yourself. Who understands what giving means must laugh at the idea of sacrifice. Nor can he fail to recognize the many forms which sacrifice may take. He laughs as well at pain and loss, at sickness and at grief, at poverty, starvation and at death. He recognizes sacrifice remains the one idea that stands

behind them all, and in his gentle laughter are they healed (workbook, pp. 345f).

Thus, regardless of the behavior we seek to espouse, whether it be for pleasure (material salvation) or pain (religious salvation), or behavior in others we find objectionable, our task remains the same: to bring our concern or desire to the Holy Spirit, asking His help to look at the issue as being but a manifestation of an internal thought. And it is that thought that needs correction. The principle is simple; its universal application, however, is difficult, for we are here talking about the total undoing of the defensive system *we* identified as necessary for salvation. Each and every circumstance in our lives that concerns us becomes an opportunity for returning to the root of that concern. Only an uncompromising non-dualistic metaphysics can present such a simple plan for salvation:

> How simple is salvation! All it says is what was never true is not true now, and never will be. The impossible has not occurred, and can have no effects. And that is all (text, p. 600).

It is a plan that has no exceptions, and thus there is no order of difficulty in miracles: They are all the same because there is likewise no hierarchy in illusions; they are all the same as well:

> One problem, one solution. Salvation is accomplished.... It is in this that the simplicity of salvation lies (workbook, p. 141).

Therefore, it is not the world that needs redemption, preservation, or plans for peace, but the mind that believes in a world that needs redemption. This, then is the new morality of *A Course in Miracles*: act not out of concern or misplaced empathy, but out of the love of God that knows not of pain or suffering. And from that place of love within our minds, love itself will act, gently guiding our bodies to an interaction with the world devoid of ego, and so devoid of problems. It is an interaction such as Jesus demonstrated when he walked the earth; an interaction with others and the world that was invested only with the Father's love: a love that literally does nothing, but simply is.[23]

From this new moral position regarding injustice we can deduce similar conclusions regarding the traditional spiritual emphases on asceticism and detachment from the world and the body. Clearly, if there is no body to begin with, what is there to detach *from*? Moreover, to practice any form of asceticism, believing that it is rooting out "the

---

23. For further discussion, see *Forgiveness and Jesus*, pp. 76-109.

world, the flesh, and the devil," merely reinforces the body's reality, thus fulfilling the ego's plan for its salvation. We recall part of the quotation from page 20 in the text: "It is not necessary to protect the mind by denying the unmindful [the body]." The more ascetically successful spiritual aspirants are, the more they are deluded into believing that they have actually accomplished something (by "denying the unmindful"), while all the time their unconscious guilt remains safe and secure behind the body's armor, requiring still greater effort to undo it. The Course comments on this in two places. In the text it says:

> It is extremely difficult to reach Atonement by fighting against sin. Nor is a lifetime of contemplation and long periods of meditation aimed at detachment from the body necessary. All such attempts will ultimately succeed because of their purpose. Yet the means are tedious and very time consuming, for all of them look to the future for release from a state of present unworthiness and inadequacy (text, p. 363).

With our sense of unworthiness and inadequacy made real, these ascetic practices become almost self-defeating. Workbook lesson 155 provides practical guidelines for one's life in the world, advocating the middle path indicated above between asceticism and libertinism. The lesson speaks to all would-be teachers of God:

> If truth demanded they give up the world, it would appear to them as if it asked the sacrifice of something that is real. Many have chosen to renounce the world while still believing its reality. And they have suffered from a sense of loss, and have not been released accordingly. Others have chosen nothing but the world, and they have suffered from a sense of loss still deeper, which they did not understand.
> Between these paths there is another road that leads away from loss of every kind, for sacrifice and deprivation both are quickly left behind. This is the way appointed for you now (workbook, p. 284).

Thus, choosing to fight against the body, or choosing to indulge the body, end up as opposite sides of the same coin:

> The body does appear to be the symbol of sin while you believe that it can get you what you want. While you believe that it can give you pleasure, you will also believe that it can bring you pain. . . . It is impossible to seek for pleasure through the body and not find pain. It is essential that this relationship be understood, for it is one the ego sees as proof of sin. It is not really punitive at all. It is but the inevitable result of equating yourself with the body, which is the invitation to pain. . . . It [the body] will share the pain of all illusions,

and the illusion of pleasure will be the same as pain (text, pp. 384,386f).

The "middle path" of *A Course in Miracles* has nothing to do with behavior, neither ascetic withdrawal nor physical or psychological attraction. It deals only with the absence of guilt in one's mind, leading inevitably to absence of projection in the world. These teachers of God, therefore, look no different from anyone else, and do nothing different from anyone else. The difference comes from the peace they feel within:

> There is a way of living in the world that is not here, although it seems to be. You do not change appearance, though you smile more frequently. Your forehead is serene; your eyes are quiet. And the ones who walk the world as you do recognize their own.... You walk this path as others walk, nor do you seem to be distinct from them, although you are indeed (workbook, p. 284).

An earlier lesson makes the same point:

> The body is your only savior. . . . This is the universal belief of the world you see. Some hate the body, and try to hurt and humiliate it. Others love the body, and try to glorify and exalt it. But while the body stands at the center of your concept of yourself, you are attacking God's plan for salvation... that you may not hear the Voice of truth and welcome It as a Friend (workbook, p. 123).

Therefore the true students of the Course who learn and live its lessons will look and act normally. They will not necessarily give up certain foods, sexuality, enjoying a pretty sunset, etc.; their clothing will usually not be different. What does change, however, is the purpose given to these and other human activities. The forms remain the same; the content changes. If their forms shift, it is only to fulfill the content of love that has been guiding them. We shall discuss the teacher of God again in Part III.

PART III

SUMMARY AND CONCLUSIONS

INTRODUCTION TO PART III

Our journey is almost complete. Having traversed large terrains of theoretical speculation and spiritual experience, we are better able to understand the nature of the mind and its relation to the physical world. It has been a journey, not of distance nor even time, but of a vertical descent through the layers of fog that have concealed the truth. Truth's light shines more brightly now, for we no longer believe we are the victims of external conditions beyond our control. Our minds are indeed the ruler of the world we see and experience, and indeed, have made. Thus is the cause of the world returned to its source, where it can be gently undone at last. In this concluding Part of the book, we re-examine *A Course in Miracles* in the light of the ancient traditions of Platonism, Christianity, and Gnosticism, realizing the ultimate purpose of our study: learning how to live in this illusory world without becoming trapped in the thought that it is really there. Thus does the Holy Spirit's gentle thought of love correct the ego's thought of hate, and we are home, where we have always been and where God "would have us be" (text, p. 622).

Throughout the dream's expansion into time and space, the shining presence of perfect love that we call the Holy Spirit has continually illuminated the Son's mind, made accessible to that mind whenever its individual fragments chose to listen. In this book we have limited our discussion of the manifestations of this truth to the development (or counter-development) of the non-dualistic aspect of Western philosophy and theology. However, it is worth reiterating that it would be a glaring example of the error of spiritual specialness, to be reconsidered in Chapter 19, to limit expressions of the Holy Spirit *only* to these spiritual teachings. Love is the content that is beyond all forms, and only that *abstract* presence in our minds is true. As was mentioned in the Preface, the Hindus teach that truth is one but the sages know it by many names. The specific names used in this study are merely a few among "many thousands."

Returning to our myth, we recall the Son's unquestioning acceptance of the ego's tale of sin, guilt, and fear, which acceptance was the *cause* of the world and all the suffering that has been experienced ever since. Thus, salvation is ultimately complete when the Son accepts the Holy Spirit's message, undoing the ego's underlying thought system. Jesus is the name we give to the concrete manifestation of this one thought of acceptance and undoing--the principle of the Atonement--and we have seen how traditional Christianity greatly distorted his teaching. In the Western tradition, Jesus' non-dualistic message of salvation was prefigured, albeit in a flawed manner, in the work of the pre-Socratics and Platonists, carried forward--still flawed--by the great Gnostic teachers, the Neoplatonist Plotinus, and others, and finally brought to fruition in *A Course in Miracles*. It might be hypothesized, incidentally, that figures like Socrates, Plato, Valentinus, and Plotinus, to name just a few, might have themselves been very advanced teachers, presenting truth to the world in the form and at a level acceptable to their particular age. Thus, while a later age such as ours may look back to the flaws of their respective systems, such flaws may simply have been expressions of a limitation commensurate with the needs of their time period, and not necessarily reflective of ego limitations in the teachers themselves.

The orienting theme of this book has been what we have referred to as the God-world paradox. We have seen that all Platonists, beginning with Plato himself, agonized over the issue of how the perfect Good, One, or God, could have extended into the obviously imperfect and flawed material world of multiplicity. Orthodox Christians perceived no problem, for they found no contradiction between God and His created material world. The Gnostics, too, saw no contradiction in their position of God not creating the world, yet the world being at the same time real and powerful enough to imprison them.

Thus, from the perspective of *A Course in Miracles*, each tradition in its own way has fallen into the trap of making the error real. It is the unique contribution of the Course to avoid that trap, at the same time providing a metaphysics *and* a guide for living in the body that does justice to both levels of discourse. The Course's use of psychodynamic theory is the means whereby this integration of truth and our individual experience is consummated. In Part III we review our earlier discussions and present the full implications of the Course's position. We also consider, in a separate chapter, the various errors observed in students of *A Course in Miracles*, in which the ego has attempted to divert attention from the Course's truth, even while appearing to uphold its teachings. Interestingly enough, most of these errors parallel those historical ones we have already pointed out.

Chapter 18

A COURSE IN MIRACLES RE-EXAMINED

The journey through the Platonic-Christian-Gnostic world has illustrated the strange compromises the ego has devised to protect its thought system, even in the face of experience and thoughts that contradict it. This is what we have been referring to, again, as the God-world paradox: the incongruity of the perfect God coexisting with, if not causing--directly or indirectly--the imperfect world; stated another way, it is the paradox of holding as equally real--materially and/or psychologically--the unified and undifferentiated spiritual perfection of God, and the fragmented and differentiated material imperfection of the world. Our study has demonstrated the struggles that non-orthodox Christian theologians and "pagan" philosophers alike have experienced in dealing with this paradox, while never successfully resolving it, either from a theoretical or pragmatic point of view. The orthodox Christian of course, handled this paradox by outrightly denying any problem at all, as we have seen.

Let us begin by restating the basic cosmogonic premise of this study: The physical universe was made by the split-off part of the mind (the ego), attempting to solidify its own illusory existence by rooting its identity in a fortress called the body and the world. This separated self now appeared to be prey to forces outside its control, forever doomed to a victimized existence within a victimizing and threatening world. As a cover for this cosmic subterfuge, the ego continually speaks of the world's and body's reality to the part of our minds that chooses to believe in it. Part of the ego's tricks of "magic" and "sleight of hand" (workbook, p. 291) is the development of philosophies and theologies that ultimately support this belief by placing the world's creation in the Mind of God. This of course has nothing whatsoever to do with the true God, whose truth has now become hidden by the "divine" belief system that properly belongs to the ego, as is discussed in "The Laws of Chaos" in the text of *A Course in Miracles*. Once the thought that God created this world is accorded truth, the ego can safely rest. Whatever inconsistencies may from time to time appear within the consciousness of individuals are quickly disposed of, either by the ego's "appeal to 'mysteries,' insisting that you must accept the meaningless to save yourself" (text, p. 157), or by repression. Once pushed out of awareness, these inconsistent thoughts are no longer accessible to question and revision:

> The ego has no real answer to this [the mind's question of the ego's

inconsistency] because there is none, but it does have a typical solution. It obliterates the question from the mind's awareness. Once out of awareness the question can and does produce uneasiness, but it cannot be answered because it cannot be asked (text, p. 60).

Indeed, one of the thoughts the ego would violently oppose is found in these lines from *A Course in Miracles*:

There is no statement that the world is more afraid to hear than this:

"I do not know the thing I am, and therefore do not know what I am doing, where I am, or how to look upon the world or on myself."

Yet in this learning is salvation born. And What you are will tell you of Itself (text, p. 614, italics omitted).

Stages of the Myth

We turn now to the seven stages of the myth presented in Part II, discussing them within the specific context of the God-world paradox we have been exploring from the beginning of the book. This will enable us to discuss *A Course in Miracles* in the light of the other three traditions, showing how the Course alone within the Western tradition exemplifies the purity of this ancient message of Atonement. Thus we review all that we have traversed, bringing, as the Course would state, the illusions of past mistakes to the truth. We group some of the stages together for ease of discussion, beginning with the first three that represent the Course's metaphysics.

1. Stages One, Two, and Three

The first stage of the story involves the nature of God and His creation. The key to our whole discussion rests at this pre-cosmic level, because the premises implicit here directly affect what is to come. We have seen how non-dualistic apophaticism contrasts sharply with dualistic thinking; the latter begins by making evil real, coexisting with God, which evil must then be defeated or at least defended against. However, the war against this enemy can never be successful because the *thought* of evil remains within the mind, to be continually projected out and fought where the thought can never be undone. In a pure non-dualism, such as we find in *A Course in Miracles*, this evil or sinful thought *cannot* occur, and therefore *has not* occurred in reality. There is no compromise in this position. We have seen that the other non-dualisms, such as exist in certain strands of Christian mysticism or in Plotinus, end up compromising their teachings by attributing reality or even divinity to non-spiritual being, evil or otherwise. Thus, while the Course is in agreement with many Christian mystics and Neoplatonists about the nature of God, the origin of the physical world remains a point of serious divergence; it is really only with the Gnostics that there is virtual agreement about God's purely acosmic nature.

The separation or fall from God is the watershed that divides *A Course in Miracles* from all the spiritualities we have been considering in this book. The Course keeps the thought of separation *outside* the Mind and Will of God, and therefore it is outside reality and in the realm of illusion. Following the principle "Ideas leave not their source," all the ideas resulting from this thought, such as the physical world, must also be illusory and outside reality.

We have seen that Valentinus, of all the Gnostic theologians, came closest to this understanding of the fundamental unreality of the world, though without developing a full-blown psychological context for his insights. Nonetheless, the seeds of the Course's twentieth-century system can be found latent in the work of the Valentinian school. In passages quoted from "The Gospel of Truth" we have seen reference to the "terror and disturbance and instability and doubt and division" that led to the "many illusions at work . . . empty fictions, as if they were sunk in sleep . . . in disturbing dreams." And yet upon waking, the dreamers "see nothing," for "all these disturbances . . . are nothing" (GT I.29.30, in *NHL*, p. 43). The Valentinian author of this startling passage, let alone Valentinus himself, would clearly not have gone as far as *A Course in Miracles* in declaring the absolute unreality of the physical world, along with the ethical consequences of this position. However, he powerfully depicts the experience and knowledge of its psychological unreality, within the larger anti-cosmic Gnostic framework.

Plotinus' heart is in the right place when he describes the absolute undifferentiation of the One as compared with the gradual emanations and declinations from it. And yet to him everything that comes from the One is ultimately real, regardless of his struggles with the baseness and "non-being" of matter. Thus on one level we can observe that the Course's description of the ego's process of fragmentation parallels Plotinus' tale of the downward emanation. In this sense we can say that *A Course in Miracles* is Neoplatonism psychologized: It takes the declination from the One, which is ultimately a negative event for Plotinus, his rationalizations to the contrary, and explains from a psychological point of view--i.e., from the dynamics of the separated mind of sin, guilt, and fear--how and why this seemed to occur.

Thus, we can see again how the Course is an amalgam of different approaches, yet a successful integration of them: It is *Neoplatonic* in terms of describing the downward procession (or projection) from the One; *Gnostic* in its clarity on the world not coming from the Divine at all, exposing the ego's trickery in back of it; and *Christian*, not only in its language, but through its recognizing a benevolent presence of God experienced in the world--the memory of His love (the Holy Spirit) in the split mind--not to mention the central place accorded to Jesus. Through its integration of the metaphysical and practical levels, *A Course in Miracles* is able to retain a metaphysical purity, at the same time providing a gentle and loving correction for the mind's errors and miscreations. Jesus as its source and teacher is the Course's great symbol for the loving gentleness of God, thus bridging the gap between our abstract, undifferentiated, and utterly impersonal Source, and our childlike need for a loving Father and Mediator while we remain imprisoned in our minds' dreams.

We are thus speaking about an almost unique approach and attitude towards the phenomenal universe. The closest parallel is found in certain non-dualistic (advaita) Hindu systems, as seen in Sankara, for example, the great eighth-century A.D. Indian mystic and scholar. There, the absolute Reality, Brahman, is understood to be totally unrelated to the phenomenal world, as is the Course's God in relation to the ego and its world. However, in most other forms of Eastern thought, which nonetheless see the world as illusory, matter and form are still conceived of--to use Neoplatonic language--as being implicit in the Absolute undifferentiated unity of the Godhead; the phenomenal world being a reflection of the non-material Ideas, from which they are ultimately derived. As Bede Griffiths observes, speaking of the total transcendence yet immanence of the Divine Reality:

> . . . the absolute Reality is beyond words and thought . . . totally transcendent . . . [yet] totally immanent. The one Reality is manifesting itself in every particle of matter, in every living thing, in every human being (Griffiths, p. 83).

We are not far at all from the same paradox we have been considering throughout the book: how the pure oneness of reality can be manifest in the imperfect multiplicity of the world of forms and bodies.

Yet we see in the Course many passages sharing the Gnostic and Platonic expressions of rejection of the physical world:

> You do not want the world. The only thing of value in it is whatever part of it you look upon with love. This gives it the only reality it will ever have. Its value is not in itself, but yours is in you. . . . For this world *is* the opposite of Heaven, being made to be its opposite, and everything here takes a direction exactly opposite of what is true (text, pp. 212,317).

"God's Name reminds me that I am His Son,
Not slave to time, unbound by laws which rule
The world of sick illusions . . ."
(workbook, p. 379, italics omitted)

In light of this totally *a*cosmic stance, however, we also note that unlike the Gnostic position, *A Course in Miracles* is not *anti*-cosmic. To refer back to the sophisticated psychological base we have been examining, we see that it makes no sense to fight against something that has not been created by God and so is not real. To see the world or the body as the locus of sin is simply to fall into the trap of making the error real. As the Course states:

Everyone who follows the world's curriculum, and everyone here does follow it until he changes his mind, teaches solely to convince himself that he is what he is not. Herein is the purpose of the world (manual, p. 1).

The world was made as an attack on God. It symbolizes fear. And what is fear except love's absence? Thus the world was meant to be a place where God could enter not, and where His Son could be apart from Him. . . . [Illusions'] aim is to fulfill the purpose which the world was made to witness and make real (workbook, p. 403).

Therefore the Course urges us to look at the world benevolently: since we believe we are here, the world can be seen as kind, offering us itself as a classroom in which we learn the lessons that will lead us beyond the world entirely:

The real purpose of this world is to use it to correct your unbelief [i.e., not believing in the unreality of a world of time and space]. . . . The only purpose worthy of your mind this world contains is that you pass it by, without delaying to perceive some hope where there is none (text, p. 11; workbook, p. 227).

The purpose of time is to enable you to learn how to use time constructively. It is thus a teaching device and a means to an end. Time will cease when it is no longer useful in facilitating learning. . . . The Holy Spirit interprets time's purpose as rendering the need for time unnecessary. He regards the function of time as temporary, serving only His teaching function, which is temporary by definition (text, pp. 2,230).

These lines echo the spirit of Origen, for whom the world was also a classroom. This idea, however, would have been anathema to almost all Gnostics, who of course saw absolutely nothing redeeming about the world.

527

2. Stage Four

We can thus see that implicit in the Course's presentation of the dynamics of the ego thought system--which underlie our physical existence in this world--is the view that the separated mind and hence the body are a far cry from our divine and spiritual nature. In this respect *A Course in Miracles* is quite Gnostic, and we can hear the angry voice of Plotinus inveighing against its teachings with the same vehemence he directed against the Gnostics who "infiltrated" his lecture rooms. There is, however, a major difference that distinguishes the Course not only from the Gnostics but also, ironically enough, from the attitude or tone of Plotinus, not to mention Plato. Despite the Course's insistence on the unreality of the body, it never makes the mistake of attacking the body that ensnared the Platonists and Gnostics alike, who perceived the body as repulsive. Rather, to the Course, the body is perceived as neutral--"My body is a wholly neutral thing" (workbook, p. 435)--neither to be venerated or rejected, but simply to be used for learning purposes as long as we believe we are in it.

The central aspect to the ego's life in the body is of course the special relationship, and it is interesting to note, as was done in Part II, the statements in "The Gospel of Truth" and Plotinus that so insightfully foreshadow the teachings on special relationships found in *A Course in Miracles*. These should come as no surprise as it is precisely the Valentinian and Plotinian schools that on another level most closely approximate the spirit and insights of the Course, both metaphysically and psychologically. The Gnostic tract describes the same double dream layer of the ego that is found in the Course: victim *and* victimizer. Note these two passages, presented successively here, though separated by almost eighteen centuries of time:

> Either (there is) a place to which they are fleeing . . . or they are involved in striking blows, or they are receiving blows themselves, or they have fallen from high places. . . . Again, sometimes (it is as) if people were murdering them . . . or they themselves are killing their neighbors, for they have been stained with their blood (GTI.29.11-26, in *NHL*, p. 43).

> A brother separated from yourself, an ancient enemy, a murderer who stalks you in the night and plots your death . . . of this you dream. Yet underneath this dream is yet another, in which you become the murderer, the secret enemy, the scavenger and the destroyer of your brother and the world alike (text, p. 5·12).

And from Plotinus we read, again, of our deficiency or lack--the foundation of the special relationship--and the illusion of loving what is external:

This universe. . . . is many and divided into a multiplicity, and one part stands away from another and is alien to it, and there is not only friendship but also enmity because of the separation, and in their deficiency one part is of necessity at war with another. . . . by which it is preserved (*Enn.* III.2.2).

So therefore when we look outside that on which we depend we do not know that we are one. . . . as long as it is in that which has the impression received by the senses [i.e., what has form: the body], the lover is not yet in love. . . . But if he [the lover] should come to understand that one must change to that which is more formless [i.e., what is "not perceptible by the senses"], he would desire that; for his experience from the beginning was love of a great light from a dim glimmer (*Enn.* VI.5.7; 7.33).

Paralleling its Platonic ancestor, the Course first describes the "army of the powerless," silently afraid and alone in the world:

They are indeed a sorry army, each one as likely to attack his brother or turn upon himself. . . . In hatred they have come together, but have not joined each other (text, p. 431).

[For] Fear . . . is love's replacement. . . . [and] is both a fragmented and fragmenting emotion. It seems to take many forms. . . . [in which a very] serious effect lies in the fragmented perception from which the behavior stems. No one is seen complete (text, p. 347).

As for the search without for what can only be found within:

Seek not outside yourself. . . . Heaven cannot be found where it is not, and there can be no peace excepting there. . . . For all your pain comes simply from a futile search for what you want, insisting where it must be found (text, p. 573).

You see the flesh or recognize the spirit. There is no compromise between the two. . . . If you choose flesh, you never will escape the body as your own reality. . . . But choose the spirit, and all Heaven bends to touch your eyes and bless your holy sight . . . (text, p. 614).

Let us briefly consider now the traditional Christian and Platonic conception of the body which, though at times an object of derision and disgust, was nonetheless seen as part of the divine creation. The framework of our brief discussion is the chapter by Verbeke on "Man as a 'Frontier'," treating St. Thomas Aquinas' theology of man within the Platonic tradition.

To Plato, humanity must choose between its spiritual and corporeal selves, as we have discussed at length. Aquinas, on the other hand, understands that the choice is not so much between two oppositional realities, as it is a choice of which of the two is to be dominant:

> ... man is considered to be a subject where the spiritual and the corporeal, the temporal and the eternal are ... closely united ... and they constitute one single substance.... He is neither alienated from the world nor from the intelligible nor from the purely spiritual because he encompasses everything.... his activities always imply a dual nature, they never completely go beyond the corporeal and temporal nature (Verbeke, p. 215).

Plato and his followers believed that some amount of force was needed to reconcile these oppositional elements, as in the image from the *Phaedrus* of the charioteer and the two horses. The Gnostics also believed in the opposition of body and spirit; yet this opposition could *never* be reconciled. Aquinas, however, saw the issue as being more one of cooperation. Rather than advocating the ultimate repudiation of the physical self, Aquinas idealized its integration with the spiritual:

> As man is on the frontier of the spiritual and the corporeal he should not strive to eliminate one of the two dimensions but to combine them and develop into a harmonious symbiosis ... (Verbeke, pp. 222f).

A Course in Miracles, interestingly enough, agrees with both positions, but in a manner obviously quite different from each. On what we have called Level I (the metaphysical), the Course agrees with the Platonic and Gnostic notions of two contradictory realities, but states that only one is true. On Level II (based in our experience of the illusory world), on the other hand, the Course calls for the integration (or correction) of the ego's "lower" mind within the Holy Spirit's "higher" mind. Thus the ego dimension of our lives--our physical identification--is not denied or repudiated, but reinterpreted. In the end this identification too will disappear. However, as long as we believe we are in this world, we are challenged not to deny our experience here but to shift our perception of this experience.

Thus there is a double duality: the difference between our spiritual and ego-body selves, and the difference between two interpretations of this ego-body self. It is in this integration of Levels I and II that the Platonic, Christian, and Gnostic traditions are ultimately reconciled in *A Course in Miracles.*

3. Stages Five and Six

A Course in Miracles' internal process of salvation is directly antithetical to the Christian *and* many Gnostic theologies. The Christian theologian makes sin real, and then saves us through atonement and sacrifice, as discussed in Chapter 17, while the Course sees sin as illusory right from the beginning, and therefore requires "atonement" through corrected thinking. Thus the Course is closer to the Platonic and Neoplatonic insistence on the cultivation of virtue (in which category we can include the training of the mind). The focus is not on placing one's faith in an external salvation figure who will magically undo our egos for us. Rather, we are urged to place our faith in the process whereby we bring the illusions within our own minds to the loving presence of the Holy Spirit's truth. It is this *process* of changing our minds that is truly salvific, for it reflects our acceptance of the healing that has *already* occurred and is present within us, patiently waiting, as it were, our return to it. Likewise, Valentinus' teachings, as reflected in "The Gospel of Truth" especially, and almost unique in the Gnostic corpus, emphasize the *mental* process of knowledge correcting the deficiency. In a passage quoted from earlier, we read:

> Since the deficiency came into being because the Father was not known, therefore when the Father is known, from that moment on the deficiency will no longer exist. As with the ignorance of a person, when he comes to have knowledge his ignorance vanishes of itself, as the darkness vanishes when light appears, so also the deficiency vanishes in the perfection (GT I.24.28-25.2, in *NHL*, p. 41).

While it appears that *A Course in Miracles* is talking about the same concept of God and the Holy Spirit as are traditional Christians, in reality its view is quite different. As we have frequently seen, the Course's purpose of correcting illusions before totally undoing them leads it to speak often of the benevolent and personal aspects of the Creator. Thus, God as our loving friend, and *not* a vengeful enemy to be feared, is certainly a central theme in *A Course in Miracles*. This is not the case with the Gnostic or Christian message, where God is both loving *and* vengeful: the Final Judge who rewards the good and punishes the bad. Needless to say, since the Neoplatonic God is abstract and impersonal, any discussion of God in anthropomorphic terms would be irrelevant; the thought would have been scandalous to Plotinus. We thus see once again the importance of the distinction made between the Course's metaphysical teachings on one level, and their presentation within a context that meets us at our level of experience and understanding.

Likewise, the Course's treatment of the redeemer figure, whether spoken of as the Holy Spirit or Jesus, often strikes the reader as similar to the traditional Christian one. Yet on closer examination the Course is really much nearer to the Platonic notion. Jesus is actually a shining example and paradigm of Plato's philosopher king, Philo's lover of genuine philosophy, and Plotinus' Sage--all different expressions that describe the ideal teacher of God of *A Course in Miracles*. We shall return to this concept at the end of this chapter. Thus, the Holy Spirit is not a person of God who *acts* in this world, nor is Jesus the Son whom God sent to save us; quite the contrary: the Holy Spirit is the abstract and unchanging presence of God's love in our minds' memory that is as a shining light, whose brilliance continually reminds us of our choice between darkness or light, while Jesus is a symbol for us within the dream of what the light looks like when it is chosen over the ego's darkness. Both figures therefore serve the same function as do Plato's Ideas, or Plotinus' ongoing, formless, and abstract Call of the One; in fact, these are but differing expressions of the Divine Presence that has been buried within our separated minds by the ego. Thus, one of the purposes of this book has been to present the Platonic position as an aid to understanding the principles (content) expressed beneath the Course's language (form).

Interestingly enough, the Gnostic view of Jesus is, in this regard at least, closer to the orthodox Church, for not a single Christian Gnostic saw Jesus as being other than divine. For the Gnostic, therefore, he was ontologically different from the rest of humanity (the sole exception to this position, as we have seen, is Origen who, however, never identified himself with the Gnostics at all).

A specific expression of this difference between the Course's and the orthodox Christian's views of Jesus is in the understanding of the resurrection. We have observed that this was a point of real contention between the Gnostics and the orthodox Church, the roots of which go back as far as the middle of the first century, as witnessed to by Paul's first letter to the Corinthians. The position of *A Course in Miracles*, as previously discussed, is strikingly similar to the Gnostic. Jesus says, for example:

> I am *your* resurrection and *your* life. You live in me because you live in God. . . . Believe in the resurrection because it has been accomplished, and it has been accomplished in you. This is as true now as it will ever be, for the resurrection is the Will of God, which knows no time and no exceptions. But make no exceptions yourself, or you will not perceive what has been accomplished for you. For we ascend unto the Father together, as it was in the beginning, is now and ever shall be, for such is the nature of God's Son as his Father created him (text, p. 193).

The focus of the orthodox Church on the *physical* resurrection of Jesus is senseless from the perspective of the Course. It misses the whole point by shifting the focus of salvation to the *body*, obscuring the changing of the *mind* that is the only saving agent. It places the saving act as being not only within the physical realm but, through its identification with the death and resurrection of Jesus as historical events, also places it within the past. Yet, if the present is the only time there is, a saving event that occurred in the past can have no meaning or relevance. The reader can recall Basilides' Jesus, laughing in a tree while the crowd watched Simon's crucifixion. We can therefore see that the shift in focus from the mind to the body is another example of the Apostles' "upside-down thinking" Jesus refers to in the Course (text, p. 87). We shall return to the further implications of this shift in the next chapter.

4. Stage Seven

While *A Course in Miracles* inhabits the same metaphysical world as do most Gnostics, albeit a more sophisticated one, with very few exceptions they part company when it comes to their religious practices and ethical teachings. We have noted this several times before in this book, and now explore the Course's position regarding the spiritual life and its practice in this world, in contrast to the other traditions.

We have seen the important role that sacrament and ritual played in many Gnostic systems, not to mention in the orthodox Church. In addition to the more obvious sacraments and rituals, we can include the orthodox Christian's reliance on the Bible as a *sacred* book, and the regular (daily, weekly, seasonal) times of worship. In all of these the underlying premise is that the world is real, God is present in it--at least in certain places and at certain times--and that our spiritual progress is enhanced by manipulating the world in some way, pleasing God in the process. Thus we find the same confusion between the real and unreal: viewing the perfect, eternal, and infinite God as somehow involved in the imperfect, temporal, and finite world. This is the trap fallen into by the Course's Neoplatonic and Gnostic predecessors, not to mention orthodox Christians: making the error real by seeing some aspect of our experience here as evil and to be escaped from or, at best, a problem to be solved here, whether through divine intervention or the pursuit of a virtuous, ascetic life.

Therefore, to state the point again, while the Course appears to agree with traditional Christian thinking on seeking the help of the Holy Spirit (or God, Jesus, or Christ), this agreement is really only on the level of form or language. Its content or meaning is much closer to the Neoplatonic and Valentinian philosophers, who were clear about not seeking outside (divine) aid for problems that must be resolved at their own level: in the mind.

This emphasis on the reinterpretation of the forms of the world--shifting the ego's content of separation and attack to the Holy Spirit's meaning of joining through forgiveness--is essential to understanding some of the differences between the Course on the one hand, and Gnosticism and Christianity on the other. Stating that the world is illusory is not to say that it is sinful. Thus unlike these two other systems, *A Course in Miracles* does not teach that the world, the flesh, and the devil are to be avoided, indulged in, or fought against. Rather, its central teaching is to forgive the world, loving it *for* its gift of forgiveness. In a passage frequently misunderstood, the Course states:

> The statement "For God so loved the world that He gave His only begotten Son, that whosoever believeth in Him should not perish but have everlasting life" [Jn 3:16] needs only one slight correction to be meaningful in this context; "He gave it *to* His only begotten Son" (text, pp. 28f).

The context of this quotation is the Atonement purpose of time (and therefore the world). The world that God gave "to" us is the real world, which reflects the Holy Spirit's purpose in helping us shift from the ego's purpose for being here--hatred and separation--to the Holy Spirit's of forgiveness and joining. Thus, we are encouraged to feel grateful for our experiences in the illusory world, for they serve as the classroom in which we can truly learn that the world and its underlying thought system *are* illusory. An important passage from the Course, used twice before in this book, succinctly summarizes the Course's metaphysical view and its attitude towards the phenomenal and illusory world:

> The body was not made by love. Yet love does not condemn it and can use it lovingly, respecting what the Son of God has made and using it to save him from illusions (text, p. 359).

It is here that we see the central divergence of the Course from practically every other spirituality that has been taught, for it reflects a purely non-dualistic metaphysics that nonetheless does not denigrate, dismiss, nor deify the physical world. Thus, any Gnostic would agree, as did Plato and Plotinus, that this material world is not our home. However, the means for remembering and returning to our true home differs markedly among the Platonists, Gnostics, and *A Course in Miracles*. The Platonists and the Course, as we have seen, are similar in their emphasis on seeking within, rather than outside oneself for truth. However, the Platonic focus on pursuing a life of study, contemplation, and virtue as the means of attaining truth stands in sharp contrast to that of the Course, which focuses on changing one's mind within the context of interpersonal relationships. When properly understood, the Course's central message of forgiveness does not make the error of believing in the reality of the phenomenal world, which must inevitably follow from the Platonic and Gnostic hatred of the body. On the metaphysical level (Level I), there is nobody out there to forgive. However, on the level of our experience (Level II), our projected internal guilt appears to be present in another person. And so it is with that experience that we must begin the process of forgiveness.

We thus may conclude that the paradox between the Platonic and Gnostic philosophy/theology and personal experience results from a not-fully-integrated spirituality, reflecting the ego's unconscious need and investment to perpetuate at least some semblance of belief in the reality of the material world and the body.

The Course's goal for its students is that they become teachers of God which, as observed earlier, is roughly analogous to Plato's and Philo's philosopher and Plotinus' enlightened Sage. Each of these is asked to be fully present to the world and its citizens, to be a messenger and model. The remembrance of the truth, once attained, becomes the goal for all people. Just as Plato's prisoner must return from the light to awaken his fellow prisoners still chained in darkness, so are we asked by *A Course in Miracles* to be instruments of that light's extension for the world:

> In your [holy] relationship you have joined with me [Jesus] in bringing Heaven to the Son of God, who hid in darkness. You have been willing to bring the darkness to light, and this willingness has given strength to everyone who would remain in darkness.... You who are now the bringers of salvation have the function of bringing light to darkness.... And from this light will the Great Rays [of Christ] extend back into darkness and forward unto God, to shine away the past and so make room for His eternal Presence, in which everything is radiant in the light (text, p. 354).

While the Gnostic revealer of many of the texts that we have considered urges the Gnostics to give the saving message to the world, the context is almost always a polemic one. The reader never comes away from these texts with the feeling of a genuine Gnostic concern for others, truly caring about the benighted ones to whom they are to deliver the saving *gnosis*. Rather, the feeling is: "Here is my message of truth; take it or leave it, but at your own risk." As we have seen earlier, an exception to this insensitivity appears to be the Valentinian moderateness, most apparent in the gentle teaching of Ptolemaeus in his letter to Flora.

A principal difference between the Platonists and Course on the one hand, and the traditional Christians and most Gnostics on the other, can be found in how the ideal person is seen. The more religiously oriented--Gnostic and Christian alike--see themselves in the role of savior, whose mission is to save the world. Those who do not accept the saving message are condemned to death and hell, to be punished for their benightedness in the final conflagration. The philosophers, however, and we can include *A Course in Miracles* in this category, see their role primarily as a teacher, with there being no rewards or punishments from on high, other than those *internal* experiences of joy or pain that inevitably follow from the acceptance or denial of the truth. The Course is thus strictly consistent in its emphasis on seeing *all* problems and concerns as existing only within our minds. The problem is never "out there," but always within our own thoughts and perceptions. Therefore, only by totally accepting the correction for the *belief* in the world's reality can one be truly freed from it. It is this consistency of metaphysical principles with practical application that is the Course's unique contribution to contemporary spirituality.

Chapter 19

ERRORS AND MISCONCEPTIONS

We turn now to the errors of practice that have sprung up around *A Course in Miracles*, still in its early infancy, and actually have been common throughout the histories of almost all spiritualities. Even more specifically, we find interesting parallels between students of the Course and the Gnostics of the early Christian centuries, not to mention the orthodox Christians themselves. We can group these errors into three general categories:

1) *spiritual specialness*: believing that one's self or group is somehow ontologically different or better than others, if not more beloved by God.

2) *making the error real*: establishing the world and the body as real by assigning them negative or positive values; forms of this mistake involve spiritualizing matter, developing ethical or moral systems of asceticism, libertinism, or moderateness, and believing that spiritual practices have meaning and power in and of themselves.

3) *minimizing our investment in the ego's thought system*: believing that any spiritual path is easy and requires little or no effort, for one need only hear the Voice of the Holy Spirit.

In these three categories we will see that the misunderstandings of its students have led to conclusions, both theoretical and practical, directly opposite to what *A Course in Miracles* actually teaches. On one level we should not expect otherwise. Following upon the basic premises of this book and of the Course itself, we recognize the tremendous investment our egos have in holding to the beliefs that 1) separation and thus specialness is real; 2) this world of error is real and created by a power outside our own mind; and 3) our guilt and fear are not the awesome "truth" about ourselves we have made them out to be, and can easily be handled by the ego's plan. To remove our investment in these three "facts" of the ego's world is to undo the very foundation of the ego system.

Thus, in general, we can understand these errors to be defenses against the truth that is found in the Course. As *A Course in Miracles* points out, and as has been mentioned several times already, when the ego is confronted by the loving truth of the Holy Spirit it becomes afraid, for the truth of our reality as God's Son is the greatest threat to the integrity of its thought system. The Course explains:

> The ego is ... particularly likely to attack you when you react lovingly, because it has evaluated you as unloving and you are going against its judgment.... This is when it will shift abruptly from suspiciousness to viciousness, since its uncertainty is increased.... It remains suspicious as long as you despair of yourself. It shifts to viciousness when you decide not to tolerate self-abasement and seek relief. Then it offers you the illusion of attack as a "solution." ... When the ego experiences threat, its only decision is whether to attack now or to withdraw to attack later.... Even the faintest hint of your reality literally drives the ego from your mind, because you will give up all investment in it.... The ego will make every effort to recover and mobilize its energies against your release (text, pp. 164,166).

Therefore, if the ego cannot attack directly--because the Son would find that totally unacceptable--then it "withdraws" to attack later through distortion; its form of passive resistance. Thus the ego follows the axiom: "If you can't lick 'em, join 'em." Unable to convince us *not* to pursue *A Course in Miracles*, the ego nonetheless is able to distort the Course's teachings sufficiently to allow its truth to be clouded over, protecting the ego's belief system from ever being looked at openly and honestly. Jesus asks each of us in the Course to "Be very honest with yourself ... for we must hide nothing from each other" (text, p. 56). Thus we must openly look at these errors and bring them to his love, *after* which they can be released. Without such honest examination, the truth will continue to be obstructed, and its light "forbidden" entry into the hidden portals of the ego's darkened mind, where it would surely heal our mistaken thoughts.

This fear of the truth leading to the defense of distortion has striking parallels to the early history of Christianity, where the followers of Jesus quite clearly changed his teachings to suit their own fear and guilt. As Jesus comments in the text, specifically referring to the aforementioned "upside-down" interpretations given to his crucifixion:

> If you interpret the crucifixion in any other way [i.e., than a loving and *un*sacrificial act], you are using it as a weapon for assault rather than as the call for peace for which it was intended. The Apostles often misunderstood it, and for the same reason that anyone misunderstands it. Their own imperfect love made them vulnerable to projection, and out of their own fear they spoke of the "wrath of God" as His retaliatory weapon. Nor could they speak of the crucifixion entirely without anger, because their sense of guilt had made them angry.... I do not want you to allow any fear to enter into the thought system toward which I am guiding you (text, pp. 87f).

Finally, we may recall again the Course's statement that

> To learn this course requires willingness to question every value that you hold. Not one can be kept hidden and obscure but it will jeopardize your learning (text, p. 464).

This important teaching refers to our willingness to generalize the Course's principles totally, without exception. To hold out any situation or belief from its uncompromising non-dualism is to make some aspect of the illusory world real. A serious student of *A Course in Miracles* recognizes the absoluteness of its thought system. To quote again one of the Course's statements about itself:

> This course will be believed entirely or not at all. For it is wholly true or wholly false, and cannot be but partially believed (text, p. 440).

Almost all mistakes students make regarding the Course result from what we have earlier called level confusion; namely, not understanding the important distinction *and* interface between the metaphysical (Level I) and practical (Level II) levels on which *A Course in Miracles* is written. It is from the metaphysical absoluteness of the Course's thought system that its practical teachings of forgiveness derive their power and meaning.

We must therefore be careful not to bring the truth to the illusion, but rather to bring our illusory beliefs to the truth *A Course in Miracles* holds out to us. This requires an openness within ourselves to examine our investments in perpetuating the ego's thought system. The errors we shall be discussing ultimately result from the unconscious unwillingness to bring our fears to the Holy Spirit's love and truth.

Spiritual Specialness

In Chapter 8 we explored the expression of spiritual specialness in orthodox Christianity and Gnosticism, where it was seen that such specialness was inherent in the theologies themselves. This is clearly not the case with the teachings of *A Course in Miracles*, whose whole message specifically corrects this kind of specialness. Nonetheless, many of the Course's students have not entirely escaped this subtle trap.

The we-they battlefield of the first two centuries between the orthodox Church and the Gnostics--hating and attacking the other group--that we explored in Chapter 3 is also finding its way into the "community" already beginning to crop up around the Course. Thus its students often confuse form with content, and forget Jesus' statement in the text that "All my brothers are special" (text, p. 10), and that the

Course is only one path among "many thousands" (manual, p. 3). We can see these errors occurring on two levels: First, students of *A Course in Miracles* sometimes join together *as if* they were a group unto themselves, part of a family or network, this groupiness somehow making them and the Course special. Second, factions develop within the Course community itself. We briefly examine these now.

1) To begin with, what truly unites people as a family is their common Source, which is only of spirit. Our worldly families--biological, ethnic, religious, local community, country, sports allegiances, etc.-- are nothing more than classes we have chosen to attend, in which to learn that there is in truth only one Family: Christ. Referring to our only Name, the workbook lesson "The Name of God is my inheritance" states:

> You live by symbols. You have made up names for everything you see. Each one becomes a separate entity, identified by its own name. By this you carve it out of unity. By this you designate its special attributes, and set it off from other things by emphasizing space surrounding it. This space you lay between all things to which you give a different name; all happenings in terms of place and time; all bodies which are greeted by a name (workbook, p. 336).

Rather, we are asked to

> accept the Name for all reality, and realize the many names ... [we] gave its aspects have distorted what . . . [we] see, but have not interfered with truth at all. One Name we bring into our practicing. One Name we use to unify our sight.
> And though we use a different name for each awareness of an aspect of God's Son, we understand that they have but one Name, Which He has given them (workbook, p. 338).

And so we pray:

> "Father, our Name is Yours. In It we are united with all living things, and You Who are their one Creator. What we made and call by many different names is but a shadow we have tried to cast across Your Own Reality.... Your Name unites us in the oneness which is our inheritance and peace. Amen" (workbook, p. 338, italics omitted).

However, we are certainly not asked by the Course to deny our specific affiliations in this world. Instead, we are urged not to take them seriously as realities to be upheld, justified, and defended, but

simply to be used for the Holy Spirit's teaching purpose. Recall an earlier quoted passage:

> You have need to use the symbols of the world a while. But be you
> not deceived by them as well. They do not stand for anything at all.
> ... They become but means by which you can communicate in ways
> the world can understand, but which you recognize is not the unity
> where true communication can be found (workbook, p. 337).

By now it should be clear to the reader that *A Course in Miracles* is not
the first spiritual thought system to have explored these metaphysical
issues, although it is certainly the first to have integrated psychology
and spirituality in the way that it has, thus leaving us with a consistent
message from start to finish. Yet this consistency does not make its
teachings nor its students ultimately any better or more deserving of
Heaven's blessing. The Course is quite clear about the dangers of
believing that a certain group is a more special recipient of the Holy
Spirit's love:

> Salvation cannot seek to help God's Son be more unfair than he has
> sought to be. If miracles, the Holy Spirit's gift, were given specially
> to an elect and special group, and kept apart from others as less
> deserving, then is He ally to specialness. What He cannot perceive He
> bears no witness to. And everyone is equally entitled to His gift of
> healing and deliverance and peace (text, p. 502).

The biblical text "For many are called, but few are chosen" (Mt 22:14),
a clear statement of specialness on the part of a God who chooses only
certain of His children, is corrected in the Course to place the responsibility onto us: "All are called, but few choose to listen" (text, p. 39).

2) Students of the Course factionalize among themselves, as did the
early churches. Opposing camps of interpretation arise, battling with
each other over whose understanding of the Course is more correct, or
more faithful to the teachings, or to Jesus, etc. The point here again is
not to deny that differences among students do in fact exist, but to
avoid making the differences into an issue that divides and attacks.
The early history of Christianity, recounted in Chapter 3, should serve
as a model for how differences in interpretation or theology should *not*
be handled. It is silly for students to use *A Course in Miracles*, based on
principles of forgiveness and unity, as a weapon against other students, simply because of differing interpretations or practices.

In general, these inter- and intra- mural divisions rest on the confusion of form with content, the same confusion we have explored
earlier. Such confusion, in fact, is the heart of the ego's defensive

system of protecting its special relationships, as we see in these excerpts from passages already cited:

> Whenever any form of special relationship tempts you to seek for love in ritual, remember love is content, and not form of any kind. The special relationship is a ritual of form, aimed at raising the form to take the place of God at the expense of content (text, p. 319).

And of the ego's laws of chaos, grouped around the belief in specialness, the Course adds:

> And yet, how can it be that laws like these can be believed? There is a strange device that makes it possible. Nor is it unfamiliar; we have seen how it appears to function many times before.... No law of chaos could compel belief but for the emphasis on form and disregard of content (text, p. 458).

Differences are inevitable in a world that was founded on differences, the world originating with the thought that there was a difference between God and His Son. In a physical universe such differences are the norm, and *A Course in Miracles*, again, does not ask us to deny our physical experience in this world. It is the underlying investment in maintaining the thought of separation that is the issue. Similarly, judgments are unavoidable here; for example, I must have made a judgment to write this book and not some other; you, the reader, likewise have made a judgment to read this book and not some other. When the Course says not to judge, it means not to condemn. Therefore, while on the one hand we must inevitably identify with our groups of preference (the form), we must on the other hand be vigilant against the special love and/or hate judgments (content) that almost as inevitably creep into our group identifications. In other words, differences in understanding and presentation of the Course's teachings will inevitably arise, and should be honored and respected, though not necessarily agreed with. However, these differences need not carry with them an emotional investment, a taking seriously which can be expressed through opposition, for example. Rather, we "remember ... to laugh" at the silliness of making differences ultimately important. Moreover, very often it can be a helpful experience to learn how to differ with another *without* becoming upset, and not letting the ego make the difference into a major symbol of separation, attack, and guilt.

Another issue that frequently arises from this underlying belief in specialness is making certain people associated with *A Course in Miracles*, historically or currently, special or more holy than others. This inevitably places them on the special love pedestal, whose outcome of hate is obvious. The "special" person of the Course is Jesus or the Holy Spirit; that is, the internal presence of God's love that, again, leads Jesus to state that all his "brothers are special."

One final point regarding groups centering on *A Course in Miracles*: The central process of studying the Course and following its particular spiritual path is an individualized one. There can be no escaping the work and dedication involved in *individually* studying and re-studying the text, as well as doing the workbook exercises during the one-year training program that is integral to the Course's educational process. All too often, joining a group or class can subtly interfere with this responsibility of the student, substituting the form of joining with the group for the content of joining with the Holy Spirit *within one's own mind*. Thus again we see the error of mistaking form for content. The joining with each other emphasized by *A Course in Miracles* comes from undoing the barriers of separation that exist within our *minds*. This process can occur regardless of whether or not we are in the presence of others. External joining is an example of magic, if the value of salvation is placed upon it; the joining in our minds through forgiveness is the miracle. Our problems cannot be solved through the magical use of external situations, but only through the use of the miracle's ability to heal our thoughts. Only on the level of the mind can true joining occur, because it was only on the mind's level that the separation occurred.

It is thus only a short step from the magical belief in the efficacy of Course groups meeting together, to the investment in *A Course in Miracles* organizations and networks. And before you know it we are on the familiar road that leads to religious institutionalization and churches, factionalism, judgments, and persecutions. To state the central point again, the issue is not that groups in and of themselves are mistakes, but rather that investment in their form as being necessary, meaningful, or salvific is a mistake. The history of Christianity serves as a glaring example of the unfortunate consequences of *not* recognizing the great potential for specialness inherent in forming groups, cloaking the specialness in spiritual clothing.

Making the Error Real

This particular error of making the error real clearly strikes at the heart of this book's theme, for we have seen its presence in all the philosophical and religious systems we have explored. Within the Platonic and Christian traditions the error is inherent in the systems themselves. The Platonic and Christian belief in the reality of the physical world is an important part of their respective traditions, though we have seen the paradox inherent there as well. In most of the Gnostic systems, however, the error is *implicit*, and was expressed psychologically, without being consciously recognized by the Gnostics themselves. As was discussed earlier, the Gnostics were clear that God did not create the world. However, they then proceeded to establish the world's and body's psychological reality by making them the object of derision, ridicule, and attack.

With students of *A Course in Miracles* we find a similarly unconscious error. We have discussed at length the tremendous investment the ego has in maintaining its thought system, which is predicated on the belief in the reality of the separated and physical world. This world's origin is usually ascribed to God or, in many secular systems, to forces outside the mind. To doubt these cosmogonies is to raise the question: If God (or other forces) did not create the world, who did? The answer strikes sheer terror in our minds, for to recall the world's origin in the ego mind, and its purpose as a defense against God, is to confront our own guilt and accept responsibility for the separation. The ego has convinced us that such acceptance brings us face to face with our own destruction at the hands of our vengeful Creator. It therefore should come as no surprise that many students of *A Course in Miracles* strongly resist accepting completely what the Course is teaching. Therefore, what creeps into these students' understanding and practice of the Course are subtle ways of making the world and the body real, thereby "protecting" the ego's existence. Let us examine some of these now.

There are many, many passages in the Course--some of which we have presented in earlier chapters--that clearly state that God did not and could not have created the physical world. Believing He did, directly flies against the integrity of the Course's thought system, a basic premise of which is that God could not create a being (or anything) unlike Himself. Nonetheless, many students of *A Course in Miracles* change its teachings to read that God did not create a world of pain, but did create a world of physical beauty, not to mention a body that can be improved upon and even made immortal. In this regard we can see the close parallels--psychologically if not always philosophically--with the Platonic tradition, wherein the physical beauty of the universe is extolled, while the pain and sufferings of the body are abhorred. One of the purposes of this book has been to help students recognize the Platonic soil in which the Course has its philosophical roots, and to distinguish the Course's teachings from the God-world paradox that is inherent within this Platonic tradition. Understanding this background can then, it is hoped, alert the student of the Course to this error.

As has been emphasized, it is the Course's uncompromising metaphysical absoluteness that is deeply problematic for many people. One of its stated goals, therefore, is to effect a total transfer of learning, for "the impairment of the ability to generalize is a crucial learning failure" (text, p. 210). As the workbook states in its introduction:

The purpose of the workbook is to train your mind in a systematic way to a different perception of everyone and everything in the world. The exercises are planned to help you generalize the lessons. ... [If] Transfer of training in true perception.... has been achieved in connection with any person, situation or event, total transfer to everyone and everything is certain (workbook, p. 1).

Because of this ego investment in our maintaining belief in the reality of the illusory, it is difficult to accept the full implications of the Course's statements about God not creating the world. These implications include not according reality *at all* to any aspect of the physical and/or psychological world (one and the same really), including perceptions of "pain and loss ... sickness and ... grief ... poverty, starvation and ... death" (workbook, p. 346). These implications likewise include not according efficacy to any of the world's methods of healing or alleviating pain, traditional and non-traditional alike. Certain New Age practices of visualizing healing, or sending light to diseased bodies or to conflicted situations in the world, also fall into the same trap of making the error real. Why would you send light or visualize healing unless you believed there were a real darkness outside of you that needed healing? As we have emphasized, the only problem is the darkness of guilt in *our* minds that believe that darkness is real outside. To restate this important teaching: ".... seek not to change the world, but choose to change your *mind* about the world" (text, p. 415, my italics).

What heals my pain or sickness is not the "healing energies" of another or the universe, nor the arousal of the energy within myself (kundalini), but the only true "healing energy" which is the correction of my thoughts of guilt through forgiveness. Physical or mental energies can certainly affect the body's electromagnetic field, thereby bringing physical or mental relief, but we are still within the domain of the ego/body world and dealing with effects, not the cause. Imputing spiritual properties to matter, be it Mother Earth or certain minerals such as crystals, likewise reflects the same error.

One would not think, moreover, that study of *A Course in Miracles* would lend itself to rituals, given its clear statements about form and content. However, as we have seen, a student's practice of the workbook can easily turn into a ritual that *must* be performed, and performed properly with the "required" amount of repetitions of the day's idea successfully carried out. The truth and beauty of the Course's teaching, the loving gentleness of Jesus that comes through its words, also can lead to a transfer of these *thoughts* to the actual books themselves, wherein people may believe that the mere touch of the blue cover (green in the United Kingdom), or the running of one's hands over its pages, promotes healing, or that the simple repetition of its words magically infuses the message into one's self, without the necessity of challenging one's thought system and changing it. In addition, once groups form, it is quite easy to fall into informal rituals that soon evolve into practices that, when not performed, lead to anxiety and discomfort, if not feelings of deprivation and anger.

Once again, the relevant issue here is not the use of, or belief in, such practices, but the attempt to combine them with the teachings of *A Course in Miracles*. Such attempts, conscious or otherwise, are subtle ego ploys to minimize the radicalness of the Course and blur its distinctiveness from other systems. This leads us to the next important way in which the ego attempts to dilute the clarity of the Course's message: claiming that the Course is "just like" other spiritualities. To discuss this at any length would take us away from our central theme, but very few contemporary or even ancient spiritualities have been exempt from such attempts. These have included: Classical Hinduism and Buddhism, Christian Science, Science of Mind, Unity, the Urantia material, the writings of Edgar Cayce, Joel Goldsmith, and C. G. Jung, transpersonal psychology, and an absolute plethora of contemporary channeled writings. (Traditional Christianity--Roman Catholic and mainstream Protestantism--and Gnosticism have of course also been included in these "just like" statements.)

To be sure, many other spiritualities deal with forgiveness, the importance of our mind's power, and faith in a loving and non-punitive God. However, none presents these ideas in the metaphysical/psychological framework as does *A Course in Miracles*, as seen, for example, in the important statement quoted earlier: "The world was made as an attack on God" (workbook, p. 403). Combining the Course with other paths also blurs its unique teaching. As discussed in the Preface, and again in this chapter, many students of *A Course in Miracles* confuse its asking us not to judge with denying the differences that certainly do exist within the illusory world. Thus, one can recognize and accept differences among the many world spiritualities without judging against certain ones, or playing the game of spiritual specialness. Thus, to state it still once again, to teach that the Course is different from these other spiritualities is not to judge against them.

Our final example of how students of the Course have made the body real falls under the three ethical categories we discussed in Chapters 10 and 17: asceticism, libertinism, and moderateness. Again, despite the Course's strong and consistent teaching of the fundamental unreality of the body, which literally does not exist and therefore does not get sick or well, live or die, many students cannot avoid the Gnostic error of making the body psychologically real. This is done by seeing the body as the problem that has to be addressed through the development of certain ethical or behavioral norms. Let us take them in turn, first the ascetic.

As with the Gnostics, asceticism is by far the most common form of this error into which students of *A Course in Miracles* fall. Passages in the Course, already quoted above, that point out our investment in the body, or describe *our* guilty and fearful experience of our bodies, are wrenched from their context to suggest that the body should be avoided or denied because it is sinful, evil, and the predominant obstacle to achieving unity with God. Sexuality, food, and money, not surprisingly, are the most widely used specific expressions of this belief that the body is the problem. Thus, a thought system that was given to help us learn how not to make the error real or, stated another way, how not to take the ego's world seriously, is transposed to say that the body is to be taken very seriously. Followers of the Course, therefore, are urged, among other things, to be celibate, thin, or vegetarian, not to drink coffee, smoke cigarettes, or earn large amounts of money, or not to charge money for activities relating to *A Course in Miracles*. The underlying premise here, not always stated, is that sexuality, certain foods, and money are inherently unspiritual. In one sense, to be sure, that is true, for *everything* in the physical realm is unspiritual, being made, as we have seen over and over again, to keep the spiritual out of our awareness and memory. To isolate certain bodily functions or aspects of the material world, however, as being particularly unholy is to fall into the trap of the first law of chaos; namely, that there is a hierarchy of illusions, wherein some aspects of the illusory world are seen to be holier or better than others. Such differentiation, in and of itself, nicely serves the ego's purpose of establishing *its* creation (or miscreation) as real, and God's undifferentiated creation as not real.

Another form of the same error, though more subtle, is the notion that the body can be immortal. The underlying premise of course is that the body's death is somehow bad, and is a fate that can and should be overcome. The body thus has been made real (for as we saw when we discussed the resurrection, if the body can live forever it *must* be real) by placing a value on eternal *physical* life. This error also results from the ego's effective use of denial, so that we forget that the body was made to keep the immortal hidden, immortality being a characteristic totally beyond the ego:

> Eternalness [immortality] is the one function the ego has tried to develop, but has systematically failed to achieve. The ego compro-

mises with the issue of the eternal, just as it does with all issues touching on the real question in any way (text, p. 60).

Still another form of making the error real comes, in true Gnostic spirit, through detaching oneself from the world that is perceived as evil and contaminating. Some of the forms taken by this error of denigrating the physical world are professing indifference to world events by avoiding radio or television news, or newspapers and news magazines, saying, in effect: "I will not pollute my mind with the world's negativity or violence by allowing the news in. What goes on around me does not concern me because it is too negative and might disrupt my positive thinking and peace of mind." Clearly, salvation does not depend on one's being kept abreast of world affairs. However, the feeling of repulsion often present in such "detachment" gives the ego away, for it has first convinced us that the world is real by virtue of its negative valence, and then provides its own solution to a problem that *it* has established.

If one is genuinely uninterested in the world news, so be it; the lack of interest needs no justification. If one feels a sense of abhorrence to the world or the body, so be it as well; this abhorrence needs no justification either. What the latter does need, however, is an absence of justification based upon so-called spiritual ideals. This justification is the problem, a shadow of the original problem of compounding the error by witnessing to the separated world's reality and justifying the defense against it. Feeling an abhorrence is a mistake, to be sure, for one can only dislike something that has first been judged as real. However, the mistake's *correction* is prevented by 1) taking the mistake seriously and calling it a sin, and 2) justifying its defense through projection and elevating the feeling of abhorrence to a spiritual principle. It is much wiser and healthier to accept the negative emotion without judgment of oneself. Then we are eventually able to bring its cause of fear to the Holy Spirit's love, at which point the negative investment disappears.

The second ethical form of the mistake of making the error real is libertinism. Here, students of *A Course in Miracles* take the teaching that the world and body are illusory as a justification for doing whatever they wish, especially in the areas of sexuality and aggression. I myself have been quoted, totally out of context, as having said in workshops that if you have no guilt in your mind, then anything that you do will be loving. The true meaning of this principle echoes St. Augustine's aforementioned dictum: "Love and do what you will." However, misapplication of this principle, rather than giving honor to the process of being an extension of the Holy Spirit's love, unfettered by our thoughts of guilt, results in excusing the practice of sexual or sociopathic acting out, all done in the name of the spirituality of *A Course in*

Miracles: the illusory world has no meaning for me and therefore it does not matter what I do. A variation of this libertinism, which also comes close to the old Gnostic libertines, is the flouting of societal rules judged as being ego-based. Thus, in arguments we are already familiar with, one may practice the Course in a provocative manner, attempting to demonstrate one's freedom by not adhering to certain societal conventions. On rare occasions one can even note a striking similarity of Course students, not only in content but in form, to the Adamites we cited earlier. These Gnostics removed their clothes (the encumbrance to the innocence of Eden--hence their name) when they prayed, so that they could manifest a pure spirituality that would take them closer to God.

Similarly, it has not been unusual for students of *A Course in Miracles* to demonstrate their "spirituality" or advancement in the Course by divesting themselves of other symbols of society. Thus, they might refrain from locking cars or house doors, carrying medical or life insurance, etc., not because they are truly indifferent to the concerns that "normal" people have. Rather, their actions are often motivated by the need to force upon themselves the *form* of what they believe to be signs of spiritual advancement, magically hoping that the *content* of ego-freedom would infuse their minds through their behavior. Thus they can avoid the at times painful process of having to look within at the guilt and fear that is present, for now these have been covered over by this veneer of holiness. Thus, still again, we can see here the unconscious (and sometimes not so unconscious) flouting of the evil and unspiritual society through these defiant activities. The Gnostic error has never been too far from our door. A more benign variation of this same theme of judging spirituality by externals was demonstrated by a very sincere young man who approached me after a workshop, saying: "I know you must be a very holy person because you don't smoke cigarettes, don't drink coffee, and don't keep running to the bathroom." How he observed the final part of this trinity I still do not understand, but it would be wonderful if one's salvation were dependent only on satisfying these three criteria for spiritual advancement.

Finally, we find those students who assume a moderate ethical position so as to *avoid* the mistakes of either the ascetic or libertine extreme. While the *form* of this middle path appears consistent to what would be advocated by the Course, the underlying *content* of the fear of falling into a trap reflects having *already* done so by making the body and behavior real. Readers may remind themselves at this point of the psychoanalytic joke that suggests that one can never win, no matter what is done: Patients who come early for sessions are anxious, those who come late are resistant, while those who are on time are compulsive. However, as discussed in Chapter 17, the Course's morality is not behavioral, but is rather based on an attitude within the mind, i.e., the motivation for what we do.

Minimizing the Ego

As we have seen, one of the prominent Gnostic characteristics was the belief in the availability of the *gnosis* or revelation only to certain special people. This obviously meant that these Gnostics were beyond their egos--hence their self-designation as the "perfect ones." It was of course this boast that was a particular thorn in the side of the orthodox Church, for how can you rationally deal with someone claiming to have a special connection to Heaven? One finds, interestingly enough, the same phenomenon existing today, where it seems that almost everyone, and his or her second cousin, is hearing or channeling the Holy Spirit. In the phrase of Irenaeus, these "channelers" seem to be sprouting up like mushrooms.

This recent infusion of an experienced "voice" that is claimed to be the Holy Spirit has been widespread in the Pentecostal and Charismatic Renewal movements within the Protestant and Catholic churches respectively. Almost as a rebellion to the hierarchical suppression of people's religious experience in the name of Church authority, the faithful now were allowed and encouraged by these movements to experience God for themselves, and to interpret scripture without the benefit or at times even the blessing of a minister or priest. Clearly, the removal of the domain of spiritual experience from the sole proprietorship of the Church elite is a positive event; however, the point here is the mistake in believing that the easiest thing in the world is to set aside the ego and allow God's Voice to speak to you. This particular phenomenon has found an almost consummate expression in students of *A Course in Miracles*.

This error among Course students finds its justification by many lifting out of their context those passages, most often in the workbook, that suggest an ease in listening to the Holy Spirit. Thus, lesson 49 states: "God's Voice speaks to me all through the day," and begins:

> It is quite possible to listen to God's Voice all through the day without interrupting your regular activities in any way (workbook, p. 78).

A later lesson tells us:

> If you will lay aside the ego's voice, however loudly it may seem to call . . . then you will hear the mighty Voice of truth. . . . Listen and hear your Father speak to you through His appointed Voice. . . . Hear

and be silent. He would speak to you. . . . Hear Him today, and listen
to the Word which lifts the veil that lies upon the earth. . . . Ask and
expect an answer (workbook, pp. 187f).

And one lesson even has us address God Himself, asking Him

to reveal His plan to us. Ask Him very specifically:

> "What would You have me do?"
> "Where would You have me go?"
> "What would You have me say, and to whom?"

> Give Him full charge . . . and let Him tell you what needs to be done
> by you in His plan for your salvation (workbook, p. 121, italics
> omitted).

In view of passages such as these, torn from the fabric of the entire
curriculum of the Course, it is understandable that students spend
their days believing that they are in constant communication with
Heaven's Voice. Thus they are "told" when to get up in the morning,
what to wear, eat, and where to go; what God's plan is, not only for
themselves, but also for everyone else ranging from world leaders to
friends and family members, fellow students and non-students alike.
Given the weight accorded such passages by these students, the
overall thrust of *A Course in Miracles* is lost. This thrust, as repeatedly
discussed above, emphasizes the tremendous unconscious investment
our minds have in holding on to the ego thought system, and the
remarkably ingenious ways we perpetuate this world of specialness
we have constructed. One passage in particular is easily overlooked:

> Only very few can hear God's Voice at all. . . . Do not forget that truth
> can come only where it is welcomed without fear (manual, p. 30).

And how many walk this earth without fear?

A Course in Miracles is a unified curriculum, and the three books need
to be studied and used as a set, even though the actual sequence of
study is left to the individual student and the Holy Spirit--"The
curriculum is highly individualized, and all aspects are under the Holy
Spirit's particular care and guidance" (manual, p. 67). The workbook,
therefore, is not meaningful without the text:

> A theoretical foundation such as the text provides *is necessary as a*
> *framework to make the exercises in this workbook meaningful* (workbook,
> p. 1, my italics).

And in a passage cited earlier, the workbook clarifies its purpose:

> . . . to train your mind to think along the lines the text sets forth (workbook, p. 1).

On the other hand, the workbook provides the practical application of the principles of the text:

> . . . it is doing the exercises that will make the goal of the course possible. An untrained mind can accomplish nothing (workbook, p. 1).

The workbook is meant to be a one-year training program; it is not meant to supply the theoretical substance of the curriculum, which is the purpose of any textbook. Part of the world's curriculum, the undoing of which is the goal of *A Course in Miracles*, is the aforementioned belief that only a certain few--the religious elite--can be in communication with God. Only these few are seen to be worthy and chosen by their Creator, while the sinfulness and deserved guilt of the rest of the world's population prevent such an open and loving relationship with God. Such a belief clearly reinforces the ego's tale of sin, guilt, and fear of Heaven's retributive wrath. And so it is the reversal of this belief at which much of the workbook aims. It accomplishes this by beginning the process of training our minds to believe that the love of God is not absent from us, at least not by His Will. Since it is *our* wills--in consort with the ego--to banish God from the kingdom of our minds, it is also our changed wills that welcome Him back in.

In many passages, therefore, the workbook, as well as the text, places this decision before us, emphasizing that the ego system can be changed in a single instant (since there is no time, but only the illusion of time that our guilt demands is required before our sin can be redeemed, there is in reality only the one instant). However, such teachings can be very much misunderstood when removed from the context of the overriding message of the Course, which is to help us understand the enormity of the ego thought system in terms of its investment in proving the Holy Spirit wrong. For example, the manual discusses the apparent hopelessness of escaping the ego's battlefield of murder:

> There is a way in which escape is possible. It can be learned and taught, but it requires patience and *abundant* willingness (manual, p. 43, my italics).

It is interesting to note the Course's departure here from its usual use of the adjective "little" to modify "willingness." "Abundant" emphasizes to the reader the full extent of the ego thought system, and our need to exercise vigilance against our investment in it. Of the six stages in the development of trust, moreover, which are discussed in the opening pages of the manual, we find that four of them contain elements of discomfort. These are described with words such as "painful," "difficult," "It takes great learning," "enormous conflict," and "anticipated grief." In the fifth stage, the "period of unsettling," we are told that we must "attain a state [the anticipated sixth stage, "a period of achievement"] that may remain impossible to reach for a long, long time" (manual, pp. 9f).

It is clear, if only from these brief excerpts, that the curriculum of *A Course in Miracles* is a lifelong one, helping its students to embark upon a journey that requires great diligence and consistent application. We are told by Jesus early in the text that we "are much too tolerant of mind wandering, and are passively condoning . . . [our] mind's miscreations" (text, p. 25). One of the important messages to be learned from the text is the respect we should accord our ego thought system, not because it is true, but because we believe in it. Thus we can also state that the process of learning the Course involves growing in the discernment of knowing to which voice we are listening. It is to help facilitate this discernment of the ego's voice, obviously based upon recognizing it, that the text describes in graphic and sometimes painful detail, in passage after passage, the intricacies of the insane thought system we have elevated to the throne of reason and truth. The central teaching of *A Course in Miracles*, therefore, is not the love and unity that is our reality in Heaven, but rather the identifying and undoing of the guilt and fear--"protected" by our special relationships--that we believe to be our reality on earth:

> Be not afraid to look upon the special hate relationship, for freedom lies in looking at it. . . . In looking at the special relationship, it is necessary first to realize that it involves a great amount of pain. Anxiety, despair, guilt and attack all enter into it, broken into by periods in which they seem to be gone. All these must be understood for what they are. Whatever form they take, they are always an attack on the self to make the other guilty (text, pp. 313,317).

And so

> The course does not aim at teaching the meaning of love, for that is beyond what can be taught. It does aim, however, at removing the blocks to the awareness of love's presence, which is your natural inheritance (text, intro.).

And later, again in the context of the special relationship, the Course reiterates:

> Your task is not to seek for love, but merely to seek and find all of the barriers within yourself that you have built against it. It is not necessary to seek for what is true, but it *is* necessary to seek for what is false (text, p. 315).

Thus, we may fail to recognize that the central teaching of *A Course in Miracles* is helping us to remember that the one problem of the world is guilt, as expressed through the special relationship, and that its undoing comes through forgiveness. This is very clearly and succinctly stated, using slightly different terms, in two successive workbook lessons, partially cited above: "Let me recognize the problem so it can be solved," and "Let me recognize my problems have been solved":

> The problem of separation, which is really the only problem, has already been solved [through the Holy Spirit]. . . . Your one central problem has been answered, and you have no other. . . . Salvation thus depends on recognizing this one problem, and understanding that it has been solved. One problem, one solution (workbook, pp. 139,141).

Yet this problem cannot be easily recognized, let alone understood, because our whole existence in this physical world is predicated on *not* recognizing it.

Another unfortunate result of this process of denial is the confusion regarding the role of the Holy Spirit in our Atonement path. Coincident with the magical idea that all one need do to be free of the ego is have the wish that this be so (without dealing with the underlying attraction to its thought system), is the equally magical idea of the Holy Spirit as the Great Provider. We have already discussed this in some detail above, and so only briefly mention it here. Displacing our one need of undoing our belief in scarcity onto material lack, we also displace the solution for such lack onto the Holy Spirit. Rather than looking to His love as the means for undoing our faulty belief system, He now becomes the one to solve magically our pseudo-problems by providing rent money, parking spaces, good health, world peace, etc., etc., etc. The profound and truly healing message of *A Course in Miracles* thus becomes relegated to the trivial and superficial, much as the ancient spiritual wisdom of the *I Ching* has become reduced, in the hands of some, to a mere fortune-telling device.

Further, many followers of the Course identify the Holy Spirit with the ego self. Thus, we subtly replicate the original error of displacing God with our own self, and so exclude the Holy Spirit's presence from our awareness. Asking the Holy Spirit for solutions to our external concerns usurps His role, for such requests presuppose *our* understanding what our needs are, *without first consulting Heaven's wisdom*. Again, we have taken His place by presuming to know *by ourselves* our problems and their solutions. As the Course emphasizes:

> There is another advantage,--and a very important one,--in refer-
> ring decisions to the Holy Spirit with increasing frequency. . . . To
> follow the Holy Spirit's guidance is to let yourself be absolved of
> guilt. It is the essence of the Atonement. It is the core of the curricu-
> lum. The imagined usurping of functions not your own is the basis
> of fear. The whole world you see reflects the illusion that you have
> done so, making fear inevitable. To return the function to the One to
> Whom it belongs is thus the escape from fear. And it is this that lets
> the memory of love return to you (manual, p. 67).

Thus, again, by believing--*on our own*--that we have real problems external to our minds that require solutions--*that we determine*--we fall into the trap of making the error real.

Finally, we may note that the errors we have been discussing inevitably lead to the previously mentioned lack of discernment between the voice of the ego and the Voice for God; for example, anything I hear is the Holy Spirit, because my intention is holy. Moreover, even if we do "hear" right--namely our guidance is not coming from the voice of guilt--the Holy Spirit's message is often meant for us personally, filtered through our own need system. The message itself need not necessarily apply to the whole world, let alone to certain individuals we may choose to single out as beneficiaries of our revelation. Thus we are reminded by the Course to "Trust not your good intentions. They are not enough. But trust implicitly your willingness . . ." (text, p. 355). This willingness reflects our truly turning over to the Holy Spirit our *investment* to be holy, good, or helpful.

And so the overriding purpose of *A Course in Miracles* is not only to teach us that our true Identity is Christ and not the ego, but to help us understand the massive defensive structure *we* have built to defend against this truth. The Course thus provides us with the means of changing our mind and choosing again. Overly emphasizing the lovely truth about ourselves short circuits the process of undoing by placing our sleeping guilt under the heavy blanket of denial, where it then can never be brought to the healing truth of forgiveness. To assert that the central teaching of *A Course in Miracles* is love and oneness is not only to fly in the face of the Course's own words, but also to deny ourselves access to the healing opportunity it offers us.

In this regard, students of *A Course in Miracles* fall into the same category of "bliss-ninnyhood" into which many well-intentioned contemporary spiritual seekers have unfortunately fallen. These otherwise sincere seekers end up hiding the pain of their own experience within a blissful cloud of denial, to no one's benefit, least of all their own. This cloud of denial then often leads a person to profess love and unity while really denying the unconscious guilt and projecting it onto others, never truly recognizing what is being done. Thus in recent years we have observed the lack of peace and concord in individuals professing this same peace and concord. Activists of any kind, be they for racial integration, world peace or inner peace, or anti-abortionists claiming to be pro-life, all end up witnessing to the underlying ego thought system of separation, victimized attack, and death, which their conscious protestations appear to be against. Indeed, "the lady doth protest too much."

A word should be mentioned here, recalled from this book's Preface and Chapter 16, about the Course's use of language. At times *A Course in Miracles* speaks metaphorically, as when it speaks of God's loneliness, weeping, or state of incompletion:

> God is lonely without His Sons, and they are lonely without Him. ... God Himself is lonely when His Sons do not know Him (text, pp. 19,120).

> God weeps at the "sacrifice" of His children who believe they are lost to Him (text, p. 82).

> "God Himself is incomplete without me." ... For by it [sin] God Himself is changed, and rendered incomplete (text, pp. 165,375, italics omitted).

Clearly, since God is abstract and does not have a body, He does not get lonely, nor weep; as He is the All, He cannot be incomplete. Further, the very idea that He could be any of those things clearly implies that the separation of His Son from Himself has actually happened, and this of course is directly antithetical to the Course's teachings. The point that is being made, therefore, has to be understood on the level of the *content* of God's love for His children (itself of course an anthropocentric metaphor), expressed through the *form* of an earthly father's love for his child. Since we are still very much children in the spiritual life--"You are very new in the ways of salvation" (text, p. 339), *A Course in Miracles* tells us--the Course's use of language at this level is more than appropriate.

Many times *A Course in Miracles* will say something meaningful within a particular context, and yet when removed from that context the words appear inconsistent or even contradictory to its larger teachings. A good example involves the Course's teachings on time, which emphasize its non-linear as well as illusory nature. However, in many passages time is talked of *as if* it were real, paralleling our personal experience of time's reality. We have already discussed this particular teaching in Chapter 17.

Another example comes in the section "The Incorruptible Body," where some students wrench the title from its context of the body's inherent illusoriness--"The body no more dies than it can feel. It does nothing. Of itself it is neither corruptible nor incorruptible. It *is* nothing. It is the result of a tiny, mad idea of corruption that can be corrected" (text, p. 389)--to justify the teaching of *other* spiritual systems that the body can indeed become immortal, a teaching totally antithetical to the principles of *A Course in Miracles*.

We may cite one final example. On page 19 in the text we are told that "To speak of 'a miracle of healing' is to combine two orders of reality inappropriately. Healing is not a miracle." And yet on page 529 the text speaks of "A miracle of healing." The apparent inconsistency is resolved by recognizing that in the first reference Jesus is emphasizing that the miracle is a means, while healing is the result. This teaching purpose was not present later in the text, and so the more poetic expression, "a miracle of healing," could be used.

Thus, if a person's ego wishes to invalidate the authority of *A Course in Miracles*, it can easily find "cause" by pointing to these seeming incongruities. Similarly, people seeking to change the Course's teachings around to suit their own needs can also find innumerable passages to "support" their position. As a safeguard against making these mistakes, a student should always evaluate any particular statement in the Course in the light of its overall teaching.

To summarize, the errors that students of *A Course in Miracles* fall into are very similar in form to the errors to which the Gnostics fell prey. But despite the similarity in form, which is specifically relevant to this book, there is a similarity in content that underlies *all* spiritual errors: the ego's fear of our recognizing the insanity of its position, and accepting, finally, the sanity of the Holy Spirit's. With the fear of God's wrath finally examined and smiled at, the need for the defense against it disappears as well. And so the world will disappear, back into the nothingness from which it came.

Thus it is precisely this ego fear of what *A Course in Miracles* teaches that causes its students very often to attempt to change what it says. As Franz Liszt wrote in an 1870 letter--a reference I unfortunately cannot locate--regarding Wagner's beautiful though lengthy music-drama, *Die Walkuere:*

> Great works should be embraced entire, body and soul, form and thought, spirit and life. One ought not to carp at Wagner for his lengths - *it is better to expand one's scale to his* (my italics).

The ego's fearful message thus gets through to us, who still prefer the ego's story over the Holy Spirit's, and our statement to ourselves, "I do not *want* to see what this is saying," becomes: "The Course is *not* saying this." And so the message is given to our brains to change *A Course in Miracles* to mean something other than what it is truly saying.

Thus, instead of bringing our illusions to the Course's truth, we end up dragging down the Course's truth to conform to our illusions. Paraphrasing Liszt, instead of expanding our scale to the Course, we scale the Course down to ourselves, finding all manner of justifications for doing so. These include attempts to change the masculine terminology on the grounds the Course is unfair to women, or to remove the offensive Christian language on the grounds that the Course is unfair to Jews, or even to de-emphasize the religious language in general on the grounds that the Course excludes Buddhists and other practitioners of non-Western spiritualities. Channeled writings have already appeared--some of which purport to be from Jesus--stating not only that their source is the author of *A Course in Miracles*, but also claiming to improve on the original by correcting, elucidating, simplifying, or even transcending the Course. All of these, not surprisingly, de-emphasize, distort, or simply ignore the Course's non-dualistic metaphysics as being irrelevant at best, or non-existent at worst.

This de-emphasis on the metaphysics of *A Course in Miracles* has given rise to a strong anti-intellectual movement regarding the Course, not too dissimilar from a more general movement that can be noted in our society today. This movement has also been associated with the overemphasis on experience and feelings that has overrun psychology, a movement whose contemporary roots date back to the post-World War II period. Students of *A Course in Miracles* may therefore argue that understanding its theory is irrelevant, and that study of the text is a waste of time, clearly ignoring this warning at the end of the first chapter:

> This is a course in mind training. All learning involves attention and study at some level. Some of the later parts of the course rest too heavily on these earlier sections not to require their careful study. You will also need them for preparation. Without this, you may become much too fearful of what is to come to make constructive use of it. However, as you study these earlier sections, you will begin to see some of the implications that will be amplified later on (text, p. 13).

One then sees many students emphasizing the workbook at the expense of the text, rather than viewing each book as a companion to the other. The error here is similar to what we have already discussed. It reflects the same unconscious Gnostic error of believing that our ego identification is weak and can be easily discarded, leaving our minds open to receive--instantaneously and joyously--the Word of God. This anti-intellectual stance is thus in many cases the expression of a fear of looking at the ego thought system in all its ugliness. As we have commented before, no one really wants to deal with the horrifying sin and guilt our egos have convinced us is our reality.

Thus, rather than carefully reading the text--which lays out the brutal nature of the ego thought system, necessitating our dealing with it--a student may dismiss such discussions of the ego as not being important. Again, this misses the whole point of the Course's efficacy as a spiritual teaching, and discounts the inherent unity of its curriculum, which does depend on understanding and recognizing our investment in perpetuating the ego's thought system, precisely by *not* looking at it. As we have already discussed, it is in not looking at the ego that it is allowed to survive as a thought system in our minds. To be sure, *A Course in Miracles* is not always easy to understand, let alone practice. Yet the ultimate difficulty does not really lie on a conceptual or intellectual level, but rather is found within the teaching itself. This teaching, as we have discussed throughout this book, strikes terror in minds which still identify with the ego self. And it is this very ego self that is so threatened by what the Course presents to us.

Finally, we should underscore that the attempt to dismiss the Course's teachings also reflects a denial of what *A Course in Miracles* is. It *is* an intellectual system, at least in form. In fact, the scribe Helen Schucman had exclaimed to Jesus at the close of the dictation: "Thank God there is at last something [on the spiritual life] for the intellectual." There already exist many fine spiritual systems--ancient and contemporary--that are non-intellectual. All these are as valid as the Course in their potential to lead their serious students to God. To deny the Course its particular uniqueness is to diminish its contribution, just as forcing a non-intellectual approach into a Procrustean bed of the intellect would wreak equal havoc on that system. Moreover, it is important to realize that working through the Course's intellectual presentation leads one to an *experience* of peace, and that experience, not a mere intellectual understanding, is the goal of the Course.

Therefore, students should pay careful attention to the Course's teachings on the ego, and should resist the temptation to change the form to suit their personal requirements. Above all, one should have humility as one stands before it. The Course urges us to "Be humble before Him, and yet great *in* Him" (text, p. 288), meaning that we are great because of our Identity as God's Son, and yet we are humble because He is our Creator and Source, and we need His help (through the Holy Spirit) to awaken to our reality as His Son. Likewise, we should feel the humility of recognizing the learning we need accomplish before we can remember our Identity as Christ. Trying to change, distort, or scale *A Course in Miracles* down to our size is an expression of the ego's arrogance. One would do well to remember a statement made by Bruno Walter, perhaps the greatest Mozart conductor of this century.

> It needs some maturity to understand the depth of emotion which speaks in Mozart's seeming tranquillity and measure. . . . I was . . . fifty when for the first time I was audacious enough to perform the G Minor [Symphony]. I . . . had such a feeling of responsibility and of the difficulty to perform it. . . . And I wondered at all the young conductors who, without any qualms, just went ahead and conducted all these works which asked for such depth of feeling and such maturity of technique. (From an unpublished interview.)

Clearly, people do not have to be fifty before they can feel they have understood *A Course in Miracles*, or are prepared to teach it. However, we should be able to accept with humility the need to learn from this wonderful gift from Heaven, rather then to allow the ego's arrogance to tell us that, since the love of God is all that we now experience, we have already learned everything the Course can teach. True humility, in the spirit of Dr. Walter's attitude towards Mozart, would have us welcome gladly the truth that in this world we have much to learn, and so we gratefully accept the spiritual tool and inner Guide that would teach us how to remove "the blocks to the awareness of love's presence" (text, intro.), and return home to that Love.

EPILOGUE

Helmut Koester has commented on the newly discovered Nag Hammadi texts ("new texts"):

> We must rewrite Christian theology to reflect a more radical newness. . . . Our old schemes of categorization, developed by the last century of scholarship, are not adequate for the new texts. We must not simply fit the new evidence into the old schemes but rather develop new schemes, to be discarded in their turn (Layton, p. 351).

A Course in Miracles is such a rewrite of Christian theology, in the context of the Neoplatonic and Gnostic traditions, cleansed and expanded by the insights of twentieth-century psychology. Thus the old wine of traditional Christianity has been reconstituted in new wineskins, its "old schemes" looked at freshly, and presented anew to eyes and ears receptive to the form of its message. Indeed, the Course can be thought of as the zenith of Western philosophical and religious thought, reconciling the paradox that has virtually imprisoned us in thought systems that reflected our conflicted experience in a world from which we could not truly escape. Holding the key that unlocks this prison door, the Course heals these conflicts of the past, freeing us to build upon its foundation a new beginning, turning the corner on a journey that will carry us ever closer to our God.

At the end of the third edition of *The Gnostic Religion,* Jonas posed a challenge to philosophy regarding "a third road" that bridges the gap between our dualistic experience in the world and the truth of our transcendent reality:

> The disruption between man and total reality is at the bottom of nihilism. The illogicality of the rupture, that is, of a dualism without metaphysics, makes its fact no less real, nor its seeming alternative any more acceptable: the stare at isolated selfhood, to which it condemns man, may wish to exchange itself for a monistic naturalism which, along with the rupture, would abolish also the idea of man as man. Between that Scylla and this her twin Charybdis, the modern mind hovers. Whether a third road is open to it--one by which the dualistic rift can be avoided and yet enough of the dualistic insight saved to uphold the humanity of man—philosophy must find out (Jonas, p. 340).

It has been one of the prime motivations of this book to set forth the integration of these two roads--a non-dualistic metaphysics alongside our dualistic experience here--and illustrate how *A Course in Miracles*

561

provides that middle ground of which Jonas speaks: a philosophical teaching that does full justice both to our experience within the physical world, and our awareness of the reality that is totally transcendent to our experience here. In this regard, then, the reader has been urged *not* to change the Course, but, seeking to grow into its vision, to accept it on *its* terms in order to understand the gift it is offering. Thus, in the context of students working with the Course, we may repeat here the words of Krishnamurti in continually reminding his audiences of the importance of truly listening to his teaching message: *Pay attention.*

Recognizing the philosophical and theological soil from which *A Course in Miracles* derives the context for its ultimately trans-contextual message can be a helpful tool in one's study and practice of its teachings. Thus, this book has also addressed those who would find explication of such a context advantageous to their study. The in-depth look at the Course's resolution of the God-world paradox highlights the uniqueness of *A Course in Miracles* as a contemporary spiritual tool. However, whether or not individuals decide it is their particular spiritual path, it is hoped at least that such decision is an informed one, rather than one made--for or against--on the basis of misunderstanding and fear.

Thus we can, finally, speak of the Course as being the great middle path--Jonas' "third road"--that steers clear of the twin dangers of irrelevant and impractical metaphysics on the one hand, and superficial and groundless practical application on the other. By blending together both roads, *A Course in Miracles* forges a spirituality for our day that meets us in our ego's depths, at the same time lifting us to the gate of Heaven. We recall this previously quoted passage from the workbook:

> Our Love awaits us as we go to Him, and walks beside us showing us the way. He fails in nothing. He the end we seek, and He the means by which we go to Him (workbook, p. 440).

Joined once again with the love of Heaven, we are free to walk through this world of seeming imprisonment and pain, with God's gentle presence of truth flowing unhindered through us. Our eyes have opened to reality; and despite our apparent presence within the illusory world, our minds have remembered their Source, and rest peacefully within His love. The nightmare has ended, replaced by happy dreams of forgiveness whose message of hope and freedom has been finally received. Our grateful hearts open to God's Call, and our arms extend in fond embrace to all living things. Jesus' name sings through our lips, softly touching all the world whose ears have yearned for sounds they thought were forever lost. Now does the song of Heaven's love reverberate through every mind, and our journey speeds mightily along as we rejoin our loved ones, reunited in Christ, for Christ, as Christ. One Son again, we are safely home and can rest at last.

APPENDIX

THE GOSPEL OF TRUTH

This tractate is reprinted here from The Nag Hammadi Library, *first edition, translation by George W. MacRae. Textual signs have been retained except for line dividers and numbers. Square brackets [] indicate a lacuna in the manuscript; when the text could not be reconstructed, three dots were placed within the brackets, regardless of the size of the lacuna. Pointed brackets <> indicate a correction of a scribal omission or error. Braces {} indicate superfluous letters or words added by the scribe. Parentheses () indicate material supplied by the editor or translator.*

The gospel of truth is a joy for those who have received from the Father of truth the gift of knowing him, through the power of the Word that came forth from the pleroma--the one who is in the thought and the mind of the Father, that is, the one who is addressed as the Savior, (that) being the name of the work he is to perform for the redemption of those who were ignorant of the Father, while the name [of] the gospel is the proclamation of hope, being discovery for those who search for him.

Indeed the all went about searching for the one from whom it (pl.) had come forth, and the all was inside of him, the incomprehensible, inconceivable one who is superior to every thought. Ignorance of the Father brought about anguish and terror. And the anguish grew solid like a fog so that no one was able to see. For this reason error became powerful; it fashioned its own matter foolishly, not having known the truth. It set about making a creature, with (all its) might preparing, in beauty, the substitute for the truth.

This was not, then, a humiliation for him, the incomprehensible, inconceivable one, for they were nothing--the anguish and the oblivion and the creature of lying--while the established truth is immutable, imperturbable, perfect in beauty. For this reason, despise error.

Being thus without any root, it fell into a fog regarding the Father, while it was involved in preparing works and oblivions and terrors in order that by means of these it might entice those of the middle and capture them. The oblivion of error was not revealed. It is not a [...] under the Father. Oblivion did not come into existence under the Father, although it did indeed come into existence because of him. But what comes into existence in him is knowledge, which appeared in order that oblivion might vanish and the Father might be known. Since oblivion came into existence because the Father was not known, then if the Father comes to be known, oblivion will not exist from that moment on.

This <is> the gospel of the one who is searched for, which <was> revealed to those who are perfect through the mercies of the Father--

567

the hidden mystery, Jesus, the Christ. Through it he enlightened those who were in darkness. Out of oblivion he enlightened them, he showed (them) a way. And the way is the truth which he taught them.

For this reason error grew angry at him, persecuted him, was distressed at him, (and) was brought to naught. He was nailed to a tree; he became a fruit of the knowledge of the Father, which did not, however, become destructive because it <was> eaten, but to those who ate it it gave (cause) to become glad in the discovery. For he discovered them in himself, and they discovered him in themselves, the incomprehensible, inconceivable one, the Father, the perfect one, the one who made the all, while the all is within him and the all has need of him, since he retained its (pl.) perfection within himself which he did not give to the all. The Father was not jealous. What jealousy indeed (could there be) between himself and his members? For if the aeon had thus [received] their [perfection], they could not have come [...] the Father, since he retained their perfection within himself, granting it to them as a return to him and a knowledge unique in perfection. It is he who fashioned the all, and the all is within him and the all had need of him.

As in the case of one of whom some are ignorant, who wishes to have them know him and love him, so--for what did the all have need of if not knowledge regarding the Father?--he became a guide, restful and leisurely. He went into the midst of the schools (and) he spoke the word as a teacher. There came the wise men--in their own estimation--putting him to the test. But he confounded them because they were foolish. They hated him because they were not really wise.

After all these, there came the little children also, those to whom the knowledge of the Father belongs. Having been strengthened, they learned about the impressions of the Father. They knew, they were known; they were glorified, they glorified. There was revealed in their heart the living book of the living--the one written in the thought and the mind [of the] Father, and which from before the foundation of the all was within the incomprehensible (parts) of him--that (book) which no one was able to take since it is reserved for the one who will take it and will be slain. No one could have appeared among those who believed in salvation unless that book had intervened. For this reason the merciful one, the faithful one, Jesus, was patient in accepting sufferings until he took that book, since he knows that his death is life for many.

Just as there lies hidden in a will, before it <is> opened, the fortune of the deceased master of the house, so (it is) with the all, which lay hidden while the Father of the all was invisible, the one who is from himself, from whom all spaces come forth. For this reason Jesus appeared; he put on that book; he was nailed to a tree; he published the

edict of the Father on the cross. O such great teaching! He draws
himself down to death though life eternal clothes him. Having
stripped himself of the perishable rags, he put on imperishability,
which no one can possibly take away from him. Having entered the
empty spaces of terrors, he passed through those who were stripped
naked by oblivion, being knowledge and perfection, proclaiming the
things that are in the heart of the [Father] in order to [...] teach those
who will receive teaching.

But those who are to receive teaching [are] the living who are
inscribed in the book of the living. They receive teaching about
themselves. They receive it (pl.) from the Father, turning again to him.
Since the perfection of the all is in the Father, it is necessary for the all
to ascend to him. Then, if one has knowledge, he receives what are his
own and draws them to himself. For he who is ignorant is in need, and
what he lacks is great since he lacks that which will make him perfect.
Since the perfection of the all is in the Father and it is necessary for the
all to ascend to him and for each one to receive what are his own, he en-
rolled them in advance, having prepared them to give to those who
came forth from him.

Those whose name he knew in advance were called at the end, so
that one who has knowledge is the one whose name the Father has
uttered. For he whose name has not been spoken is ignorant. Indeed,
how is one to hear if his name has not been called? For he who is
ignorant until the end is a creature of oblivion, and he will vanish along
with it. If not, how is it that these miserable ones have no name, (how
is it that) they do not have the call? Therefore if one has knowledge, he
is from above. If he is called, he hears, he answers, and he turns to him
who is calling him, and ascends to him. And he knows in what manner
he is called. Having knowledge, he does the will of the one who called
him, he wishes to be pleasing to him, he receives rest.

Each one's name comes to him. He who is to have knowledge in this
manner knows where he comes from and where he is going. He knows
as one who having become drunk has turned away from his drunkenness, (and) having returned to himself, has set right what are his own.
He has brought many back from error. He has gone before them to
their places, from which they had moved away when they received
error, on account of the depth of the one who encircles all spaces while
there is none that encircles him. It was a great wonder that they were
in the Father, not knowing him, and (that) they were able to come forth
by themselves, since they were unable to comprehend or to know the
one in whom they were. If his will had not thus emerged from him--
for he revealed it in view of a knowledge in which all its emanations
concur.

This is the knowledge of the living book which he revealed to the
aeons to the last of its [letters], revealing how they are not vowels nor

are they consonants, so that one might read them and think of something foolish, but they are letters of the truth which they alone speak who know them. Each letter is a complete <thought> like a complete book, since they are letters written by the Unity, the Father having written them for the aeons in order that by means of his letters they should know the Father. His wisdom contemplates the Word, his teaching utters it, his knowledge has revealed <it>. His forbearance is a crown upon it, his gladness is in harmony with it, his glory has exalted it, his image has revealed it, his repose has received it into itself, his love has made a body over it, his fidelity has embraced it. In this way the Word of the Father goes forth in the all, as the fruit [of] his heart and an impression of his will. But it supports the all; it chooses it (pl.) and also receives the impression of the all, purifying it (pl.), bringing it (pl.) back into the Father, into the Mother, Jesus of the infiniteness of gentleness.

The Father reveals his bosom--now his bosom is the Holy Spirit. He reveals what is hidden of him--what is hidden of him is his Son--so that through the mercies of the Father the aeons may know him and cease laboring in search of the Father, resting there in him, knowing that this is rest. Having filled the deficiency, he abolished the form--the form of it is the world, that in which he served. For the place where there is envy and strife is a deficiency, but the place where (there is) Unity is a perfection. Since the deficiency came into being because the Father was not known, therefore when the Father is known, from that moment on the deficiency will no longer exist. As with the ignorance of a person, when he comes to have knowledge his ignorance vanishes of itself, as the darkness vanishes when light appears, so also the deficiency vanishes in the perfection. So from that moment on the form is not apparent, but it will vanish in the fusion of Unity, for now their works lie scattered. In time Unity will perfect the spaces. It is within Unity that each one will attain himself; within knowledge he will purify himself from multiplicity into Unity, consuming matter within himself like fire, and darkness by light, death by life.

If indeed these things have happened to each one of us, then we must see to it above all that the house will be holy and silent for the Unity. (It is) as in the case of some people who moved out of dwellings where there were jars that in spots were not good. They would break them, and the master of the house does not suffer loss. Rather <he> is glad because in place of the bad jars there are full ones which are made perfect. For such is the judgment which has come from above. It has passed judgment on everyone; it is a drawn sword, with two edges, cutting on either side. When the Word came into the midst, the one that is within the heart of those who utter it--it is not a sound alone but it became a body--a great disturbance took place among the jars because some had been emptied, others filled; that is, some had been supplied, others poured out, some had been purified, still others broken up. All the spaces were shaken and disturbed because they had no order nor stability. Error was upset, not knowing what to do; it was grieved, in mourning, afflicting itself because it knew nothing. When knowledge drew near it--this is the downfall of (error) and all its emanations--error is empty, having nothing inside.

Truth came into the midst; all its emanations knew it. They greeted the Father in truth with a perfect power that joins them with the Father. For everyone loves the truth because the truth is the mouth of the Father; his tongue is the Holy Spirit. He who is joined to the truth is joined to the Father's mouth by his tongue, whenever he is to receive the Holy Spirit. This is the manifestation of the Father and his revelation to his aeons: he manifested what was hidden of him; he explained it. For who contains if not the Father alone? All the spaces are his emanations. They have known that they came forth from him like children who are from a grown man. They knew that they had not yet received form nor yet received a name, each one of which the Father begets. Then when they receive form by his knowledge, though truly within him, they do not know him. But the Father is perfect, knowing every space within him. If he wishes, he manifests whomever he wishes by giving him form and giving him a name, and he gives a name to him and brings it about that those come into existence who before they come into existence are ignorant of him who fashioned them.

I do not say, then, that they are nothing (at all) who have not yet come into existence, but they are in him who will wish that they come into existence when he wishes, like the time that is to come. Before all things appear, he knows what he will produce. But the fruit which is not yet manifest knows nothing, nor does it do anything. Thus also every space which is itself in the Father is from the one who exists, who established it from what does not exist. For he who has no root has no fruit either, but though he thinks to himself, "I have come into being," yet he will perish by himself. For this reason, he who did not exist at all will never come into existence. What, then, did he wish him to think of himself? This: "I have come into being like the shadows and phantoms of the night." When the light shines on the terror which that person had experienced, he knows that it is nothing.

Thus they were ignorant of the Father, he being the one whom they did not see. Since it was terror and disturbance and instability and doubt and division, there were many illusions at work by means of these, and (there were) empty fictions, as if they were sunk in sleep and found themselves in disturbing dreams. Either (there is) a place to which they are fleeing, or without strength they come (from) having chased after others, or they are involved in striking blows, or they are receiving blows themselves, or they have fallen from high places, or they take off into the air though they do not even have wings. Again, sometimes (it is as) if people were murdering them, though there is no one even pursuing them, or they themselves are killing their neighbors, for they have been stained with their blood. When those who are going through all these things wake up, they see nothing, they who were in the midst of all these disturbances, for they are nothing. Such is the way of those who have cast ignorance aside from them like sleep, not esteeming it as anything, nor do they esteem its works as solid things either, but they leave them behind like a dream in the night. The knowledge of the Father they value as the dawn. This is the way each one has acted, as though asleep at the time when he was ignorant. And this is the way he has come to knowledge, as if he had awakened. {And} Good for the man who will come to and awaken. And blessed is he who has opened the eyes of the blind. And the Spirit ran after him, hastening from waking him up. Having extended his hand to him who lay upon the ground, he set him up on his feet, for he had not yet risen. He gave them the means of knowing the knowledge of the Father and the revelation of his Son.

For when they had seen him and had heard him, he granted them to taste him and to smell him and to touch the beloved Son. When he had appeared instructing them about the Father, the incomprehensible one, when he had breathed into them what is in the mind, doing his will, when many had received the light, they turned to him. For the material ones were strangers and did not see his likeness and had not known him. For he came by means of fleshly appearance while nothing blocked his course because it was incorruptibility (and) irresistibility. Again, speaking new things, still speaking about what is in the heart of the Father, he brought forth the flawless word. Light spoke through his mouth, and his voice gave birth to life. He gave them thought and understanding and mercy and salvation and the powerful spirit from the infiniteness and the gentleness of the Father. He made punishments and tortures cease, for it was they which were leading astray from his face some who were in need of mercy, in error and in bonds; and with power he destroyed them and confounded them with knowledge. He became a way for those who were lost and knowledge for those who were ignorant, a discovery for those who were searching, and a support for those who were wavering, immaculateness for those who were defiled.

He is the shepherd who left behind the ninety-nine sheep which were not lost. He went searching for the one which was lost. He rejoiced when he found it, for 99 is a number that is in the left hand which holds it. But when the one is found, the entire number passes to the right (hand). Thus (it is with) him who lacks the one; that is, the entire right which draws what was deficient and takes it from the left-hand side and brings (it) to the right, and thus the number becomes 100. It is the sign of the one who is in their sound; it is the Father. Even on the Sabbath, he labored for the sheep which he found fallen into the pit. He gave life to the sheep, having brought it up from the pit in order that you might know interiorly--you, the sons of interior knowledge--what is the Sabbath, on which it is not fitting for salvation to be idle, in order that you may speak from the day from above, which has no night, and from the light which does not sink because it is perfect. Say, then, from the heart that you are the perfect day and in you dwells the light that does not fail.

Speak of the truth with those who search for it, and (of) knowledge to those who have committed sin in their error. Make firm the foot of those who have stumbled and stretch out your hands to those who are ill. Feed those who are hungry and give repose to those who are weary, and raise up those who wish to rise, and awaken those who sleep. For you are the understanding that is drawn forth. If strength acts thus, it becomes even stronger. Be concerned with yourselves; do not be concerned with other things which you have rejected from yourselves. Do not return to what you have vomited to eat it. Do not be moths, do not be worms, for you have already cast it off. Do not become a (dwelling) place for the devil, for you have already destroyed him. Do not strengthen (those who are) obstacles to you who are collapsing, as though (you were) a support (for them). For the unjust one is someone to treat ill rather than the just one. For the former does his works as an unjust person; the latter as a righteous person does his works among others. So you, do the will of the Father, for you are from him.

For the Father is gentle and in his will there are good things. He took cognizance of the things that are yours that you might find rest in them. For by the fruits does one take cognizance of the things that are yours because the children of the Father are his fragrance, for they are from the grace of his countenance. For this reason the Father loves his fragrance and manifests it in every place, and if it mixes with matter he gives his fragrance to the light and in his repose he causes it to surpass every form (and) every sound. For it is not the ears that smell the fragrance, but (it is) the breath that has the sense of smell and attracts the fragrance to itself and is submerged in the fragrance of the Father. It shelters it, then, takes it to the place where it came from, the first fragrance which is grown cold. It is something in a psychic form, being like cold water which has [...], which is on earth that is not solid, of which those who see it think it is earth; afterwards it dissolves again. If a breath draws it, it gets hot. The fragrances therefore that are cold are from the division. For this reason [faith] came; it did away with the division, and it brought the warm pleroma of love in order that the cold should not come again but there should be the unity of perfect thought.

This <is> the word of the gospel of the discovery of the pleroma, for those who await the salvation which is coming from on high. While their hope which they are waiting for is waiting--they whose image is light with no shadow in it--then at that time the pleroma is about to come. The deficiency of matter has not arisen through the limitlessness of the Father, who is about to bring the time of the deficiency, although no one could say that the incorruptible one will come in this way. But the depth of the Father was multiplied and the thought of error did not exist with him. It is a thing that falls, it is a thing that easily stands upright (again) in the discovery of him who has come to him whom he shall bring back. For the bringing back is called repentance.

For this reason incorruptibility breathed forth; it pursued the one who had sinned in order that he might rest. For forgiveness is what remains for the light in the deficiency, the word of the pleroma. For the physician runs to the place where a sickness is because that is his will that is in him. He who has a deficiency, then, does not hide it, because one has what the other lacks. So with the pleroma, which has no deficiency; it fills up his deficiency--(it is) that which he provided for filling up what he lacks, in order that therefore he might receive the grace. When he was deficient he did not have the grace. That is why there was diminution existing in the place where there is no grace. When that which was diminished was received, he revealed what he lacked, as a pleroma; that is the discovery of the light of truth which rose upon him because it is immutable.

That is why Christ was spoken of in their midst, so that those who were disturbed might receive a bringing back, and he might anoint them with the ointment. The ointment is the mercy of the Father who will have mercy on them. But those whom he has anointed are the ones who have become perfect. For full jars are the ones that are usually anointed. But when the anointing of one (jar) is dissolved, it is emptied, and the reason for there being a deficiency is the thing through which its ointment goes. For at that time a breath draws it, one by the power of the one with it. But from him who has no deficiency no seal is removed, nor is anything emptied. But what he lacks the perfect Father fills again. He is good. He knows his plantings because it is he who planted them in his paradise. Now his paradise is his place of rest.

This is the perfection in the thought of the Father, and these are the words of his meditation. Each one of his words is the work of his one will in the revelation of his Word. While they were still in the depth of his thought, the Word which was first to come forth revealed them along with a mind that speaks the one Word in silent grace. It (masc.)

was called thought since they were in it (fem.) before being revealed. It came about, then, that it was first to come forth at the time that was pleasing to the will of him who willed. And the will is what the Father rests in and is pleased with. Nothing happens without him, nor does anything happen without the will of the Father, but his will is incomprehensible. His trace is the will, and no one will know it, nor is it possible for one to scrutinize it in order to grasp it. But when he wills, what he wills is this--even if the sight does not please them in any way--before God (it is) the will, the Father. For he knows the beginning of all of them and their end. For at their end he will question them directly (?). Now the end is receiving knowledge about the one who is hidden, and this is the Father, from whom the beginning came forth, to whom all will return who have come forth from him. And they have appeared for the glory and the joy of his name.

Now the name of the Father is the Son. It is he who first gave a name to the one who came forth from him, who was himself, and he begot him as a son. He gave him his name which belonged to him; he is the one to whom belongs all that exists around him, the Father. His is the name; his is the Son. It is possible for him to be seen. But the name is invisible because it alone is the mystery of the invisible which comes to ears that are completely filled with it. For indeed the Father's name is not spoken, but it is apparent through a Son.

In this way, then, the name is a great thing. Who therefore will be able to utter a name for him, the great name, except him alone to whom the name belongs and the sons of the name in whom rested the name of the Father, (who) in turn themselves rested in his name? Since the Father is unengendered, he alone is the one who begot a name for himself before he brought forth the aeons in order that the name of the Father should be over their head as lord, that is, the name in truth, which is firm in his command through perfect power. For the name is not from (mere) words, nor does his name consist of appellations, but it is invisible. He gave a name to himself since he sees himself, he alone having the power to give himself a name. For he who does not exist has no name. For what name is given to him who does not exist? But the one who exists exists also with his name, and he knows himself. And to give himself a name is (the prerogative of) the Father. The Son is his name. He did not therefore hide it in the work, but the Son existed; he alone was given the name. The name therefore is that of the Father, as the name of the Father is the Son. Where indeed would mercy find a name except with the Father?

But no doubt one will say to his neighbor, "Who is it who will give a name to him who existed before himself, as if offspring did not receive a name from those who begot them?" First, then, it is fitting for us to reflect on this matter: what is the name? It is the name in truth;

it is not therefore the name from the father, for it is the one which is the proper name. Therefore he did not receive the name on loan as (do) others, according to the form in which each one is to be produced. But this is the proper name. There is no one else who gave it to him. But he is unnameable, indescribable, until the time when he who is perfect spoke of himself. And it is he who has the power to speak his name and to see it.

When therefore it pleased him that his name which is uttered should be his Son, and he gave the name to him, that is, him who came forth from the depth, he spoke about his secret things, knowing that the Father is a being without evil. For that very reason he brought him forth in order to speak about the place and his resting-place from which he had come forth, and to glorify the pleroma, the greatness of his name and the gentleness of the Father. About the place each one came from he will speak, and to the region where he received his essential being he will hasten to return again, and to be taken from that place--the place where he stood--receiving a taste from that place and receiving nourishment, receiving growth. And his own resting-place in his pleroma.

Therefore all the emanations of the Father are pleromas, and the root of all his emanations is in the one who made them all grown up in himself. He assigned them their destinies. Each one then is apparent in order that through their own thought [...]. For the place to which they send their thought, that place (is) their root, which takes them up in all the heights to the Father. They possess his head which is rest for them and they hold on close to him, as though to say that they have participated in his face by means of kisses. But they do not appear in this way, for they did not surpass themselves nor lack the glory of the Father nor think of him as small nor that he is harsh nor that he is wrathful, but a being without evil, imperturbable, gentle, knowing all spaces before they have come into existence, and having no need to be instructed.

This is the manner of those who possess (something) from above of the immeasurable greatness, as they stretch out after the one alone and the perfect one, the one who is there for them. And they do not go down to Hades nor have they envy nor groaning nor death within them, but they rest in him who is at rest, not striving nor being involved in the search for truth. But they themselves are the truth; and the Father is within them and they are in the Father, being perfect, being undivided in the truly good one, being in no way deficient in anything, but they are set at rest, refreshed in the Spirit. And they will heed their root. They will be concerned with those (things) in which he will find his root and not suffer loss to his soul. This is the place of the blessed; this is their place.

For the rest, then, may they know, in their places, that it is not fitting for me, having come to be in the resting-place, to speak of anything else. But it is in it that I shall come to be, to be concerned at all times with the Father of the all and the true brothers, those upon whom the love of the Father is poured out and in whose midst there is no lack of him. They are the ones who appear in truth since they exist in true and eternal life and speak of the light which is perfect and filled with the seed of the Father, and which is in his heart and in the pleroma, while his Spirit rejoices in it and glorifies the one in whom it existed because he is good. And his children are perfect and worthy of his name, for he is the Father: it is children of this kind that he loves.

TABLE OF DATES

GLOSSARY

anamnesis - the process whereby the imprisoned soul, through reason and education, remembers its true home in the intelligible world.

cosmos - the entire physical universe created by the Demiurge (Plato), Divine Mind (Philo), or Soul (Plotinus); seen as a "living god." See also under Gnosticism, and "world" under *A Course in Miracles*.

Craftsman - See: *Demiurge*

Demiurge - the fashioner or Craftsman of the material world; a positive figure in Plato. See also under Gnosticism.

evil - inherent in matter; what is not spiritual or good.

Good - Plato's God, the Source of the Ideas.

hyle - "matter"; a given in Platonic thought; uncreated, the lowest in the chain of being; unformed and irrational until shaped by the Demiurge (Mind, Soul).

hypostasis - in Plotinus, one of three Divine Beings: One, Mind, Soul.

Ideas (Forms) - the perfect, immutable, and ideal models, of which everything found in the material world is but an imperfect copy; part of reality.

Intelligible - Platonic word for spiritual, as in the intelligible (non-material) world.

Logos - Philo's term, roughly equivalent to Plato's Ideas, through which God creates the world.

matter - See: *hyle*.

Middle Platonism - the revival of Platonism in the second century B.C. through the first century A.D.

mimesis - imitation; the activity wherein the soul imitates the purity of the Ideas and attains virtue.

Mind - Middle Platonic term, roughly equivalent to Plato's Good; in Plotinus, the middle part of the Triad and the home of the Divine Ideas, giving rise to the Soul.

Monism - philosophical doctrine of one original principle of being; non-dualism.

Neoplatonism - the extension of Platonism beginning in the third century A.D.; Plotinus was its foremost representative.

nous - "mind"; seen as divine and thus roughly equivalent to the spirit.

nurse - in Plato, the receptacle for matter, later to be fashioned into the world by the Demiurge.

One - in Plotinus, the first part of the Triad and thus equivalent to God; totally unified and undifferentiated.

ontology - study of being; usually referring to ultimate origins, as in the ontological instant of separation.

reason - Plato's "salvation" principle, the means whereby the soul remembers its reality.

soul - in Plato, consists of reason, emotion, and the appetites; is immortal and yet is trapped in the world of shadows and must be freed to return to the world of light; also spoken of as the mediator between these two worlds; in Plotinus, the third part of the Triad and creator of the world, and also the mediator between the Ideas and the world; when spelled in lower case, refers to the split off part of the Soul that became trapped in matter and needs to return to its Self. See also under GNOSTICISM.

ORTHODOX CHRISTIANITY

Apocrypha (New Testament) - the Christian writings that remained outside of the Church canon (non-canonical), some of which nonetheless remained unofficially sanctioned by the Church.

apophaticism - the theological teaching that God is totally beyond our understanding and knowledge.

canon - "rule"; the set of writings, established by the orthodox Church, that came to be exclusively identified as the New Testament.

Christ - Second Person of the Trinity, exclusively identified with Jesus, God's only Son. See also under *A COURSE IN MIRACLES*.

Christology - the theology of Christ (Jesus); "low" Christology refers to the Synoptic Jesus who is born to the Virgin Mary; "high" Christology refers to the Johannine Jesus who coexists with God from the beginning--the cosmic Christ--and through whom the world is created.

deutero-Paul - "second Paul"; the unknown author of New Testament letters attributed to Paul, but written after his death.

docetism - Gnostic heresy; see under GNOSTICISM.

eschatology - theology of the "End Times"; almost always concerned with the Last Judgment.

Fathers of the Church - the theologians of the early Christian centuries, whose writings shaped Church theology.

God - See: *Trinity*; more popularly thought of as the First Person of the Trinity; Creator of both Heaven and the material universe; Father of Jesus Christ, His only Son. See also under *A COURSE IN MIRACLES*.

heresiologists - the Church Fathers who devoted themselves to defending the Church against those deemed as heretics.

Holy Spirit - Third Person of the Trinity, coexistent with the Father and the Son. See also under *A COURSE IN MIRACLES*.

Jesus - See: *Christ*. See also under *A COURSE IN MIRACLES*.

Johannine - denoting the gospel and three epistles of John.

Logos - in John's gospel the creative principle of God, equated solely with Jesus Christ, the Second Person of the Trinity.

Pelagianism - a Christian heresy that held that God is not necessary for salvation; opposed by St. Augustine's doctrine of grace.

rational beings - Origen's term for God's original creation, the spiritual Self, that "falls," after which the rational being is referred to as the soul.

regula fidei - "rule of faith"; the divinely inspired norm for the "true" interpretation of the gospel.

soteriology - the doctrine of salvation.

synoptic gospels - gospels written with the "same eye"-- Matthew, Mark, Luke--which share many similarities with each other, and all different from the gospel of John.

Subordinationism - a Christian heresy, expressed by Origen, that described the downward procession of the Trinity, wherein the Second and Third Persons are inferior to the First.

Trinity - the Three Persons of the Godhead, consisting of God the Father, God the Son, and God the Holy Spirit.

GNOSTICISM

aeons - "worlds"; divine beings or emanations of God; part of the Pleroma.

archons - the evil rulers of the world who seek to imprison the Gnostics.

Christ - one of the original aeons, very close to the Creator; manifested in this world as Jesus. See also under CHRISTIANITY and *A COURSE IN MIRACLES*.

cosmos - the entire physical universe; seen by the Gnostics as negative; the product of the false god and ruled by evil archons seeking to imprison humanity. See also under PLATONISM.

cosmogony - study of the origin of the world.

cosmology - study of the nature of the world.

Cross - See: *Limit*

Demiurge - taken from Plato, offspring of Sophia and fashioner of the world; almost always portrayed in negative terms, at best as neutral. See also under PLATONISM.

deficiency - the Valentinian term for the state of lack that followed Sophia's folly; remedied only by knowledge *(gnosis)*; comparable to the scarcity principle of *A Course in Miracles*.

Docetism - from the Greek *dokein*, meaning "appear"; a branch of Gnosticism, teaching that Jesus merely *appeared* to inhabit a body.

dualism - the principle of coexisting precosmic states of light and darkness, good and evil, that establishes evil as real.

epiphenomenon - what is secondary to, or derived from, something else; e.g., the world is the epiphenomenon of Sophia's folly.

First Father - term for God, the Creator; sometimes denotes the Demiurge or Ialdabaoth.

Gnosis, Gnosticism - "Knowledge."

God - the true Creator and source of life; in most Gnostic systems He is unknowable and ineffable; also known as Fore-Father. See also under CHRISTIANITY and *A COURSE IN MIRACLES*.

hylic - part of the threefold division of humanity, corresponding to the body; the hylics represented those who were already damned and lost.

Ialdabaoth - the equivalent to the Demiurge, also known by other names and spellings; Sophia's offspring, mockingly depicted as the Old Testament creator God.

Jesus Splendor - in Manicheism, a mythological figure of light and redemption; also known as the Luminous Jesus. Limit (Cross) - in Valentinian *Gnosis*, created after Sophia's fall to separate out the lower from the higher Sophia, casting the lower out of the Pleroma, thus protecting the other aeons.

Luminous Jesus - See: *Jesus Splendor*

mana - in Mandeanism, the divinity in humanity.

Manda - in Mandeanism, "Knowledge"; the equivalent of "Gnosticism."

Manda dHaiye - in Mandeanism, "Knowledge of Life"; the savior of the Mandeans, sent to the world by the Great Life.

non-dualism - the principle that in the beginning there existed only light or good, with darkness or evil coming later; in its pure form the non-dualistic position holds that *only* light is real, with darkness being illusory; other non-dualisms make the light primary, yet evil real nonetheless.

Ogdoad - the first two tetrads, comprising the first eight aeons.

Ormuzd - in Manicheism, Primal Man trapped in the world and requiring salvation.

Pleroma - "Fullness"; the Gnostic Heaven, home of God and the aeons.

pneuma - part of the threefold division of humanity, corresponding to the spiritual self, unaffected by the body; the pneumatics represented the Gnostics, already saved.

psychic - part of the threefold division of humanity, corresponding to the mind; the psychics represented the orthodox church, who had to choose between heaven and the world.

Ptahil - in Mandeanism, the Uthra who made the material world; etymologically derived from the Egyptian artisan-god Ptah and the Hebrew "el," meaning God.

Ruha - in Mandeanism, "Spirit"; the evil mother of the seven planets.

Self - the divinity in humanity; not part of the physical world. See also under *A COURSE IN MIRACLES*.

Sh'Kina - in Mandeanism, "Habitation"; connoting the glorious light surrounding the Uthras like a dwelling.

soul - what has been split off from the Self and therefore in need of redemption. See also under PLATONISM.

Sophia - "wisdom"; in Valentinian *Gnosis* the last aeon to be created; tries to create like her Father, and her failure ultimately leads to the making of the world.

Tibil - in Mandeanism, "Earth."

uthra - in Mandeanism, "Wealth"; divine beings who emanate from the Great Mana or Life.

A COURSE IN MIRACLES

Atonement - the Holy Spirit's plan of correction to undo the ego's belief in separation; it came into being with the Holy Spirit after the dream of separation began.

body - the embodiment of the ego's thought of separation, giving seeming witness to the reality of the separation; to the ego it is a symbol of guilt and attack; to the Holy Spirit it is the instrument or classroom of salvation, through which we learn forgiveness.

Christ - Second Person of the Trinity; the one Son of God that God created as Himself: spirit; our true Self; not to be exclusively identified with Jesus. See also under CHRISTIANITY.

creation - the extension of God's being: Christ.

creations - the extension of Christ's being; as extensions of Christ, the creations are part of the Second Person of the Trinity, and have no connection to, or expression in the material world.

dream - the post-separation state in which the sleeping Son of God dreams a world of sin, guilt, and fear.

ego - the belief in the reality of the separated self, made as substitute for the Self which God created; a thought system based on sin, guilt, fear, and attack as "protection" against the Voice of the Holy Spirit.

face of Christ - symbol of forgiveness; the face of innocence seen in another when we are free from our projections of guilt; not to be confused with the face of Jesus.

fear - the emotion originating in the expected punishment from God for our sins, which our guilt demands.

forgiveness - our special function that shifts perception of others as enemies to friends, removing all projections of guilt from them and therefore from ourselves.

God - First Person of the Trinity; the Creator and Source of all being and life; is not the creator of the material universe. See also under CHRISTIANITY.

guilt - the feeling experienced in relation to sin; includes all the negative feelings and beliefs we have about ourselves; gives rise to fear, and will always be projected onto others in the form of attack, or onto our bodies in the form of sickness.

happy dream - the Holy Spirit's correction for the ego's dream of pain; the dream of forgiveness in which the real world is ultimately perceived and salvation attained.

holy relationship - the Holy Spirit's means to undo the goal of the special relationship by shifting the goal to forgiveness; occurs within the mind, though in the context of a relationship in which two people perceived as separate now join together.

Holy Spirit - Third Person of the Trinity; God's Answer to the separation and the communication link between God and His separated Son; the abstract memory of God's love that is present in the Son's split mind. See also under CHRISTIANITY.

illusion - the belief that the separation from God is real, upon which rest all the manifestations of the physical world, all equally unreal.

Jesus - the first person or "I" of *A Course in Miracles*; the one who first completed his part of the Atonement; though different from us in time, he is the same as we in eternity; not to be exclusively identified with Christ. See also under CHRISTIANITY.

knowledge - synonym for Heaven, or the pre-separation world of God.

magic - the attempt to solve a problem where it is not; the ego's strategy to keep the real problem of the mind--the belief in separation--from the Holy Spirit by projecting its guilt onto the world.

Mind - the aspect of God through which His spirit creates. See also under *Platonism*.

mind - the agent of choice between the ego and the Holy Spirit, roughly equivalent to the Neoplatonic soul; not to be confused with the brain, which simply carries out the wishes of the mind.

miracle - the change of mind that shifts our perception from the ego's attack to the Holy Spirit's forgiveness; not to be confused with the traditional understanding of changes in external phenomena.

projection - the fundamental law of mind; what we see inwardly determines what we see outside of ourselves; reinforces guilt by placing it onto someone else, attacking it there and denying its presence in our own mind.

real world - the state of mind in which, through forgiveness, the world is released from the projections of guilt we had placed upon it; thus, it is the mind that has changed, not the world; the happy dream that is the end of the Atonement.

scarcity principle - an aspect of guilt; the belief that we lack what we need, leading us to seek special relationships to fill the scarcity we experience within ourselves; comparable to the Valentinian concept of deficiency.

Self - See: *Christ*. See also under GNOSTICISM.

separation - the belief in sin that affirms an identity separate from our Creator; real in time, though unknown in eternity, it is projected out and gives rise to a world of separation.

sin - the belief in the reality of our separation from God, which is seen by the ego as an attack on God who can never forgive us; gives rise to guilt which in turn demands our punishment.

Son of God - in Heaven, the Second Person of the Trinity, the Christ who is our true Self; in the world, our identity as separated Sons, or the Son of God as an ego.

special relationship - relationships onto which we project our guilt, substituting them for the love of God; special hate justifies the projection of guilt by attack; special love conceals the attack within the illusion of love, where we believe our needs are met by special people; as these relationships retain guilt, they reinforce belief in the scarcity principle, which is their source.

spirit - the nature of our true reality which, being of God, is changeless and eternal; its energy is activated by the Mind, to which it is roughly equivalent.

teacher of God - at the instant we decide to join with another, we become teachers of God; teaching forgiveness we learn it for ourselves, recognizing the Holy Spirit as our true Teacher.

world - the thought of separation projected out and given form; being the expression of the belief in time and space, it was not created by the eternal and formless God; to the ego it serves to reinforce belief in itself; to the Holy Spirit it becomes a classroom in which forgiveness teaches us ultimately that there is no world. See also *"cosmos"* under PLATONISM and GNOSTICISM.

WORKS CITED

Allberry, C. R. C., ed. See: *A Manichaean Psalm-Book.*

Aristotle. *The Basic Works of Aristotle.* Edited by Richard McKeon. New York: Random House, 1941.

_____. *Problems* I. Trans. by W. S. Hett. Cambridge: Harvard Univ. Loeb Classical Library, 1961.

Armstrong, A. H. *An Introduction to Ancient Philosophy.* Third Edition. Totowa, NJ: Rowman & Allanheld, 1981. First published in 1947 by Methuen & Co. Ltd., London.

Aurelius, Marcus. *Meditations. To Himself.* In *Essential Works of Stoicism.* Edited with Introduction by Moses Hadas. New York: Bantam Books, 1961.

Bréhier, Emile. *The Philosophy of Plotinus.* Trans. by Joseph Thomas. Chicago: The Univ. of Chicago Press, 1958.

Baer, Richard A., Jr. *Philo's Use of the Categories Male and Female.* Leiden: E. J. Brill, 1970.

Bourke, Vernon, ed. *The Essential Augustine.* New York: New American Library, 1964.

Brown, Raymond. *The Birth of the Messiah.* New York: Doubleday, 1977.

_____. *The Community of the Beloved Disciple.* New York: Paulist Press, 1979.

Bultmann, Rudolf. *Primitive Christianity In Its Contemporary Setting.* Trans. by Reginald H. Fuller. Philadelphia: Fortress Press, 1980.

Callahan, John F. *Four Views of Time in Ancient Philosophy.* Revised Edition. Westport, CN: Greenwood Press, 1968.

Course in Miracles, A. Tiburon, CA: Foundation for Inner Peace, 1975.

Dillon, John. "The Descent of the Soul in Middle Platonic and Gnostic Theory." In *The Rediscovery of Gnosticism.* Proceedings of the International Conference on Gnosticism at Yale, 1978. Vol. One: *The School of Valentinus.* Edited by Bentley Layton. Leiden: E. J. Brill, 1980.

Encyclopedia of Religion and Ethics. James Hastings, ed. Twelve Vols. & Index Vol. Compiled 1908-1926. Edinburgh. New York: Scribners.

Foerster, Werner, ed. *Gnosis: A Selection of Gnostic Texts.* Vol. I: *Patristic Evidence.* Vol. II: *Coptic and Mandean Sources.* Oxford: Oxford University Press, 1972, 1974.

Forgotten Books of Eden, The. Rutherford H. Platt, Jr., ed. New York: Bell, 1980.

Graham, Dom Aelred. *The End of Religion.* New York: Harcourt Brace and Jovanovich, 1971.

Grant, Robert M. *Gnosticism and Early Christianity.* New York: Columbia Univ. Press, 1966.

_____, ed. *Gnosticism: A Source Book of Heretical Writings from the Early Christian Period.* New York: Harper & Brothers, 1961.

Griffiths, Bede, O.S.B., Cam. "The Emerging Universal Consciousness and the Mystical Traditions of Asia." *Cistercian Studies,* XXII (1987:1), 76-87.

Guitton, Jean. *Great Heresies and Church Councils*. New York: Harper & Row, 1965.

Haardt, Robert. *Gnosis: Character and Testimony*. Trans. by J. F. Hendry. Leiden: E. J. Brill, 1971.

Hanratty, Gerald. "The Early Gnostics." "The Early Gnostics II." *Irish Theological Quarterly*. Vol. 51, 3 (1985), 209-224, Vol. 51, 4 (1985), 289-299.

Jerusalem Bible, The. New York: Doubleday, 1966.

Joachim of Fiore. *The Article of Belief*. In *Apocalyptic Spirituality*. Bernard McGinn, ed. New York: Paulist Press, 1979.

Jonas, Hans. *The Gnostic Religion: The Message of the Alien God and the Beginnings of Christianity*. Second edition, revised. Boston: Beacon Press, 1963.

Krishnamurti, J. *The Awakening of Intelligence*. San Francisco: Harper & Row, 1987.

Layton, Bentley, ed. *The Rediscovery of Gnosticism*. Proceedings of the International Conference on Gnosticism at Yale, New Haven, Conn., March 28-31, 1978. Vol. One: *The School of Valentinus*. Leiden: E. J. Brill, 1980.

Lossky, Vladimir. *The Mystical Theology of the Eastern Church*. New York: St. Vladimir's Seminary Press, 1976.

Lost Books of the Bible, The. New York: Bell Publishing Co., 1979. Reprint of the 1926 ed. published by World Pub. Co., Cleveland. Trans. by Jones, Wake, 1820.

MacKenna, Stephen. Introduction to *Plotinus: The Enneads*. Second Edition revised by B. S. Page. New York: Pantheon Books, 1956.

Manichaean Psalm-Book, A. Part II. Manichaean Manuscripts in the Chester Beatty Collection II. Edited by C. R. C. Allberry. Stuttgart: W. Kohlhammer, 1938.

Mansel, Henry Longueville. *The Gnostic Heresies of the First and Second Centuries*. London: John Murray, 1875.

McGinn, Bernard. *See* Joachim of Fiore.

Merton, Thomas. *Cables to the Ace or Familiar Liturgies of Misunderstanding*. New York: New Directions, 1967.

Nag Hammadi Library in English, The. Edited by James Robinson. San Francisco: Harper & Row, 1977.

New Testament Apocrypha. Edited by Edgar Hennecke and Wilhelm Schneemelcher. English translation edited by R. McL. Wilson. Vol. One: *Gospels and Related Writings*. Vol. Two: *Writings Relating to the Apostles; Apocalypses and Related Subjects*. Index to Volumes One and Two. Philadelphia: Westminster Press, 1963, 1965.

Nigg, Walter. *The Heretics*. New York: Alfred Knopf, 1962.

Origen: An Exhortation to Martyrdom, Prayer, First Principles: Book IV, Prologue to the Commentary on the Song of Songs, Homily XXVII on Numbers. Trans. and Introduction by Rowan A. Greer. New York: Paulist Press, 1979.

Origen. *On First Principles*. Trans., Introduction, Notes by G. W. Butterworth.

Introduction to Torchbook edition by Henri DeLubac. New York: Harper Torchbooks, 1966.

Oxford Dictionary of Quotations. 3rd Edition. New York: Oxford Univ. Press, 1979.

Pagels, Elaine. *The Gnostic Gospels.* New York: Vintage Books, Random House, 1979.

Perkins, Pheme. *The Gnostic Dialogue: The Early Church and the Crisis of Gnosticism.* New York: Paulist Press, 1980.

Philo. Ten Volumes and Two Supplementary Volumes. Trans. by F. H. Colson, Rev. G. H. Whitaker, Ralph Marcus. Cambridge: Harvard Univ. Loeb Classical Library, 1929-1953.

Philo of Alexandria: The Contemplative Life, The Giants, And Selections. Translation and Introduction by David Winston. New York: Paulist Press, 1981.

Plato. *The Collected Dialogues of Plato, Including the Letters.* Edited by Edith Hamilton and Huntington Cairns. New York: Bollingen Foundation, 1961.

_____. *The Republic.* Translation and Introduction by Desmond Lee. New York: Penguin Books, 1955.

_____. *Timaeus and Critias.* Trans. with Introduction, Appendix by Desmond Lee. New York: Penguin Books, 1971.

Plotinus: The Enneads. Seven Volumes. Trans. by A. H. Armstrong. Cambridge: Harvard Univ. Loeb Classical Library, 1966-1988.

"Psychotherapy: Purpose, Process and Practice." Tiburon, CA: Foundation for Inner Peace, 1976.

Puech, Henri-Charles. "Gnosis and Time." In *Man and Time.* Vol. 3 Eranos Yearbooks. Edited by Joseph Campbell. New York: Pantheon Books, 1957.

Rudolph, Kurt. *Gnosis: The Nature and History of Gnosticism.* Translation edited by Robert McLochlan Wilson. San Francisco: Harper & Row, 1983.

Sahakian, William and Mabel. *Plato.* Boston: Twayne, 1977.

St. Augustine. *The Confessions of St. Augustine.* Translation with Introduction and Notes by John K. Ryan. New York: Doubleday Image Books, 1960.

St. John of the Cross. *The Collected Works of St. John of the Cross.* Trans. by Kieran Kavanaugh, O.C.D., and Otilio Rodgriguez, O.C.D. Washington: Institute of Carmelite Studies, 1964.

Schucman, Helen. *The Gifts of God.* Tiburon, CA: Foundation for Inner Peace, 1982.

"Song of Prayer, The." Tiburon, CA: Foundation for Inner Peace, 1978.

Tresmontant, Claude. *The Origins of Christian Philosophy.* New York: Hawthorn Books, 1963.

Verbeke, Gerard and D. Verhelst, eds. *Aquinas and Problems of His Time.* Leuven: Leuven Univ. Press, 1976.

Wapnick, Gloria and Kenneth. *Awaken From the Dream.* Roscoe, NY: Foundation for "A Course in Miracles," 1987.

Wapnick, Kenneth. *Absence From Felicity: The Story of Helen Schucman, and Her Scribing of* A Course in Miracles. Roscoe, NY: Foundation for "A Course in Miracles," 1990.

____. "Christian Psychology in *A Course in Miracles*." Roscoe, NY: Foundation for "A Course in Miracles," 1978.

____. *Forgiveness and Jesus: The Meeting Place of* A Course in Miracles *and Christianity*. Roscoe, NY: Foundation for "A Course in Miracles," 1983.

____. *Glossary-Index for* A Course in Miracles. Second edition, enlarged. Roscoe, NY: Foundation for "A Course in Miracles," 1982.

____. *Vast Illusion, A: Time According to* A Course in Miracles. Roscoe, NY: Foundation for "A Course in Miracles," 1990.

Weisheipl, James A., O.P. *Friar Thomas D'Aquino. His Life, Thought, and Works*. Washington: The Catholic Univ. of America Press, 1983.

Wilson, R. McL. *Gnosis and the New Testament*. Philadelphia: Fortress Press, 1968.

Yamauchi, Edwin M. *Pre-Christian Gnosticism. A Survey of the Proposed Evidences*. Second Edition. Grand Rapids, MI: Baker Book House, 1983.

SELECTED BIBLIOGRAPHY

GNOSTICISM

Foerster, Werner, ed. *Gnosis: A Selection of Gnostic Texts.* Vol. I: *Patristic Evidence.* Vol. II: *Coptic and Mandean Sources.* Oxford: Oxford University Press, 1972, 1974.

Haardt, Robert. *Gnosis: Character and Testimony.* Trans. by J. F. Hendry. Leiden: E. J. Brill, 1971.

Jonas, Hans. *The Gnostic Religion: The Message of the Alien God and the Beginnings of Christianity.* Second edition, revised. Boston: Beacon Press, 1963.

Layton, Bentley, ed. *The Rediscovery of Gnosticism.* Proceedings of the International Conference on Gnosticism at Yale, New Haven, Conn., March 28-31, 1978. Vol. One: *The School of Valentinus.* Leiden: E. J. Brill, 1980.

Manichaean Psalm-Book, A. Part II. Manichaean Manuscripts in the Chester Beatty Collection II. Edited by C. R. C. Allberry. Stuttgart: W. Kohlhammer, 1938.

Nag Hammadi Library in English, The. Edited by James Robinson. San Francisco: Harper & Row, 1977.

Rudolph, Kurt. *Gnosis: The Nature and History of Gnosticism.* Translation edited by Robert McLochlan Wilson. San Francisco: Harper & Row, 1983.

CHRISTIANITY

Bourke, Vernon, ed. *The Essential Augustine.* New York: New American Library, 1964.

Forgotten Books of Eden, The. Rutherford H. Platt, Jr., ed. New York: Bell, 1980.

Jerusalem Bible, The. New York: Doubleday, 1966.

Lost Books of the Bible, The. New York: Bell Publishing Co., 1979. Reprint of the 1926 ed. published by World Pub. Co., Cleveland. Trans. by Jones, Wake, 1820.

New Testament Apocrypha. Edited by Edgar Hennecke and Wilhelm Schneemelcher. English translation edited by R. McL. Wilson. Vol. One: *Gospels and Related Writings.* Vol. Two: *Writings Relating to the Apostles; Apocalypses and Related Subjects.* Index to Volumes One and Two. Philadelphia: Westminster Press, 1963, 1965.

Origen. *An Exhortation to Martyrdom, Prayer, First Principles: Book IV, Prologue to the Commentary on the Song of Songs, Homily XXVII on Numbers.* Translation and Introduction by Rowan A. Greer. NY: Paulist Press, 1979.

St. Augustine. *The Confessions of St. Augustine.* Translation with Introduction and Notes by John K. Ryan. New York: Doubleday, 1960.

PHILOSOPHERS

Armstrong, A. H. *An Introduction to Ancient Philosophy*. Third Edition. Totowa, NJ: Rowman & Allanheld, 1981. First published in 1947 by Methuen & Co. Ltd., London.

Bréhier, Emile. *The Philosophy of Plotinus*. Trans. by Joseph Thomas. Chicago: Univ. of Chicago Press, 1958.

Philo. Ten Volumes and Two Supplementary Volumes. Trans. by F. H. Colson, Rev. G. H. Whitaker, Ralph Marcus. Cambridge: Harvard Univ. Loeb Classical Library, 1929-1953.

Plato. *The Collected Dialogues of Plato, Including the Letters*. Edited by Edith Hamilton and Huntington Cairns. New York: Bollingen Foundation, 1961.

Plotinus: The Enneads. Seven Volumes. Trans. by A. H. Armstrong. Cambridge: Harvard Univ. Loeb Classical Library, 1966-1988.

A COURSE IN MIRACLES

A Course in Miracles. Tiburon, CA: Foundation for Inner Peace, 1975.

"Psychotherapy: Purpose, Process and Practice." Tiburon, CA: Foundation for Inner Peace, 1976.

"Song of Prayer, The." Tiburon, CA: Foundation for Inner Peace, 1978.

Wapnick, Kenneth and Gloria. *Awaken From the Dream*. Roscoe, NY: Foundation for "A Course in Miracles," 1987.

Wapnick, Kenneth. *Forgiveness and Jesus: The Meeting Place of* A Course in Miracles *and Christianity*. Roscoe, NY: Foundation for "A Course in Miracles," 1983.

____. *Glossary-Index for* A Course in Miracles. Second edition, enlarged. Roscoe, NY: Foundation for "A Course in Miracles," 1982.

INDICES

WRITINGS OF CHURCH FATHERS

Irenaeus

Epiphanius

Epiphanius (continued)

Clement of Alexandria

Hippolytus

Hippolytus (continued)

Tertullian

PLOTINUS

PLOTINUS (continued)

THE NAG HAMMADI LIBRARY

THE NAG HAMMADI LIBRARY (continued)

MANDEAN SOURCES

*Books are cited in roman, individual sections and/or paragraphs in arabic numerals,
with references to translations used in Foerster, Vol. II.*

MANDEAN SOURCES (continued)

A COURSE IN MIRACLES

Text

Text (continued)

320 484	404 467,494	542 498,528
327 466	407 488	543 451
333 449	415 512,545	544 415,433,514
339 556	416 420	545 461-62,514
347 428,529	431 529	546 462
348 426,432,458	440 431,539	551 441
352 444	442 489	552 462
354 535	455 43	553 435,461,463
355 555	456 424,459	554 421
359 6,413,455,534	458 508,542	559 297,452-53
361 451	459 451	560 452
362 451	464 512,539	563 481
363 10,471,516	484 497	570 413
364 420,450	486 469	572 426
367 432	492 297,509	573 448,529
368 432	493 511	576 424
369 466	494 511	584 458
374 491	502 541	593 491
375 490,512,556	505 450	594 491
376 489	511 435,437	600 515
378 467	512 421,436	601 429
383 485	513 436	610 460,486
384 485,517	515 412	611 486
385 450	518 509	612 486
386 517	519 209	613 486
387 517	525 486	614 524,529
389 557	526 486	620 462
395 502	528 491	621 196
398 467	529 557	622 521
401 297,429	538 428	

Workbook

1 ..... 504,545,551, 552	121 551	188 551
3 504	123 517	193 467
34 430,463	139 554	194 467
78 550	141 515,554	197 504
105 502	159 454	227 527
112 445	164 504	237 472
120 446	165 504,505,506	247 493
	187 551	284 516,517

Workbook (continued)

Manual for Teachers

"The Song of Prayer"

"Psychotherapy: Purpose Process and Practice"

INDEX OF NAMES

Old and New Testament figures and writers, and figures from Gnostic myths are listed in the Subject Index. A Course in Miracles is abbreviated as ACIM.

603

SUBJECT INDEX

This index is not exhaustive; only the main references for each entry have been included. Platonism, Christianity, and Gnosticism appear as subentries under other headings. A Course in Miracles (abbreviated as ACIM) appears as a main heading for a few specific references; all other references are in subentries.